SOUTH AMERICA

Pages 72–73

75

74

AFRICA

Pages 48–49

50–51

47

NORTH AMERICA

58–59

56–57

60–61

64–65

66

66

67

62–63

69

70

GENERAL MAPS

AUSTRALASIA

Pages 32–33

34

35

CITY PLANS

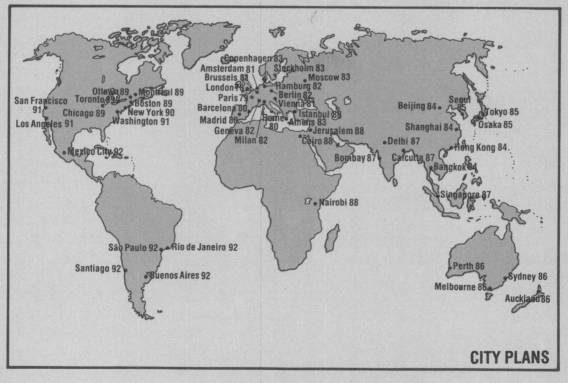

Copenhagen 83
Amsterdam 81
Brussels 81
Stockholm 83
Moscow 83
Hamburg 82
London 78
Paris 79
Berlin 82
Vienna 81
Ottawa 89
Montreal 89
Toronto 89
Boston 89
San Francisco 91
Chicago 89
New York 90
Barcelona 80
Madrid 80
Beijing 84
Seoul 85
Tokyo 85
Istanbul 88
Los Angeles 91
Washington 91
Geneva 82
Rome 80
Athens 83
Shanghai 84
Osaka 85
Milan 82
Jerusalem 88
Cairo 88
Delhi 87
Hong Kong 84
Mexico City 92
Bombay 87
Calcutta 87
Bangkok 84
Singapore 87
Nairobi 88
São Paulo 92
Rio de Janeiro 92
Santiago 92
Buenos Aires 92
Perth 86
Sydney 86
Melbourne 86
Auckland 86

THE TIMES

ATLAS OF THE WORLD

FAMILY EDITION

TIMES BOOKS

A Division of HarperCollinsPublishers

Published in 1992 by
TIMES BOOKS
A Division of HarperCollins *Publishers*
77-85 Fulham Palace Road
Hammersmith
London W6 8JB

First edition 1988
Reprinted 1988
Reprinted with revisions 1989, 1990, 1991
Second edition 1992

Copyright © Times Books and
Bartholomew 1992

Maps and index prepared by
Bartholomew, Edinburgh

Geographical Dictionary prepared by
Professor B.W. Atkinson

Physical Earth Maps
Duncan Mackay

Design
Ivan Dodd

Printed and bound in Italy by
Mondadori, Verona.

*The Publishers would like to extend
their grateful thanks to the following:*

Mrs J Candy, Geographical Research
   Associates, Maidenhead
Cosmographics, Watford
Flag information provided and authenticated
   by the Flag Institute, Chester
Additional information from the Flag
   Research Center, Massachusetts, USA
Mr. P.J.M Geelan, Place-name consultant
Mr Michael Hendrie, Astronomy
   Correspondent, *The Times*, London
Mr H.A.G. Lewis OBE, Geographical
   consultant to *The Times*
Mr R. Muhs, School of Slavonic & East
   European Studies, University of London
Swanston Graphics, Derby
Thames Cartographic Services, Maidenhead

*British Library Cataloguing in
Publication Data*
The Times atlas of the world.
  Family edition – 2nd ed.
  911

ISBN 0-7230-0490-0

This, *The Times Atlas of the World, Family Edition*, has been extensively revised since it was first published in 1988. This is the second edition of this popular atlas. It is a reference work for use in the home, office or school, for those who travel the world and also those, like Francis Bacon, who journey only "in map and chart".

An index of no fewer than 30,000 entries, keyed to the main map plates, will aid those who, whilst familiar with the name of a place, are uncertain of just where it lies on the map.

It is by no means always easy to ascertain the correct title and status of a country as distinct from its everyday name used on maps. The list of states and territories gives in addition to name, title and status, the population and area, the national currency, the major religions and the national flag.

Maps, being an efficient way of storing and displaying information, are used to amplify the list of states and territories and the geographical comparisons of continents, oceans, lakes and islands. They form the basis of the section on earthquakes, volcanoes, economic minerals, vegetation, temperature, rainfall and population.

Maps are also, by nature, illustrative and a 14-page section shows the world's major physical features in the way they appear from space but with the names of the features added.

Amongst the statistical data contained in the Atlas is a listing of the major metropolitan areas with their populations. For the past several decades there has been, throughout the world, an accelerating flow of people from the land to towns and cities and especially the major cities, some of which now contain the bulk of the national population. Growth in air travel has turned those same cities into centres of tourism. Influx of population and the demands of tourism have enhanced the status of cities. Generous space has, therefore, been allocated to maps of major cities and their environs.

Geographical names in this Atlas are given in their anglicized (conventional) form where such a form is in current use. Other names are given in their national Roman alphabet or else converted into English by transliteration (letter-to-letter) or transcription (sound-to-sound). Because Roman alphabet letters, sometimes modified, are pronounced in a variety of ways, a brief guide to pronunciation has been included. The whole is supplemented by a dictionary of geographical terms.

In the names, in the portrayal of international boundaries and in the list of states and territories, the aim has been to show the situation as it pertains in the area at the time of going to press. This must not be taken as endorsement by the publishers of the status of the territories concerned. The aim throughout has been to show things as they are. In that way the Atlas will best serve the reader to whom, it is hoped, it will bring interest, benefit and continuing pleasure.

H.A.G. Lewis, OBE
Geographical Consultant to *The Times*

CONTENTS

AFGHANISTAN

STATUS: Republic
AREA: 652,225 sq km (251,773 sq miles)
POPULATION: 16,433,000
ANNUAL NATURAL INCREASE: 2.4%
CAPITAL: Kabul
LANGUAGE: Pushtu, Dari (Persian dialect)
RELIGION: 90% Sunni and 9% Shia
Muslim
CURRENCY: afghani (AFA)
ORGANISATIONS: UN, Col. Plan

Afghanistan is a mountainous landlocked country in south-west Asia with a climate of extremes. In summer the lowland south-west reaches a temperature of over 40°C (104°F); in winter this may drop to −26°C (−15°F) in the northern mountains. Rainfall varies between 10 and 40cm (4–16in). The country is one of the poorest in the world with hardly 10% of the land suitable for agriculture. Main crops are wheat, fruit and vegetables. Sheep and goats are the main livestock. Mineral resources are rich but underdeveloped with natural gas, coal and iron ore deposits predominating. The main industrial area is centred on Kabul.

ALAND

STATUS: Self-governing Island Province
of Finland
AREA: 1,505 sq km (581 sq miles)
POPULATION: 24,231

ABBREVIATIONS	
ANZUS	Australia, New Zealand, United States Security Treaty
ASEAN	Association of South East Asian Nations
CACM	Central American Common Market
CARICOM	Caribbean Community and Common Market
CFA	(Communauté Financière Africaîne
CFP	or Pacific franc (Communauté Française du Pacifique)
CIS	Commonwealth of Independent States
Col. Plan	Colombo Plan
Comm.	Commonwealth
ECOWAS	Economic Community of West African States
EC	European Community
EFTA	European Free Trade Association
G7	Group of Seven Industrial Nations (Canada, France, Germany, Italy, Japan, UK, USA)
NATO	North Atlantic Treaty Organisation
OAS	Organisation of American States
OAU	Organisation of African Unity
OECD	Organisation for Economic Co-operation and Development
OIEC	Organisation for International Economic Co-operation
OPEC	Organisation of Petroleum Exporting Countries
UN	United Nations
WEU	Western European Union

Codes, given in brackets, following the name of a currency are those issued by the International Standards Organisation.

ALBANIA

STATUS: Republic
AREA: 28,750 sq km (11,100 sq miles)
POPULATION: 3,250,000
ANNUAL NATURAL INCREASE: 2.1%
CAPITAL: Tirana (Tiranë)
LANGUAGE: Albanian (Tosk, Gheg)
RELIGION: Religion officially banned from
1967-1990. Formerly 70% Muslim,
20% Orthodox and 10% Roman Catholic
CURRENCY: lek (ALL)
ORGANISATIONS: UN

Albania is situated on the eastern seaboard of the Adriatic. With the exception of a coastal strip, most of the territory is mountainous and largely unfit for cultivation. The country possesses considerable mineral resources, notably chrome, copper, iron ores and nickel, with rich deposits of coal, oil and natural gas. After decades of self-imposed political and economic isolation Albania shook off its own peculiar variant of communism in 1990. Administrative chaos and a massive fall in production ensued, notably in the (as yet collectivised) agricultural sector. Acute food shortages and economic backwardness have generated a desire for emigration among the younger members of the fast-growing population.

ALEUTIAN ISLANDS

STATUS: Territory of USA
AREA: 17,665 sq km (6,820 sq miles)
POPULATION: 6,730

ALGERIA

STATUS: Republic
AREA: 2,381,745 sq km (919,355 sq miles)
POPULATION: 24,960,000
ANNUAL NATURAL INCREASE: 3.1%
CAPITAL: Algiers (El-Djezaïr)
LANGUAGE: Arabic, French, Berber
RELIGION: Muslim
CURRENCY: Algerian dinar (DZD)
ORGANISATIONS: UN, Arab League, OAU, OPEC

Physically the country is divided between the coastal Atlas mountain ranges of the north and the Sahara to the south. Arable land occupies small areas of the northern valleys and coastal strip, with wheat, barley and vines the leading crops. Sheep, goats and cattle are the most important livestock. Although oil from the southern deserts dominates the economy, it is now declining. Economic policy has concentrated on encouraging smaller manufacturing and service industries. Tourism is a growth industry and now earns important foreign exchange.

ANDORRA

STATUS: Principality under Franco-Spanish
sovereignty
AREA: 465 sq km (180 sq miles)
POPULATION: 52,000
CAPITAL: Andorra la Vella
LANGUAGE: Spanish (Castilian, Catalan), French
RELIGION: mainly Roman Catholic
CURRENCY: French francs (FRF), Andorran
peseta (ADP)

Andorra is a tiny alpine state high in the Pyrenees between France and Spain. Agriculture and tourism are the main occupations. Tobacco and potatoes are the principal

crops, sheep and cattle the main livestock. Important sources of revenue are the sale of hydro-electricity, stamps and duty-free goods.

ANGOLA

STATUS: Republic
AREA: 1,246,700 sq km (481,225 sq miles)
POPULATION: 10,020,000
ANNUAL NATURAL INCREASE: 2.5%
CAPITAL: Luanda
LANGUAGE: Portuguese, tribal dialects
RELIGION: mainly traditional beliefs. Large
Roman Catholic and Protestant minorities

CURRENCY: new kwanza (AON)
ORGANISATIONS: UN, OAU

Independent from the Portuguese since 1975, Angola is a large country south of the equator in south-western Africa. Much of the interior is savannah plateaux with rainfall varying from 25cm (10in) in the north to 60cm (24in) in the south. Most of the population is engaged in agriculture producing cassava, maize and coffee, but Angola is very rich in minerals. Petroleum, diamonds, iron ore, copper and manganese are exported with petroleum accounting for at least 50% of earnings. The small amount of industry is concentrated around Luanda. Most consumer products and textiles are imported.

ANGUILLA

STATUS: UK Dependent Territory
AREA: 91 sq km (35 sq miles)
POPULATION: 7,019
CAPITAL: The Valley

ANTIGUA & BARBUDA

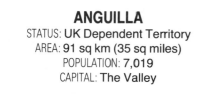

STATUS: Commonwealth State
AREA: 442 sq km (171 sq miles)
POPULATION: 85,000
ANNUAL NATURAL INCREASE: 0.4%
CAPITAL: St John's (on Antigua)
LANGUAGE: English
RELIGION: Anglican Christian majority
CURRENCY: East Caribbean dollar (XCD)
ORGANISATIONS: Comm, UN, CARICOM, OAS

The country consists of two main islands in the Leeward group in the West Indies. Tourism is the main activity but local agriculture is being encouraged to reduce food imports. The production of rum is the main manufacturing industry.

ARGENTINA

STATUS: Republic
AREA: 2,766,889 sq km (1,068,302 sq miles)
POPULATION: 32,610,000
ANNUAL NATURAL INCREASE: 1.4%
CAPITAL: Buenos Aires
LANGUAGE: Spanish
RELIGION: 90% Roman Catholic, 2% Protestant, Jewish minority
CURRENCY: peso
ORGANISATIONS: UN, OAS

The country stretches over 30 degrees of latitude from the thick sub-tropical forests of the north through the immense flat grass plains of the pampas to the cool desert plateaux of Patagonia in the south. The economy of Argentina was long dominated by the produce of the rich soils of the pampas, beef and grain. Agricultural products account for over 60% of export revenue with grain crops pre-dominating, although the late 1980s saw a decline due to competition and falling world grain prices. Beef exports, the mainstay of the economy from 1850, decreased by over 50% between 1970 and 1983, again due to strong competition from western Europe. Industry has also declined during the last decade. Shortages of raw materials and foreign aid debts have meant lower production, unemployment and a strong decline in domestic demand. The expansion of the oil and gas industry and the steady growth of coal, hydro-electricity and nuclear power, is providing a base for industrial growth but internal inflation has not yet allowed this expansion.

ARMENIA

STATUS: Republic
AREA: 30,000 sq km (11,580 sq miles)
POPULATION: 3,300,000
CAPITAL: Yerevan
LANGUAGE: Armenian, Russian
RELIGION: Russian Orthodox, Armenian Apostolic
CURRENCY: rouble
ORGANISATIONS: CIS

Smallest of the 15 republics of the former USSR, Armenia is a rugged and landlocked country with hot, dry summers and severe winters. Arable land is limited but fertile. Extensive mountain pastures support cattle, sheep and goats. Industry is mainly concerned with machine-building, chemicals and textiles. Conflict with neighbouring Azerbaijan looks set to cast a cloud over the immediate future.

ARUBA

STATUS: Self-governing Island of Netherlands Realm
AREA: 193 sq km (75 sq miles)
POPULATION: 62,500
CAPITAL: Oranjestad

ASCENSION

STATUS: Island Dependency of St Helena
AREA: 88 sq km (34 sq miles)
POPULATION: 1,007
CAPITAL: Georgetown

AUSTRALIA

STATUS: Federal Nation
AREA: 7,682,300 sq km (2,965,370 sq miles)
POPULATION: 17,086,197
ANNUAL NATURAL INCREASE: 1.5%
CAPITAL: Canberra
LANGUAGE: English
RELIGION: 75% Christian. Aboriginal beliefs. Jewish minority
CURRENCY: Australian dollar (AUD)
ORGANISATIONS: Comm, UN, ANZUS, Col. Plan, OECD

AUSTRALIAN CAPITAL TERRITORY (CANBERRA)
STATUS: Federal Territory
AREA: 2,432 sq km (939 sq miles)
POPULATION: 284,985
CAPITAL: Canberra

NEW SOUTH WALES
STATUS: State
AREA: 801,430 sq km (309,350 sq miles)
POPULATION: 5,827,373
CAPITAL: Sydney

NORTHERN TERRITORY
STATUS: Territory
AREA: 1,346,200 sq km (519,635 sq miles)
POPULATION: 157,304
CAPITAL: Darwin

QUEENSLAND
STATUS: State
AREA: 1,727,000 sq km (666,620 sq miles)
POPULATION: 2,906,838
CAPITAL: Brisbane

SOUTH AUSTRALIA
STATUS: State
AREA: 984,380 sq km (79,970 sq miles)
POPULATION: 1,439,157
CAPITAL: Adelaide

TASMANIA
STATUS: State
AREA: 68,330 sq km (26,375 sq miles)
POPULATION: 456,663
CAPITAL: Hobart

VICTORIA
STATUS: State
AREA: 227,600 sq km (87,855 sq miles)
POPULATION: 4,379,981
CAPITAL: Melbourne

WESTERN AUSTRALIA

STATUS: State
AREA: 2,525,500 sq km (974,845 sq miles)
POPULATION: 1,633,896
CAPITAL: Perth

Australia is both a continent and a country and is the sixth largest country in terms of area. The centre and the west, over 50% of the land area, are desert and scrub with less than 25 cm (10 in) of rain. Only in the sub-tropical north and the eastern highlands does rainfall exceed 100 cm (39 in) annually. The majority of the population live in cities concentrated along the south-east coast. Australia is rich in both agricultural and natural resources. Wool, wheat, meat, sugar and dairy products account for over 40% of export revenue despite the immense growth in mineral exploitation. The country has vast reserves of coal, oil, natural gas, nickel, iron ore, bauxite and uranium ores. Gold, silver, lead, zinc and copper ores are also exploited. In 1989 minerals accounted for about 42% of export revenue. Recent high deficits in balance of trade have been caused by fluctuations in world demand, competition from the E.C. and recent unfavourable climatic conditions affecting agricultural surpluses. Increasing trade with eastern Asia, and Japan in particular, has opened up new areas of commerce to counteract the sharp decline in Europe as a market.

AUSTRALIAN ANTARCTIC TERRITORY

STATUS: Territory
AREA: 6,120,000 sq km (2,320,000 sq miles)
POPULATION: No permanent population

AUSTRIA

STATUS: Federal Republic
AREA: 83,855 sq km (32,370 sq miles)
POPULATION: 7,761,700
ANNUAL NATURAL INCREASE: 0.1%
CAPITAL: Vienna (Wien)
LANGUAGE: German
RELIGION: 89% Roman Catholic, 6% Protestant
CURRENCY: schilling (ATS)
ORGANISATIONS: UN, Council of Europe, EFTA, OECD

Austria is an alpine, land-locked country in central Europe. The mountainous Alps which cover 75% of the land consist of a series of east-west ranges enclosing lowland basins. The climate is continental with cold winters and warm summers. About 25% of the country, in the north and north-east, is lower foreland or flat land containing most of Austria's fertile farmland. Half is arable and the remainder is mainly for root or fodder crops. Manufacturing and heavy industry, however, account for the majority of export revenue, particularly pig-iron, steel, chemicals and vehicles. Over 70% of the country's power is hydroelectric. Tourism and forestry are also important to the economy.

AZERBAIJAN

STATUS: Republic
AREA: 87,000 sq km (33,580 sq miles)
POPULATION: 7,100,000
CAPITAL: Baku
LANGUAGE: Azeri (a Turkish dialect), Armenian, Russian
RELIGION: Muslim (Shia), Armenian Apostolic, Orthodox
CURRENCY: rouble
ORGANISATIONS: CIS

Azerbaijan gained independence on the break-up of the USSR in 1991. The country includes two autonomous regions: Nakhichevan, from which it is cut off by a strip of intervening Armenian territory, and Nagorny Karabakh. Long-standing tensions over the latter escalated into civil war in 1992. Azerbaijan benefits from a dry subtropical climate with mild winters and long, hot summers. Traditional customs have largely disappeared under the impact of modernisation and urbanisation. Originally based on petroleum extraction and oil refining, industrial development in Azerbaijan has been supplemented by manufacturing, engineering and chemicals. Arable land accounts for less than 10% of the total area, with raw cotton the leading product. Tobacco ranks as the second most valuable crop, followed by grapes. The challenge facing the economy of adaptation to post-communist market conditions is exacerbated by political uncertainty.

BAHAMAS

STATUS: Commonwealth State
AREA: 13,865 sq km (5,350 sq miles)
POPULATION: 254,685
ANNUAL NATURAL INCREASE: 1.9%
CAPITAL: Nassau
LANGUAGE: English
RELIGION: mainly Anglican Christian, Baptist and Roman Catholic
CURRENCY: Bahamian dollar (BSD)
ORGANISATIONS: Comm, UN, CARICOM, OAS

About 700 islands and over 2000 coral sand cays (reefs) constitute the sub-tropical Commonwealth of the Bahamas. The island group extends from the coast of Florida to Cuba and Haiti in the south. Only 29 islands are inhabited. Most of the 100cm (39in) of rainfall falls in the summer. The tourist industry is the main source of income and, although fluctuating through recession, still employs over 70% of the working population. Recent economic plans have concentrated on reducing imports by developing fishing and domestic agriculture. Other important sources of income are ship registration (the world's third largest open-registry fleet), income generated by offshore finance and banking, and export of rum, salt and cement.

BAHRAIN

STATUS: State
AREA: 661 sq km (225 sq miles)
POPULATION: 503,000
ANNUAL NATURAL INCREASE: 4.3%
CAPITAL: Manama (Al Manamah)
LANGUAGE: Arabic, English
RELIGION: 60% Shia and 40% Sunni Muslim. Christian minority
CURRENCY: Bahraini dinar (BHD)
ORGANISATIONS: UN, Arab League

The sheikdom is a barren island in the Persian Gulf with less than 8cm (3in) rainfall. Summer temperatures average 32°C (89°F). Bahrain was the first country in the Arabian

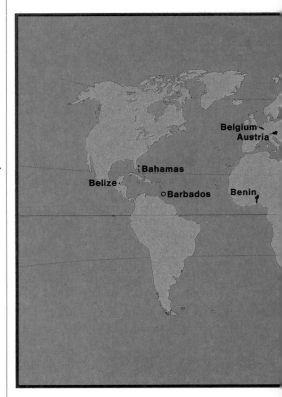

peninsula to strike oil, in 1932. In 1985, oil accounted for 65% of revenue, but a decline in value of the product and lower production is now causing the government to diversify the economy with expansion of light and heavy industry and chemical plants, and the subsequent encouragement of trade and foreign investment.

BANGLADESH

STATUS: Republic
AREA: 144,000 sq km (55,585 sq miles)
POPULATION: 109,291,000
ANNUAL NATURAL INCREASE: 2.8%
CAPITAL: Dhaka

LANGUAGE: Bengali (Bangla), Bihari, Hindi, English
RELIGION: 85% Muslim. Hindu, Buddhist and Christian minorities
CURRENCY: taka (BDT)
ORGANISATIONS: Comm, UN, Col. Plan

Bangladesh is one of the poorest and most densely populated countries of the world. Most of the territory of Bangladesh, except for bamboo-forested hills in the south-east, comprises the vast river systems of the Ganges and Brahmaputra which drain from the Himalayas into the Bay of Bengal, frequently changing course and flooding the flat delta plain. This land is, however, extremely fertile and attracts a high concentration of the population. The climate is tropical, and agriculture is dependent on monsoon rainfall. When the monsoon fails there is drought. 82% of the population of Bangladesh are farmers, the main crops being rice and jute. There are no extensive mineral deposits, although large reserves of natural gas under the Bay of Bengal are beginning to be exploited.

BARBADOS

STATUS: Commonwealth State
AREA: 430 sq km (166 sq miles)
POPULATION: 257,082
ANNUAL NATURAL INCREASE: 0.3%
CAPITAL: Bridgetown
LANGUAGE: English
RELIGION: Anglican Christian majority. Methodist and Roman Catholic minorities
CURRENCY: Barbados dollar (BBD)
ORGANISATIONS: Comm, UN, CARICOM, OAS

The former British colony of Barbados in the Caribbean is the easternmost island of the Antilles chain. The gently rolling landscape of the island is lush and fertile, the temperature

ranging from 25°–28°C(77°–82°F) with 127–190cm(50–75in) rainfall per year. Sugar and its by-products, molasses and rum, form the mainstay of the economy. Tourism has become a growing industry in recent years.

BELGIUM

STATUS: Kingdom
AREA: 30,520 sq km (11,780 sq miles)
POPULATION: 9,845,000
ANNUAL NATURAL INCREASE: 0.0%
CAPITAL: Brussels (Bruxelles/Brussel)
LANGUAGE: French, Dutch (Flemish), German
RELIGION: Roman Catholic majority. Protestant, Jewish minorities
CURRENCY: Belgian franc (BEF)
ORGANISATIONS: UN, Council of Europe, EC, NATO, OECD, WEU

Belgium is situated between the hills of Northern France and the North European plain. Over two thirds of the country comprises the Flanders plain, a flat plateau covered by fertile wind-blown loess which extends from the North Sea coast down to the forested mountains of the Ardennes in the south, which rise to a height of 692m(2270ft). The climate is mild and temperate, although the country's proximity to the Atlantic means that low pressure fronts bring changeable weather and frequent rainfall (72–120cm or 28–47in per annum). Over half the country is intensively farmed – cereals (mainly wheat), root crops, vegetables and flax are the main crops. Extensive pastureland ensures that Belgium is self-sufficient in meat and dairy products. Belgium lacks mineral resources, except for coal, but its metal and engineering industries account for nearly one third of its exports. The Flanders region is famous for its textiles. Most of Belgium's trade passes through the North sea port of Antwerp, and an efficient communications network links the port with the rest of Europe.

BELIZE

STATUS: Commonwealth State
AREA: 22,965 sq km (8,865 sq miles)
POPULATION: 188,000
ANNUAL NATURAL INCREASE: 2.8%
CAPITAL: Belmopan
LANGUAGE: English, Spanish, Maya
RELIGION: 60% Roman Catholic, 40% Protestant
CURRENCY: Belizean dollar (BZD)
ORGANISATIONS: Comm, UN, CARICOM, OAS

Bordering the Caribbean Sea, sub-tropical Belize is dominated by its dense forest cover. Principal crops for export are sugar-cane, fruit, rice, maize and timber products. Since

independence from Britain in 1973 the country has developed agriculture to lessen reliance on imported food products. Fish is a staple diet and also provides valuable foreign exchange.

BELORUSSIA

STATUS: Republic
AREA: 208,000 sq km (80,290 sq miles)
POPULATION: 10,200,000
CAPITAL: Minsk
LANGUAGE: Belorussian, Russian
RELIGION: Roman Catholic, Uniate
CURRENCY: rouble
ORGANISATIONS: UN, CIS

Belorussia achieved independence in 1991. The country is mainly flat with forests covering more than one-third of the area. Swamps and marshlands cover large areas but, when drained, the soil is very fertile. The climate varies from maritime to continental with mild winters and high humidity. Grain, flax, potatoes and sugar beet are the main crops but livestock production accounts for more than half the value of agricultural output. Large areas of Belorussia are thinly populated; most people live in the central area. The republic is comparatively poor in mineral resources and suffered terrible devastation during the Second World War. Post-war industrialisation has been based on imported raw materials and semi-manufactured goods, concentrating on the production of trucks, tractors, agricultural machinery and other heavy engineering equipment. The capital, Minsk, serves as the administrative centre for the Commonwealth of Independent States, the successor organisation to the Soviet Union.

BENIN

STATUS: Republic
AREA: 112,620 sq km (43,470 sq miles)
POPULATION: 188,000
ANNUAL NATURAL INCREASE: 3.2%
CAPITAL: Porto Novo
LANGUAGE: French, Fon, Adja
RELIGION: traditional beliefs majority, 15% Roman Catholic and 13% Muslim
CURRENCY: CFA franc (W Africa) (XOF)
ORGANISATIONS: UN, ECOWAS, OAU

Benin, formerly Dahomey, is a small strip of country descending from the wooded savannah hills of the north to the forested and cultivated lowlands fringing the Bight of Benin. The economy is dominated by agriculture, with palm oil, cotton, coffee, groundnuts and copra as main exports. The developing off-shore oil industry has proven reserves of over 20 million barrels.

BERMUDA

STATUS: Self-governing UK Crown Colony
AREA: 54 sq km (21 sq miles)
POPULATION: 61,000
CAPITAL: Hamilton

BHUTAN

STATUS: Kingdom
AREA: 46,620 sq km (17,995 sq miles)
POPULATION: 1,517,000
ANNUAL NATURAL INCREASE: 2.1%
CAPITAL: Thimphu
LANGUAGE: Dzongkha, Nepali, English
RELIGION: Mahayana Buddhist. Hindu minority
CURRENCY: ngultrum (BTN), Indian rupee (INR)
ORGANISATIONS: UN, Col. Plan

The country spreads across the Himalayan foothills between China and India east of Nepal. Rainfall is high at over 300cm (118in) per year but temperatures vary between extreme cold of the northern ranges to a July average of 27°C (81°F) in the southern forests. Long isolated, the economy of Bhutan is dominated by agriculture and small local industries. All manufactured goods are imported.

BIOKO (FERNANDO PÓO)

STATUS: Island province of Equatorial Guinea
AREA: 2,034 sq km (785 sq miles)
POPULATION: 57,190
CAPITAL: Malabo

BOLIVIA

STATUS: Republic
AREA: 1,098,575 sq km (424,050 sq miles)
POPULATION: 7,400,000
ANNUAL NATURAL INCREASE: 2.8%
CAPITAL: La Paz
LANGUAGE: Spanish, Quechua, Aymara
RELIGION: Roman Catholic majority
CURRENCY: boliviano (BOB)
ORGANISATIONS: UN, OAS

With an average life expectancy of 51 years, Bolivia is one of the world's poorest nations. Landlocked and isolated, the country stretches from the eastern Andes across high cool plateaux before dropping to the dense forest of the Amazon basin and the grasslands of the south-east. Development of the economy relies on the growth of exploitation of mineral resources as subsistence agriculture occupies the majority of the population. Crude oil, natural gas, tin, zinc and iron ore are the main mineral deposits.

BONAIRE

STATUS: Self-governing Island of Netherlands Antilles
AREA: 288 sq km (111 sq miles)
POPULATION: 10,797
CAPITAL: Kralendijk

BONIN ISLANDS (OGASAWARA-SHOTO)

STATUS: Islands of Japan
AREA: 104 sq km (40 sq miles)
POPULATION: 200

BOTSWANA

STATUS: Republic
AREA: 582,000 sq km (224,652 sq miles)
POPULATION: 1,291,000
ANNUAL NATURAL INCREASE: 3.4%
CAPITAL: Gaborone
LANGUAGE: Setswana, English
RELIGION: traditional beliefs majority. Christian minority
CURRENCY: pula (BWP)
ORGANISATIONS: Comm, UN, OAU

The arid high plateau of Botswana, with its poor soils and low rainfall, supports little arable agriculture, but over 2.3 million cattle graze the dry grasslands. Diamonds, copper, nickel and gold are mined in the east and are the main mineral exports. The growth of light industries around the capital has stimulated trade with neighbouring countries.

BOUGAINVILLE ISLAND

STATUS: Part of Papua New Guinea
AREA: 10,620 sq km (4,100 sq miles)
POPULATION: 159,100
CAPITAL: Arawa

BRAZIL

STATUS: Federal Republic
AREA: 8,511,965 sq km (3,285,620 sq miles)
POPULATION: 155,600,000
ANNUAL NATURAL INCREASE: 2.2%
CAPITAL: Brasilia
LANGUAGE: Portuguese
RELIGION: 90% Roman Catholic. Protestant minority
CURRENCY: cruzeiro (BRC)
ORGANISATIONS: UN, OAS

Brazil is not only the largest country in South America but also has the fastest growing economy. Brazil is now an industrial power

but with development limited to the heavily populated urban areas of the eastern coastal lowlands. The Amazon basin tropical rain forest covers roughly one third of the country; savannah grasslands of the centre west give way to light forest – now much cleared – of the eastern Brazilian Highlands, and the cool southern plateau of the south. This varied landscape is dominated by three river systems of the Amazon, São Francisco and Paraguay/Paraná. Economic variety reflects the changing landscape. In agricultural production Brazil is one of the world's leading exporters with coffee, soya beans, sugar, bananas, cocoa, tobacco, rice and cattle major commodities. Mineral resources, except for iron ore, at the moment do not play a significant role in the economy, but recent economic policies have concentrated on developing the industrial base – road and rail communications, on light and heavy industry and expansion of energy resources, particularly hydro-electric power harnessed from the great river systems.

BRUNEI

STATUS: Sultanate
AREA: 5,765 sq km (2,225 sq miles)
POPULATION: 266,000
ANNUAL NATURAL INCREASE: 3.3%
CAPITAL: Bandar Seri Begawan
LANGUAGE: Malay, English, Chinese
RELIGION: 65% Sunni Muslim. Buddhist and Christian minorities
CURRENCY: Brunei dollar (BND)
ORGANISATIONS: Comm, UN, ASEAN

The Sultanate of Brunei is situated on the north-west coast of Borneo. Its tropical climate is hot and humid with annual rainfall ranging from 250cm (98in) on the thin coastal strip to

500cm(197in) in the mountainous interior. Oil, both on-shore and off-shore is the mainstay of the Brunei economy. Other exports include natural gas, which is transported to Japan, rubber and timber. Apart from oil, most other industries are local.

BULGARIA

STATUS: Republic
AREA: 110,910 sq km (42,810 sq miles)
POPULATION: 9,011,000
ANNUAL NATURAL INCREASE: 0.2%
CAPITAL: Sofia (Sofiya)
LANGUAGE: Bulgarian, Turkish

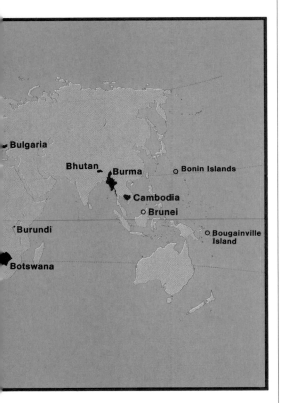

RELIGION: Eastern Orthodox majority, Muslim
CURRENCY: lev (BGL)
ORGANISATIONS: UN, OIEC

Bulgaria occupies the south-eastern portion of the Balkan peninsula and its landscape exhibits great variety, ranging from the fertile Danubian plain in the north and the mountainous central and southern parts with their high ranges, deep river gorges and extensive upland basins, to the Black Sea coastal region on the eastern fringe of the country. The climate is of the continental type with hot summers and cold winters. Bulgaria is not rich in natural resources but the Black Sea resorts contain much potential for development, as does the production and export of tobacco and wine. However, the communist regime has left the country with a disastrous ecological legacy. The political institutions of post-communist Bulgaria are still in a state of flux, and its society is undergoing a prolonged and painful crisis of transformation.

BURKINA

STATUS: Republic
AREA: 274,122 sq km (105,811 sq miles)
POPULATION: 9,001,000
ANNUAL NATURAL INCREASE: 2.6%
CAPITAL: Ouagadougou
LANGUAGE: French, Moré (Mossi), Dyula
RELIGION: 60% animist, 30% Muslim, 10% Roman Catholic
CURRENCY: CFA franc, (W Africa) (XOF)
ORGANISATIONS: UN, ECOWAS, OAU

Situated on the southern edge of the Sahara, Burkina is a poor, landlocked country with thin soils supporting savannah grasslands. Frequent droughts, particularly in the north, seriously affect exports of cattle and cotton and the economy which is mainly subsistence agriculture. There is virtually no industry.

BURMA

STATUS: Union of states and divisions
AREA: 678,030 sq km (261,720 sq miles)
POPULATION: 39,300,000
ANNUAL NATURAL INCREASE: 2.0%
CAPITAL: Rangoon (Yangon)
LANGUAGE: Burmese
RELIGION: 85% Buddhist. Animist, Muslim, Hindu and Christian minorities
CURRENCY: kyat (BUK)
ORGANISATIONS: UN, Col. Plan

Much of Burma is covered by tropical rainforest divided by the central valley of the Irrawaddy, the Sittang and the Salween rivers. The western highlands are an extension of the Himalayas; hills to the east and south are a continuation of the Yunnan plateau of China. The economy is based on the export of the rice and forestry products. The irrigated central basin and the coastal region to the east of the Irrawaddy delta are the main rice-growing areas. Hardwoods, particularly teak, cover the highlands. There is potential for greater exploitation of tin, copper, oil and natural gas deposits. The small amount of industry concentrates on food processing.

BURUNDI

STATUS: Republic
AREA: 27,835 sq km (10,745 sq miles)
POPULATION: 5,458,000
ANNUAL NATURAL INCREASE: 2.9%

CAPITAL: Bujumbura
LANGUAGE: French, Kirundi, Swahili
RELIGION: 60% Roman Catholic. Large animist minority
CURRENCY: Burundi franc (BIF)
ORGANISATIONS: UN, OAU

This central African republic is one of the world's poorest nations. Manufacturing industry is almost non-existent and the population barely produce enough food for itself. Burundi is close to the equator but because of its altitude temperatures range between 17° and 23°C (63° and 74°F). The poverty has two basic causes – repeated droughts and slow recovery from tribal conflicts.

CAMBODIA

STATUS: State
AREA: 181,000 sq km (69,865 sq miles)
POPULATION: 8,246,000
ANNUAL NATURAL INCREASE: 2.3%
CAPITAL: Phnom Penh
LANGUAGE: Khmer
RELIGION: Buddhist majority. Roman Catholic and Muslim minorities
CURRENCY: riel (KHR)
ORGANISATIONS: UN, Col. Plan

Cambodia is a potentially rich country in S.E. Asia whose economy has been damaged since the 1970's by the aftermath of the Vietnam War. The central plain of the river Mekong covers over 70% of the country and provides ideal conditions for rice production and harvesting of fish. Over 50% of Cambodia is covered by monsoon rain forest.

CAMEROON

STATUS: Republic
AREA: 475,500 sq km (183,545 sq miles)
POPULATION: 11,834,000
ANNUAL NATURAL INCREASE: 3.2%
CAPITAL: Yaoundé
LANGUAGE: English, French
RELIGION: 40% Christian, 39% traditional beliefs, 21% Muslim
CURRENCY: CFA franc (C Africa) (XAF)
ORGANISATIONS: UN, OAU

Cameroon is situated on the coast of West Africa just north of the equator. Coastal lowlands rise to densely forested plateaux. Rainfall varies from over 1000 to only 50cm per year. The majority of the population are farmers with agricultural products accounting for over 80% of export revenue. Coffee and cocoa are the main cash crops. Mineral resources are underdeveloped but Cameroon already is one of Africa's major producers of bauxite, aluminium ore. Oil exploitation is playing an increasing role in the economy.

CANADA

STATUS: Commonwealth Nation
AREA: 9,922,385 sq km (3,830,840 sq miles)
POPULATION: 26,800,000
ANNUAL NATURAL INCREASE: 1.0%
CAPITAL: Ottawa
LANGUAGE: English, French
RELIGION: 46% Roman Catholic, Protestant and Jewish minority
CURRENCY: Canadian dollar (CAD)
ORGANISATIONS: Comm, UN, Col. Plan, NATO, OECD, OAS, G7

ALBERTA
STATUS: Province
AREA: 661,190 sq km (255,220 sq miles)
POPULATION: 2,468,000
CAPITAL: Edmonton

BRITISH COLUMBIA
STATUS: Province
AREA: 948,595 sq km (366,160 sq miles)
POPULATION: 3,168,000
CAPITAL: Victoria

MANITOBA
STATUS: Province
AREA: 650,090 sq km (250,935 sq miles)
POPULATION: 1,096,000
CAPITAL: Winnipeg

NEW BRUNSWICK
STATUS: Province
AREA: 73,435 sq km (28,345 sq miles)
POPULATION: 723,000
CAPITAL: Fredericton

NEWFOUNDLAND AND LABRADOR
STATUS: Province
AREA: 404,520 sq km (156,145 sq miles)
POPULATION: 573,000
CAPITAL: St. John's

NORTHWEST TERRITORIES
STATUS: Territory
AREA: 3,379,685 sq km (1,304,560 sq miles)
POPULATION: 54,000
CAPITAL: Yellowknife

NOVA SCOTIA
STATUS: Province
AREA: 55,490 sq km (21,420 sq miles)
POPULATION: 897,000
CAPITAL: Halifax

ONTARIO
STATUS: Province
AREA: 1,068,630 sq km (412,490 sq miles)
POPULATION: 9,880,000
CAPITAL: Toronto

PRINCE EDWARD ISLAND
STATUS: Province
AREA: 5,655 sq km (2,185 sq miles)
POPULATION: 132,000
CAPITAL: Charlottetown

QUEBEC
STATUS: Province
AREA: 1,540,680 sq km (594,705 sq miles)
POPULATION: 6,779,000
CAPITAL: Quebec

SASKATCHEWAN
STATUS: Province
AREA: 651,900 sq km (251,635 sq miles)
POPULATION: 1,005,000
CAPITAL: Regina

YUKON TERRITORY
STATUS: Territory
AREA: 482,515 sq km (186,250 sq miles)
POPULATION: 27,000
CAPITAL: Whitehorse

Canada is the world's second largest country stretching from the great barren islands of the Arctic north to the vast grasslands of the central south, and from the Rocky Mountain chain of the west to the farmlands of the Great Lakes in the east. This huge area experiences great climatic differences but basically a continental climate prevails with extremes of heat and cold particularly in the central plains. The Arctic tundra of the far north provides summer grazing for caribou. Further south coniferous forests grow on the thin soils of the ancient shield landscape and on the extensive foothills of the Rocky Mountains. In contrast, the rich soils of the central prairies support grasslands and grain crops. The Great Lakes area provides fish, fruit, maize, root crops and dairy products; the prairies produce over 20% of the world's wheat; and the grasslands of Alberta support a thriving beef industry. Most minerals are mined and exploited in Canada with oil and natural gas, iron ore, bauxite, nickel, zinc, copper, gold and silver the major exports. The country's vast rivers provide huge amounts of hydro-electric power but most industry is confined to the Great Lakes and St Lawrence margins. The principal manufactured goods for export are steel products, motor vehicles, and paper for newsprint. Despite economic success, Canada still remains one of the world's most under-exploited countries so vast are the potential mineral resources and areas of land for agricultural development.

CANARY ISLANDS
STATUS: Island Provinces of Spain
AREA: 7,275 sq km (2,810 sq miles)
POPULATION: 1,589,403
CAPITAL: Las Palmas (Gran Canaria) and Santa Cruz (Tenerife)

CAPE VERDE

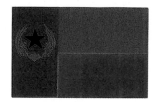

STATUS: Republic
AREA: 4,035 sq km (1,560 sq miles)
POPULATION: 370,000
ANNUAL NATURAL INCREASE: 2.5%
CAPITAL: Praia
LANGUAGE: Portuguese, Creole
RELIGION: 98% Roman Catholic
CURRENCY: Cape Verde escudo (CVE)
ORGANISATIONS: UN, ECOWAS, OAU

Independent since 1975, the ten inhabited volcanic islands of the republic are situated in the Atlantic 500km (310 miles) west of Senegal. Rainfall is low but irrigation encourages growth of sugar-cane, coconuts, fruit and maize. Fishing accounts for about 70% of export revenue. All consumer goods are imported and trading links continue to be maintained with Portugal.

CAYMAN ISLANDS
STATUS: UK Dependent Territory
AREA: 259 sq km (100 sq miles)
POPULATION: 27,000
CAPITAL: George Town

CENTRAL AFRICAN REPUBLIC

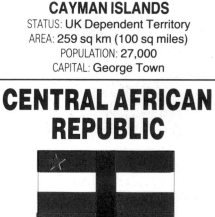

STATUS: Republic
AREA: 624,975 sq km (241,240 sq miles)
POPULATION: 3,039,000
ANNUAL NATURAL INCREASE: 2.7%
CAPITAL: Bangui
LANGUAGE: French, Sango (national)
RELIGION: Animist majority. 33% Christian. Muslim minority
CURRENCY: CFA franc (C Africa) (XAF)
ORGANISATIONS: UN, OAU

The republic is landlocked and remote from both east and west Africa. In size it rivals France, its former colonial power. It has a tropical climate with little variation in temperature. Savannah covers the rolling plateaux with rainforest in the south-east. To the north lies the Sahara Desert. Most farming is at subsistence level with a small amount of crops grown for export – cotton, coffee, timber and tobacco. Diamonds and uranium ore are the major mineral exports along with some small quantities of gold. Hardwood forests in the south-west provide timber for export.

CEUTA
STATUS: Spanish External Province
AREA: 19.5 sq km (7.5 sq miles)
POPULATION: 68,970

CHAD

STATUS: Republic
AREA: 1,284,000 sq km (495,625 sq miles)
POPULATION: 5,679,000
ANNUAL NATURAL INCREASE: 2.4%
CAPITAL: Ndjamena
LANGUAGE: French, Arabic, local languages

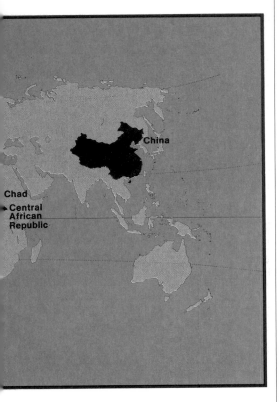

RELIGION: 50% Muslim, 45% animist,
5% Christian
CURRENCY: CFA franc (C Africa) (XAF)
ORGANISATIONS: UN, OAU

Chad, one of the world's poorest countries, is a vast state of central Africa stretching deep into the Sahara. The economy is based on agriculture but only the south, with 100 cm (39 in) of rainfall, can support crops for export – cotton, rice and groundnuts. Severe droughts, increasing desertification and border disputes have severely restricted development. Life expectancy at birth is still only 43 years. Salt is mined around Lake Chad where the majority of the population live.

CHANNEL ISLANDS
STATUS: British Crown Dependency
AREA: 194 sq km (75 sq miles)
POPULATION: 138,668
CAPITAL: St Helier (Jersey),
St Peter Port (Guernsey)

CHILE

STATUS: Republic
AREA: 751,625 sq km (290,125 sq miles)
POPULATION: 13,173,000
ANNUAL NATURAL INCREASE: 1.7%
CAPITAL: Santiago
LANGUAGE: Spanish
RELIGION: 85% Roman Catholic. Protestant
minority
CURRENCY: Chilean peso (CLP)
ORGANISATIONS: UN, OAS

Chile is a long thin country on the west coast of South America stretching throughout 38° degrees of latitude from the Atacama desert of the north to the ice deserts of Tierra del Fuego. Apart from a thin coastal strip of lowland, the country is dominated by the Andes mountains. The economy is based upon the abundance of mineral resources with copper (the world's largest reserve), iron ore, nitrates, coal, oil and gas all major exports. Most energy is provided by hydro-electric power. Light and heavy industries are based around Concepción and Santiago.

CHINA

STATUS: People's Republic
AREA: 9,597,000 sq km (3,704,440 sq miles)
POPULATION: 1,088,870,000
ANNUAL NATURAL INCREASE: 1.3%
CAPITAL: Beijing (Peking)
LANGUAGE: Mandarin Chinese, regional
languages
RELIGION: Confucianist, Buddhist, Taoist. Small
Christian and Muslim minority
CURRENCY: Yuan Renminbi (CNY)
ORGANISATIONS: UN

ANHUI (ANHWEI)
STATUS: Province
AREA: 139,900 sq km (54,000 sq miles)
POPULATION: 53,770,000
CAPITAL: Hefei

BEIJING (PEKING)
STATUS: Municipality
AREA: 17,800 sq km (6,870 sq miles)
POPULATION: 10,819,407

FUJIAN (FUKIEN)
STATUS: Province
AREA: 123,000 sq km (47,515 sq miles)
POPULATION: 28,450,000
CAPITAL: Fuzhou

GANSU (KANSU)
STATUS: Province
AREA: 530,000 sq km (204,580 sq miles)
POPULATION: 21,360,000
CAPITAL: Lanzhou

GUANGDONG (KWANGTUNG)
STATUS: Province
AREA: 231,400 sq km (89,320 sq miles)
POPULATION: 59,280,000
CAPITAL: Guangzhou (Canton)

GUANGXI-ZHUANG (KWANGSI-CHUANG)
STATUS: Autonomous Region
AREA: 220,400 sq km (85,075 sq miles)
POPULATION: 40,880,000
CAPITAL: Nanning

GUIZHOU (KWEICHOW)
STATUS: Province
AREA: 174,000 sq km (67,165 sq miles)
POPULATION: 31,270,000
CAPITAL: Guiyang

HAINAN
STATUS: Province
AREA: 34,965 sq km (13,500 sq miles)
POPULATION: 6,280,000
CAPITAL: Haikou

HEBEI (HOPEI)
STATUS: Province
AREA: 202,700 sq km (78,240 sq miles)
POPULATION: 57,950,000
CAPITAL: Shijiazhuang

HEILONGJIANG (HEILUNGKIANG)
STATUS: Province
AREA: 710,000 sq km (274,060 sq miles)
POPULATION: 34,660,000
CAPITAL: Harbin

HENAN (HONAN)
STATUS: Province
AREA: 167,000 sq km (64,460 sq miles)
POPULATION: 80,940,000
CAPITAL: Zhengzhou

HUBEI (HUPEH)
STATUS: Province
AREA: 187,500 sq km (72,375 sq miles)
POPULATION: 51,850,000
CAPITAL: Wuhan

HUNAN (HUNAN)
STATUS: Province
AREA: 210,500 sq km (81,255 sq miles)
POPULATION: 58,900,000
CAPITAL: Changsha

JIANGSU (KIANGSU)
STATUS: Province
AREA: 102,200 sq km (39,450 sq miles)
POPULATION: 64,380,000
CAPITAL: Nanjing (Nanking)

JIANGXI (KIANGSI)
STATUS: Province
AREA: 164,800 sq km (63,615 sq miles)
POPULATION: 36,090,000
CAPITAL: Nanchang

JILIN (KIRIN)
STATUS: Province
AREA: 290,000 sq km (111,940 sq miles)
POPULATION: 23,730,000
CAPITAL: Changchun

LIAONING
STATUS: Province
AREA: 230,000 sq km (88,780 sq miles)
POPULATION: 38,200,000
CAPITAL: Shenyang

NEI MONGOL (INNER MONGOLIA)
STATUS: Autonomous Region
AREA: 450,000 sq km (173,700 sq miles)
POPULATION: 20,940,000
CAPITAL: Hohhot

NINGXIA HUI (NINGHSIA HUI)
STATUS: Autonomous Region
AREA: 170,000 sq km (65,620 sq miles)
POPULATION: 4,450,000
CAPITAL: Yinchuan

QINGHAI (CHINGHAI)
STATUS: Province
AREA: 721,000 sq km (278,305 sq miles)
POPULATION: 4,340,000
CAPITAL: Xining

SHAANXI (SHENSI)
STATUS: Province
AREA: 195,800 sq km (75,580 sq miles)
POPULATION: 31,350,000
CAPITAL: Xian

SHANDONG (SHANTUNG)
STATUS: Province
AREA: 153,300 sq km (59,175 sq miles)
POPULATION: 80,610,000
CAPITAL: Jinan

SHANGHAI
STATUS: Municipality
AREA: 5,800 sq km (2,240 sq miles)
POPULATION: 13,341,896

SHANXI (SHANSI)
STATUS: Province
AREA: 157,100 sq km (60,640 sq miles)
POPULATION: 27,550,000
CAPITAL: Taiyuan

SICHUAN (SZECHWAN)
STATUS: Province
AREA: 569,000 sq km (219,635 sq miles)
POPULATION: 105,760,000
CAPITAL: Chengdu

TIANJIN (TIENTSIN)
STATUS: Municipality
AREA: 4,000 sq km (1,545 sq miles)
POPULATION: 8,785,402

XINJIANG UYGUR (SINKIANG UIGHUR)
STATUS: Autonomous Region
AREA: 1,646,800 sq km (635,665 sq miles)
POPULATION: 14,260,000
CAPITAL: Urumqi

XIZANG (TIBET)
STATUS: Autonomous Region
AREA: 1,221,600 sq km (471,540 sq miles)
POPULATION: 2,120,000
CAPITAL: Lhasa

YUNNAN (YUNNAN)
STATUS: Province
AREA: 436,200 sq km (168,375 sq miles)
POPULATION: 35,940,000
CAPITAL: Kunming

ZHEJIANG (CHEKIANG)
STATUS: Province
AREA: 101,800 sq km (39,295 sq miles)
POPULATION: 41,700,000
CAPITAL: Hangzhou

With population over one billion and vast mineral and agricultural resources China has made a tremendous effort during the late 1970's and 80's to erase the negative economic effects of the collectivisation policy implemented from 1955, and the cultural revolution of the late 1960's.

The land of China is one of the most diverse on Earth. The majority of the people live in the east where the economy is dictated by the great drainage basins of the Huang He and the Chang Jiang (Yangtze). Here, intensive irrigated agriculture produces one third of the world's rice as well as wheat, maize, sugar, soya beans and oil seeds. Pigs are reared and fish caught throughout China. The country is basically self-sufficient in cereals, livestock and fish.

Western and northern China are far less densely populated areas as cultivation is restricted to oases and sheltered valleys. In the south-west, the Tibetan plateau averages 4,900 m (16,000 ft) and supports scattered sheep herding. To the north are Sinkiang and the desert basins of Tarim and Dzungaria, and bordering Mongolia the vast dry Gobi desert. In the far north only in Manchuria does the rainfall allow extensive arable cultivation, mainly wheat, barley and maize.

The natural mineral resources of China are immense, varied and under-exploited. The Yunnan Plateau of the south-east is rich in tin, copper, and zinc; Manchuria possesses coal and iron ore; and oil is extracted from beneath the Yellow Sea. The main industrial centres are situated close to the natural resources and concentrate on the production of iron, steel, cement, light engineering and textile manufacturing. The economy is being built on this industrial base, with stable and adequate food production and increasing trade with the United States, Western Europe and Japan.

CHRISTMAS ISLAND
STATUS: External Territory of Australia
AREA: 135 sq km (52 sq miles)
POPULATION: 2,000

COCOS (KEELING) ISLANDS
STATUS: External Territory of Australia
AREA: 14 sq km (5 sq miles)
POPULATION: 616

COLOMBIA

STATUS: Republic
AREA: 1,138,915 sq km (439,620 sq miles)
POPULATION: 32,987,000
ANNUAL NATURAL INCREASE: 2.1%
CAPITAL: Bogotá
LANGUAGE: Spanish, Indian languages
RELIGION: 95% Roman Catholic. Small Protestant and Jewish minorities
CURRENCY: Colombian peso (COP)
ORGANISATIONS: UN, OAS

Colombia is bounded in the north by the Caribbean Sea and in the west by the Pacific Ocean. The Andes chain runs from north to south through the country. The eastern part of the country consists of the headwaters of the Amazon and Orinoco basins. Two-thirds of Colombia is covered by tropical rainforest. The fertile river valleys in the uplands produce most of the famous Colombian coffee. Bananas, tobacco, cotton, sugar and rice are grown at lower altitudes. Coffee has always been the major export crop, but manufacturing industry and mining of coal, iron ore, copper and precious stones are becoming more dominant in the economy. Immense illegal quantities of cocaine are exported to the US and elsewhere.

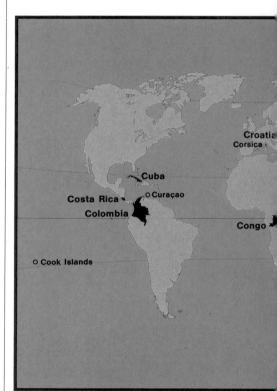

COMOROS

STATUS: Federal Republic
AREA: 1,860 sq km (718 sq miles)
POPULATION: 551,000
ANNUAL NATURAL INCREASE: 3.7%
CAPITAL: Moroni
LANGUAGE: French, Arabic, Comoran
RELIGION: large Muslim majority. Christian minority
CURRENCY: Comoro franc (KMF)
ORGANISATIONS: UN, OAU

The Comoro Islands, comprising Moheli, Grand Comore, and Anjouan, are situated between Madagascar and the east African coast. In 1974, the island of Mayotte voted in referenda

to remain a French dependency. A cool, dry season alternates with hot, humid monsoon weather between November and April, and annual rainfall ranges from 100–114cm(40–45in). Mangoes, coconuts and bananas are grown around the coastal lowlands. The island's economy is based on the export of coffee, vanilla, copra, sisal, cacao and cloves. Timber and timber products are important to local development. There is no manufacturing.

CONGO

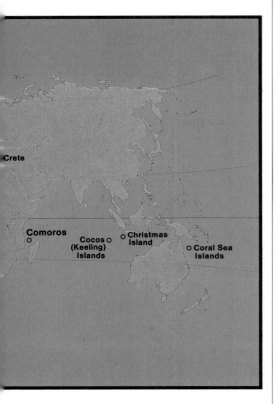

STATUS: People's Republic
AREA: 342,000 sq km (132,010 sq miles)
POPULATION: 2,271,000
ANNUAL NATURAL INCREASE: 3.4%
CAPITAL: Brazzaville
LANGUAGE: French, Kongo, Teke, Sanga
RELIGION: 50% traditional beliefs, 30% Roman Catholic. Small Protestant and Muslim minority
CURRENCY: CFA franc (C Africa) (XAF)
ORGANISATIONS: UN, OAU

The Congo, Africa's first communist state still has strong economic ties with the west, especially France, its former colonial ruler. Situated on the coast of West Africa, it contains over two-thirds swamp and forest, with wooded savannah on the highlands of the Batéké plateau near the Gabon border. Its climate is hot and humid with average rainfall of 122-128cm (48-50in). Over 60% of the population are employed in subsistence farming, the main crops being plantains, maize and cassava, while coffee, groundnuts and cocoa are all exported. Timber and timber products account for 60% of

all Congo's exports. Its mineral resources are considerable including industrial diamonds, gold, lead, zinc and extensive coastal oilfields. Manufacturing industry is concentrated in the major towns and is primarily food processing and textiles.

COOK ISLANDS
STATUS: Self-governing Overseas Territory in free association with New Zealand
AREA: 233 sq km (90 sq miles)
POPULATION: 19,000
CAPITAL: Avarua

CORAL SEA ISLANDS
STATUS: External Territory of Australia
AREA: 22 sq km (8.5 sq miles)
POPULATION: No permanent population

CORSICA
STATUS: Island Region of France
AREA: 8,680 sq km (3,350 sq miles)
POPULATION: 246,000
CAPITAL: Ajaccio

COSTA RICA

STATUS: Republic
AREA: 50,900 sq km (19,650 sq miles)
POPULATION: 2,994,000
ANNUAL NATURAL INCREASE: 2.3%
CAPITAL: San Jose
LANGUAGE: Spanish
RELIGION: 95% Roman Catholic
CURRENCY: Costa Rican colón (CRC)
ORGANISATIONS: UN, CACM, OAS

Costa Rica is a narrow country, situated between Nicaragua and Panama, with both a Pacific and a Caribbean coastline. The mountain chains that run the length of the country form the fertile uplands where coffee (one of the main crops and exports) and cattle flourish. Bananas are grown on the Pacific coast. Although gold, silver, iron ore and bauxite are mined, the principal industries are food processing and manufacture of textiles and chemicals, fertilizers and furniture.

CRETE
STATUS: Island Region of Greece
AREA: 8,330 sq km (3,215 sq miles)
POPULATION: 501,082
CAPITAL: Iráklion

CROATIA

STATUS: Republic
AREA: 56,540 sq km (21,825 sq miles)
POPULATION: 4,726,000
CAPITAL: Zagreb
LANGUAGE: Croat
RELIGION: Roman Catholic majority
CURRENCY: Croatian dinar

Croatia is an oddly-shaped country, which runs in a narrow strip along the Adriatic coast and extends inland in a broad curve. The fertile plains of central and eastern Croatia are intensively farmed and provide the country with surplus crops, meat and dairy products. The mountainous and barren littoral has been developed for tourism. Croatia used to be the most highly developed part of Yugoslavia, concentrating on electrical engineering, metalworking and machine-building, chemicals and rubber. All of this could mean future prosperity but the disruption of Croatia's trade with other parts of Yugoslavia and with the former Eastern Bloc has severely harmed the economy. The military conflict over the right to secession and for control of Serbian areas of settlement has caused further damage, with tourism all but collapsing in 1991.

CUBA

STATUS: Republic
AREA: 114,525 sq km (44,205 sq miles)
POPULATION: 10,617,000
ANNUAL NATURAL INCREASE: 0.9%
CAPITAL: Havana (Habana)
LANGUAGE: Spanish
RELIGION: Roman Catholic majority
CURRENCY: Cuban peso (CUP)
ORGANISATIONS: UN, OIEC

Cuba, consisting of one large island and over fifteen hundred small ones, dominates the entrance to the Gulf of Mexico. It is a mixture of fertile plains, mountain ranges and gentle countryside with temperatures ranging from 22°-28°C (72°–82°F) and an average annual rainfall of 120cm (47in). Being the only communist state in the Americas, most of Cuba's trade relations are with the former USSR and Comecon countries. Sugar, tobacco and nickel are the main exports and the mining of manganese, chrome, copper and oil is expanding. Cuba has enough cattle and coffee for domestic use but many other food products are imported.

CURAÇAO
STATUS: Self-governing Island of Netherlands Antilles
AREA: 444 sq km (171 sq miles)
POPULATION: 146,096
CAPITAL: Willemstad

CYPRUS

STATUS: Republic
AREA: 9,250 sq km (3,570 sq miles)
POPULATION: 707,000
ANNUAL NATURAL INCREASE: 1.1%
CAPITAL: Nicosia
LANGUAGE: Greek, Turkish, English
RELIGION: Greek Orthodox majority, Muslim minority
CURRENCY: Cyprus pound (CYP), Turkish Lira (TL)
ORGANISATIONS: Comm, UN, Council of Europe

Cyprus is a prosperous Mediterranean island. The summers are very hot (38°C, 100°F) and dry, and the winters warm and wet. About two-thirds of the island is under cultivation and produces citrus fruit, potatoes, barley, wheat and olives. Sheep, goats and pigs are the principal livestock. The main exports are minerals (including copper and asbestos), fruit, wine and vegetables. Tourism is also an important source of foreign exchange, despite Turkish occupation of the north. Most industry consists of local manufacturing.

CZECHOSLOVAKIA

STATUS: Federal Republic
AREA: 127,870 sq km (49,360 sq miles)
POPULATION: 15,678,000
ANNUAL NATURAL INCREASE: 0.3%
CAPITAL: Prague (Praha)
LANGUAGE: Czech, Slovak
RELIGION: 70% Roman Catholic, 8% Protestant
CURRENCY: koruna (CSK)
ORGANISATIONS: UN, OIEC, Council of Europe

At the heart of central Europe, Czechoslovakia is fringed by forested uplands in the west and the Carpathians to the east. Winters are cold and wet, while summers are hot and humid with frequent thundery showers. In spite of limited raw materials, Czechoslovakia has long been one of the more advanced European economies, a position which it managed to retain through the communist period. The country boasts a very productive and efficient agricultural sector as well as a comparatively healthy industrial base. Engineering is the largest branch of production, and Czechoslovakia used to be the most important supplier of machinery to the Eastern Bloc. It is also a significant exporter of armaments and explosives, but with the end of the Cold War and the collapse of communism, the country is now facing severe problems of adaptation. Moreover, the mounting tension between Czechs and Slovaks has been threatening to lead to a break-up of the country into two separate states.

DENMARK

STATUS: Kingdom
AREA: 43,075 sq km (16,625 sq miles)
POPULATION: 5,140,000
ANNUAL NATURAL INCREASE: 0.0%
CAPITAL: Copenhagen (København)
LANGUAGE: Danish
RELIGION: 94% Lutheran. Roman Catholic minority
CURRENCY: Danish krone (DKK)
ORGANISATIONS: UN, Council of Europe, NATO, OECD, EC

Denmark, the smallest of the Scandinavian countries, acts as a bridge between Germany and Scandinavia. It consists of the Jutland Peninsula and over 400 islands of which only about one quarter are inhabited. The low-lying landscape was scarred by retreating glaciers leaving distinctive 'moraines' (accumulations of earth and stones carried by glaciers). The climate is mild, especially in the North Sea area, with rainfall all year round, mostly in the summer and autumn. Meat and dairy products – beef, butter, cheese, eggs, bacon and pork are exported but not in such great quantities as in the past. An extensive fishing industry is centred on the shallow lagoons which have formed along the indented western coastline. Recently the fishing industry has had problems with over-fishing and disputes over quotas. Over 30% of the total workforce are involved in industry, with manufactured goods being the main export. Denmark has few mineral resources.

DJIBOUTI

STATUS: Republic
AREA: 23,000 sq km (8,800 sq miles)
POPULATION: 409,000
ANNUAL NATURAL INCREASE: 3.5%
CAPITAL: Djibouti
LANGUAGE: French, Somali, Dankali, Arabic
RELIGION: mainly Muslim. Roman Catholic minority
CURRENCY: Djibouti franc (DJF)
ORGANISATIONS: UN, Arab League, OAU

The former French colony of Djibouti, strategically situated at the mouth of the Red Sea, acts as a trade outlet for Ethiopia, as well as serving Red Sea shipping. Its climate is extremely hot and arid – average annual temperatures are 30°C(86°F) and the annual rainfall on the coast is as low as 38cm(15in), and there is consequently very little cultivation. Cattle, hides and skins are the main exports. The port of Djibouti is an important transit point for Red Sea trade.

DOMINICA

STATUS: Commonwealth State
AREA: 751 sq km (290 sq miles)
POPULATION: 81,200
ANNUAL NATURAL INCREASE: 1.4%
CAPITAL: Roseau
LANGUAGE: English, French patois
RELIGION: 80% Roman Catholic
CURRENCY: East Caribbean dollar (XCD)
ORGANISATIONS: Comm, UN, CARICOM, OAS

Dominica is located in the Windward Islands of the east Caribbean between Martinique and Guadeloupe. Tropical rainforest covers the island which obtains foreign revenue from sugar cane, bananas, coconuts, soap, vegetables and citrus fruits. Tourism is the most rapidly expanding industry.

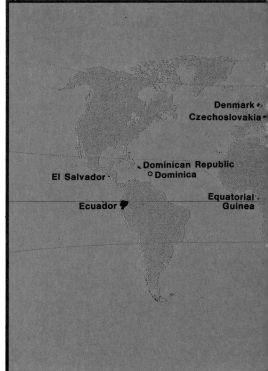

DOMINICAN REPUBLIC

STATUS: Republic
AREA: 48,440 sq km (18,700 sq miles)
POPULATION: 7,170,000
ANNUAL NATURAL INCREASE: 2.3%
CAPITAL: Santo Domingo
LANGUAGE: Spanish
RELIGION: 90% Roman Catholic. Small Protestant and Jewish minority
CURRENCY: Dominican peso (DOP)
ORGANISATIONS: UN, OAS

The Caribbean island of Hispaniola is divided between Haiti and the Dominican Republic. The landscape is dominated by a series of mountain ranges, thickly covered with rain forest, reaching up to 3000m(9840ft). To the south there is a coastal plain where the capital, Santo Domingo, lies. The annual rainfall exceeds 100cm(40in). Agriculture forms the backbone of the economy – sugar, coffee, cocoa and tobacco are the staple crops. Minerals include bauxite, nickel, gold and silver.

ECUADOR

STATUS: Republic
AREA: 461,475 sq km (178,130 sq miles)
POPULATION: 10,782,000

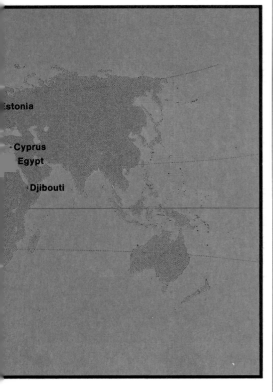

ANNUAL NATURAL INCREASE: 2.7%
CAPITAL: Quito
LANGUAGE: Spanish, Quechua, other Indian languages
RELIGION: 90% Roman Catholic
CURRENCY: sucre (ECS)
ORGANISATIONS: UN, OAS, OPEC

Ecuador falls into two distinctive geographical zones, the coastal lowlands which border the Pacific Ocean and inland, the Andean highlands. The highlands stretch about 400km (250 miles) north–south, and here limited quantities of maize, wheat and barley are cultivated. Ecuador's main agricultural exports – bananas, coffee and cocoa, are all grown on the fertile coastal lowlands. The rapidly growing fishing industry, especially shrimps, is becoming more important. Large resources of crude oil have been found in the thickly-forested lowlands on the eastern border. Ecuador is now South America's second largest oil producer after Venezuela. Mineral reserves include silver, gold, copper and zinc.

EGYPT

STATUS: Republic
AREA: 1,000,250 sq km (386,095 sq miles)
POPULATION: 53,153,000
ANNUAL NATURAL INCREASE: 2.6%
CAPITAL: Cairo (El Qâhira)
LANGUAGE: Arabic, Berber, Nubian, English, French
RELIGION: 80% Muslim (mainly Sunni), Coptic Christian minority
CURRENCY: Egyptian pound (EGP)
ORGANISATIONS: UN, Arab League, OAU

The focal point of Egypt, situated on the Mediterranean coast of north-east Africa, is the fertile, irrigated Nile Valley, sandwiched between two deserts. Egypt is virtually dependent on the River Nile for water as average rainfall varies between only 20cm (8 in) in the north and zero in the deserts. Cotton and Egyptian clover are the two most important crops, with increasing cultivation of cereals, fruits, rice, sugar cane and vegetables. Agriculture is concentrated around the Nile flood plain and delta. In spite of this, however, Egypt has to import over half the food it needs. Buffalo, cattle, sheep, goats and camels are the principal livestock. Tourism is an important source of revenue together with tolls from the Suez Canal. Major manufactures include cement, cotton goods, iron and steel, and processed foods. The main mineral deposits are phosphates, iron ore, salt, manganese and chromium.

EL SALVADOR

STATUS: Republic
AREA: 21,395 sq km (8,260 sq miles)
POPULATION: 5,252,000
ANNUAL NATURAL INCREASE: 1.4%
CAPITAL: San Salvador
LANGUAGE: Spanish
RELIGION: 80% Roman Catholic
CURRENCY: El Salvador colón (SVC)
ORGANISATIONS: UN, CACM, OAS

Independent from Spain since 1821, El Salvador is a small, densely populated country on the Pacific coast of Central America. Most of the population live around the lakes in the central plain. Temperatures range from 24° to 26°C (75°–79°F) with an average, annual rainfall of 178cm (70 in). Coffee and cotton are important exports and the country is the main producer of balsam. Industry has expanded considerably with the production of textiles, shoes, cosmetics, cement, processed foods, chemicals and furniture. Mineral resources are negligible.

EQUATORIAL GUINEA

STATUS: Republic
AREA: 28,050 sq km (10,825 sq miles)
POPULATION: 348,000
ANNUAL NATURAL INCREASE: 5.1%
CAPITAL: Malabo
LANGUAGE: Spanish, Fang, Bubi, other tribal languages
RELIGION: 96% Roman Catholic. 4% animist
CURRENCY: CFA franc (C Africa) (XAF)
ORGANISATIONS: UN, OAU

Independent from Spain since 1968, Equatorial Guinea is made up of two separate provinces – mainland Mbini with hot, wet climate and dense rain forest but little economic development, and the volcanic island of Bioko. Agriculture is the principal source of revenue. Cocoa and coffee from the island plantations are the main exports with wood products, fish and processed foods manufactured near the coast in Mbini.

ESTONIA

STATUS: Republic
AREA: 45,100 sq km (17,413 sq miles)
POPULATION: 1,600,000
CAPITAL: Tallinn
LANGUAGE: Estonian, Russian
RELIGION: Lutheran, Roman Catholic and Orthodox minorities
CURRENCY: rouble, kroon (1992)
ORGANISATIONS: UN

With the mainland situated on the southern coast of the Gulf of Finland and encompassing a large number of islands, Estonia is the smallest and most northerly of the Baltic States. The generally flat or undulating landscape is characterised by extensive forests and many lakes. The country's mean altitude is only 49m (160ft) above sea level and nowhere exceeds 305m (1000ft). The climate is temperate. Estonia is poor in natural resources, the only deposits of importance being oil shale and phosphorite. The land is difficult to farm and agriculture, mainly livestock production, accounts for less than 20% of the gross national product. Industries include engineering and metalworking. Timber production, woodworking and textiles are also important. The economy is currently undergoing a profound transformation from central planning and state-ownership to a free market system based on private enterprise. Incorporated into the Soviet Union in 1940 Estonia, after a protracted struggle, was able to regain its independence in 1991.

ETHIOPIA

STATUS: Republic
AREA: 1,023,050 sq km (394,895 sq miles)
POPULATION: 50,774,000
ANNUAL NATURAL INCREASE: 2.9%
CAPITAL: Addis Ababa (Adis Abeba)
LANGUAGE: Amharic, English, Arabic
RELIGION: Ethiopian Orthodox, Muslim and animist
CURRENCY: birr (ETB)
ORGANISATIONS: UN, OAU

Situated on the Red Sea coast, the landscape of Ethiopia consists of heavily dissected plateaux and plains of arid desert. Rainfall in these latter areas is minimal and unreliable. Drought and starvation are an ever-present problem. Farming, in the high rural areas, accounts for 90% of export revenue with coffee as the principal crop and main export together with fruit and vegetables, oil-seeds, hides and skins. Gold and salt are mined on a small scale. The most important industries are cotton textiles, cement, canned foods, construction materials and leather goods. These are concentrated around the capital, and Asmara in the north. Difficulty of communication has hindered development. In recent years the economy has been devastated by droughts and civil wars.

FAEROES
STATUS: Self-governing Island Region of Denmark
AREA: 1,399 sq km (540 sq miles)
POPULATION: 47,663
CAPITAL: Tórshavn

FALKLAND ISLANDS
STATUS: UK Crown Colony
AREA: 12,175 sq km (4,700 sq miles)
POPULATION: 2,000
CAPITAL: (Port) Stanley

FIJI

STATUS: Republic
AREA: 18,330 sq km (7,075 sq miles)
POPULATION: 765,000
ANNUAL NATURAL INCREASE: 1.8%
CAPITAL: Suva
LANGUAGE: Fijian, English, Hindi
RELIGION: 51% Methodist Christian, 40% Hindu, 8% Muslim
CURRENCY: Fiji dollar (FJD)
ORGANISATIONS: UN, Col. Plan

A country of some 320 tropical islands, of which over 100 are inhabited, the Republic of Fiji is located in the south central Pacific Ocean. Fiji's economy is geared to production of sugar-cane, coconut oil, bananas and rice. Main industries are sugar processing, gold-mining, copra processing and fish canning. Important livestock are cattle, goats, pigs and poultry.

FINLAND

STATUS: Republic
AREA: 337,030 sq km (130,095 sq miles)
POPULATION: 4,986,000
ANNUAL NATURAL INCREASE: 0.4%
CAPITAL: Helsinki
LANGUAGE: Finnish, Swedish
RELIGION: 90% Evangelical Lutheran. Eastern Orthodox minority
CURRENCY: markka (Finnmark) (FIM)
ORGANISATIONS: UN, EFTA, OECD, Council of Europe

Finland is a flat land of lakes and forests. The soils are thin and poor on the ice-scarred granite plateau, but 80% of the country supports coniferous forest. Timber and timber products and dairy goods make up most of Finnish exports. Because of the harsh northern climate most of the population live in towns in the far south. Manufacturing industry has been developing rapidly in recent years.

FRANCE

STATUS: Republic
AREA: 543,965 sq km (209,970 sq miles)
POPULATION: 56,556,000
ANNUAL NATURAL INCREASE: 0.4%
CAPITAL: Paris
LANGUAGE: French
RELIGION: 90% Roman Catholic. Protestant, Muslim and Jewish minorities
CURRENCY: French franc (FRF)
ORGANISATIONS: UN, Council of Europe, EC, OECD, WEU, NATO, G7

France encompasses a great variety of landscapes, a series of high plateaux, mountain ranges and lowland basins. The Pyrenees form the border with Spain in the south-west, and the Jura mountains form a border with Switzerland. The highest mountain range is the Alps, south of the Jura.

The highest plateau is the Massif Central which rises to 1886m(6188ft). The Vosges plateau borders the plain of Alsace, and the third major plateau, Armorica, occupies the Brittany peninsula.

The French climate is moderated by proximity to the Atlantic, and is generally mild. The south has a Mediterranean climate with hot dry summers, the rest of the country has rain all year round. Much of the French countryside is agricultural. France is self-sufficient in cereals, dairy products, meat, fruit and vegetables, and a leading exporter of wheat, barley and sugarbeet. Wine is also a major export. France has reserves of coal, oil and natural gas, and is one of the world's leading producers of iron ore. It has large steel-making and chemical refining industries. Its vehicle, aeronautical and armaments industries are among the world's most

important. Leading light industries are fashion, perfumes and luxury goods. Most of its heavy industry is concentrated in the major industrial zone of the north-east.

FRANZ JOSEF LAND
STATUS: Islands of Russia
AREA: 16,575 sq km (6,400 sq miles)
POPULATION: No reliable figure available

FRENCH GUIANA
STATUS: Overseas Department of France
AREA: 91,000 sq km (35,125 sq miles)
POPULATION: 93,540
CAPITAL: Cayenne

FRENCH POLYNESIA
STATUS: Overseas Territory of France
AREA: 3,940 sq km (1,520 sq miles)
POPULATION: 188,814
CAPITAL: Papeete

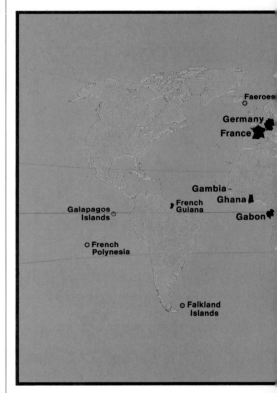

FRENCH SOUTHERN AND ANTARCTIC TERRITORIES
STATUS: Overseas Territory of France
AREA: 439,580 sq km (169,680 sq miles)
POPULATION: 180

GABON

STATUS: Republic
AREA: 267,665 sq km (103,320 sq miles)
POPULATION: 1,172,000
ANNUAL NATURAL INCREASE: 3.7%
CAPITAL: Libreville
LANGUAGE: French, Bantu dialects, Fang
RELIGION: 60% Roman Catholic
CURRENCY: CFA franc (C Africa) (XAF)

ORGANISATIONS: UN, OAU, OPEC

Gabon, which lies on the equator, consists of the Ogooúe river basin covered with tropical rain forest. It is hot and wet all year with average annual temperatures of 25°C(77°F). It is one of the most prosperous states in Africa with valuable timber and mineral resources.

GALAPAGOS ISLANDS
STATUS: Archipelago Province of Ecuador
AREA: 7,845 sq km (3,030 sq miles)
POPULATION: 7,954

GAMBIA, THE

STATUS: Republic

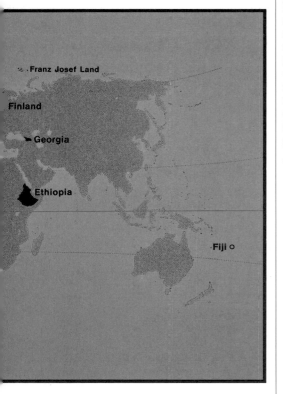

AREA: 10,690 sq km (4,125 sq miles)
POPULATION: 861,000
ANNUAL NATURAL INCREASE: 3.3%
CAPITAL: Banjul
LANGUAGE: English, Madinka, Fula, Wolof
RELIGION: 85% Muslim. Christian and
animist minorities
CURRENCY: dalasi (GMD)
ORGANISATIONS: Comm, UN, ECOWAS, OAU

The Gambia is the smallest country in Africa and, apart from its Atlantic coastline, is entirely surrounded by Senegal. It is 470km(292 miles) long, averages 24km(15 miles) wide and is divided by the Gambia river. The climate has two distinctive seasons. November to May is dry but July to October sees monsoon rainfall up to 130cm(51in). The temperatures average about 23°–27°C(73°–81°F) throughout the year. Groundnuts and subsidiary products are the mainstay of the economy but tourism is developing rapidly. The production of cotton, livestock, fish and rice is increasing to change the present economic reliance on groundnuts.

GEORGIA

STATUS: Republic
AREA: 69,700 sq km (26,905 sq miles)
POPULATION: 5,400,000
CAPITAL: Tbilisi
LANGUAGE: Georgian, Armenian, Russian
RELIGION: Orthodox Christian
CURRENCY: rouble

Georgia, situated south of the Caucasus, is a mountainous country with forests covering one-third of its area. The climate ranges from sub-tropical on the shores of the Black Sea, to perpetual ice and snow on the Caucasian crests. Rich deposits of coal, petroleum and manganese, and considerable water-power resources, have led to industrialisation successfully concentrated on metallurgy and machine-building. With the exception of the fertile plain of Kolkhida, agricultural land is in short supply and difficult to work. This is partly compensated by the cultivation of labour-intensive and profitable crops such as tea, grapes, tobacco and citrus fruit. The question of regional autonomy for the Abkhaz, Adzhar and South Ossetian minorities has repeatedly led to violent ethnic conflict in recent years. The break-up of the Soviet Union brought independence for Georgia in 1991.

GERMANY

STATUS: Federal Republic
AREA: 356,840 sq km (137,740 sq miles)
POPULATION: 78,500,000
ANNUAL NATURAL INCREASE: 0.2%
CAPITAL: Berlin
SEAT OF GOVERNMENT: Bonn, moving to Berlin
LANGUAGE: German
RELIGION: 45% Protestant (mostly Lutheran),
40% Roman Catholic
CURRENCY: Deutsch Mark (DEM)
ORGANISATIONS: UN, EC, NATO, OECD, WEU,
Council of Europe, G7

Geographically, Germany divides into three main areas: the Northern plain, stretching from the rivers Oder and Neisse in the east to the Dutch border; the central uplands with elevated plateaux intersected by river valleys and relieved by isolated mountains, gradually getting higher towards the south and rising to peaks of up to nearly 1500m (5000ft) in the Black Forest: finally the Bavarian Alps straddling the Austrian border. With the exception of the Danube, all German river systems run north and issue into the North or the Baltic Seas. The climate in Germany is predominantly continental with cold, wet winters and moderately warm summers. Only in the north-western corner of the country does the weather become more oceanic in character. Germany as a whole has large stretches of very fertile farmland.

Politically, the division of Germany, a product of the post-1945 Cold War between the victorious Allies against Hitler, was rapidly overcome after the collapse of communism in Eastern Europe, and the unification of the two German states was effected in 1990. Economically, the legacy of 40 years of socialist rule in the East ensures that, in terms of both structure and performance, Germany will encompass two vastly different halves for a long time to come. Having lost its captive markets in what used to be the Soviet Bloc, the eastern economy then all but collapsed under the weight of superior western competition. The task of reconstruction is proving more difficult, more protracted and, most of all, more costly than expected. In the West, the Ruhr basin, historically the industrial heartland of Germany, with its emphasis on coal mining and iron and steel works, has long since been overtaken by more advanced industries elsewhere, notably in the Rhine-Maine area and further south in the regions around Stuttgart and Munich. The rapidly expanding services sector apart, the German economy is now dominated by the chemical, pharmaceutical, mechanical engineering, motor and high-tech industries. To lessen the country's dependence on oil imports, an ambitious nuclear energy programme has been adopted. Although poor in minerals and other raw materials with the exception of lignite and potash, Germany has managed to become one of the world's leading manufacturers and exporters of vehicles, machine tools, electrical and electronic products and of consumer goods of various description, in particular textiles. But the massive balance of trade surplus West Germany used to enjoy has now disappeared due to the sucking in of imports by, and the redistribution of output to, the newly acquired territories in the East.

GHANA

STATUS: Republic
AREA: 238,305 sq km (91,985 sq miles)
POPULATION: 15,028,000
ANNUAL NATURAL INCREASE: 3.4%
CAPITAL: Accra
LANGUAGE: English, tribal languages
RELIGION: 42% Christian
CURRENCY: cedi (GHC)
ORGANISATIONS: Comm, UN, ECOWAS, OAU

Ghana, the West African state once known as the Gold Coast, gained independence from Britain in 1957. The landscape varies from tropical rain forest to dry scrubland, with the annual rainfall ranging from over 200cm(79in) to less than 100cm(40in). The temperature averages 27°C(81°F) all year. Cocoa is the principal crop and chief export but although most Ghanaians farm, there is also a thriving industrial base around Tema,where local bauxite is smelted into aluminium, the largest artificial harbour in Africa. Other exports include gold and diamonds and principal imports are fuel and manufactured goods.

GIBRALTAR
STATUS: UK Crown Colony
AREA: 6.5 sq km (2.5 sq miles)
POPULATION: 30,689

GREECE

STATUS: Republic
AREA: 131,985 sq km (50,945 sq miles)
POPULATION: 10,269,074
ANNUAL NATURAL INCREASE: 0.4%
CAPITAL: Athens (Athínai)
LANGUAGE: Greek
RELIGION: 97% Greek Orthodox
CURRENCY: drachma (GRD)
ORGANISATIONS: UN, Council of Europe, EC,
NATO, OECD

Mainland Greece and the many islands are dominated by mountains and sea. The climate is predominantly Mediterranean with hot, dry summers and mild winters. Poor irrigation and drainage mean that much of the agriculture is localised but the main crop, olives, is exported and agricultural output generally is increasing. The surrounding seas are important, providing two-thirds of Greece's fish and supporting an active merchant fleet. Athens is the manufacturing base and at least one-quarter of the population live there. Greece is a very popular tourist destination which helps the craft industries in textiles, metals and ceramics and other local products.

GREENLAND
STATUS: Self-governing Island Region of
Denmark
AREA: 2,175,600 sq km (839,780 sq miles)
POPULATION: 55,558
CAPITAL: Godthåb (Nuuk)

GRENADA

STATUS: Commonwealth State
AREA: 345 sq km (133 sq miles)
POPULATION: 99,205
ANNUAL NATURAL INCREASE: 0.8%
CAPITAL: St George's
LANGUAGE: English, French patois
RELIGION: Roman Catholic majority
CURRENCY: E. Caribbean dollar (XCD)
ORGANISATIONS: Comm, UN, CARICOM, OAS

The Caribbean island of Grenada is the southernmost of the Windward Islands. It is mountainous and thickly forested, with a settled warm climate (average temperature of 27°C or 81°F), which ensures that its tourist industry continues to expand. Bananas are the main export, although the island is also famous for its spices, especially nutmeg and cloves. Cocoa is also exported.

GUADELOUPE
STATUS: Overseas Department of France
AREA: 1,780 sq km (687 sq miles)
POPULATION: 344,000
CAPITAL: Basse-Terre

GUAM
STATUS: Unincorporated Territory of USA
AREA: 450 sq km (174 sq miles)
POPULATION: 132,726
CAPITAL: Agaña

GUATEMALA

STATUS: Republic
AREA: 108,890 sq km (42,030 sq miles)
POPULATION: 9,197,000
ANNUAL NATURAL INCREASE: 2.9%
CAPITAL: Guatemala City
LANGUAGE: Spanish, Indian languages
RELIGION: 75% Roman Catholic,
25% Protestant
CURRENCY: quetzal (GTQ)
ORGANISATIONS: UN, CACM, OAS

The central American country of Guatemala has both a Pacific and a Caribbean coastline. The mountainous interior, with peaks reaching up to 4000m (13,120ft), covers two-thirds of the country; in addition there are coastal lowlands and a thickly forested mainland to the north known as the Petén. Agricultural products form the bulk of Guatemala's exports, notably coffee, sugar-cane and bananas. Mineral resources including nickel, antimony, lead, silver and, in the north, crude oil, are only just beginning to be exploited.

GUINEA

STATUS: Republic
AREA: 245,855 sq km (94,900 sq miles)
POPULATION: 5,756,000
ANNUAL NATURAL INCREASE: 2.5%
CAPITAL: Conakry
LANGUAGE: French, Susu, Manika (Official
languages: French and 8 others)
RELIGION: mainly Muslim, some animist,
1% Roman Catholic
CURRENCY: Guinea franc (GNF)
ORGANISATIONS: UN, ECOWAS, OAU

Guinea, a former French colony is situated on the West African coast. Its drowned coastline, lined with mangrove swamps contrasts strongly with its interior highlands containing the headwaters of the Gambia, Niger and Senegal rivers. Agriculture occupies 80% of the workforce, the main exports being coffee, bananas, pineapple and palm products. Guinea has some of the largest resources of bauxite (aluminium ore) in the world as well as gold and diamonds. Both bauxite and aluminium are exported.

GUINEA-BISSAU

STATUS: Republic
AREA: 36,125 sq km (13,945 sq miles)
POPULATION: 965,000
ANNUAL NATURAL INCREASE: 1.9%
CAPITAL: Bissau
LANGUAGE: Portuguese, Crioulo,
Guinean dialects
RELIGION: Animist and Muslim majorities.
Roman Catholic minority
CURRENCY: Guinea-Bissau peso (GWP)
ORGANISATIONS: UN, ECOWAS, OAU

Guinea-Bissau, on the West African coast was once a centre for the Portuguese slave trade. The coast is swampy and lined with mangroves, and the interior consists of a low-lying plain densely covered with rain forest. The coast is

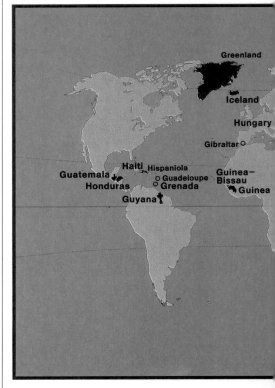

hot and humid with annual rainfall of 200–300cm (79–118in) a year, although the interior is cooler and drier. 80% of the country's exports comprise groundnuts, groundnut oil, palm kernels and palm oil. Fish, fish products and coconuts also make an important contribution to trade.

GUYANA

STATUS: Co-operative Republic
AREA: 214,970 sq km (82,980 sq miles)
POPULATION: 990,000
ANNUAL NATURAL INCREASE: 0.6%
CAPITAL: Georgetown
LANGUAGE: English, Hindi, Urdu,
Amerindian dialects

RELIGION: mainly Christian, Muslim and Hindu
CURRENCY: Guyana dollar (GYD)
ORGANISATIONS: Comm, UN, CARICOM

The ex-British colony of Guyana borders both Venezuela and Brazil. Its Atlantic coast, the most densely-populated area, is flat and marshy, while towards the interior the landscape gradually rises to the Guiana Highlands – a region densely covered in rain forest. Sugar, molasses and rum, once Guyana's main exports, are now being outstripped by bauxite.

HAITI

STATUS: Republic
AREA: 27,750 sq km (10,710 sq miles)
POPULATION: 6,486,000

ANNUAL NATURAL INCREASE: 1.8%
CAPITAL: Port-au-Prince
LANGUAGE: French, Creole (90%)
RELIGION: 80% Roman Catholic. Some Voodoo folk religion
CURRENCY: gourde (HTG)
ORGANISATIONS: UN, OAS

Haiti occupies the western part of the island of Hispaniola in the Caribbean. It is the poorest country in Central America. The country is mountainous with three main ranges, the highest reaching 2680m (8793 ft). Agriculture is restricted to the plains which divide the ranges. The climate is tropical. 90% of the workforce are farmers, and coffee is the main export. Light manufacturing industries are concentrated around the capital.

HISPANIOLA
STATUS: Island of the West Indies comprising Haiti and Dominican Republic
AREA: 76,170 sq km (29,400 sq miles)
POPULATION: 12,154,000

HOKKAIDO
STATUS: Island of Japan
AREA: 78,460 sq km (30,285 sq miles)
POPULATION: 5,671,000

HONDURAS

STATUS: Republic
AREA: 112,085 sq km (43,265 sq miles)
POPULATION: 5,105,000
ANNUAL NATURAL INCREASE: 3.5%
CAPITAL: Tegucigalpa
LANGUAGE: Spanish, Indian dialects
RELIGION: large Roman Catholic majority
CURRENCY: lempira (HNL) or peso
ORGANISATIONS: UN, CACM, OAS

The Central American republic of Honduras is a poor, sparsely populated country which consists substantially of rugged mountains and high plateaux with, on the Caribbean coast, an area of hot and humid plains, densely covered with tropical vegetation. These low-lying plains are subject to high annual rainfall, an average of 250 cm (98 in), and it is in this region that bananas and coffee, accounting for half the nation's exports, are grown. Other crops include sugar, rice, maize, beans and tobacco. Exploitation of lead, iron, tin and oil may lead, however, to a change in the traditional agriculture-based economy. Most industries are concerned with processing local products. Lead, silver and zinc are exported.

HONG KONG
(INCLUDING KOWLOON AND THE NEW TERRITORIES)
STATUS: UK Dependent Territory
AREA: 1,067 sq km (412 sq miles)
POPULATION: 5,448,000

HONSHU
STATUS: Main Island of Japan
AREA: 230,455 sq km (88,955 sq miles)
POPULATION: 98,352,000

HUNGARY

STATUS: Republic
AREA: 93,030 sq km (35,910 sq miles)
POPULATION: 10,352,000
ANNUAL NATURAL INCREASE: –0.1%
CAPITAL: Budapest
LANGUAGE: Hungarian (Magyar)
RELIGION: 60% Roman Catholic, 20% Hungarian Reformed Church, Lutheran and Orthodox minorities
CURRENCY: forint (HUE)
ORGANISATIONS: UN, OIEC, Council of Europe

The undulating fertile plains of Hungary are bisected vertically by the Danube. Hungary is bordered by Czechoslovakia in the north, by Romania and Ukraine in the east, by Austria and Slovenia in the west, and by Croatia and Yugoslavia (Serbia) in the south. Winters in Hungary are severe, though in summer the enclosed plains can become very hot. Bauxite is Hungary's only substantial mineral resource, and less than 15% of the gross national product is now derived from agriculture. The massive drive for industrialisation has fundamentally transformed the structure of the economy in the period since 1945. Both capital and consumer goods industries were developed, and during the 1980s engineering accounted for more than half the total industrial output. After a series of more or less unsuccessful attempts to introduce market elements into what remained in essence a centrally planned and largely state-owned economy, the communist regime finally gave up in 1989/90. However, their democratically-elected successors have yet to prove that privatisation and free competition will eventually bring general prosperity as well as political stability to what is now a profoundly troubled society.

ICELAND

STATUS: Republic
AREA: 102,820 sq km (39,690 sq miles)
POPULATION: 255,000
ANNUAL NATURAL INCREASE: 1.1%
CAPITAL: Reykjavík
LANGUAGE: Icelandic
RELIGION: 93% Evangelical Lutheran
CURRENCY: Icelandic krona (ISK)
ORGANISATIONS: UN, Council of Europe, EFTA, NATO, OECD

The northernmost island in Europe, Iceland is 850km (530 miles) away from Scotland, its nearest neighbour. The landscape is entirely volcanic – compacted volcanic ash has been eroded by the wind and there are substantial ice sheets and lava fields as well as many still active volcanoes, geysers and hot springs. The climate is cold, with average summer temperatures of 9°–10°C(48°–50°F), and vegetation is sparse. An average of 950,000 tonnes of fish are landed each year and 95% of Iceland's exports consist of fish and fish products.

INDIA

STATUS: Federal Republic
AREA: 3,166,830 sq km (1,222,395 sq miles)
POPULATION: 843,930,861
ANNUAL NATURAL INCREASE: 2.1%

CAPITAL: New Delhi
LANGUAGE: Hindi, English, regional languages
RELIGION: 83% Hindu, 11% Muslim
CURRENCY: Indian rupee (INR)
ORGANISATIONS: Comm, UN, Col. Plan

India has the world's second largest population. This vast country contains an extraordinary variety of landscapes, climates and resources. The Himalaya in the north is the world's highest mountain range with many peaks reaching over 6000km (19,685 ft). The Himalayan foothills are covered with lush vegetation, water is in abundant supply (rainfall in Assam reaches 1,070cm or 421in a year) and the climate is hot, making this region a centre for tea cultivation. To the south lies the vast expanse of the Indo-Gangetic plain, 2500km (1550 miles) east-west, divided by the Indus, Ganges and Brahmaputra rivers. This is one of the world's most fertile regions, although it is liable to flooding, and failure of monsoon rainfall (June to September) can result in severe drought. In the pre-monsoon season the heat becomes intense – average temperatures in New Delhi reach 38°C (100°F). Rice, wheat, cotton, jute, tobacco and sugar are the main crops. To the south lies the Deccan plateau. India's natural resources are immense – timber, coal, iron ore and nickel, and oil has been discovered in the Indian Ocean. There has been a rapid expansion of light industry and the manufacturing of consumer goods. Tourism is a valuable source of revenue. Nevertheless, 70% of the population live by subsistence farming. Main exports by value are precious stones and jewellery, engineering goods, clothing, leather goods, chemicals and cotton.

INDONESIA

STATUS: Republic
AREA: 1,919,445 sq km (740,905 sq miles)
POPULATION: 179,321,641
ANNUAL NATURAL INCREASE: 2.1%
CAPITAL: Jakarta
LANGUAGE: Bahasa Indonesian, Dutch
RELIGION: 78% Muslim, 11% Christian,
11% Hindu and Buddhist
CURRENCY: rupiah (IDR)
ORGANISATIONS: UN, ASEAN, Col. Plan, OPEC

Indonesia consists of an arc of thousands of islands along the equator which includes Kalimantan (the central and southern parts of Borneo), Sumatra, Irian Jaya (the western part of New Guinea), Sulawesi and Java. Most of its people live along the coasts of the islands or in the river valleys. It is a Muslim nation and has the fourth largest population in the world. Most people live on Java, leaving parts of the other islands virtually uninhabited. The climate is tropical: hot, wet and subject to monsoons. Over three-quarters of the people live in villages and farm, but the crops produced are hardly enough for the increasing population and the fishing industry needs developing. Timber and oil production are becoming very important as sources of foreign exchange and there are also rich mineral deposits, as yet not fully exploited. Tourism is increasing.

IRAN

STATUS: Republic
AREA: 1,648,000 sq km (636,130 sq miles)
POPULATION: 56,031,000
ANNUAL NATURAL INCREASE: 3.0%
CAPITAL: Tehran
LANGUAGE: Farsi, Kurdish, Arabic, Baluchi, Turkic
RELIGION: Shia Muslim majority. Sunni Muslim and Armenian Christian minorities
CURRENCY: Iranian rial (IRR)
ORGANISATIONS: UN, Col. Plan, OPEC

Iran is a large mountainous country situated between the Caspian Sea and the Persian Gulf. The climate is one of extremes with temperatures ranging from –20 to 55°C (–4 to 131°F) and rainfall varying from 200cm (79 in) to almost zero. Iran is rich in oil and gas and the revenues have been used to improve communications and social conditions generally. The war with Iraq between 1980 and 1988 seriously restricted economic growth and particularly affected the Iranian oil industry in the Persian Gulf. Agricultural conditions are poor except around the Caspian Sea and wheat is the main crop though fruit (especially dates) and nuts are grown and exported. The main livestock is sheep and goats. Iran has substantial mineral deposits relatively underdeveloped.

IRAQ

STATUS: Republic
AREA: 438,317 sq km (169,235 sq miles)
POPULATION: 18,920,000
ANNUAL NATURAL INCREASE: 3.6%
CAPITAL: Baghdad
LANGUAGE: Arabic, Kurdish, Turkoman
RELIGION: 50% Shia, 45% Sunni Muslim
CURRENCY: Iraqi dinar (IQD)
ORGANISATIONS: UN, Arab League, OPEC

Iraq is mostly marsh and mountain, but there are substantial areas of fertile land between the Tigris and the Euphrates. The two great rivers join and become the Shatt al-Arab which flows into the Persian Gulf. The climate is mainly arid with small and unreliable rainfall, less than 50cm (20 in). Summers are very hot and winters cold. Iraq has a very short coastline making Basra the principal port with oil the major export. Light industry is situated around Baghdad, the capital, and there are major petro-chemical complexes around the Basra and Kirkuk oilfields. The war with Iran (1980-88) and the recent Gulf conflict (1991) have placed great strains on the economy with exports of oil and natural gas severely restricted. Iraq will take some time to recover from the damage caused to its infrastructure.

IRELAND (EIRE)

STATUS: Republic
AREA: 68,895 sq km (26,595 sq miles)
POPULATION: 3,503,000
ANNUAL NATURAL INCREASE: 0.4%
CAPITAL: Dublin (Baile Atha Cliath)
LANGUAGE: Irish, English
RELIGION: 95% Roman Catholic, 5% Protestant
CURRENCY: punt or Irish pound (IEP)
ORGANISATIONS: UN, Council of Europe, EC, OECD

The Irish Republic forms 80% of the island of Ireland. It is a country where the cool, damp climate makes for rich pastureland, and livestock farming predominates. Meat and dairy produce is processed in the small market towns where there are also breweries and mills.

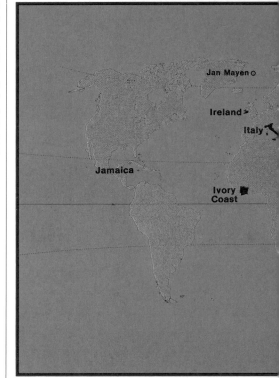

Large-scale manufacturing is centred round Dublin, the capital and main port. Ireland also possesses reserves of oil and natural gas, peat and deposits of lead and zinc.

ISRAEL

STATUS: State
AREA: 20,770 sq km (8,015 sq miles)
POPULATION: 4,822,000
ANNUAL NATURAL INCREASE: 1.7%
CAPITAL: Jerusalem
LANGUAGE: Hebrew, Arabic, Yiddish
RELIGION: 85% Jewish, 13% Muslim
CURRENCY: shekel (ILS)
ORGANISATIONS: UN

This narrow country on the eastern Mediterranean littoral contains a varied landscape – a coastal plain bounded by foothills in the south and the Galilee Highlands in the north; a deep trough extending from the River Jordan to the Dead Sea, and the Negev, a desert region in the south extending to the Gulf of Aqaba. Economic development in Israel is the most advanced in the Middle East. Manufacturing, particularly diamond finishing and electronics, and mining are the most important industries although Israel also has a flourishing agricultural industry exporting fruit, flowers and vegetables to Western Europe.

ITALY

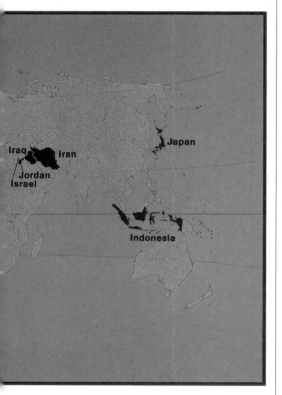

STATUS: Republic
AREA: 301,245 sq km (116,280 sq miles)
POPULATION: 57,690,000
ANNUAL NATURAL INCREASE: 0.2%
CAPITAL: Rome (Roma)
LANGUAGE: Italian, German, French
RELIGION: 90% Roman Catholic
CURRENCY: Italian lira (ITL)
ORGANISATIONS: UN, Council of Europe, EC NATO, OECD, WEU, G7

Over 75% of the landscape of Italy is hill or mountain, with the north dominated by the flat plain of the River Po rising to the high Alps. Climate varies from hot summers and mild winters in the south and lowland areas, to mild summers and cold winters in the Alps. Agriculture flourishes with cereals, vegetables, olives and vines the principal crops. Italy is the world's largest wine producer. Cheese is also an important commodity. In spite of the lack of mineral and power resources textiles, manufacturing industry: cars, machine tools, textile machinery and engineering, mainly in the north, are

expanding rapidly and account for nearly 50% of the work force. This is increasing the imbalance between the north and south where the average income is far less per head, and where investment is lacking.

IVORY COAST

STATUS: Republic
AREA: 322,465 sq km (124,470 sq miles)
POPULATION: 11,998,000
ANNUAL NATURAL INCREASE: 4.0%
CAPITAL: Yamoussoukro
LANGUAGE: French, tribal languages
RELIGION: 65% traditional beliefs, 23% Muslim 12% Roman Catholic
CURRENCY: CFA franc (W Africa) (XOF)
ORGANISATIONS: UN, ECOWAS, OAU

Independent from the French since 1960, the Ivory Coast is divided between the low plains of the south and the plateaux of the north. The climate is tropical with rainfall all year round in the south. Much of the population is engaged in agriculture producing rice, cassava, maize, sorghum, plantains and yams. Exports include coffee, timber and cocoa. The main industrial area and leading port is centred on Abidjan. Important industries are food-processing, textiles and timber products.

JAMAICA

STATUS: Commonwealth State
AREA: 11,425 sq km (4,410 sq miles)
POPULATION: 2,420,000
ANNUAL NATURAL INCREASE: 1.3%
CAPITAL: Kingston
LANGUAGE: English, local patois
RELIGION: Anglican Christian majority. Rastafarian minority
CURRENCY: Jamaican dollar (JMD)
ORGANISATIONS: Comm, UN, CARICOM, OAS

Jamaica, part of the Greater Antilles chain of islands in the Caribbean is formed from the peaks of a submerged mountain range. The climate is tropical with an annual rainfall of over 500cm(197in) on the high ground. There is a plentiful supply of tropical fruits such as melons, bananas and guavas. Principal crops include sugar-cane, bananas and coffee. Jamaica is rich in bauxite which provides over half foreign-exchange earnings. Main manufacturing industries are food processing, textiles, cement and agricultural machinery.

JAN MAYEN
STATUS: Island Territory of Norway
AREA: 380 sq km (147 sq miles)
POPULATION: No permanent population

JAPAN

STATUS: Constituential monarchy
AREA: 369,700 sq km (142,705 sq miles)
POPULATION: 123,612,000
ANNUAL NATURAL INCREASE: 0.6%
CAPITAL: Tokyo
LANGUAGE: Japanese
RELIGION: Shintoist, Buddhist, Christian minority
CURRENCY: yen (JPY)
ORGANISATIONS: UN, Col. Plan, OECD, G7

Japan consists of the main islands of Hokkaido, Honshu, Shikoku and Kyushu which stretch over 1,600km (995 miles). The land is mountainous and heavily forested with small, fertile patches and a climate ranging from harsh to tropical. The highest mountain is Mt Fuji 3,776m (12,388 ft). The archipelago is also subject to monsoons, earthquakes, typhoons and tidal waves. Very little of the available land is cultivable and although many of the farmers only work part-time Japan manages to produce enough rice for the growing population. Most food has to be imported but the Japanese also catch and eat a lot of fish. The Japanese fishing fleet is the largest in the world. Japan is a leading economic power and most of the population are involved in industry. Because of the importance of trade, industry has grown up round the major ports especially Yokohama and Osaka and Tokyo, the capital. The principal exports are electronic, electrical and optical equipment. To produce these goods Japan relies heavily on imported fuel and raw materials and is developing the country's nuclear power resources to reduce this dependence. Production of coal, oil and natural gas is also being increased.

JORDAN

STATUS: Kingdom
AREA: 90,650 sq km (35,000 sq miles)
POPULATION: 3,170,000
ANNUAL NATURAL INCREASE: 3.7%
CAPITAL: Amman
LANGUAGE: Arabic
RELIGION: 90% Sunni Muslim, Christian and Shia Muslim minorities
CURRENCY: Jordanian dinar (JOD)
ORGANISATIONS: UN, Arab League

Jordan is one of the few remaining kingdoms in the middle east. It is mostly desert, but has fertile pockets. Temperatures rise to 49°C(120°F) in the valleys but it is cooler and wetter in the east. Fruit and vegetables account for 20% of Jordan's exports and phosphate, the most valuable mineral, accounts for over 40% of export revenue. Amman is the manufacturing centre, processing bromide and potash from the Dead Sea. Other important industries are food processing and textiles.

KAZAKHSTAN

STATUS: Republic
AREA: 2,717,300 sq km (1,048,880 sq miles)
POPULATION: 16,700,000
CAPITAL: Alma-Ata
LANGUAGE: Kazakh, Russian
RELIGION: mainly Muslim
CURRENCY: rouble
ORGANISATIONS: CIS

Stretching across central Asia, Kazakhstan is Russia's southern neighbour. Consisting of lowlands, hilly plains and plateaux, with a small mountainous area, the country has a continental climate with hot summers alternating with equally extreme winters. Exceptionally rich in raw materials, extractive industries have played a major role in the country's economy. Rapid industrialisation in recent years has focussed on iron and steel, cement, chemicals, fertilizers and consumer goods. Although three-quarters of all agricultural land is used for pasture, the nomadic ways of the Kazakh people have all but disappeared. Economic development during the Soviet period brought a massive influx of outside labour which swamped the indigenous population. The proportion of Kazakhs employed in the industrial sector has, until recently, been small, but with the move to the towns and better training, this balance is starting to be redressed. Since Kazakhstan's independence in 1991, its economic prospects appear favourable; but the Soviet legacy includes environmental problems, such as the ruthless exploitation of the Aral Sea for irrigation, which have to be faced.

KENYA

STATUS: Republic
AREA: 582,645 sq km (224,900 sq miles)
POPULATION: 24,032,000
ANNUAL NATURAL INCREASE: 3.8%
CAPITAL: Nairobi
LANGUAGE: Kiswahili, English, Kikuyu, Luo
RELIGION: traditional beliefs majority, 25% Christian, 6% Muslim
CURRENCY: Kenya shilling (KES)
ORGANISATIONS: Comm, UN, OAU

Kenya lies on the equator but as most of the country is on a high plateau the temperatures range from 10° to 27°C (50° to 81°F). Rainfall varies from 76 to 250cm(30 to 98in) depending on altitude. Poor soil and a dry climate mean that little of the land is under cultivation but exports are nonetheless dominated by farm products – coffee, tea, sisal and meat. Nairobi and Mombasa are the manufacturing centres. The tourist industry is growing. Electricity is generated from both geothermal sources and hydro-electric power stations on the Tana river.

KIRGIZIA

STATUS: Republic
AREA: 198,500 sq km (76,620 sq miles)
POPULATION: 4,400,000
CAPITAL: Bishkek
LANGUAGE: Kirgizian, Russian
RELIGION: Muslim
CURRENCY: rouble
ORGANISATIONS: CIS

Located in the heart of Asia, Kirgizia is a mountainous country. Traditionally an agrarian-based economy, with stock raising prevalent, the country underwent rapid industrialisation during the Soviet period and is now a major producer of machinery and hydro-electric power. Coal, antimony and mercury are mined. The cultivation of cotton, sugar beet, tobacco and opium poppies is expanding and provides the basis for a growing processing industry. Independence came unexpectedly in 1991, although Kirgizia had long wanted to control its own affairs.

KIRIBATI

STATUS: Republic
AREA: 717 sq km (277 sq miles)
POPULATION: 66,000
ANNUAL NATURAL INCREASE: 1.9%
CAPITAL: Bairiki (in Tarawa Atoll)
LANGUAGE: I-Kiribati, English
RELIGION: Christian majority
CURRENCY: Australian dollar (AUD)
ORGANISATIONS: Comm

Kiribati consists of sixteen Gilbert Islands, eight Phoenix Islands, three Line Islands and Ocean Island. These four groups are spread over 5 million sq km(1,930,000 sq miles) in the central and west Pacific. The temperature is a constant 27° to 32°C (80° to 90°F). The islanders grow coconut, breadfruit, bananas and babai (a coarse vegetable). Copra is the only major export. Main imports are machinery and manufactured goods.

KOREA, NORTH

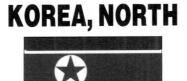

STATUS: Republic
AREA: 122,310 sq km (47,210 sq miles)
POPULATION: 21,773,000
ANNUAL NATURAL INCREASE: 1.2%
CAPITAL: Pyŏngyang
LANGUAGE: Korean
RELIGION: mainly Buddhist, Confucianist, Daoist and Chundo Kyo

CURRENCY: North Korean won (KPW)
ORGANISATIONS: UN, OIEC

High, rugged mountains and deep valleys typify North Korea. Climate is extreme with severe winters and warm, sunny summers. Cultivation is limited to the river valley plains where rice, millet, maize and wheat are the principal crops. North Korea is rich in minerals including iron ore, coal and copper and industrial development has been expanding. Further potential exists in the exploitation of the plentiful resources of hydro-electricity. Main exports are metal ores and metal products.

KOREA, SOUTH

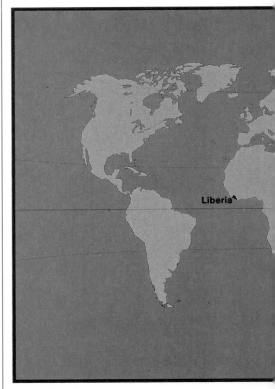

STATUS: Republic
AREA: 98,445 sq km (38,000 sq miles)
POPULATION: 43,201,000
ANNUAL NATURAL INCREASE: 1.6%
CAPITAL: Seoul (Sŏul)
LANGUAGE: Korean
RELIGION: 26% Mahayana Buddhism, 22% Christian. Confucianist minority, Daoism, Chundo Kyo
CURRENCY: won (KRW)
ORGANISATIONS: UN, Col. Plan

The terrain of South Korea is less rugged than the north and the climate is less extreme. The majority of the population live in the arable river valleys and along the coastal plain. Agriculture is very primitive, with rice the principal crop. Tungsten, coal and iron ore are the main mineral deposits. The country is a major industrial nation with iron and steel, chemicals, machinery, shipbuilding, vehicles and electronics dominating. South Korea builds more ships than any other nation except Japan. Oil and industrial materials have to be imported.

KUWAIT

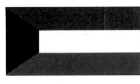

STATUS: State
AREA: 24,280 sq km (9,370 sq miles)
POPULATION: 1,000,000 (approx.)
ANNUAL NATURAL INCREASE: 4.3%
CAPITAL: Kuwait (Al Kuwayt)
LANGUAGE: Arabic, English
RELIGION: 95% Muslim, 5% Christian and Hindu
CURRENCY: Kuwaiti dinar (KWD)
ORGANISATIONS: UN, Arab League, OPEC

Situated at the mouth of the Gulf, Kuwait comprises low, undulating desert, with summer temperatures as high as 52°C (126°F). Annual rainfall fluctuates between 1 and 37 cm (½–15 in). Since the discovery of oil Kuwait has been

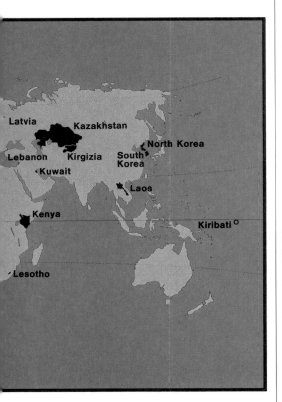

transformed into one of the world's wealthiest nations, exporting oil to Japan, France, The Netherlands and the UK since 1946. The natural gas fields have also been developed. Other industries include fishing (particularly shrimp), food processing, chemicals and building materials. In agriculture, the aim is to produce half the requirements of domestic vegetable consumption by expanding the irrigated area. The invasion and attempted annexation of Kuwait by Iraq in 1990-91 has had severe effects on the country's economy.

LAOS

STATUS: Republic

AREA: 236,725 sq km (91,375 sq miles)
POPULATION: 4,139,000
ANNUAL NATURAL INCREASE: 2.7%
CAPITAL: Vientiane (Viangchan)
LANGUAGE: Lao, French, tribal languages
RELIGION: Buddhist majority, Christian and animist minorities
CURRENCY: kip (LAK)
ORGANISATIONS: UN, Col. Plan

Laos is a poor, landlocked country in Indo-China. Temperatures range from 15°C (59°F) in winter, to 32°C (90°F) before the rains, and 26°C (79°F) during the rainy season from May to October. Most of the sparse population are farmers growing small amounts of rice, maize, sweet potatoes and tobacco. The major exports are tin and teak, the latter floated down the Mekong river. Almost constant warfare since 1941 has hindered any possible industrial development. Main exports are timber products and coffee.

LATVIA

STATUS: Republic
AREA: 63,700 sq km (24,590 sq miles)
POPULATION: 2,700,000
CAPITAL: Riga
LANGUAGE: Latvian, Lithuanian, Russian
RELIGION: Lutheran, Roman Catholic and Orthodox minorities
CURRENCY: rouble (lat 1992)
ORGANISATIONS: UN

Latvia is situated on the shores of the Baltic Sea and the Gulf of Riga. Forests cover more than a third of the total territory, a second third being made up of meadows, swamps and wasteland. Farmland supports dairy and meat production and grain crops. The climate is oceanic: windy, cloudy and humid. The country possesses no mineral resources of any value. Industrial development has been sustained by a massive influx of Russian labour since Latvia's incorporation into the Soviet Union in 1940. Machine building and metal engineering are the chief manufacturing activities. Under the Soviets, Latvia was assigned the production of consumer durables such as refrigerators and motorcycles as well as ships, rolling stock and power generators. Environmental damage, commercial unprofitability and the collapse of communism necessitate fundamental reform. Latvia regained its independence in 1991.

LEBANON

STATUS: Republic
AREA: 10,400 sq km (4,015 sq miles)
POPULATION: 2,701,000
ANNUAL NATURAL INCREASE: 2.1%
CAPITAL: Beirut (Beyrouth)
LANGUAGE: Arabic, French, English

RELIGION: 58% Shia and Sunni Muslim, 42% Roman Catholic and Maronite Christian
CURRENCY: Lebanese pound (LBP)
ORGANISATIONS: UN, Arab League

Physically, Lebanon can be divided into four main regions: a narrow coastal plain; a narrow, fertile, interior plateau; the west Lebanon and Anti-Lebanon mountains. The climate is of Mediterranean type with an annual rainfall ranging between 92cm (36in) on the coast and 230cm (91in) in the mountains. Trade and tourism have been severely affected by civil war since 1975. Agriculture accounts for nearly half the employed people. Cement, fertilisers, jewellery, sugar and tobacco products are all manufactured on a small scale.

LESOTHO

STATUS: Kingdom
AREA: 30,345 sq km (11,715 sq miles)
POPULATION: 1,774,000
ANNUAL NATURAL INCREASE: 2.7%
CAPITAL: Maseru
LANGUAGE: Sesotho, English
RELIGION: 80% Christian
CURRENCY: loti (LSL), S African rand (ZAR)
ORGANISATIONS: Comm, UN, OAU

Lesotho, formerly Basutoland, is completely encircled by South Africa. This small country is rugged and mountainous, and southern Africa's highest mountain, Thabana Ntlenyana (3482m or 11,424ft) is to be found in the east Drakensberg. Because of the terrain, agriculture is limited to the lowlands and foothills. Sorghum, wheat, barley, maize, oats and legumes are the main crops. Cattle, sheep and goats graze on the highlands.

LIBERIA

STATUS: Republic
AREA: 111,370 sq km (42,990 sq miles)
POPULATION: 2,607,000
ANNUAL NATURAL INCREASE: 3.1%
CAPITAL: Monrovia
LANGUAGE: English, tribal languages
RELIGION: Christian majority, 5% Muslim
CURRENCY: Liberian dollar (LRD)
ORGANISATIONS: UN, ECOWAS, OAU

The West African republic of Liberia is the only nation in Africa never to have been ruled by a foreign power. The hot and humid coastal plain with its savannah vegetation and mangrove swamps rises gently towards the Guinea Highlands, and the interior is densely covered by tropical rain forest. Rubber, formerly Liberia's main export has now been supplemented by iron, discovered in the Bomi Hills. Liberia has the world's largest merchant fleet of over 2,500 ships due to its flag of convenience tax regime.

LIBYA

STATUS: Republic
AREA: 1,759,180 sq km (679,180 sq miles)
POPULATION: 4,545,000
ANNUAL NATURAL INCREASE: 4.2%
CAPITAL: Tripoli (Ṭarābulus)
LANGUAGE: Arabic, Italian, English
RELIGION: Sunni Muslim
CURRENCY: Libyan dinar (LYD)
ORGANISATIONS: UN, Arab League, OAU, OPEC

Libya is situated on the lowlands of North Africa which rise southwards from the Mediterranean Sea. 95% of its territory is hot and dry desert or semi-desert with average rainfall of less than 13cm(5in). The coastal plains, however, have a moister Mediterranean climate with rainfall of 20–61cm(8–24in), and this is the most densely populated region. In these areas, a wide range of crops are cultivated including grapes, groundnuts, oranges, wheat and barley. Dates are grown in the desert oases. Only 30 years ago Libya was classed as one of the world's poorest nations but the exploitation of oil has transformed Libya's economy and now accounts for over 95% of its exports. Most imported goods come from Italy.

LIECHTENSTEIN

STATUS: Principality
AREA: 160 sq km (62 sq miles)
POPULATION: 29,000
ANNUAL NATURAL INCREASE: 1.1%
CAPITAL: Vaduz
LANGUAGE: Alemannish, German
RELIGION: 87% Roman Catholic
CURRENCY: Franken (Swiss franc) (CHF)
ORGANISATIONS: UN, Council of Europe, EFTA

Situated in the central Alps between Switzerland and Austria, Liechtenstein is one of the smallest states in Europe. Its territory is divided into two zones – the flood plains of the Rhine to the north and Alpine mountain ranges to the south where cattle are reared. Liechtenstein's other main sources of revenue comprise light industry chiefly the manufacture of precision instruments, also textile production, food products and tourism.

LITHUANIA

STATUS: Republic
AREA: 65,200 sq km (25,165 sq miles)

POPULATION: 3,700,000
CAPITAL: Vilnius
LANGUAGE: Lithuanian, Russian, Polish
RELIGION: mainly Roman Catholic
CURRENCY: rouble (lat to be introduced in 1992)
ORGANISATIONS: UN

Lying on the shores of the Baltic Sea, Lithuania is bounded by Latvia to the north, by Belorussia to the east and south, and in the southwest by Poland and the Kaliningrad (Königsberg) district, a territorial exclave belonging to Russia. The whole country consists of a low-lying plain, the climate being transitional between the oceanic type of western Europe and the continental conditions prevailing further east. After almost 50 years' involuntary incorporation into the Soviet Union, Lithuania led the renewed Baltic struggle for freedom, and in 1991 was able to win back its independence. However, the social and economic problems with which the country is beset defy an easy solution. The massive drive for industrialisation during the Soviet period has done enormous damage to the environment but failed to create competitive enterprises that can survive under market conditions. This has led to a dramatic fall in production in the recent past and to rising unemployment. Lithuania's agriculture, with its emphasis on meat and dairy products, still awaits decollectivisation.

LUXEMBOURG

STATUS: Grand Duchy
AREA: 2,585 sq km (998 sq miles)
POPULATION: 378,000
ANNUAL NATURAL INCREASE: 0.4%
CAPITAL: Luxembourg
LANGUAGE: Letzeburgish, French, German
RELIGION: 95% Roman Catholic
CURRENCY: Luxembourg franc (LUF),
Belgian franc (BEF)
ORGANISATIONS: UN, Council of Europe, EC
NATO, OECD, WEU

The Grand Duchy of Luxembourg is strategically situated between France, Belgium and Germany. In the north the Oesling region is an extension of the Ardennes which are cut through by thickly forested river valleys. The Gutland to the south is an area of rolling lush pastureland. The climate is mild and temperate with rainfall ranging from 70–100cm(28–40in) a year. Just over half the land is arable, mainly cereals, dairy produce and potatoes, and wine is produced in the Moselle Valley. Iron ore is found in the south and is the basis of the thriving steel industry. Other major industries are textiles, chemicals, metal goods and pharmaceutical products.

MACAU
STATUS: Overseas Territory of Portugal
AREA: 16 sq km (6 sq miles)
POPULATION: 479,000
CAPITAL: Macau

MADAGASCAR

STATUS: Republic
AREA: 594,180 sq km (229,345 sq miles)
POPULATION: 11,197,000
ANNUAL NATURAL INCREASE: 2.8%
CAPITAL: Antananarivo
LANGUAGE: Malagasy, French, English
RELIGION: 57% animist, 40% Christian,
3% Muslim
CURRENCY: Malagasy franc (MGF)
ORGANISATIONS: UN, OAU

Madagascar is the world's fourth largest island, situated 400 km (250 miles) east of the Mozambique coast. The terrain consists largely of a high plateau reaching 1500m (4920ft), with

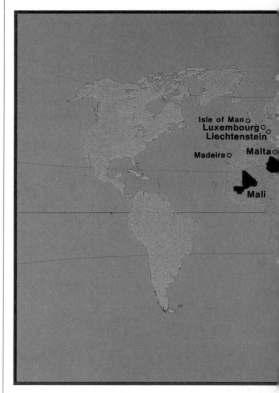

steppe and savannah vegetation and desert in the south. The mountains of the Tsaratanana Massif to the north reach up to 2876m (9435ft). Much of the hot humid east coast is covered by tropical rainforest – here rainfall reaches 150-200cm (59-79 in) per annum. Although farming is the occupation of about 85% of the population, only 3% of the land is cultivated. Coffee, rice and cassava are the main products. Much of Madagascar's plant and animal life is unique to the island. However, habitats are under increasing threat due to widespread deforestation, caused by the rapid development of forestry, and soil erosion.

MADEIRA
STATUS: Self-governing Island Region
of Portugal
AREA: 796 sq km (307 sq miles)
POPULATION: 273,200
CAPITAL: Funchal

MALAWI

STATUS: Republic
AREA: 94,080 sq km (36,315 sq miles)
POPULATION: 8,289,000
ANNUAL NATURAL INCREASE: 3.4%
CAPITAL: Lilongwe
LANGUAGE: Chichewa, English
RELIGION: traditional beliefs majority,
10% Roman Catholic, 10% Protestant
CURRENCY: kwacha (MWK)
ORGANISATIONS: Comm, UN, OAU

Malawi is located at the southern end of the East African Rift Valley. The area around Lake Malawi is hot and humid with swampy vegeta-

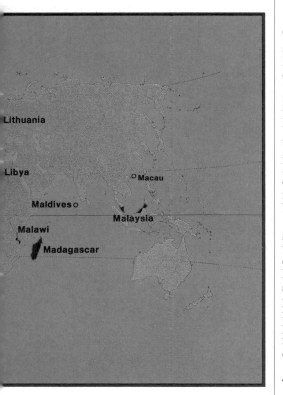

tion, gradually supplemented by highlands to the west and south-east, where conditions are cooler. Malawi has an intensely rural economy – 96% of the population work on the land. Maize is the main subsistence crop, and tea, tobacco, sugar and groundnuts are the main exports. Malawi has deposits of both coal and bauxite, but they are under-exploited at present. Manufacturing industry concentrates on consumer goods and building and construction materials. All energy is produced by hydro-electric power.

MALAYSIA

STATUS: Federation
AREA: 332,965 sq km (128,525 sq miles)

POPULATION: 17,861,000
ANNUAL NATURAL INCREASE: 2.6%
CAPITAL: Kuala Lumpur
LANGUAGE: Bahasa Malaysia, English
RELIGION: 53% Muslim, 25% Buddhist, Hindu,
Christian and animist minorities
CURRENCY: Malaysian dollar or ringgit (MYR)
ORGANISATIONS: Comm, UN, ASEAN, Col. Plan

PENINSULAR MALAYSIA
STATUS: States
AREA: 131,585 sq km (50,790 sq miles)
POPULATION: 14,005,000

SABAH
STATUS: State
AREA: 76,115 sq km (29,380 sq miles)
POPULATION: 1,342,631
CAPITAL: Kota Kinabalu

SARAWAK
STATUS: State
AREA: 124,965 sq km (48,235 sq miles)
POPULATION: 1,550,000
CAPITAL: Kuching

The federation of Malaysia consists of two separate parts; West Malaysia is located on the Malay Peninsula, while East Malaysia consists of Sabah and Sarawak on the island of Borneo 700 km (435 miles) across the South China Sea. Despite this distance, both areas share a similar landscape, which is mountainous and covered with lush tropical rainforest. The climate is tropical, hot and humid all the year round, with annual average rainfall of 250 cm (98 in). Malaysia is one of the world's main tin producers, and also produces over 40% of the world's rubber, and is also a leading source of palm oil, bauxite and gold.

Chief exports by value are manufactured goods, rubber, crude oil, palm oil, timber and timber products and tin. Most industries are concerned with production and processing of local products – palm oil, furniture, food processing and petroleum products. Most of the population are engaged in agriculture for local needs but crops grown for export include pineapples, tobacco, cocoa and spices. Livestock is important to the home economy with pigs, cattle, goats, buffaloes and sheep predominant.

MALDIVES

STATUS: Republic
AREA: 298 sq km (115 sq miles)
POPULATION: 214,139
ANNUAL NATURAL INCREASE: 3.4%
CAPITAL: Malé
LANGUAGE: Divehi
RELIGION: Sunni Muslim majority
CURRENCY: rufiyaa (MVR)
ORGANISATIONS: Comm, UN, Col. Plan

The Maldive Islands are listed as one of the world's poorest nations. They consist of a series of coral atolls stretching 885km(550 miles) across the Indian Ocean. Although there are

2000 islands, only about 215 are inhabited. The main island, Malé, is only 1½ miles long. Fishing is the main activity and fish and coconut fibre are both exported. Most staple foods have to be imported but coconuts, millet, cassava, yams and fruit are grown locally. Tourism is developing.

MALI

STATUS: Republic
AREA: 1,240,140 sq km (478,695 sq miles)
POPULATION: 8,156,000
ANNUAL NATURAL INCREASE: 2.5%
CAPITAL: Bamako
LANGUAGE: French, native languages
RELIGION: 65% Muslim, 30% traditional beliefs
5% Christian
CURRENCY: CFA franc (W Africa) (XOF)
ORGANISATIONS: UN, ECOWAS, OAU

Mali is one of the world's most undeveloped countries. Over half the area is barren desert. South of Tombouctou the savannah-covered plains support a wide variety of wildlife. Most of the population live in the Niger valley and grow cotton, oil seeds and groundnuts. Fishing is important. Mali has few mineral resources. Recent droughts have taken their toll of livestock and agriculture. Main exports are cotton and livestock. There is no industry.

MALTA

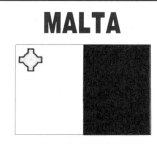

STATUS: Republic
AREA: 316 sq km (122 sq miles)
POPULATION: 356,000
ANNUAL NATURAL INCREASE: –0.6%
CAPITAL: Valletta
LANGUAGE: Maltese, English, Italian
RELIGION: Great majority Roman Catholic
CURRENCY: Maltese lira (MTL)
ORGANISATIONS: Comm, UN, Council of Europe

Malta lies about 96km(60 miles) south of Sicily, and consists of three islands; Malta, Gozo and Comino. Malta has a Mediterranean climate with mild winters, hot dry summers and an average rainfall of 51cm(20in). About 40% of the land is under cultivation with wheat, potatoes, tomatoes and vines the main crops. The large natural harbour at Valletta has made it a major transit port. Tourism is also an important source of revenue. Principal exports are machinery, beverages, tobacco, flowers, wine, leather goods and potatoes.

MAN, ISLE OF
STATUS: British Crown Dependency
AREA: 572 sq km (221 sq miles)
POPULATION: 64,000
CAPITAL: Douglas

MARIANA ISLANDS, NORTHERN
STATUS: Self-governing commonwealth territory of USA
AREA: 471 sq km (182 sq miles)
POPULATION: 20,591

MARSHALL ISLANDS
STATUS: Self-governing State in Compact of Free Association with USA
AREA: 181 sq km (70 sq miles)
POPULATION: 40,609
CAPITAL: Majuro

MARTINIQUE
STATUS: Overseas Department of France
AREA: 1,079 sq km (417 sq miles)
POPULATION: 359,000
CAPITAL: Fort-de-France

MAURITANIA

STATUS: Republic
AREA: 1,030,700 sq km (397,850 sq miles)
POPULATION: 2,025,000
ANNUAL NATURAL INCREASE: 2.6%
CAPITAL: Nouakchott
LANGUAGE: Arabic, French
RELIGION: Muslim
CURRENCY: ouguiya (MRO)
ORGANISATIONS: UN, ECOWAS, Arab League, OAU

Situated on the west coast of Africa, Mauritania consists of savannah, steppes and desert with high temperatures, low rainfall and frequent droughts. There is very little arable farming except in the Senegal river valley where millet and dates are grown. Most Mauritanians raise cattle, sheep, goats or camels. The country has only one railway which is used to transport the chief export, iron ore, from the mines to the coast at Nouadhibou. Severe drought during the last decade decimated the livestock population and forced many nomadic tribesmen into the towns. Coastal fishing contributes nearly 50% of foreign earnings. Exports are almost exclusively confined to iron ore, copper and fish products.

MAURITIUS

STATUS: Commonwealth State
AREA: 1,865 sq km (720 sq miles)
POPULATION: 1,075,000
ANNUAL NATURAL INCREASE: 1.0%
CAPITAL: Port Louis
LANGUAGE: English, French Creole, Hindi, Bhojpuri

RELIGION: 51% Hindu, 31% Christian 17% Muslim
CURRENCY: Mauritian rupee (MUR)
ORGANISATIONS: Comm, UN, OAU

Mauritius is a mountainous island in the Indian Ocean. It has a varied climate with temperatures ranging from 7° to 36°C(45° to 97°F) and annual rainfall of between 153 and 508cm(60 to 200in). Sugar-cane and its by-products are the mainstay of the economy and tourism is developing rapidly.

MAYOTTE
STATUS: French 'Territorial Collectivity', claimed by Comoros
AREA: 376 sq km (145 sq miles)
POPULATION: 77,300
CAPITAL: Dzaoudzi

MELILLA
STATUS: Spanish External Province
AREA: 12.5 sq km (4.8 sq miles)
POPULATION: 62,569

MEXICO

STATUS: Federal Republic
AREA: 1,972,545 sq km (761,400 sq miles)
POPULATION: 86,154,000
ANNUAL NATURAL INCREASE: 2.2%
CAPITAL: Mexico City
LANGUAGE: Spanish
RELIGION: 96% Roman Catholic
CURRENCY: Mexican peso (MXP)
ORGANISATIONS: UN, OAS

The landscape of Mexico consists mainly of mountain ranges and dissected plateaux. The only extensive flat lands are in the Yucatan Peninsula. As much of the land is above 500 m (1640 ft) temperature and rainfall are modified by altitude and the landscape. The north is arid but the south is humid and tropical. The land requires irrigation to support agriculture. Maize and beans are grown for local consumption. The population has outstripped food production and many Mexicans have moved to the cities. Minerals, especially silver, uranium and gold, are the main source of Mexico's wealth but the mines are mostly foreign-owned and Mexico aims to lessen this dependence on foreign investment as the country develops. Oil, natural gas and coal all have considerable reserves and are gradually becoming more important. Main exports are crude oil and machinery, along with coffee and frozen shrimps. Tourism brings in important foreign revenue.

MICRONESIA
STATUS: Self-governing Federation of States in Free Association with USA
AREA: 330 sq km (127 sq miles)
POPULATION: 109,000
CAPITAL: Kolonia

MOLDAVIA

STATUS: Republic
AREA: 33,700 sq km (13,010 sq miles)
POPULATION: 4,400,000
CAPITAL: Kishinev
LANGUAGE: Romanian, Russian
RELIGION: Orthodox
CURRENCY: rouble
ORGANISATIONS: CIS

A country of hilly plains, Moldavia enjoys a warm and dry climate with relatively mild winters. Given its very fertile soil, arable farming dominates agricultural output with viticulture, fruit and vegetables especially important. Sunflower seeds are the main industrial crop; wheat and maize the chief grain crops. Tradi-

tionally, food processing has been the major industry but recently machine-building and engineering have been expanding. Although Moldavia has close ethnic, linguistic and historic ties with neighbouring Romania, any moves towards re-unification have been fiercely resisted by the Russian minority in the east.

MONACO

STATUS: Principality
AREA: 1.6 sq km (0.6 sq miles)
POPULATION: 29,876
ANNUAL NATURAL INCREASE: 1.4%
CAPITAL: Monaco-ville
LANGUAGE: French, Monegasque, Italian, English

RELIGION: 90% Roman Catholic
CURRENCY: French franc (FRF)

The tiny Principality is the world's smallest independent state after the Vatican City. It occupies a thin strip of the French Mediterranean coast near the Italian border and is backed by the Maritime Alps. It comprises the towns of Monaco, la Condamine, Fontvieille and Monte Carlo. Most revenue comes from tourism, casinos and light industry. Land has been reclaimed from the sea to extend the area available for commercial development.

MONGOLIA

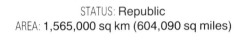

STATUS: Republic
AREA: 1,565,000 sq km (604,090 sq miles)

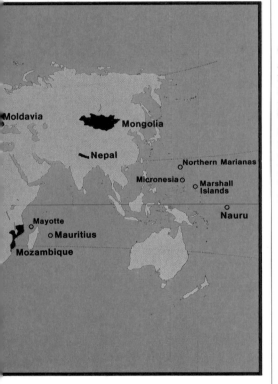

POPULATION: 2,095,000
ANNUAL NATURAL INCREASE: 2.8%
CAPITAL: Ulan Bator (Ulaanbaatar)
LANGUAGE: Khalkha Mongolian
RELIGION: some Buddhist Lamaism
CURRENCY: tugrik (MNT)
ORGANISATIONS: UN, OIEC

Situated between China and the Russian Federation, Mongolia has one of the lowest population densities in the world. Much of the country consists of a high undulating plateau (1500 m or 4920 ft) covered with grassland. To the north, mountain ranges reaching 4231 m (13,881 ft) bridge the border with the Russian Federation, and to the south is the large expanse of the Gobi desert where rainfall averages only 10-13 cm (4-5 in) a year. The climate is very extreme with January temperatures falling to –34°C (–29°F). Mongolia is predominantly a farming economy, its main exports being cattle and horses, and wheat, barley, millet and oats are also grown. Its natural resources include some oil, coal, iron ore, gold, tin and copper.

MONTSERRAT
STATUS: UK Crown Colony
AREA: 160 sq km (41 sq miles)
POPULATION: 13,000
CAPITAL: Plymouth

MOROCCO

STATUS: Kingdom
AREA: 710,895 sq km (274,414 sq miles)
POPULATION: 25,061,000
ANNUAL NATURAL INCREASE: 2.7%
CAPITAL: Rabat
LANGUAGE: Arabic, French, Spanish, Berber
RELIGION: Muslim majority, Christian and Jewish minorities
CURRENCY: Moroccan dirham (MAD)
ORGANISATIONS: UN, Arab League

One third of Morocco, on the north-west coast of Africa, consists of the Atlas Mountains reaching 4165 m (13,665 ft). Between the Atlas and the Atlantic coastal strip is an area of high plateau bordered on the south by the Sahara. The north of the country has a Mediterranean climate and vegetable, and west-facing slopes of the Atlas have high annual rainfall and are thickly forested. Morocco has the world's largest phosphate deposits. The main crops are wheat and barley, and tourism is a major industry.

MOZAMBIQUE

STATUS: Republic
AREA: 784,755 sq km (302,915 sq miles)
POPULATION: 15,656,000
ANNUAL NATURAL INCREASE: 2.7%
CAPITAL: Maputo
LANGUAGE: Portuguese, tribal languages
RELIGION: mainly traditional beliefs, 15% Christian, 15% Muslim
CURRENCY: metical (MZM)
ORGANISATIONS: UN, OAU

The ex-Portuguese colony of Mozambique consists of a large coastal plain, rising towards the interior to the plateaux and mountain ranges which border Malawi, Zambia and Zimbabwe. The highlands in the north reach 2436m (7992ft). The climate is tropical on the coastal plain, although high altitudes make it cooler inland. Over 90% of the population are subsistence farmers cultivating coconuts, cashews, cotton, maize and rice. Mozambique also acts as an entrepôt, handling exports from South Africa, and landlocked Zambia and Malawi. Coal is the main mineral deposit and there are large reserves. Other underexploited minerals are iron ore, bauxite and gold.

NAMIBIA

STATUS: Republic
AREA: 824,295 sq km (318,180 sq miles)
POPULATION: 1,781,000
ANNUAL NATURAL INCREASE: 3.2%
CAPITAL: Windhoek
LANGUAGE: Afrikaans, German, English, regional languages
RELIGION: 90% Christian
CURRENCY: South African rand (ZAR)
ORGANISATIONS: Comm, UN, OAU

The south-west African country of Namibia is one of the driest in the world. The Namib desert on the coast has less than 5cm (2in) average rainfall a year, the Kalahari to the north-east 10-25cm (4-10in). The vegetation is sparse. Maize and sorghum are grown in the northern highlands and sheep are reared in the south. Namibia is, however, rich in mineral resources, with large deposits of diamonds, lead, tin and zinc, and the world's largest uranium mine. Once a trust territory under the auspices of the United Nations, Namibia achieved independence in 1990.

NAURU

STATUS: Republic
AREA: 21 sq km (8 sq miles)
POPULATION: 10,000
ANNUAL NATURAL INCREASE: –0.3%
CAPITAL: Yaren
LANGUAGE: Nauruan, English
RELIGION: Nauruan Protestant majority
CURRENCY: Australian dollar (AUD)
ORGANISATIONS: Comm (special member)

Nauru is one of the smallest republics in the world. Its great wealth has been entirely derived from phosphate deposits. The flat coastal lowlands encircled by coral reefs rise gently to the central plateau where the phosphate is mined. Most phosphate is exported to Australasia and Japan. Deposits may soon be exhausted.

NEPAL

STATUS: Kingdom
AREA: 141,415 sq km (54,585 sq miles)
POPULATION: 18,916,000
ANNUAL NATURAL INCREASE: 2.6%
CAPITAL: Kathmandu
LANGUAGE: Nepali, Maithir, Bhojpuri

RELIGION: 90% Hindu, 5% Buddhist, 3% Muslim
CURRENCY: Nepalese rupee (NPR)
ORGANISATIONS: UN, Col. Plan

Nepal is a Himalayan kingdom sandwiched between China and India. The climate changes sharply with altitude from the southern Tarai plain to the northern Himalayas. Central Kathmandu varies between 2°C(35°F) and 30°C(86°F). Most rain falls between June and October and can reach 250cm(100in). Agriculture concentrates on rice, maize and cattle, buffaloes, sheep and goats. The small amount of industry processes local products.

NETHERLANDS

STATUS: Kingdom
AREA: 33,940 sq km (13,105 sq miles)
POPULATION: 15,010,000
ANNUAL NATURAL INCREASE: 0.5%
CAPITAL: Amsterdam (seat of Government: The Hague)
LANGUAGE: Dutch
RELIGION: 40% Roman Catholic 30% Protestant. Jewish minority
CURRENCY: gulden (guilder) or florin (NLG)
ORGANISATIONS: UN, Council of Europe, EC, NATO, OECD, WEU

The Netherlands is situated at the western edge of the North European plain. The country is exceptionally low-lying, and about 25% of its territory has been reclaimed from the sea. The wide coastal belt consists of flat marshland, mud-flats, sand-dunes and dykes. Further inland, the flat alluvial plain is drained by the Rhine, Maas and Ijssel. A complex network of dykes and canals prevents the area from flooding. To the south and east the land rises. Flat and exposed to strong winds, the Netherlands has mild winters and cool summers.

The Dutch are leading world producers of dairy goods and also cultivate crops such as wheat, barley, oats and potatoes. Lacking mineral resources, much of the industry of the Netherlands is dependent on natural gas. Most manufacturing industry has developed around Rotterdam. Here are oil refineries, steel-works and chemical and food processing plants.

NETHERLANDS ANTILLES
STATUS: Self-governing part of Netherlands Realm
AREA: 800 sq km (308 sq miles)
POPULATION: 192,866
CAPITAL: Willemstad

NEW BRITAIN
STATUS: Island, part of Papua New Guinea
AREA: 36,500 sq km (14,090 sq miles)
POPULATION: 268,400

NEW CALEDONIA
STATUS: Overseas Territory of France
AREA: 19,105 sq km (7,375 sq miles)
POPULATION: 144,051
CAPITAL: Nouméa

NEW GUINEA
STATUS: Island comprising Irian Jaya and part of Papua New Guinea
AREA: 808,510 sq km (312,085 sq miles)
POPULATION: 3,763,300

NEW ZEALAND

STATUS: Commonwealth Nation
AREA: 265,150 sq km (102,350 sq miles)
POPULATION: 3,390,000
ANNUAL NATURAL INCREASE: 0.8%
CAPITAL: Wellington
LANGUAGE: English, Maori
RELIGION: 35% Anglican Christian, 22% Presbyterian, 16% Roman Catholic
CURRENCY: New Zealand dollar (NZD)
ORGANISATIONS: Comm, UN, ANZUS, Col. Plan, OECD

The two main islands that make up New Zealand lie in the South Pacific Ocean. The Southern Alps run the length of South Island with a narrow coastal strip in the west and a broader plain to the east. Stewart Island lies beyond the Foreaux Strait to the south. North Island is less mountainous. Most of the country enjoys a temperate climate. Nearly 20% of the land is forested and 50% pasture. New Zealand is one of the world's leading exporters of beef, mutton and wool. Most exploited minerals are for industrial use – clay, iron sand, limestone, sand and coal. Manufacturing industries and tourism are of increasing importance. New trading links are developing with countries bordering the Pacific.

NICARAGUA

STATUS: Republic
AREA: 148,000 sq km (57,130 sq miles)
POPULATION: 3,871,000
ANNUAL NATURAL INCREASE: 3.4%
CAPITAL: Managua
LANGUAGE: Spanish
RELIGION: Roman Catholic
CURRENCY: cordoba-oro (NIO)
ORGANISATIONS: UN, CACM, OAS

Nicaragua is the largest of the Central American republics south of Mexico situated between the Caribbean and the Pacific. Active volcanic mountains parallel the western coast. The south is dominated by Lakes Managua and Nicaragua. Climate is tropical with rains May to October. Agriculture is the main occupation with cotton, coffee, sugar-cane and fruit the main exports. Gold, silver and copper are mined.

NIGER

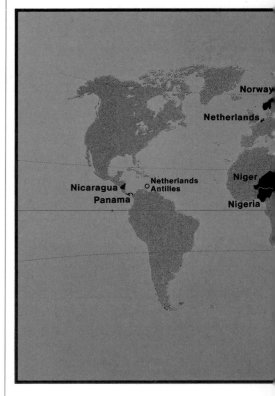

STATUS: Republic
AREA: 1,186,410 sq km (457,955 sq miles)
POPULATION: 7,732,000
ANNUAL NATURAL INCREASE: 3.5%
CAPITAL: Niamey
LANGUAGE: French, Hausa and other local languages
RELIGION: 85% Muslim, 15% animist
CURRENCY: CFA franc (W Africa) (XOF)
ORGANISATIONS: UN, ECOWAS, OAU

Niger is a vast landlocked south Saharan republic with rainfall gradually decreasing from 56cm(22in) in the south to near zero in the north. Temperatures are above 35°C(95°F) for

much of the year. Most of the population are farmers particularly cattle, sheep and goat herders. Recent droughts have affected both cereals and livestock. Large deposits of uranium ore and phosphates are being exploited. The economy depends largely on foreign aid.

NIGERIA

STATUS: Federal Republic
AREA: 923,850 sq km (356,605 sq miles)
POPULATION: 88,500,000
ANNUAL NATURAL INCREASE: 3.3%
CAPITAL: Abuja
LANGUAGE: English, Hausa, Yoruba, Ibo

RELIGION: **Muslim majority, 35% Christian, animist minority**
CURRENCY: **naira (NGN)**
ORGANISATIONS: **Comm, UN, ECOWAS, OAU, OPEC**

The most populous nation in Africa, Nigeria is bounded to the north by the Sahara and to the west, east and south-east by tropical rain forest. The southern half of the country is dominated by the Niger and its tributaries, the north by the interior plateaux. Temperature averages 32°C(90°F) with high humidity. From a basic agricultural economy, Nigeria is slowly being transformed by oil discoveries in the Niger delta which account for 95% of exports.

NIUE
STATUS: **Self-governing Overseas Territory in Free Association with New Zealand**
AREA: **259 sq km (100 sq miles)**
POPULATION: **2,267**
CAPITAL: **Alofi**

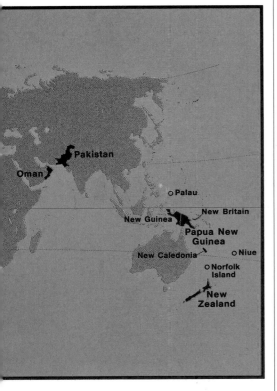

NORFOLK ISLAND
STATUS: **External Territory of Australia**
AREA: **36 sq km (14 sq miles)**
POPULATION: **1,977**
CAPITAL: **Kingston**

NORWAY

STATUS: **Kingdom**
AREA: **323,895 sq km (125,025 sq miles)**
POPULATION: **4,242,000**
ANNUAL NATURAL INCREASE: **0.3%**
CAPITAL: **Oslo**

LANGUAGE: **Norwegian (Bokmal and Nynorsk), Lappish**
RELIGION: **92% Evangelical Lutheran Christian**
CURRENCY: **Norwegian krone (NOK)**
ORGANISATIONS: **UN, Council of Europe, EFTA, NATO, OECD**

Norway is a mountainous country stretching from 58° to 72°N. The climate on the indented western coast is modified by the Gulf Stream with high rainfall and relatively mild winters with temperatures averaging −3.9°C(25°F) in January and 17°C(63°F) in July. Rainfall may be as high as 196cm(79in). Most settlements are scattered along the fjords, the coast and around Oslo in the south. Norway is rich in natural resources. Coal, petroleum, natural gas predominate in exports but are supplemented by forestry products and fishing. By value, the most important exports are crude oil and natural gas, food manufacturing and machinery. The advanced production of hydro-electric power has helped develop industry, particularly chemicals, metal products and paper.

OMAN

STATUS: **Sultanate**
AREA: **271,950 sq km (104,970 sq miles)**
POPULATION: **2,000,000**
ANNUAL NATURAL INCREASE: **4.7%**
CAPITAL: **Muscat (Masqat)**
LANGUAGE: **Arabic, English**
RELIGION: **75% Ibadi Muslim, 25% Sunni Muslim**
CURRENCY: **rial Omani (OMR)**
ORGANISATIONS: **UN, Arab League**

The Sultanate occupies the north-east coast of Arabia with a detached portion overlooking the Straits of Hormuz. The desert landscape consists of a coastal plain and low hills rising to plateau in the interior. The two fertile areas are the Batinah in the north and Dhofar in the south. The main crop is dates. Oil provides over 95% of export revenue.

PAKISTAN

STATUS: **Republic**
AREA: **803,940 sq km (310,320 sq miles)**
POPULATION: **112,050,000**
ANNUAL NATURAL INCREASE: **3.2%**
CAPITAL: **Islamabad**
LANGUAGE: **Urdu, Punjabi, Sindhi, Pushtu, English**
RELIGION: **90% Muslim**
CURRENCY: **Pakistani rupee (PKR)**
ORGANISATIONS: **Comm, UN, Col. Plan**

The landscape and the economy of Pakistan are dominated by the river Indus and its tributaries which flow south flanked by the plateau of Baluchistan and the Sulaiman mountains to the west and the Thar desert to the east. The climate is dry and hot averaging 27°C(80°F). Rainfall reaches 90cm(36in) in the northern mountains. Over 50% of the population are engaged in agriculture which is confined to the irrigated areas near the great rivers. Main crops are wheat, cotton, maize, rice and sugarcane. There are many types of low-grade mineral deposits, such as coal and copper, but these are little developed. Main industries are food-processing and metals but these only contribute about 20% to the economy.

PALAU
STATUS: **UN Trustee Territory under US Administration**
AREA: **497 sq km (192 sq miles)**
POPULATION: **14,106**
CAPITAL: **Koror**

PANAMA

STATUS: **Republic**
AREA: **78,515 sq km (30,305 sq miles)**
POPULATION: **2,315,000**
ANNUAL NATURAL INCREASE: **2.2%**
CAPITAL: **Panama**
LANGUAGE: **Spanish, English**
RELIGION: **large Roman Catholic majority**
CURRENCY: **balboa (PAB), US dollar (USD)**
ORGANISATIONS: **UN, OAS**

Panama is situated at the narrowest part of Central America and has both Pacific and Caribbean coastlines. The climate is tropical with little variation throughout the year – average temperature 27°C(80°F). The rainy season is from April to December. Panama probably has the world's largest copper reserves but these are hardly developed. Most foreign revenue is earned from the Panama Canal, and export of petroleum products.

PAPUA NEW GUINEA

STATUS: **Commonwealth Nation**
AREA: **462,840 sq km (178,655 sq miles)**
POPULATION: **3,699,000**
ANNUAL NATURAL INCREASE: **2.4%**
CAPITAL: **Port Moresby**
LANGUAGE: **Pidgin English, English, native languages**
RELIGION: **Pantheist, Christian minority**
CURRENCY: **kina (PGK)**
ORGANISATIONS: **Comm, UN, Col. Plan**

Papua New Guinea (the eastern half of New Guinea and neighbouring islands) is a mountainous country. It has an equatorial climate with temperatures of 21° to 32°C(70° to 90°F) and annual rainfall of over 200cm(79in). Copper is the major mineral deposit with large reserves on Bougainville, one of the neighbouring islands. Sugar and beef-cattle are developing areas of production. Major exports are copra, timber, coffee, rubber and tea.

PARAGUAY

STATUS: Republic
AREA: 406,750 sq km (157,005 sq miles)
POPULATION: 4,277,000
ANNUAL NATURAL INCREASE: 3.2%
CAPITAL: Asunción
LANGUAGE: Spanish, Guarani
RELIGION: 90% Roman Catholic
CURRENCY: guarani (PYG)
ORGANISATIONS: UN, OAS

Paraguay is a landlocked country in South America with temperatures which average 15°C(59°F) all year. The country divides into lush, fertile plains and heavily forested plateau east of the River Paraguay and marshy scrubland (the Chaco) west of the river. Cassava, cotton, soyabeans and maize are the main crops but the rearing of livestock – cattle, horses, pigs and sheep – and food processing, dominate the export trade. The largest hydro-electric dam in the world is at Itaipú. This was constructed as a joint project with Brazil and will eventually have a capacity of 12.6 million kw.

PERU

STATUS: Republic
AREA: 1,285,215 sq km (496,095 sq miles)
POPULATION: 22,332,000
ANNUAL NATURAL INCREASE: 2.2%
CAPITAL: Lima
LANGUAGE: Spanish, Quechua, Aymara
RELIGION: large Roman Catholic majority
CURRENCY: new sol (PEN)
ORGANISATIONS: UN, OAS

Peru divides into three geographical regions. The coastal region is very dry but fertile oases produce cotton, sugar, fruit and fodder crops. This is the most prosperous and heavily populated area which includes the industrial centres around Lima. In the ranges and plateaux of the Andes and the Amazon lowlands the soil is thin but the inhabitants depend on cultivation and grazing. Poor communications have hindered the development of Peru and there are great differences between rich and poor. Peru has rich mineral deposits of copper, lead, zinc and silver. There are oil reserves in the interior.

PHILIPPINES

STATUS: Republic
AREA: 300,000 sq km (115,800 sq miles)
POPULATION: 62,868,000
ANNUAL NATURAL INCREASE: 2.4%
CAPITAL: Manila
LANGUAGE: Pilipino (Tagalog), English, Spanish, Cebuano
RELIGION: 90% Christian, 7% Muslim
CURRENCY: Philippine peso (PHP)
ORGANISATIONS: UN, ASEAN, Col. Plan

The Philippines consist of three main island groups, Luzon and its neighbours, the Visayas and Mindanao, including the Sulus. The archipelago is subject to earthquakes and typhoons. It has a monsoon climate and over 40% of the country is covered by rainforest. Fishing is important but small farms dominate the economy, producing rice and copra for domestic consumption and other coconut and sugar products for export. Forestry is becoming increasingly important. Main exports are textiles, fruit and electronic products. High unemployment and emigration are problems to be faced.

PITCAIRN ISLAND
STATUS: UK Dependent Territory
AREA: 45 sq km (17.25 sq miles)
POPULATION: 59
CAPITAL: Adamstown

POLAND

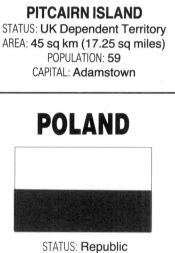

STATUS: Republic
AREA: 312,685 sq km (120,695 sq miles)
POPULATION: 38,180,000
ANNUAL NATURAL INCREASE: 0.8%
CAPITAL: Warsaw (Warszawa)
LANGUAGE: Polish
RELIGION: 90% Roman Catholic
CURRENCY: zloty (PLZ)
ORGANISATIONS: UN, OIEC

Poland occupies most of the southern coast of the Baltic Sea. Part of the North European Plain, the flat well-drained landscape rises gently towards the foothills of the Carpathians in the far south. The climate is continental with long severe winters. Average winter temperatures are below freezing point; rainfall averages between 52 and 73cm(21 and 29in). Both agriculture and natural resources play an important part in the economy and Poland is nearly self-sufficient in cereals sugar-beet and potatoes. There are large reserves of coal, copper, sulphur and natural gas. Major industries are ship-building in the north and production of metals and chemicals in the major mining centres in the south.

PORTUGAL

STATUS: Republic
AREA: 91,630 sq km (35,370 sq miles)
POPULATION: 10,525,000
ANNUAL NATURAL INCREASE: 0.6%
CAPITAL: Lisbon (Lisboa)
LANGUAGE: Portuguese
RELIGION: large Roman Catholic majority
CURRENCY: escudo (PTE)
ORGANISATIONS: UN, Council of Europe, EC, NATO, OECD, WEU

Portugal occupies the western, Atlantic coast of the Iberian Peninsula. The Mediterranean climate is modified by westerly winds and the Gulf Stream. This is reflected in the lusher mixed

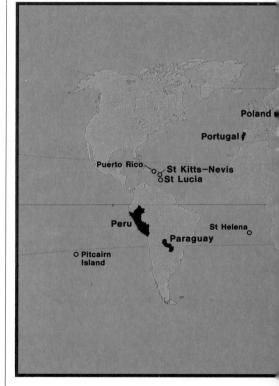

deciduous/coniferous forest in the northern mountains and the Mediterranean scrub in the far south. The hills along the coast rise to the interior plateaux. A quarter of the population are farmers growing vines, olives, wheat, maize and beans. Mineral deposits include coal, copper, kaolinite and uranium.

PUERTO RICO
STATUS: Self-governing Commonwealth Territory of USA
AREA: 8,960 sq km (3,460 sq miles)
POPULATION: 3,599,000
CAPITAL: San Juan

QATAR

STATUS: State
AREA: 11,435 sq km (4,415 sq miles)
POPULATION: 368,000

ANNUAL NATURAL INCREASE: 5.2%
CAPITAL: Doha (Ad Dawhah)
LANGUAGE: Arabic, English
RELIGION: Muslim
CURRENCY: Qatari Riyal (QAR)
ORGANISATIONS: UN, Arab League, OPEC

The country occupies all of the Qatar peninsula which reaches north from the north-east Arabian coast into the Persian Gulf. The land is flat and dry desert; the climate is hot and humid. July temperatures average 37°C (98°F) and annual rainfall averages 62mm (2.5in). Irrigation schemes are expanding production of fruit and vegetables for home consumption. The main source of revenue is from the exploitation of oil and gas reserves. The N.W. Dome oilfield contains 12% of known world gas reserves.

RÉUNION

STATUS: Overseas Department of France
AREA: 2,510 sq km (969 sq miles)
POPULATION: 596,000
CAPITAL: Saint-Denis

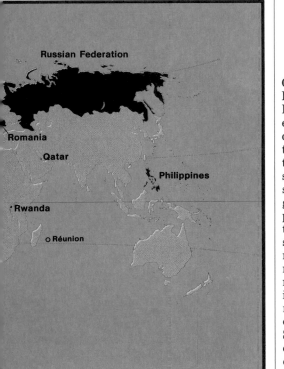

ROMANIA

STATUS: Republic
AREA: 237,500 sq km (91,675 sq miles)
POPULATION: 23,490,000
ANNUAL NATURAL INCREASE: 0.4%
CAPITAL: Bucharest (Bucuresti)
LANGUAGE: Romanian, Magyar
RELIGION: 65% Orthodox, 8% Roman Catholic, 3% Protestant
CURRENCY: leu (ROL)
ORGANISATIONS: UN, OIEC

The landscape of Romania is dominated by the great curve of the Carpathians. Lowlands to the west, east and south contain rich agricultural land. The climate in continental with variable

rainfall, hot summers and cold winters. Forced industrialisation had taken the economy from one based on agriculture to one dependent on heavy industry, notably chemicals, metal processing and machine-building. Political and economic prospects for the future look bleak.

RUSSIAN FEDERATION

STATUS: Federation
AREA: 17,078,005 sq km (6,592,110 sq miles)
POPULATION: 148,100,000
CAPITAL: Moscow (Moskva)
LANGUAGE: Russian
RELIGION: Russian Orthodox, Jewish and Muslim minorities
CURRENCY: rouble
ORGANISATIONS: UN, CIS

Covering much of eastern and north-eastern Europe and all of northern Asia, the Russian Federation (Russia) displays an enormous variety of landforms and climates. The Arctic deserts of the north give way to the wastes of the tundra and taiga which cover two-thirds of the country. In the far south, beyond the steppes some areas assume sub-tropical and semi-desert landscapes. Almost all of Russia's great rivers flow north. The majority of the population live west of the north–south spine of the Urals but in recent decades there has been a substantial migration eastwards to the Siberian basin in order to exploit its vast natural resources. Oil and gas pipelines link Siberia to refineries further west in Russia and elsewhere in Europe. Russia's extraordinary wealth of natural resources has been a key factor in the country's speedy industrialisation during the Soviet period. Heavy industry still plays a decisive role in the economy, while light and consumer industries have remained relatively backward and under developed. Agricultural land covers one-sixth of Russia's territory but there remains great potential for increase through drainage and clearance. By the mid-1980s the Soviet system was finally acknowledged to have reached an impasse, and the failure of the 'perestroika' programme for reform precipitated the disintegration of the Soviet Union, which finally broke up in 1991. The future is fraught with political and economic uncertainty.

RWANDA

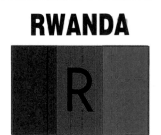

STATUS: Republic
AREA: 26,330 sq km (10,165 sq miles)
POPULATION: 7,181,000

ANNUAL NATURAL INCREASE: 3.3%
CAPITAL: Kigali
LANGUAGE: French, Kinyarwanda (Bantu), tribal languages
RELIGION: 50% animist, 50% Roman Catholic
CURRENCY: Rwanda franc (RWF)
ORGANISATIONS: UN, OAU

Small and isolated Rwanda supports a high density of population on the moist plateaux east of the Rift Valley. Agriculture is basically subsistence with coffee the major export. Few minerals have been discovered, and manufacturing is confined to food processing and construction materials.

ST HELENA

STATUS: UK Dependent Territory
AREA: 122 sq km (47 sq miles)
POPULATION: 5,564
CAPITAL: Jamestown

ST KITTS (ST CHRISTOPHER)-NEVIS

STATUS: Commonwealth State
AREA: 262 sq km (101 sq miles)
POPULATION: 44,000
ANNUAL NATURAL INCREASE: −0.9%
CAPITAL: Basseterre
LANGUAGE: English
RELIGION: Christian
CURRENCY: E. Caribbean dollar (XCD)
ORGANISATIONS: Comm, UN, CARICOM, OAS

St Kitts-Nevis, in the Leeward Islands, comprises two volcanic islands: St Christopher (St Kitts) and Nevis. The climate is tropical and humid with temperatures between 16°C and 33°C (61°F and 91°F) and an average annual rainfall of 140cm (55in). Main exports are sugar and molasses and cotton. Tourism is an important source of revenue.

ST LUCIA

STATUS: Commonwealth State
AREA: 616 sq km (238 sq miles)
POPULATION: 146,600
ANNUAL NATURAL INCREASE: 2.0%
CAPITAL: Castries
LANGUAGE: English, French patois
RELIGION: 80% Roman Catholic
CURRENCY: E. Caribbean dollar (XCD)
ORGANISATIONS: Comm, UN, CARICOM, OAS

Independent since 1979 this small tropical Caribbean island in the Lesser Antilles grows coconuts, cocoa, citrus fruit and bananas. Most of the population are small farmers. Main industries are food and drink processing and all consumer goods are imported. There are no commercial mineral deposits. Tourism is a rapidly developing industry.

ST PIERRE & MIQUELON

STATUS: 'Territorial Collectivity'of France
AREA: 241 sq km (93 sq miles)
POPULATION: 6,392
CAPITAL: St Pierre

ST VINCENT

STATUS: Commonwealth State
AREA: 389 sq km (150 sq miles)
POPULATION: 113,950
ANNUAL NATURAL INCREASE: 1.1%
CAPITAL: Kingstown
LANGUAGE: English
RELIGION: Christian
CURRENCY: E. Caribbean dollar (XCD)
ORGANISATIONS: Comm, UN, CARICOM, OAS

St Vincent in the Lesser Antilles comprises the main island and a chain of small islands called the Northern Grenadines. The climate is tropical. Most exports are foodstuffs: arrowroot, sweet potatoes, bananas, coconut products and yams. Some sugar-cane is grown for the production of rum and other drinks. Tourism is an expanding industry.

SAN MARINO

STATUS: Republic
AREA: 61 sq km (24 sq miles)
POPULATION: 24,000
ANNUAL NATURAL INCREASE: 1.2%
CAPITAL: San Marino
LANGUAGE: Italian
RELIGION: Roman Catholic
CURRENCY: Italian lira (ITL),
San Marino coinage
ORGANISATIONS: Council of Europe

An independent state within Italy, San Marino straddles a limestone peak in the Apennines south of Rimini. The economy is centred around tourism and sale of postage stamps. Most of the population are farmers growing cereals, olives and vines and tending herds of sheep and goats. Wine and textiles are exported.

SÃO TOMÉ AND PRINCÍPE

STATUS: Republic
AREA: 964 sq km (372 sq miles)
POPULATION: 115,600
ANNUAL NATURAL INCREASE: 3.0%
CAPITAL: São Tomé
LANGUAGE: Portuguese, Fang
RELIGION: Roman Catholic majority
CURRENCY: dobra (STD)
ORGANISATIONS: UN, OAU

Independent from Portugal since 1975, two large and several small islands make up this tiny state situated near the equator 200km(125 miles) off the west coast of Africa. The climate is tropical with temperatures averaging 25°C(77°F) and rainfall between 100 and 500cm (40 and 197in). Cocoa, coconuts and palm oil are the main crops grown on the rich volcanic soil. Other foods and consumer goods are imported.

SARDINIA

STATUS: Island Region of Italy
AREA: 24,090 sq km (9,300 sq miles)
POPULATION: 1,651,218
CAPITAL: Cagliari

SAUDI ARABIA

STATUS: Kingdom
AREA: 2,400,900 sq km (926,745 sq miles)
POPULATION: 12,000,000
ANNUAL NATURAL INCREASE: 5.1%
CAPITAL: Riyadh (Ar Riyād)
LANGUAGE: Arabic
RELIGION: Muslim (85% Sunni)
CURRENCY: Saudi riyal (SAR)
ORGANISATIONS: UN, Arab League, OPEC

Saudi Arabia occupies the heart of the vast arid Arabian Peninsula. There are no rivers which flow all year round. To the east, high mountains fringe the Red Sea but even here rainfall rarely exceeds 38cm (15in). Temperatures rise beyond 44°C (111°F) in the summer. The interior plateau slopes down gently eastwards to the Gulf and supports little vegetation. The south-east part of the country is well named as the 'Empty Quarter'; it is almost devoid of population. Only in the coastal strips and oases are cereals and date palms grown. Oil is the most important resource and export commodity and economic development is dependent on its revenue. Irrigation schemes and land reclamation projects are attempting to raise food production.

SENEGAL

STATUS: Republic
AREA: 196,720 sq km (75,935 sq miles)
POPULATION: 7,327,000
ANNUAL NATURAL INCREASE: 3.0%
CAPITAL: Dakar
LANGUAGE: French, native languages
RELIGION: 90% Muslim (Sunni),
5% Roman Catholic
CURRENCY: CFA franc (W Africa) (XOF)
ORGANISATIONS: UN, ECOWAS, OAU

Senegal on the coast of West Africa, is a flat, dry country cut through by the Gambia, Casamance and Senegal rivers. Rainfall rarely ex-

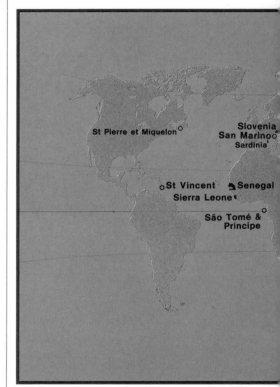

ceeds 58cm(23in) on the wetter coast. The interior savannah supports varied wildlife but little agriculture. Groundnuts, cotton and millet are the main crops, but frequent droughts have reduced their value as cash crops. Phosphate mining, ship-repairing and food processing are the major industries.

SEYCHELLES

STATUS: Republic
AREA: 404 sq km (156 sq miles)
POPULATION: 67,000
ANNUAL NATURAL INCREASE: 0.9%
CAPITAL: Victoria
LANGUAGE: English, French, Creole

RELIGION: **90% Roman Catholic**
CURRENCY: **Seychelles rupee (SCR)**
ORGANISATIONS: **Comm, UN, OAU**

This archipelago in the Indian Ocean comprises of over 100 granite or coral islands. Mahe, the largest, covers 155 sq km (60 sq miles) rising steeply to over 900 m (2953 ft). The coral islands rise only a few metres above sea level. Temperatures are a constant 24-29°C (75-84°F), and rainfall is in the range of 180-345 cm (71-135 in). Main exports are copra, coconuts and cinnamon. The staple food, rice, is imported although crops such as cassava, sweet potatoes, yams and sugar cane are grown for local consumption. Fishing is also important to the economy. Tourism has expanded greatly since the opening of the international airport in 1978.

SHIKOKU
STATUS: **Island Prefecture of Japan**
AREA: **18,755 sq km (7,240 sq miles)**
POPULATION: **4,224,000**

SIERRA LEONE

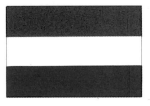

STATUS: **Republic**
AREA: **72,325 sq km (27,920 sq miles)**
POPULATION: **4,151,000**
ANNUAL NATURAL INCREASE: **2.4%**
CAPITAL: **Freetown**
LANGUAGE: **English, (also Krio Temne, Mende)**
RELIGION: **animist majority. Muslim and Christian minorities**
CURRENCY: **leone (SLL)**
ORGANISATIONS: **Comm, UN, ECOWAS, OAU**

A former British colony, the coastline of Sierra Leone is dominated by swamps broken only by the mountainous peninsula south of Freetown.

A wide coastal plain extends inland to the foothills of the interior plateaux and mountains. The land is not fertile due to the poor soils with most of the population farming at subsistence level. Mineral deposits include diamonds, iron ore and bauxite with manufacturing only developed around the capital. Oil-, rice- and timber-mills process these products for export.

SINGAPORE

STATUS: **Republic**
AREA: **616 sq km (238 sq miles)**
POPULATION: **3,002,800**
ANNUAL NATURAL INCREASE: **1.2%**
CAPITAL: **Singapore**
LANGUAGE: **Malay, Chinese (Mandarin), Tamil, English**
RELIGION: **Daoist, Buddhist, Muslim, Christian and Hindu**
CURRENCY: **Singapore dollar (SGD)**
ORGANISATIONS: **Comm, UN, ASEAN, Col. Plan**

Founded by Sir Stamford Raffles, the state of Singapore has been transformed from an island of mangrove swamps into one the world's major entrepreneurial centres. The island, connected to Peninsular Malaysia by a man-made causeway, has a hot, humid climate with 224cm(96in) of rain per year. With few natural resources, Singapore depends on manufacturing precision goods and electronic products along with financial services.

SLOVENIA

STATUS: **Republic**
AREA: **20,250 sq km (7,815 sq miles)**
POPULATION: **1,924,000**
CAPITAL: **Ljubljana**
LANGUAGE: **Slovenian**
RELIGION: **mainly Roman Catholic**
CURRENCY: **Slovenian dinar (Tolar)**

The northernmost part of the former Yugoslav federation, Slovenia has always been one of the key gateways from the Balkans to central and western Europe. Much of the country is mountainous, its heartland and main centre of population being the Ljubljana basin. Extensive mountain pastures provide profitable dairy-farming, but the amount of cultivable land is restricted. There are large mercury mines in the northwest which, in recent decades, has also developed a broad range of light industries. Combined with tourism, this has given the country a well-balanced economy. After a brief military conflict Slovenia won its independence in 1991 which status has since been internationally recognised.

SOLOMON ISLANDS

STATUS: **Commonwealth Nation**
AREA: **29,790 sq km (11,500 sq miles)**
POPULATION: **321,000**
ANNUAL NATURAL INCREASE: **3.5%**
CAPITAL: **Honiara**
LANGUAGE: **English, Pidgin English, native languages**
RELIGION: **95% Christian**
CURRENCY: **Solomon Island dollar (SBD)**
ORGANISATIONS: **Comm, UN**

Situated in the South Pacific Ocean the Solomon Islands consist of six main and many smaller islands. The mountainous large islands are covered by tropical rain forest reflecting the high temperatures and heavy rainfall. The main crops are coconuts, cocoa and rice, with copra, timber and palm oil being the main exports. This former British protectorate became independent in 1978. There are reserves of bauxite, phosphate and gold.

SOMALIA

STATUS: **Republic**
AREA: **630,000 sq km (243,180 sq miles)**
POPULATION: **7,497,000**
ANNUAL NATURAL INCREASE: **3.0%**
CAPITAL: **Mogadishu (Muqdisho)**
LANGUAGE: **Somali, Arabic, English, Italian**
RELIGION: **Muslim. Roman Catholic minority**
CURRENCY: **Somali shilling (SOS)**
ORGANISATIONS: **UN, Arab League, OAU**

Independent since 1960, Somalia, is a hot and arid country in north-east Africa. The semi-desert of the northern mountains contrasts with the plains of the south where the bush country is particularly rich in wildlife. Most of the population are nomadic, following herds of camels, sheep, goats and cattle. Little land is cultivated but cotton, maize, millet and sugar-cane are grown. Bananas are a major export. Iron ore, gypsum and uranium deposits are found but none are yet exploited.

SOUTH AFRICA

STATUS: **Republic**
AREA: **1,184,825 sq km (457,345 sq miles)**
POPULATION: **35,282,000**
ANNUAL NATURAL INCREASE: **2.4%**
CAPITAL: **Pretoria (administrative)
Cape Town (legislative)**

LANGUAGE: Afrikaans, English, various African languages
RELIGION: mainly Christian, Hindu, Jewish and Muslim minorities
CURRENCY: rand (ZAR)
ORGANISATIONS: UN

TRIBAL HOMELANDS

This includes the Bantu homelands and the South African homeland republics of Bophuthatswana, Ciskei, Transkei and Venda
POPULATION: 16,000,000 approx.

CAPE PROVINCE

STATUS: Province
AREA: 656,640 sq km (253,465 sq miles)
POPULATION: 4,901,251

NATAL

STATUS: Province
AREA: 86,965 sq km (33,570 sq miles)
POPULATION: 2,145,018

ORANGE FREE STATE

STATUS: Province
AREA: 127,990 sq km (49,405 sq miles)
POPULATION: 1,863,327

TRANSVAAL

STATUS: Province
AREA: 268,915 sq km (103,800 sq miles)
POPULATION: 7,532,179

The Republic of South Africa is the most highly developed country in Africa. Geographically, the interior consists of a plateau of over 900m(2955ft) drained by the Orange and Limpopo rivers. Surrounding the plateau is a pronounced escarpment below which the land descends by steps to the sea. Rainfall in most areas is less than 50cm(20in) becoming increasingly drier in the west. Agriculture is limited by poor soils but sheep and cattle are extensively grazed. Main crops are maize, wheat, sugar-cane, vegetables, cotton and vines. Wine is an important export commodity. South Africa abounds in minerals. Diamonds, gold, platinum, silver, uranium, copper, manganese and asbestos are mined and nearly 80% of the continent's coal reserves are in South Africa. Manufacturing and engineering is concentrated in southern Transvaal and around the ports. Most foreign revenue is earned through exports of minerals, metals, precious stones, textiles and chemicals and tobacco.

SPAIN

STATUS: Kingdom
AREA: 504,880 sq km (194,885 sq miles)
POPULATION: 38,991,000
ANNUAL NATURAL INCREASE: 0.5%
CAPITAL: Madrid
LANGUAGE: Spanish (Castilian), Catalan, Basque, Galician
RELIGION: Roman Catholic
CURRENCY: Spanish peseta (ESP)
ORGANISATIONS: UN, Council of Europe, EC, NATO, OECD, WEU

Once a great colonial power, Spain occupies most of the Iberian Peninsula. Mountain ranges fringe the meseta, a vast plateau averaging 600m(1970ft). Climate is affected regionally by latitude and proximity to the Atlantic Ocean and Mediterranean Sea. Much of the land is covered by Mediterranean scrub but wheat, barley, maize, grapes and olives are cultivated. Main cash crops are cotton, olives, tobacco and citrus fruit. Textile manufacturing in the north-east and steel, chemicals, consumer goods and vehicle manufacturing in the towns and cities has proved a magnet for great numbers of the rural population. Other major industries are cement, fishing and forestry. Main minerals are coal, iron ore, uranium and zinc. Tourism is of vital importance to the economy.

SRI LANKA

STATUS: Republic
AREA: 65,610 sq km (25,325 sq miles)
POPULATION: 16,993,000
ANNUAL NATURAL INCREASE: 1.5%
CAPITAL: Colombo
LANGUAGE: Sinhala, Tamil, English
RELIGION: 70% Buddhist, 15% Hindu. Roman Catholic and Muslim minorities
CURRENCY: Sri Lanka rupee (LKR)
ORGANISATIONS: Comm, UN, Col. Plan

Situated only 19km (12 miles) from mainland India, Sri Lanka (also called Ceylon) is an island of undulating coastal plain encircling the central highlands. The climate is divided accordingly between tropical on the coast and temperate in the hills. Annual rainfall averages only 100cm (39in) in the north and east while the south and west receive over 200cm (79in). Natural resources are limited but the rich agricultural land produces tea, rubber and coconuts. Gemstones (sapphire, ruby, beryl, topaz), graphite and salt are mined. The main industries are food processing, textiles, chemicals and rubber.

SUDAN

STATUS: Republic
AREA: 2,505,815 sq km (967,245 sq miles)
POPULATION: 25,204,000
ANNUAL NATURAL INCREASE: 3.0%
CAPITAL: Khartoum
LANGUAGE: Arabic, tribal languages
RELIGION: Muslim (Sunni) 70%, animist and Christian
CURRENCY: Sudanese pound (SDP)
ORGANISATIONS: UN, Arab League, OAU

Sudan, in the upper Nile basin, is Africa's largest country. The land is mostly flat and infertile with a hot, arid climate. The White and Blue Niles are invaluable, serving not only to irrigate cultivated land but also as a potential source of hydro-electric power. Subsistence farming accounts for 80% of the Sudan's total production. Major exports include cotton, groundnuts, sugar cane, and sesame seed. The principal activity is nomadic herding with over 40 million cattle and sheep and 14 million goats.

SURINAM

STATUS: Republic
AREA: 163,820 sq km (63,235 sq miles)
POPULATION: 422,000
ANNUAL NATURAL INCREASE: 2.5%
CAPITAL: Paramaribo

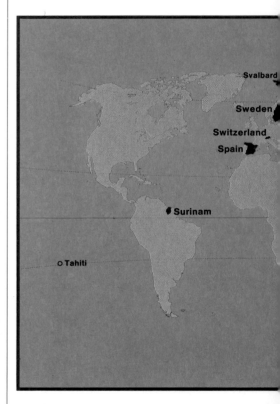

LANGUAGE: Dutch, English, Spanish, Surinamese (Sranang Tongo), Hindi and others
RELIGION: 45% Christian, 28% Hindu, 20% Muslim
CURRENCY: Surinam guilder (SRG)
ORGANISATIONS: UN, OAS

Independent from the Dutch since 1976, Surinam is a small state lying on the north-east coast in the tropics of South America. Physically, there are three main regions: a low-lying, marshy coastal strip; undulating savannah; densely forested highlands. Rice growing takes up 75% of all cultivated land. The introduction of cattle-raising for meat and dairy products is not yet complete. Bauxite accounts for 90% of Surinam's foreign earnings. Rice and timber products are also important. Timber resources are largely untapped.

SVALBARD

STATUS: Archipelago Territory of Norway
AREA: 62,000 sq km (23,930 sq miles)
POPULATION: 3,942

SWAZILAND

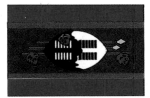

STATUS: Kingdom
AREA: 17,365 sq km (6,705 sq miles)
POPULATION: 768,000
ANNUAL NATURAL INCREASE: 3.4%
CAPITAL: Mbabane
LANGUAGE: English, SiSwati
RELIGION: 60% Christian, 40% traditional
beliefs
CURRENCY: lilangeni (SZL) S. African rand (ZAR)
ORGANISATIONS: Comm, UN, OAU

Landlocked Swaziland in southern Africa, is a sub-tropical, savannah country. It is divided into four main regions: the High, Middle and

Low Velds and the Lebombo Mountains. Rainfall is abundant promoting good pastureland for the many cattle and sheep. Major exports include sugar, meat, citrus fruits, textiles, wood products and asbestos.

SWEDEN

STATUS: Kingdom
AREA: 449,790 sq km (173,620 sq miles)
POPULATION: 8,595,000
ANNUAL NATURAL INCREASE: 0.2%
CAPITAL: Stockholm
LANGUAGE: Swedish, Finnish, Lappish
RELIGION: 95% Evangelical Lutheran

CURRENCY: Swedish krona (SEK)
ORGANISATIONS: UN, Council of Europe, EFTA
OECD

Glacial debris, glacier-eroded valleys and thick glacial clay are all dominant features of Sweden. Physically, Sweden comprises four main regions: Norrland, the northern forested mountains; the Lake District of the centre south; the southern uplands of Jönköping; and the extremely fertile Scania plain of the far south. Summers are short and hot with long, cold winters. Annual rainfall varies between 200 cm (79 in) in the west and south-west, to 50 cm (20 in) in the east and south-east.

Over half the land area is forested resulting in a thriving timber industry, but manufacturing industry, particularly cars and trucks, metal products and machine tools, is becoming increasingly dominant. Mineral resources are also rich and plentiful – iron-ore production alone exceeds 17 million tons a year. There are also deposits of copper, lead and zinc.

SWITZERLAND

STATUS: Federation
AREA: 41,285 sq km (15,935 sq miles)
POPULATION: 6,712,000
ANNUAL NATURAL INCREASE: 0.3%
CAPITAL: Bern (Berne)
LANGUAGE: German, French, Italian, Romansch
RELIGION: 44% Protestant, 48% Roman
Catholic. Jewish minority
CURRENCY: Swiss franc (CHF)
ORGANISATIONS: Council of Europe, EFTA, OECD

Switzerland is a mountainous, landlocked country in the Alps. Winters are very cold with heavy snowfall. Summers are mild with an average July temperature of 18°-19°C (64°-66°F). Rainfall is normally restricted to the summer months. Agriculture is based mainly on dairy farming. Major crops include hay, wheat, barley and potatoes. Industry plays a major role in Switzerland's economy, centred on metal engineering, watchmaking, food processing, textiles and chemicals. Switzerland's history of neutrality from armed conflict has made it an attractive location for the headquarters of several international organisations. The Swiss, on the whole, enjoy a high standard of living. Tourism is also an important source of income and employment. The financial services sector, especially banking, is also of great importance.

SYRIA

STATUS: Republic
AREA: 185,680 sq km (71,675 sq miles)

POPULATION: 12,116,000
ANNUAL NATURAL INCREASE: 3.6%
CAPITAL: Damascus (Dimashq)
LANGUAGE: Arabic
RELIGION: 80% Sunni Muslim. Christian
minority
CURRENCY: Syrian pound (SYP)
ORGANISATIONS: UN, Arab League

Syria is situated at the heart of the Middle East bordered by Turkey, Iraq, Jordan, Israel and Lebanon. Its most fertile areas lie along the coastal strip on the Mediterranean Sea which supports the bulk of its population, and in the depressions and plateaux of the north-east which are cut through by the rivers Orontes and Euphrates. In the south the Anti-Lebanon range is bordered to the east by the Syrian desert. While the coast has a Mediterranean climate with dry hot summers and mild wet winters, the interior becomes increasingly hot and arid – average summer temperatures in the desert reach 43°C (109°F). Rainfall varies between 22 and 40 cm (9 and 16 in). Cotton is Syria's main export crop, and wheat and barley are also grown. Cattle, sheep and goats are the main livestock. Although traditionally an agriculturally-based economy, the country is rapidly becoming industrialised as oil, natural gas and phosphate resources are exploited. Salt and gypsum are mined, oil and oil products, food and textiles are also exported.

TAHITI
STATUS: Main Island of French Polynesia
AREA: 1,042 sq km (402 sq miles)
POPULATION: 115,820

TAIWAN

STATUS: Island Republic of China
AREA: 35,990 sq km (13,890 sq miles)
POPULATION: 19,700,000
ANNUAL NATURAL INCREASE: 1.5%
CAPITAL: Taipei
LANGUAGE: Mandarin Chinese
RELIGION: Buddhist majority. Muslim, Daoist
and Christian minorities
CURRENCY: New Taiwan dollar (TWD)

Taiwan is separated from mainland China by the Taiwan Strait (the former Formosa Channel) in which lie the Pescadores. Two-thirds of Taiwan is mountainous, the highest point attaining 3,950 m (12,959 ft). The flat to rolling coastal plain in the western part of the island accommodates the bulk of the population and the national commerce, industry and agriculture. Climate is tropical, marine, with persistent cloudy conditions. The monsoon rains fall in June to August, annual average 260 cm (102 in). Main crops are rice, tea, fruit, sugar cane and sweet potatoes. Industry is light and heavy, principal exports are textiles, electrical goods and services. Natural resources are limestone, marble, asbestos, copper and sulphur. Natural gas is extracted from the Strait.

TAJIKISTAN

STATUS: Republic
AREA: 143,100 sq km (55,235 sq miles)
POPULATION: 5,200,000
CAPITAL: Dushanbe
LANGUAGE: Tajik, Uzbek, Russian
RELIGION: Muslim
CURRENCY: rouble
ORGANISATIONS: CIS

Situated in the mountainous heart of Asia, more than half the territory of Tajikistan lies above 3000 m (10,000 ft). The major settlement areas are related to the junction between mountain and steppe and to the principal rivers. The climate varies from continental to subtropical according to elevation and shelter. Extensive irrigation, without which agriculture would be severely limited, has made it possible for cotton growing to develop into the leading branch of agriculture, and on that basis textiles have become the largest industry in the country. Tajikistan is rich in mineral and fuel deposits, the exploitation of which became a major feature of economic development during the Soviet era. Preceding full independence in 1991 there was an upsurge of, sometimes violent, Tajik nationalism as a result of which many Russians and Uzbeks have left the country.

TANZANIA

STATUS: Republic
AREA: 939,760 sq km (362,750 sq miles)
POPULATION: 25,635,000
ANNUAL NATURAL INCREASE: 3.5%
CAPITAL: Dodoma
LANGUAGE: Swahili, English
RELIGION: 40% Christian, 35% Muslim
CURRENCY: Tanzanian shilling (TZS)
ORGANISATIONS: Comm, UN, OAU

Much of this East African country consists of high interior plateaux covered by scrub and grassland, bordered to the north by the volcanic Kilimanjaro region, to the east by Lake Tanganyika, and by highlands to the south. Despite its proximity to the equator, the altitude of much of Tanzania means that temperatures are reduced, and only on the narrow coastal plain is the climate truly tropical. Average temperatures vary between 19° and 28°C (67° and 82°F), and rainfall 57 to 106 cm (23 to 43 in). Subsistence farming is the main way of life, although coffee, cotton, sisal, cashew nuts and tea are exported. Industry is limited, but gradually growing in importance, and involves textiles, food processing and tobacco. Tourism could be a future growth area.

THAILAND

STATUS: Kingdom
AREA: 514,000 sq km (198,405 sq miles)
POPULATION: 54,532,000
ANNUAL NATURAL INCREASE: 1.9%
CAPITAL: Bangkok (Krung Thep)
LANGUAGE: Thai
RELIGION: Buddhist, 4% Muslim
CURRENCY: baht (THB)
ORGANISATIONS: UN, ASEAN, Col. Plan

Thailand consists of a flat undulating central plain, containing the Chao Phraye River, fringed by mountains and by a plateau in the north-east drained by the Mekong River. From May to October, monsoon rains are heavy with an annual average rainfall of 150 cm (59 in). The climate is tropical with temperatures reaching 36°C (97°F). Over 50% of the country is covered by dense rainforest. The central plain is well-served with irrigation canals which supply the paddy fields. Rice is the main export crop, although maize, beans, coconuts and groundnuts are also grown. Thailand is one of the world's largest producers of rubber and tin. A small-scale petrochemical industry has been developed.

TOGO

STATUS: Republic
AREA: 56,785 sq km (21,920 sq miles)
POPULATION: 3,531,000
ANNUAL NATURAL INCREASE: 3.5%
CAPITAL: Lomé
LANGUAGE: French, Kabre, Ewe
RELIGION: 60% animist, 25% Christian 7.5% Muslim
CURRENCY: CFA franc (W Africa) (XOF)
ORGANISATIONS: UN, ECOWAS, OAU

Togo, formerly a German protectorate and French colony, is situated between Ghana and Benin in West Africa. A long narrow country, it has only 65 km (40 miles) of coast. The interior consists of mountains and high infertile tableland. The climate is tropical with an average temperature of 27°C (81°F). Most of Togo's farmers grow maize, cassava, yams, groundnuts and plantains, and the country is virtually self-sufficient in food-stuffs. Phosphates account for a half of export revenue. Cotton, cocoa and coffee are also exported.

TOKELAU ISLANDS
STATUS: Overseas Territory of New Zealand
AREA: 10 sq km (4 sq miles)
POPULATION: 1,690

TONGA

STATUS: Kingdom
AREA: 699 sq km (270 sq miles)
POPULATION: 95,000
ANNUAL NATURAL INCREASE: 0.4%
CAPITAL: Nuku'alofa
LANGUAGE: Tongan, English
RELIGION: Christian
CURRENCY: pa'anga (TOP)
ORGANISATIONS: Comm

Tonga consists of an archipelago of 169 islands in the Pacific 180km(112 miles) north of New Zealand. There are seven groups of islands, but the most important are Tongatapu, Ha'apai and Vava'u. All the islands are covered with dense tropical vegetation, and temperatures

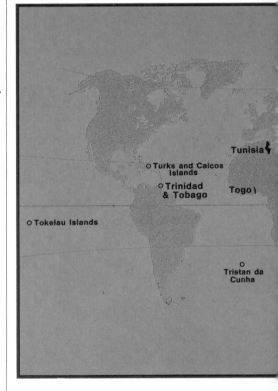

range from 11° to 29°C(52° to 84°F). Main exports are coconut products and bananas.

TRINIDAD & TOBAGO

STATUS: Republic
AREA: 5,130 sq km (1,980 sq miles)
POPULATION: 1,234,388
ANNUAL NATURAL INCREASE: 1.7%
CAPITAL: Port of Spain
LANGUAGE: English
RELIGION: 60% Christian, 25% Hindu, 6% Muslim
CURRENCY: Trinidad & Tobago dollar (TTD)
ORGANISATIONS: Comm, UN, CARICOM, OAS

These Caribbean islands lie only 11 and 30km(7 and 19 miles) respectively from the Venezuelan coast. Both islands have mountainous interiors – the central range of Trinidad reaches 940m(3084ft) – and are densely covered with tropical rain forest. Sugar was once the mainstay of the economy but oil is now the leading source of revenue.

TRISTAN DA CUNHA
STATUS: Dependency of St Helena
AREA: 98 sq km (38 sq miles)
POPULATION: 306

TUNISIA

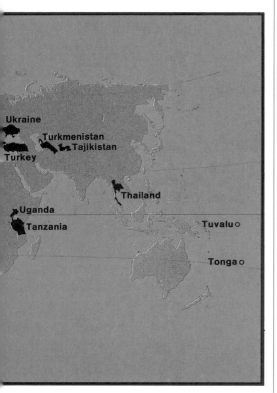

STATUS: Republic
AREA: 164,150 sq km (63,378 sq miles)
POPULATION: 8,180,000
ANNUAL NATURAL INCREASE: 2.5%
CAPITAL: Tunis
LANGUAGE: Arabic, French
RELIGION: Muslim
CURRENCY: Tunisian dinar (TND)
ORGANISATIONS: UN, Arab League, OAU

Tunisia is fringed to the north and west by the eastern end of the Atlas mountain range. Salt lakes are scattered throughout the central plains and to the south lies the Sahara. Average annual temperature ranges from 10° to 27℃ (50° to 81°F) and while the coastal area has Mediterranean scrub, the interior is desert. The majority of the population live along the north-east coast. Wheat, barley, olives and citrus fruit are the main crops and oil, natural gas and sugar refining are the main industries. The tourist industry is expanding and is becoming increasingly important to the economy.

TURKEY

STATUS: Republic
AREA: 779,450 sq km (300,870 sq miles)
POPULATION: 58,687,000
ANNUAL NATURAL INCREASE: 2.3%
CAPITAL: Ankara
LANGUAGE: Turkish, Kurdish
RELIGION: Sunni Muslim, Christian minority
CURRENCY: Turkish lira (TRL)
ORGANISATIONS: UN, Council of Europe, NATO, OECD

Turkey has always occupied a strategically important position linking Europe and Asia. The central Anatolian plateau is bordered to the north and south by mountain ranges which converge in the eastern Anatolian mountains crowned by Mt Ararat 5165m(16,945ft). The north, south and west coastlines are fringed by Mediterranean vegetation and have short, mild and wet winters and long, hot summers. The interior is arid with average rainfall less than 25cm(10in). The main crops are wheat and barley, but tobacco, olives, sugar-beet, tea and fruit are also grown, and sheep, goats and cattle are raised. Turkey is becoming increasingly industrialised and now leads the Middle East in the production of iron, steel, chrome, coal and lignite. Tourism is a rapidly growing industry.

TURKMENISTAN

STATUS: Republic
AREA: 488,100 sq km (188,405 sq miles)
POPULATION: 3,600,000
CAPITAL: Ashkhabad
LANGUAGE: Turkmen, Russian
RELIGION: Muslim
CURRENCY: rouble
ORGANISATIONS: CIS

Situated in the far south of the former Soviet Union, Turkmenistan is a land of deserts and oases; only in the south do hills and mountains emerge. The continental climate is responsible for great fluctuations in temperature, both during the day and the year. Traditionally nomads, the Turkmen tribes under the Soviet regime, turned from pastoral farming to cotton-growing, made possible by extensive irrigation. Rich in minerals and chemicals, its industrial growth was forcibly developed by the Russians, resulting in ethnic-outsiders making up the majority of the urban population.

TURKS & CAICOS ISLANDS
STATUS: UK Dependent Territory
AREA: 430 sq km (166 sq miles)
POPULATION: 11,696
CAPITAL: Cockburn Town

TUVALU

STATUS: State
AREA: 24.6 sq km (9.5 sq miles)
POPULATION: 10,000
ANNUAL NATURAL INCREASE: 1.5%
CAPITAL: Funafuti
LANGUAGE: Tuvaluan, English
RELIGION: 98% Protestant
CURRENCY: Australian dollar (AUD), Tuvaluan coinage
ORGANISATIONS: Comm (special member)

Tuvalu consists of nine dispersed coral atolls, north of Fiji, in the Pacific Ocean. The climate is tropical; hot, with heavy annual rainfall (c.300cm or 118in). Fish is the staple food but coconuts and bread-fruit are cultivated.

UGANDA

STATUS: Republic
AREA: 236,580 sq km (91,320 sq miles)
POPULATION: 18,795,000
ANNUAL NATURAL INCREASE: 3.2%
CAPITAL: Kampala
LANGUAGE: English, tribal languages
RELIGION: 60% Christian. Muslim minority
CURRENCY: Uganda shilling (UGX)
ORGANISATIONS: Comm, UN, OAU

Uganda is bordered to the west by the African Rift valley and to the east by Kenya. The central high plateau is savannah, while the area around Lake Victoria has been cleared for cultivation. To the west are mountain ranges reaching 5110m(16,765ft). The climate is warm (21°–24°C or 70°–75°F), and rainfall ranges from 75–150cm(30–59in). The main export crop is coffee. Lake Victoria has great supplies of freshwater fish.

UKRAINE

STATUS: Republic
AREA: 603,700 sq km (233,030 sq miles)
POPULATION: 51,800,000
CAPITAL: Kiev
LANGUAGE: Ukrainian, Russian
RELIGION: Russian Orthodox, Uniate
CURRENCY: rouble (temporary coupon currency, new currency to be introduced in 1992)
ORGANISATIONS: UN, CIS

Ukraine consists mainly of level plains and mountainous border areas. The landscape is, however, diverse, with marshes, forests, wooded and treeless steppe. Deposits of 'black earth', among the most fertile soils, cover about 65% of Ukraine. Grain, potatoes, vegetables and fruits, industrial crops (notably sugar beets and sunflower seeds) and fodder crops are grown. Food processing is important to the economy, and southern regions are renowned for wines. Ukraine is rich in mineral resources, such as iron ore, coal and lignite, and has large reserves of petroleum and gas. Extensive mining, metal production, machine-building, engineering and chemicals dominate Ukraine industry, most of it is located in the Donets basin and the Dnepr lowland. These two regions account for four-fifths of the urban population. Natural wealth and advanced industrial development make Ukraine well-equipped for adaptation to free market conditions.

UNITED ARAB EMIRATES (UAE)

STATUS: Federation of 7 emirates
AREA: 75,150 sq km (29,010 sq miles)
POPULATION: 1,600,000
ANNUAL NATURAL INCREASE: 4.6%
CAPITAL: Abu Dhabi
LANGUAGE: Arabic, English
RELIGION: Sunni Muslim
CURRENCY: UAE dirham (AED)
ORGANISATIONS: UN, Arab League, OPEC

ABU DHABI
STATUS: Emirate
AREA: 64,750 sq km (24,995 sq miles)
POPULATION: 670,125

ÁJMĀN
STATUS: Emirate
AREA: 260 sq km (100 sq miles)
POPULATION: 64,318

DUBAI
STATUS: Emirate
AREA: 3,900 sq km (1,505 sq miles)
POPULATION: 419,104

FUJAIRAH
STATUS: Emirate
AREA: 1,170 sq km (452 sq miles)
POPULATION: 54,425

RAS AL-KHAIMAH
STATUS: Emirate
AREA: 1,690 sq km (652 sq miles)
POPULATION: 116,470

SHARJAH
STATUS: Emirate
AREA: 2,600 sq km (1,005 sq miles)
POPULATION: 268,722

UMM AL QAIWAIN
STATUS: Emirate
AREA: 780 sq km (300 sq miles)
POPULATION: 29,229

Seven emirates stretched along the south eastern shores of the Persian Gulf constitute this oil rich Arab state. Flat deserts cover most of the landscape rising to the Hajar mountains of the Musandam Peninsula. Summer temperatures reach 40°C(104°F) and winter rainfall 13cm(5in). Only the desert oases are fertile, producing fruit and vegetables. Trade is dominated by exports of oil and natural gas.

UNITED KINGDOM OF GREAT BRITAIN & NORTHERN IRELAND (UK)

STATUS: Kingdom
AREA: 244,755 sq km (94,475 sq miles)
POPULATION: 55,514,500
ANNUAL NATURAL INCREASE: 0.2%
CAPITAL: London
LANGUAGE: English, Welsh, Gaelic
RELIGION: Protestant majority. Roman Catholic Jewish, Muslim and Hindu minorities
CURRENCY: Pound Sterling (GBP)
ORGANISATIONS: Comm, UN, Col. Plan, Council of Europe, NATO, OECD, WEU, EC, G7

ENGLAND
STATUS: Constituent Country
AREA: 130,360 sq km (50,320 sq miles)
POPULATION: 46,170,300
CAPITAL: London

NORTHERN IRELAND
STATUS: Constituent Region
AREA: 14,150 sq km (5,460 sq miles)
POPULATION: 1,589,000
CAPITAL: Belfast

SCOTLAND
STATUS: Constituent Country
AREA: 78,750 sq km (30,400 sq miles)
POPULATION: 4,957,000
CAPITAL: Edinburgh

WALES
STATUS: Principality
AREA: 20,760 sq km (8,015 sq miles)
POPULATION: 2,798,200
CAPITAL: Cardiff

The United Kingdom is part of the British Isles which are situated off the coast of north-west Europe separated from France by the English Channel and from Belgium, the Netherlands and Scandinavia by the North Sea. There are two main islands: the larger, Great Britain, comprises England, Scotland and Wales; the other, the island of Ireland separated from Britain by the Irish Sea, comprises Northern Ireland and the Irish Republic.

The Highland zone of Britain consists of ancient uplifted rocks which now form the mountainous dissected and glaciated areas of the Lake District in the north-west, and Wales, the Southern Uplands and Grampians of Scotland which rise to the highest point in the UK to

1344m (4409ft) at Ben Nevis. The latter are divided by the wide Central Lowland rift valley.

Central England is dominated by the Pennine mountain chain which stretches southwards from the Southern Uplands down the centre of England to the river Trent. The landscape of the south-west consists of the ancient uplifted granite domes of Dartmoor and Bodmin Moor.

Lowland Britain is a very contrasting landscape. Limestone and sandstone hills are separated by flat clay vales, east of a line joining the rivers Humber and Exe. Here is found both the richest agricultural land and the densest population.

The climate of the British Isles is mild, wet and variable. Summer temperatures average 13°–17°C (55°–63°F), and winter temperatures 5°–7°C (41°–45°F). Annual rainfall varies between 65 and 500cm (26 and 200in) with the highest in the central Lake District and the lowest on the coasts of East Anglia.

Although a tiny percentage of the nation's workforce are employed in agriculture, farm produce is important to both home and export

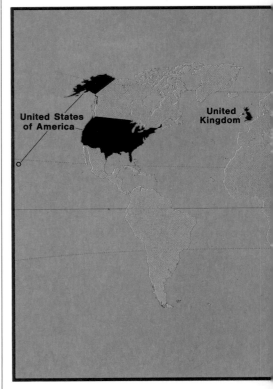

markets. 76% of the total UK land area is farmland. The main cereal crops are wheat, barley and oats. Potatoes, sugar-beet and green vegetable crops are widespread.

About 20% of the land is permanent pasture for raising of dairy and beef stock; and 28% of the land, mainly hill and mountain areas, is used for rough grazing of sheep. Pigs and poultry are widespread in both England and lowland Britain. The best fruit-growing areas are the south-east, especially Kent, and East Anglia and the central Vale of Evesham for apples, pears and soft fruit. Both forestry and fishing industries contribute to the economy.

The major mineral resources of the UK are coal, oil and natural gas. Coal output, mostly from the fields of South Wales, Central Scotland, North-East England, Yorkshire and the Midlands, goes towards the generation of electricity but oil and natural gas from the North Sea, and to a lesser extent nuclear power, are divided between the needs of industry and the consumer. Iron ore, once mined sufficiently to satisfy industry, is now imported to support the iron and steel manufacturing sector.

The UK produces a great range of industrial goods for home consumption and export. Heavy industry particularly the production of iron and steel is traditionally located close to fuel sources (coal) in South Wales, the North-East at Tees-side and South Yorkshire. The majority of iron ore is imported. The main shipbuilding areas are Clydeside in western Scotland, Belfast in Northern Ireland and Tyneside in the North-East. Other heavy industrial goods, vehicles, engines and machinery are produced on Merseyside, Derby and Nottingham in the North Midlands, Birmingham in the West Midlands, Cardiff in South Wales, Clydeside and Belfast.

General and consumer good manufacturing is located in all heavy industrial areas but the London area, West Midlands and Lancashire and Merseyside predominate. Main products are food and drinks, chemicals, light engineering products, cotton and woollen textiles, electrical and electronic goods.

The UK is a trading nation. The balance of trade has changed during the last 30 years because of stronger economic, military and

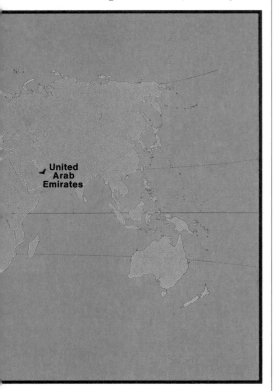

political ties within Europe – the EC and NATO – and consequently reduced trading links with former colonies particularly in Australasia. Major exports are cereals, meat, dairy products, beverages, tobacco products, textiles, metalliferous ores, petroleum and petroleum products, chemicals, pharmaceutical goods, plastics, leather goods, rubber, paper, iron and steel, other metal goods, engines and vehicles, machinery, electrical goods and transport equipment.

The UK has a highly developed transport network to move goods and services. Motorways, trunk roads and principal roads total over 50,000 km (31,070 miles). The railway network covers 16,730 km (10,395 miles) and now carries over 140 million tonnes of freight annually. The inland waterway system, once a major freight carrier, totals only 563 navigable kilometres (350 miles) but still carries over 4 million tonnes of goods annually.

UNITED STATES OF AMERICA (USA)

STATUS: Federal Republic
AREA: 9,363,130 sq km (3,614,170 sq miles)
POPULATION: 248,709,873
ANNUAL NATURAL INCREASE: 1.0%
CAPITAL: Washington, DC
LANGUAGE: English, Spanish
RELIGION: Christian majority. Jewish minority
CURRENCY: US dollar (USD)
ORGANISATIONS: UN, ANZUS, Col. Plan, NATO OECD, OAS, G7

ALABAMA
STATUS: State
AREA: 131,485 sq km (50,755 sq miles)
POPULATION: 3,984,000
CAPITAL: Montgomery

ALASKA
STATUS: State
AREA: 1,478,450 sq km (570,680 sq miles)
POPULATION: 546,000
CAPITAL: Juneau

ARIZONA
STATUS: State
AREA: 293,985 sq km (113,480 sq miles)
POPULATION: 3,619,000
CAPITAL: Phoenix

ARKANSAS
STATUS: State
AREA: 134,880 sq km (52,065 sq miles)
POPULATION: 2,337,000
CAPITAL: Little Rock

CALIFORNIA
STATUS: State
AREA: 404,815 sq km (156,260 sq miles)
POPULATION: 29,279,000
CAPITAL: Sacramento

COLORADO
STATUS: State
AREA: 268,310 sq km (103,570 sq miles)
POPULATION: 3,272,000
CAPITAL: Denver

CONNECTICUT
STATUS: State
AREA: 12,620 sq km (4,870 sq miles)
POPULATION: 3,227,000
CAPITAL: Hartford

DELAWARE
STATUS: State
AREA: 5,005 sq km (1,930 sq miles)
POPULATION: 658,000
CAPITAL: Dover

DISTRICT OF COLUMBIA
STATUS: Federal District
AREA: 163 sq km (63 sq miles)
POPULATION: 575,000
CAPITAL: Washington

FLORIDA
STATUS: State
AREA: 140,255 sq km (54,140 sq miles)
POPULATION: 12,775,000
CAPITAL: Tallahassee

GEORGIA
STATUS: State
AREA: 150,365 sq km (58,040 sq miles)
POPULATION: 6,387,000
CAPITAL: Atlanta

HAWAII
STATUS: State
AREA: 16,640 sq km (6,425 sq miles)
POPULATION: 1,095,000
CAPITAL: Honolulu

IDAHO
STATUS: State
AREA: 213,455 sq km (82,390 sq miles)
POPULATION: 1,004,000
CAPITAL: Boise

ILLINOIS
STATUS: State
AREA: 144,120 sq km (55,630 sq miles)
POPULATION: 11,325,000
CAPITAL: Springfield

INDIANA
STATUS: State
AREA: 93,065 sq km (35,925 sq miles)
POPULATION: 5,499,000
CAPITAL: Indianapolis

IOWA
STATUS: State
AREA: 144,950 sq km (55,950 sq miles)
POPULATION: 2,767,000
CAPITAL: Des Moines

KANSAS
STATUS: State
AREA: 211,805 sq km (81,755 sq miles)
POPULATION: 2,467,000
CAPITAL: Topeka

KENTUCKY
STATUS: State
AREA: 102,740 sq km (39,660 sq miles)
POPULATION: 3,665,000
CAPITAL: Frankfort

LOUISIANA
STATUS: State
AREA: 115,310 sq km (44,510 sq miles)
POPULATION: 4,181,000
CAPITAL: Baton Rouge

MAINE
STATUS: State
AREA: 80,275 sq km (30,985 sq miles)
POPULATION: 1,218,000
CAPITAL: Augusta

MARYLAND
STATUS: State
AREA: 25,480 sq km (9,835 sq miles)
POPULATION: 4,733,000
CAPITAL: Annapolis

MASSACHUSETTS
STATUS: State
AREA: 20,265 sq km (7,820 sq miles)
POPULATION: 5,928,000
CAPITAL: Boston

MICHIGAN
STATUS: State
AREA: 147,510 sq km (56,940 sq miles)
POPULATION: 9,179,000
CAPITAL: Lansing

MINNESOTA
STATUS: State
AREA: 206,030 sq km (79,530 sq miles)
POPULATION: 4,359,000
CAPITAL: St Paul

MISSISSIPPI
STATUS: State
AREA: 122,335 sq km (47,220 sq miles)
POPULATION: 2,535,000
CAPITAL: Jackson

MISSOURI
STATUS: State
AREA: 178,565 sq km (68,925 sq miles)
POPULATION: 5,079,000
CAPITAL: Jefferson City

MONTANA
STATUS: State
AREA: 376,555 sq km (145,350 sq miles)
POPULATION: 794,000
CAPITAL: Helena

NEBRASKA
STATUS: State
AREA: 198,505 sq km (76,625 sq miles)
POPULATION: 1,573,000
CAPITAL: Lincoln

NEVADA
STATUS: State
AREA: 284,625 sq km (109,865 sq miles)
POPULATION: 1,193,000
CAPITAL: Carson City

NEW HAMPSHIRE
STATUS: State
AREA: 23,290 sq km (8,990 sq miles)
POPULATION: 1,103,000
CAPITAL: Concord

NEW JERSEY
STATUS: State
AREA: 19,340 sq km (7,465 sq miles)
POPULATION: 7,617,000
CAPITAL: Trenton

NEW MEXICO
STATUS: State
AREA: 314,255 sq km (121,300 sq miles)
POPULATION: 1,490,000
CAPITAL: Santa Fe

NEW YORK
STATUS: State
AREA: 122,705 sq km (47,365 sq miles)
POPULATION: 17,627,000
CAPITAL: Albany

NORTH CAROLINA
STATUS: State
AREA: 126,505 sq km (48,830 sq miles)
POPULATION: 6,553,000
CAPITAL: Raleigh

NORTH DAKOTA
STATUS: State
AREA: 179,485 sq km (69,280 sq miles)
POPULATION: 634,000
CAPITAL: Bismarck

OHIO
STATUS: State
AREA: 106,200 sq km (40,995 sq miles)
POPULATION: 10,778,000
CAPITAL: Columbus

OKLAHOMA
STATUS: State
AREA: 177,815 sq km (68,635 sq miles)
POPULATION: 3,124,000
CAPITAL: Oklahoma City

OREGON
STATUS: State
AREA: 249,115 sq km (96,160 sq miles)
POPULATION: 2,828,000
CAPITAL: Salem

PENNSYLVANIA
STATUS: State
AREA: 116,260 sq km (44,875 sq miles)
POPULATION: 11,764,000
CAPITAL: Harrisburg

RHODE ISLAND
STATUS: State
AREA: 2,730 sq km (1,055 sq miles)
POPULATION: 989,000
CAPITAL: Providence

SOUTH CAROLINA
STATUS: State
AREA: 78,225 sq km (30,195 sq miles)
POPULATION: 3,272,000
CAPITAL: Columbia

SOUTH DAKOTA
STATUS: State
AREA: 196,715 sq km (75,930 sq miles)
POPULATION: 693,000
CAPITAL: Pierre

TENNESSEE
STATUS: State
AREA: 106,590 sq km (41,145 sq miles)
POPULATION: 4,822,000
CAPITAL: Nashville

TEXAS
STATUS: State
AREA: 678,620 sq km (261,950 sq miles)
POPULATION: 16,825,000
CAPITAL: Austin

UTAH
STATUS: State
AREA: 212,570 sq km (82,050 sq miles)
POPULATION: 1,711,000
CAPITAL: Salt Lake City

VERMONT
STATUS: State
AREA: 24,900 sq km (9,612 sq miles)
POPULATION: 560,000
CAPITAL: Montpelier

VIRGINIA
STATUS: State
AREA: 102,835 sq km (39,695 sq miles)
POPULATION: 6,128,000
CAPITAL: Richmond

WASHINGTON
STATUS: State
AREA: 172,265 sq km (66,495 sq miles)
POPULATION: 4,827,000
CAPITAL: Olympia

WEST VIRGINIA
STATUS: State
AREA: 62,470 sq km (24,115 sq miles)
POPULATION: 1,783,000
CAPITAL: Charleston

WISCONSIN
STATUS: State
AREA: 140,965 sq km (54,415 sq miles)
POPULATION: 4,870,000
CAPITAL: Madison

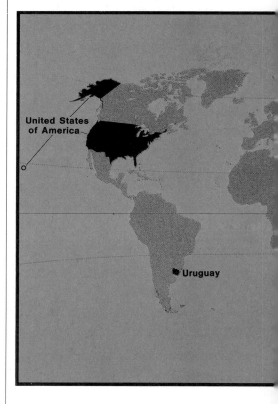

United States of America

Uruguay

WYOMING
STATUS: State
AREA: 251,200 sq km (96,965 sq miles)
POPULATION: 450,000
CAPITAL: Cheyenne

The United States of America is the world's third largest country after Canada and China, with the world's fourth largest population. The 19th and 20th centuries have brought 42 million immigrants to its shores, and the population of the USA now has the highest living standard of any country in the world. The large land area covers a huge spectrum of different landscapes, environments and climates. The eastern coast of New England where the European settlers first landed, is rocky, mountainous and richly wooded. South of New England is the Atlantic coastal plain, rising to the west towards the Appalachian mountain system. Beyond the Appalachians lie the central lowlands, a large undulating plain cut through by the Mississippi and Ohio rivers. Further west lie the Great Plains crossed by the Mis-

souri, Red and Arkansas rivers and rising gently towards the mighty Rockies, a spine of mountains running south from Alaska. The highest point is Mt. Whitney in California, at 4418 m (14,495 ft). Beyond the Rockies lies the Great Valley of California and the Pacific coast.

Climatic variety within this vast region is enormous, ranging from the Arctic conditions of Alaska to the desert of the south-west – winter temperatures in Alaska plummet to –28°C (–19°F), whereas in Florida they maintain a steady 19°C (66°F). In California the weather varies little, being constantly mild with a range of only 9°C (16°F), whereas in the central lowlands winters are severe and the summers very hot. The centre of the continent is dry, but both the north-west Pacific and the New England Atlantic coast are humid with heavy rainfall. Many areas of the USA fall prey to exceptional, often disastrous, weather conditions: the north-eastern seaboard is susceptible to heavy blizzards, the southern lowlands are vulnerable to spring thaw flooding and the Mississippi valley is prone to tornadoes.

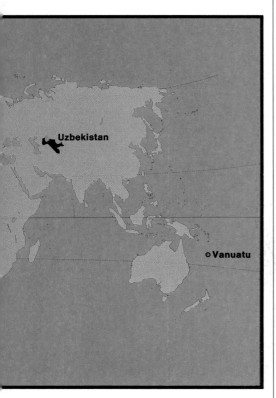

The natural vegetation of the USA reflects its climatic diversity. The north-west coast is rich in coniferous forest, especially Douglas fir, while the Appalachian mountain region is well endowed with hardwoods, notably maple and oak. In the arid south-west, vegetation is limited to desert scrub whereas the Gulf and South Atlantic coast are fringed with swampy wetlands. The central lowlands are endowed with rich black-earth soils (the agricultural heartland), gradually supplanted – towards the Rockies, by tall-grass prairie. The north-eastern states of Illinois, Iowa, Indiana and Nebraska form the so-called corn belt, whereas further west wheat supplements corn as the main crop. Spring wheat is grown in the northern states of North and South Dakota and Minnesota. The north-eastern corner of the USA is predominantly dairy country, and the states of the deep south are famous for their cotton, though cotton cultivation is declining. Rice is grown in Texas, California and Louisiana, and fruit and vegetables in Florida, Texas and California.

The USA consumes 25% of all the world's energy resources but is well endowed with energy reserves. There are substantial coal resources in Pennsylvania, the Appalachian region, the Dakotas and Wyoming, and oil and natural gas regions in Texas, Louisiana, Alaska, and off-shore, in the Gulf of Mexico. The vast resources of America's great rivers have been harnessed extensively for hydro-electric power. In the west, mineral deposits include copper, lead, zinc and silver, and there is iron ore around Lake Superior. Most specialist industrial minerals are imported. Diamonds, tin, chromite, nickel, asbestos, platinum, manganese, mercury, tungsten, cobalt, antimony and cadmium are not found in sufficient quantities for home demand. Main non-metallic minerals extracted within the USA are cement, clays, gypsum, lime, phosphate, salt, sand, gravel and sulphur.

About one fifth of the land area of the USA is covered with commercially usable coniferous and deciduous forest. Exploitation and re-planting are closely controlled. Atlantic and Pacific fishing, particularly around Alaska, is mainly carried out within the 200 mile fishery zone.

America's first industrialised area lies to the south of the Great Lakes, and has gradually extended south and west to form one of the largest industrial zones in the world. Chicago is the main steel-producing town, while Pennsylvania and Pittsburgh are famous for their steel and chemical industries. Manufacturing industries are more predominant towards the east of this zone.

Most of the fastest growing industrial areas are along the west coast. These stretch from Seattle and Portland in the north to San Francisco, Oakland and San Jose in central California and to Los Angeles, Anaheim, Santa Ana and San Diego in the south. The main industries are vehicle manufacture, armaments, machinery, electrical goods, electronics, textiles and clothing and entertainment.

URUGUAY

STATUS: Republic
AREA: 186,925 sq km (72,155 sq miles)
POPULATION: 3,094,000
ANNUAL NATURAL INCREASE: 0.6%
CAPITAL: Montevideo
LANGUAGE: Spanish
RELIGION: Roman Catholic
CURRENCY: Uruguayan peso (UYP)
ORGANISATIONS: UN, OAS

Situated on the south-east coast of South America, Uruguay is the smallest country in South America. It consists of a narrow coastal plain with rolling hills inland. Maximum elevation is around 200 m (656 ft). The temperate climate and adequate rainfall provide good argicultural potential but most of the land is given over to the grazing of sheep and cattle. The entire economy relies on the production of meat and wool. Most industry is devoted to food processing. 87% of the land area is farmed. There are few mineral resources.

UZBEKISTAN

STATUS: Republic
AREA: 447,400 sq km (172,695 sq miles)
POPULATION: 20,300,000
CAPITAL: Tashkent
LANGUAGE: Uzbek, Russian
RELIGION: Muslim
CURRENCY: rouble
ORGANISATIONS: CIS

Established in 1924 as a constituent republic of the Soviet Union, Uzbekistan became an independent state in 1991. The majority of the country consists of flat, sun-baked lowlands with mountains in the south and east. The climate is markedly continental and very dry with an abundance of sunshine and mild, short winters. The southern mountains are of great economic importance providing ample supplies of water for hydro-electric plants and irrigation schemes. The mountain regions also contain substantial reserves of natural gas, oil, coal, iron and other metals. With its fertile soils (when irrigated) and good pastures Uzbekistan is well situated for cattle raising and for producing cotton. Uzbekistan is the largest producer of machines and heavy equipment in central Asia, and has been specialising mainly in machinery for cotton cultivation and harvesting, machines for irrigation projects, for road-building and textile processing. During the Soviet period the urban employment market became increasingly dominated by Russians and other outsiders. The gradual emergence of better educated and better trained Uzbeks has generated fiercely nationalist sentiments. The country's future development will be severely hampered by the damage done to the natural environment under communism.

VANUATU

STATUS: Republic
AREA: 14,765 sq km (5,700 sq miles)
POPULATION: 147,000
ANNUAL NATURAL INCREASE: 2.9%
CAPITAL: Port Vila
LANGUAGE: Bislama (national), English, French, many Melanesian languages
RELIGION: Christian
CURRENCY: Vatu (VUV)
ORGANISATIONS: Comm, UN

Vanuatu is a chain of densely forested, mountainous, volcanic islands in the South Pacific. Climate is tropical and cyclonic. Copra, cocoa and coffee are grown mainly for export. Fish, pigs and sheep are important for home consumption as well as yam, taro, manioc and bananas. Manganese is the only mineral.

VATICAN CITY

STATUS: Ecclesiastical State
AREA: 0.44 sq km (0.17 sq miles)
POPULATION: 766
LANGUAGE: Italian, Latin
RELIGION: Roman Catholic
CURRENCY: Italian lira (ITL), Papal coinage

The headquarters of the Roman Catholic church, the Vatican in Rome is the world's smallest independent state. The papal residence since the 5th century AD, it is the destination for pilgrims and tourists from all over the world. Most income is derived from voluntary contributions and interest on investments. The only industries are those connected with the Church.

VENEZUELA

STATUS: Republic
AREA: 912,045 sq km (352,050 sq miles)
POPULATION: 19,735,000
ANNUAL NATURAL INCREASE: 2.8%
CAPITAL: Caracas
LANGUAGE: Spanish
RELIGION: Roman Catholic
CURRENCY: bolivar (VEB)
ORGANISATIONS: UN, OAS, OPEC

Venezuela, one of the richest countries of Latin America, is divided into four topographic regions: the continuation of the Andes in the west; the humid lowlands around Lake Maracaibo in the north; the savannah-covered central plains (llanos), and the extension of the Guiana Highlands covering almost half the country. The climate varies between tropical in the south to warm temperate along the northern coasts. The majority of the population live along the north coast. The economy is built around oil production in the Maracaibo region; over three-quarters of export revenue comes from oil. Bauxite and iron ore are also important. The majority of employment is provided by industrial and manufacturing developments.

VIETNAM

STATUS: Republic
AREA: 329,566 sq km (127,246 sq miles)

POPULATION: 66,200,000
ANNUAL NATURAL INCREASE: 2.3%
CAPITAL: Hanoi
LANGUAGE: Vietnamese, French, Chinese
RELIGION: Buddhist
CURRENCY: dong (VND)
ORGANISATIONS: UN, OIEC

A long narrow country in South-East Asia, Vietnam has a mountainous backbone and two extensive river deltas: the Song Hong (Red River) in the north and the Mekong in the south. Monsoons bring 150cm (59in) of rain every year and rainforest covers most of the central mountainous areas. Rice is grown extensively throughout the north along with coffee and rubber in other parts of the country. Vietnam possesses a wide range of minerals including coal, lignite, anthracite, iron ore and tin. Industry is expanding rapidly, but decades of warfare and internal strife have impeded development.

VIRGIN ISLANDS (UK)

STATUS: UK Dependent Territory
AREA: 153 sq km (59 sq miles)
POPULATION: 13,000
CAPITAL: Road Town

VIRGIN ISLANDS (USA)

STATUS: External Territory of USA
AREA: 345 sq km (133 sq miles)
POPULATION: 117,000
CAPITAL: Charlotte Amalie

WALLIS & FUTUNA ISLANDS

STATUS: Self-governing Overseas Territory of France
AREA: 274 sq km (106 sq miles)
POPULATION: 15,400
CAPITAL: Mata-Utu

WESTERN SAMOA

STATUS: Commonwealth State
AREA: 2,840 sq km (1,095 sq miles)
POPULATION: 170,000
ANNUAL NATURAL INCREASE: 0.3%
CAPITAL: Apia
LANGUAGE: English, Samoan
RELIGION: local beliefs
CURRENCY: talà (dollar) (WST)
ORGANISATIONS: Comm, UN

Nine volcanic tropical islands constitute this south Pacific state, of which only four are populated – Savaii, Upolu, Manono and Apolima. Annual rainfall is often 250cm(100in) per year. Temperatures average 26°C(79°F) for most months. Main exports are copra, timber, taro, cocoa and fruit. The only industries are food processing and timber products. Main imports are food products, consumer goods, machinery and animals.

WRANGEL ISLAND

STATUS: Island Territory of Russia
AREA: 7,250 sq km (2,800 sq miles)
POPULATION: No permanent population

YEMEN

STATUS: Republic
AREA: 477,530 sq km (184,325 sq miles)
POPULATION: 12,000,000
ANNUAL NATURAL INCREASE: 3.0%
CAPITAL: San'a
LANGUAGE: Arabic
RELIGION: Sunni and Shia Muslim

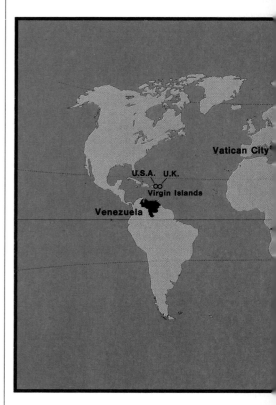

CURRENCY: Yemeni rial (YER)
ORGANISATIONS: UN, Arab League

The Yemen Arab Republic and the People's Democratic Republic of Yemen were unified in 1990 to form a single state with its capital at San'a. Situated in the southern part of the Arabian peninsula the country comprises several contrasting physical landscapes. The north is mainly mountainous and relatively wet with rainfall reaching 89cm (35in) in inland areas which helps to irrigate the cereals, cotton, fruits and vegetables which are grown on the mountain sides and along the coast. The south coast stretches for 1100km (685 miles) from the mouth of the Red Sea to Oman. The narrow southern coastal plain fringes the wide irrigated Hadhramaut valley in which are grown sorghum, millet, wheat and barley. To the north of the Hadhramaut lies the uninhabitated Arabian Desert. The majority of the people live in the west of the country where the climate is more suited to agriculture. A large proportion of the population are farmers and nomadic herders; the main livestock are sheep,

goats, cattle and poultry. The only commercial mineral being exploited is salt and the discovery of oil in the Marib area in 1984 and the beginning of exports in 1986 are making a vital contribution to the economy. Industrial output is mainly confined to small-scale manufacturing. A small amount of cotton and fish are exported; food and live animals are imported.

YUGOSLAVIA

STATUS: Federation
AREA: 255,805 sq km (98,740 sq miles)
POPULATION: 23,898,000

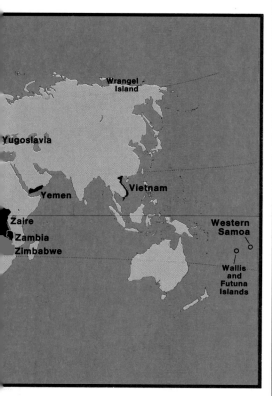

ANNUAL NATURAL INCREASE: 0.7%
CAPITAL: Belgrade (Beograd)
LANGUAGE: Serbian, Albanian, Macedonian, Slovene, Hungarian
RELIGION: 40% Orthodox Christian, 30% Roman Catholic, 10% Muslim
CURRENCY: dinar (YUN)
ORGANISATIONS: UN

BOSNIA & HERCEGOVINA

AREA: 51,130 sq km (19,735 sq miles)
POPULATION: 4,795,000
ETHNIC COMPOSITION: 44% Muslim, 31% Serbian, 18% Croatian

MACEDONIA

AREA: 25,715 sq km (9,925 sq miles)
POPULATION: 2,193,000
ETHNIC COMPOSITION: 70% Macedonian, 20% Albanian, 5% Turkish

MONTENEGRO

AREA: 13,810 sq km (5,330 sq miles)
POPULATION: 664,000
ETHNIC COMPOSITION: 70% Montenegrin, 13% Muslim, 8% Albanian

SERBIA

AREA: 88,360 sq km (34,105 sq miles)
POPULATION: 9,815,000
ETHNIC COMPOSITION: 70% Serbian, 15% Albanian, 5% Hungarian

The Yugoslav state, as first created in 1918 and reconstituted as a federation after 1945, had long been suffering from ethnic conflict and tensions between its component republics. It finally disintegrated in 1991 when, in the face of fierce opposition from the Serbian-dominated centre, Slovenia and Croatia managed to break away. Bosnia & Hercegovina and Macedonia have also declared their independence but have not yet gained international recognition. Yugoslavia may therefore be reduced to Montenegro and Serbia which are committed to staying together. On the other hand, Serbia has laid claim to various territories outside its present boundaries, which are wholly or partly inhabited by Serbs. Internally, it has abolished the autonomous status previously enjoyed by the provinces of Kosovo, with its overwhelmingly Albanian population, and Vojvodina which has a large proportion of ethnic Hungarians. The secession of the more advanced northern republics has dealt a very severe blow to the Yugoslav economy, as the majority of industrial installations are situated in this area, and the costly military campaign to stop secession, has wrought further havoc, with the currency becoming all but worthless in the process. Future potential revenue from tourism along the Adriatic coast has now been lost to Slovenia and Croatia. So whatever the outcome of the political crisis, the economic future of what is left of Yugoslavia looks bleak.

ZAIRE

STATUS: Republic
AREA: 2,345,410 sq km (905,330 sq miles)
POPULATION: 35,562,000
ANNUAL NATURAL INCREASE: 3.1%
CAPITAL: Kinshasa
LANGUAGE: French, Kiswahili, Tshiluba, Kikongo, Lingala
RELIGION: traditional beliefs, 48% Roman Catholic, 13% Protestant
CURRENCY: zaïre (ZRZ)
ORGANISATIONS: UN, OAU

Zaire, formerly the Belgian Congo, is Africa's third largest country after Sudan and Algeria and is dominated by the drainage basin of the Zaire River. Tropical rainforest covers most of the basin. The climate is very variable but basically equatorial with high temperatures and high rainfall. Soils are poor with the majority of the population engaged in shifting agriculture. Cassava, cocoa, coffee, cotton, millet, rubber and sugar-cane are grown. 60% of

exports are minerals – copper, cobalt, diamonds, gold, manganese, uranium and zinc, with copper being the most important and accounting for 40% of total foreign exchange earnings. The country is the world's largest source of cobalt. Zaire has abundant wildlife and tourism is becoming important.

ZAMBIA

STATUS: Republic
AREA: 752,615 sq km (290,510 sq miles)
POPULATION: 7,818,447
ANNUAL NATURAL INCREASE: 3.7%
CAPITAL: Lusaka
LANGUAGE: English, African languages
RELIGION: 70% Christian, animist minority
CURRENCY: kwacha (ZMK)
ORGANISATIONS: Comm, UN, OAU

Mineral-rich Zambia, situated in the interior of south-central Africa, consists mainly of high rolling plateaux. Altitude moderates the potentially tropical climate so that the summer temperature averages only 13°-27°C (55°-81°F). The north receives over 125cm (49in) of rain per annum, the south, less. Most of the country is grassland with some forest in the north. Farming is mainly at subsistence level. Copper is still the mainstay of the country's economy although reserves are fast running out. Lead, zinc, cobalt and tobacco are also exported. Wildlife is diverse and abundant and contributes to expanding tourism.

ZIMBABWE

STATUS: Republic
AREA: 390,310 sq km (150,660 sq miles)
POPULATION: 9,369,000
ANNUAL NATURAL INCREASE: 3.6%
CAPITAL: Harare
LANGUAGE: English, Chishona, Sindebele
RELIGION: traditional beliefs, 20% Christian
CURRENCY: Zimbabwe dollar (ZWD)
ORGANISATIONS: Comm, UN, OAU

Landlocked Zimbabwe (formerly Rhodesia) consists of rolling plateaux (the high veld) 1,200-1,500m (3940-4920ft) and the low veld (the valleys of the Zambezi and Limpopo rivers). Altitude moderates the tropical climate of the high veld to temperate with low humidity. Mineral deposits include chrome, nickel, platinum and coal with gold and asbestos especially important. Maize is the most important crop as it is the staple food of a large proportion of the population. Tobacco, tea, sugar-cane and fruit are also grown. Manufacturing industry is slowly developing and now provides a wide range of consumer products.

North and Central America
25 349 000
9 785 000

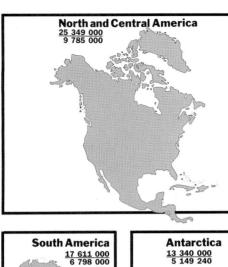

South America
17 611 000
6 798 000

Antarctica
13 340 000
5 149 240

CONTINENTS

land area ▨ = 1 000 000 sq kms / 386 000 sq miles

Europe
10 498 000
4 052 000

Asia
43 608 000
16 833 000

Europe

Asia

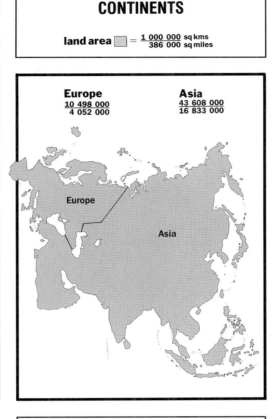

Africa
30 335 000
11 709 000

Australasia
8 923 000
3 444 278

METROPOLITAN AREAS

Population	City	Country
2,168,000	**Abidjan**	Ivory Coast
1,891,000	**Addis Ababa**	Ethiopia
3,646,000	**Ahmadabad**	India
3,684,000	**Alexandria**	Egypt
3,033,000	**Algiers**	Algeria
1,151,300	**Alma-Ata**	Kazakhstan
1,062,000	**Amsterdam**	Netherlands
3,022,236	**Ankara**	Turkey
2,517,080	**Anshan**	China
3,097,000	**Athens**	Greece
2,737,000	**Atlanta**	USA
864,700	**Auckland**	New Zealand
4,044,000	**Baghdad**	Iraq
1,780,000	**Baku**	Azerbaijan
2,342,000	**Baltimore**	USA
4,993,000	**Bangalore**	India
5,832,843	**Bangkok**	Thailand
1,677,699	**Barcelona**	Spain
10,819,407	**Beijing (Peking)**	China
1,500,000	**Beirut**	Lebanon
1,575,000	**Belgrade**	Yugoslavia
3,615,234	**Belo Horizonte**	Brazil
3,400,000	**Berlin**	Germany
2,310,900	**Birmingham**	UK
4,851,000	**Bogotá**	Colombia
11,169,000	**Bombay**	India
2,845,000	**Boston**	USA
1,803,478	**Brasília**	Brazil
970,501	**Brussels**	Belgium
2,194,000	**Bucharest**	Romania
2,115,000	**Budapest**	Hungary
12,604,018	**Buenos Aires**	Argentina
13,300,000	**Cairo**	Egypt
11,835,000	**Calcutta**	India
310,000	**Canberra**	Australia
2,310,000	**Cape Town**	South Africa
4,092,000	**Caracas**	Venezuela
3,213,000	**Casablanca**	Morocco
2,214,000	**Changchun**	China
1,362,000	**Changsha**	China
1,143,000	**Chelyabinsk**	Russian Federation
3,004,000	**Chengdu**	China
6,216,000	**Chicago**	USA
3,151,000	**Chongqing**	China
1,337,114	**Copenhagen**	Denmark
2,543,000	**Dalian**	China
3,766,000	**Dallas – Fort Worth**	USA
2,049,000	**Damascus**	Syria
1,657,000	**Dar-es-Salaam**	Tanzania
8,766,000	**Delhi**	India
4,352,000	**Detroit**	USA
6,646,000	**Dhaka**	Bangladesh
926,000	**Dublin**	Republic of Ireland
2,745,700	**Essen – Dortmund**	Germany
1,420,000	**Fushun**	China
373,000	**Geneva**	Switzerland
2,846,720	**Guadalajara**	Mexico
3,671,000	**Guangzhou (Canton)**	China
1,600,000	**Hamburg**	Germany

Population	City	Country
1,412,000	**Hangzhou**	China
1,088,862	**Hanoi**	Vietnam
2,966,000	**Harbin**	China
2,099,000	**Havana**	Cuba
5,448,000	**Hong Kong**	UK colony
3,247,000	**Houston**	USA
3,535,000	**Hyderabad**	India
6,665,000	**Istanbul**	Turkey
9,253,000	**Jakarta**	Indonesia
508,000	**Jerusalem**	Israel
1,327,000	**Jilin**	China
2,415,000	**Jinan**	China
1,714,000	**Johannesburg**	South Africa
2,000,000	**Kābul**	Afghanistan
7,702,000	**Karachi**	Pakistan
1,947,000	**Khartoum**	Sudan
2,624,000	**Kiev**	Ukraine
3,505,000	**Kinshasa**	Zaire
1,711,000	**Kuala Lumpur**	Malaysia
4,100,000	**Lagos**	Nigeria
4,092,000	**Lahore**	Pakistan
1,566,000	**Lanzhou**	China
6,404,500	**Lima**	Peru
1,603,000	**Lisbon**	Portugal
9,092,024	**London**	UK
10,845,000	**Los Angeles**	USA
5,702,000	**Madras**	India
2,991,200	**Madrid**	Spain
2,590,500	**Manchester**	UK
8,475,000	**Manila – Quezon City**	Philippines
1,585,000	**Medellín**	Colombia
3,081,000	**Melbourne**	Australia
18,748,000	**Mexico City**	Mexico
1,814,000	**Miami**	USA
2,388,000	**Minneapolis – St Paul**	USA
1,637,000	**Minsk**	Belorussia
2,521,697	**Monterrey**	Mexico
1,197,000	**Montevideo**	Uruguay
3,084,100	**Montréal**	Canada
9,000,000	**Moscow**	Russian Federation
1,631,000	**Munich**	Germany
2,160,000	**Nagoya**	Japan
1,503,000	**Nairobi**	Kenya
1,415,000	**Nanchang**	China
2,265,000	**Nanjing**	China
16,198,000	**New York**	USA
1,436,000	**Novosibirsk**	Russian Federation
1,115,000	**Odessa**	Ukraine
8,520,000	**Osaka-Kobe**	Japan
458,364	**Oslo**	Norway
885,300	**Ottawa**	Canada
9,060,000	**Paris**	France

Population	City	Country
4,920,000	**Philadelphia**	USA
2,030,000	**Phoenix**	USA
2,094,000	**Pittsburg**	USA
2,906,472	**Pôrto Alegre**	Brazil
1,294,000	**Prague**	Czechoslovakia
3,875,000	**Pusan**	South Korea
2,230,000	**Pyôngyang**	North Korea
622,000	**Quebec**	Canada
2,010,000	**Qingdao**	China
1,281,849	**Quito**	Ecuador
3,295,000	**Rangoon**	Burma
2,814,795	**Recife**	Brazil
915,000	**Riga**	Latvia
11,205,567	**Rio de Janeiro**	Brazil
1,975,000	**Riyadh**	Saudi Arabia
3,051,000	**Rome**	Italy
1,385,000	**Sacramento**	USA
3,237,000	**Saigon (Ho Chi Minh)**	Vietnam
2,424,878	**Salvador**	Brazil
2,370,000	**San Diego**	USA
5,028,000	**San Francisco**	USA
1,390,000	**San Juan**	Puerto Rico
4,734,000	**Santiago**	Chile
2,203,000	**Santo Domingo**	Dominican Republic
17,112,712	**São Paulo**	Brazil
10,979,000	**Seoul**	South Korea
13,341,896	**Shanghai**	China
4,763,000	**Shenyang**	China
2,723,000	**Singapore**	Singapore
1,190,000	**Sofia**	Bulgaria
2,467,000	**St Louis**	USA
5,035,000	**St Petersburg** (formerly Leningrad)	Russian Federation
1,662,000	**Stockholm**	Sweden
2,383,000	**Surabaya**	Indonesia
3,657,000	**Sydney**	Australia
2,518,000	**Taegu**	South Korea
2,961,000	**Taipei**	Taiwan
2,199,000	**Taiyuan**	China
482,000	**Tallinn**	Estonia
2,100,000	**Tashkent**	Uzbekistan
1,264,000	**Tbilisi**	Georgia
6,773,000	**Tehran**	Iran
1,029,700	**Tel Aviv**	Israel
8,785,402	**Tianjin**	China
11,935,700	**Tokyo**	Japan
3,822,400	**Toronto**	Canada
2,062,000	**Tripoli**	Libya
1,586,600	**Vancouver**	Canada
1,531,000	**Vienna**	Austria
582,000	**Vilnius**	Lithuania
1,655,100	**Warsaw**	Poland
3,734,000	**Washington DC**	USA
325,700	**Wellington**	New Zealand
648,500	**Winnipeg**	Canada
3,921,000	**Wuhan**	China
2,859,000	**Xian**	China
1,300,000	**Yerevan**	Armenia
1,174,512	**Zagreb**	Croatia
2,400,000	**Zibo**	China

MOUNTAIN HEIGHTS

metres	feet	Mountain	Location
8,848	29,028	**Everest (Qomolangma Feng)**	*China–Nepal*
8,611	28,250	**K2 (Qogir Feng) (Godwin Austen)**	*India–China*
8,598	28,170	**Kangchenjunga**	*India–Nepal*
8,481	27,824	**Makalu**	*China–Nepal*
8,217	26,958	**Cho Oyu**	*China–Nepal*
8,167	26,795	**Dhaulagiri**	*Nepal*
8,156	26,758	**Manaslu**	*Nepal*
8,126	26,660	**Nanga Parbat**	*India*
8,078	26,502	**Annapurna**	*Nepal*
8,088	26,470	**Gasherbrum**	*India–China*
8,027	26,335	**Xixabangma Feng (Gosainthan)**	*China*
7,885	25,869	**Distaghil Sar**	*Kashmir, India*
7,820	25,656	**Masherbrum**	*India*
7,817	25,646	**Nanda Devi**	*India*
7,788	25,550	**Rakaposhi**	*India*
7,756	25,446	**Kamet**	*China–India*
7,756	25,447	**Namjagbarwa Feng**	*China*
7,728	25,355	**Gurla Mandhata**	*China*
7,723	25,338	**Muztag**	*China*
7,719	25,325	**Kongur Shan (Kungur)**	*China*
7,690	25,230	**Tirich Mir**	*Pakistan*
7,556	24,790	**Gongga Shan**	*China*
7,546	24,757	**Muztagata**	*China*
7,495	24,590	**Pik Kommunizma**	*Tajikistan*
7,439	24,406	**Pik Pobedy (Tomur Feng)**	*Kirgizia–China*
7,313	23,993	**Chomo Lhari**	*Bhutan–Tibet*
7,134	23,406	**Pik Lenina**	*Kirgizia*
6,960	22,834	**Aconcagua**	*Argentina*
6,908	22,664	**Ojos del Salado**	*Argentina–Chile*
6,872	22,546	**Bonete**	*Argentina*
6,800	22,310	**Tupungato**	*Argentina–Chile*
6,770	22,211	**Mercedario**	*Argentina*
6.768	22,205	**Huascarán**	*Peru*
6,723	22,057	**Llullaillaco**	*Argentina–Chile*
6,714	22,027	**Kangrinboqê Feng (Kailas)**	*Tibet, China*
6,634	21,765	**Yerupaja**	*Peru*
6,542	21,463	**Sajama**	*Bolivia*
6,485	21,276	**Illampu**	*Bolivia*
6,425	21,079	**Coropuna**	*Peru*
6,402	21,004	**Illimani**	*Bolivia*
6,310	20,702	**Chimborazo**	*Ecuador*
6,194	20,320	**McKinley**	*USA*
6,050	19,849	**Logan**	*Canada*
5,896	19,344	**Cotopaxi**	*Ecuador*
5,895	19,340	**Kilimanjaro**	*Tanzania*
5,800	19,023	**Sa. Nevada de Sta. Marta (Cristobal Colon)**	*Columbia*
5,775	18,947	**Bolivar**	*Venezuela*
5,699	18,697	**Citlaltépetl (Orizaba)**	*Mexico*
5,642	18,510	**El'brus**	*Russian Federation*
5,601	18,376	**Damāvand**	*Iran*
5,489	18,008	**Mt St. Elias**	*Canada*
5,227	17,149	**Mt Lucania**	*Canada*
5,200	17,058	**Kenya (Kirinyaga)**	*Kenya*
5,165	16,945	**Ararat (Büyük Ağri Daği)**	*Turkey*
5,140	16,860	**Vinson Massif**	*Antarctica*
5,110	16,763	**Stanley (Margherita)**	*Uganda–Zaire*
5,029	16,499	**Jaya (Carstensz)**	*Indonesia*
5,005	16,421	**Mt Bona**	*USA*
4,949	16,237	**Sandford**	*USA*
4,936	16,194	**Mt Blackburn**	*Canada*
4,808	15,774	**Mont Blanc**	*France–Italy*
4,750	15,584	**Klyuchevskaya Sopka**	*Russian Federation*
4,634	15,203	**Monte Rosa (Dufour)**	*Italy–Switzerland*
4,620	15,157	**Ras Dashen**	*Ethiopia*
4,565	14,979	**Meru**	*Tanzania*
4,545	14,910	**Dom (Mischabel group)**	*Switzerland*
4,528	14,855	**Kirkpatrick**	*Antarctica*
4,508	14,790	**Wilhelm**	*Papua, New Guinea*
4,507	14,786	**Karisimbi**	*Rwanda–Zaire*
4,477	14,688	**Matterhorn**	*Italy–Switzerland*
4,418	14,495	**Whitney**	*USA*
4,398	14,431	**Elbert**	*USA*
4,392	14,410	**Rainier**	*USA*
4,351	14,275	**Markham**	*Antarctica*
4,321	14,178	**Elgon**	*Kenya–Uganda*
4,307	14,131	**Batu**	*Ethiopia*
4,169	13,677	**Mauna Loa**	*USA, Hawaii*
4,165	13,644	**Toubkal**	*Morocco*
4,095	13,435	**Cameroon (Caméroun)**	*Cameroon*
4,094	13,431	**Kinabalu**	*Malaysia*
3,794	12,447	**Erebus**	*Antarctica*
3,776	12,388	**Fuji**	*Japan*
3,764	12,349	**Cook**	*New Zealand*
3,718	12,198	**Teide**	*Canary Is*
3,482	11,424	**Thabana Ntlenyana**	*Lesotho*
3,482	11,424	**Mulhacén**	*Spain*
3,415	11,204	**Emi Koussi**	*Chad*
3,323	10,902	**Etna**	*Italy, Sicily*
2,743	9,000	**Mt Balbi**	*Bougainville, Papua, New Guinea*
2,655	8,708	**Gerlachovsky stit (Tatra)**	*Czechoslovakia*
2,230	7,316	**Kosciusko**	*Australia*

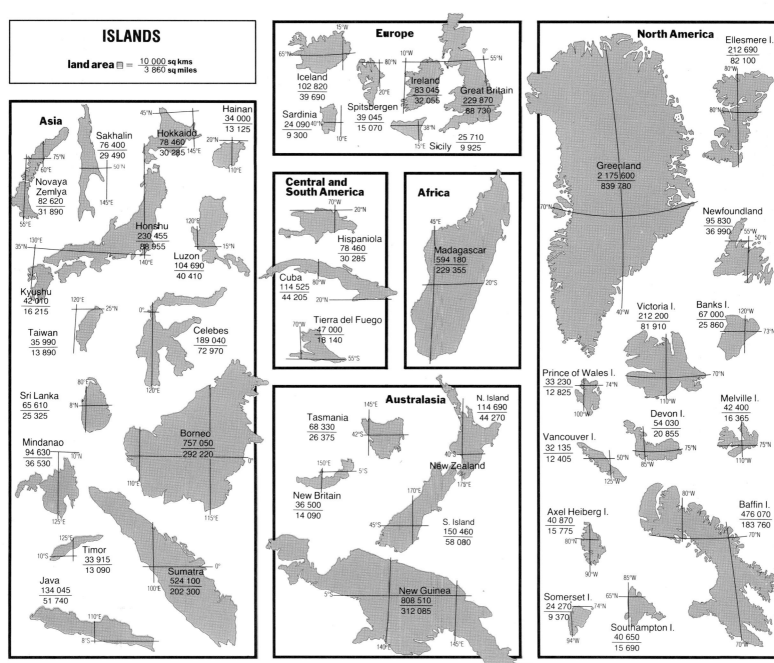

ISLANDS

land area ☐ = 10 000 sq kms / 3 860 sq miles

Asia

Sakhalin 76 400 / 29 490
Hainan 34 000 / 13 125
Hokkaido 78 460 / 30 285
Novaya Zemlya 82 620 / 31 890
Honshu 230 455 / 88 955
Luzon 104 690 / 40 410
Kyushu 42 010 / 16 215
Taiwan 35 990 / 13 890
Celebes 189 040 / 72 970
Sri Lanka 65 610 / 25 325
Mindanao 94 630 / 36 530
Borneo 757 050 / 292 220
Timor 33 915 / 13 090
Java 134 045 / 51 740
Sumatra 524 100 / 202 300

Europe

Iceland 102 820 / 39 690
Ireland 83 045 / 32 055
Great Britain 229 870 / 88 730
Sardinia 24 090 / 9 300
Spitsbergen 39 045 / 15 070
Sicily 25 710 / 9 925

Central and South America

Hispaniola 78 460 / 30 285
Cuba 114 525 / 44 205
Tierra del Fuego 47 000 / 18 140

Africa

Madagascar 594 180 / 229 355

Australasia

Tasmania 68 330 / 26 375
N. Island 114 690 / 44 270
New Britain 36 500 / 14 090
S. Island 150 460 / 58 080
New Guinea 808 510 / 312 085

North America

Ellesmere I. 212 690 / 82 100
Greenland 2 175 600 / 839 780
Newfoundland 95 830 / 36 990
Victoria I. 212 200 / 81 910
Banks I. 67 000 / 25 860
Prince of Wales I. 33 230 / 12 825
Devon I. 54 030 / 20 855
Melville I. 42 400 / 16 365
Vancouver I. 32 135 / 12 405
Axel Heiberg I. 40 870 / 15 775
Baffin I. 476 070 / 183 760
Somerset I. 24 270 / 9 370
Southampton I. 40 650 / 15 690

45

OCEANS AND SEAS

water area ▨ = $\frac{1\,000\,000 \text{ sq km}}{386\,000 \text{ sq miles}}$

OCEAN FACTS AND FIGURES

The area of the Earth covered by sea is estimated to be 361,740,000 sq km (139,670,000 sq miles), or 70.92% of the total surface. The mean depth is estimated to be 3554 m (11,660 ft), and the volume of the oceans to be 1,285,600,000 cu. km (308,400,000 cu. miles).

INDIAN OCEAN

Mainly confined to the southern hemisphere, and at its greatest breadth (Tasmania to Cape Agulhas) 9600 km. Average depth is 4000 m; greatest depth is the Amirante Trench (9000 m).

ATLANTIC OCEAN

Commonly divided into North Atlantic (36,000,000 sq km) and South Atlantic (26,000,000 sq km). The greatest breadth in the North is 7200 km (Morocco to Florida) and in the South 9600 km (Guinea to Brazil). Average depth is 3600 m; the greatest depths are the Puerto Rico Trench 9220 m, S. Sandwich Trench 8264 m, and Romansh Trench 7728 m.

PACIFIC OCEAN

Covers nearly 40% of the world's total sea area, and is the largest of the oceans. The greatest breadth (E/W) is 16,000 km and the greatest length (N/S) 11,000 km. Average depth is 4200 m; also the deepest ocean. Generally the west is deeper than the east and the north deeper than the south. Greatest depths occur near island groups and include Mindanao Trench 11,524 m, Mariana Trench 11,022 m, Tonga Trench 10,882 m, Kuril-Kamchatka Trench 10,542 m, Philippine Trench 10,497 m, and Kermadec Trench 10,047 m.

Comparisons (where applicable)	greatest distance N/S (km)	greatest distance E/W (km)	maximum depth (m)
Indian Ocean	—	9600	9000
Atlantic Ocean	—	9600	9220
Pacific Ocean	11,000	16,000	11,524
Arctic Ocean	—	—	5450
Mediterranean Sea	960	3700	4846
S. China Sea	2100	1750	5514
Bering Sea	1800	2100	5121
Caribbean Sea	1600	2000	7100
Gulf of Mexico	1200	1700	4377
Sea of Okhotsk	2200	1400	3475
E. China Sea	1100	750	2999
Yellow Sea	800	1000	91
Hudson Bay	1250	1050	259
Sea of Japan	1500	1100	3743
North Sea	1200	550	661
Red Sea	1932	360	2246
Black Sea	600	1100	2245
Baltic Sea	1500	650	460

EARTH'S SURFACE WATERS

Total volume	c.1400 million cu. km
Oceans and seas	1370 million cu. km
Ice	24 million cu. km
Interstitial water (in rocks and sediments)	4 million cu. km
Lakes and rivers	230 thousand cu. km
Atmosphere (vapour)	c.140 thousand cu. km

to convert metric to imperial measurements:
1 m = 3.281 feet
1 km = 0.621 miles
1 sq km = 0.386 sq miles

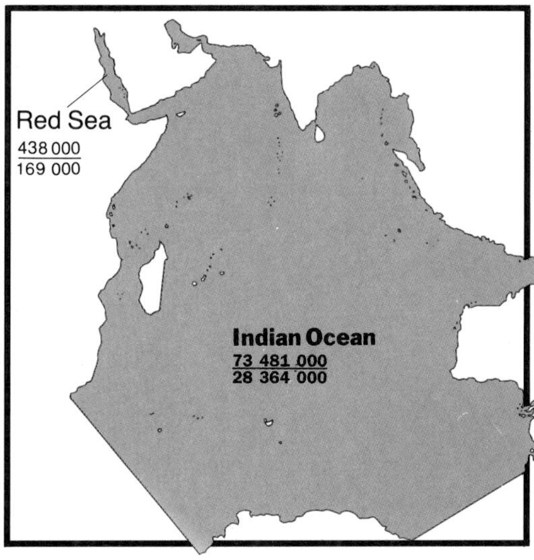

Red Sea
438 000
169 000

Indian Ocean
73 481 000
28 364 000

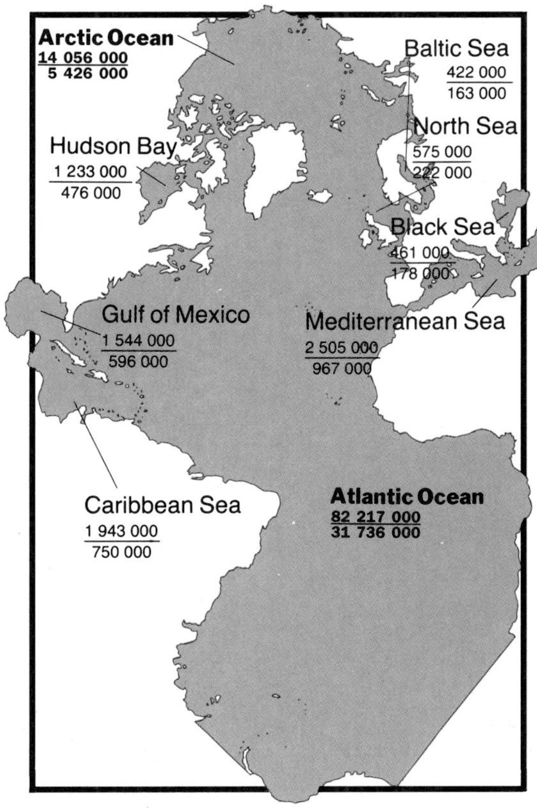

Arctic Ocean
14 056 000
5 426 000

Baltic Sea
422 000
163 000

North Sea
575 000
222 000

Hudson Bay
1 233 000
476 000

Black Sea
461 000
178 000

Gulf of Mexico
1 544 000
596 000

Mediterranean Sea
2 505 000
967 000

Caribbean Sea
1 943 000
750 000

Atlantic Ocean
82 217 000
31 736 000

FEATURES OF THE OCEAN BASIN

The majority of land drainage occurs in the Atlantic, yet this is the most saline ocean due to interchange of waters with its marginal seas. The continental margins (21% of ocean floors) are the most important economic areas.

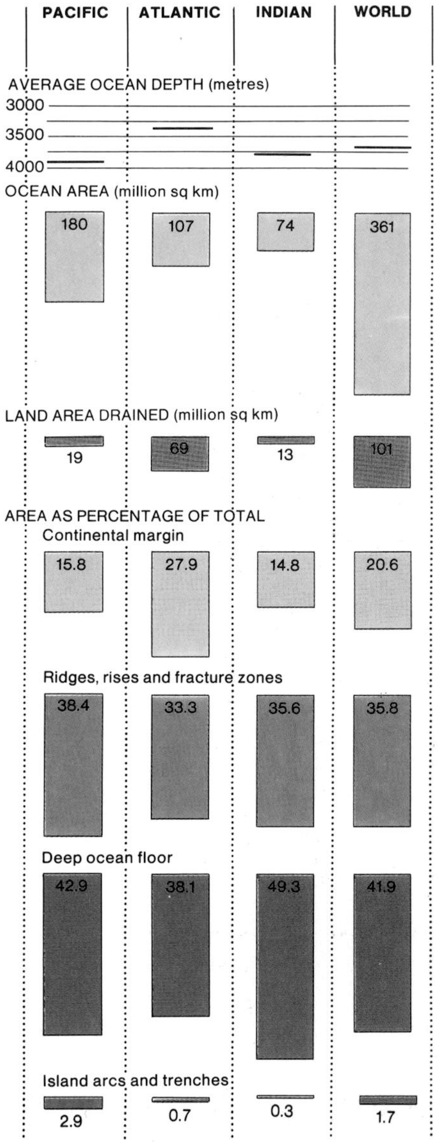

	PACIFIC	ATLANTIC	INDIAN	WORLD
AVERAGE OCEAN DEPTH (metres)				
OCEAN AREA (million sq km)	180	107	74	361
LAND AREA DRAINED (million sq km)	19	69	13	101
AREA AS PERCENTAGE OF TOTAL				
Continental margin	15.8	27.9	14.8	20.6
Ridges, rises and fracture zones	38.4	33.3	35.6	35.8
Deep ocean floor	42.9	38.1	49.3	41.9
Island arcs and trenches	2.9	0.7	0.3	1.7

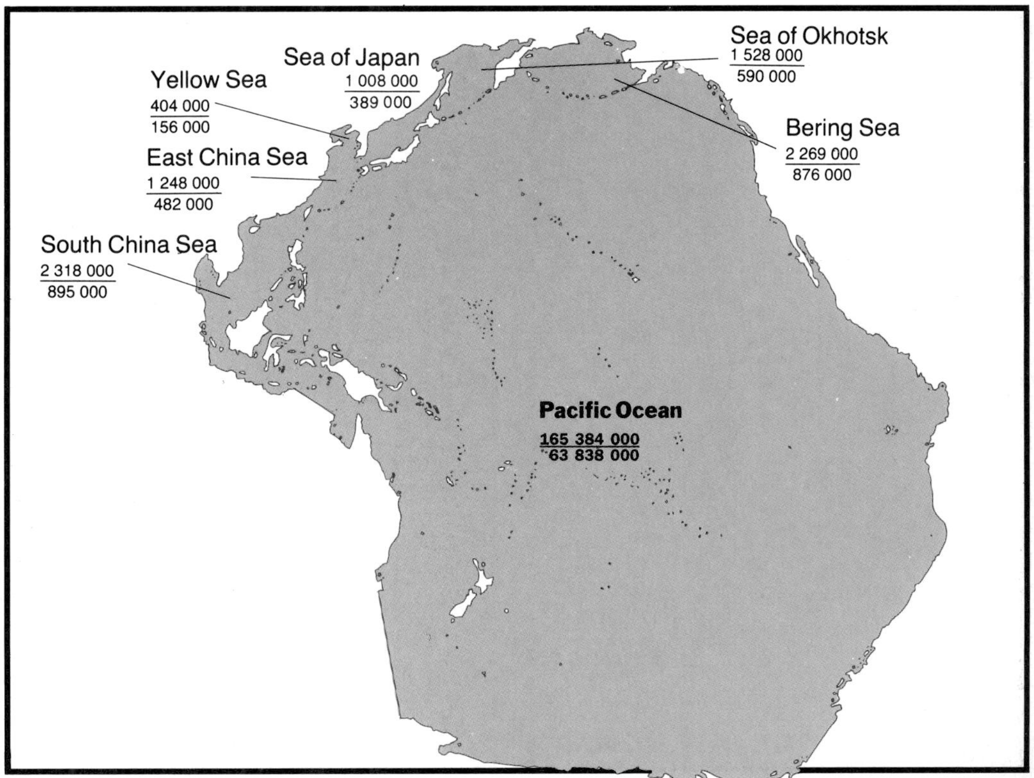

Sea of Japan
1 008 000
389 000

Sea of Okhotsk
1 528 000
590 000

Yellow Sea
404 000
156 000

Bering Sea
2 269 000
876 000

East China Sea
1 248 000
482 000

South China Sea
2 318 000
895 000

Pacific Ocean
165 384 000
63 838 000

RIVER LENGTHS

km	miles		
6,695	4,160	**Nile**	*Africa*
6,515	4,050	**Amazon**	*South America*
6,380	3,965	**Yangtze (Chang Jiang)**	*Asia*
6,019	3,740	**Mississippi-Missouri** *North America*	
5,570	3,460	**Ob'-Irtysh**	*Asia*
5,550	3,450	**Yenisei-Angara**	*Asia*
5,464	3,395	**Yellow River (Huang He)** *Asia*	
4,667	2,900	**Congo (Zaire)**	*Africa*
4,500	2,800	**Paraná**	*South America*
4,440	2,775	**Irtysh**	*Asia*
4,425	2,750	**Mekong**	*Asia*
4,416	2,744	**Amur**	*Asia*
4,400	2,730	**Lena**	*Asia*
4,250	2,640	**Mackenzie**	*North America*
4,090	2,556	**Yenisei**	*Asia*
4,030	2,505	**Niger**	*Africa*
3,969	2,466	**Missouri**	*North America*
3,779	2,348	**Mississippi**	*North America*
3,750	2,330	**Murray-Darling**	*Australasia*
3,688	2,290	**Volga**	*Europe*
3,218	2,011	**Purus**	*South America*
3,200	1,990	**Madeira**	*South America*
3,185	1,980	**Yukon**	*North America*
3,180	1,975	**Indus**	*Asia*
3,078	1,913	**Syrdar'ya**	*Asia*
3,060	1,901	**Salween**	*Asia*
3,058	1,900	**St Lawrence**	*North America*
2,900	1,800	**São Francisco** *South America*	
2,870	1,785	**Rio Grande**	*North America*
2,850	1,770	**Danube**	*Europe*
2,840	1,765	**Brahmaputra**	*Asia*
2,815	1,750	**Euphrates**	*Asia*
2,750	1,710	**Pará-Tocantins** *South America*	
2,750	1,718	**Tarim**	*Asia*
2,650	1,650	**Zambezi**	*Africa*
2,620	1,630	**Amudar'ya**	*Asia*
2,620	1,630	**Araguaia**	*South America*
2,600	1,615	**Paraguay**	*South America*
2,570	1,600	**Nelson-Saskatchewan** *North America*	

km	miles		
2,534	1,575	**Ural**	*Asia*
2,513	1,562	**Kolyma**	*Asia*
2,510	1,560	**Ganges (Ganga)**	*Asia*
2,500	1,555	**Orinoco**	*South America*
2,490	1,550	**Shabeelle**	*Africa*
2,490	1,550	**Pilcomayo**	*South America*
2,348	1,459	**Arkansas**	*North America*
2,333	1,450	**Colorado**	*North America*
2,285	1,420	**Dneper**	*Europe*
2,250	1,400	**Columbia**	*North America*
2,150	1,335	**Irrawaddy**	*Asia*
2,129	1,323	**Pearl River (Xi Jiang)**	*Asia*
2,032	1,270	**Kama**	*Europe*
2,000	1,240	**Negro**	*South America*
1,923	1,195	**Peace**	*North America*
1,899	1,186	**Tigris**	*Asia*
1,870	1,162	**Don**	*Europe*
1,860	1,155	**Orange**	*Africa*
1,809	1,124	**Pechora**	*Europe*
1,800	1,125	**Okavango**	*Africa*
1,609	1,000	**Marañón**	*South America*
1,609	1,095	**Uruguay**	*South America*
1,600	1,000	**Volta**	*Africa*
1,600	1,000	**Limpopo**	*Africa*
1,550	963	**Magdalena** *South America*	
1,515	946	**Kura**	*Asia*
1,480	925	**Oka**	*Europe*
1,480	925	**Belaya**	*Europe*
1,445	903	**Godavari**	*Asia*
1,430	893	**Senegal**	*Africa*
1,410	876	**Dnester**	*Europe*
1,400	875	**Chari**	*Africa*
1,368	850	**Fraser**	*North America*
1,320	820	**Rhine**	*Europe*
1,314	821	**Vyatka**	*Europe*
1,183	735	**Donets**	*Europe*
1,159	720	**Elbe**	*Europe*
1,151	719	**Kizilirmak**	*Asia*

km	miles		
1,130	706	**Desna**	*Europe*
1,094	680	**Gambia**	*Africa*
1,080	675	**Yellowstone**	*North America*
1,049	652	**Tennessee**	*North America*
1,024	640	**Zelenga**	*Asia*
1,020	637	**Duena**	*Europe*
1,014	630	**Vistula (Wisła)**	*Europe*
1,012	629	**Loire**	*Europe*
1,006	625	**Tagus (Tejo)**	*Europe*
977	607	**Tisza**	*Europe*
925	575	**Meuse (Maas)**	*Europe*
909	565	**Oder**	*Europe*
761	473	**Seine**	*Europe*
354	220	**Severn**	*Europe*
346	215	**Thames**	*Europe*
300	186	**Trent**	*Europe*

DRAINAGE BASINS

sq km	sq miles		
7,050,000	2,721,000	**Amazon**	*South America*
3,700,000	1,428,000	**Congo**	*Africa*
3,250,000	1,255,000	**Mississippi-Missouri** *North America*	
3,100,000	1,197,000	**Paraná**	*South America*
2,700,000	1,042,000	**Yenisei**	*Asia*
2,430,000	938,000	**Ob'**	*Asia*
2,420,000	934,000	**Lena**	*Asia*
1,900,000	733,400	**Nile**	*Africa*
1,840,000	710,000	**Amur**	*Asia*
1,765,000	681,000	**Mackenzie**	*North America*
1,730,000	668,000	**Ganges-Brahmaputra** *Asia*	
1,380,000	533,000	**Volga**	*Europe*
1,330,000	513,000	**Zambezi**	*Africa*
1,200,000	463,000	**Niger**	*Africa*
1,175,000	454,000	**Yangtze**	*Asia*
1,020,000	394,000	**Orange**	*Africa*
980,000	378,000	**Yellow River**	*Asia*
960,000	371,000	**Indus**	*Asia*
945,000	365,000	**Orinoco**	*South America*
910,000	351,000	**Murray-Darling** *Australasia*	
855,000	330,000	**Yukon**	*North America*
815,000	315,000	**Danube**	*Europe*
810,000	313,000	**Mekong**	*Asia*
225,000	86,900	**Rhine**	*Europe*

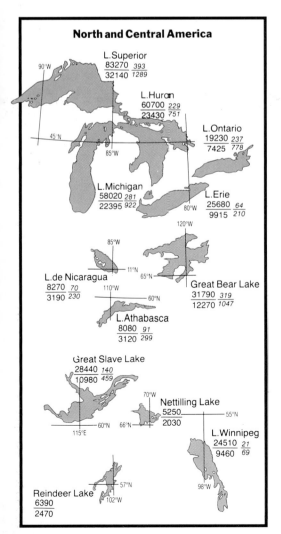

North and Central America

L.Superior
83270 *393*
32140 *1289*

L.Huron
60700 *229*
23430 *751*

L.Ontario
19230 *237*
7425 *778*

L.Michigan
58020 *281*
22395 *922*

L.Erie
25680 *64*
9915 *210*

L.de Nicaragua
8270 *70*
3190 *230*

Great Bear Lake
31790 *319*
12270 *1047*

L.Athabasca
8080 *91*
3120 *299*

Great Slave Lake
28440 *140*
10980 *459*

Nettilling Lake
5250
2030

L.Winnipeg
24510 *21*
9460 *69*

Reindeer Lake
6390
2470

water surface area ▨ = 1 000 sq km / 386 sq miles

deepest point 229 metres / 751 feet

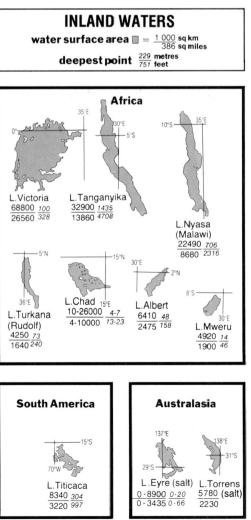

Africa

L.Victoria
68800 *100*
26560 *328*

L.Tanganyika
32900 *1435*
13860 *4708*

L.Nyasa (Malawi)
22490 *706*
8680 *2316*

L.Turkana (Rudolf)
4250 *73*
1640 *240*

L.Chad
10-26000 *4-7*
4-10000 *13-23*

L.Albert
6410 *48*
2475 *158*

L.Mweru
4920 *14*
1900 *46*

South America

L.Titicaca
8340 *304*
3220 *997*

Australasia

L.Eyre (salt)
0 - 8900 *0-20*
0 - 3435 *0-66*

L.Torrens
5780 (salt)
2230

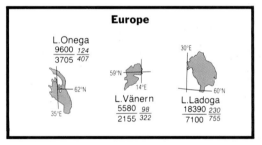

Europe

L.Onega
9600 *124*
3705 *407*

L.Vänern
5580 *98*
2155 *322*

L.Ladoga
18390 *230*
7100 *755*

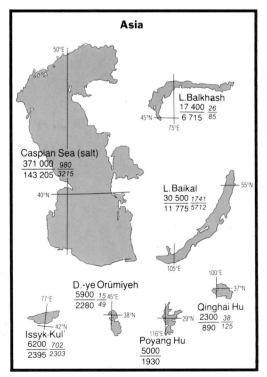

Asia

L.Balkhash
17 400 *26*
6 715 *85*

Caspian Sea (salt)
371 000 *980*
143 205 *3215*

L.Baikal
30 500 *1741*
11 775 *5712*

D.-ye Orūmiyeh
5900 *15*
2280 *49*

Issyk-Kul'
6200 *702*
2395 *2303*

Qinghai Hu
2300 *38*
890 *125*

Poyang Hu
5000
1930

SIBERIA

Lena

Kolyma

Laptev
Sea

New Siberian
Islands

ARCTIC

OCEAN

East
Siberian
Sea

Honshu

Sakhalin

Hokkaido

Sea of Okhotsk

Kuril Islands

Kamchatka

Anadyr

Wrangel
Island

Chukchi
Sea

Chukotskiy
Peninsula

Bering

Sea

Bering Strait

Brooks Range

Point Barrow

Beaufort
Sea

Melville
Island

Banks
Island

Victoria

Aleutian Islands

Yukon

Alaska Range
Mount
McKinley

Aleutian Range

Mackenzie Mountains

Mackenzie

Great
Bear
Lake

Kodiak Island

Gulf
of
Alaska

Coast Mountains

Great
Slave Lake

NORTH

Sandwich Islands

Lake
Athabasca

ROCKY

Athabasca

PACIFIC

Hawaiian Islands

Queen
Charlotte
Islands

Fraser

Saskatchewan

Vancouver
Island

MOUNTAINS

OCEAN

Mount Rainier
Mount St Helens

Cascade Range

Columbia

Snake

Coast Ranges

Sierra Nevada

Great Salt
Lake

Mount
Whitney

Colorado

Gulf of California

Lower California

Sierra Madre Occidental

A Ob'
Urals
Kara
Sea
Novaya
Zemlya
Barents
Sea
Severnaya
Zemlya
North Cape
S C A N D I N A V I A
Baltic Sea
Black Sea
Franz
Josef
Land
Bear
Island
Limit of permanent pack ice
Svalbard
Norwegian
Sea
North
Sea
Mediterranean Sea
NORTH POLE
Wandell
Sea
Jan Mayen
Greenland Sea
BRITISH
ISLES
Bay
of
Biscay
N O R T H   A F R I C A
Lincoln
Sea
Ellesmere
Island
G r e e n l a n d
Denmark Strait
Iceland
Axel
Heiburg
Island
Queen
Elizabeth
Islands
Parry Islands
Devon
Island
Baffin Bay
Davis Strait
Madeira
Somerset
Island
Prince of
Wales Island
Island
Cape Farewell
N O R T H
Canary
Islands
Baffin Island
Nettiling
Lake
Azores
Foxe
Basin
Labrador
Sea
Southampton
Island
Hudson Strait
Cape Chidley
Hudson
Bay
Labrador
Reindeer
Lake
Churchill
Churchill
Southern
Indian
Lake
Nelson
La Grande Rivière
Laurentian
Highlands
Newfoundland
Cape Race
A T L A N T I C
James
Bay
Rupert
Lake
Winnipeg
Nova
Scotia
Lake
Manitoba
Lake
of the
Woods
Lake Superior
St. Lawrence
Missouri
Mississippi
Lake Michigan
Lake
Huron
Lake Ontario
Cape Cod
G r e a t
Platte
Lake Erie
A p p a l a c h i a n   M o u n t a i n s
Bermuda
O C E A N
P l a i n s
Ohio
Ozark
Plateaus
Cape Hatteras
Appalachian
Tennessee
Arkansas
Mississippi
Savannah
Red River
Florida
The
Bahamas
Sierra Madre Oriental
Rio Grande
Gulf of Mexico
W e s t   I n d i e s
Yucatan
C a r i b b e a n   Sea
Orinoco

Mississippi

Rio Grande

GULF
OF
MEXICO

Florida

W
C
U

GREA

Gulf of California

Lower California

Sierra Madre Occidental

Sierra Madre Oriental

Gulf of Campeche

Yucatan

Popocatépetl ▲

Sierra Madre del Sur

Gulf
of
Honduras

Islas Revillagigedo

Lake
Nicaragua

Clipperton
Island

Isthmus of

Gulf
of
Panama

P A C I F I C

Isla del Coco

Isla de Malpelo

Cotopaxi

Chimborazo ▲

Galapagos Islands

O C E A N

Galapagos Islands

San Félix   San Ambrosio

Aconcagua

Juan Fernández

SOUTH

Sala y Gómez

Easter Island

PACIFIC

OCEAN

Ducie Island

Henderson Island

Pitcairn Island

A
N
D
E
S

Gran Chaco

Pampas

Pilcomayo

Bermejo

Salado

Paraná

Uruguay

Plate

Colorado

Negro

Chubut

Chico

Deseado

Patagonia

Falkland
Islands

Tierra del
Fuego

Cape Horn

Drake   Passage

Elephant Island

South
Shetland
Islands

King
George I.

Graham Land

Palmer Land

ANTARCTIC PENINSULA

Peter I Island

Bellingshausen
Sea

Ronne

Ellsworth
Land

Amundsen
Sea

Lesser
Antarctica

A N T

Marie Byrd
Land

Rockefeller
Plateau

Ross
Ice
Shelf

Ross

Sea

TRANSANTARCTIC MOUNTAINS

Mount Erebus

Scott Island

Oates
Land

Chatham
Islands

Balleny Islands

Bounty
Islands

Antipodes

New
Zealand

Campbell Island

St Helena

S O U T H

Tristan da Cunha

Cunene

Gough Island

Orange River

Kalahari
Desert

South Georgia

South
Sandwich
Islands

Cape
of
Good Hope

Limpopo

A T L A N T I C

South Orkney
Islands

Bouvet Island

Madagascar

Weddell

Sea

Prince Edward
Islands

Lazarev
Sea

Limit of permanent pack ice

O C E A N

Ice Shelf

Queen Maud Land

Îles Crozet

A R C T I C A

Antarctica

Enderby Land

Greater

Îles Kerguelen

Macdonald Islands
Heard Island

St Paul
Amsterdam Island

• SOUTH POLE

George V
Land

Wilkes Land

OCEAN

Mediterra

Azores

Strait of Gibralter

Chott
Melrhir

El Jerid

Gulf of
Sirte

Madeira

ATLAS MOUNTAINS

Libyan

Canary Islands

NORTH

ATLANTIC

OCEAN

Hoggar

S   A   H   A   R   A

Tibesti

Jebel
Marra

Los Faguibine

Senegal

S   A   H   E   L

Lake
Chad

Cape Verde
Islands

Cape
Verde

Gambia

Niger

Benue

Adam
Highlands

Ubangi

Mbele

Lake
Volta

Slave Coast

Grain Coast

Ivory Coast

Gold Coast

Bight of
Benin

Mouths
of the Niger

Sanaga

Bioko

Zaire

Gulf of Guinea

Principe

Lac
Mai-Ndombe

St Paul Rocks

São Tomé

Pagalu

Congo

Kasai

S   O   U   T   H

SOUTH AMERICA

Ascension

Cuango

St Helena

A   T   L   A   N   T   I   C

Cubango

Okavango

Cunene

Etosha Pan

Okavango

N A

Lake
Ngami

Namib Desert

Kalahari

Walvis
Bay

Desert

Orange River

54

Great
Karoo

Cape of Good Hope

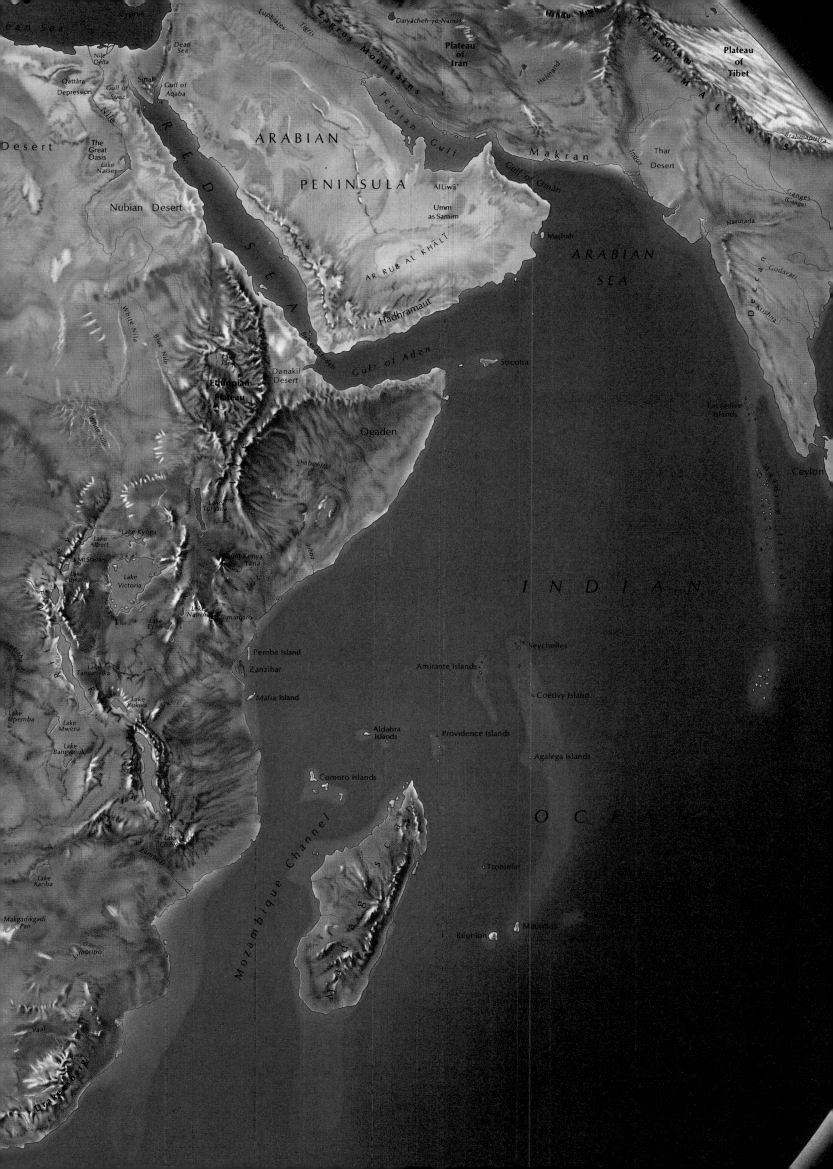

NORTH POLE .

ARCTIC

Ellesmere Island

Greenland
Sea

Svalbard

Hudson Bay

Baffin Island

Davis Strait

Greenland

Jan Mayen

Bear
Island

Norwegian

LABRADOR

Denmark Strait

Sea

Cape Farewell

Iceland

Faeroe Islands

N O R T H

Shetland

Orkney

SCANDIN

Rockall

British
Isles

Grampians

North

Lake
Vänern

Lake
Vättern

A T L A N T I C

Irish Sea

Sea

Ba

Elbe

Oder

Severn

Thames

Rhine

N O R

Ne

English Channel

Seine

Danub

Loire

O C E A N

Bay
of
Biscay

Massif
Central

Mt. Blanc

A L P S

Po

Azores

Cantabrian Mts

Garonne

Rhône

Adriatic

Pyrenees

Corsica

Apennines

Dinar

Sea

Tagus

Ebro

Balearic Islands

Sardinia

Guadalquivir

M E D I T E R

Strait of Gibraltar

Sicily

Madeira

R

A T L A S   M O U N T A I N S

Malta

Chott Melrhir

R

Canary Islands

El Jerid

OCEAN

Limit of permanent pack ice

Franz
Josef
Land

Spitsbergen

*Kara
Sea*

Novaya
Zemlya

Severnaya
Zemlya

*Barents
Sea*

North Cape

Lena

C E N T R A L
S I B E R I A N
P L A T E A U

Nizhnyaya Tunguska
Lena

Yenisey

W E S T

S I B E R I A N

P L A I N

Angara

Lake
Baikal

White
Sea

Pechora

U R A L   M O U N T A I N S

Ob'

Ob'

Irtysh

Gulf of Bothnia

Severnaya Dvina

Lake
Onega

P L A I N

Lake
Ladoga

Gulf of Finland

E U R O P E A N

Volga

Lake
Balkhash

tic Sea

Dvina

Central

Russian

Uplands

K I R G H I Z   S T E P P E

Vistula

Ural

Lake
Balkhash

CARPATHIANS

Dnieper

K I

Volga

Aral
Sea

Syrdar'ya

Dniester

Don

Kyzylkum

Hungarian Plain

Sea of Azov

C a u c a s u s

C a s p i a n

Amudar'ya

Tisza

Karakumy

Danube

Balkan Mountains

Black   Sea

S e a

Alps

Rhodope

Thrace

Bosporus

Araxes

Lake
Van

Lake
Urmia

Elbruz Mts

Daryācheh-ye-Namak

Pindus

Dardanelles

Sea of
Marmara

ASIA MINOR

Kizil Irmak

Z a g r o s   M o u n t a i n s

Plateau
of
Iran

Aegean
Sea

Tuz
Gölü

T a u r u s

M e s o p o t a m i a

Cyprus

Tigris

Euphrates

A N E A N   S E A

Crete

Jordan

Syrian Desert

Dead Sea

P e r s i a n

G u l f

Gulf
of
Oman

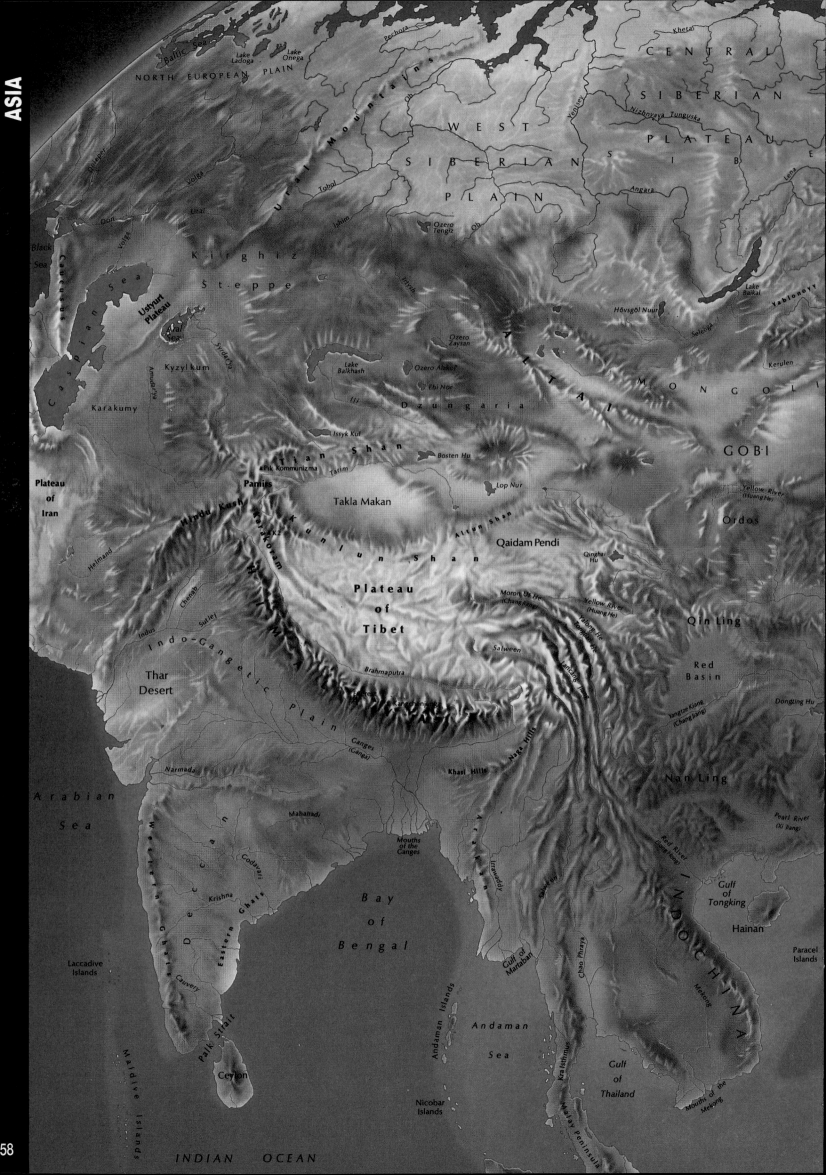

Baltic
Sea
Lake
Ladoga
Lake
Onega
NORTH EUROPEAN PLAIN
Pechora
Kheta
C E N T R A L
S I B E R I A N
P L A T E A U
Ob
Nizhnyaya Tunguska
S I B
E
Ural Mountains
W E S T
S I B E R I A N
P L A I N
Yenisey
Angara
Nizhnyaya Tunguska
Lena
Dnieper
Volga
Tobol
Ural
Ishim
Ob
Irtysh
Ozero
Tengiz
Angara
Lena
Black
Sea
Caucasus
Don
Volga
K i r g h i z
S t e p p e
Lake
Baikal
Yablonovy
Caspian Sea
Ustyurt
Plateau
Aral
Sea
Syrdar'ya
Amudar'ya
Kyzylkum
Ozero
Zaysan
Ozero Alakol'
Ebi Nor
Hövsgöl Nuur
A L T A I
M O N G O L I
Kerulen
Karakumy
I l i
D z u n g a r i a
Lake
Balkhash
Selenga
Plateau
of
Iran
Issyk Kul
T i a n   S h a n
Bosten Hu
G O B I
Pik Kommunizma
Tarim
Lop Nur
Yellow River
(Huang He)
Pamirs
Takla Makan
Ordos
Hindu Kush
Karakoram
AK2
K u n l u n   S h a n
Altun Shan
Qaidam Pendi
Qinghai
Hu
Helmand
H
Moron Us He
(Chang Jiang)
Yellow River
(Huang He)
Qin Ling
Chenab
Sutlej
I
P l a t e a u
o f
T i b e t
Yalong He
Tongtian He
Lancang Jiang
Indus
Sutlej
M
Salween
Red
Basin
Indo-Gangetic
Brahmaputra
Thar
Desert
A
Everest
Kanchenjunga
Yangtze Kiang
(Chang Jiang)
Dongting Hu
L
Naga Hills
P l a i n
Ganges
(Ganga)
Nan Ling
Narmada
Khasi Hills
Pearl River
(Xi Jiang)
Arabian
Sea
Mahanadi
Deccan
Western Ghats
Godavari
Eastern Ghats
Krishna
Arakan
Mouths
of the
Ganges
Red River
(Song Hong)
Gulf
of
Tongking
Hainan
B a y
o f
B e n g a l
Irrawaddy
Salween
I N D O C H I N A
Paracel
Islands
Laccadive
Islands
Cauvery
Gulf of
Martaban
Chao Phraya
Mekong
Palk Strait
Andaman
Islands
A n d a m a n
S e a
Kra Isthmus
Gulf
of
Thailand
Mouths of the
Mekong
Maldive Islands
Ceylon
Nicobar
Islands
Malay Peninsula

INDIAN   OCEAN

Nicobar
Islands

South
China
Sea

B o r n e o

Celebes

Sea

NORT

Malay Peninsula

Strait of Malacca

Molucca

Halmahera

S u m a t r a

E

Celebes

Seram

Makassar Strait

J a v a
Sea

B a n d a
Sea

A

Java

Bali   Sumbawa   Flores

Arafura

Sea

S

Sumba

Timor

Christmas Island

T I N D I E S

Timor
Sea

Cocos–Keeling Island

Arnhem Land

C

Victoria

Barkly Tableland

I N D I A N

Fitzroy

Kimberley
Plateau

Tanami
Desert

Great
Sandy
Desert

Lake
Mackay

Macdonnell Ranges

Ashburton

Gibson
Desert

Lake
Amadeus

Simpson
Desert

Gascoyne

Finke

Murchison

Great Victoria Desert

Lake
Eyre

Lake
Barlee

Lake
Torrens

Lake
Moore

Nullarbor Plain

Lake
Gairdner

O C E A N

Great Australian Bight

Spencer
Gulf

Amsterdam Island

St Paul

Kerguelen

Heard Island
Macdonald Islands

A N T A R C T I C A

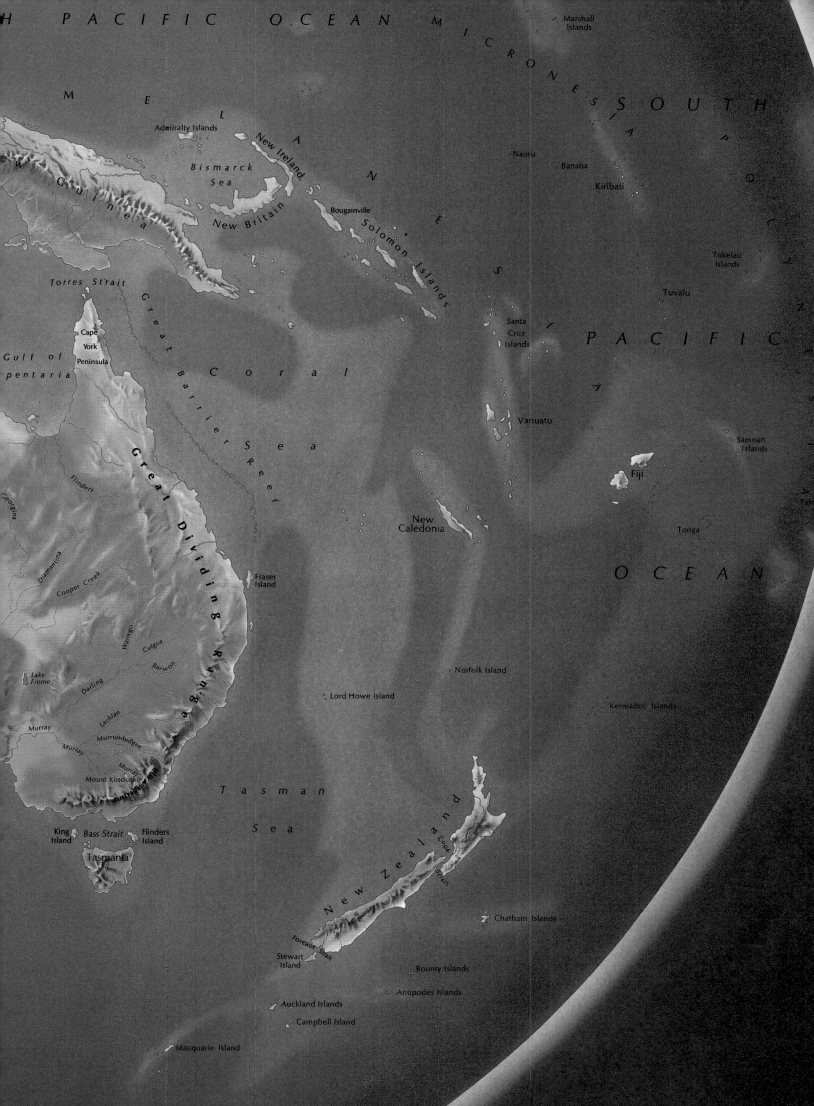

H PACIFIC OCEAN MICRONESIA SOUTH

M E L A N E S I A P O L Y N E S I A

Marshall
Islands

Admiralty Islands

Bismarck
Sea

New Ireland

New Guinea

New Britain

Bougainville

Solomon Islands

Nauru

Banaba

Kiribati

Tokelau
Islands

Tuvalu

PACIFIC

Santa
Cruz
Islands

Torres Strait

Great Barrier Reef

Cape
York
Peninsula

Gulf of
Carpentaria

Coral

Sea

Vanuatu

Samoan
Islands

Fiji

Tahiti

Great Dividing Range

Flinders

Georgina

Diamantina

Cooper Creek

Lake
Frome

Warrego

Culgoa

Barwon

Darling

Lachlan

Murrumbidgee

Murray

Murray

Murray

Mount Kosciusko

Australian Alps

New Caledonia

Tonga

OCEAN

Fraser
Island

Norfolk Island

Lord Howe Island

Kermadec Islands

Tasman

Sea

King
Island

Bass Strait

Flinders
Island

Tasmania

New Zealand

Cook Strait

Chatham Islands

Foveaux Strait

Stewart
Island

Bounty Islands

Antipodes Islands

Auckland Islands

Campbell Island

Macquarie Island

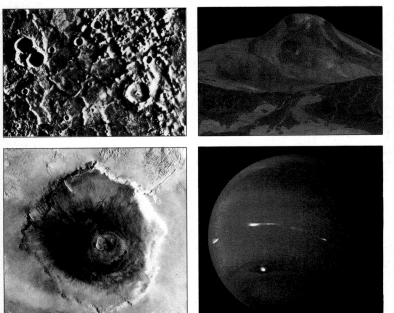

Far left The Caloris basin of Mercury is the largest impact feature on the planet.
Left Radar mapping of Venus has provided this computer-generated image of the volcano, Maat Mons.
Top right Io (left) and Europa are clearly visible as they cross the face of Jupiter.

Far left Olympus Mons on Mars is the largest known volcano in the solar system. It is 550 km across at the base and more than 26 km high.
Right The rings of Saturn lie in the equatorial plane and consist of countless ice-covered particles, perhaps up to several metres across.
Left Voyager 2 produced this false-colour image of Neptune in August 1989. A planet-wide haze (red) and white clouds are visible.

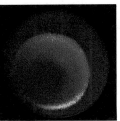

Left This image of Uranus in false-colour was taken from 9.1 million km by Voyager 2. The atmosphere is deep, cold and remarkably clear, but the false colours enhance the polar region. Here, the suggestion is that a brownish haze of smog is concentrated over the pole.

Current theory suggests that the solar system condensed from a primitive solar nebula of gas and dust during an interval of a few tens of millions of years about 4600 million years ago. Gravity caused this nebula to contract, drawing most of its mass into the centre. Turbulence gave the original cloud a tendency to rotate faster and faster, forcing the remainder of the cloud into a disc shape.

The centre of the cloud heated up as it compressed, and so eventually became hot enough for the Sun to begin to shine, through nuclear energy released at its core. Meanwhile the surrounding disc of cloud cooled, allowing material to condense into solid form. Particles stuck together as they collided and progressively larger bodies were built up. These swept up most of the debris to form the planets, which now orbit the Sun.

EARTHLIKE PLANETS

Mercury is the nearest planet to the Sun, spinning three times for every two orbits around the Sun. It has an exceptionally large metallic core which may be responsible for Mercury's weak magnetic field. Mercury is an airless world subject to vast extremes of temperature, from −180°C (−292°F) at night to 430°C (806°F) near the middle of its long day. The Mariner 10 space probe, during the mid-1970s, revealed the surface to be dominated by heavily cratered areas.

Venus has a dense atmosphere with a surface pressure 90 times that of the Earth. Made up of 96% carbon dioxide, the lower layers are rich in sulphur dioxide while sulphuric acid droplets populate the higher clouds. The clouds maintain a mean surface temperature of about 480°C (896°F). The hidden surface has been mapped by radar from orbiting probes and shows a rugged surface with some volcanoes, possibly still active.

Mars has a thin atmosphere of about 96% carbon dioxide mixed with other minor gasses. The polar caps consist of semi-permanent water-ice and solid carbon dioxide. Day and night surface temperatures vary between about −120°C (−184°F) and −20°C (−4°F). Mars has two small satellites, Phobos and Deimos, each less than about 25km (15.5 miles) across, probably captured asteroids.

Mars also shows evidence of erosional processes. The effect of winds is seen in the form of the deposition of sand dunes. Dust storms frequently obscure the surface. The large channels, such as the 5000km (3107 miles) long Valles Marineris, may have been cut by flowing water. Water is abundant in the polar caps and may be widespread, held in as permafrost.

GAS GIANTS

Jupiter has at least 16 satellites and a debris ring system about 50,000km (31,070 miles) above the cloud tops. The outer atmosphere is all that can be directly observed of the planet itself. It is mostly hydrogen with lesser amounts of helium, ammonia, methane and water vapour. Jupiter's rapid rotation causes it to be flattened towards the poles. This rotation and heat flow from the interior cause complex weather patterns. Where cloud systems interact vast storms can occur in the form of vortices. Some last only a few days, but the most persistent of these, the Great Red Spot, has been present since it was first detected in the 17th century.

Saturn is the least dense of the planets. It has a stormy atmosphere situated above a 30,000km (18,640 miles) layer of liquid hydrogen and helium distorted by rotation.

The rings of Saturn are thought to be mostly made of icy debris, from 10m (33 ft) down to a few microns in size, derived from the break-up of a satellite. The rings are less than 1km thick.

Uranus, consisting mainly of hydrogen, was little known until Voyager 2 flew by it in 1986. The probe discovered ten new satellites and provided images of the planet's eleven icy rings of debris.

Neptune was visited by Voyager 2 in 1989. Six new satellites were discovered, one larger than Nereid, the smaller of the two known satellites. Triton, the largest satellite, was found to be smaller than previous estimates. The turbulent atmosphere is a mixture of hydrogen, helium and methane.

Pluto is now 4500 million km from the Sun, closer than Neptune until 1999, but its eccentric orbit will take it to 7500 million km by 2113. A tenuous atmosphere has been found above a surface of frozen methane. Charon, the satellite, is half Pluto's diameter.

	SUN	MERCURY	VENUS	EARTH	(MOON)	MARS	JUPITER	SATURN	URANUS	NEPTUNE	PLUTO
Mass (Earth = 1)	333 400	0.055	0.815	1 (5.97 10²⁴kg)	0.012	0.107	317.8	95.2	14.5	17.2	0.003
Volume (Earth = 1)	1 306 000	0.06	0.88	1	0.020	0.150	1 323	752	64	54	0.007
Density (water = 1)	1.41	5.43	5.24	5.52	3.34	3.94	1.33	0.70	1.30	1.64	2.0
Equatorial diameter (km)	1 392 000	4878	12 104	12 756	3476	6 794	142 800	120 000	52 000	48 400	2 302
Polar flattening	0	0	0	0.003	0	0.005	0.065	0.108	0.060	0.021	0
'Surface' gravity (Earth = 1)	27.9	0.37	0.88	1	0.16	0.38	2.69	1.19	0.93	1.22	0.05
Number of satellites greater than 100 km diameter	—	0	0	1	—	0	7	13	7	6	1
Total number of satellites	—	0	0	1	—	2	16	17	15	8	1
Period of rotation (in Earth days)	25.38	58.65	−243 (retrograde)	23hr 56m 4 secs	27.32	1.03	0.414	0.426	−0.74 (retrograde)	0.67	−6.39 (retrograde)
Length of year (in Earth days and years)	—	88 days	224.7 days	365.26 days	—	687 days	11.86 years	29.46 years	84.01 years	164.8 years	247.7 years
Distance from Sun (mean) Mkm	—	57.9	108.9	149.6	—	227.9	778.3	1 427	2 870	4 497	5 900

EARTH STRUCTURE

Internally, the Earth may be divided broadly into crust, mantle and core (*see right*).

The crust is a thin shell constituting only 0.2% of the mass of the Earth. The continental crust varies in thickness from 20 to 90km (12 to 56 miles) and is less dense than ocean crust. Two-thirds of the continents are overlain by sedimentary rocks of average thickness less than 2km (1.2 miles). Ocean crust is on average 7km (4.4 miles) thick. It is composed of igneous rocks, basalts and gabbros.

Crust and mantle are separated by the Mohorovičić Discontinuity (Moho). The mantle differs from the crust. It is largely igneous. The upper mantle extends to 350km (218 miles). The lower mantle has a more uniform composition. A sharp discontinuity defines the meeting of mantle and core. The inability of the outer core to transmit seismic waves suggests it is liquid. It is probably of metallic iron with other elements – sulphur, silicon, oxygen, potassium and hydrogen have all been suggested. The inner core is solid and probably of nickel-iron. Temperature at the core-mantle boundary is about 3700°C (5430°F) and 4000°–4500°C (7230°–8130°F) in the inner core.

THE ATMOSPHERE

The ancient atmosphere lacked free oxygen. Plant life added oxygen to the atmosphere and transferred carbon dioxide to the crustal rocks and the hydrosphere. The composition of air today at 79% nitrogen and 20% oxygen remains stable by the same mechanism.

Solar energy is distributed around the Earth by the atmosphere. Most of the weather and climate processes occur in the troposphere at the lowest level. The atmosphere also shields the Earth. Ozone exists to the extent of 2 parts per million and is at its maximum at 30km (19 miles). It is the only gas which absorbs ultra-violet radiation. Water-vapour and CO_2 keep out infra-red radiation.

Above 80km (50 miles) nitrogen and oxygen tend to separate into atoms which become ionized (an ion is an atom lacking one or more of its electrons). The ionosphere is a zone of ionized belts which reflect radio waves back to Earth. These electrification belts change their position dependent on light and darkness and external factors.

Beyond the ionosphere, the magnetosphere extends to outer space. Ionized particles form a plasma (a fourth state of matter, ie. other than solid, liquid, gas) held in by the Earth's magnetic field.

ORIGIN AND DEVELOPMENT OF LIFE

Primitive life-forms (blue-green algae) are found in rocks as old as 3500Ma (million years) and, although it cannot yet be proved, the origin of life on Earth probably dates back to about 4000Ma. It seems likely that the oxygen levels in the atmosphere increased only slowly at first, probably to about 1% of the present amount by 2000Ma. As the atmospheric oxygen built up so the protective ozone layer developed to allow organisms to live in shallower waters. More highly developed photosynthesising organisms led to the development of oxygen breathing animals. The first traces of multicellular life occur about 1000Ma; by 700Ma complex animals, such as jellyfish, worms and primitive molluscs, had developed.

Organisms developed hard parts that allowed their preservation as abundant fossils at about 570Ma. This coincided with a

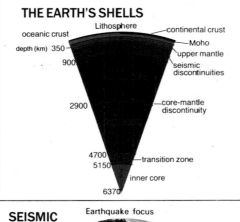

THE EARTH'S SHELLS

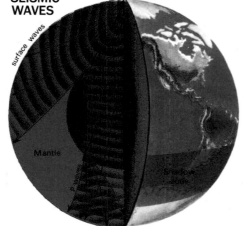

SEISMIC WAVES

Earthquake focus

Above In an earthquake the shock generates vibrations, or seismic waves, which radiate in all directions from the focus. Surface waves travel close to the surface of the Earth. They cause most damage in the ground and most damage to structures.

Other waves known as body waves pass through the body of the Earth. Primary (P) waves are compressional. They are able to travel through solids and fluids and cause the particles of the Earth to vibrate in the direction of travel. Secondary (S) waves are transverse, or shear, waves. They can only pass through solids.

period of explosive evolution of marine life. Fishes appeared about 475Ma and by 400Ma land plants had developed. Between 340 and 305Ma dense vegetation covered the land, amphibians emerged from the sea, and by about 250Ma had given rise to reptiles and the first mammals. These expanded hugely about 65Ma.

EARTHQUAKES

Earthquakes are the manifestation of a slippage at a geological fault. The majority occur at tectonic plate boundaries. The interior of a plate tends to be stable and less subject to earthquakes. When plates slide past each other strain energy is suddenly released. Even though the amount of movement is very small the energy released is colossal. It

is transferred in shock waves.

Most earthquakes originate at not very great depths – 5km (3 miles) or so. Some, however, may be as deep as 700km (435 miles). The precise cause of these very deep earthquakes is not known. The point from which the earthquake is generated is the focus and the point on the surface immediately above the focus is the epicentre.

The Richter Scale is used to define the magnitude of earthquakes. In the Scale each unit is ten times the intensity of the next lower on the scale. The intensity is recorded by seismographs. There is no upper limit but the greatest magnitude yet recorded is 8.9.

VOLCANOES

Almost all the world's active volcanoes, numbering 500–600 are located at convergent plate boundaries. Those are the volcanoes which give spectacular demonstrations of volcanic activity. Yet far greater volcanic activity continues unnoticed and without cessation at mid-ocean ridges where magma from the upper mantle is quietly being extruded on to the ocean floor to create new crustal material.

Chemical composition of magmas and the amount of gas they contain determine the nature of a volcanic eruption. Gas-charged basalts produce cinder cones. Violent eruptions usually occur when large clouds of lava come into contact with water to produce fine-grained ash. When andesites are charged with gas they erupt with explosive violence.

Nuées ardentes (burning clouds) are extremely destructive. They are produced by magmas which erupt explosively sending molten lava fragments and gas at great speeds down the mountain sides.

In spite of the destructiveness of many volcanoes people still live in their vicinity because of the fertile volcanic soils. Geothermal energy in regions of volcanic activity is another source of attraction.

GRAVITY AND MAGNETISM

The Earth is spheroidal in form because it is a rotating body. Were it not so it would take the form of a sphere. The shape is determined by the mass of the Earth and its rate of rotation. Centrifugal force acting outwards reduces the pull of gravity acting inwards so that gravity at the equator is less than at the poles. Uneven distribution of matter within the Earth distorts the shape taken up by the mean sea-level surface (the geoid). Today the belief is that electric currents generated in the semi-molten outer core are responsible for the magnetic field. The Earth's magnetic poles have experienced a number of reversals, the north pole becoming the south and vice-versa.

ROCK AND HYDROLOGICAL CYCLES

Right In the most familiar cycle rain falls onto the land, drains to the sea, evaporates, condenses into cloud and is precipitated onto the land again. Water is also released and recirculated. In the rock cycle rocks are weathered and eroded, forming sediments which are compacted into rocks that are eventually exposed and then weathered again.

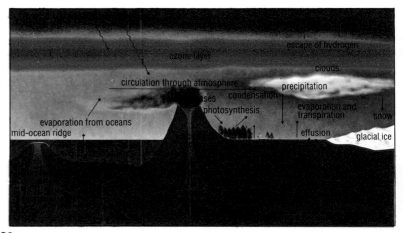

EARTHQUAKES AND VOLCANOES

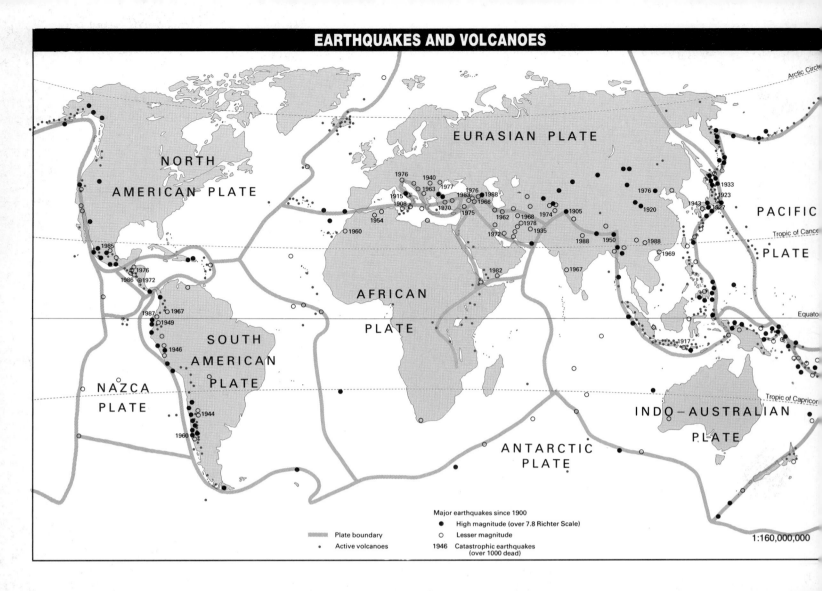

EURASIAN PLATE

NORTH AMERICAN PLATE

PACIFIC PLATE

AFRICAN PLATE

SOUTH AMERICAN PLATE

NAZCA PLATE

INDO-AUSTRALIAN PLATE

ANTARCTIC PLATE

Arctic Circle
Tropic of Cancer
Equator
Tropic of Capricorn

Major earthquakes since 1900
● High magnitude (over 7.8 Richter Scale)
○ Lesser magnitude
1946 Catastrophic earthquakes (over 1000 dead)

▭ Plate boundary
• Active volcanoes

1:160,000,000

ECONOMIC MINERALS

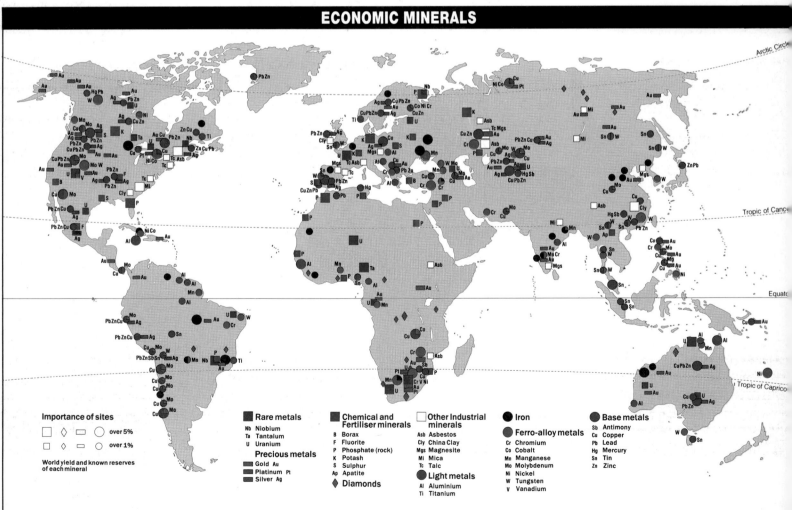

Arctic Circle
Tropic of Cancer
Equator
Tropic of Capricorn

Importance of sites

▭ ◇ ▭ ○ over 5%
▭ ◇ ▭ ○ over 1%

World yield and known reserves of each mineral

■ **Rare metals**
Nb Niobium
Ta Tantalum
U Uranium

Precious metals
Au Gold
Pt Platinum
Ag Silver

■ **Chemical and Fertiliser minerals**
B Borax
F Fluorite
P Phosphate (rock)
K Potash
S Sulphur
Ap Apatite

◆ **Diamonds**

□ **Other Industrial minerals**
Asb Asbestos
Cly China Clay
Mgs Magnesite
Mi Mica
Tc Talc

● **Light metals**
Al Aluminium
Ti Titanium

● **Iron**

● **Ferro-alloy metals**
Cr Chromium
Co Cobalt
Mn Manganese
Mo Molybdenum
Ni Nickel
W Tungsten
V Vanadium

● **Base metals**
Sb Antimony
Cu Copper
Pb Lead
Hg Mercury
Sn Tin
Zn Zinc

1:160,000,000

64

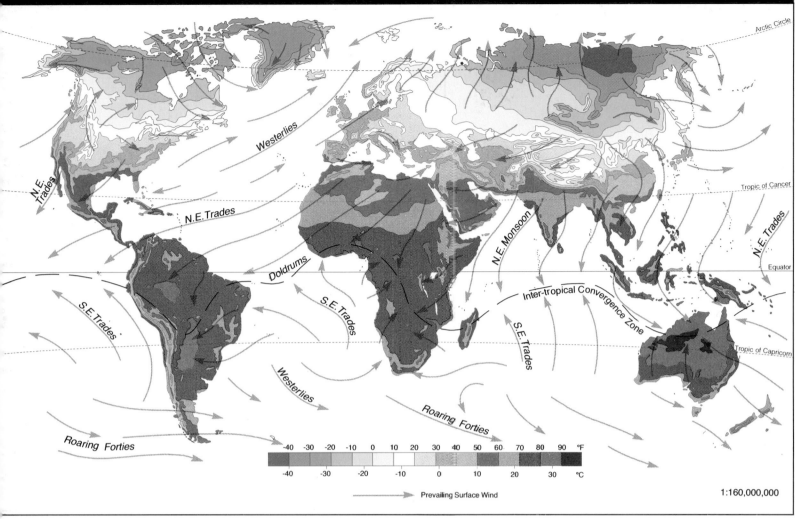

Arctic Circle

Westerlies

N.E. Trades

N.E. Trades

N.E. Trades

Tropic of Cancer

N.E. Monsoon

Equator

Doldrums

S.E. Trades

Inter-tropical Convergence Zone

S.E. Trades

S.E. Trades

S.E. Trades

Tropic of Capricorn

Westerlies

Roaring Forties

Roaring Forties

-40 -30 -20 -10 0 10 20 30 40 50 60 70 80 90 °F

-40   -30   -20   -10   0   10   20   30   °C

Prevailing Surface Wind

1:160,000,000

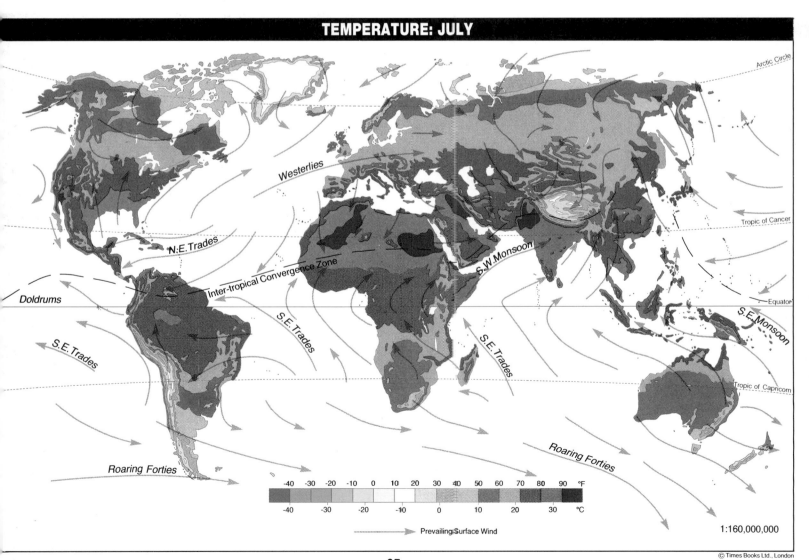

Arctic Circle

Westerlies

Westerlies

N.E. Trades

Tropic of Cancer

S.W. Monsoon

Doldrums

Inter-tropical Convergence Zone

Equator

S.E. Monsoon

S.E. Trades

S.E. Trades

S.E. Trades

Tropic of Capricorn

Roaring Forties

Roaring Forties

-40 -30 -20 -10 0 10 20 30 40 50 60 70 80 90 °F

-40   -30   -20   -10   0   10   20   30   °C

Prevailing Surface Wind

1:160,000,000

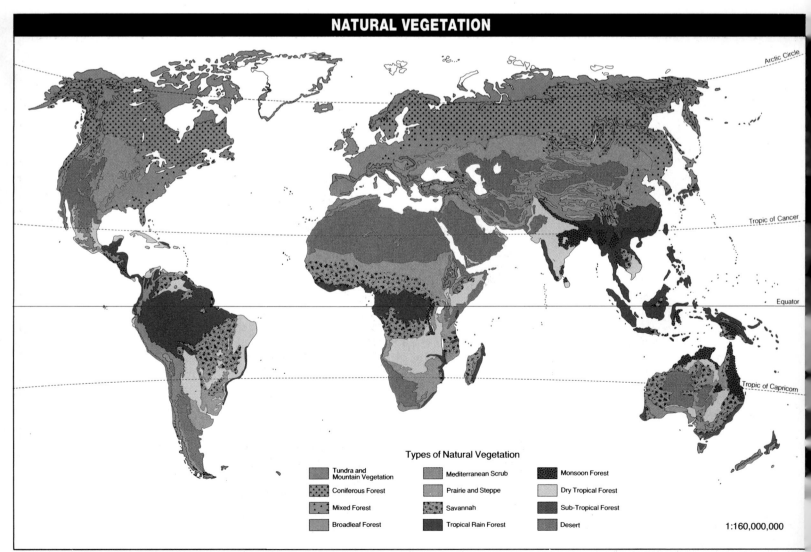

Mean Annual Precipitation

0	100	200	400	600	1000	2000	4000 millimetres
0	3·9	7·9	15·7	23·6	39·4	78·7	157·5 inches

1:160,000,000

NATURAL VEGETATION

Types of Natural Vegetation

Tundra and Mountain Vegetation	Mediterranean Scrub	Monsoon Forest
Coniferous Forest	Prairie and Steppe	Dry Tropical Forest
Mixed Forest	Savannah	Sub-Tropical Forest
Broadleaf Forest	Tropical Rain Forest	Desert

1:160,000,000

POPULATION DENSITY

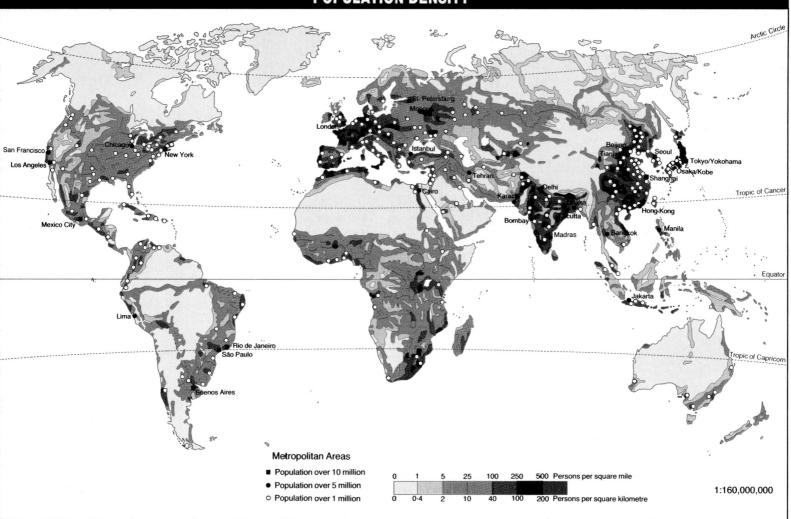

Metropolitan Areas

■ Population over 10 million
● Population over 5 million
○ Population over 1 million

| 0 | 1 | 5 | 25 | 100 | 250 | 500 | Persons per square mile |
| 0 | 0·4 | 2 | 10 | 40 | 100 | 200 | Persons per square kilometre |

San Francisco
Los Angeles
Chicago
New York
Mexico City
Lima
Rio de Janeiro
São Paulo
Buenos Aires

London
Moscow
St. Petersburg
Istanbul
Tehran
Cairo
Karachi
Delhi
Bombay
Calcutta
Madras
Dhaka

Beijing
Tianjin
Seoul
Tokyo/Yokohama
Osaka/Kobe
Shanghai
Hong Kong
Bangkok
Manila
Jakarta

1:160,000,000

POPULATION CHANGE

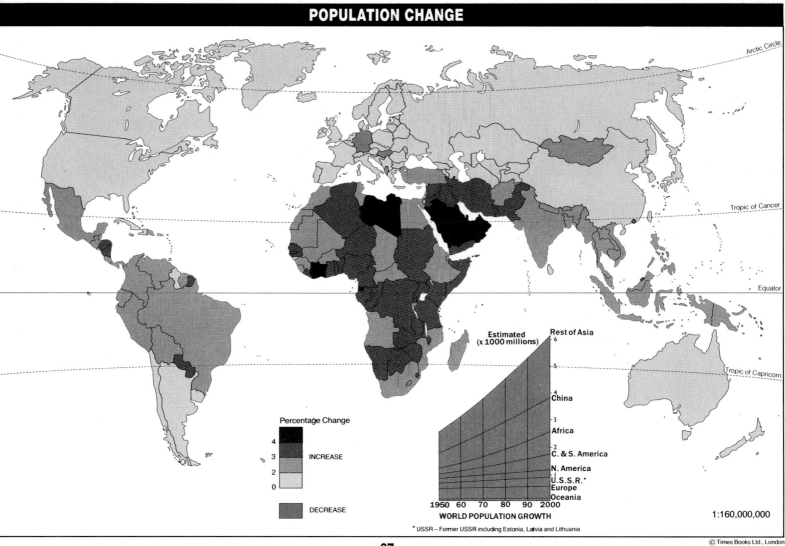

Percentage Change

4
3   INCREASE
2
0

DECREASE

Estimated
(x 1000 millions)

Rest of Asia
China
Africa
C. & S. America
N. America
U.S.S.R.*
Europe
Oceania

1950 60 70 80 90 2000
WORLD POPULATION GROWTH

* USSR – Former USSR including Estonia, Latvia and Lithuania

1:160,000,000

TIME ZONES

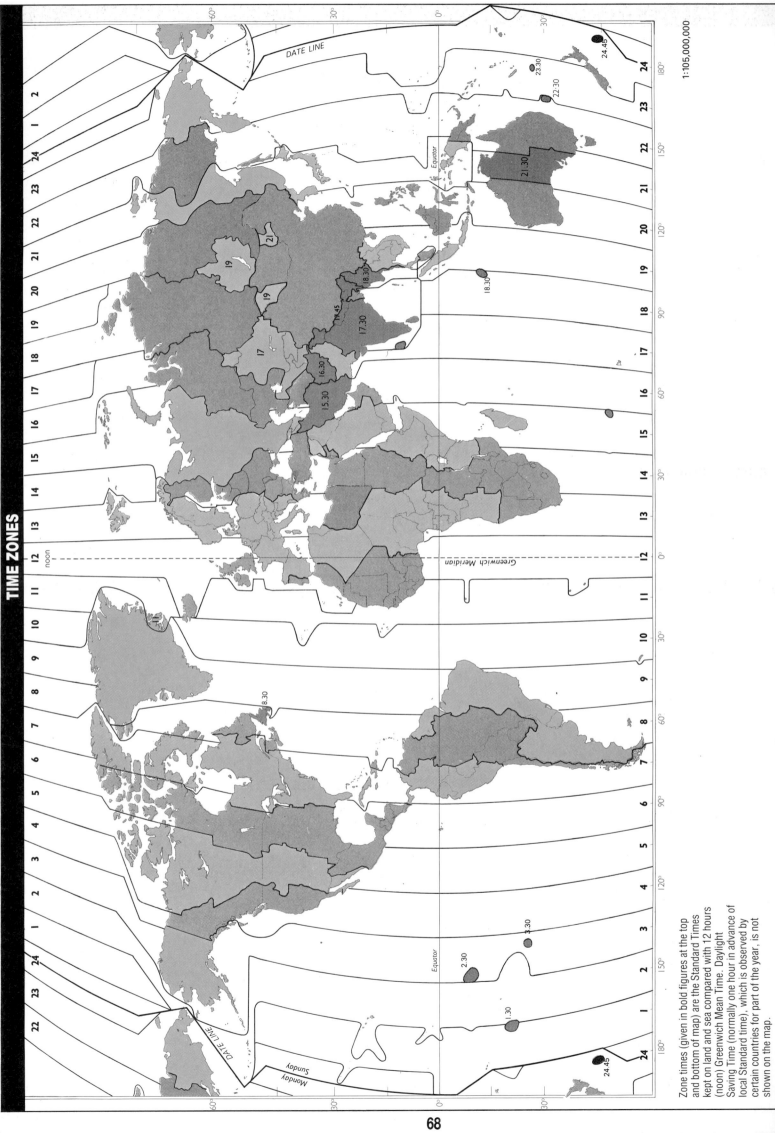

Zone times (given in bold figures at the top and bottom of map) are the Standard Times kept on land and sea compared with 12 hours (noon) Greenwich Mean Time. Daylight Saving Time (normally one hour in advance of local Standard time), which is observed by certain countries for part of the year, is not shown on the map.

1:105,000,000

This page explains the main symbols, lettering style and height/depth colours used on the reference maps on pages 2 to 76. The scale of each map is indicated at the foot of each page. Abbreviations used on the maps appear at the beginning of the index.

BOUNDARIES

———————	International
— — — —	International under Dispute
· · · · · · · ·	Cease Fire Line
———————	Autonomous or State
———————	Administrative
— — — = —	Maritime (National)
— — — —	International Date Line

COMMUNICATIONS

———————	Motorway/Express Highway
=========	Under Construction
———————	Major Highway
———————	Other Roads
— — — —	Under Construction
- - - - - -	Track
→- - - - -←	Road Tunnel
- - - - - -	Car Ferry
——•———	Main Railway
———————	Other Railway
— — — —	Under Construction
→- - - -—	Rail Tunnel
- - - - - -	Rail Ferry
—+——+—	Canal
⊕	International Airport
✈	Other Airport

LAKE FEATURES

	Freshwater
	Saltwater
	Seasonal
	Salt Pan

LANDSCAPE FEATURES

	Glacier, Ice Cap
	Marsh, Swamp
	Sand Desert, Dunes

OTHER FEATURES

	River
	Seasonal River
≍	Pass, Gorge
	Dam, Barrage
	Waterfall, Rapid
→- - - -—	Aqueduct
	Reef
▴4231	Summit, Peak
.217	Spot Height, Depth
⌣	Well
Δ	Oil Field
▲	Gas Field
—Gas/Oil—	Oil/Natural Gas Pipeline
Gemsbok Nat. Pk	National Park
∴UR	Historic Site

LETTERING STYLES

CANADA	Independent Nation
FLORIDA	State, Province or Autonomous Region
Gibraltar (U.K.)	Sovereignty of Dependent Territory
Lothian	Administrative Area
LANGUEDOC	Historic Region
Loire *Vosges*	Physical Feature or Physical Region

TOWNS AND CITIES

Square symbols denote capital cities. Each settlement is given a symbol according to its relative importance, with type size to match.

■	●	**New York**	Major City
■	●	**Montréal**	City
□	○	Ottawa	Small City
■	●	Québec	Large Town
□	○	St John's	Town
□	○	Yorkton	Small Town
□	○	Jasper	Village
			Built-up-area

Height

	6000m
	5000m
	4000m
	3000m
	2000m
	1000m
	500m
	200m
0	0 Sea Level
	200m
	2000m
	4000m
	6000m
	8000m
	Depth

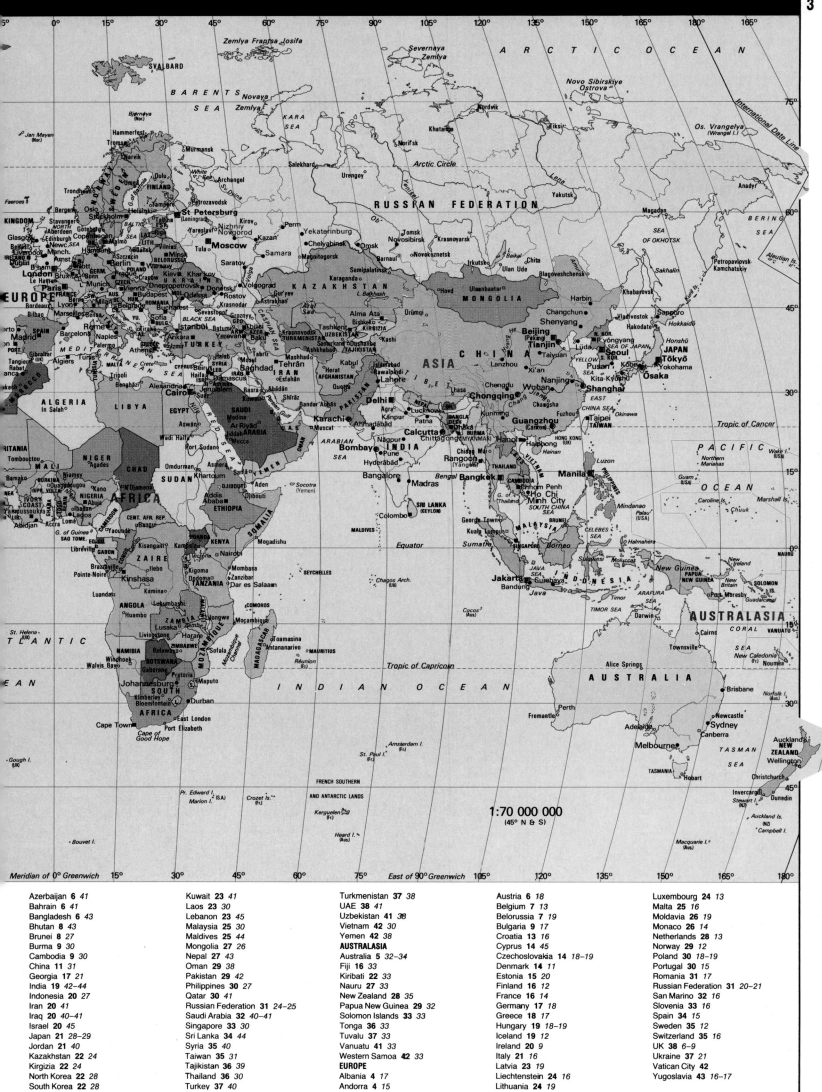

1:70 000 000
(45° N & S)

1:15M

200   400   600 km
100   200   300 mils

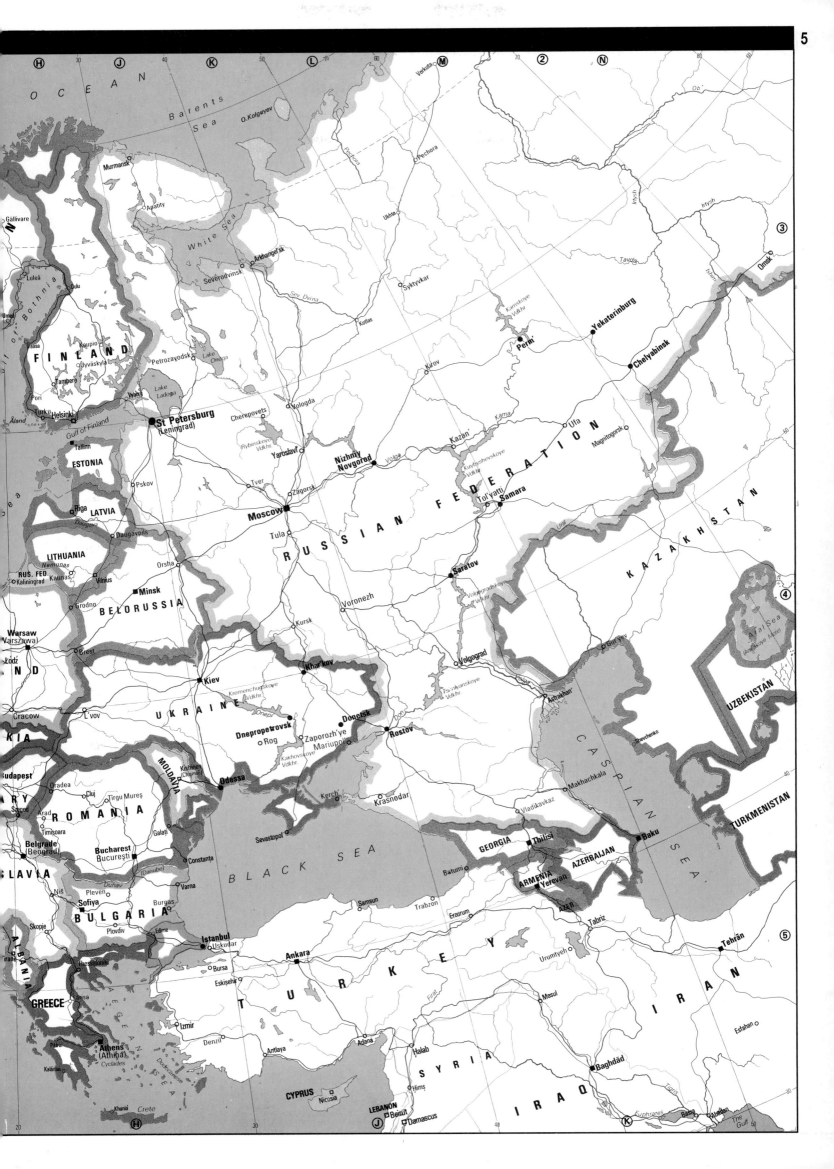

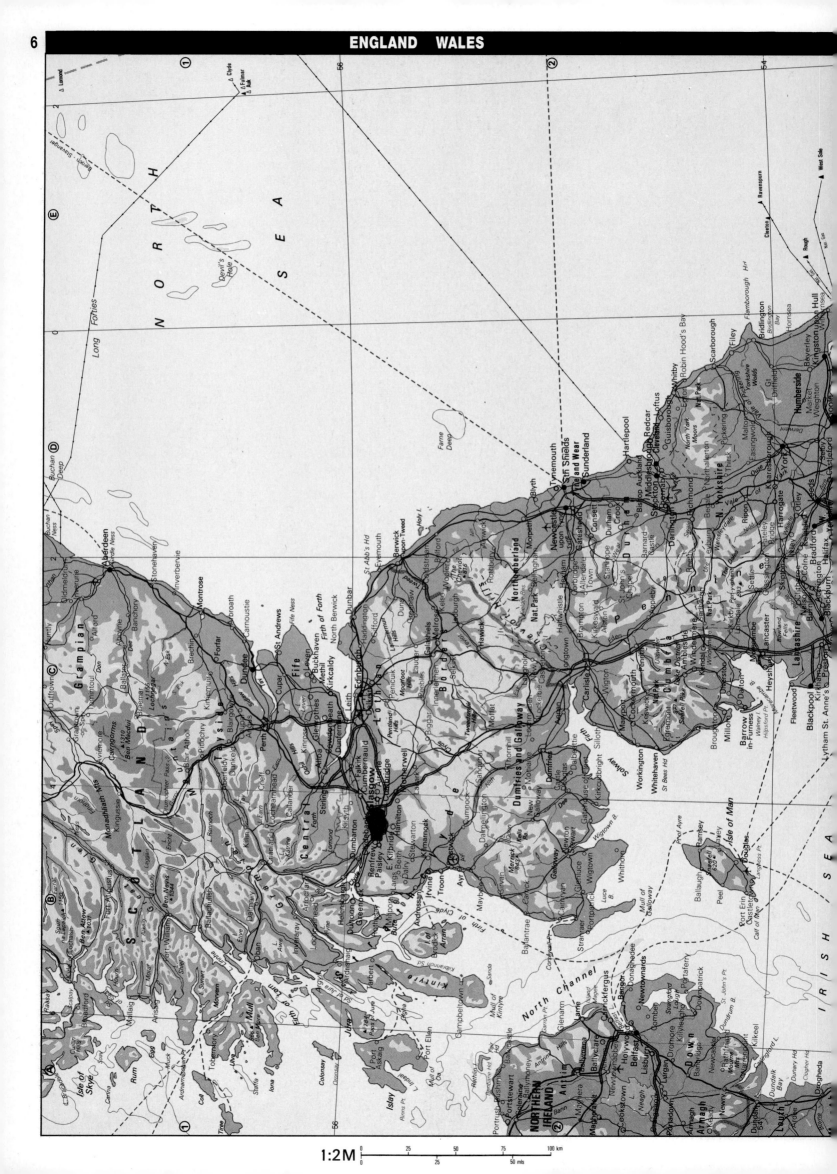

1:2M

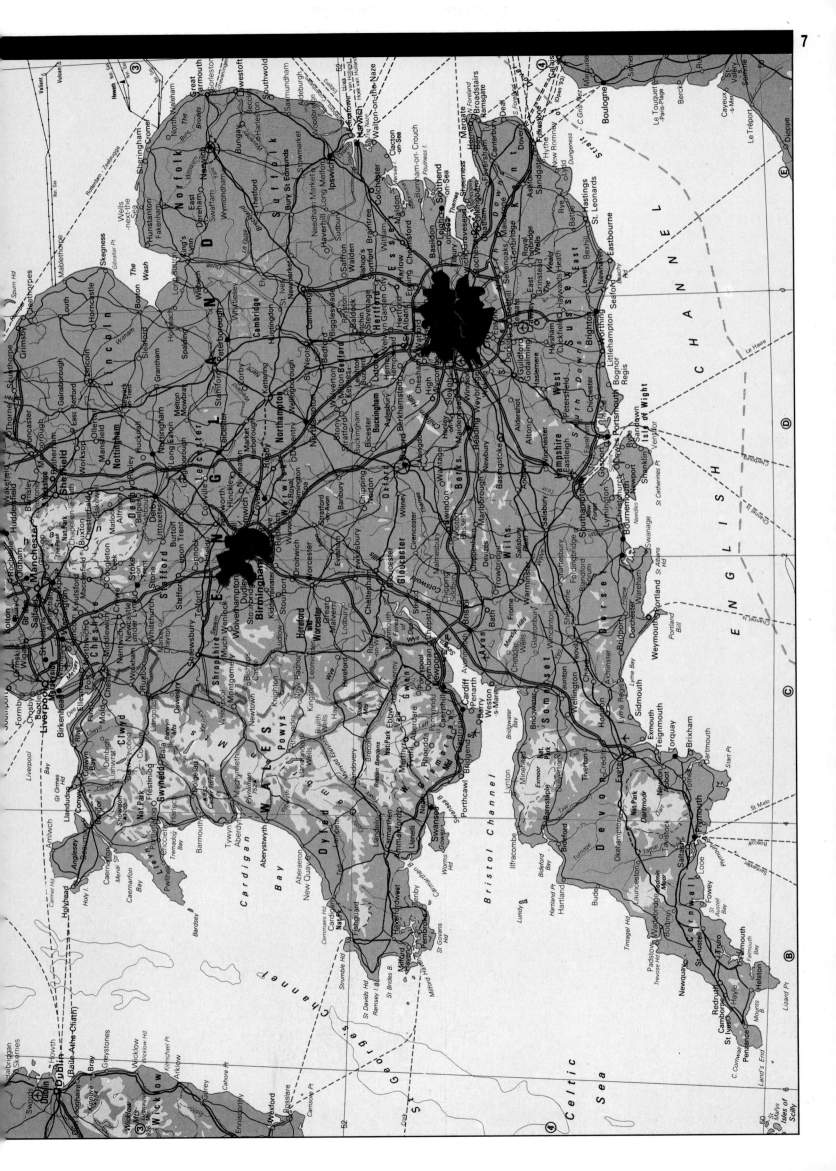

1:2M

1:2M

25   50   75   100 km

25

50 mls

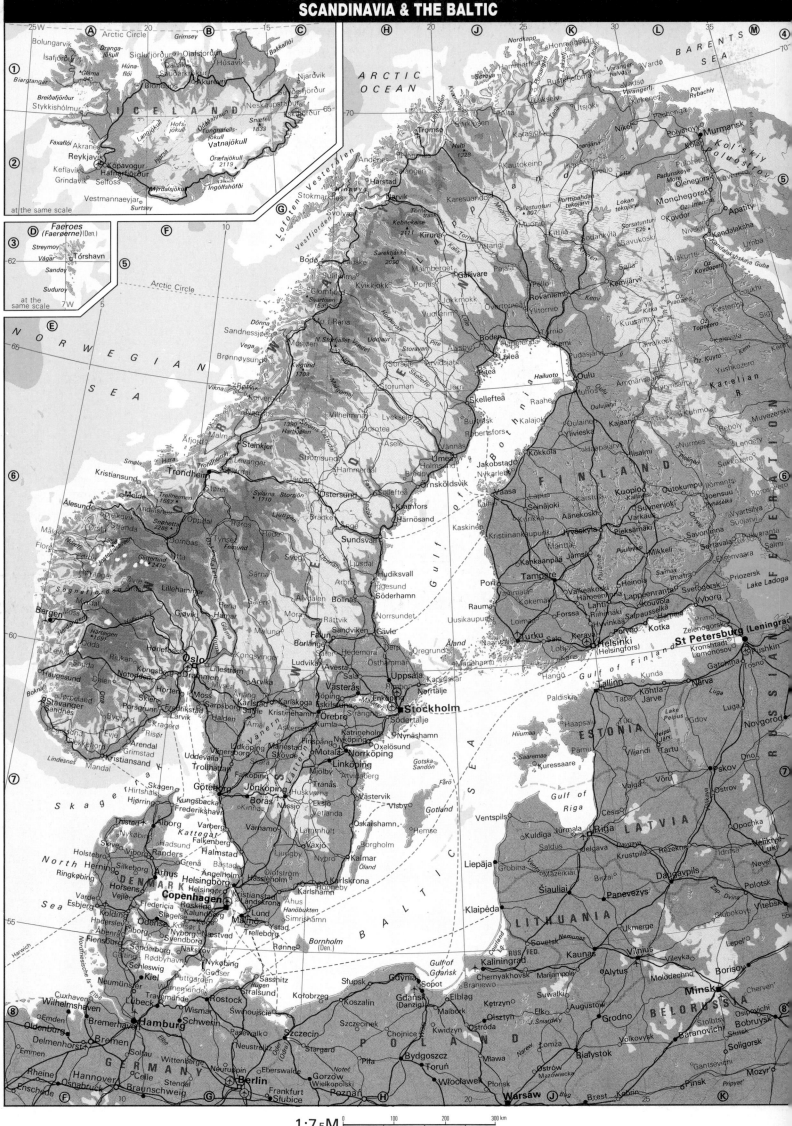

1:7.5M

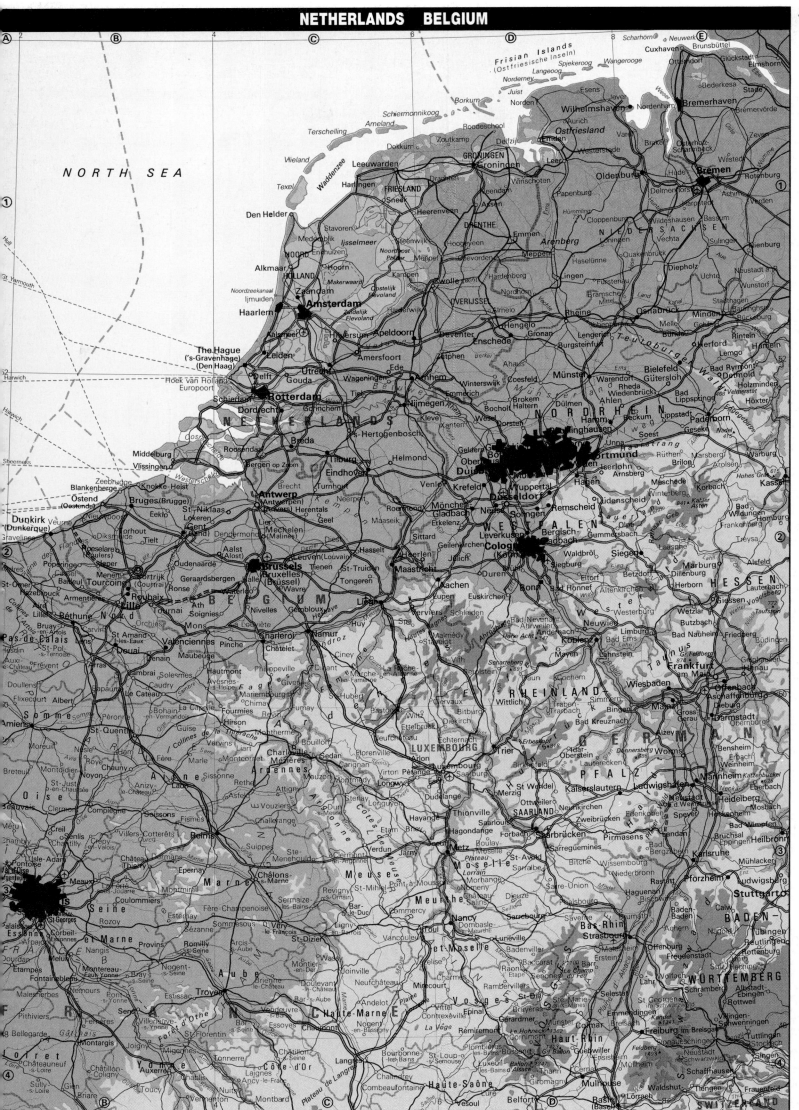

1:2.5M

| 25 | 50 | 75 | 100 km |
| 25 | 50 mls |

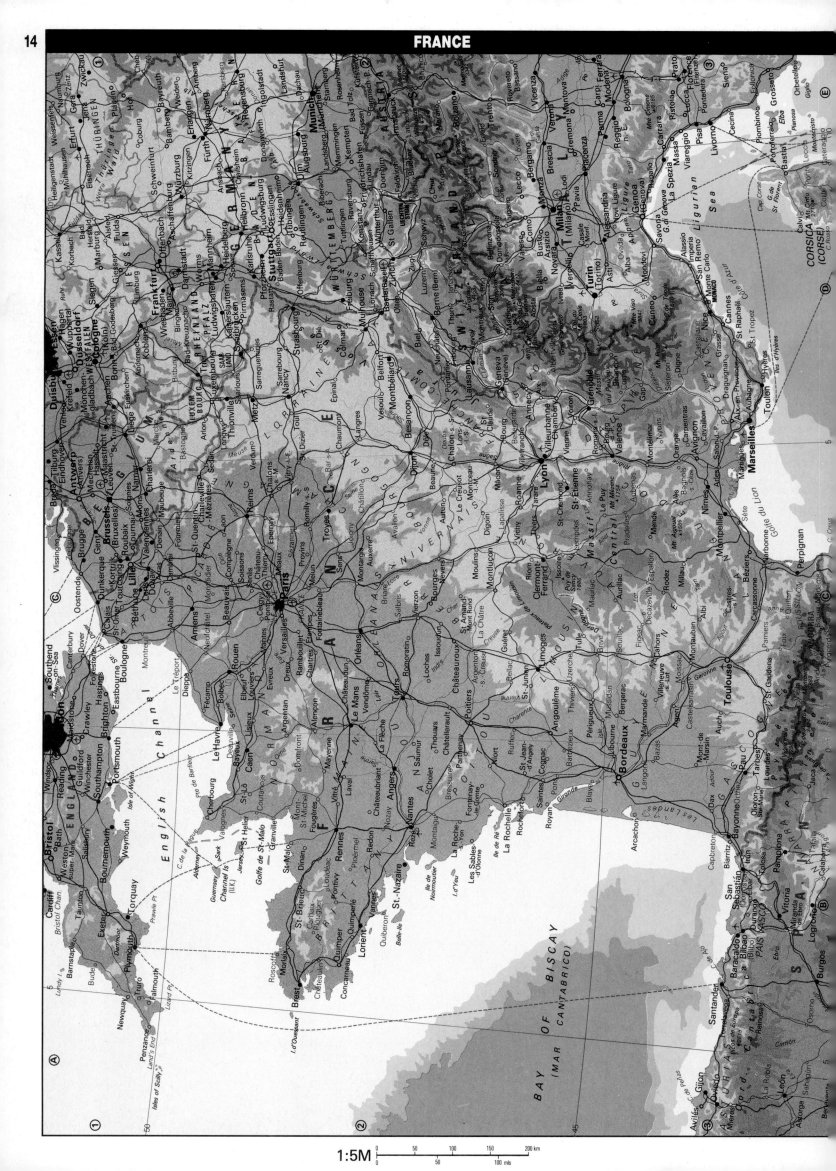

1:5M
0 50 100 150 200 km
0 50 100 mls

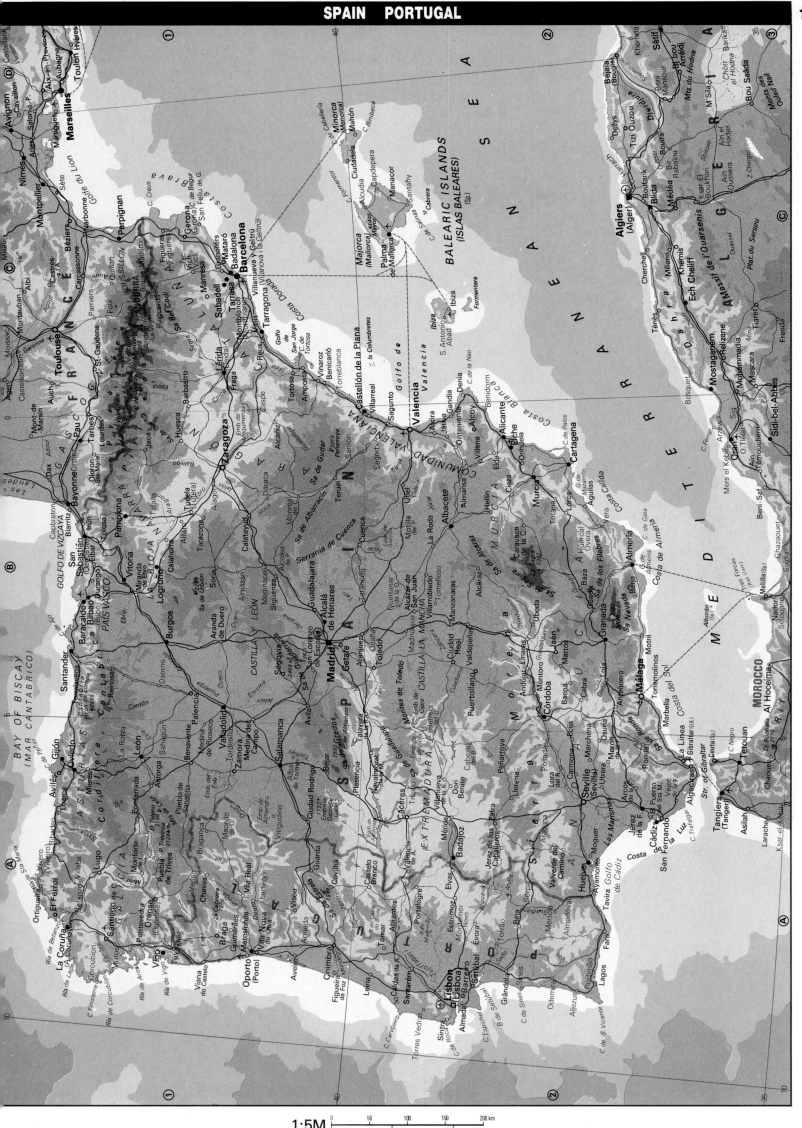

1:5M

| 0 | 50 | 100 | 150 | 200 km |
| 0 | | 50 | 100 mls |

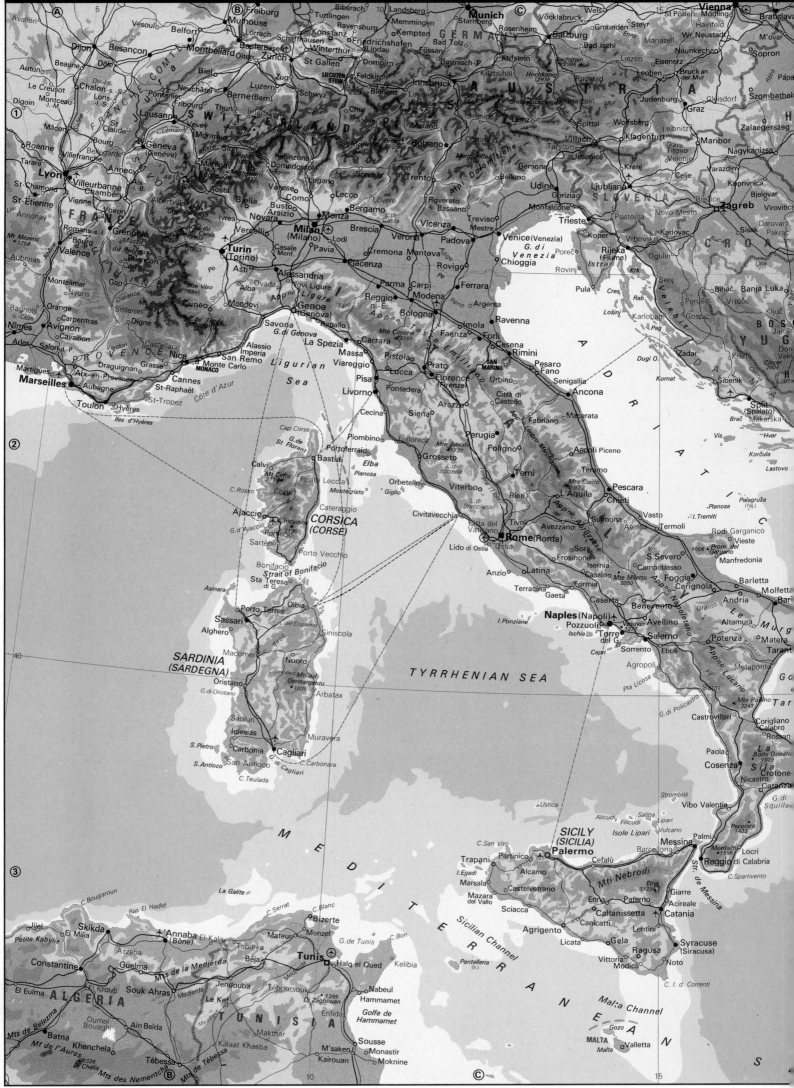

1:5M

1:5M

NORTH

SEA

BALT

SWEDEN

Göteborg
Jönköping
Borås
HusKvarna
Eksjö
Hultsfred
Västervik
Nässjö
Värnamo
Vetlanda
Oskarshamn
Mönsteras
Ålem
Borgholm
Öland
Växjö
Kalmar
Ljungby
Markaryd
Nybro
Älmhult
Ronneby
Halmstad
Hässleholm
Karlshamn
Ängelholm
Karlskrona
Båstad
Kristianstad
Helsingborg
Landskrona
Helsingør
Simrishamn
Lund
Copenhagen
(København)
Malmö
Ystad
Trelleborg
Hanöbukten
Køge
Roskilde
Bornholm
Sjælland
Rønne

Hirtshals
Skagen
Mölndal
Kungsbacka
Åby
Hjørring
Thisted
Frederikshavn
Varberg
Falkenberg
Ålborg
Nykøbing
Skive
Hadsund
Hobro
Viborg
Randers
Grenå
Anholt
Herning
Silkeborg
Åbenrå
Brande
Kattegat
Læsø
DENMARK
Jylland
(Jutland)
Varde
Vejle
Kolding
Kalundborg
Odense
Fredericia
Assens
Fyn
Nyborg
Korsør
Svendborg
Vordingborg
Nakskov
Lolland
Falster
Nykøbing
Gedser
Esbjerg
Haderslev
Sønderborg
Als
Rømø
Sylt
Westerland
Flensburg

Ostende
Zeebrugge
Vlissingen
Breda
Bruges
Gent
Antwerp
(Antwerpen)
(Anvers)
BELGIUM
Brussels
(Bruxelles)
(Brüssel)
Mechelen
Leuven
Tournai
Mons
Namur
Charleroi
Liège
Maastricht
Aachen
Lille
Roubaix
Béthune
Douai
Valenciennes
Denain
Maubeuge
Cambrai
Arras
St-Quentin
Fourmies
Laon
Soissons
Compiègne
Château-Thierry
Reims
Épernay
Sézanne
Provins
Sens
Joigny
Auxerre
Avallon
Troyes
Chaumont
Langres
Châtillon
Dijon
Besançon
Montbéliard
Belfort
Mulhouse
Basle
(Basel)
Zürich
Winterthur
St Gallen
Dornbirn
Feldkirch
Vaduz
LIECHTENSTEIN
SWITZERLAND
Bern (Berne)
Biel
Luzern
Zug
Schwyz
Glarus
Chur
Lausanne
Geneva
(Genève)
Léman
Montreux
Sion
Brig
Locarno
Lugano
Bellinzona
Domodossola
Varese
Como
Lecco
Bergamo
Brescia
Milan
(Milano)
Lodi
Pavia
Placenza
Cremona
Mantova
ITALY

Lyon
St-Chamond
St-Étienne
Villeurbanne
Vienne
Annonay
Valence
Montélimar

FRANCE
LORRAINE
Metz
Nancy
Épinal
Toul
Verdun
Bar-le-Duc
Vitry-le-F.
Chalons-s.-M.
Saarlouis
Saarbrücken
Saargemünd
Sarrebourg
Strasbourg
Colmar
Freiburg
Mulhouse

NORTH SEA
Harwich

NEDERLAND
Den Helder
Alkmaar
Haarlem
Leiden
The Hague
('s-Gravenhage)
(Den Haag)
Rotterdam
Dordrecht
Vlissingen
Hilversum
Amsterdam
Utrecht
Amersfoort
Apeldoorn
Arnhem
Nijmegen
Zwolle
Deventer
Enschede
Hengelo
Leeuwarden
Sneek
Heerenveen
Assen
Emmen
Groningen
Emden
Leer
Meppen
Lingen
Rheine
Münster
Osnabrück
Bielefeld
Coesfeld
Bocholt
Wesel
NORDRHEIN
WESTFALEN
Duisburg
Essen
Dortmund
Hamm
Krefeld
Mönchengladbach
Düsseldorf
Wuppertal
Hagen
Cologne
(Köln)
Bonn
Bad Godesberg
Siegen
Aachen

GERMANY
Cuxhaven
Wilhelmshaven
Bremerhaven
Stade
Bremen
Oldenburg
NIEDERSACHSEN
Nienburg
Diepholz
Langenhagen
Hannover
Hildesheim
Celle
Wolfsburg
Braunschweig
Salzgitter
Göttingen
Kassel
Paderborn
Münden
Korbach
Bad Hersfeld
Marburg
Giessen
HESSEN
Fulda
Alsfeld
Limburg
Koblenz
RHEINLAND
PFALZ
Frankfurt
am Main
Wiesbaden
Mainz
Offenbach
Darmstadt
Aschaffenburg
Worms
Mannheim
Heidelberg
Ludwigshafen
Kaiserslautern
Pirmasens
Speyer
Karlsruhe
Pforzheim
Heilbronn
Crailsheim
BADEN
WÜRTTEMBERG
Stuttgart
Ludwigsburg
Esslingen
Baden-Baden
Rastatt
Offenburg
Tübingen
Reutlingen
Ulm
Biberach
Schwäbisch
Ravensburg
Memmingen
Kempten
Lindau
Friedrichshafen
Konstanz

Elmshorn
Heide
Rendsburg
Kiel
Neumünster
SCHLESWIG-HOLSTEIN
Schleswig
Oldenburg
Puttgarden
Fehmarn
Lübeck
Travemünde
Hamburg
Lüneburg
Lauenburg
Rotenburg
Uelzen
Salzwedel
Wittenberge
Stendal
MECKLENBURG-VORPOMMERN
Wismar
Schwerin
Rostock
Warnemünde
Stralsund
Greifswald
Rügen
Sassnitz
Neustadt
Mecklenburger
Bucht
Kieler
Bucht
Malchin
Anklam
Neubrandenburg
Neustrelitz
Ludwigslust
Prenzlau
Pritzwalk
Neuruppin
Oranienburg
Rathenow
Nauen
Brandenburg
BRANDENBURG
Berlin
Potsdam
Frankfurt
an-der-Oder
Eberswalde
Fürstenwalde
Luckenwalde
Jüterbog
Magdeburg
Burg
SACHSEN-ANHALT
Aschersleben
Bernburg
Dessau
Bitterfeld
Wittenberg
Halle
Nordhausen
Heiligenstadt
Mühlhausen
Erfurt
Weissenfels
Naumburg
Zeitz
Jena
Gera
THÜRINGEN
Eisenach
Thüringer
Wald
Coburg
Schweinfurt
Würzburg
Kitzingen
Bamberg
Bayreuth
Weiden
Erlangen
Fürth
Nürnberg
Ansbach
Amberg
Regensburg
BAYERN
Ingolstadt
Donauwörth
Augsburg
Landsberg
Munich
(München)
Dachau
Starnberg
Rosenheim
Landshut
Mühldorf
Passau
Freistadt
Schärding
Bad Tölz
Füssen
Garmisch-P.
Kufstein
Innsbruck
Kitzbühel

Wittstock
Genthin
Torgau
Riesa
Meissen
Dresden
SACHSEN
Chemnitz
Zwickau
Plauen
Hof
Marktredwitz
Cheb
Karlovy
Vary
Kladno
Prague
(Praha)
Plzeň
Most
Teplice
Ústí n.-L.
Liberec
Zittau
Görlitz
Bautzen
Finsterwalde
Elsterwerda
Cottbus
Guben
Forst
Nowa Sól
Żary
Sagan

POLSKA
Szczecin
Świnoujście
Kołobrzeg
Koszalin
Sławno
Słupsk
Świdwin
Białogard
Szczecinek
Goleniów
Stargard
Wałcz
Choszczno
Piła
Jastrowie
Myśliborz
Gorzów Wlkp.
Kostrzyn
Skwierzyna
Pniewa
Poznań
Oborniki
Świebodzin
Zielona Góra
Głogów
Leszno
Wschowa
Szprotawa
Bolesławiec
Legnica
Wrocław
Jelenia
Góra
Wałbrzych
Świdnica
Dzierżoniów
Kłodzko
Jabłonec
n.-N.
Mladá
Boleslav
Hradec
Králové
Pardubice
Kolín
Kutná Hora
Benešov
Tábor
Písek
České
Budějovice
ČESKÉ ZEMĚ
Brandýs-nad-L.
Český
Svitavy
Olomouc
Přerov
Vyškov
Jihlava
Třebíč
Brno
Znojmo
Mikulov
Hodonín
Břeclav
AUSTRIA
Linz
Wels
Steyr
Gmunden
Vöcklabruck
Salzburg
Bad Ischl
Bischofshofen
Hochkönig
2938
Radstadt
Liezen
Schladming
Dachstein
2996
Tauern
Spittal
Villach
Klagenfurt
Wolfsberg
Judenburg
Leoben
Bruck an
der Mur
Graz
Leibnitz
Gleisdorf

Vienna
(Wien)
Stockerau
Klosterneuburg
Korneuburg
Mödling
Wr. Neustadt
Neunkirchen
St Pölten
Hainfeld
Bratislava
M'óvár
Sopron
Szombathely
Zalaegerszeg
Nagykanizsa
Maribor
Varaždin
Zagreb
CROATIA
SLOVENIA
Ljubljana
Kranj
Celje
Velenje
Koper
Trieste
Rijeka
(Fiume)
Istra
Gorizia
Udine
Pordenone
Belluno
Cortina
Dolomiten
Bolzano
Merano
Brunico
Lienz
Tarvisio
Gemona
Monfalcone
Treviso
Mestre
Venice
(Venezia)
G. di
Venezia
Padova
Vicenza
Verona
Rovigo
Chioggia
Mantova
Este
Ferrara

Turin
(Torino)
Asti
Alessandria
Casale Monf.
Novara
Vercelli
Biella
Ivrea
Aosta
Bustō
Arsizio
Monza
Bergamo
Lodi
Cremona
Mantova
Rovigo
Piacenza
Brescia
Verona
Padova

50   100   150   200 km
50   100 mls

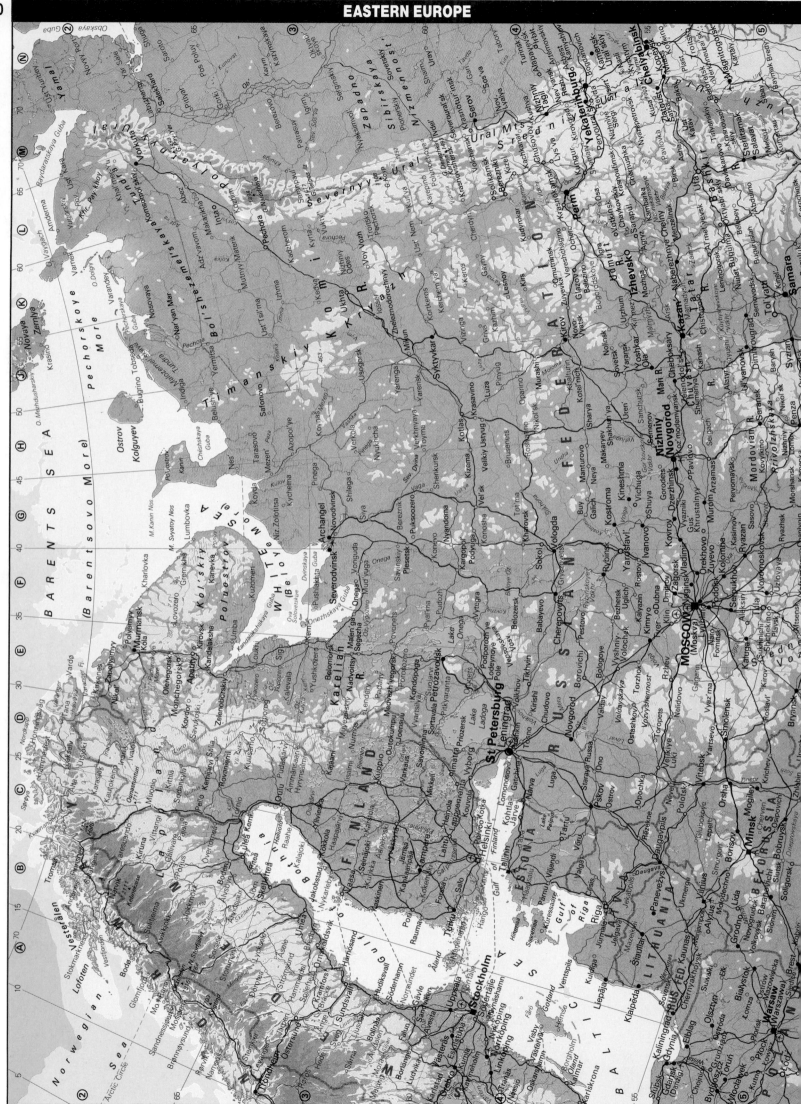

1:10M

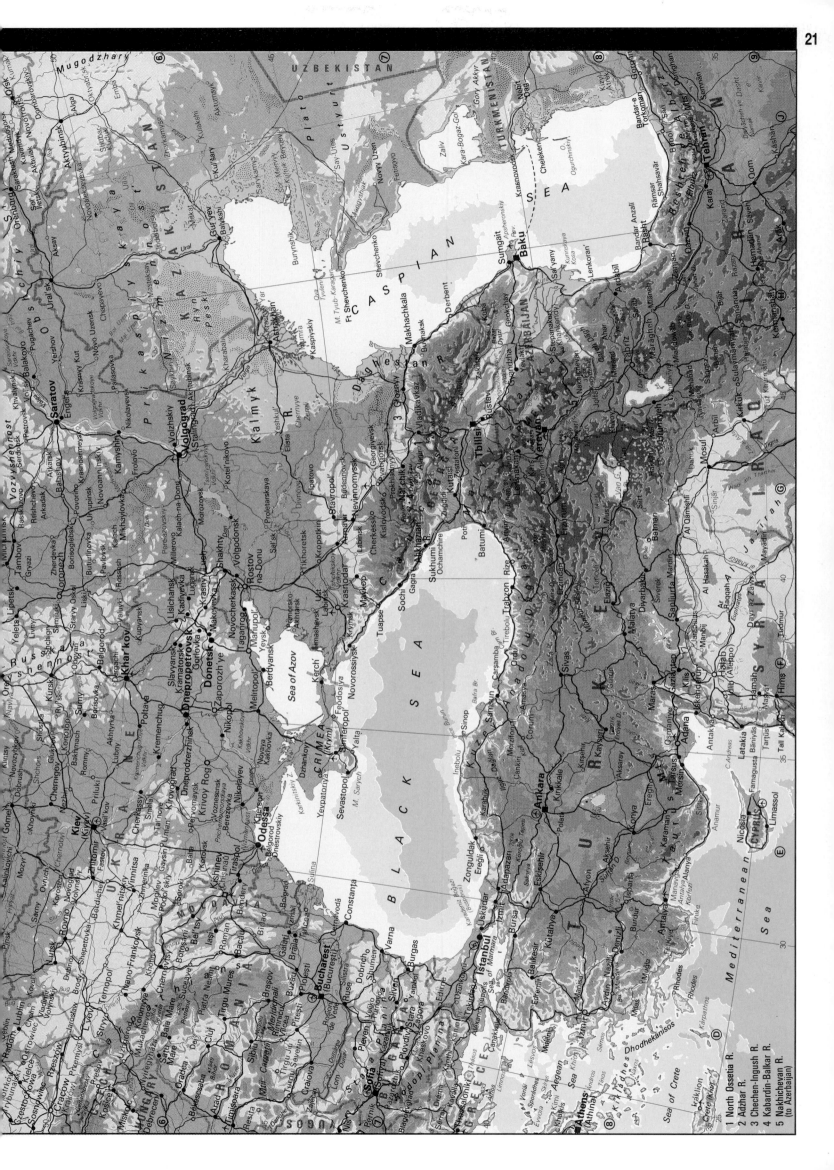

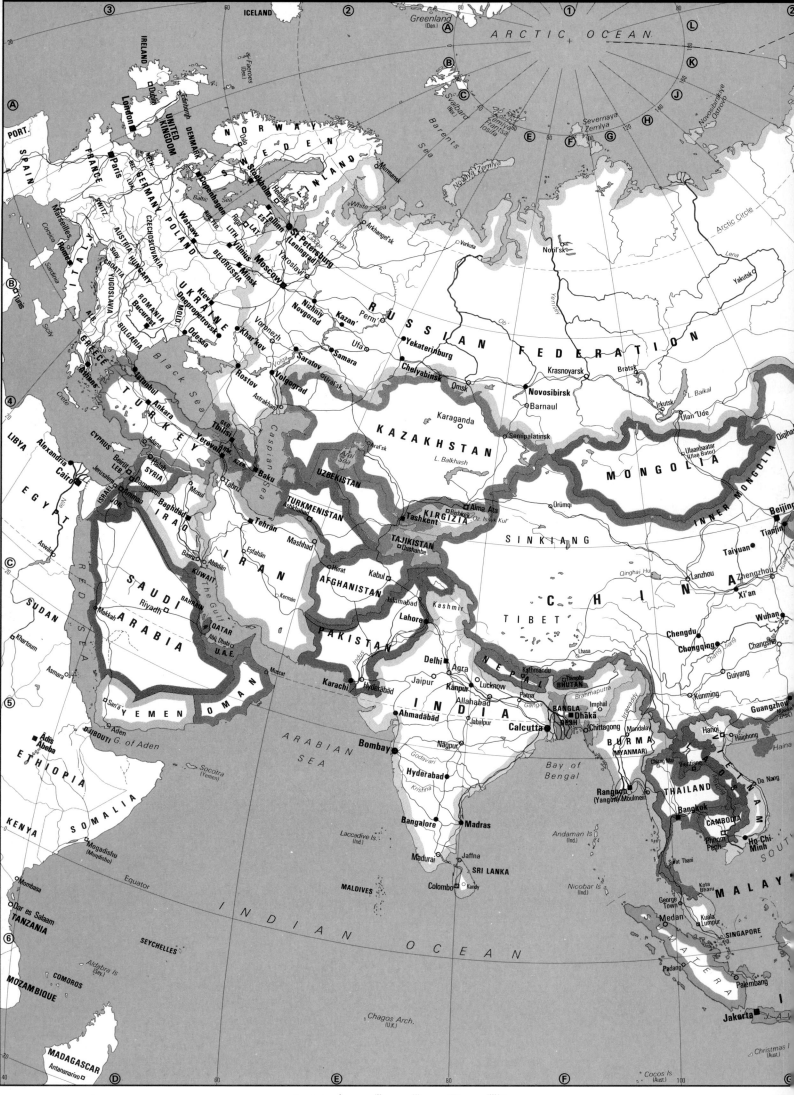

21

1:40M

0   400   800   1200   1600 km
0   400   800 mils

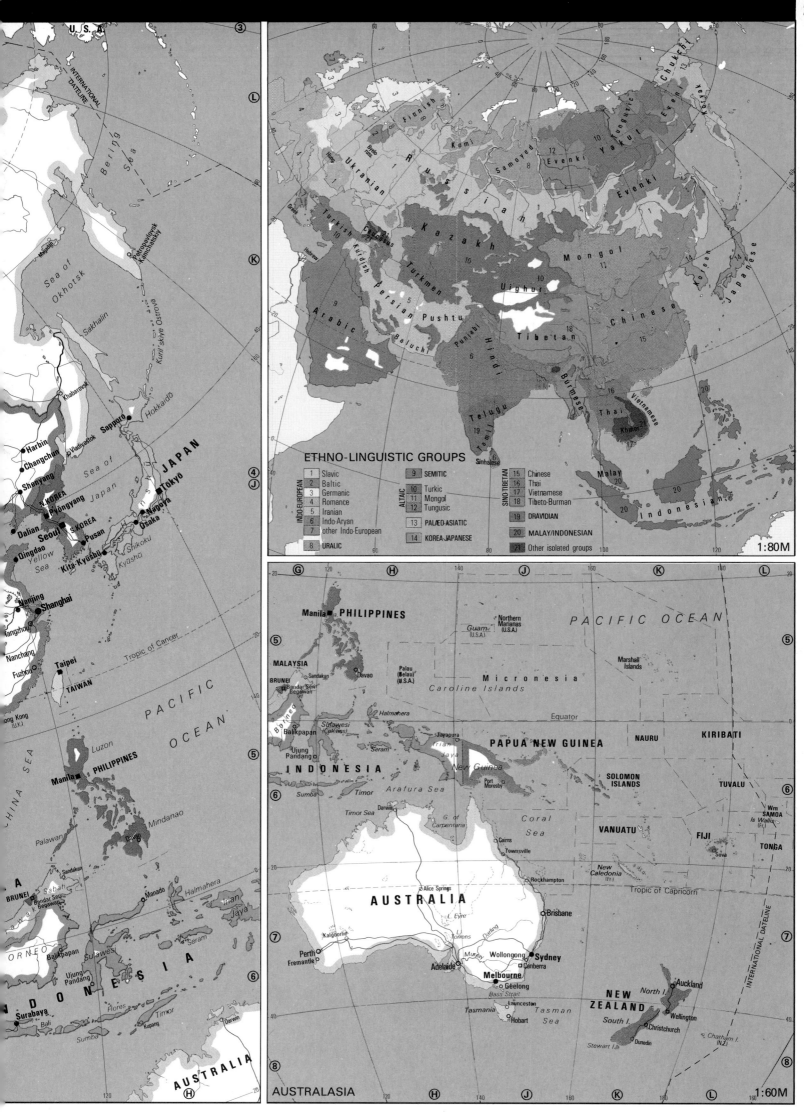

ETHNO-LINGUISTIC GROUPS

INDO-EUROPEAN
1 Slavic
2 Baltic
3 Germanic
4 Romance
5 Iranian
6 Indo-Aryan
7 other Indo-European

8 URALIC

ALTAIC
9 SEMITIC
10 Turkic
11 Mongol
12 Tungusic

13 PALÆO-ASIATIC

14 KOREA-JAPANESE

SINO-TIBETAN
15 Chinese
16 Thai
17 Vietnamese
18 Tibeto-Burman

19 DRAVIDIAN

20 MALAY/INDONESIAN

21 Other isolated groups

1:80M

AUSTRALASIA

1:60M

NORTHERN ASIA

RUSSIAN FEDERATION
1 Chuvash R.
2 Chechen-Ingush R.
3 North Ossetia R.
4 Kabardin- Balkar R.

GEORGIA
5 Abkhaz R.
6 Adzhar R.

AZERBAIJAN
7 Nakhichevan R.

1:20M

0   200   400   600   800 km
0   200   400 mls

1:20M

| 0 | 200 | 400 | 600 | 800 km |
| 0 | | 200 | 400 mils |

Ⓐ Ⓑ Ⓒ

Kailu
Muren Sum
Tongliao
Changchun
Jilin
Jiaohe
Xinzhan
Dongning
Mikhaylovka
Ussuriysk

Baixingt
Wafang
Shuangliao
Dongliao He
Huaide
Chaluhe
Yitong
Shuangyang
Huangnihe
Dunhua
Chunyang
Tianqiaoling
Guandi
Razdol'noye
Artem
Sergeyevka

Horqin Zuoyi Hougu
Sanjiangkou
Siping
Liaoyangwopu
CHINA
Yantongshan
Badaohe
Liangbingtai
Wangqing
Chunhua
Uglovoye
Vladivostok

Naiman Qi
Hure Qi
Bamianchong
Changtu
Xifeng
Liaoyuan
Huinan
Panshi
Shan
Narhong
Huadian
Jingyu
Longgang
Jiang
Yanji
Helong
Longjing
Kaishantun
Tumen
Hunchun
Kraskino
Pos'yet
Barabash
Bol'shoy
Kamen
Partizansk

Kangping
Kaiyuan
Tieling
Hailong
Jilin
Antu
Erdaobaihe
Zaliv
Petra Velikogo
Dunay
Nakhodka

Ⓐ②
Fuxin
Xinlitun
Xinmin
Gaotaishan
Fushun
Nahzamu
Gangou
Changbai
Paegam
254
Kwanmo
Samcha
Hoeryŏng
Unggi
Najin

Beipiao
Heishan
Dahongqi
Inchengzi
Tonghua
Xinbin
Laoling
Huch'ang
2205
Hyesan
Kapsan
Musan
Puryŏng
Khasan

Yi Xian
Beizhen
Dahushan
Fushun
Benxi
Huanren
Hwapyong
Samsu
Manp'o
Nangnim
Kimso
Pungsan
Myonggan
Myongchon
Ch'ŏngjin
Nanam
Kyŏngsŏng
Orang

Jinzhou
Mu'erhe
Shenyang
Benxi
Linjiatai
Ji'an
Chasong
Chonchon
Hochon
Ŏdaejin

Liaoyang
Tongyuanpu
Kuandian
Pyŏktong
Kanggye
Songgan
Changjin
Pukch'ong
Kilchu
Musu-dan
Hwadae

Yingkou
Qian Shan
Bandao
Linjiatai
Kujang
Taechung
Sinp'o
Kimch'aek

Liaodong Wan
Yingkou
Haicheng
Fengcheng
Chosan
Koin
Lagusha
Tongshang
T'aech'ŏn
Unsan
Kaech'ŏn
Nyongwŏn
Hamhŭng
Hamhŭng
Riwon
Ch'aho
Tanch'ŏn

Gai Xian
Shagang
Xiuyan
Dandong
Okkang-dong
Hŭich'ŏn
Pukch'in
Yŏngwŏn
Pukch'ŏng
Hongwon

Xiongyuecheng
Xujiatun
Zhuanghe
Sinŭiju
Ŭiju
Sŏnch'ŏn
Kusŏng
Taedong-do
Chŏngju
Anju
Sunch'ŏn
Maengsan
Yŏnghŭng
Chongpyong
SEA
40
Fuzhoucheng
Dawa
Niuzhuang
Qingduizi
Donggou
Gushan
Sŏnch'ŏn
Ch'ŏngju
Sukch'ŏn
Gunan
Sŏngch'ŏn
Kowŏn
Hŭngnam
Tongjosŏn-man

Wudao
Fu Xian
Xinjin
Changhai
Chengzitan
Chŏngju
Chŭngsan
Namp'o
Suan
P'yŏngyang
Sinp'yŏng
Kosan
Hoeyang
Kŭmgang
Kosŏng
NORTH
KOREA

Jin Xian
Dalian
Lüshun
Korea
Bay
Changnyŏng
Chaeryŏng
Sariwŏn
Sohŭng
Koksan
Sep'o
Ch'ŏrwŏn
Kŭmhwa
Kimhwa
Kansong
Taegang-got
Yŏnghŭng-man
Amnyong-dan

③
Yantai
Weihai
Muping
Wendeng
Rongcheng
Rushan
Shidao
Changyŏn
Ongjin
Yŏnan
Kaesŏng
P'anmunjŏm
Munsan
Yŏngsan
Ich'ŏn
Ch'ŏrwŏn
Hwach'ŏn
Yanggu
Sokcho
Yangyang

Haeju
Kanghwa
Ŭijŏngbu
Kap'yŏng
Ch'unch'ŏn
Hongch'ŏn
Kangnŭng
Ullŭng-do
Todong
Tok-do
(Take-shima)
(Liancourt Rocks)

Seoul
(Sŏul)
Inch'ŏn
Kopo-ri
Suwŏn
Ryoju
Wŏnju
Hoengsŏng
Ch'ŏngsŏn
Samch'ŏk

Asan-man
Changhowan-ri
Yŏngt'aek
Ch'ŏngju
Chech'ŏn
Nyongwŏl
Ulchin
SOUTH
KOREA
J
A

Sosan
Onyang
Ch'ŏnan
Ch'ungju
Tanyang
Ch'unyang
Yongju
Yŏngyang
Pyŏnggok-dong

Anhŭng
Hongsong
Ch'ŏngju
Choch'iwŏn
Mun'gyŏng
Andong
Uisŏng
Yŏngdŏk

Taech'on
Kongju
Sanju
Yŏngch'ŏn
Yŏngil-man

Taejŏn
Chŭngni
Kimch'ŏn
Waegwan
P'ohang
Oki-shotō
Nishino-shima
Dōzen
Chiburi-jima

Sŏch'ŏn
Changhang
Nonsan
Iri
Okch'ŏn
Songju
Taegu
Kyŏngju
Matsue
Taisha
Izumo
Oda

Kunsan
Kimje
Ch'ŏnju
Koryong
Kyŏngsan
Ulsan
Gotsu
Hamada

Puan
Chŏngŭp
Imsil
Anui
Hapch'ŏn
Ch'ŏngdo
Miryang
Yangsan
Tongnae
Masuda
Hiroshima

YELLOW SEA
Kochang
Namwŏn
Koksong
Chinju
Ŭiryŏng
Kimhae
Pusan
Mi-shima
Susa
Hagi
Nagato
Shobara
Miyoshi

35
(HUANG HAI)
Yŏnggwang
Sago-ri
Hadong
Masan
Chinhae
Sach'ŏn
Kimhae
Tsushima
Izuhara suidō
Wakuni
Yamaguchi
Hōfu
Kure
Imabari
Matsuyama
Saij

Songjong
Naju
Kwangju
Hwasun
Kwangyang
Sunch'ŏn
Samch'ŏnp'o
Koje
Ch'ungmu
KOREA STRAIT
(TSUSHIMA-KAIKYŌ)
Higashi-suidō
Iki
Nakama
Negata
Shimonoseki
Kita-Kyūshū
Ube
Suō-nada
Tokuyama
nada

Mokp'o
Changhŭng
Posong
Yŏsu
Tolsan-do
Kŭmo-do
Nishi-suidō
Tsushima
Izuhara suidō
Kōfukuoka
Iizuka
Usa
Kitsuki
Beppu

Usuyong
Haenam
Kohŭng
Ch'o-do
Soan
kundo
Cheju haehyŏp
Tosu
Karatsu
Nakatsu
Ōita
Uwajima
Nakamur

Wando
Chindo
Kŭmnyŏng
Songsan-ni
Cheju
Hirado-shima
Uku-jima
Hirado
Imari
Saga
Kurume
Yanagawa
Takeo
Aso
Kuju-san
1791
Taketa
Saiki
Tosashimizu

④
1950
Halla-san
Cheju do
Sŏgwi-ri
Hirado
Sasebo
Ōmura
Isahaya
Omuta
Kumamoto
Nobeoka

Fukue
Fukue
Tomie
Gotō-rettō
Nagasaki
Nomo-saki
Shimabara
Yatsushiro
Hiroyoshi
Hyūga
Ashizuri
misaki

Minamata
Takanabe
Senda
Akune
Kobayashi
Miyazaki

KYŪSHŪ
Kagoshima
Fukuyama
Miyakonojō
Kushima
Kanoya
Makurazaki
Yamagawa

Ⓐ Ⓑ Ⓒ
125 130

RUS. FED.

Arkhipovka
Yangou
Lazo
Ol'ga
Margaritovo

continued on inset

Asahikawa
Takikawa
Fukagawa
Akabira
Sunagawa
Ashibetsu
Bibai
Iwamizawa
Furano
Asahi dake 2298
Kutcharo-ko
Teshikaga

Shakotan-misaki
Furubira
Ishikari-wan
Yubari
Kushiro
Ikeda
Nemuro

Iwanai
Sapporo
Ebetsu
Obihiro
Tokachi
HOKKAIDŌ

Suttsu
Kutchan
Chitose
Tomakomai
Mukawa
Hidaka-sammyaku

Oshamambe
Date
Noboribetsu
Taiki

Setana
Yakumo
Uchiura-wan
Muroran
Urakawa
Samani
Hiroo
Erimo-misaki
②

Okushiri-tō
Mori
Komaga take 1133
Esashi

Matsumae
Kikonai
Hakodate
Ōhata
Shiriya-saki
Ōma-saki
Esan-misaki
Mutsu

Tsugaru-kaikyō
Kodomari-misaki
Minmaya
Aomori
Mutsu-wan
Ōminato
Nobeji

Goshogawara
Ajigasawa
Iwaki-san 1625
Kuroishi
Towada
Hachinohe

Henashi-zaki
Hirosaki
Towada-ko
Kuji
Mi-zaki
40

Odate

Noshiro
Oga
Koma
Morioka
Miyako

Akita
Tazawa-ko
Tazawako
Morioka
Yamada

Honjō
Hanamaki
Yokote
Tono
Kamaishi

Kitakami
Mizusawa
Ōfunato

Tobi-shima
Sakata
Shinjō
Yuzawa
Yokobori
Chōkai-san 2230
Ichinoseki
Rikuzen-Tanaka
Kesennuma

Tsuruoka
Narudo
Furukawa
Ishinomaki

Ōbanazawa
Mogami
Higashine
Sendai
Shiogama

Awa-shima
Tendō
Yamagata
Nataro

Hajiki-saki
Murakami
Nagai
Kaminoyama
Kakuda

Sado-shima
Ayato
Yonezawa
Sōma

Aikawa
Ryōtsu
Niigata
Shibata
Fukushima
Haramachi

Mano-wan
Niitsu
Iide-san 2105
Kitakata
Nihommatsu

Teradomari
Sanjō
Aizu-Wakamatsu
Kōriyama

Hegura-jima
Nagaoka
Ojiya
Shirakawa
Sukagawa
Taira
Iwaki

Nanatsu-jima
Kashiwazaki
Koide
Kuroiso
Otawara
③

Suzu-misaki
Wajima
Naoetsu
Takada
Tokamachi
Nikkō
Imaichi

Noto
Suzu
Arai
Nakano
Shirane-san 2360
Utsunomiya
Hitachi
Hitachi-Ota

Hakui
Nanao
Itoigawa
Numata
Mito
Katsuta

hantō
Himi
Toyama-wan
Kurobe
Suzaka
Maebashi
Kiryū
Nakaminato

Takaoka
Shimminato
Toyama
Ōmachi
Shibukawa
Ashikaga
Ishioka
Hok

Kanazawa
Tsubata
Nagano
Ueda
Takasaki
Koga
Tsuchiura

Komatsu
Kaga
Hakusan 2702
Matsumoto
Ōta
Kumagaya
Konosu
Sawara
Chōshi

Fukui
Katsuyama
Okaya
Suwa
Chichibu
Ōmiya
Narita
Inube-saki

Dōgo
Saigō
Nakano-shima
Sabae
Takayama
Chino
Kawagoe
Urawa
TOKYO
Funabashi

Takefu
Ōno
Ontake-san 3063
Agematsu
Enzan
Kawaguchi
Chiba

Kasumi
Shirotori
Hachiman
Kōfu
Hachiōji
Kawasaki
Bōsō-

Sakaiminato
Kuroyoka
Obama
Nakatsu
Iida
Fuji-Yoshida
Yokohama
hantō

Kurayoshi
Amino
Wakasa-wan
Tsuruga
Gifu
Akaishi-san 3120
Fujisawa
Kisarazu
Mobara

Yonago
Tottori
Miyazu
Kinomoto
Ichinomiya
Shirane-san 3192
Fujinomiya
Odawara
Mihara
Katsuura

Matsue
Fukuchiyama
Hikone
Seto
Toyota
Fuji
Numazu
Tateyama
Kamogawa

Niimi
Chizu
Ōtsu
Kusatsu
Yokkaichi
Nagoya
Shimizu
Atami
Nojima-zaki

Tsuyama
Biwa-ko
Kameyama
Okazaki
Shizuoka
Ito

Tatsuno
Nishiwaki
Kyōto
Uji
Nara
Toyohashi
Shimada
Yaizu
Sagami-nada

Takahashi
Aioi
Himeji
Kōbe
Toyonaka
Tsu
Handa
Hamamatsu
Suruga-wan
Ō-shima

Okayama
Kakogawa
Akashi
Ōsaka
Suzuka
Matsusaka
Toyohashi
Shimoda

Kurashiki
Sakai
Nabari
Ise-wan
Ōmae-zaki
To-shima

Fukuyama
Tamano
Kishiwada
Izumi-Sano
Ise
Toba
Iro-zaki

Onomichi
Marugame
Awaji-shima
Wakayama
Nagashima
Nii-jima

Sakaidō
Takamatsu
Sumoto
Kainan
Owase
Kōzu-shime

Niihama
Naruto
Komatsushima
Gobo
Kumano
Miyake-jima

Shikoku-sanchi
Tokushima
Anan
Ōnohara-jima
Mikura-jima

Kōchi
Nankoku
Hiwasa
Tanabe
Hikigawa
Shingū

Tosa
Aki
Yoshino
Kushimoto
Shiono-misaki

Tosa-wan
Muroto
Muroto-zaki

SHIKOKU

PACIFIC

JAPAN

Inset (lower right):

Wakkanai
Sōya-misaki
145 at the same scale
①

Rebun-tō
Rishiri-tō
Hama-Tombetsu

Kitami-Esashi

Oteineppu
Ōmu
Okoppe
Mombetsu
HOKKAIDŌ
Shiretoko-misaki
M.Dokuchayevo
Rudnaya

Yagishiri-tō
Teuri-tō
Uryū-ko
Nayoro
Soroma-ko
Abashiri-wan
O. Kunashir
(Rus. Fed. admin./claimed by Japan)

Rumoi
Takinoue
Engaru
Teshio dake 1558
Abashiri
Shari
Rausu
Golovnino

Shibetsu
Kitami

②
Takikawa
Fukagawa
Asahikawa
Shibetsu

Shakotan-misaki
Sunagawa
Akabira
Ashibetsu
Asahi dake 2290
Kutcharo-ko
Teshikaga
Nemuro-kaikyō

Furubira
Bibai
Iwamizawa
Furano
Me-akan dake
Shibetsu

Iwanai
Otaru
Yubari
Kushiro
②

Sapporo
Ebetsu
Eniwo
Obihiro
Ikeda
Nemuro

1:10M

100   200   300   400 km

100   200 mils

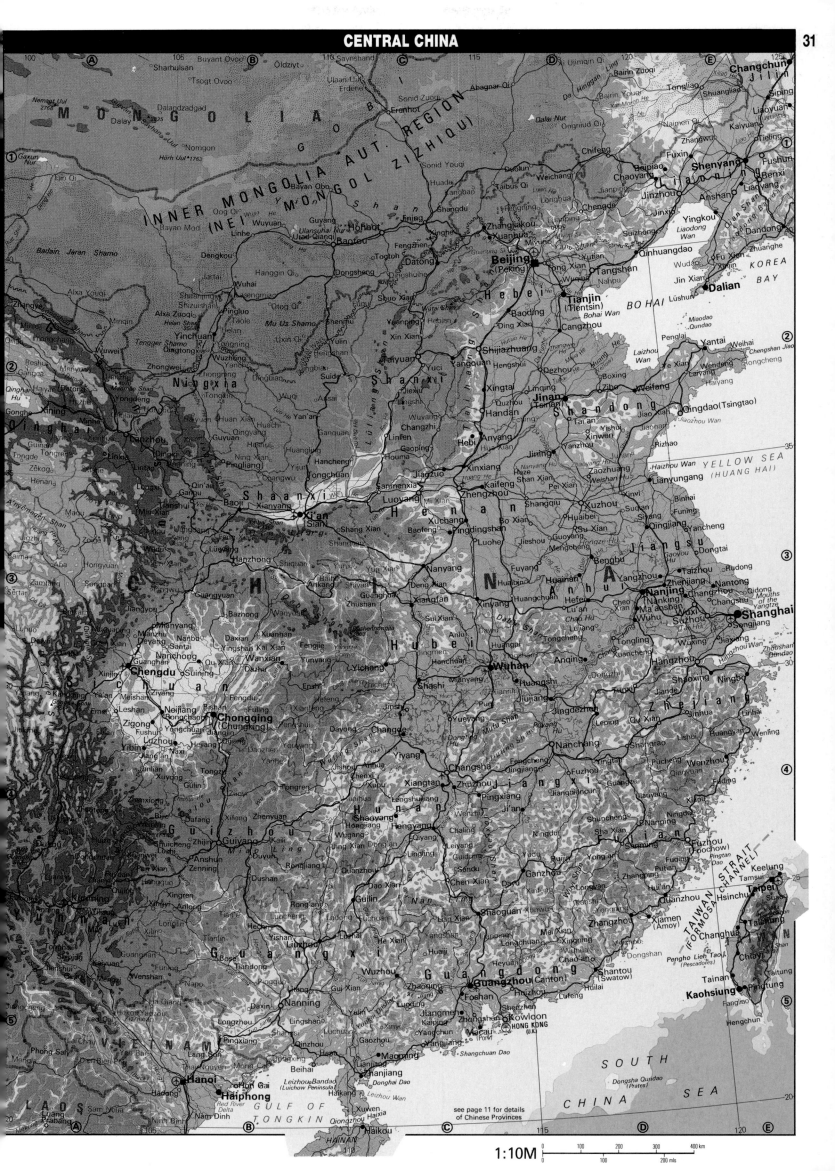

1:10M

see page 11 for details
of Chinese Provinces

1:20M

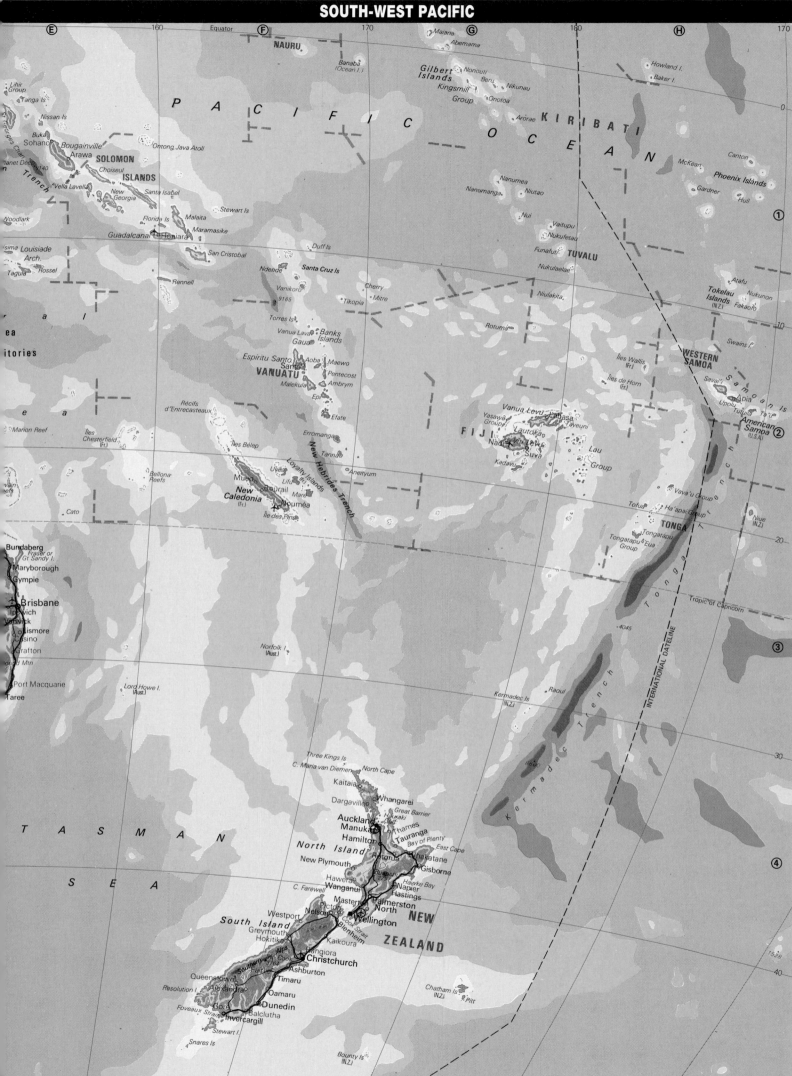

1:7.5M

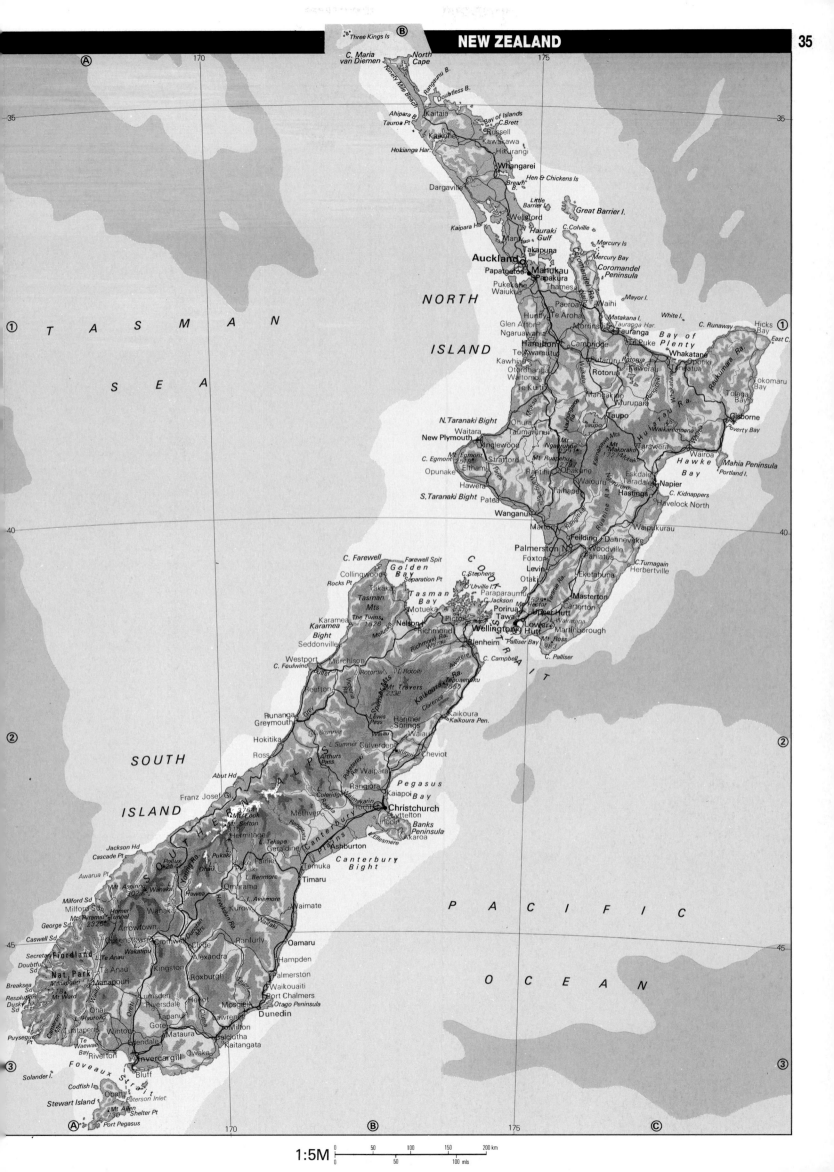

Three Kings Is

C. Maria
van Diemen
North
Cape

Rangaunu B.

Doubtless B.

Ahipara B.
Tauroa Pt
Kaitaia

Bay of Islands
C.Brett
Russell
Kawakawa

Kaikohe
Hikurangi
Hokianga Har.
Whangarei
Dargaville
Hen & Chickens Is
Bream
B.

Little
Barrier I.
Wellsford
Great Barrier I.

Kaipara Har.
Maunu
C.Colville
Hauraki
Gulf
Mercury Is

Takapuna
Mercury Bay

Auckland
Coromandel
Peninsula

Papatoetoe
Manukau
Papakura
Pukekohe
Thames
Mayor I.

Waiuku
Paeroa
Waihi

NORTH
Huntly
Te Aroha
White I.
C. Runaway
Hicks
Bay

Glen Afton
Morrinsville
Matakana I.
East C.

Ngaruawahia
Tauranga Har.
Tauranga

ISLAND
Hamilton
Cambridge
Te Puke
Bay
of
Plenty
Whakatane

Te Awamutu
Putaruru
Rotorua
Opotiki
Kawerau

Kawhia
Otorohanga
Rotorua
Tokomaru
Bay

Waitomo
Tolaga
Bay

Te Kuiti
Mangakino
Murupara

Taupo
Gisborne

Ohura
Taumarunui
Mt
Ngauruhoe
Makorako
Tarawera
Poverty Bay

N. Taranaki Bight
Waitara
L.Taupo
Wairoa

New Plymouth
Inglewood
Mt
Ruapehu
Eskdale
Mahia Peninsula

Mt Egmont
Stratford
Ohakune
Taradale
Portland I.

C. Egmont
Eltham
Raetihi
Waiouru
Napier

Opunake
Hawera
Taihape
Hastings
C. Kidnappers

S. Taranaki Bight
Patea
Havelock North

Wanganui
Marton
Waipukurau

Feilding
Dannevirke

COOK
Palmerston N.
Woodville

C. Farewell
Farewell Spit
Foxton
Pahiatua
C.Turnagain
Herbertville

Collingwood
Golden
Bay
Separation Pt
Levin
Eketahuna

Rocks Pt
C. Stephens
Otaki

Takaka
D'Urville I.
Paraparaumu
Masterton

Tasman
Mts
Tasman
Bay
C.Jackson
Carterton
Upper Hutt

The Twins
1826
Motueka
Picton
Tawa
Porirua

Karamea
Nelson
Wellington
Lower Hutt
Martinborough

Karamea
Bight
Richmond
Blenheim
Palliser Bay
Mt.Ross
883

Seddonville
Richmond Ra.
Wairau

Westport
Murchison
Awatere
C. Campbell
C. Palliser

C. Foulwind
Buller
Mt Travers
2338

Reefton
Kaikoura
Ra.

Runanga
Lewis
Pass
Hanmer
Springs
Kaikoura

Greymouth
Clarence
Kaikoura Pen.

Hokitika
Waiau

Ross
L.Sumner
Culverden
Cheviot

Arthurs
Pass
Waipara

Abut Hd
Rangiora
Pegasus
Bay

Franz Josef Gl.
Kaiapoi

Coleridge
Waimakariri
Christchurch

Mt Cook
3764
Methven
Lyttelton

Mt Sefton
Lincoln
Banks
Peninsula

Hermitage
Geraldine
Akaroa

Jackson Hd
Temuka
L.Ellesmere

Cascade Pt
L. Tekapo
Ashburton

Awarua Pt
Canterbury
Plains
Canterbury
Bight

Mt Aspiring
2035
L.
Wanaka
Timaru

Milford Sd
Homer
Tunnel
L.Ohau
Omarama

Mt Pyramid
2326
Wanaka
L. Benmore

George Sd
Arrowtown
L. Aviemore
Waimate

Caswell Sd
Queenstown
Cromwell
Oamaru

Secretary I.
Wakatipu
Clyde

Fiordland
L.Te Anau
Alexandra
Hampden

Doubtful
Nat. Park
Te Anau
Roxburgh
Palmerston

Breaksea
Sd
Manapouri
Waikouaiti

Resolution
I.
Mt Ward
Tapanui
Port Chalmers

Dusky
Sd
Lumsden
Riversdale
Lawrence
Otago Peninsula

Puysegur
Pt
L.Hauroko
Heriot
Mosgiel
Dunedin

Wintons
Gore
Milton

Te
Waewae
Bay
Mataura
Balclutha

Riverton
Edendale
Kaitangata

Invercargill
Owaka

Foveaux Strait

Bluff

Solander I.

Codfish I.
Oban

Paterson Inlet

Stewart Island

Mt Allen
980
Shelter Pt

Port Pegasus

TASMAN
SEA

SOUTH
ISLAND

PACIFIC
OCEAN

SOUTHERN
ALPS

1:5M

0   50   100   150   200 km

0   50   100 mils

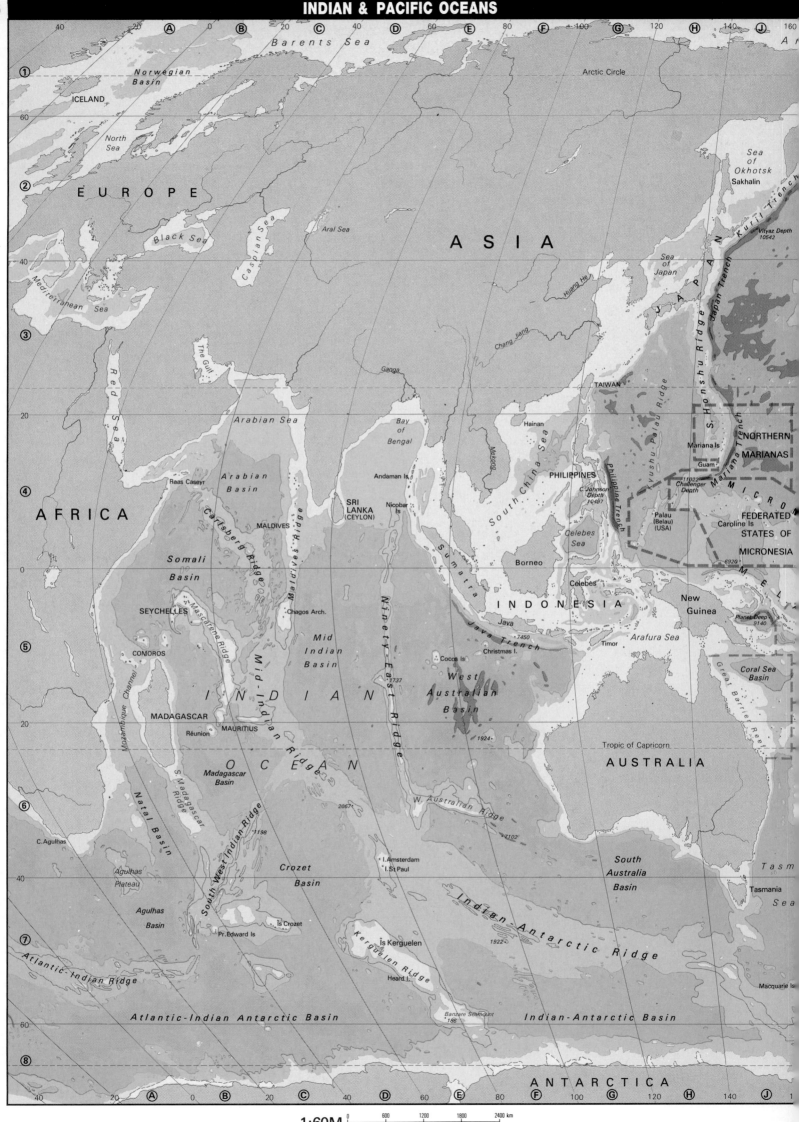

Barents Sea

Norwegian Basin

Arctic Circle

ICELAND

North Sea

E U R O P E

A S I A

Black Sea

Caspian Sea

Aral Sea

Sea of Okhotsk

Sakhalin

Vityaz Depth 10542

Mediterranean Sea

J A P A N

Kuril Trench

Japan Trench

Sea of Japan

The Gulf

Huang He

Ganga

Chang Jiang

TAIWAN

S. Honshu Ridge

Mariana Trench

Red Sea

Arabian Sea

Bay of Bengal

Hainan

South China Sea

Kyushu-Palau Ridge

Mariana Is

NORTHERN MARIANAS

Raas Caseyr

Arabian Basin

Andaman Is

PHILIPPINES

Guam

Philippine Trench

MICRO

A F R I C A

Carlsberg Ridge

MALDIVES

SRI LANKA (CEYLON)

Nicobar Is

C. Johnson Depth 10497

Challenger Depth 11022

FEDERATED

Somali Basin

Maldives Ridge

Celebes Sea

Palau (Belau) (USA)

Caroline Is

STATES OF MICRONESIA

SEYCHELLES

Mascarene Ridge

Chagos Arch.

Sumatra

Borneo

Celebes

I N D O N E S I A

New Guinea

6920

COMOROS

Mid Indian Basin

Ninety-East Ridge

Java

7450

Planet Deep 9140

M E L

I N D I A N

Mid-Indian Ridge

Java Trench

Christmas I.

Timor

Arafura Sea

Coral Sea Basin

MADAGASCAR

MAURITIUS

Cocos Is

West Australian Basin

Réunion

7737

Great Barrier Reef

O C E A N

Madagascar Basin

2067

1924

Tropic of Capricorn

AUSTRALIA

S. Madagascar Ridge

South West Indian Ridge

W. Australian Ridge

7102

South Australia Basin

Tas

Natal Basin

1198

C. Agulhas

Crozet Basin

I. Amsterdam

I. St Paul

Indian-Antarctic Ridge

Tasmania Sea

Agulhas Plateau

Agulhas Basin

Is Crozet

Pr. Edward Is

Kerguelen Ridge

Is Kerguelen

1922

Macquarie Is

Atlantic-Indian Ridge

Heard I.

Atlantic-Indian Antarctic Basin

Banzare Seamount 186

Indian-Antarctic Basin

A N T A R C T I C A

1:60M

600   1200   1800   2400 km

600   1200 mils

To enhance the ocean features, the 3000m contour has been added, and over 5000m is shown by an extra tint.

K 180   L 160   M 140   N 120   O 100   P 80   Q 60   R 40   S 20   0

①

GREENLAND

ICELAND

Arctic Ocean

Bering Sea

Hudson Bay

C. Farewell

Labrador Basin

Atlantic

②

Aleutian Is

7822

Aleutian Trench

Newfoundland

Ocean

Grand Banks

40

Emperor Seamount Chain

NORTH

AMERICA

North American

Bermuda

③

Basin

Van

18

104

Midway Is

Mendocino Seascarp

2926

Murray Seascarp

Gulf of

Mexico

Hawaiian Islands

Tropic of Cancer

C. Falso

CUBA

West Indies

20

Mid-Pacific Mountains

1477

P

Is Revilla Gigedo

Middle America Trench

Cayman Tr.

Caribbean Sea

Clarion Fracture Zone

East Pacific Rise

④

MARSHALL ISLANDS

O

Line Is

L

Marshall Is

A

C

I

F

I

C

Cocos Ridge

Y

Equator

Is Galápagos

0

NAURU

KIRIBATI

N

O

C

E

A

N

SOUTH

AMERICA

SOLOMON ISLANDS

6150

TUVALU

Phoenix Is

E

Tokelau

Is Marquises

East Pacific Ridge

⑤

S

American Samoa

Wallis & Futuna

Wn Samoa

Samoa

French Polynesia

Peru Basin

S.W. Peru or Nazca Ridge

ANUATU

I

FIJI

A

TONGA

Niue

Cook Is

Samoa

Is de la Société

Tahiti

Is Tuamotu

S

A

Peru-Chile Trench

8066

New Caledonia

Tonga Trench

Is Gambier

20

Is Tubuai

5537

S.Ambrosio

S.Félix

Horizon Depth 10882

Pitcairn

1344

Sala y Gómez

⑥

Norfolk I.

10047

Easter I. (I. de Pascua)

S. Fiji Basin

Kermadec Trench

Norfolk I. Ridge

INTERNATIONAL DATE LINE

Is Juan Fernández

N. Cape

South West

Pacific

Basin

Rise

NEW ZEALAND

Argentine Basin

40

Chatham Is

New Zealand Plateau

Pacific-Antarctic Ridge

Falkland Is

⑦

uckland Is

Campbell I.

6240

732

N Scotia Ridge

S. Georgia

C. Horn

Scotia Sea

South East Pacific Basin

Drake Passage

S.Sandwich Is

S. Sandwich Trench

5486

S.Orkney Is

60

alleny Is

Scott Is

Antarctic Peninsula

Antarctic Circle

⑧

Weddell Sea

K 180   L 160   M 140   N 120   O 100   P 80   Q 60   R 40   S 20   0

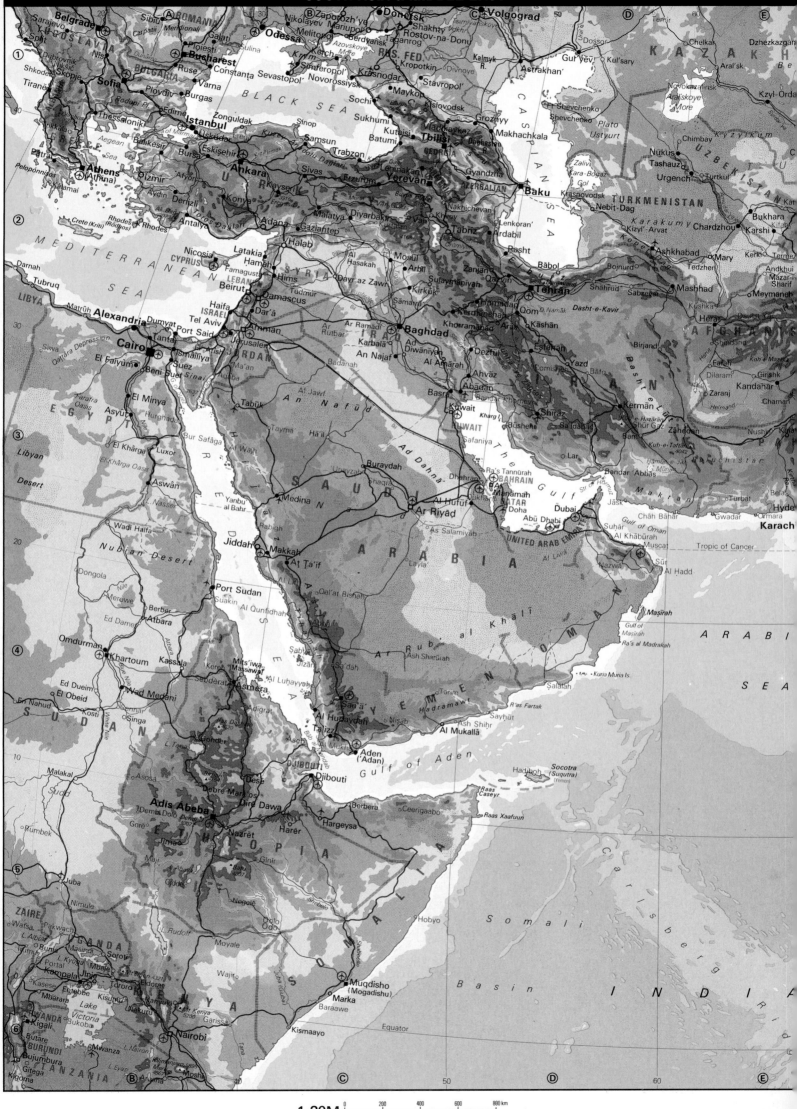

1:20M

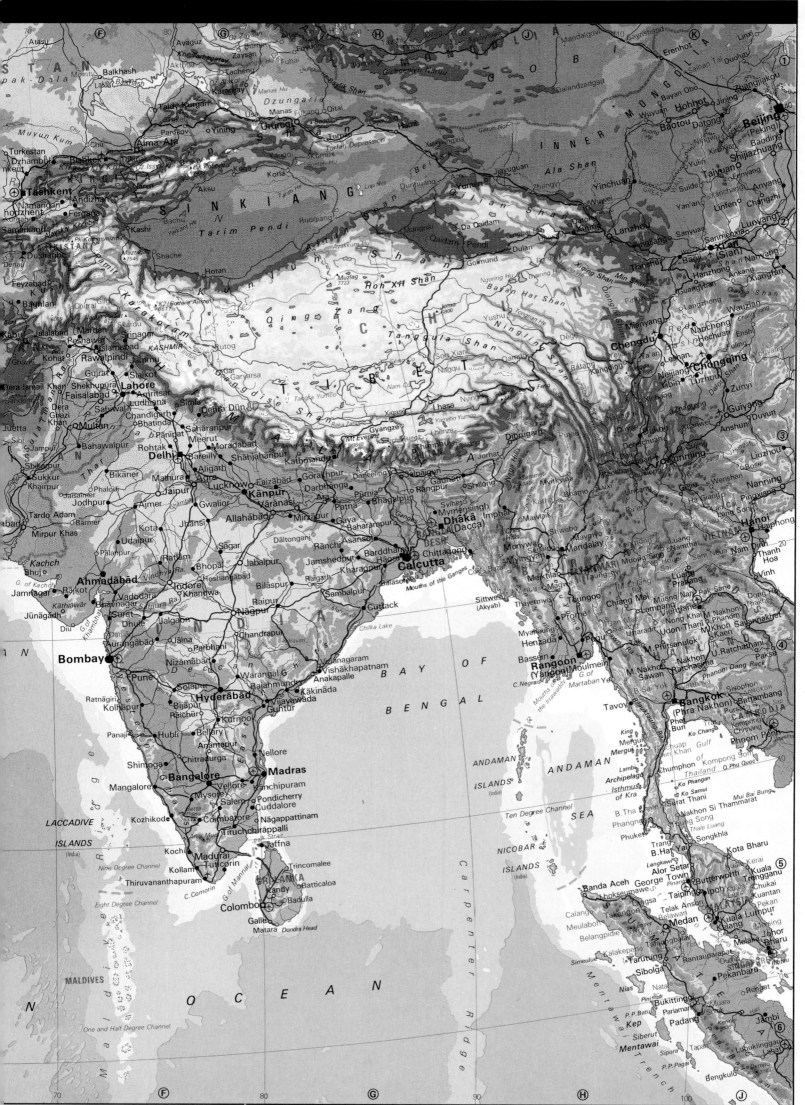

1:7.5M

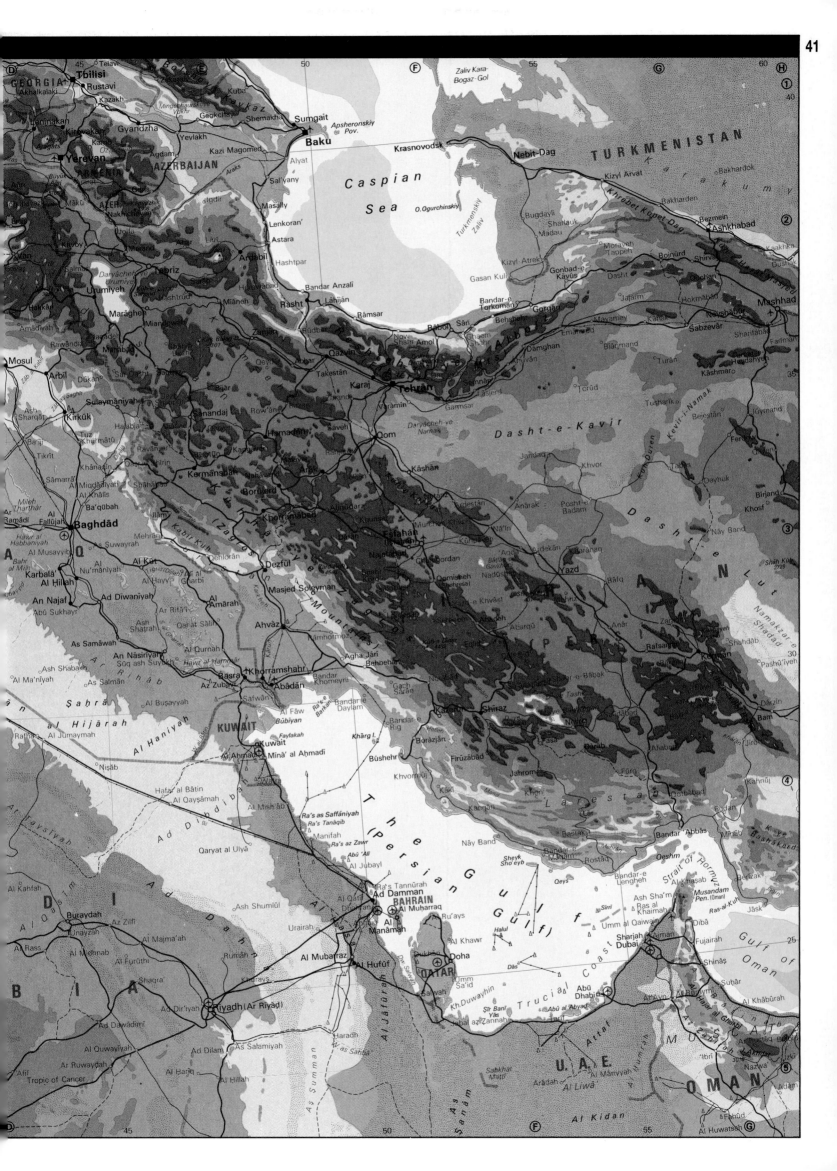

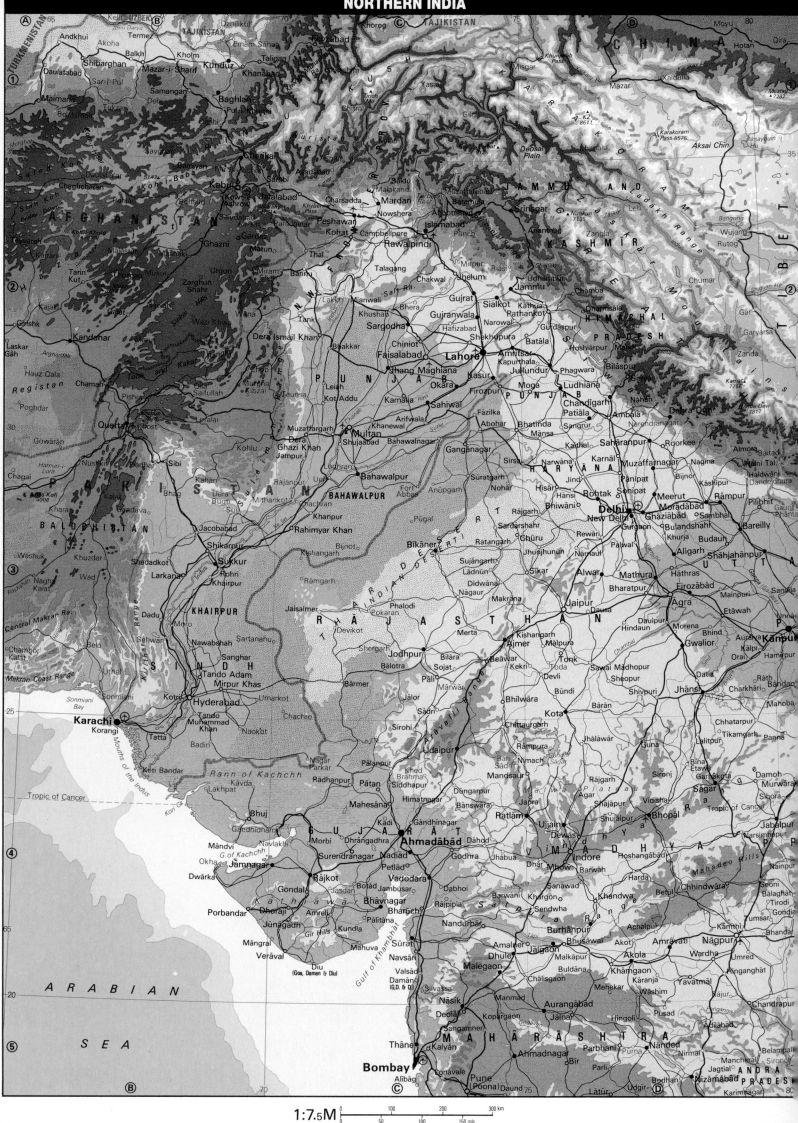

1:7.5M

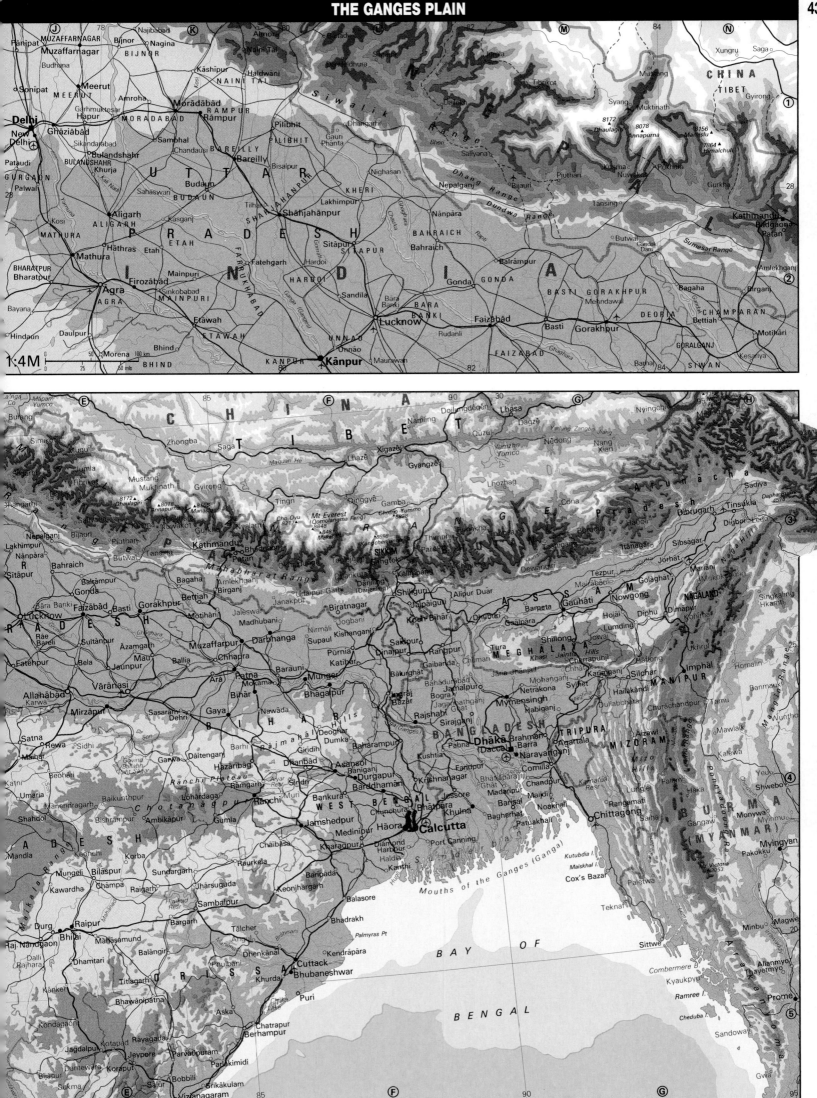

1:7.5M

0   100   200   300 km
0   50   100   150 mls

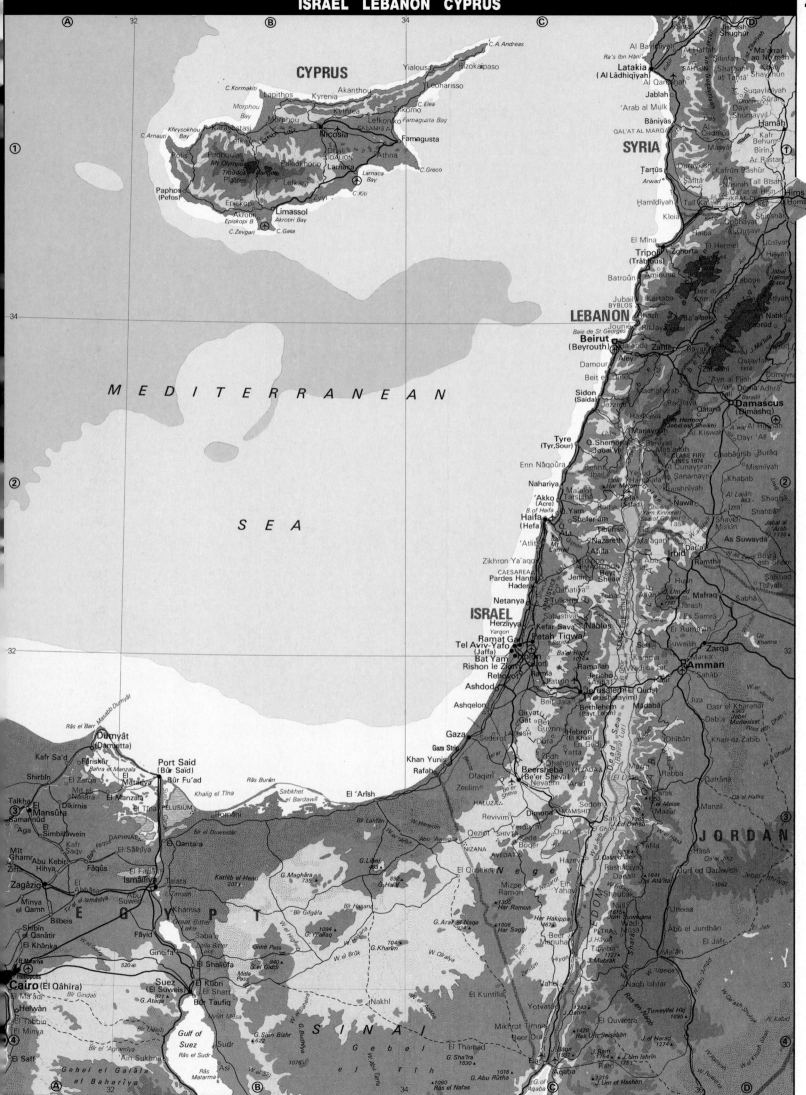

1:40M

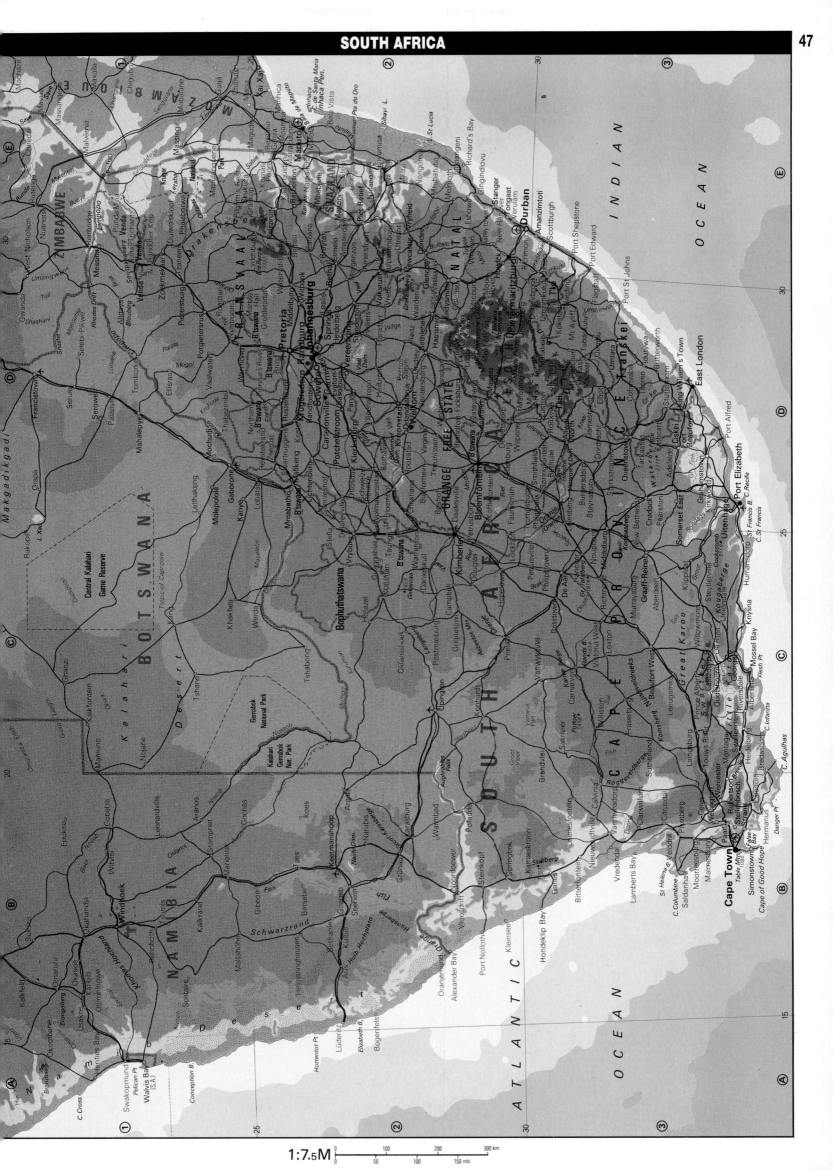

1:15M

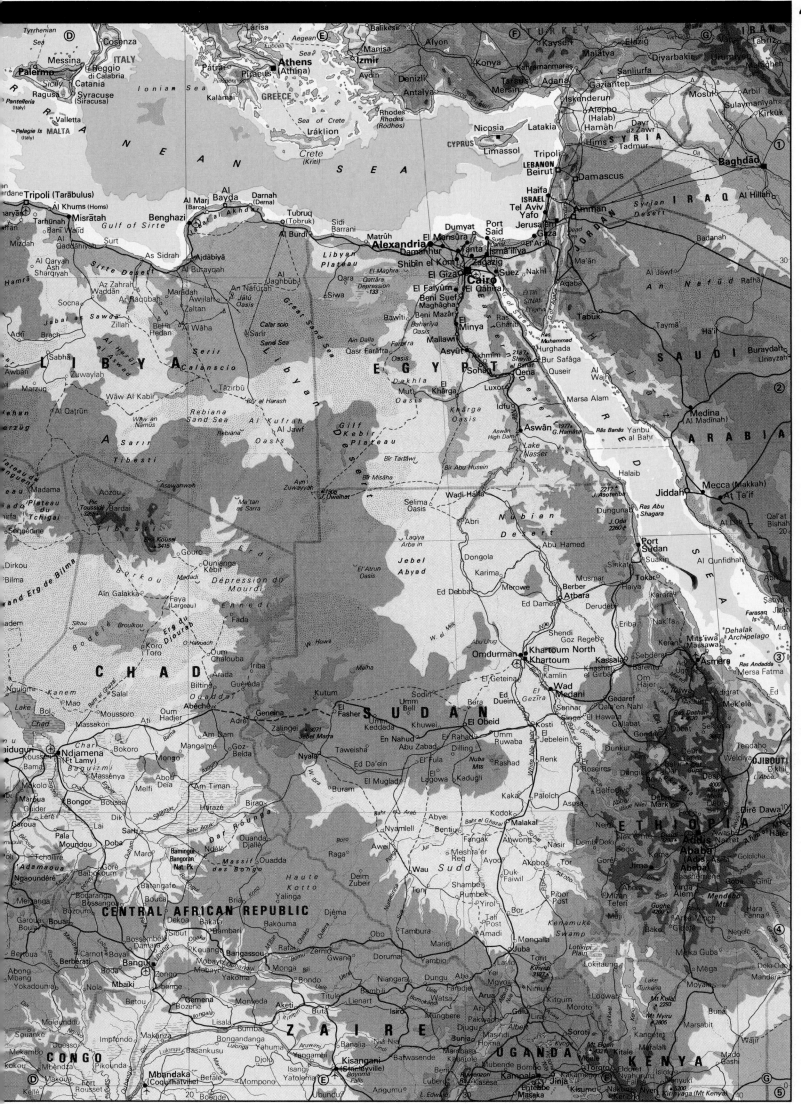

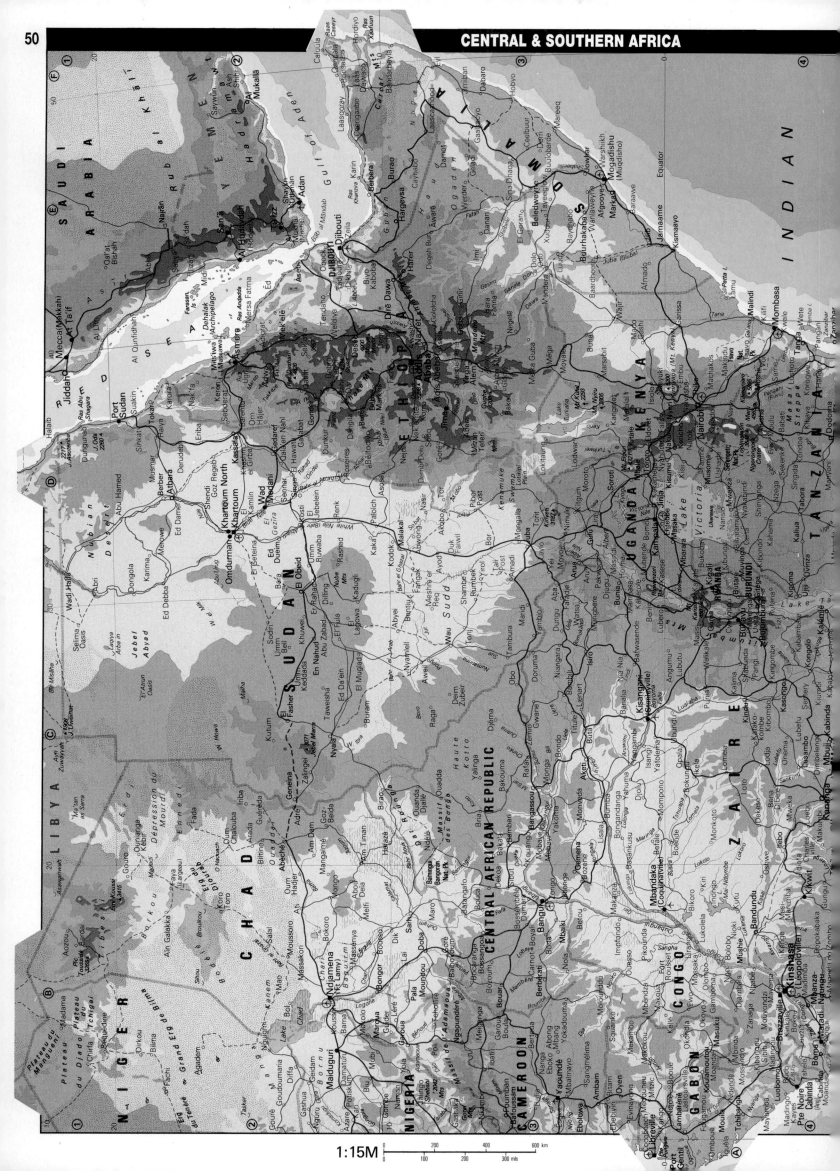

1:15M

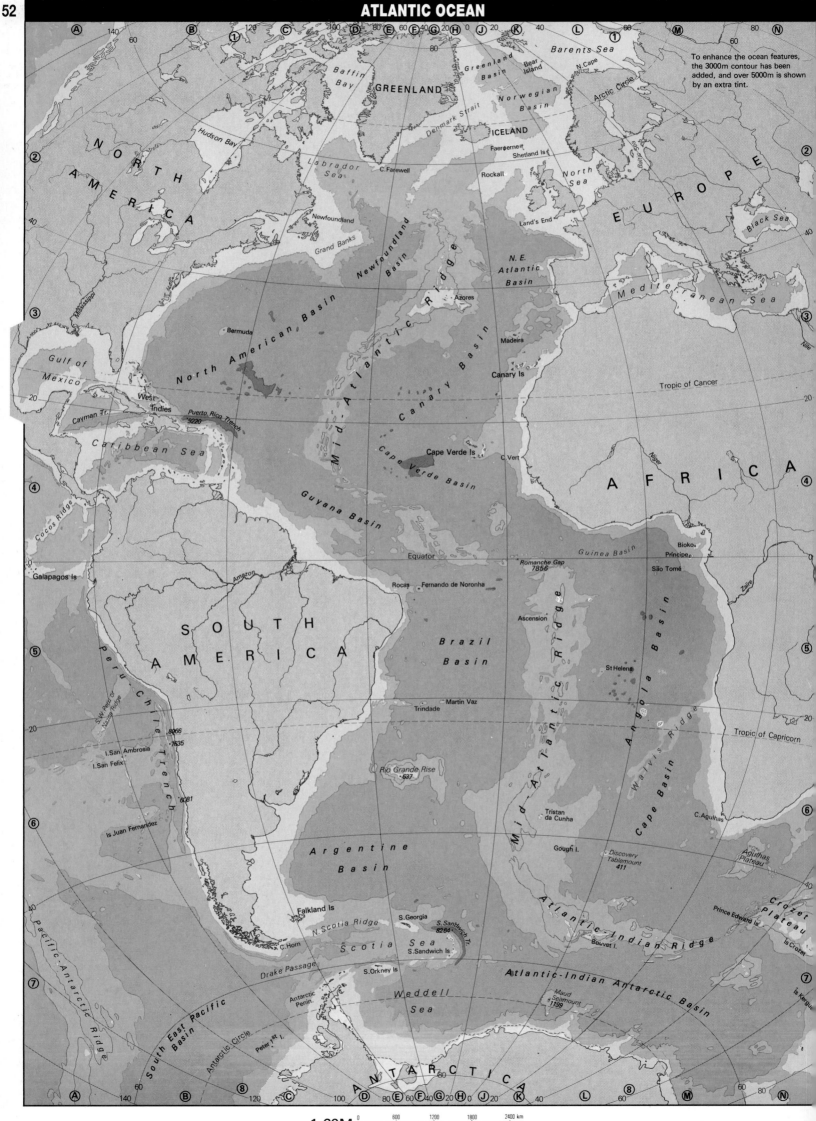

To enhance the ocean features, the 3000m contour has been added, and over 5000m is shown by an extra tint.

NORTH AMERICA

EUROPE

AFRICA

SOUTH AMERICA

ANTARCTICA

GREENLAND

ICELAND

Baffin Bay

Hudson Bay

Labrador Sea

Barents Sea

Greenland Basin

Bear Island

Norwegian Basin

N. Cape

Arctic Circle

Denmark Strait

Faeroerne

Shetland Is

C. Farewell

Rockall

Land's End

North Sea

Black Sea

Mediterranean Sea

Newfoundland

Grand Banks

Newfoundland Basin

N.E. Atlantic Basin

Azores

Madeira

Bermuda

North American Basin

Mid-Atlantic Ridge

Canary Basin

Canary Is

Tropic of Cancer

Gulf of Mexico

West Indies

Cayman Tr.

Puerto Rico Trench ·9220

Caribbean Sea

Cocos Ridge

Cape Verde Is

C. Vert

Cape Verde Basin

Guyana Basin

Galapagos Is

Amazon

Equator

Romanche Gap 7856

Guinea Basin

Bioko

Príncipe

São Tomé

Niger

Zaïre

Rocas

Fernando de Noronha

Ascension

Mid-Atlantic Ridge

Brazil Basin

St Helena

Angola Basin

Peru-Chile Trench

S.W. Perú or Nazca Ridge

·8066

·7635

I.San Ambrosia

I.San Felix

Martin Vaz

Trindade

·6081

Rio Grande Rise ·637

Tropic of Capricorn

Walvis Ridge

Cape Basin

Is Juan Fernandez

Tristan da Cunha

Gough I.

Discovery Tablemount 411

Agulhas Plateau

C. Agulhas

Crozet Plateau

Prince Edward Is

Argentine Basin

Falkland Is

N. Scotia Ridge

S. Georgia

S. Sandwich Tr. 8264

Atlantic-Indian Ridge

Bouvet I.

Is Crozet

C. Horn

Scotia Sea

S. Sandwich Is

Pacific-Antarctic Ridge

Drake Passage

S. Orkney Is

Atlantic-Indian Antarctic Basin

Maud Seamount 1199

Antarctic Penin.

Weddell Sea

South East Pacific Basin

Antarctic Circle

Peter I st I.

Mississippi

1:60M

600   1200   1800   2400 km

600   1200 mls

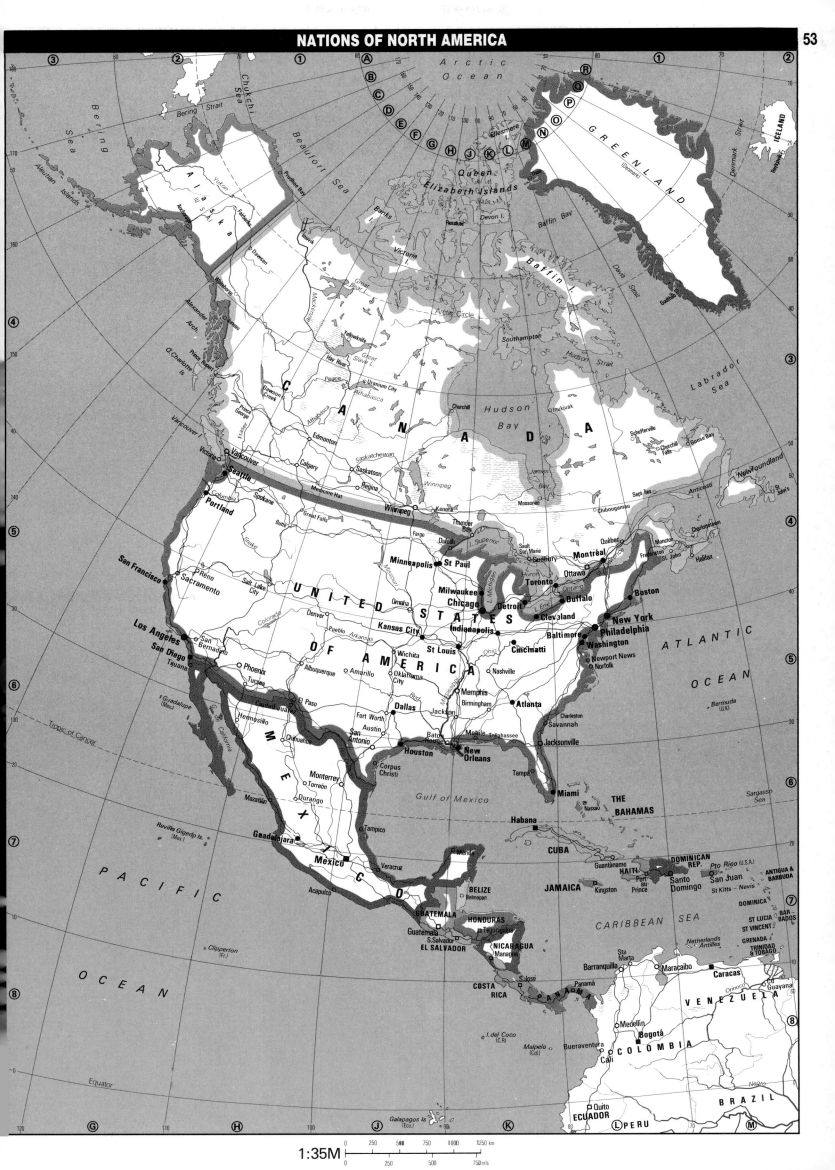

1:35M

Arctic Ocean

ICELAND
Reykjavik

G R E E N L A N D
(Denmark)

Bering Sea

Chukchi Sea

Bering Strait

Beaufort Sea

Prudhoe Bay

Aleutian Islands

Alaska
Yukon

Fairbanks

Inuvik

Dawson

Whitehorse

Juneau

Alexander Arch.

Prince Rupert

Q. Charlotte Is

Vancouver I.

Ellesmere I.

Resolute

Queen Elizabeth Islands

Victoria I.

Banks I.

Devon I.

Baffin Bay

Baffin I.

Davis Strait

Denmark Strait

Godthab

Arctic Circle

Yellowknife

Great Bear L.

Great Slave L.

Hay River

Southampton I.

Hudson Strait

Labrador Sea

C A N A D A

Churchill

Inukjuak

Hudson Bay

James Bay

Moosonee

Schefferville

Churchill Falls

Goose Bay

Newfoundland

St John's

Anticosti I.

Sept-Iles

Chibougamau

Charlottetown

Prince George

Dawson Creek

Uranium City

Athabasca

L. Athabasca

Peace

Fraser

Mackenzie

Edmonton

Calgary

Saskatoon

Regina

Saskatchewan

Medicine Hat

L. Winnipeg

Victoria
Vancouver
Seattle
Portland
Columbia
Spokane

Great Falls

Butte

Snake

Fargo

Duluth

Winnipeg

Kenora

Thunder Bay

L. Superior

Sault Ste Marie

Sudbury

Québec

Moncton

Fredericton

St. John

Halifax

St Lawrence

Montréal

Ottawa

Toronto

L. Huron

L. Michigan

L. Ontario

Buffalo

Boston

San Francisco
Reno
Sacramento
Salt Lake City

Minneapolis
St Paul

Milwaukee
Chicago

Detroit
Cleveland

L. Erie

New York

Philadelphia

U N I T E D   S T A T E S

Omaha

Denver

Colorado

Pueblo

Arkansas

Kansas City

St Louis

Indianapolis

Cincinnati

Baltimore
Washington
Newport News
Norfolk

ATLANTIC OCEAN

O F   A M E R I C A

Los Angeles
San Bernadino
San Diego
Tijuana

Phoenix

Tucson

Albuquerque

Wichita

Amarillo

Oklahoma City

Red

Nashville

Memphis

Ohio

Mississippi

Birmingham

Atlanta

Charleston

Savannah

Bermuda (U.K)

Ciudad Juárez

El Paso

Hermosillo

Guadalupe (Mex.)

Chihuahua

Fort Worth

Dallas

Austin

San Antonio

Jackson

Baton Rouge

Mobile

Tallahassee

Jacksonville

Houston

New Orleans

Corpus Christi

Tampa

Miami

M E X I C O

Monterrey

Torreón

Durango

Mazatlán

Revilla Gigedp Is. (Mex.)

Tropic of Cancer

California

Gulf of Mexico

THE BAHAMAS

Nassau

Sargasso Sea

Habana

CUBA

DOMINICAN REP.

Pto Rico (U.S.A)

San Juan

ANTIGUA & BARBUDA

Guadalajara

Mexico

Veracruz

Tampico

Mérida

Acapulco

BELIZE
Belmopan

Guantánamo

HAITI

Port au Prince

JAMAICA

Kingston

Santo Domingo

St Kitts – Nevis

DOMINICA

ST LUCIA
ST VINCENT

BARBADOS

GRENADA

TRINIDAD & TOBAGO

P A C I F I C

GUATEMALA
Guatemala
S.Salvador
EL SALVADOR

HONDURAS
Tegucigalpa

NICARAGUA
Managua

CARIBBEAN SEA

Netherlands Antilles

Sta Marta

Barranquilla

Maracaibo

Caracas

Guayana

O C E A N

Clipperton (Fr.)

I. del Coco (C.R)

COSTA RICA

S.José

PANAMA

Panamá

V E N E Z U E L A

Medellín

Bogotá

Orinoco

Malpelo (Col.)

Bucraventura

Cali

C O L O M B I A

Galapagos Is (Ecu.)

Quito

ECUADOR

PERU

B R A Z I L

Negro

Equator

0 250 500 750 1000 1250 km

0 250 500 750 mls

Names underlined indicate
Province/State capitals

1:15M

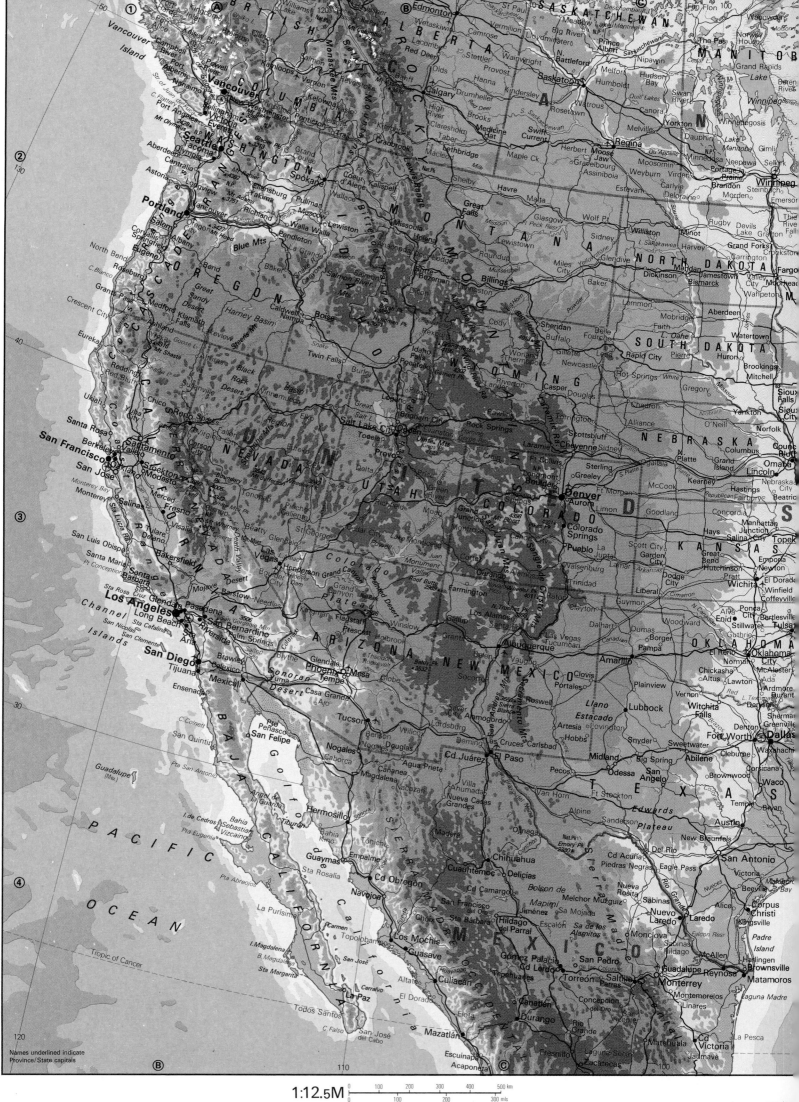

1:12.5M

0 100 200 300 400 500 km
0   100   200   300 mls

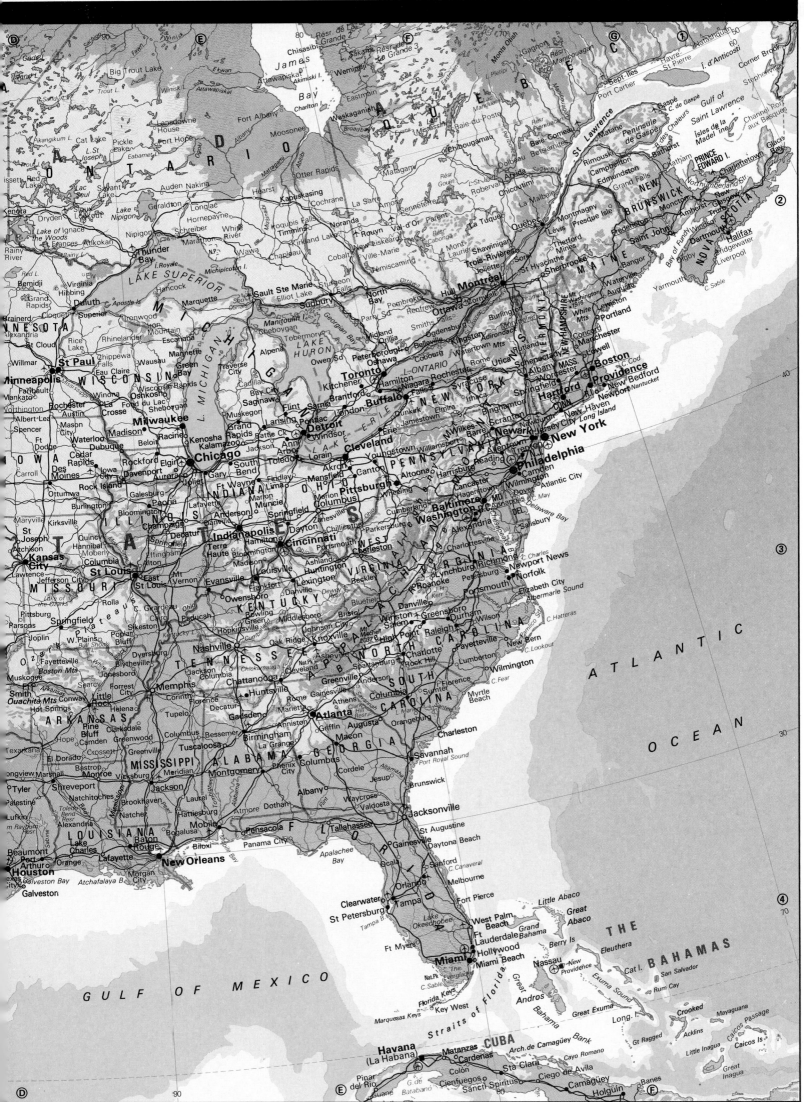

1:5M

| 0 | 50 | 100 | 150 | 200 km |
| 0 | | 50 | | 100 mls |

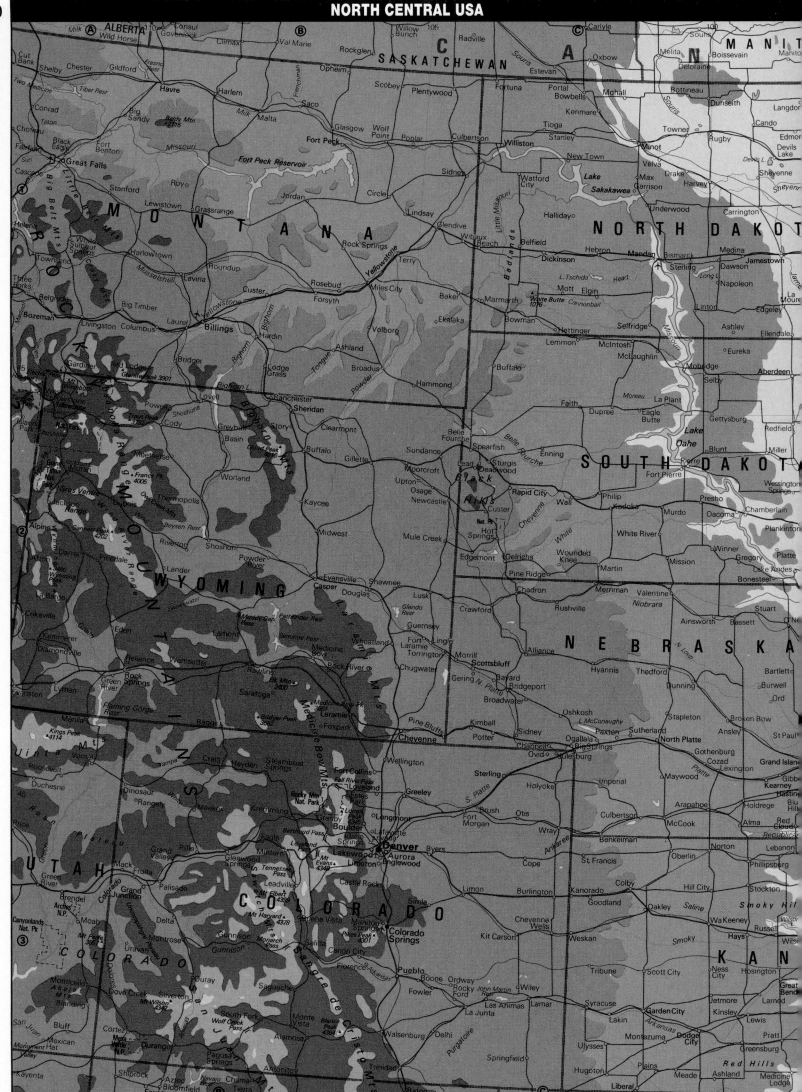

1:5M

| 0 | 50 | 100 | 150 | 200 km |
| 0 | | 50 | | 100 mls |

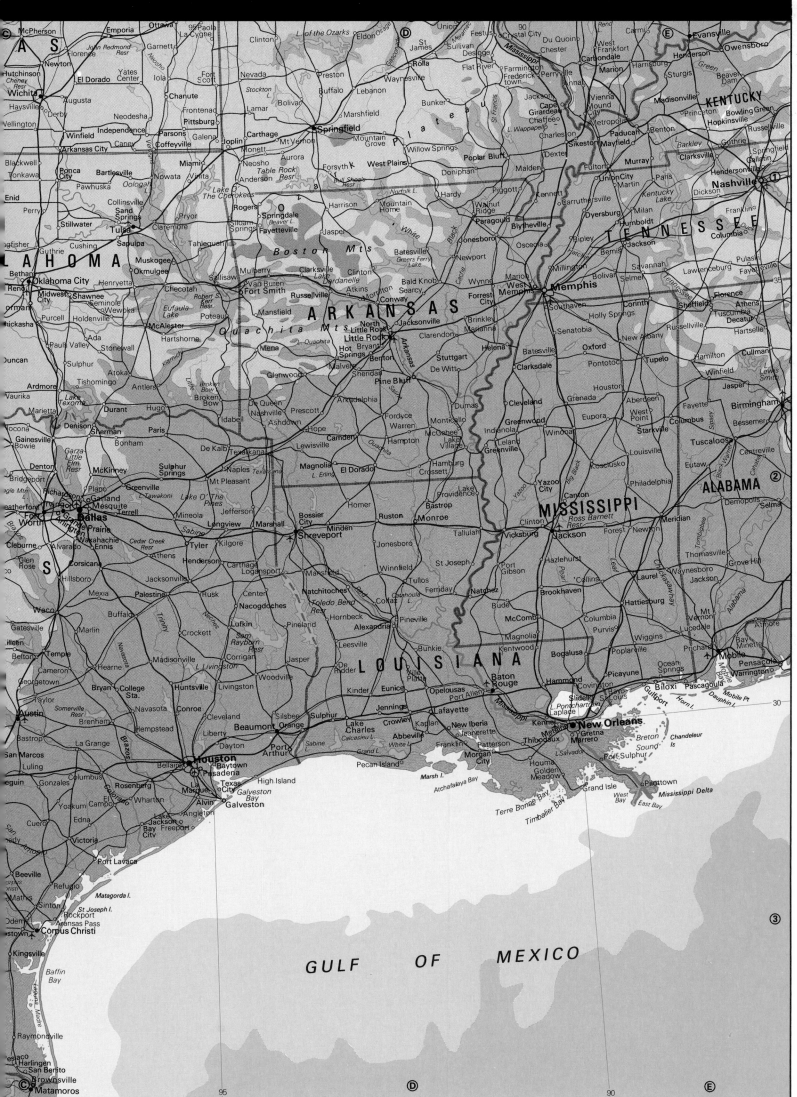

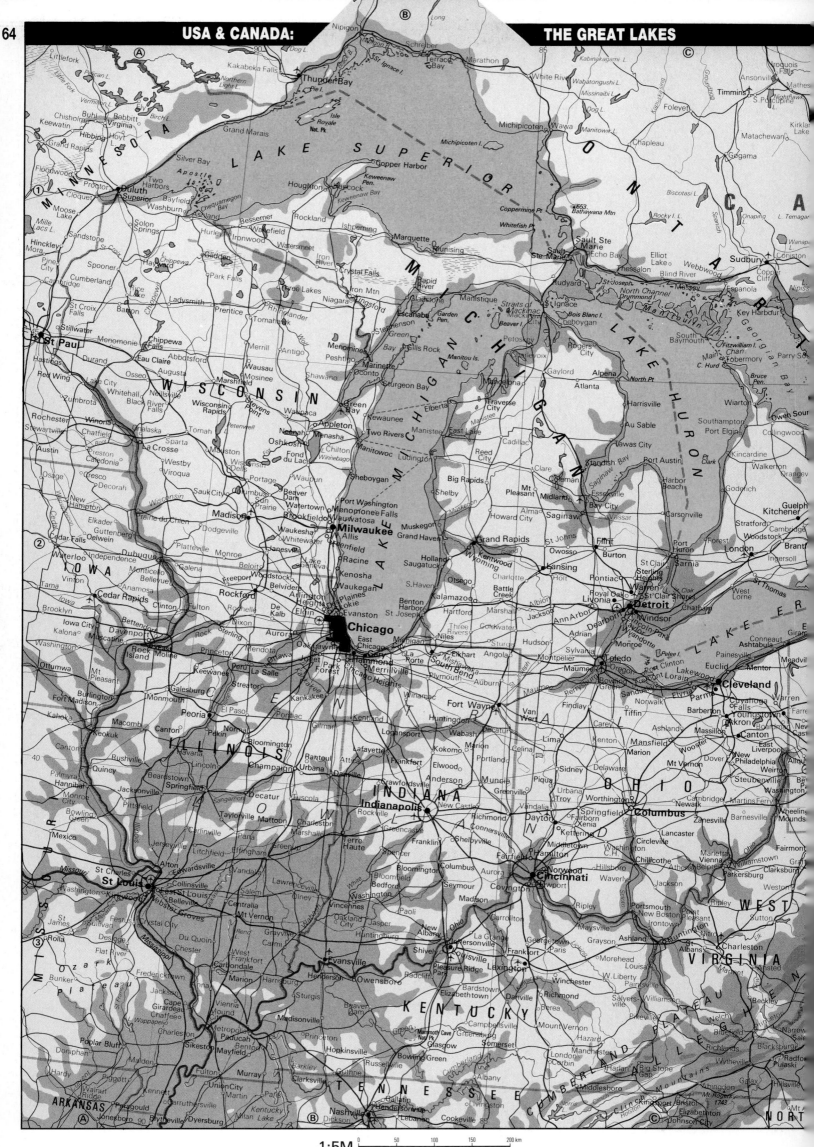

1:5M

0   50   100   150   200 km
0   50   100 mls

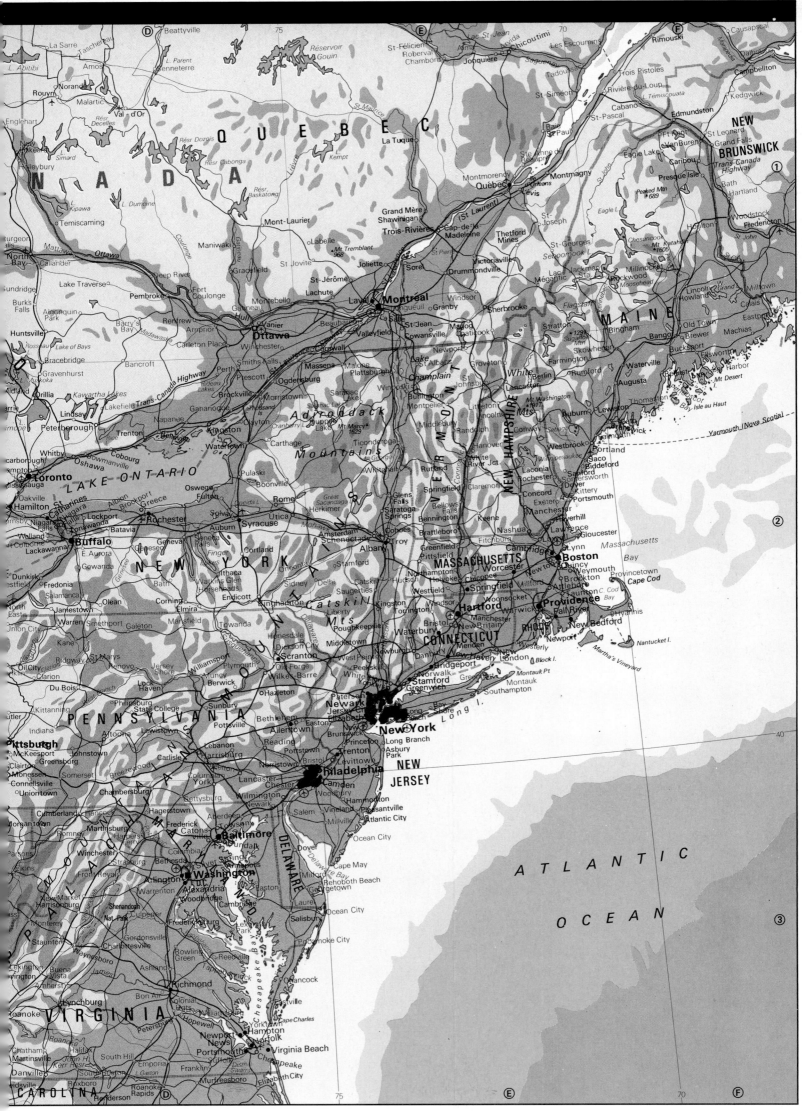

USA, HAWAII

1:5M

1:2.5M

ATLANTIC

OCEAN

GULF OF

MEXICO

THE BAHAMAS

1:5M

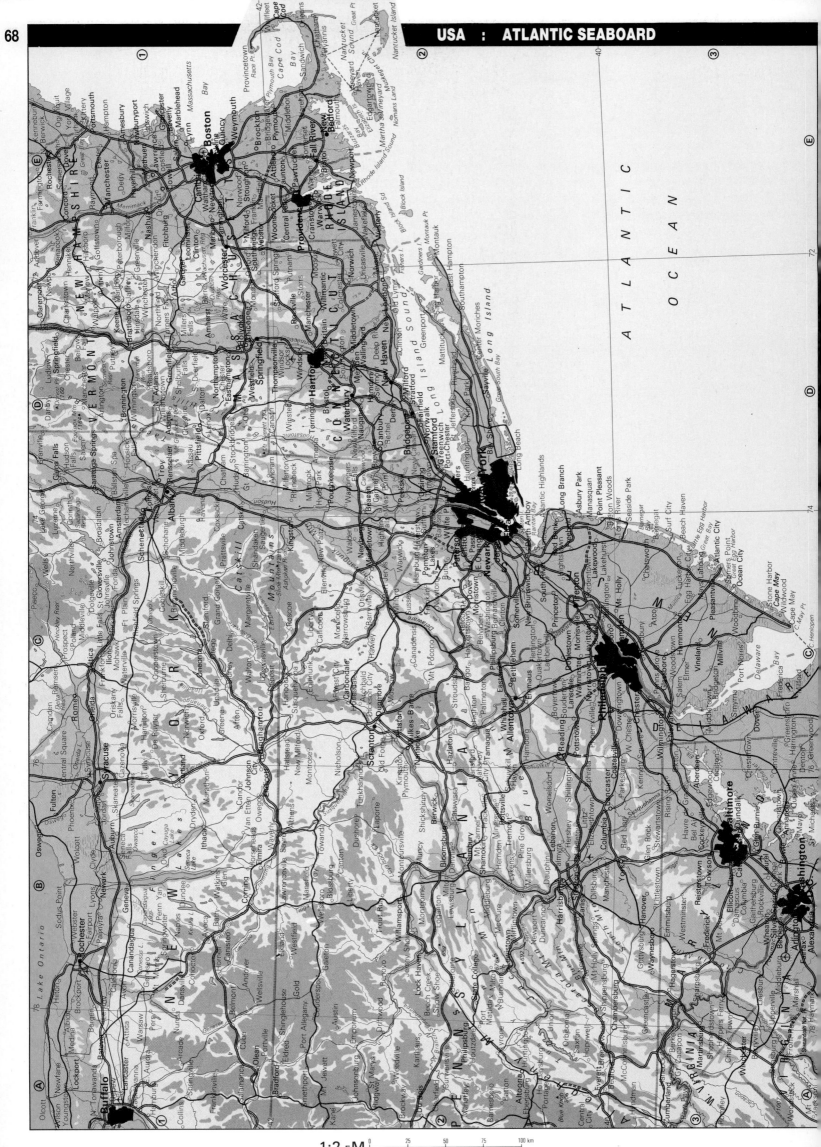

1:2.5M

TRINIDAD (L)

1:2.5 M

Port of Spain, San Fernando, Galera Pt, Matura Bay, St. Joseph, Arima, Upper Tunapuna, Princes Town, Rio Claro, Debe, Guayaguayare, Galeota Pt, Chupara Pt, Northern Mts Aripo Range, San Juan, Chaguanas, Gulf of Paria, Point Fortin, Fullarton

DOMINICA (Q)

1:2.5 M

Portsmouth, Roseau, C. Melville, Marigot, Pte. Rosalie, Vieille Case Diablotin 1447, Grand Bay

BARBADOS (R)

1:2.5 M

Bridgetown, North Pt, Speightstown, Holetown, Mt Hillaby 340, Ragged Pt, Blackman's, South Pt, 59°30′, 13°15′

ST LUCIA (P)

1:2.5 M

Gros Islet, Castries, Soufrière, Vieux Fort, Cap Pt, Dennery, C. Moule à Chique

ST VINCENT (N)

1:2.5 M

Barrouallie, Kingstown, Georgetown, Porter Pt, Soufrière 1237, 61°15′ Johnston Pt, 13°15′

GRENADA (M)

1:2.5 M

St George's, Grenville, Bedford Pt, Sauteurs, Mt St Catherine 840, Pt Saline, Prickly Pt, 61°45′, 12°

TOBAGO (K)

1:2.5 M

Charlotteville, Speyside, Scarborough, Crown Pt, Canaan, Plymouth, 60°30′, 11°15′

JAMAICA (H/J)

1:2.5 M

Montego Bay, Falmouth, St Ann's Bay, Ocho Rios, Pt Antonio, Annotto Bay, Spanish Town, Kingston, Port Royal, The Blue Mtns Blue Mtn Pk 2256, Chapelton, May Pen, Mandeville, Cambridge, Wakefield, The Cockpit Country, Mt Denham 986, Salt River, Southfield, Savanna la Mar, Black River, Galina Pt, Morant Bay, Morant Pt, Portland Pt, Long Bay, Dry Harbour Mts, S. Negril Point

ATLANTIC OCEAN

BAHAMAS

Palm Beach, L. Worth, Delray Beach, Pompano Beach, Ft Lauderdale, Hollywood, Miami, Key West, Naples, Belle Glade, The Everglades, FLORIDA, Marquesas Keys, Florida Keys, Tropic of Cancer, Straits of Florida, Cay Sal, Grand Bahama, Freeport, Marsh Harbour, Great Abaco, Dunmore Town, Nassau, New Providence, Eleuthera, Great Bahama Bank, Andros, Great Exuma, Cat I., New Bight, Long I., San Salvador, Rum Cay, Little Inagua, Great Inagua, Mayaguana, Acklins, Crooked I., Matthew Town, Deadman's Cay, Kemps Bay, Nicholl's Town, Anguilla Cays, Bahama, Ragged I.

CUBA

Havana, Guanabacoa, Matanzas, Güines, San Antonio, Pinar del Río, C. San Antonio, Nueva Gerona, I. de la Juventud (I. de Pinos), Batabanó, G. de Batabanó, Cienfuegos, Santa Clara, Sancti Spíritus, Ciego de Ávila, Morón, Camagüey, Arch. de Camagüey, Nuevitas, Victoria de las Tunas, Holguín, Banes, Palma Soriano, Santiago de Cuba, Manzanillo, Bayamo, Guantánamo, Baracoa, Sagua de Tánamo, Sta Cruz del Sur, Jardines de la Reina, Golfo de Guacanayabo, C. Cruz, Sagua la Grande, Esmeralda, Cayman Islands (U.K.), Grand Cayman, Little Cayman, Cayman Brac

PUERTO RICO (U.S.A.)

San Juan, Arecibo, Caguas, Mayagüez, Aguadilla, Ponce, Pico de Punta 1338, Mona Passage, I. Mona

HAITI / DOMINICAN REPUBLIC

Cap-Haïtien, Port-de-Paix, Gonaïves, Port-au-Prince, Les Cayes, Jacmel, Anse d'Hainault, La Gonâve, I. de la Gonâve, Massif de la Hotte, Golfe de la Gonâve, Massif de la Selle 2680, Santiago, S. Francisco, Puerto Plata, Samaná, La Romana, San Pedro, Santo Domingo, Cordillera Central Pico Duarte 3175, Baní, Barahona, I. Beata, C. Beata, Windward Passage, Jamaica Channel

Hispaniola

VENEZUELA

Caracas, Maiquetía, Maracay, Valencia, Pto Cabello, Barcelona, Cumaná, Guanta, Pto la Cruz, Carúpano, Maturín, El Tigre, Cd Bolívar, Cd Guayana, Tucupita, Güiria, Barquisimeto, Acarigua, Guanare, S. Felipe, San Juan, San Fernando, San Carlos, Calabozo, El Baúl, El Sombrero, Coro, Dabajuro, Pto Fijo, G. de Venezuela, Maracaibo, Cabimas, Lago de Maracaibo, Valledupar, Pen. de la Guajira, Riohacha, Trujillo, Valera, Mérida, Sierra Nevada Pico Bolívar 5007, San Cristóbal, Barinas, Isla Margarita, La Asunción, Porlamar, I. de Coche, I. Los Testigos, Los Roques (Ven.), La Blanquilla (Ven.), Isla la Tortuga, La Orchila, Los Hermanos

COLOMBIA

Barranquilla, Cartagena, Santa Marta, Ciénaga, Sierra Nevada de Sta Marta 5775, Soledad, Sabanalarga, Plato, El Banco, Sincelejo, Montería, Sincé, S. Onofre, Gulf of Darién, Acandí

Netherlands Antilles

Aruba (Neth.), Curaçao (Neth.), Bonaire (Neth.), Willemstad, Oranjestad

Lesser Antilles / Leeward Islands / Windward Islands

Anguilla (U.K.), St Martin (Fr. & Neth.), St Kitts & Nevis, Antigua & Barbuda (U.K.), Barbuda, Montserrat (U.K.), Guadeloupe (Fr.), Pointe-à-Pitre, Basse Terre, Marie Galante, Dominica, Roseau, Martinique (Fr.), Fort-de-France, St Lucia, Castries, St Vincent, Kingstown, The Grenadines, Grenada, St George's, Barbados, Bridgetown, Virgin Is U.S.A. & U.K., St Croix, Windward Islands, PUERTO RICO TRENCH

TRINIDAD AND TOBAGO

Port of Spain, San Fernando, Trinidad, Tobago, Scarborough

CARIBBEAN SEA

PANAMA

Colón, Panamá, La Chorrera, Panama Canal, Arch. de las Perlas, Penonomé, David, Pto Armuelles

COSTA RICA

San José, Cartago, Alajuela, Heredia, Limón, B. de Coronado

NICARAGUA

Bluefields, Puerto Cabezas, Rio Grande, Prinzapolca, San Juan del Norte, Cabo Gracias á Dios, Cayos Miskito, I. del Maíz (Nic. & U.S.A.), Corn Is, à I. de San Andrés (Col.), à I. de Providencia (Col.)

HONDURAS

Cayos Cabezas, Caratasca, Brus Laguna, Laguna de Caratasca, Swan I. (Hond.)

1:10M

0 100 200 300 400 km

0 100 200 mls

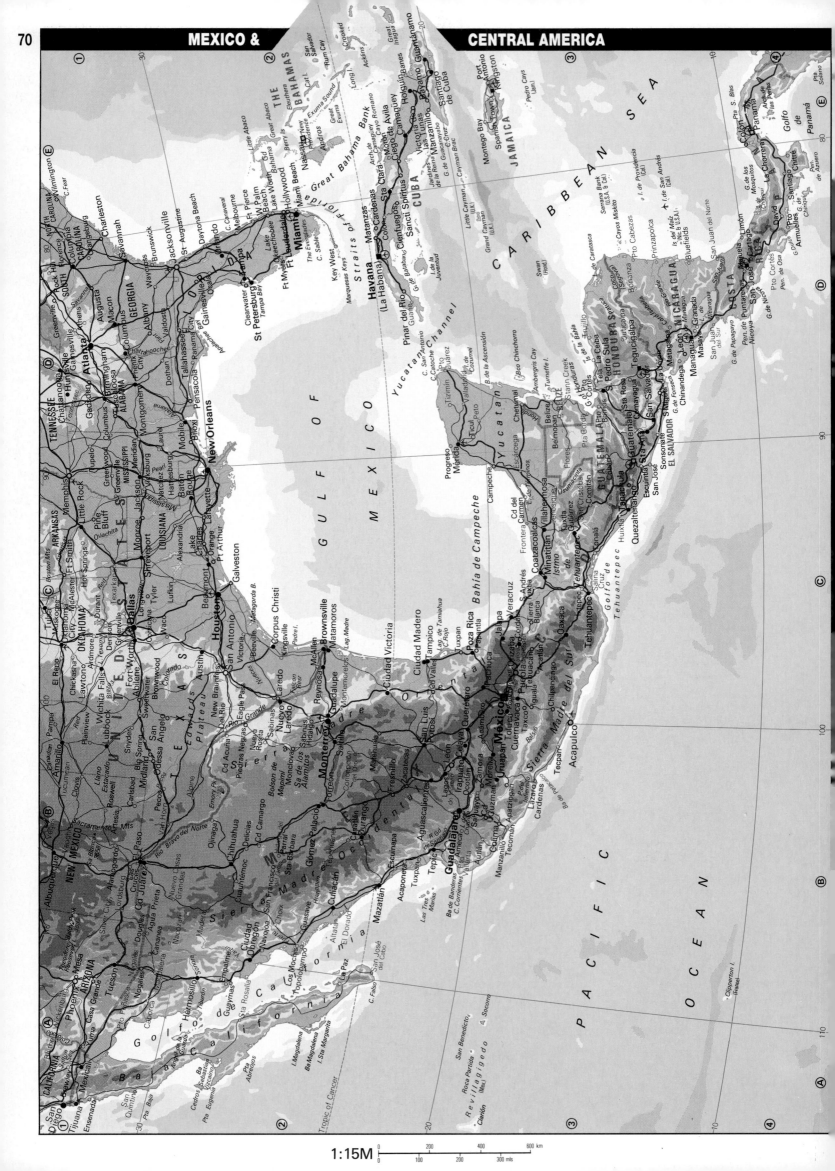

1:15M

0   200   400   600 km
0   100   200   300 mts

Gulf of Mexico

① Tropic of Cancer ①

U.S.A.
● Miami

THE BAHAMAS

● Habana

● Mérida

CUBA

○ Guantanamo

MEXICO

□ **BELIZE**
Belmopan

GUATEMALA
□ Guatemala
□ **HONDURAS**
□ **S.Salvador** Tegucigalpa
□ **EL SALVADOR**

② Santiago de Cuba

DOMINICAN REP.
○ Santiago
○ Santo Domingo

JAMAICA
○ Kingston

○ Port au Prince
HAITI

Pto Rico (U.S.A.)
□ San Juan
St Kitts – Nevis

ANTIGUA & BARBUDA
Guadeloupe (Fr.)

DOMINICA
Martinique (Fr.)

ST LUCIA
ST VINCENT

BARBADOS

GRENADA

NICARAGUA
● Managua

COSTA RICA
○ S.José
□ Colón
□ Panamá
PANAMA

I. del Coco (C.R.)

C A R I B B E A N   S E A

○ Sta Marta
○ Barranquilla
○ Cartagena

● Maracaibo ● **Caracas**
○ Barcelona
○ Barquisimeto

Port of Spain
TRINIDAD & TOBAGO

○ S.Cristóbal
Orinoco
○ Cd. Bolívar
○ Cd. Guayana

Malpelo (Col.)

③ Buenaventura

○ Medellín
○ Manizales
● **Bogotá**
○ Cali
○ Popayán
Pasto ○

VENEZUELA

Georgetown
□ **GUYANA**
Paramaribo □
SURINAM
Cayenne □
FR. GUIANA

③

COLOMBIA

○ Boa Vista
Branco

○ S.Lorenzo

Equator 0

Galapagos Is (Ecu.)

Quito ●
ECUADOR

Putumayo

Negro

Macapá ○
I. de Marajó
Amazon

S.Pedro e S.Paulo (Braz.)

Equator 0

○ Guayaquil
○ Iquitos

Marañón

Juruá

Manaus ○
○ Santarém

● Belém

São Luís ○
Codó ○
○ Sobral
○ Teresina

○ Fortaleza
Rocas

I. Fernando de Noronha (Braz.)

④ ○ Piura
Ucayali
Purus
Amazon
Xingu
Tapajós
Madeira
Tocantins

○ Natal
○ João Pessoa
● **Recife**

④

○ Chiclayo
○ Trujillo
○ Chimbote

PERU

○ Rio Branco
Pto Velho ○

○ Juazeiro

Maceió ○
○ Aracajú

B R A Z I L

○ Callao
● **Lima**
○ Huancayo

Pto Maldonado ○

São Francisco

○ Alagoinhas
● **Salvador**

⑤ ○ Cuzco

○ Arequipa

● La Paz
○ Oruro
BOLIVIA
○ Cochabamba
○ Sucre
○ Sta Cruz

○ Cáceres
○ Cuiabá

○ Goiânia
□ Brasília

○ Ilhéus

○ Montes Claros

⑤

○ Arica
○ Iquique

○ Corumbá

○ Campo Grande
○ Dourados

○ Ribeirão Prêto
○ Corinto
● **Belo Horizonte**

○ Vitória

S O U T H

P A C I F I C

O C E A N

⑥ ○ Antofagasta
Tropic of Capricorn

PARAGUAY
○ Concepción

○ Campinas
□ Juiz de Fora
○ Campos

Trindade (Braz.)

S.Félix (Chile)

○ Salta
Salado

○ Asunción
○ Foz do Iguacu

○ Ponta Grossa
● **São Paulo**
○ Santos
● **Rio de Janeiro**

C H I L E

○ S.Miguel de Tucumán
○ Resistencia

○ Posadas

○ Curitiba

Juan Fernández Is. (Chile)

Paraná

○ Florianópolis

⑥

○ Córdoba
○ Rivera

A R G E N T I N A

○ Santa Fe
○ Paraná
Paraná

○ Paysandú
URUGUAY

○ Pelotas
○ Rio Grande

○ Pto Alegre

S O U T H

⑦ ○ Viña del Mar
○ Valparaíso
● **Santiago**

○ Mendoza

○ Rosario

● **Buenos Aires**
○ Montevideo

R. de la Plata

A T L A N T I C

O C E A N

⑦

○ Talca
○ Concepción

Colorado

○ Bahía Blanca
○ Mar del Plata

Negro

○ Temuco
○ Valdivia

○ Pto Montt

Chico

○ Cmd. Rivadavia
G. San Jorge

Deseado

⑧ Falkland Is (U.K.)
○ Stanley

⑧

○ Rio Gallegos

○ Pto Natales
○ Punta Arenas
Tierra del Fuego
Cape Horn

S.Georgia (U.K.)

S.Shetland Is (U.K.)

S.Orkney Is (U.K.)

S.Sandwich Is (U.K.)

Ⓓ Ⓔ Ⓕ Ⓖ Ⓗ

Ⓒ

Ⓑ

ANTARCTICA

Ⓐ

⑨

1:35M

0   250   500   750   1000   1250 km

0   250   500   750 mls

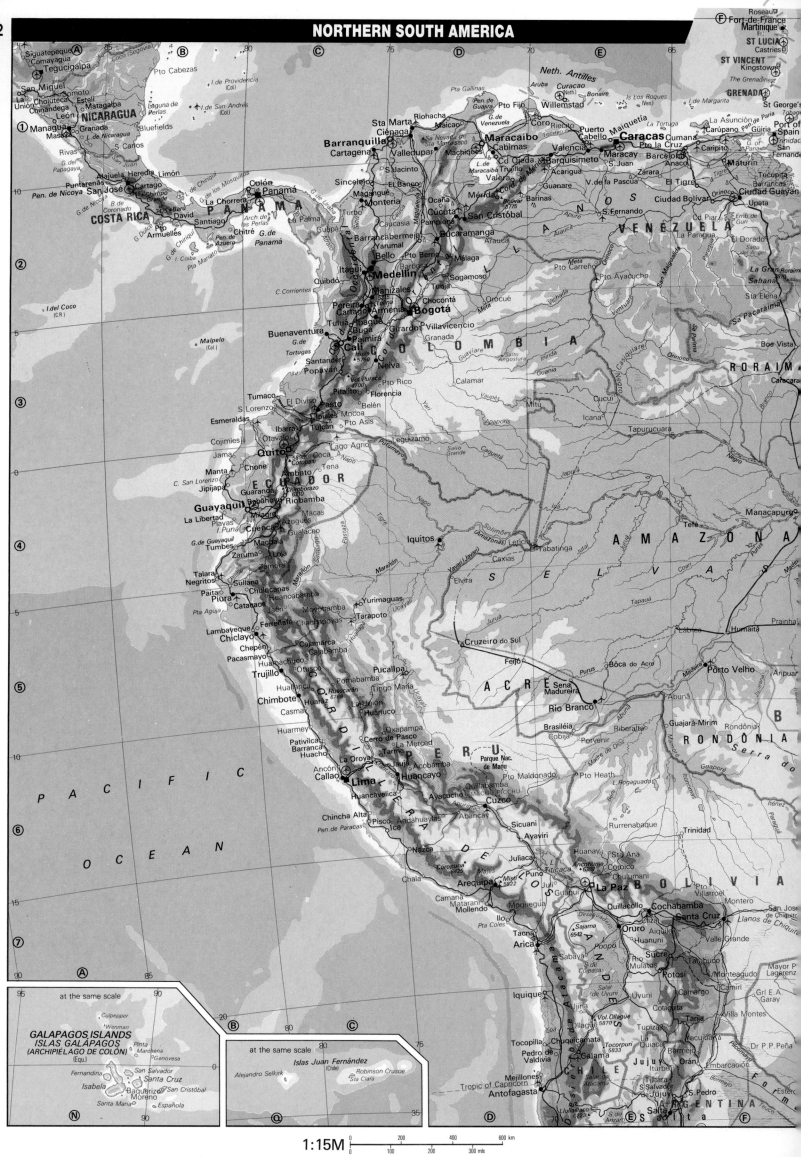

GALAPAGOS ISLANDS
ISLAS GALÁPAGOS
(ARCHIPIÉLAGO DE COLÓN)
(Equ.)

at the same scale

Islas Juan Fernández
(Chile)

at the same scale

1:15M

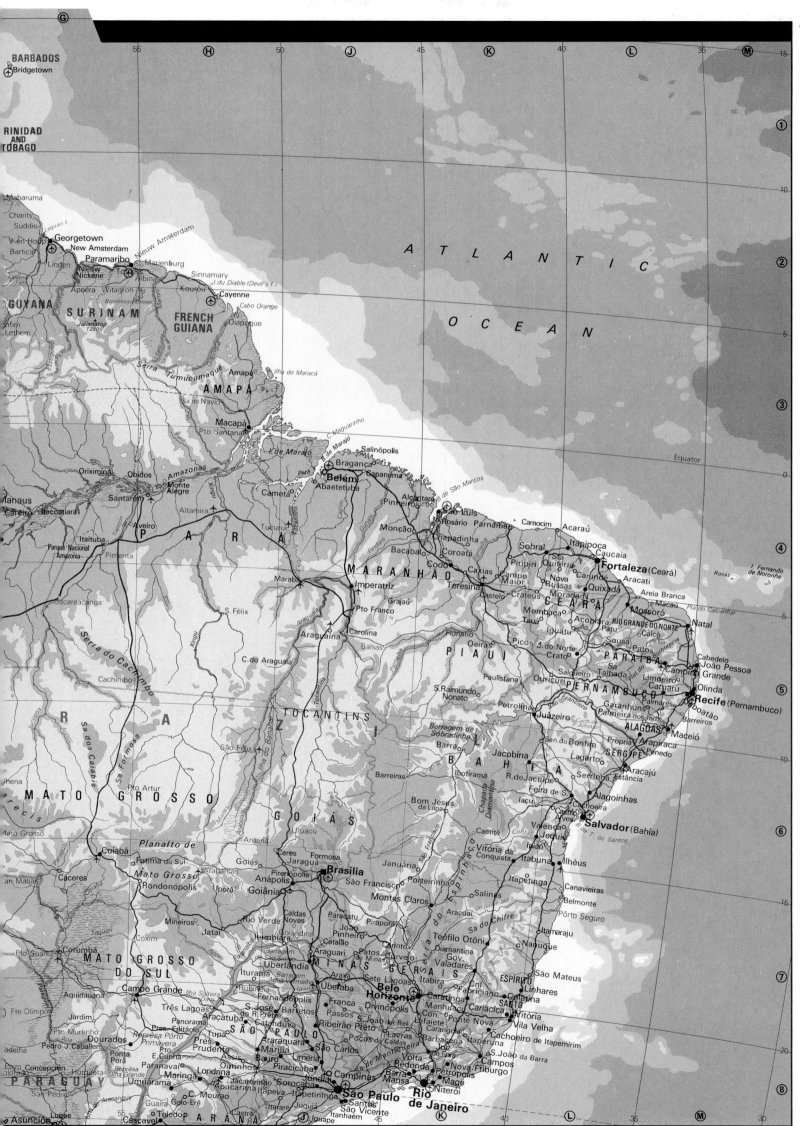

1:15M

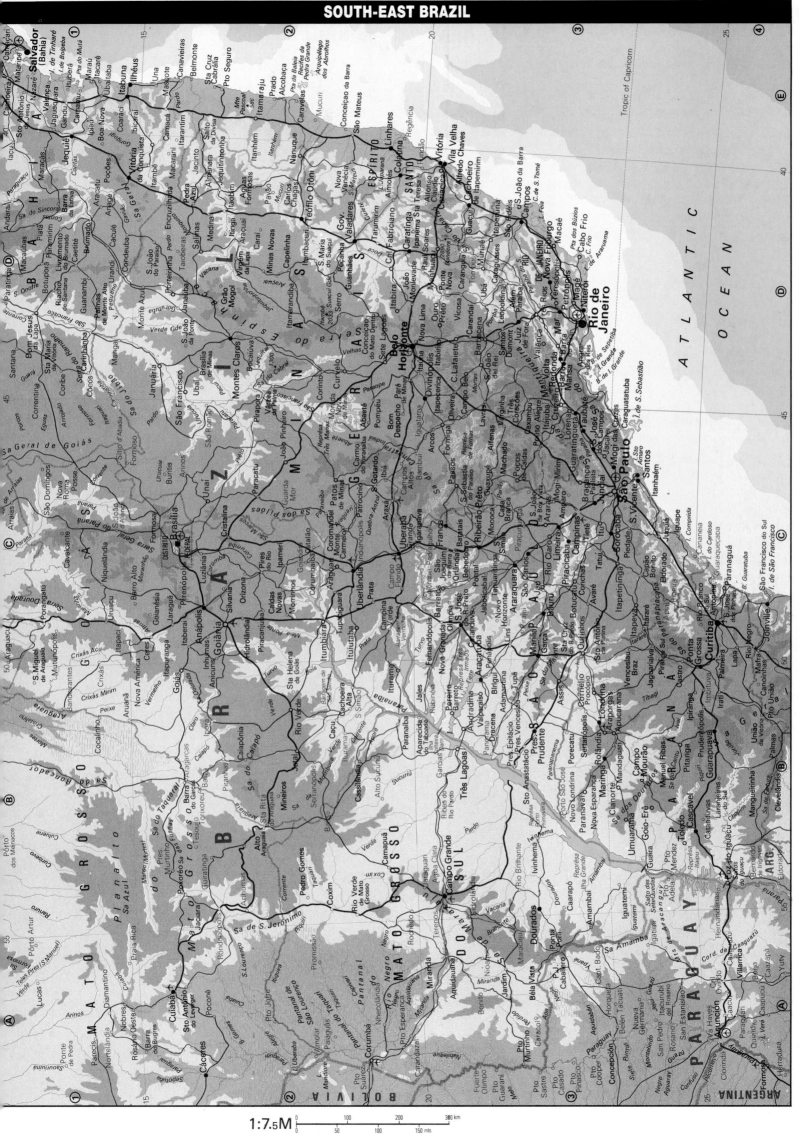

1:7.5M

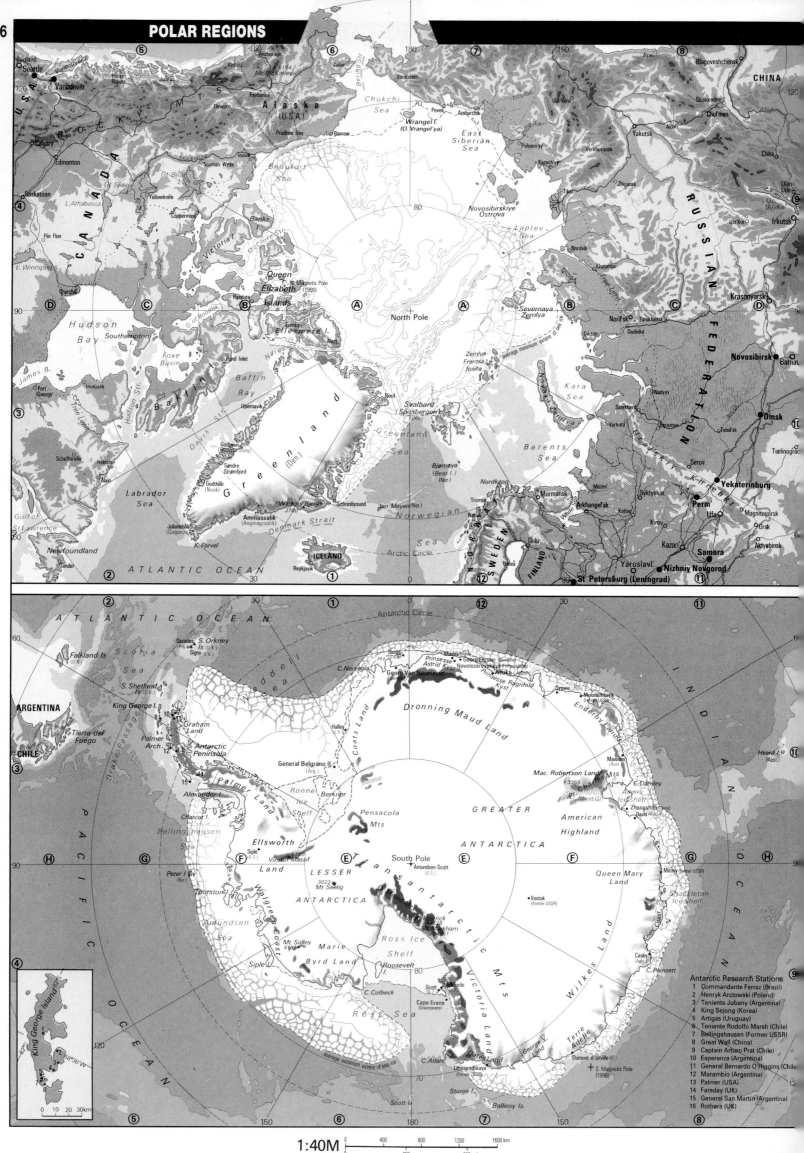

Antarctic Research Stations
1 Commandante Ferraz (Brazil)
2 Henryk Arctowski (Poland)
3 Teniente Jubany (Argentina)
4 King Sejong (Korea)
5 Artigas (Uruguay)
6 Teniente Rodolfo Marsh (Chile)
7 Bellingshausen (Former USSR)
8 Great Wall (China)
9 Captain Arturo Prat (Chile)
10 Esperanza (Argentina)
11 General Bernardo O'Higgins (Chile)
12 Marambio (Argentina)
13 Palmer (USA)
14 Faraday (UK)
15 General San Martin (Argentina)
16 Rothera (UK)

1:40M

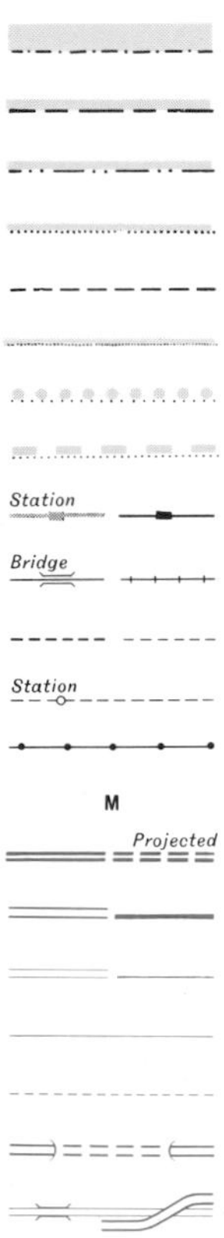

International Boundary
State Boundary
Department Boundary
City Limits
Borough, District Boundary
Military Zones
Armistice, Ceasefire Line
Demilitarised Zone
Station Main Railways
Bridge Other Railways
Projected Railways
Station Underground Railway
Aerial Cableway, Funicular
M Metro Stations
Projected Special Highway
Main Road
Secondary Road
Other Road, Street
Track
Road Tunnel
Bridge, Flyover

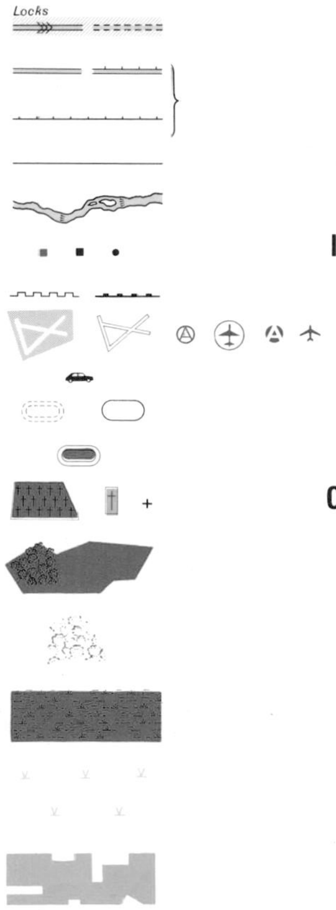

Locks Seaway
Canals
Drainage Canal
Waterfalls, Rapids
Important Buildings
Historic Walls
Airports
Car Ferry
Racecourses
Stadium
Cemetery, Churches
Woodland, Park
Jungle
Mangrove Swamp
Farmland
Built-up Area

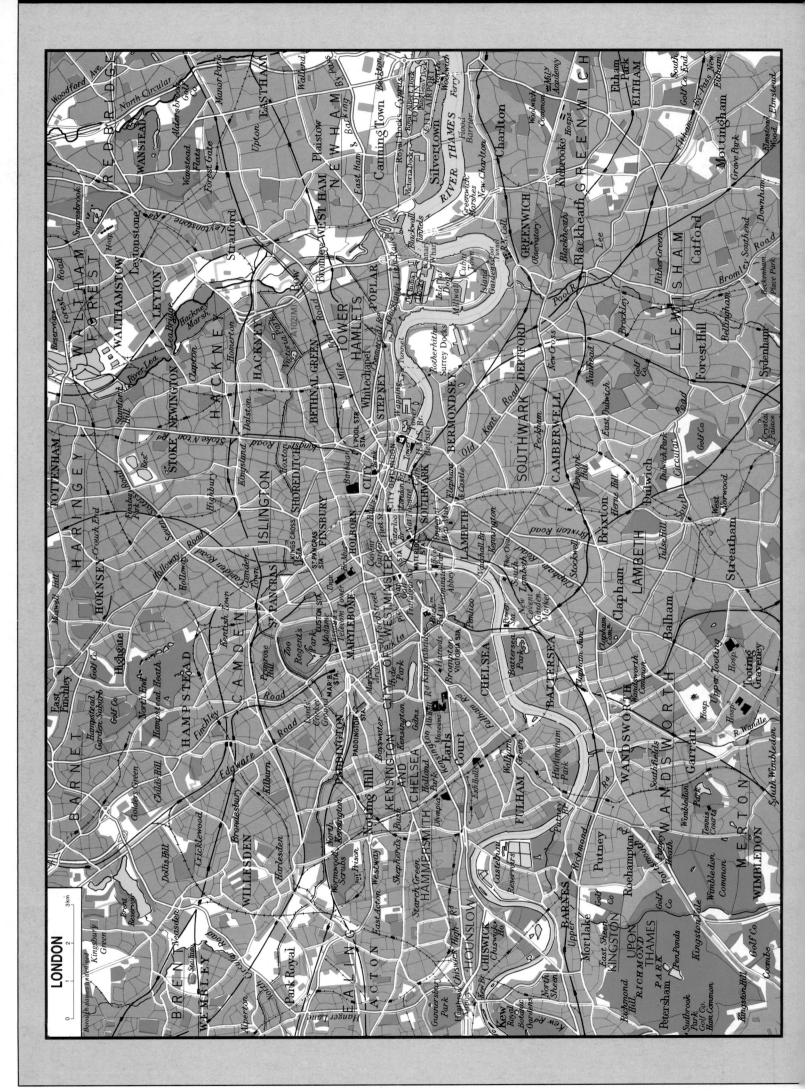

LONDON

3 km
2
1
0

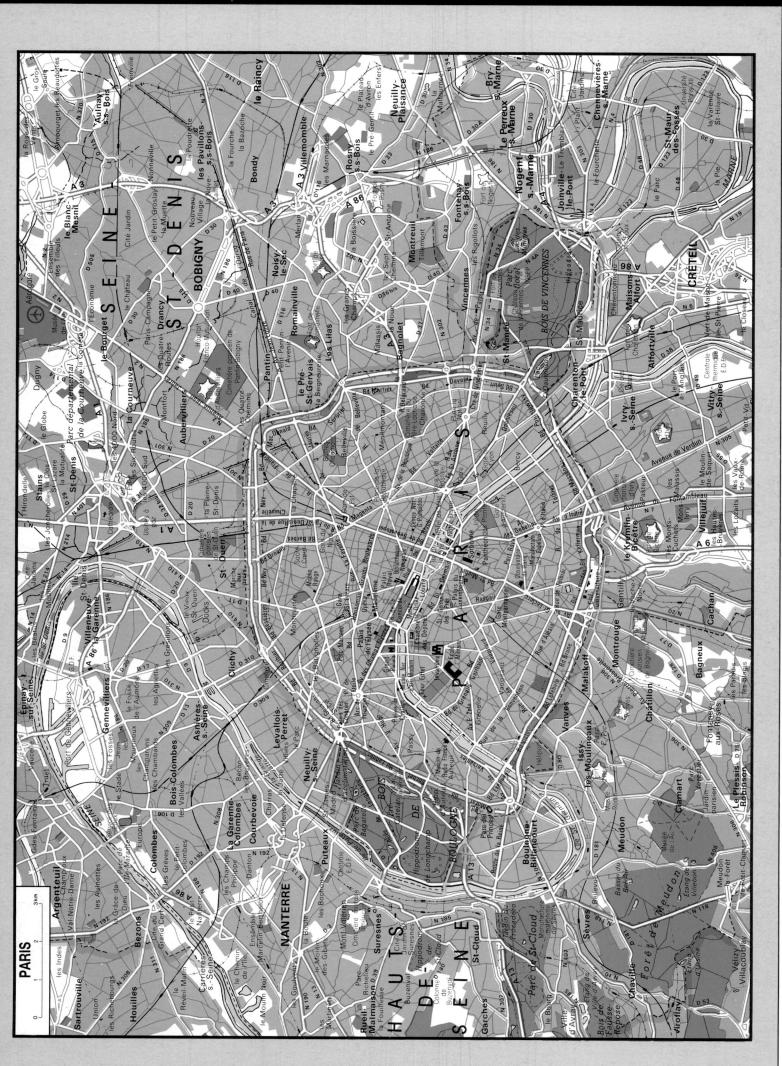

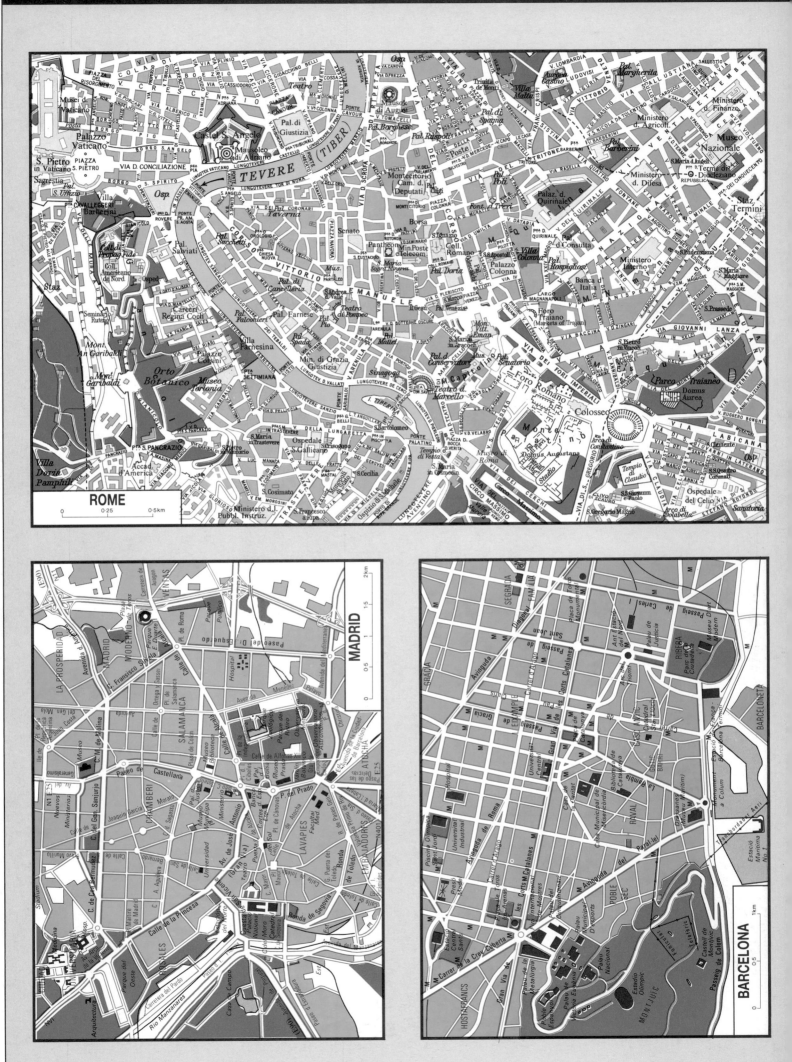

ROME

0   0·25   0·5km

MADRID

0   0·5   1   1·5   2km

BARCELONA

0   0·5   1km

VIENNA

0   0·25   0·5km

AMSTERDAM

BRUSSELS

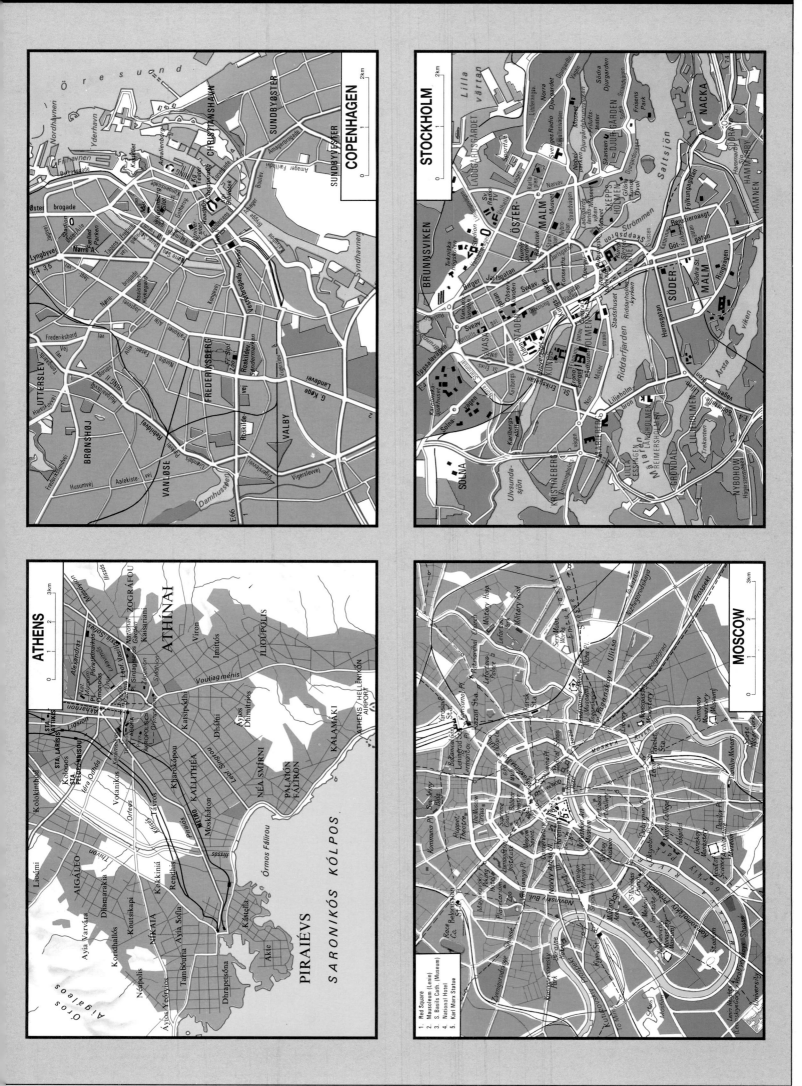

COPENHAGEN

STOCKHOLM

ATHENS

MOSCOW

1. Red Square
2. Mausoleum (Lenin)
3. S. Basils Cath. (Museum)
4. National Hotel
5. Karl Marx Statue

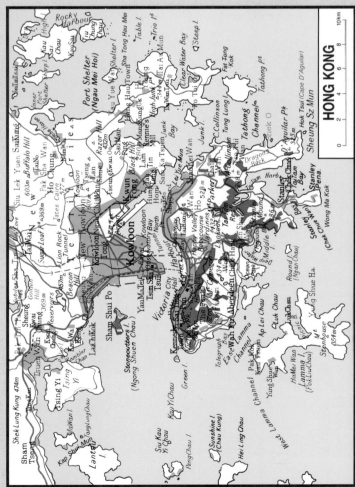

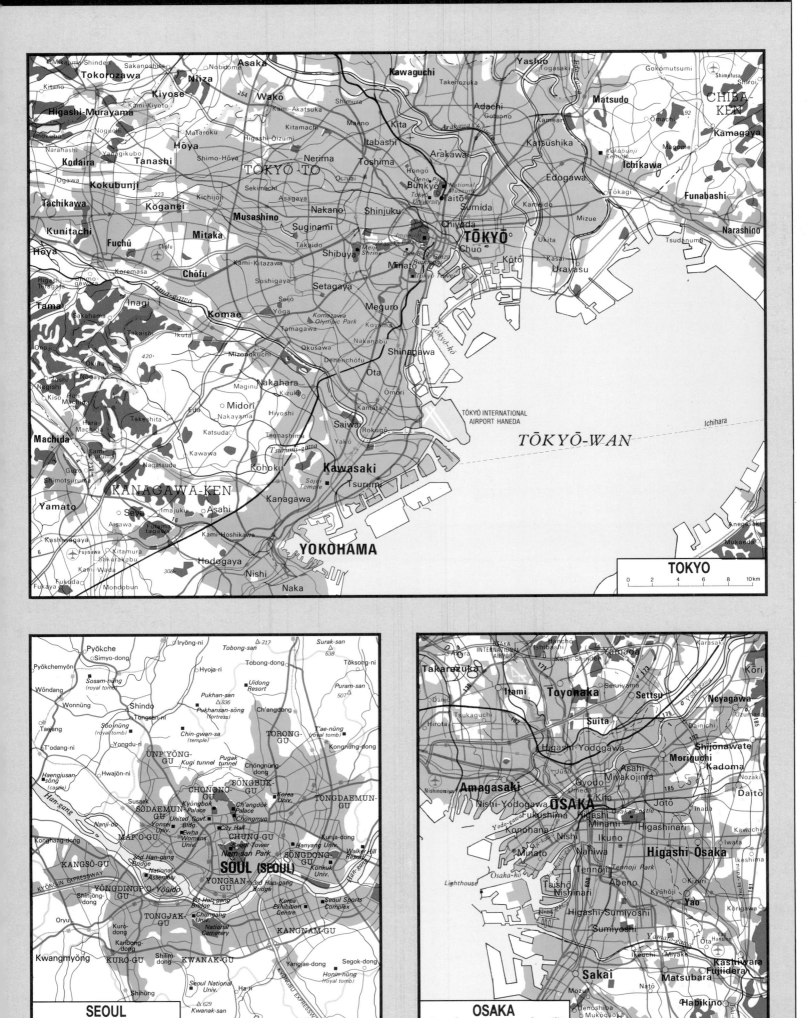

TOKYO

TŌKYŌ-WAN

TŌKYŌ INTERNATIONAL
AIRPORT HANEDA

0 2 4 6 8 10km

SEOUL

0 2 4 6 8 10km

OSAKA

0 2 4 6 8 10km

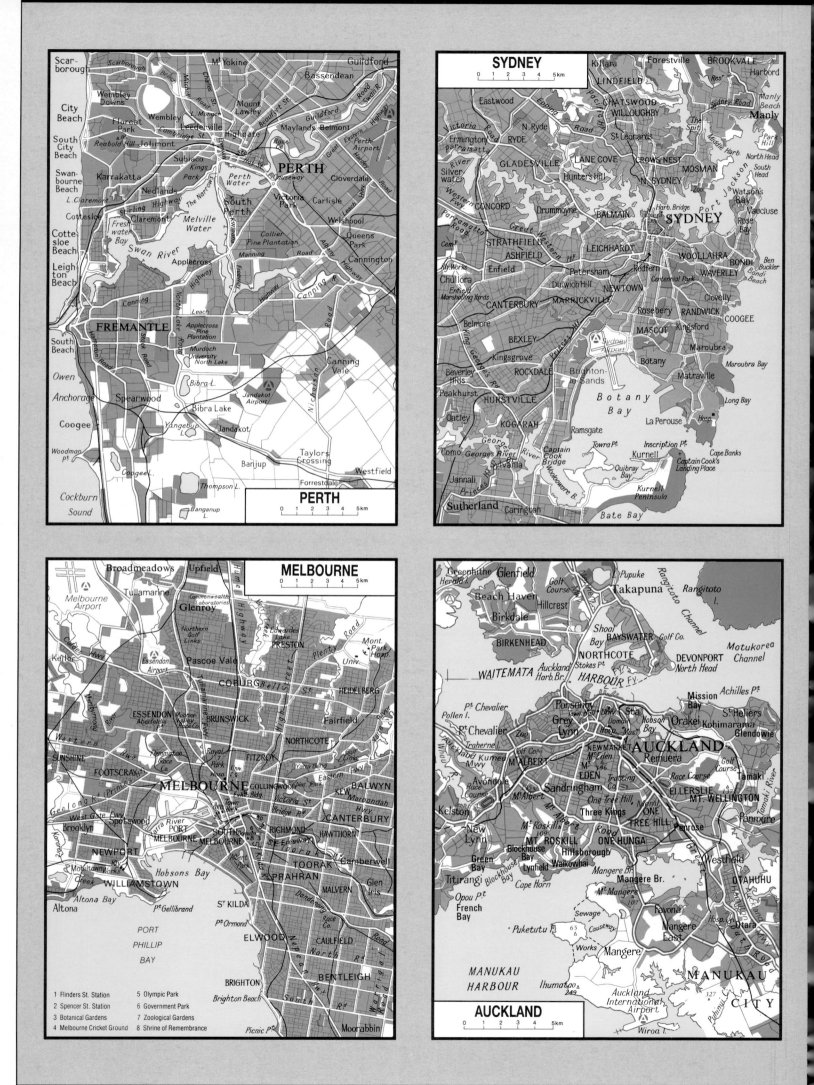

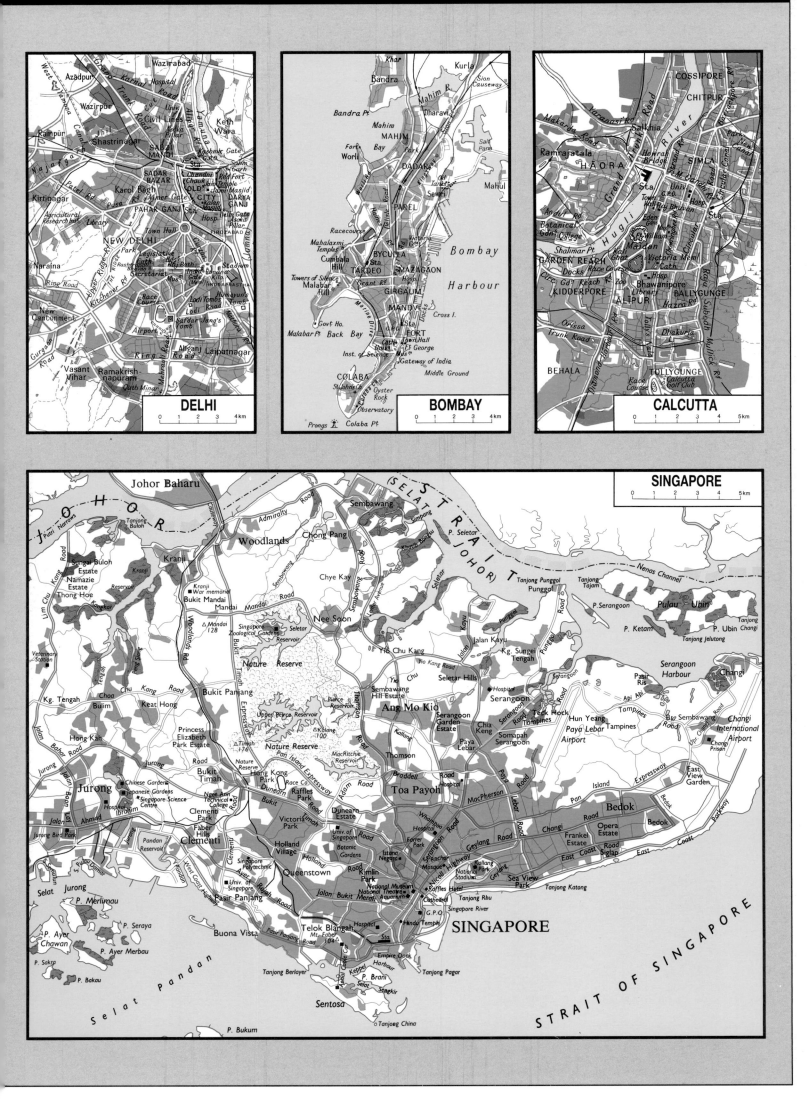

DELHI

0 1 2 3 4km

BOMBAY

0 1 2 3 4km

CALCUTTA

0 1 2 3 4 5km

SINGAPORE

0 1 2 3 4 5km

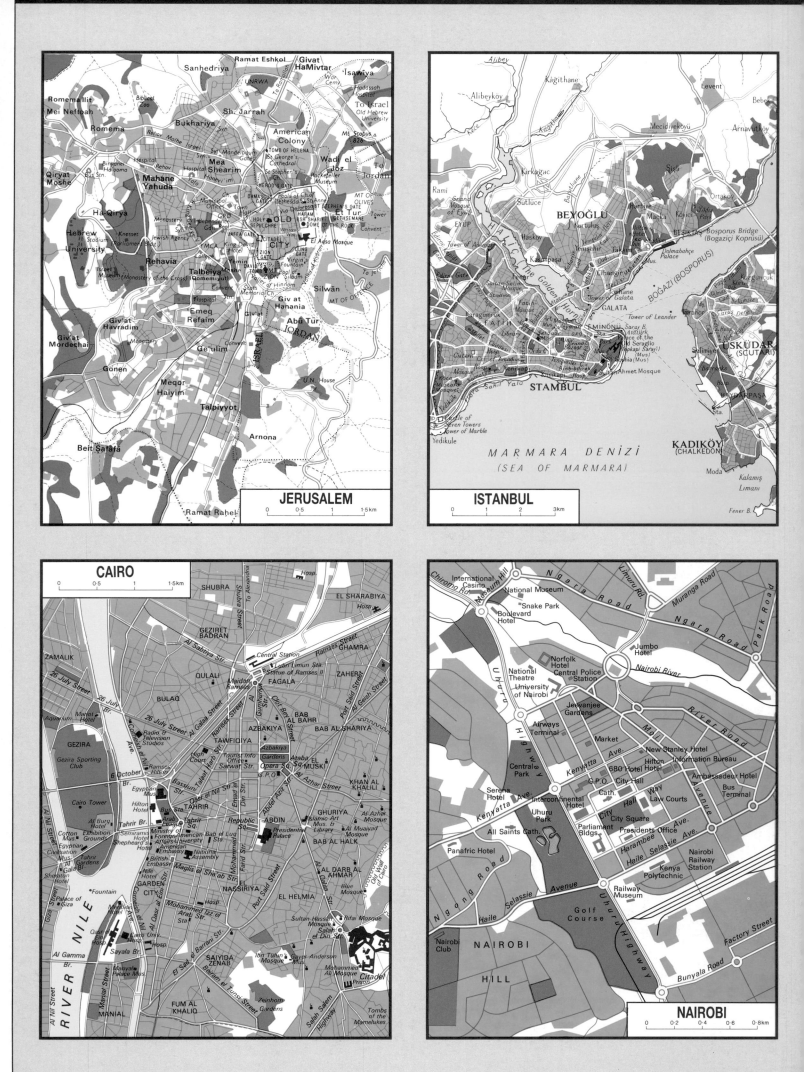

JERUSALEM

Romema llit
Mei Neftoah
Romema
Qiryat Moshe
Ha-Qirya
Hebrew University
Rehavia
Talbeiya (Qomemiyut)
Giv'at Havradim
Giv'at Mordechai
Gonen
Meqor Haiyim
Talpiyyot
Beit Safafa
Arnona
Ramat Rahel

Ramat Eshkol
Sanhedriya
UNRWA
Sh. Jarrah
Bukhariya
American Colony
Mea Shearim
Mahane Yahuda
Emeq Refaim
Giv'at Hanania
Abu Tur
Ge'ulim
Silwan

Ramat HaMivtar
Isawiya
War Cem.
Hadassah Hospital
To Israel Old Hebrew University
Wadi el Joz
Et Tur
MT. OF OLIVES
MT OF OFFENCE
JORDAN
ISR-EL
To Jordan

OLD CITY
DOME OF THE ROCK
El Aqsa Mosque

0   0.5   1   1.5km

ISTANBUL

Alibey
Kağıthane
Levent
Alibeyköy
Bebek
Mecidiyeköy
Arnavutköy
Kirkağaç
Şişli
Rami
BEYOĞLU
Ortaköy
EYÜP
BEŞİKTAŞ
Bosporus Bridge (Boğaziçi Köprüsü)
Hasköy
Sütlüce
Kasımpaşa
GALATA
BOGAZİ (BOSPORUS)
Üsküdar (SCUTARI)
FATİH
Tower of Leander
EMİNÖNÜ
STAMBUL
HAYDARPAŞA Sta.
KADIKÖY (CHALKEDON)
Yedikule
Moda
Kalamış Limanı

MARMARA DENİZİ
(SEA OF MARMARA)

0   1   2   3km

Fener B.

CAIRO

0   0.5   1   1.5km

SHUBRA
EL SHARABIYA
GEZIRET BADRAN
GHAMRA
ZAMALIK
QULALI
FAGALA
ZAHERI
BULAQ
AZBAKIYA
BAB AL BAHR
BAB AL SHARIYA
GEZIRA
TAWFIQIYA
KHAN AL KHALILI
TAHRIR
GHURIYA
ABDIN
Republic Sq.
EL MUSKI
Al Azhar Mosque
BAB AL HALK
GARDEN CITY
NASSIRIYA
EL HELMIA
AL DARB AL AHMAR
MANIAL
SAIYIDA ZENAB
FUM AL KHALIQ
Citadel
Tombs of the Mamelukes

RIVER NILE

NAIROBI

International Casino
Chiromo Rd
Museum Hill
National Museum
Snake Park
Boulevard Hotel
Ngara Road
Limuru Rd.
Muranga Road
Jumbo Hotel
Norfolk Hotel
Central Police Station
Nairobi River
River Road
National Theatre
University of Nairobi
Jeevanjee Gardens
Airways Terminal
Market
New Stanley Hotel
Hilton Hotel
Information Bureau
Central Park
Ambassadeur Hotel
Bus Terminal
Serena Hotel
Intercontinental Hotel
Uhuru Park
City Hall
Law Courts
City Square
Parliament Bldgs.
Presidents Office
All Saints Cath.
Harambee Ave.
Panafric Hotel
Nairobi Railway Station
Kenya Polytechnic
Railway Museum
Golf Course
NAIROBI HILL
Nairobi Club
Bunyala Road
Factory Street
Uhuru Highway

0   0.2   0.4   0.6   0.8km

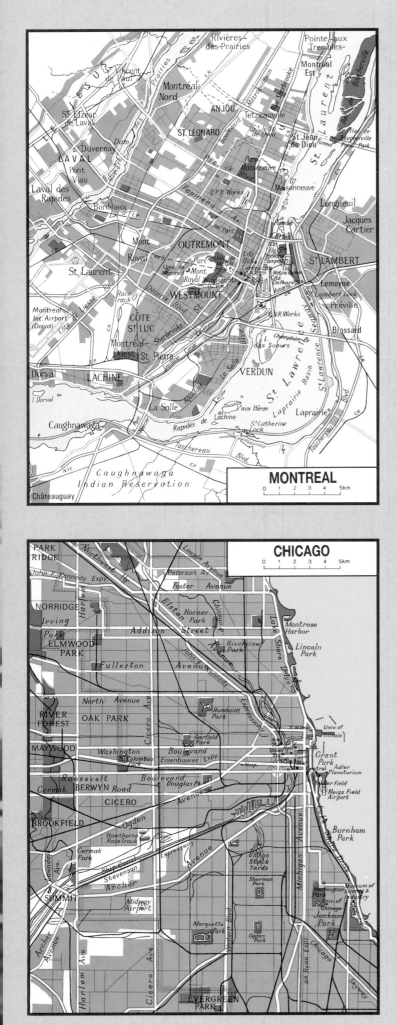

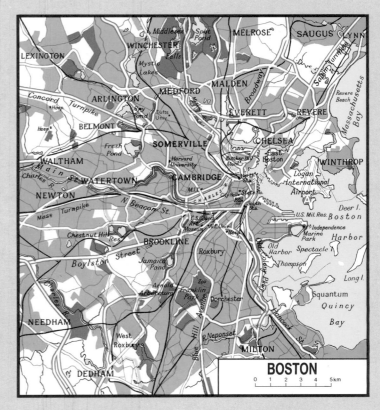

OTTAWA

0 1 2 3 4 5km

MONTREAL

0 1 2 3 4 5km

TORONTO

0 1 2 3 4 5km

CHICAGO

0 1 2 3 4 5km

BOSTON

0 1 2 3 4 5km

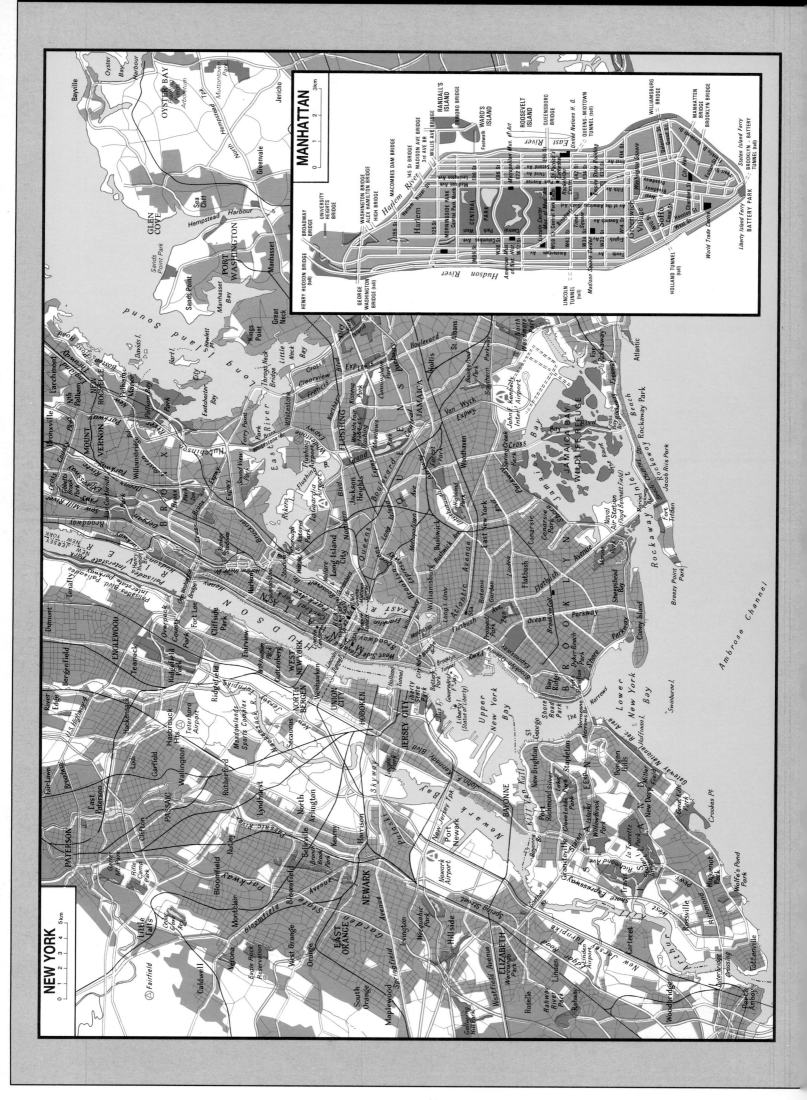

MANHATTAN

0 1 2 3km

BROADWAY BRIDGE
WASHINGTON BRIDGE
ALEX. HAMILTON BRIDGE
HIGH BRIDGE
MACOMBES DAM BRIDGE
145 St BRIDGE
MADISON AVE BRIDGE
3rd AVE BR
WILLIS AVE BRIDGE
RANDALL'S ISLAND
TRIBORO BRIDGE
WARD'S ISLAND
Footwalk
Metropolitan Mus. of Art
ROOSEVELT ISLAND
QUEENSBORO BRIDGE
QUEENS-MIDTOWN TUNNEL (toll)
United Nations H.Q.
WILLIAMSBURG BRIDGE
MANHATTEN BRIDGE
BROOKLYN BRIDGE

UNIVERSITY HEIGHTS BRIDGE
HENRY HUDSON BRIDGE (toll)
GEORGE WASHINGTON BRIDGE (toll)

Harlem River

East River

155 St
Harlem
MORNINGSIDE PARK
CENTRAL PARK
Empire State Building
Rockefeller Center
Lincoln Center (Mus. & Art)
American Mus. of Nat. Hist.
Madison Square Garden
Greenwich Village
SoHo
City Hall
Washington Square

LINCOLN TUNNEL (toll)
HOLLAND TUNNEL (toll)

Hudson River

World Trade Center
Liberty Island Ferry
Staten Island Ferry
BATTERY PARK
BROOKLYN – BATTERY TUNNEL (toll)

NEW YORK

0 1 2 3 4 5km

(Detailed metropolitan map of the New York – Manhattan area, showing Oyster Bay, Glen Cove, Port Washington, Long Island Sound, The Bronx, Mount Vernon, New Rochelle, Flushing, Jamaica, La Guardia Airport, John F. Kennedy Intnl. Airport, Jamaica Bay Wildlife Refuge, Queens, Brooklyn, Coney Island, Rockaway, Paterson, Newark, Elizabeth, Jersey City, Hoboken, Bayonne, Staten Island, Upper New York Bay, Lower New York Bay, Ambrose Channel, and surrounding communities.)

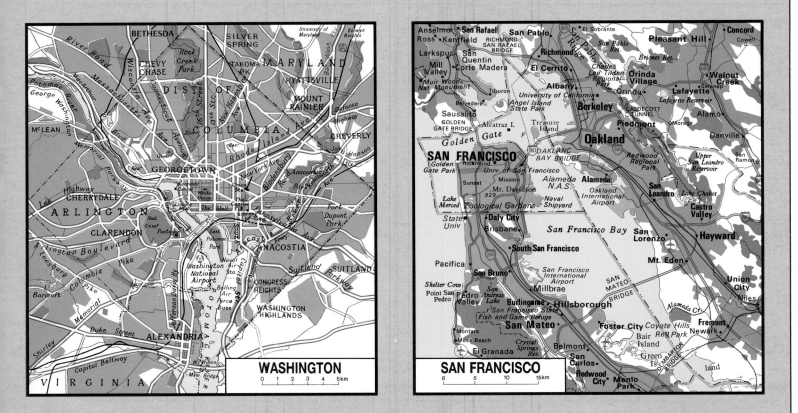

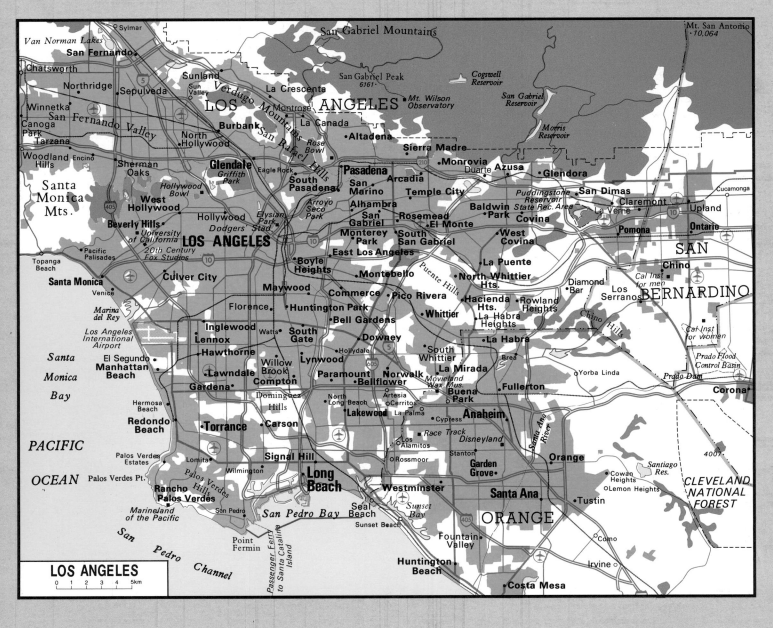

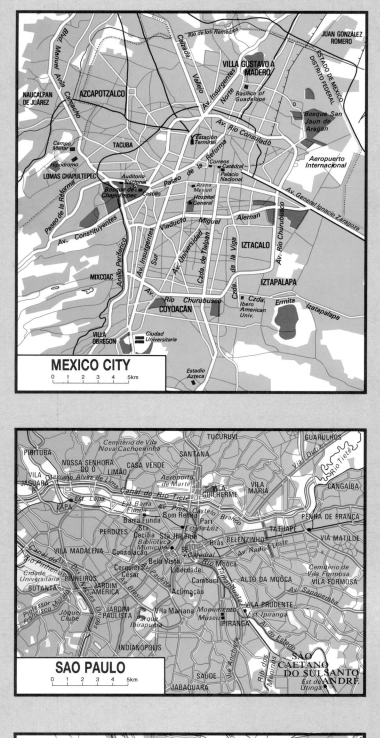

MEXICO CITY

0 1 2 3 4 5km

SAO PAULO

0 1 2 3 4 5km

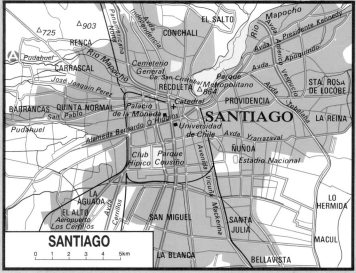

SANTIAGO

0 1 2 3 4 5km

RIO DE JANEIRO

0 2 4 6 8 10km

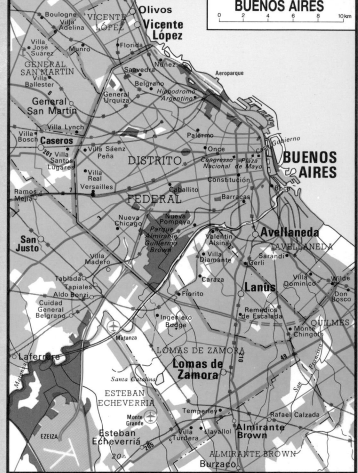

BUENOS AIRES

0 2 4 6 8 10km

The roman alphabet is used world-wide. Yet the sounds of Latin from which it was inherited were far too few to allow the alphabet to be applied unaltered to the languages of the world. As a result numerous modifications have been made by adding supplementary letters, by changing the original letters or by adding accents or other diacritical signs.

This brief guide is intended to give no more than an indication of the English language equivalents of the more important letters or combinations of letters in the various alphabets used in the Atlas. An English word is added in brackets to illustrate the sound intended.

FRENCH
There are four nasal vowels:
am an aen em en aon   ã
aim ain en eim ein im in   ē
om on   ō
um un   ẽũ are like a in hart; e in met; o in corn;
oo in book pronounced nasally.
au, eau = o (no); é = ay (lay); è, ê, = e (met);
oi oî = wa (wand)
c + a = k; c + e or i = ç = s (sit)
ch = sh (fresh); g + a, o or u = g (got)
g + e or i = j = zh*; gn = ni (onion)
gu = g (got); gü = gw (iguana)
ll = l or y; qu = k; th = t
u = between e in few and oo in too

SPANISH
c + a, o or u = k; c + e or i = th (thin) or s (sit)
ch = ch (cheese); g + a, o or u = g (got)
g + e or i = kh*; gu + a, o or u = gw (iguana)
gu + e or i = g (got); j = kh*; ñ = ny (canyon);
ll = y (yes)
qu + a, o or u = kw (quick); qu + e or i = k (kite)
y = y (yes); z = th (thin) or z depending on dialect

ITALIAN
c + a, o or u = k; c + e or i = ch (cheese)
ch = k
g + a, o or u = g (got); g + e or i = j (jet)
gh = g (got); gli = lli (million)
qu = kw (quick); z = ts or dz

ROMANIAN
ă = a in relative
â = i in ravine
c + a, o or u = k
c + e or i = ch (cheese); ch = k
g + a, o or u = g (got); g + e or i = j (jet)
ş = sh (fresh); ţ = ts (sits)

PORTUGUESE
ã, ãe = French ē
õa, õe = French ō
c + a, o or u = k; c + e or i = s
ç = s; ch = sh (fresh)
ih = lli (million)
x = sh (fresh); z = z but = zh when final

GERMAN
ä = e (met); au = ow (down)
äu = oy (boy); c = ts (sits)
ch = kh*; ei, ey = eye (= y in why)
eu = oy (boy); g = g (got)
ie = ie (retrieve); j = y (yes)
ö = oo (book); s = z but s when final
sch = sh (fresh); sp, st = shp, sht
ü = French u; v = f; w = v; z = ts (sits)

DUTCH
aa ee are long vowels
c + e or i or z = s, otherwise k
ij = eye (= y in why)

SCANDINAVIAN
å = aw (law); ä = e (met)
ø = oo (book); øj = oy (boy)
j = y (yes)

ICELANDIC
ð = dh = th (then)
hv = kw; ll = tl; p = th

FINNISH
ay = eye (= y in why)
j = y; y = French u; w = v

HUNGARIAN
a = aw (law); cs = ch (cheese); ccs = chch;
gy = d + y (dew)
j = y; ny = ny (canyon)
s = sh (fresh); ss = shsh
sz = s (sit); ty = t + y (yes)
zs = zh*
ai = e (met); av = au or av
dh = th (then); th = th (thin)
kh = kh*; oi = i (ravine)
ou = oo (too)

TURKISH
c = j (jet); ç = ch (cheese)
ö = oo (book); ş = sh
ü = French u
ı and i = i (ravine)

RUSSIAN
ay = a + y (yes)
e = e or ye
ë = yaw; ëy = yoy
ch = ch (cheese); sh = sh (fresh)
sh ch = sh ch (fresh cheese)
ts = ts (sits)
ya = ya (yam); z = z (zoo)
zh = zh (measure)
' = sound of y (yes)
" = silent

OTHER SLAVONIC

§S-C	Pol	Cz		
c	c	c	=	ts (sits)
	ć		=	ts + y (yes)
č	cz	č	=	ch (cheese)
ć			=	t + y (yes)
đ		ď	=	d + y (yes)
		ě	=	e (mother)
h	ch	ch	=	kh*
j	j	j	=	y (yes)
		ł	=	w (wood)
nj	ń	ň	=	ny (canyon)
		ř	=	rzh*
š	sz	š	=	sh (fresh)
		ť	=	t + y (yes)
ž	ž, rz, ź	ž	=	zh*

ARABIC
long vowels have a macron (bar), ā
dh = th (then)
h = h (hat); j = (jet)
gh = French r, pronounce as g (got)
kh = kh* q = g (got)
' and ' are best treated as glottal stops
ḍ ḥ ṣ ṭ ẓ = d, h, s, t, z
Note: 1. in Egypt and Sudan g = g (got)
2. in NW Africa Dj = j (jet)
ou = w (wadi)

FARSI (IRAN)
Can be read as Arabic above. Stress is on the last syllable.

SOMALI
long vowels are aa, ee, ii, oo, uu
c is silent = glottal stop
dh = th (then)
g = g (got); q = k (kite)
sh = sh (fresh); w = w (wadi)
x = kh*

MALAY – INDONESIAN
As English except
c = ch (cheese)

CHINESE (PINYIN)
q = ch (church); c = ts (sits)
x = hs = h + s

---

*zh = s in measure;
*kh = ch in Scottish loch
    = German ch in achtung

§**S-C** = Serbo-Croat
  Pol = Polish
  Cz = Czech

A

ABLATION The loss of water from ice and snow surfaces, by melting and run-off, calving of icebergs, evaporation and snow-blowing.

ABRASION The wearing down or away of rocks by friction.

ABSOLUTE HUMIDITY The amount of water vapour in a specified amount of air, frequently expressed as grams of water vapour per kilogram of dry air containing the vapour.

ABYSSAL Usually applied to the very deep parts of the oceans, over 3km below the surface.

ACCRETION The growth of objects by collection of additional material, usually of smaller size. Ice particles in the atmosphere can grow by this process.

ACID PRECIPITATION Rain and snow with a pH of less than 5.6.

ADVECTION Movement of a property in air and water by their motion. Usually applied to horizontal rather than vertical motion.

AEOLIAN Related to winds. Thus aeolian geomorphology is concerned with the processes whereby wind removes, distributes and deposits materials of the earth's surface.

AGGLOMERATE A rock made of small pieces of lava that have been fused by heat.

AGGRADATION The building up of a land surface by deposition of material by wind, water or ice.

AGGREGATE A loose collection of rock fragments.

ALLUVIAL PLAIN A plain, usually at low altitude, made of alluvium.

ANTICYCLONE An extensive region of relatively high atmospheric pressure, usually a few thousand kilometres across, in which the low level winds spiral outwards, clockwise in the northern hemisphere and anticlockwise in the southern hemisphere.

ARCHIPELAGO A sea or lake containing numerous islands, such as the area between Sumatra and the Philippines.

ARTESIAN WELL A well which taps water held under pressure in rocks below the surface. The pressure results in a well water level higher than the highest part of the water-bearing rocks.

ATOLL A coral reef surrounding a lagoon found in the tropical oceans.

AURORA BOREALIS (Northern Lights) Flashing lights in the atmosphere some 400km above polar regions caused by solar particles being trapped in the earth's magnetic field.

AVALANCHE The sudden and rapid movement of ice, snow, earth and rock down a slope.

AZIMUTH Horizontal angle between two directions.

B

BADLANDS Highly dissected landscapes, usually associated with poorly consolidated materials and sparse vegetation cover.

BAR A usually sandy feature, lying parallel to the coast and frequently underwater.

BARCHAN A crescentic sand dune whose horns point in the direction of dune movement.

BAROGRAPH An instrument for recording atmospheric pressure. The output is a graph of pressure changes through time.

BAROMETER An instrument for measuring atmospheric pressure. The reading is either by measuring the height of a column of mercury or by the compression or expansion of a series of vacuum chambers.

BARRIER REEF A coral reef characterized by the presence of a lagoon or body of water between it and the associated coastline.

BASALT A fine-grained and dark coloured igneous rock.

BASE LEVEL The lower limit to the operation of erosional processes generating on land – usually defined with reference to the role of running water. Sea level is the most general form of base level.

BASIN An area of land encompassing the water flow into any specific river channel – hence usually known as a drainage basin.

BATHOLITH A large mass of intrusive igneous rock.

BATHYMETRY Measurement of water depth.

BAUXITE The main ore of aluminium.

BEACH A coastal accumulation of various types of sediment, usually sands and pebbles.

BEAUFORT SCALE A scale of wind speed devised by Admiral Sir Francis Beaufort based on effects of winds on ships. Later modified to include land-based phenomena.

BENCH MARK A reference point used in the measurement of land height in topographic surveying.

BENTHIC Relating to plants, animals and other organisms that inhabit the floors of lakes, seas and oceans.

BERGSCHRUND The crevasse existing at the head of a glacier because of the movement of glacier ice away from the rock wall.

BIGHT A bend in a coast forming an open bay, or the bay itself.

BIOMASS The mass of biological material present per plant or animal, per community or per unit area.

BIOME A mixed community of plants and animals occupying a large area of continental size.

BIOSPHERE The zone at the interface of the earth's surface, ocean and atmosphere where life is found.

BIOTA The entire collection of species or organisms, plants and animals found in a given region.

BISE A cold, dry northerly to north-easterly wind occurring in the mountains of Central Europe in winter.

BLACK EARTH A black soil rich in humus, found extensively in temperate grasslands such as the Russian Steppes.

BLOW HOLE Vertical shaft leading from a sea cave to the surface. Air and water are frequently forced through it by advancing seas.

BORE A large solitary wave which moves up funnel-shaped rivers and estuaries.

BOREAL A descriptive term, usually of climate and forest, to characterize conditions in middle to high latitudes.

BOURNE A river channel on chalk terrain that flows after heavy rain.

BUTTE A small, flat-topped and often steep-sided hill standing isolated on a flat plain. *(see picture below)*

C

CALDERA A depression, usually several kilometres across.

CALVING The breaking away of a mass of ice from a floating glacier or ice shelf to form an iceberg.

CANYON A steep sided valley, usually found in semi-arid and arid areas.

CAPE An area of land jutting out into water, frequently as a peninsula or promontory.

CARDINAL POINTS The four principal compass points, north, east, south and west.

CATARACT A large waterfall over a precipice.

CHINOOK A warm, dry wind that blows down the eastern slopes of the Rocky Mountains of North America.

Above Butte, Monument Valley, Arizona USA. This type of flat-topped, steep sided hill is characteristic of the arid plateau region of the western United States.

CIRQUE OR CORRIE A hollow, open downstream but bounded upstream by a curved, steep headwall, with a gently sloping floor. Found in areas that have been glaciated.

CLIMATE The long-term atmospheric characteristics of a specified area.

CLOUD A collection of a vast number of small water droplets or ice crystals or both in the atmosphere.

COL A pass or saddle between two mountain peaks.

COLD FRONT A zone of strong horizontal temperature gradient in the atmosphere moving such that, for the surface observer, cold air replaces warm.

CONDENSATION The process of formation of liquid water from water vapour.

CONFLUENCE The 'coming together' of material

flows, most usually used in fluids such as the atmosphere and oceans.

CONGLOMERATE A rock which comprises or contains rounded pebbles more than about 2mm in diameter.

CONTINENTAL DRIFT The movement of continents relative to each other. (See *Plate Tectonics*)

CONTINENTAL SHELF A portion of the continental crust below sea level that slopes gently seaward forming an extension of the adjacent coastal plain separated from the deep ocean by the steeply sloping continental slope.

CONTINENTAL SLOPE Lies on the seaward edge of the continental shelf and slopes steeply to the ocean floor.

CONTOUR A line on a map that joins points of equal height or equal depth.

CONVECTION CURRENT A current resulting from convection which is a mode of mass transport within a fluid (especially heat) resulting in movement and mixing of properties of that fluid.

CONVERGENCE The opposite of divergence which is the outflowing mass of fluid. Hence convergence is the inflowing of such mass.

CORAL REEF Large structures fringing islands and coastlines consisting mostly of corals and algae.

CORDILLERA A system of mountain ranges consisting of a number of more or less parallel chains of mountain peaks – such as in the Rocky Mountains.

CRATER A depression at the top of a volcano where a vent carrying lava and gasses reaches the surface.

CRATON A continental area that has experienced little internal deformation in the last 600 million years.

CREVASSE A deep fissure in the surface of a body of ice.

CYCLONE A region of relatively low atmospheric pressure about 2000 km across around which air rotates anticlockwise in the northern hemisphere and clockwise in the southern.

D

DATUM LEVEL Something (such as a fixed point or assumed value) used as a basis for calculating or measuring. Frequently a height of ground relative to which other heights are assessed.

DECLINATION Angular distance north or south from the equator measured along a line of longitude.

DECIDUOUS FOREST Forest in which the trees shed their leaves at a particular time, season or growth stage. The most common manifestation is the shedding in winter.

DEFLATION The process whereby the wind removes fine materials from the surface of a beach or desert.

DEGRADATION The lowering and often flattening of a land surface by erosion.

DELTA Accumulations of sediment deposited at the mouths of rivers. The Nile and Mississippi deltas are two famous examples.

DENUDATION The laying bare of underlying rocks or strata by the removal of overlying material.

DEPOSITION The laying down of material, which, in geomorphological terms, was previously carried by wind, liquid water or ice.

DEPRESSION See *cyclone*

DESALINIZATION To take out the salt content of a material. Usually applied to the extraction of salt from sea water to give fresh water.

DESERT An area in which vegetation cover is sparse or absent and precipitation is low in amount. Deserts can be hot or cold.

DISCHARGE The volume of flow of fluid in a given time period.

DISSECTED PLATEAU A relatively flat, high level area of land which has been cut by streams.

DIURNAL Occurring everyday or having a daily cycle.

DIVERGENCE A spreading of material. Frequently found in high pressure areas (anticyclones) in the atmosphere where air spirals outwards from the centre.

DOLDRUMS A zone of light, variable winds and low atmospheric pressure near or slightly north of the equator.

DRAINAGE The flow of material (usually a fluid) over the earth's surface due to the force of gravity. Most familiarly seen as rivers.

DRIFT ICE Ice bodies drifting in ocean currents.

DROUGHT Dryness caused by lack of precipitation, most easily seen in the hot, dry desert areas of the world.

DROWNED VALLEY A valley which has been filled with water due to a rise of sea level relative to the level with which the river mouth was previously in accord.

DRUMLIN A depositional landform, usually made of glacially-derived material, which has been streamlined by the passage of overlying ice.

DRY VALLEY A valley which is seldom, if ever, occupied by a stream channel.

DUNE An accumulation of sand deposited and shaped by wind.

DUST Solid particles carried in suspension by the atmosphere.

DYKE A sheet-like intrusion of igneous rock, usually oriented vertically, which cuts across the structural planes of the host rocks.

E

EARTH PILLAR A pinnacle of soil or other unconsolidated material that is protected from erosion by the presence of a stone at the top.

EARTHQUAKE A series of shocks and tremors resulting from the sudden release of pressure along active faults and in areas of volcanic activity.

EBB TIDE Tide receding to or at its lowest point.

ECLIPSE, LUNAR The total or partial obscuring of the Moon by the Earth lying on a line between the Moon and the Sun.

ECLIPSE, SOLAR The total or partial obscuring of the Sun by the Moon lying on a line between the Sun and the Earth.

ECOLOGY A branch of science that studies the relations of plants and animals with each other and with their non-living environment.

ECOSYSTEM An entity within which ecological relations operate.

EPICENTRE The point on the earth's surface which lies directly above the focus of an earthquake.

EQUINOX The time of year when the sun is directly overhead at noon at the equator.

ERG A sand desert.

EROSION The group of processes whereby debris is loosened or dissolved and removed from any part of the earth's surface.

ERRATIC A rock that has been carried to its present location by a glacier.

ESCARPMENT A linear land form with one steep side (scarp slope) and one less steep side (dip slope).

ESKER A sinuous ridge of coarse gravel which has been deposited by a meltwater stream normally flowing underneath a glacier.

ESTUARY The sections of a river which flow into the sea and are influenced by tidal currents.

EVAPORATION The diffusion of water vapour into the atmosphere from freely exposed water surfaces.

EXFOLIATION The weathering of a rock by the peeling off of surface layers.

F

FATHOM A unit of length equal to six feet, most usually used in measuring depth of water.

FAULT A crack or fissure in rock, resulting from tectonic movement.

FAUNA Animals or animal life of an area.

FEN A low lying area partially covered by water which is characterized by accumulations of peat.

FJORD A glacially eroded valley whose floor is occupied by the sea.

FIRTH A sea inlet, particularly in Scotland.

FLORA Plants or plant life in an area.

FLUVIOGLACIAL The activity of rivers which are fed by water melted from glaciers.

FOG An accumulation of water droplets or ice crystals in the atmosphere such that visibility is reduced to 1km or less.

FÖHN WIND   A strong, gusty, warm, down-slope wind which occurs on the lee side of a mountain range.

FOLD   A bend in rock strata resulting from movement of the crustal rocks.

FOOD CHAIN   The transfer of food from one type of organism to another in a sequence.

FORD   A shallow part of a river that allows easy crossing.

FRACTURE   The splitting of material into parts: usually concerned with geological materials.

FRAZIL ICE   Fine spikes of ice in suspension in water, usually associated with the freezing of sea water.

FRONT   A transition zone between air of different density, temperature and humidity.

FROST   A situation resulting from air temperatures falling to 0°C – either in the air (air frost) or at the ground (ground frost).

FUMAROLE   A small, volcanic vent through which hot gasses are emitted.

G

GABBRO   A basic igneous rock, usually coarse grained and dark grey to black in colour.

GEEST   Ancient alluvial sediments which still cover the land surfaces on which they were originally deposited.

GEODESY   The determination of the size and shape of the earth by survey and calculation.

GEOID   The shape of the earth at mean sea level.

GEOLOGY   Science that deals with the nature and origin of the earth's rocks and sediments.

GEOMORPHOLOGY   Science that deals with the nature and origin of landforms of the earth's surface.

GEOSYNCLINE   A very large depression, tens or hundreds of kilometres across and up to ten kilometres deep, the floor of which is built up by sedimentation.

GEYSER   A spring of geothermally heated water that erupts intermittently due to pressures beneath the surface. Old Faithful in Yellowstone National Park, USA, is the most famous example.

GLACIATION   The incursion of ice into (or over) a landscape resulting in a whole suite of glacial processes operating thereupon.

GLACIER   A large body of ice, in a valley or covering a much larger area. The largest are found in polar regions.

GLEN   Valley. Term especially used in Scotland.

GNEISS   A coarse-grained igneous rock that has been metamorphosed.

GONDWANALAND   A large continent which it is thought was split very early in geological time to form parts of Africa, Australia, Antarctica, South America and India.

GORGE   A deep and narrow section of a river valley, usually with very steep sides.

GRAVEL   Loose, rounded fragments of rock.

GREAT CIRCLE   A circle formed on the surface of the earth by the intersection of a plane through the centre of the earth with the surface. Lines of longitude and the Equator are great circles.

GROUND FROST   See *frost*

GROUND WATER   All water (gaseous, liquid or solid) lying below the earth's surface and not chemically combined with the minerals present.

GROYNE   A man-made barrier running across a beach and into the sea; constructed to reduce erosion of the beach by longshore currents.

GULF   A part of the sea that is partly or almost completely enclosed by land.

GULLY   A linear depression worn in the earth by running water after rains.

GUYOT   A flat-topped mountain on the sea floor which does not reach the sea surface.

GYRE   Large circulations of water in the world's oceans, involving the major currents.

H

HAFF   A coastal lagoon separated from the open seas by a sand spit.

HAIL   Solid precipitation which falls as ice particles from cumulonimbus clouds. Contrasts markedly with snow.

HEMISPHERE   Half of the earth, usually thought of in terms of its surface. The most familiar are the northern and southern hemispheres, bounded by the Equator.

HORIZON   Apparent junction of earth and sky.

HORSE LATITUDE   The latitude belts over the oceans at latitudes of 30–35° where winds are predominantly calm or light and weather is often hot and dry.

HOT SPOT   A small area of the earth's crust where an unusually high heat flow is associated with volcanic activity.

HOT SPRING   An emission of hot water at the land surface.

HURRICANE   A severe cyclone occurring in the tropics, characterized by high wind speeds and heavy precipitation.

HYDROLOGICAL CYCLE   The continuous movement of all forms of water (vapour, liquid and solid) on, in and above the earth.

HYDROSPHERE   The earth's water – saline, fresh, gaseous, liquid and solid.

HYGROMETER   A device for measuring the relative humidity of the atmosphere.

HYPSOGRAPHIC CURVE   A generalized profile of the earth and ocean floors which represents the proportions of the area of the surface at various altitudes above or below a datum.

I

ICEBERG   A large floating mass of ice detached from a glacier, usually tens of metres deep and can be several kilometres across.

ICE-CAP   A dome-shaped glacier with a generally outward flow of ice.

ICE FLOE   A piece of floating ice which is not attached to the land and is usually 2–3 metres thick.

ICE SHELF   A floating sheet of ice attached to an embayment in the coast.

IGNEOUS ROCK   Rock formed when molten material solidifies, either within the earth's crust or at the surface.

INSELBERG   A large, residual hill which overlooks a surrounding eroded plain.

INSOLATION   The amount of solar radiation received over a specified area and a specified time.

INTERNATIONAL DATE LINE   An arbitary line, roughly along the 180° longitude line, east and west of which the date differs by one day.

INVERSION (temperature)
An increase of temperature with height.

IRRIGATION   The supply of water to land by artificial means. Usually to improve agricultural productivity.

ISLAND ARC   A chain of islands with an arcuate plan form. The islands are usually volcanic in origin.

ISOBAR   A line drawn on diagrams joining equal values of atmospheric pressure. A particular kind of isopleth.

ISOPLETH   A line drawn on diagrams joining equal values of the plotted element.

ISOSTASY   The condition of balance between the rigid crustal elements of the earth's surface and the underlying, denser and more mobile material.

Above Limestone towers in the world's most spectacular karst region – Li River near Guilin, Guangxi Province, China. The towers are the result of erosional processes.

ISTHMUS   A narrow strip of land which connects two islands or two large land masses.

J

JOINT   A fracture or crack in a rock.

JUNGLE   An area of land overgrown with dense vegetation, usually in the tropics.

K

KAME   An irregular mound of stratified sediment deposited by, in association with stagnant ice.

KARST   Limestone areas which have distinctive landforms such as caves, sinks and frequently a lack of surface water. *(see picture above)*

KELP   A mass of large brown seaweeds.

KETTLE HOLE   An enclosed depression resulting from the melting of buried ice.

KNOT A measure of speed – one nautical mile per hour (1.15 mi hr^{-1}; 0.85 km hr^{-1}).

KOPJE A small hill or rock outcrop; term used particularly in South Africa.

KRILL Small marine animals, resembling shrimps.

L

LACCOLITH A mass of intrusive rock, usually with a horizontal base and causing the doming of overlying strata.

LAGOON A shallow pool separated from a larger body of water by a bar or reef.

LANDSAT An unmanned satellite that carries sensors to record the resources of the earth.

LANDSLIDE The movement downward under the influence of gravity of a mass of rock debris.

LATERITE A red clay formed by the weathering of rock that consists especially of compounds of iron and aluminium.

LAURASIA The northern part of Pangaea, a super-continent thought to have been broken up by continental drift.

LAVA Molten rock material that emerges from volcanoes and volcanic fissures.

LEACHING The downward movement of water through soil resulting in the removal of water-soluble materials from upper layers and their accumulation in lower layers.

LEEWARD To the lee (downwind, downstream) of an obstacle lying in a flow.

LEVEE A broad, long ridge running parallel and adjacent to a river on its flood-plain.

LIGNITE A brownish black coal in which the texture of the original wood is distinct.

LITHOSPHERE The earth's crust and a portion of the upper mantle that together comprise a layer of strength relative to the more easily deformable layer below.

LITTORAL A coastal region.

LLANOS An open grassy plain in S. America.

LOAM A crumbly soil consisting of a mixture of clay, silt and sand.

LOCH A lake or narrow sea inlet in Scotland.

LOESS Unconsolidated and frequently unstratified material deposited after transport by wind.

LONGSHORE CURRENT A current that runs along a coast. It may result in longshore drift, the transport of beach material along the coast.

LOW See *cyclone*

LUNAR MONTH The period of time between two successive new moons, being about 29½ days.

M

MAGMA Fused, molten rock material beneath the earth's crust from which igneous rocks are formed.

MAGNETIC ANOMALIES Areas with local surface variations in the earth's magnetic field relative to large-scale values.

MAGNETIC FIELD The field of force exerted by the earth by virtue of its being like a giant magnet. Its most familiar manifestation is in the behaviour of a compass.

MAGNETIC REVERSAL The reversal of the earth's magnetic field, such that a north-seeking compass points toward the South Pole. Such reversals have occurred in geological time.

MANTLE The zone within the earth's interior extending from 25 to 70km below the surface to a depth of 2900km.

MAP PROJECTION A mathematical device for representing a portion of all of the earth's curved surface on a flat surface.

MAP SCALE A measure of the ratio of distances represented on a map to their true value.

MAQUIS Scrub vegetation of evergreen shrubs characteristic of the western Mediterranean.

MARL A fine grained mixture of clay and silt with a high proportion of calcium carbonate.

MASSIF A large mountainous area, often quite distinct, containing several individual substantial mountains.

MEANDER A sinuously winding portion of a river channel; also applied to similar forms within larger flows, such as the atmosphere and oceans.

MEAN SEA LEVEL The level of the sea determined from a mean of the tidal ranges over periods of several months to several years.

METAMORPHIC ROCKS Rocks in which their composition, structure and texture have been significantly altered by the action of heat and pressure greater than that produced normally by burial.

METEOROLOGY The study of the workings of the atmosphere.

MILLIBAR A unit of pressure, most widely used in meteorology. The average pressure exerted by the atmosphere on the surface of the earth is just over 1013 millibars.

MISTRAL A cold, dry, north or northwest wind affecting the Rhone Valley.

MONSOON A wind regime with marked seasonal reversal in direction, most famously found in the Indian sub-continent.

MORAINE A landform resulting from the deposition of till by glaciers, taking on several

distinctive forms depending upon the location and mode of deposition.

N

NADIR A point that is vertically below the observer.

NASA National Aeronautics and Space Administration (USA).

NEAP TIDE A tide of minimum height occurring at the first and third quarter of the moon.

NÉVÉ Snow that is being compacted into ice, as found in the birth place of glaciers.

NUNATAK A mountain completely surrounded by an ice cap or ice sheet.

O

OASIS An area within a desert region where there is sufficient water to sustain animal and plant life throughout the year.

OCEAN BASIN A large depression in the ocean floor analogous to basins on land.

OCEANIC CRUST The portion of the earth's surface crust comprising largely sima (silica-magnesia rich rocks) about 5km thick. Underlies most of the world's oceans.

OCEAN RIDGE A ridge in the ocean floor, sometimes 150 to 1500 km wide and hundreds of metres high.

OCCLUSION The coming together of warm and cold fronts in cyclones in the latest stages of its evolution.

OROGENESIS The formation of mountains, such as the Andes and Rocky Mountains. The mechanism is still uncertain but is probably related to plate tectonics.

OUTWASH PLAIN Stratified material deposited by glacio-fluvial waters beyond the ice margin.

OXBOW LAKE A lake, usually curved in plan, occupying an abandoned section of meandering river.

P

PACK ICE Ice formed on sea surface when water temperatures fall to about −2°C and floating free under the influence of currents and wind.

PAMPAS An extensive, generally grass-covered plain of temperate South America east of the Andes.

PANGAEA The name given to a postulated continental landmass which split up to produce most of the present northern hemisphere continents.

PASS A narrow passage over relatively low ground in a mountain range.

PEDIMENT A smooth, erosional land surface typically sloping from the foot of a high-land area to a local base level.

PELAGIC The part of an aquatic system that excludes its margins and substrate; it is essentially the main part of the water body.

PENEPLAIN The supposed end land form resulting from erosional processes wearing down an initially uplifted block.

PENUMBRA A region of partial darkness in a shadow surrounding the region of total darkness (umbra), such as seen in an eclipse.

PERIHELION The point in its orbit about the sun that a planet is closest to the sun.

PIEDMONT GLACIER A glacier which spreads out into a lobe as it flows onto a lowland.

PILLOW LAVA Lava that has solidified, probably under water, in rounded masses.

PLACER DEPOSIT A sediment, such as in the bed of a stream, which contains particles of valuable minerals.

PLAIN Extensive area of level or rolling treeless country.

PLANKTON Small freshwater and marine organisms that tend to move with water currents and comprise the food of larger and higher order organisms.

PLATE TECTONICS A theory which holds that the earth's surface is divided into several major rigid plates which are in motion with respect to each other and the underlying mantle. Continental drift results from plate motion and earthquakes, volcanoes and mountain-building tend to occur at the plate boundaries.

PLUTONIC ROCK Rock material that has formed at depth where cooling and crystallization have occurred slowly.

POLAR WANDERING The movements of the North and South Poles throughout geological time relative to the positions of the continents.

POLDER A low lying area of land that has been reclaimed from the sea or a lake by artificial means and is kept free of water by pumping.

PRECIPITATION The deposition of water from the atmosphere in liquid and solid form. Rain, snow, hail and dew are the most familiar forms.

PRAIRIE An extensive area of level or rolling, almost treeless grassland in North America.

PRESSURE GRADIENT The change per unit distance of pressure, perhaps most frequently met in atmospheric studies. The cause of winds.

Q

QUARTZ A crystalline mineral consisting of silicon dioxide that is a major constituent of many rocks.

QUICKSAND Water-saturated sand that is semi-liquid and cannot bear the weight of heavy objects.

R

RADAR A device that transmits radio waves and locates objects in the vicinity by analysis of the waves reflected back from them (radio detection and ranging).

RADIATION The transmission of energy in the form of electromagnetic waves and requiring no intervening medium.

RAIN SHADOW An area experiencing relatively low rainfall because of its position on the leeward side of a hill.

RAISED BEACH An emerged shoreline represented by stranded marine deposits and wave cut platforms, usually backed by former cliffs.

RANGE An open region over which livestock may roam and feed, particularly in North America.

RAVINE A narrow, steep sided valley usually formed by running water.

REEF A rocky construction found at or near sea-level; coral reefs are perhaps the most familiar type.

RELATIVE HUMIDITY The amount of water vapour in an air sample relative to the amount the sample could hold if it were saturated at the same temperature; expressed as a percentage.

REMOTE SENSING The observation and measurement of an object without touching it.

RHUMB LINE An imaginary line on the surface of the earth which makes equal oblique angles with all lines of longitude so that it forms a spiral coiling round the poles but never reaching them. This would be the course sailed by a ship following a single compass direction.

RIA An inlet of the sea formed by the flooding of river valleys by rising sea or sinking land. Contrast to fjords which are drowned glacial valleys.

RIFT VALLEY A valley formed when the area between two parallel faults sinks.

RIVER TERRACE A step like land form in the flood plain of rivers due to the river incising further into the plain and leaving remnants of its former flood plain at levels higher than the present level of the river channel.

ROARING FORTIES The area between 40° and 50°S, so called because of the high speeds of the winds occurring there. Sometimes applied to the winds themselves.

RUN-OFF The section of the hydrological cycle connecting precipitation to channel flow.

S

SALINITY The presence of salts in the waters and soils of arid, semi-arid and coastal areas.

SALT-MARSH Vegetated mud-flats found commonly on many low-lying coasts in a wide range of temperate environments.

SANDBANK A large deposit of sand, usually in a river or coastal waters.

SANDSTORM A wind storm driving clouds of sand, most usually in hot, dry deserts.

SAVANNAH A grassland region of the tropics and sub-tropics.

SCHIST Medium to coarse-grained crystalline metamorphic rock.

SEA-FLOOR SPREADING The phenomenon when tectonic plates move apart.

SEAMOUNT A mountain or other area of high relief on the sea-floor which does not reach the surface.

SEASAT A satellite especially designed to sense remotely wind and sea conditions on the oceans.

SEDIMENTARY ROCK Rock composed of the fragments of older rocks which have been eroded and the debris deposited by wind and water, often as distinct strata.

SEISMIC WAVE Wave resulting from the movements of materials in earthquakes.

SEISMOLOGY Science that deals with earthquakes and other vibrations of the earth.

SHALE A compacted sedimentary rock, usually with fine-grained particles.

SHALLOW-FOCUS EARTHQUAKE An earthquake with a focus (or centre) at a shallow level relative to the earth's surface.

SIAL The part of the earth's crust with a composition dominated by minerals rich in silicon and aluminium.

SIDEREAL DAY A period of complete rotation of the earth on its axis, about 23 hours 56 minutes.

SILL A tabular sheet of igneous rock injected along the bedding planes of sedimentary and volcanic formations.

SILT An unconsolidated material of small particles ranging in size from about 2 to 60 micrometres.

SIMA The part of the earth's crust with a composition dominated by minerals rich in silicon and magnesium.

SOIL CREEP The slow movement downslope of soil, usually resulting in thinning of soils on the upper reaches and accumulations on the lower.

SOLIFLUCTION The slow movement downslope of water saturated, seasonally thawed materials.

SOLSTICE The days of maximum declination of the sun measured relative to the equator. When

Above On May 18 1980, Mt St Helens demonstrated a plinian eruption (a kind first described by Pliny the Elder). The apparent smoke cloud is pulverised ash.

the midday sun is overhead at 23½°N it gives the longest day in the northern hemisphere and the shortest day in the southern. The reverse applies when the sun is overhead at 23½°S.

SPIT Usually linear deposits of beach material attached at one end to land and free at the other.

SPRING TIDE A tide of greater than average range occurring at or around the times of the new and full moon.

SQUALL A sudden, violent wind, often associated with rain or hail; frequently occurs under cumulonimbus clouds.

STALACTITE A deposit of calcium carbonate, rather like an icicle, hanging from the roof of a cave.

STALAGMITE A deposit of calcium carbonate growing up from the floor of a cave due to the constant drip of water from the roof.

STANDARD TIME The officially established time, with reference to Greenwich Mean Time, of a region or country.

STEPPE Mid-latitude grasslands with few trees, most typically found in USSR.

STORM SURGE Changes in sea level caused by extreme weather events, notably the winds in storms.

STRAIT A narrow passage joining two large bodies of water.

STRIAE Scratches of a rock surface due to the passage over it of another rock of equal or greater hardness.

SUBDUCTION ZONE An area where the rocks comprising the sea floor are forced beneath continental rocks at a plate margin to be reincorporated in the magma beneath the earth's crust.

SUBSEQUENT RIVER A stream which follows a course determined by the structure of the local bedrock.

SUBSIDENCE Usually applied to the sinking of air in the atmosphere or the downward movement of the earth's surface.

SUBSOIL The layer of weathered material that underlies the surface soil.

SUDD Floating vegetable matter that forms obstructive masses in the upper White Nile.

SUNSPOT Relatively dark regions on the disk of the sun with surface temperature of about 4500K compared to the more normal 6000K of the rest of the surface.

SURGE A sudden excess over the normal value, usually of a flow of material (soil, ice, water).

SWELL A long, perturbation (usually wavelike) of a water surface that continues beyond its cause (eg a strong wind).

 T

TAIGA The most northerly coniferous forest of cold temperature regions found in Canada, Alaska and Eurasia.

TECTONIC Concerned with the broad structures of the earth's rocks and the processes of faulting, folding and warping that form them.

TETHYS OCEAN An ocean formed in the Palaeozoic Era which extended from what is now the Mediterranean Sea eastwards as far as South-east Asia.

THERMOCLINE A layer of water or a lake or sea that separates an upper, warmer, oxygen-rich zone from a lower, colder, oxygen-poor zone and in which temperature decreases by 1°C for every metre of increased depth.

THRUST FAULT A low-angle reverse fault.

THUNDERSTORM A cloud in which thunder and lightning occur, usually associated with heavy precipitation and strong winds.

TIDAL BORE A large solitary wave that moves up funnel-shaped rivers and estuaries with the rising tide, especially spring tides.

TIDAL CURRENT The periodic horizontal motions of the sea, generated by the gravitational attraction of the moon and sun, typically of 1ms^{-1} on continental shelves.

TIDE The regular movements of the seas due to the gravitational attraction of the moon and sun, most easily observed as changes in coastal sea levels.

TOPOGRAPHY The configuration of a land surface, including its relief and the position of its natural and man-made features.

TOR An exposure of bedrock usually as blocks and boulders, forming an abrupt, steep sided culmination of a more gentle rise to the summits of hills. Famous tors exist on Dartmoor.

TORNADO A violent, localized rotating storm with winds of 100ms^{-1} circulating round a funnel cloud some 100m in diameter. Frequent in mid-western USA.

TRADE WIND Winds with an easterly component which blow from the subtropic high pressure areas around 30° toward the equator.

TROPICAL CYCLONE *See hurricane*

TROPOSPHERE The portion of the earth's atmosphere between the earth's surface and a height about 15–20km. This layer contains virtually all the world's weather. Mean temperatures decrease and mean wind speeds increase with height in the troposphere.

TSUNAMI Sea-surface waves caused by submarine earthquakes and volcanic activity. Popularly called tidal waves.

TURBULENCE Chaotic and apparently random fluctuations in fluid flow, familiarly seen in the behaviour of smoke, either from a cigarette, a chimney or a volcano.

TUNDRA Extensive, level, treeless and marshy regions lying polewards of the taiga.

TYPHOON A term used in the Far East to describe tropical cyclones or hurricanes.

U

UMBRA A region of total shadow, especially in an eclipse.

UPWELLING The upward movement of deeper water towards the sea surface.

V

VARVE A sediment bed deposited in a body of water within the course of one year.

VOE An inlet or narrow bay of the Orkney or Shetland Islands.

VOLCANIC ASH Ash emitted from a volcano.

VOLCANO An opening through which magma, molten rock ash or volatiles erupts onto the earth's surface. Also used to describe the landform produced by the erupted material. *(see picture below left)*

W

WADI An ephemeral river channel in deserts.

WARM FRONT An atmospheric front whereby, as it passes over an individual on the ground, warm air replaces cold.

WATERFALL A vertical or very steep descent of water in a stream.

WATERSHED A boundary dividing and separating the areas drained by different rivers.

WATERSPOUT A funnel-shaped, rotating cloud that forms occasionally over water when the atmosphere is very unstable. Akin to tornadoes which occur over land.

WATER TABLE The level below which the ground is wholly and permanently saturated with water.

WAVE HEIGHT The vertical extent of a wave.

WAVE LENGTH The horizontal extent of a wave, most easily seen as the distance along the direction of wave movement between crests or troughs.

WAVE PERIOD The time taken for a complete cycle of the oscillation occurring within a wave.

WAVE VELOCITY The velocity of a wave form, best seen by concentrating on one part of the wave such as its crest or trough.

WEATHERING The alteration by physical, chemical and biological processes of rocks and sediments in the top metres of the earth's crust. So called because this material is exposed to the effects of atmospheric and atmospherically related conditions.

WEATHER ROUTEING Choosing a route for a ship or aeroplane to minimise the deleterious effects of weather.

WESTERLIES Winds with a westerly component occurring between latitudes of about 35° and 60°. The whole regime forms a 'vortex' around each of the poles and forms a major element in world climate.

WHIRLWIND A general term to describe rotating winds of scales up to that of a tornado, usually a result of intense convection over small areas.

WILLY-WILLY Australasian term for a tropical cyclone or hurricane.

WINDSHEAR The variation of speed or direction or both of wind over a distance.

 Y

YARDANG A desert landform, usually but not always, of unconsolidated material, shaped by and lying roughly along the direction of the wind.

Z

ZENITH A point that is vertically above the observer: the opposite of nadir.

ZOOPLANKTON One of the three kinds of plankton, including mature representatives of many animal groups such as Protozoa and Crustacea.

ABBREVIATIONS	FULL FORM	ENGLISH FORM
A		
a.d.	an der	on the
Akr.	Akra, Akrotírion	cape
Appno	Appennino	mountain range
Arch.	Archipelago	
	Archipiélago	archipelago
B		
B.	1. Bahía, Baía,	bay
	Baie, Bay, Bucht,	
	Bukhta, Bugt	
	2. Ban	village
	3. Barrage,	dam
	4. Bir, Bîr, Bi'r	well
Bol.	Bol'sh, -oy	big
Br.	1. Branch	branch
	2. Bridge, Brücke	bridge
	3. Burun	cape
Brj	Baraj, -i	dam
C		
C.	Cabo, Cap, Cape	cape
Can.	Canal	canal
Cd	Ciudad	town
Chan.	Channel	channel
Ck	Creek	creek
Co., Cord.	Cordillera	mountain chain
D		
D.	1. Dağ, Dagh, Daği,	
	Dağları	mountain, range
	2. Daryācheh	lake
Dj.	Djebel	mountain
Dr.	doctor	doctor
E		
E.	East	east
Emb.	Embalse	reservoir
Escarp.	Escarpment	escarpment
Estr.	Estrecho	strait
F		
F.	Firth	estuary
Fj.	Fjord, Fjörður	fjord
Ft	Fort	fort
G		
G.	1. Gebel	mountain
	2. Göl, Gölü	lake
	3. Golfe, Golfo, Gulf	Gulf
	4. Gora, -gory	mountain, range
	5. Gunung	mountain
Gd, Gde	Grand, Grande	grand
Geb.	Gebirge	mountain range
Gl.	Glacier	glacier
Grl	General	general
Gt, Gtr	Great, Groot, -e,	
	Greater	greater
H		
Har.	Harbour, Harbor	harbour
Hd	Head	head
I		
I.	Ile, Ilha, Insel,	island
	Isla, Island, Isle	
	Isola,	
	Isole	islands
In.	1. Inner	inner
	2. Inlet	inlet
Is	Iles, Ilhas, Islands,	islands
	Isles, Islas	
Isth.	Isthmus	isthmus
J		
J.	Jabal, Jebel,	mountain
K		
K.	1. Kaap, Kap, Kapp	cape
	2. Kūh(hā)	mountain(s)
	3. Kólpos	gulf
Kep.	Kepulauan	islands
Khr.	Khrebet	mountain range
Kör.	Körfez, -i	gulf, bay
L		
L.	Lac, Lago, Lagoa,	lake
	Lake, Liman, Limni,	
	Loch, Lough	
Lag.	Lagoon, Laguna,	lagoon
	Lagune, Lagoa	
Ld.	Land	land
Lit.	Little	little

ABBREVIATIONS	FULL FORM	ENGLISH FORM
M		
M.	1. Muang	town
	2. Mys	cape
m	metre, -s	metre(s)
Mal.	Malyy	small
Mf	Massif	mountain group
Mgne	Montagne(s)	mountain(s)
Mt	Mont, Mount	mountain
Mte	Monte	mountain
Mti	Monti	mountains, range
Mtn	Mountain	mountain
Mts	Monts, Mountains,	mountains
	Montañas, Montes	
N		
N.	1. Neu-, Ny-	new
	2. Noord, Nord,	north
	Norte, North, Norra,	
	Nørre	
	3. Nos	cape
Nat.	National	national
Nat. Pk	National Park	national park
Ndr	Nieder	lower
N.E.	North East	north east
N.M.	National Monument	national
		monument
N.P.	National Park	national park
N.W.	North West	north west
O		
O.	1. Oost, Ost	east
	2. Ostrov	island
Ø	-øy	island
Oz.	Ozero, Ozera	lake(s)
P		
P.	1. Pass, Passo	pass
	2. Pic, Pico, Pizzo	peak
	3. Pulau	island
Pass.	Passage	passage
Peg.	Pegunungan	mountains
Pen.	Peninsula, Penisola	peninsula
Pk	1. Park	park
	2. Peak, Pik	peak
Plat.	Plateau, Planalto	plateau
Pov	Poluostrov	peninsula
Pr.	Prince	prince
P.P.	Pulau-pulau	islands
Pres.	Presidente	president
Promy	Promontory	promontory
Pt	Point	point
Pta	1. Ponta, Punta	point
	2. Puerta	pass
Pte	Pointe	point
Pto	Porto, Puerto	port
R		
R.	Rio, Río,	river
	River, Rivière	
Ra.	Range	range
Rap.	Rapids	rapids
Res.	Reserve, Reservation	reserve,
		reservation
Resp.	Respublika	Republic
Resr	Reservoir	reservoir
S		
S.	1. Salar, Salina	salt marsh
	2. San, São	saint
	3. See	sea, lake
	4. South, Sud	south
s.	sur	on
Sa	Serra, Sierra	mountain range
Sd	Sound, Sund	sound
S.E.	South East	south east
Sev.	Severo-, Severnaya,	north
	-nyy	peak
Sp.	Spitze	saint
St	Saint	saint
Sta	Santa	saint
Ste	Sainte	saint
Sto	Santo	strait
Str.	Strait	south west
S.W.	South West	
T		
T.	Tall, Tell	hill, mountain
Tg	Tanjung	cape
Tk	Teluk	bay
Tr.	Trench, Trough	trench, trough
U		
U.	Uad	wadi
Ug	Ujung	cape
Upr	Upper	upper

ABBREVIATIONS	FULL FORM	ENGLISH FORM
V		
V.	1. Val, Valle	valley
	2. Ville	town
Va	Villa	town
Vdkhr.	Vodokhranilishche	reservoir
Vol.	Volcán, Volcano,	volcano
	Vulkan	
Vozv.	Vozvyshennost'	upland
W		
W.	1. Wadi	wadi
	2. Water	water
	3. Well	well
	4. West	west
Y		
Yuzh.	Yuzhno-, Yuzhnyy	south
Z		
Z	1. Zaliv	gulf, bay
	2. Zatoka	
Zap.	Zapad-naya, Zapadno-,	western
	Zapadnyy	
Zem.	Zemlya	country, land

Introduction to the index

In the index, the first number refers to the page, and the following letter and number to the section of the map in which the index entry can be found.
For example, 14C2 **Paris** means that Paris can be found on page 14 where column C and row 2 meet.

Abbreviations used in the index

Arch	Archipelago
B	Bay
C	Cape
Chan	Channel
Gl	Glacier
I(s)	Island(s)
Lg	Lagoon
L	Lake
Mt(s)	Mountain(s)
P	Pass
Pass	Passage
Pen	Peninsula
Plat	Plateau
Pt	Point
Res	Reservoir
R	River
S	Sea
Sd	Sound
Str	Strait
UAE	United Arab Emirates
UK	United Kingdom
USA	United States of America
V	Valley

A

18B2 **Aachen** Germany
13C1 **Aalsmeer** Netherlands
13C2 **Aalst** Belgium
12K6 **Äänekoski** Finland
31A3 **Aba** China
48C4 **Aba** Nigeria
50D3 **Aba** Zaïre
41E3 **Abādān** Iran
41F3 **Ābādeh** Iran
48B1 **Abadla** Algeria
75C2 **Abaeté** Brazil
75C2 **Abaeté** *R* Brazil
73J4 **Abaetetuba** Brazil
31D1 **Abagnar Qi** China
59E3 **Abajo Mts** USA
48C4 **Abakaliki** Nigeria
25L4 **Abakan** Russian Federation
48C3 **Abala** Niger
48C2 **Abalessa** Algeria
72D6 **Abancay** Peru
41F3 **Abarqū** Iran
29E2 **Abashiri** Japan
29E2 **Abashiri-wan** *B* Japan
27H7 **Abau** Papua New Guinea
50D3 **Abaya, L** Ethiopia
50D2 **Abbai** *R* Ethiopia/Sudan
50E2 **Abbe, L** Djibouti/Ethiopia
14C1 **Abbeville** France
63D3 **Abbeville** Louisiana, USA
67B2 **Abbeville** S Carolina, USA
58B1 **Abbotsford** Canada
64A2 **Abbotsford** USA
42C2 **Abbottabad** Pakistan
40D2 **'Abd al 'Azīz, Jebel** *Mt* Syria
20J5 **Abdulino** Russian Federation
50C2 **Abéché** Chad
48B4 **Abengourou** Ivory Coast
18B1 **Åbenrå** Denmark
48C4 **Abeokuta** Nigeria
50D3 **Abera** Ethiopia
7B3 **Aberaeron** Wales
7C4 **Aberdare** Wales
66C2 **Aberdeen** California, USA
65D3 **Aberdeen** Maryland, USA
63E2 **Aberdeen** Mississippi, USA
47C3 **Aberdeen** South Africa
8D3 **Aberdeen** Scotland
56D2 **Aberdeen** S Dakota, USA
56A2 **Aberdeen** Washington, USA
54J3 **Aberdeen L** Canada
7B3 **Aberdyfi** Wales
8D3 **Aberfeldy** Scotland
8C3 **Aberfoyle** Scotland
7C4 **Abergavenny** Wales
7B3 **Aberystwyth** Wales
20L2 **Abez'** Russian Federation
50E2 **Abhā** Saudi Arabia
41E2 **Abhar** Iran
48B4 **Abidjan** Ivory Coast
61D3 **Abilene** Kansas, USA
62C2 **Abilene** Texas, USA
7D4 **Abingdon** England
64C3 **Abingdon** USA
55K4 **Abitibi** *R* Canada
55L5 **Abitibi,L** Canada
21G7 **Abkhazian Republic** Georgia
42C2 **Abohar** India
48C4 **Abomey** Benin
50B3 **Abong Mbang** Cameroon
50B2 **Abou Deïa** Chad
8D3 **Aboyne** Scotland
41E4 **Abqaiq** Saudi Arabia
15A2 **Abrantes** Portugal
70A2 **Abreojos, Punta** *Pt* Mexico
50D1 **'Abri** Sudan
32A3 **Abrolhos** *I* Australia
75E2 **Abrolhos, Arquipélago dos** *Is* Brazil
56B2 **Absaroka Range** *Mts* USA
41F5 **Abū al Abyaḑ** *I* UAE
41E4 **Abū 'Alī** *I* Saudi Arabia
45D3 **Abu 'Amūd, Wadi** Jordan
45C3 **Abu 'Aweigīla** *Well* Egypt
41F5 **Abū Dhabi** UAE
45C3 **Abū el Jurdhān** Jordan
50D2 **Abu Hamed** Sudan
48C4 **Abuja** Nigeria
45A3 **Abu Kebir Hihya** Egypt
72E5 **Abunã** Brazil
72E6 **Abunã** *R* Bolivia/Brazil
45C4 **Abu Rûtha, Gebel** *Mt* Egypt
41D3 **Abú Sukhayr** Iraq
45B3 **Abu Suweir** Egypt
45B4 **Abu Tarfa, Wadi** Egypt
35B2 **Abut Head** *C* New Zealand
40B4 **Abu Tig** Egypt
50D2 **Abu'Urug** *Well* Sudan
50D2 **Abuye Meda** *Mt* Ethiopia
50C2 **Abu Zabad** Sudan
50D3 **Abwong** Sudan
18B1 **Åby** Denmark
50C3 **Abyei** Sudan
65F2 **Acadia Nat Pk** USA
70B2 **Acámbaro** Mexico
69B5 **Acandí** Colombia
70B2 **Acaponeta** Mexico
70B3 **Acapulco** Mexico
73L4 **Acaraú** Brazil
72E2 **Acarigua** Venezuela
70C3 **Acatlán** Mexico
48B4 **Accra** Ghana
6C3 **Accrington** England
42D4 **Achalpur** India
74B6 **Achao** Chile
13E3 **Achern** Germany
9A3 **Achill Hd** *Pt* Irish Republic
10A3 **Achill I** Irish Republic
13E1 **Achim** Germany
25L4 **Achinsk** Russian Federation
16D3 **Acireale** Sicily, Italy
61E2 **Ackley** USA
69C2 **Acklins** *I* The Bahamas
72D6 **Acobamba** Peru
74B4 **Aconcagua** *Mt* Chile
73L5 **Acopiara** Brazil
Açores *Is* **= Azores**
A Coruña = La Coruña
Acre = 'Akko
72D5 **Acre** *State* Brazil
66C3 **Acton** USA
63C2 **Ada** USA
15B1 **Adaja** *R* Spain
41G5 **Adam** Oman
50D3 **Adama** Ethiopia
75B3 **Adamantina** Brazil
50B3 **Adamaoua** *Region* Cameroon/Nigeria
50B3 **Adamaoua, Massif de l'** *Mts* Cameroon
68D1 **Adams** USA
44B4 **Adam's Bridge** India/Sri Lanka
56A2 **Adams,Mt** USA
44C4 **Adam's Peak** *Mt* Sri Lanka
'Adan = Aden
21F8 **Adana** Turkey
21E7 **Adapazari** Turkey
76F7 **Adare,C** Antarctica
34B1 **Adavale** Australia
41E4 **Ad Dahnā'** *Region* Saudi Arabia
41F4 **Ad Damman** Saudi Arabia
41D5 **Ad Dawādimī** Saudi Arabia
41E4 **Ad Dibdibah** *Region* Saudi Arabia
41E5 **Ad Dilam** Saudi Arabia
41E5 **Ad Dir'iyah** Saudi Arabia
50D3 **Addis Ababa** Ethiopia
41D3 **Ad Dīwanīyah** Iraq
40D3 **Ad Duwayd** Saudi Arabia
61E2 **Adel** USA
32C4 **Adelaide** Australia
67C4 **Adelaide** Bahamas
76G3 **Adelaide** *Base* Antarctica
54J3 **Adelaide Pen** Canada
27G8 **Adelaide River** Australia
66D3 **Adelanto** USA
38C4 **Aden** Yemen
38C4 **Aden,G of** Somalia/Yemen
48C3 **Aderbissinat** Niger
45D2 **Adhra'** Syria
27G7 **Adi** *I* Indonesia
16C1 **Adige** *R* Italy
50D2 **Adigrat** Ethiopia
42D5 **Adilābād** India
58B2 **Adin** USA
65E2 **Adirondack Mts** USA
50D2 **Adi Ugri** Ethiopia
40C2 **Adiyaman** Turkey
17F1 **Adjud** Romania
54E4 **Admiralty I** USA
55K2 **Admiralty Inlet** *B* Canada
32D1 **Admiralty Is** Papua New Guinea
44B2 **Ādoni** India
14B3 **Adour** *R* France
48B2 **Adrar** Algeria
48C2 **Adrar** *Mts* Algeria
48A2 **Adrar** *Region* Mauritius
48A2 **Adrar Soutouf** *Region* Morocco
50C2 **Adré** Chad
49D2 **Adri** Libya
64C2 **Adrian** Michigan, USA
62B1 **Adrian** Texas, USA
16C2 **Adriatic S** Italy/Yugoslavia
50D2 **Adwa** Ethiopia
25P3 **Adycha** *R* Russian Federation
48B4 **Adzopé** Ivory Coast
20K2 **Adz'va** *R* Russian Federation
20K2 **Adz'vavom** Russian Federation
17E3 **Aegean Sea** Greece
38E2 **Afghanistan** *Republic* Asia
50E3 **Afgooye** Somalia
41D5 **'Afif** Saudi Arabia
48C4 **Afikpo** Nigeria
12G6 **Åfjord** Norway
48C1 **Aflou** Algeria
50E3 **Afmado** Somalia
48A3 **Afollé** *Region* Mauritius
68C1 **Afton** New York, USA
58D2 **Afton** Wyoming, USA
45C2 **Afula** Israel
21E8 **Afyon** Turkey
45A3 **Aga** Egypt
50B2 **Agadem** Niger
48C3 **Agadez** Niger
48B1 **Agadir** Morocco
42D4 **Agar** India
43G4 **Agartala** India
58B1 **Agassiz** Canada
48B4 **Agboville** Ivory Coast
40E1 **Agdam** Azerbaijan
29C3 **Agematsu** Japan
14C3 **Agen** France
41E3 **Agha Jārī** Iran
48B4 **Agnibilékrou** Ivory Coast
14C3 **Agout** *R* France
42D3 **Āgra** India
41D2 **Ağri** Turkey
16D2 **Agri** *R* Italy
16C3 **Agrigento** Sicily, Italy
26H5 **Agrihan** *I* Marianas
17E3 **Agrínion** Greece
16C2 **Agropoli** Italy
20J4 **Agryz** Russian Federation
55N3 **Agto** Greenland
75B3 **Agua Clara** Brazil
69D3 **Aguadilla** Puerto Rico
70B1 **Agua Prieta** Mexico
75A3 **Aguaray Guazú** Paraguay
70B2 **Aguascalientes** Mexico
75D2 **Aguas Formosas** Brazil
75C2 **Agua Vermelha, Barragem** Brazil
15A1 **Agueda** Portugal
48C3 **Aguelhok** Mali
48A2 **Agüenit** *Well* Morocco
15B2 **Águilas** Spain
72B5 **Aguja, Puerta** Peru
36C7 **Agulhas Basin** Indian Ocean
51C7 **Agulhas,C** South Africa
36C6 **Agulhas Plat** Indian Ocean
Ahaggar = Hoggar
21H8 **Ahar** Iran
13D1 **Ahaus** Germany
35B1 **Ahipara B** New Zealand
13D2 **Ahlen** Germany
42C4 **Ahmadābād** India
44A2 **Ahmadnagar** India
50E3 **Ahmar Mts** Ethiopia
67C1 **Ahoskie** USA
13D2 **Ahr** *R* Germany
13D2 **Ahrgebirge** *Mts* Germany
12G7 **Åhus** Sweden
41F2 **Āhuvān** Iran
41E3 **Ahvāz** Iran
69A4 **Aiajuela** Costa Rica
14C3 **Aigoual, Mount** France
29C3 **Aikawa** Japan
67B2 **Aiken** USA
31A5 **Ailao Shan** *Upland* China
75D2 **Aimorés** Brazil
16B3 **Aïn Beïda** Algeria
48B1 **Ain Beni Mathar** Morocco
49E2 **Ain Dalla** *Well* Egypt
15C2 **Aïn el Hadjel** Algeria
50B2 **Aïn Galakka** Chad
15C2 **Aïn Oussera** Algeria
48B1 **Aïn Sefra** Algeria
40B4 **'Ain Sukhna** Egypt
60D2 **Ainsworth** USA
15B2 **Aïn Témouchent** Algeria
29B4 **Aioi** Japan
48B2 **Aïoun Abd el Malek** *Well* Mauritius
48B3 **Aïoun El Atrouss** Mauritius
72E7 **Aiquile** Bolivia
48C3 **Aïr** *Desert Region* Niger
8D4 **Airdrie** Scotland
13B2 **Aire** France
6D3 **Aire** *R* England
13C3 **Aire** *R* France
55L3 **Airforce I** Canada
54E3 **Aishihik** Canada
13B3 **Aisne** *Department* France
14C2 **Aisne** *R* France
27H7 **Aitape** Papua New Guinea
19F1 **Aiviekste** *R* Latvia
14D3 **Aix-en-Provence** France
14D2 **Aix-les-Bains** France
43F4 **Aiyar Res** India
17E3 **Aiyion** Greece
17E3 **Aiyna** *I* Greece
43G4 **Āizawl** India
51B6 **Aizeb** *R* Namibia
29D3 **Aizu-Wakamatsu** Japan
16B2 **Ajaccio** Corsica, Italy
16B2 **Ajaccio, G d'** Corsica, Italy
49E1 **Ajdābiyā** Libya
29E2 **Ajigasawa** Japan
45C2 **Ajlūn** Jordan
41G4 **Ajman** UAE
42C3 **Ajmer** India
59D4 **Ajo** USA
15B1 **Ajo, Cabo de** *C* Spain
17F3 **Ak** *R* Turkey
29D2 **Akabira** Japan
29C3 **Akaishi-sanchi** *Mts* Japan
44B2 **Akalkot** India
45B1 **Akanthou** Cyprus
35B2 **Akaroa** New Zealand
29B4 **Akashi** Japan
21K5 **Akbulak** Russian Federation
40C2 **Akçakale** Turkey
48A2 **Akchar** *Watercourse* Mauritius
50C3 **Aketi** Zaïre
41D1 **Akhalkalaki** Georgia
40D1 **Akhalsikhe** Georgia
17E3 **Akharnái** Greece
49E1 **Akhdar, Jabal al** *Mts* Libya
41G5 **Akhdar, Jebel** *Mt* Oman
40A2 **Akhisar** Turkey
19F1 **Akhiste** Latvia
49F2 **Akhmîm** Egypt
21H6 **Akhtubinsk** Russian Federation
21E5 **Akhtyrka** Ukraine
29B4 **Aki** Japan
55K4 **Akimiski I** Canada
29E3 **Akita** Japan
48A3 **Akjoujt** Mauritius
45C2 **'Akko** Israel
54E3 **Aklavik** Canada
48B3 **Aklé Aouana** *Desert Region* Mauritius
50D3 **Akobo** Ethiopia
50D3 **Akobo** *R* Ethiopia/Sudan
42B1 **Akoha** Afghanistan
42D4 **Akola** India
42D4 **Akot** India
55M3 **Akpatok I** Canada
17E3 **Ákra Kafirévs** *C* Greece
17E4 **Ákra Líthinon** *C* Greece
17E3 **Ákra Maléa** *C* Greece
12A2 **Akranes** Iceland
17F3 **Ákra Sídheros** *C* Greece
17E3 **Ákra Spátha** *C* Greece
17E3 **Ákra Taínaron** *C* Greece
57E2 **Akron** USA
45B1 **Akrotiri** Cyprus
45B1 **Akrotiri B** Cyprus
42D1 **Aksai Chin** *Mts* China
21E8 **Aksaray** Turkey
21J5 **Aksay** Kazakhstan
42D1 **Aksayquin Hu** *L* China
40B2 **Akşehir** Turkey
40B2 **Akseki** Turkey
25N4 **Aksenovo Zilovskoye** Russian Federation
26E1 **Aksha** Russian Federation
39G1 **Aksu** China
50D2 **Aksum** Ethiopia
24J5 **Aktogay** Kazakhstan
21K6 **Aktumsyk** Kazakhstan
21K5 **Aktyubinsk** Kazakhstan
12B1 **Akureyri** Iceland
Akyab = Sittwe
24K5 **Akzhal** Kazakhstan
63E2 **Alabama** *R* USA
57E3 **Alabama** *State* USA
67A2 **Alabaster** USA
40C2 **Ala Dağlari** *Mts* Turkey
21G7 **Alagir** Russian Federation
73L5 **Alagoas** *State* Brazil
73L6 **Alagoinhas** Brazil
15B1 **Alagón** Spain
41E4 **Al Ahmadi** Kuwait
70D3 **Alajuela** Costa Rica
54B3 **Alakanuk** USA
24K5 **Alakol, Ozero** *L* Kazakhstan/Russian Federation
12L5 **Alakurtti** Russian Federation
27H5 **Alamagan** *I* Pacific Ocean
41E3 **Al Amārah** Iraq
59B3 **Alameda** USA
59C3 **Alamo** USA
62A2 **Alamogordo** USA
62C3 **Alamo Heights** USA
62A1 **Alamosa** USA
12H6 **Åland** *I* Finland
21E8 **Alanya** Turkey
67B2 **Alapaha** *R* USA
42L4 **Alapayevsk** Russian Federation
15B2 **Alarcón, Embalse de** *Res* Spain
40A2 **Alaşehir** Turkey
26D3 **Ala Shan** *Mts* China
54C3 **Alaska** *State* USA
54D4 **Alaska,G of** USA
54C3 **Alaska Range** *Mts* USA
16B2 **Alassio** Italy
20H5 **Alatyr'** Russian Federation
34B2 **Alawoona** Australia
41G5 **Al'Ayn** UAE
39F2 **Alayskiy Khrebet** *Mts* Tajikistan
25R3 **Alazeya** *R* Russian Federation
14D3 **Alba** Italy
15B2 **Albacete** Spain
15A1 **Alba de Tormes** Spain
40D2 **Al Badi** Iraq
17E1 **Alba Iulia** Romania
17D2 **Albania** *Republic* Europe
32A4 **Albany** Australia
67B2 **Albany** Georgia, USA
64B3 **Albany** Kentucky, USA
65E2 **Albany** New York, USA
56A2 **Albany** Oregon, USA
55K4 **Albany** *R* Canada
15B1 **Albarracin, Sierra de** *Mts* Spain
41G5 **Al Bātinah** *Region* Oman
27H8 **Albatross B** Australia
49E1 **Al Bayḑa** Libya
45C1 **Al Baylūlīyah** Syria
67B1 **Albemarle** USA
67C1 **Albemarle Sd** USA
15B1 **Alberche** *R* Spain
13B2 **Albert** France
54G4 **Alberta** *Province* Canada
27H7 **Albert Edward** *Mt* Papua New Guinea
47C3 **Albertinia** South Africa
50D3 **Albert,L** Uganda/Zaïre
57D2 **Albert Lea** USA
50D3 **Albert Nile** *R* Uganda
58D1 **Alberton** USA
14D2 **Albertville** France
14C3 **Albi** France
61E2 **Albia** USA
73H2 **Albina** Surinam
64C2 **Albion** Michigan, USA
61D2 **Albion** Nebraska, USA
65D2 **Albion** New York, USA
40C4 **Al Bi'r** Saudi Arabia
15B2 **Alborán** *I* Spain
12G7 **Ålborg** Denmark
13E3 **Albstadt-Ebingen** Germany
40D3 **Al Bū Kamāl** Syria
56C3 **Albuquerque** USA
41G5 **Al Buraymī** Oman
49D1 **Al Burayqah** Libya
49E1 **Al Burdī** Libya
32D4 **Albury** Australia
41E3 **Al Buşayyah** Iraq
15B1 **Alcalá de Henares** Spain
16C3 **Alcamo** Sicily, Italy
15B1 **Alcañiz** Spain
73K4 **Alcântara** Brazil
15A2 **Alcántara, Embalse de** *Res* Spain
15B2 **Alcaraz** Spain

Alcaraz, Sierra de
Aniak

15B2 **Alcaraz, Sierra de** *Mts* Spain
15B2 **Alcázar de San Juan** Spain
15B2 **Alcira** Spain
75E2 **Alcobaça** Brazil
15B1 **Alcolea de Pinar** Spain
15B2 **Alcoy** Spain
15C2 **Alcudia** Spain
46J8 **Aldabra Is** Indian Ocean
62A3 **Aldama** Mexico
25O4 **Aldan** Russian Federation
25P4 **Aldan** *R* Russian Federation
25O4 **Aldanskoye Nagor'ye** *Upland* Russian Federation
7E3 **Aldeburgh** England
14B2 **Alderney** *I* Channel Islands
7D4 **Aldershot** England
48A3 **Aleg** Mauritius
75A2 **Alegre** *R* Brazil
74E3 **Alegrete** Brazil
25Q4 **Aleksandrovsk Sakhalinskiy** Russian Federation
24J4 **Alekseyevka** Kazakhstan
20F5 **Aleksin** Russian Federation
18D1 **Älem** Sweden
75D3 **Além Paraíba** Brazil
14C2 **Alençon** France
66E5 **Alenuihaha Chan** Hawaiian Islands
21F8 **Aleppo** Syria
55M1 **Alert** Canada
14C3 **Alès** France
16B2 **Alessandria** Italy
24B3 **Ålesund** Norway
54C4 **Aleutian Ra** *Mts* USA
37L2 **Aleutian Trench** Pacific Ocean
54E4 **Alexander Arch** USA
47B2 **Alexander Bay** South Africa
67A2 **Alexander City** USA
76G3 **Alexander I** Antarctica
35A3 **Alexandra** New Zealand
74J8 **Alexandra,C** South Georgia
55L2 **Alexandra Fjord** Canada
49E1 **Alexandria** Egypt
57D3 **Alexandria** Louisiana, USA
57D2 **Alexandria** Minnesota, USA
57F3 **Alexandria** Virginia, USA
17F2 **Alexandroúpolis** Greece
45C2 **Aley** Lebanon
24K4 **Aleysk** Russian Federation
41D3 **Al Fallūjah** Iraq
15B1 **Alfaro** Spain
17F2 **Alfatar** Bulgaria
41E4 **Al Fāw** Iraq
75C3 **Alfensas** Brazil
17E3 **Alfiós** *R* Greece
75D3 **Alfonso Cláudio** Brazil
8D3 **Alford** Scotland
75D3 **Alfredo Chaves** Brazil
7D3 **Alfreton** England
41E4 **Al Furūthi** Saudi Arabia
21K6 **Alga** Kazakhstan
15A2 **Algeciras** Spain
Alger = Algiers
48B2 **Algeria** *Republic* Africa
16B2 **Alghero** Sardinia, Italy
15C2 **Algiers** Algeria
61E2 **Algona** USA
65D1 **Algonquin Park** Canada
38D3 **Al Ḩadd** Oman
40D3 **Al Hadīthah** Iraq
40C3 **Al Hadīthah** Saudi Arabia
40D2 **Al Ḩaḑr** Iraq
45D1 **Al Haffah** Syria
41G5 **Al Ḩajar al Gharbī** *Mts* Oman
40C3 **Al Hamad** *Desert Region* Jordan/Saudi Arabia
41E4 **Al Haniyah** *Desert Region* Iraq
41E5 **Al Ḩarīq** Saudi Arabia
40C3 **Al Harrah** *Desert Region* Saudi Arabia
49D2 **Al Harūj al Aswad** *Upland* Libya
41E4 **Al Hasa** *Region* Saudi Arabia
40D2 **Al Ḩasakah** Syria
40C4 **Al Hawjā'** Saudi Arabia
41E3 **Al Hayy** Iraq
45D2 **Al Hījānah** Syria
41D3 **Al Ḩillah** Iraq
41E5 **Al Ḩillah** Saudi Arabia
15B2 **Al Hoceima** Morocco
50E2 **Al Ḩudaydah** Yemen
41E4 **Al Hufūf** Saudi Arabia
41F5 **Al Humrah** *Region* UAE
41G5 **Al Huwatsah** Oman
41E2 **Alīābad** Iran
41G4 **Aliabad** Iran
17E2 **Aliákmon** *R* Greece
41E3 **Alī al Gharbī** Iraq
44A2 **Alībāg** India
15B2 **Alicante** Spain
56D4 **Alice** USA
16D3 **Alice, Punta** *Pt* Italy
32C3 **Alice Springs** Australia
16C3 **Alicudi** *I* Italy
42D3 **Aligarh** India
41E3 **Aligūdarz** Iran
42B2 **Ali-Khel** Afghanistan
17F3 **Alimniá** *I* Greece
43F3 **Alīpur Duār** India
64C2 **Aliquippa** USA
40C3 **Al' Īsawiyah** Saudi Arabia
47D3 **Aliwal North** South Africa
49E2 **Al Jaghbūb** Libya
40D3 **Al Jālamīd** Saudi Arabia
49E2 **Al Jawf** Libya
40C4 **Al Jawf** Saudi Arabia
40D2 **Al Jazīrah** *Desert Region* Iraq/Syria
15A2 **Aljezur** Portugal
41E4 **Al Jubayl** Saudi Arabia
41D4 **Al Jumaymah** Saudi Arabia
45D4 **Al Kabid** *Desert* Jordan
41D4 **Al Kahfah** Saudi Arabia
41E4 **Al Kāmil** Oman
40D2 **Al Khābūr** *R* Syria
41G5 **Al Khābūrah** Oman
41D3 **Al Khālis** Iraq
41G4 **Al Khaşab** Oman
41F4 **Al Khawr** Qatar
49D1 **Al Khums** Libya
41F5 **Al Kidan** *Region* Saudi Arabia
45D2 **Al Kiswah** Syria
18A2 **Alkmaar** Netherlands
49E2 **Al Kufrah Oasis** Libya
41E3 **Al Kūt** Iraq
Al Lādhiqīyah = Latakia
43E3 **Allahābād** India
45D2 **Al Lajāh** *Mt* Syria
54C3 **Allakaket** USA
30B2 **Allanmyo** Burma
67B2 **Allatoona L** USA
47D1 **Alldays** South Africa
65D2 **Allegheny** *R* USA
57F3 **Allegheny Mts** USA
67B2 **Allendale** USA
6C2 **Allendale Town** England
9B2 **Allen, Lough** *L* Irish Republic
35A3 **Allen,Mt** New Zealand
65D2 **Allentown** USA
44B4 **Alleppey** India
14C2 **Aller** *R* France
60C2 **Alliance** USA
50E1 **Al Līth** Saudi Arabia
41F5 **Al Liwā'** *Region* UAE
8D3 **Alloa** Scotland
34D1 **Allora** Australia
65E1 **Alma** Canada
64C2 **Alma** Michigan, USA
60D2 **Alma** Nebraska, USA
39F1 **Alma Ata** Kazakhstan
15A2 **Almada** Portugal
41E4 **Al Majma'ah** Saudi Arabia
41F4 **Al Manāmah** Bahrain
41D3 **Al Ma'nīyah** Iraq
59B2 **Almanor,L** USA
15B2 **Almansa** Spain
41F5 **Al Māriyyah** UAE
49E1 **Al Marj** Libya
75C2 **Almas** *R* Brazil
15B1 **Almazán** Spain
13E2 **Alme** *R* Germany
13D1 **Almelo** Netherlands
75D2 **Almenara** Brazil
15A1 **Almendra, Embalse de** *Res* Spain
15B2 **Almería** Spain
15B2 **Almería, Golfo de** Spain
20J5 **Al'met'yevsk** Russian Federation
18C1 **Älmhult** Sweden
41D4 **Al Midhnab** Saudi Arabia
41E3 **Al Miqdādīyah** Iraq
17E3 **Almirós** Greece
41E4 **Al Mish'āb** Saudi Arabia
15A2 **Almodôvar** Portugal
42D3 **Almora** India
41E4 **Al Mubarraz** Saudi Arabia
40C4 **Al Mudawwara** Jordan
41F4 **Al Muḩarraq** Bahrain
38C4 **Al Mukallā** Yemen
50E2 **Al Mukhā** Yemen
41D3 **Al Musayyib** Iraq
40C4 **Al Muwaylih** Saudi Arabia
8C3 **Alness** Scotland
6D2 **Aln, R** England
41E3 **Al Nu'mānīyah** Iraq
6D2 **Alnwick** England
27F7 **Alor** *I* Indonesia
30C4 **Alor Setar** Malaysia
Alost = Aalst
32E2 **Alotau** Papua New Guinea
32B3 **Aloysius,Mt** Australia
64C1 **Alpena** USA
16C1 **Alpi Dolomitiche** *Mts* Italy
59E4 **Alpine** Arizona, USA
62B2 **Alpine** Texas, USA
58D2 **Alpine** Wyoming, USA
16B1 **Alps** *Mts* Europe
49D1 **Al Qaddāhiyah** Libya
45D1 **Al Qadmūs** Syria
40D3 **Al Qā'im** Iraq
40C4 **Al Qalībah** Saudi Arabia
40D2 **Al Qāmishlī** Syria
45D1 **Al Qardāḩah** Syria
49D1 **Al Qaryah Ash Sharqiyah** Libya
40C3 **Al Qaryatayn** Syria
41D4 **Al Qasīm** *Region* Saudi Arabia
41E4 **Al Qatīf** Saudi Arabia
49D2 **Al Qatrūn** Libya
41E4 **Al Qayşāmah** Saudi Arabia
15A2 **Alquera** *Res* Portugal/Spain
40C3 **Al Qunayţirah** Syria
50E2 **Al Qunfidhah** Saudi Arabia
41E3 **Al Qurnah** Iraq
45D1 **Al Quşayr** Syria
45D2 **Al Quţayfah** Syria
41E5 **Al Quwayīyah** Saudi Arabia
18B1 **Als** *I* Denmark
14D2 **Alsace** *Region* France
13D3 **Alsace, Plaine d'** France
18B2 **Alsfeld** Germany
6C2 **Alston** England
12J5 **Alta** Norway
74D4 **Alta Gracia** Argentina
69D5 **Altagracia de Orituco** Venezuela
26B2 **Altai** *Mts* Mongolia
67B2 **Altamaha** *R* USA
73H4 **Altamira** Brazil
16D2 **Altamura** Italy
26D1 **Altanbulag** Mongolia
70B2 **Altata** Mexico
24K5 **Altay** China
25L5 **Altay** Mongolia
24K4 **Altay** *Mts* Russian Federation
13D2 **Altenkirchen** Germany
75B2 **Alto Araguaia** Brazil
51D5 **Alto Molócue** Mozambique
7D4 **Alton** England
64A3 **Alton** USA
65D2 **Altoona** USA
75B2 **Alto Sucuriú** Brazil
7C3 **Altrincham** England
39G2 **Altun Shan** *Mts* China
58B2 **Alturas** USA
62C2 **Altus** USA
40C4 **Al'Ulā** Saudi Arabia
40C4 **Al Urayq** *Desert Region* Saudi Arabia
62C1 **Alva** USA
63C2 **Alvarado** USA
12G6 **Älvdalen** Sweden
63C3 **Alvin** USA
12J5 **Älvsbyn** Sweden
49D2 **Al Wāha** Libya
40C4 **Al Wajh** Saudi Arabia
42D3 **Alwar** India
40D3 **Al Widyān** *Desert Region* Iraq/Saudi Arabia
31A2 **Alxa Youqi** China
31B2 **Alxa Zuoqi** China
41E2 **Alyat** Azerbaijan
12J8 **Alytus** Lithuania
13E3 **Alzey** Germany
50D3 **Amadi** Sudan
41D2 **Amādīyah** Iraq
55L3 **Amadjuak L** Canada
12G7 **Åmål** Sweden
25N4 **Amalat** *R* Russian Federation
17E3 **Amaliás** Greece
42C4 **Amalner** India
75A3 **Amambaí** Brazil
75B3 **Amambaí** *R* Brazil
75A3 **Amamba, Serra** *Mts* Brazil/Paraguay
26F4 **Amami** *I* Japan
26F4 **Amami gunto** *Arch* Japan
73H3 **Amapá** Brazil
73H3 **Amapá** *State* Brazil
62B1 **Amarillo** USA
21F7 **Amasya** Turkey
73H4 **Amazonas** *R* Brazil
72E4 **Amazonas** *State* Brazil
42D2 **Ambāla** India
44C4 **Ambalangoda** Sri Lanka
51E6 **Ambalavao** Madagascar
50B3 **Ambam** Cameroon
51E5 **Ambanja** Madagascar
25S3 **Ambarchik** Russian Federation
72C4 **Ambato** Ecuador
51E5 **Ambato-Boeny** Madagascar
51E5 **Ambatolampy** Madagascar
51E5 **Ambatondrazaka** Madagascar
18C3 **Amberg** Germany
70D3 **Ambergris Cay** *I* Belize
43E4 **Ambikāpur** India
51E5 **Ambilobe** Madagascar
6C2 **Ambleside** England
51E6 **Amboasary** Madagascar
51E5 **Ambodifototra** Madagascar
51E6 **Ambohimahasoa** Madagascar
Amboina = Ambon
27F7 **Ambon** Indonesia
51E6 **Ambositra** Madagascar
51E6 **Ambovombe** Madagascar
27E6 **Amboyna Cay** *I* S China Sea
51E5 **Ambre, Montagne d'** *Mt* Madagascar
51B4 **Ambriz** Angola
33F2 **Ambrym** *I* Vanuatu
50C2 **Am Dam** Chad
20L2 **Amderma** Russian Federation
70B2 **Ameca** Mexico
18B2 **Ameland** *I* Netherlands
68D2 **Amenia** USA
58D2 **American Falls** USA
58D2 **American Falls Res** USA
59D2 **American Fork** USA
76F10 **American Highland** *Upland* Antarctica
37L5 **American Samoa** *Is* Pacific Ocean
67B2 **Americus** USA
18B2 **Amersfoort** Netherlands
47D2 **Amersfoort** South Africa
61E1 **Amery** USA
76G10 **Amery Ice Shelf** Antarctica
61E2 **Ames** USA
68E1 **Amesbury** USA
17E3 **Amfilokhía** Greece
17E3 **Amfissa** Greece
25P3 **Amga** Russian Federation
25P3 **Amgal** *R* Russian Federation
26G2 **Amgu** Russian Federation
26G1 **Amgun'** *R* Russian Federation
50D2 **Amhara** *Region* Ethiopia
55M5 **Amherst** Canada
68D1 **Amherst** Massachusetts, USA
65D3 **Amherst** Virginia, USA
44B3 **Amhūr** India
16C2 **Amiata, Monte** *Mt* Italy
14C2 **Amiens** France
29C3 **Amino** Japan
45C1 **Amioune** Lebanon
46K8 **Amirante Is** Indian Ocean
62B3 **Amistad Res** Mexico
43F3 **Amlekhganj** Nepal
7B3 **Amlwch** Wales
40C3 **Amman** Jordan
7C4 **Ammanford** Wales
12K6 **Ämmänsaari** Finland
55P3 **Ammassalik** Greenland
28A3 **Amnyong-dan** *C* N Korea
41F2 **Amol** Iran
17F3 **Amorgós** *I* Greece
55L5 **Amos** Canada
Amoy = Xiamen
51E6 **Ampanihy** Madagascar
75C3 **Amparo** Brazil
51E5 **Ampasimanolotra** Madagascar
15C1 **Amposta** Spain
42D4 **Amrāvati** India
42C4 **Amreli** India
42C2 **Amritsar** India
43K1 **Amroha** India
36E6 **Amsterdam** *I* Indian Ocean
18A2 **Amsterdam** Netherlands
47E2 **Amsterdam** South Africa
65E2 **Amsterdam** USA
50C2 **Am Timan** Chad
24H5 **Amu Darya** *R* Uzbekistan
55J2 **Amund Ringnes I** Canada
54F2 **Amundsen G** Canada
76E **Amundsen-Scott** *Base* Antarctica
76F4 **Amundsen Sea** Antarctica
27E7 **Amuntai** Indonesia
26F1 **Amur** *R* Russian Federation
25N2 **Anabar** *R* Russian Federation
66C4 **Anacapa Is** USA
72F2 **Anaco** Venezuela
56B2 **Anaconda** USA
58B1 **Anacortes** USA
62C1 **Anadarko** USA
25T3 **Anadyr'** Russian Federation
25T3 **Anadyr'** *R* Russian Federation
25U3 **Anadyrskiy Zaliv** *S* Russian Federation
25T3 **Anadyrskoye Ploskogor'ye** *Plat* Russian Federation
17F3 **Anáfi** *I* Greece
75D1 **Anagé** Brazil
40D3 **'Ānah** Iraq
59C4 **Anaheim** USA
44B3 **Anaimalai Hills** India
44C2 **Anakāpalle** India
51E5 **Analalava** Madagascar
27D6 **Anambas, Kepulauan** *Is* Indonesia
64A2 **Anamosa** USA
21E8 **Anamur** Turkey
29B4 **Anan** Japan
44B3 **Anantapur** India
42D2 **Anantnag** India
73J7 **Anápolis** Brazil
41G3 **Anār** Iran
41F3 **Anārak** Iran
27H5 **Anatahan** *I* Pacific Ocean
74D3 **Añatuya** Argentina
28B3 **Anbyŏn** N Korea
54D3 **Anchorage** USA
72E7 **Ancohuma** *Mt* Bolivia
72C6 **Ancón** Peru
16C2 **Ancona** Italy
68D1 **Ancram** USA
74B6 **Ancud** Chile
74B6 **Ancud, Golfo de** *G* Chile
13C4 **Ancy-le-Franc** France
72D6 **Andahuaylas** Peru
12F6 **Åndalsnes** Norway
15A2 **Andalucia** *Region* Spain
67A2 **Andalusia** USA
39H4 **Andaman Is** India
75D1 **Andaraí** Brazil
13C3 **Andelot** France
12H5 **Andenes** Norway
18B2 **Andernach** Germany
64B2 **Anderson** Indiana, USA
63D1 **Anderson** Missouri, USA
67B2 **Anderson** S Carolina, USA
54F3 **Anderson** *R* Canada
72C5 **Andes, Cordillera de los** *Mts* Peru
44B2 **Andhra Pradesh** *State* India
17E3 **Andikíthira** *I* Greece
24J5 **Andizhan** Uzbekistan
24H6 **Andkhui** Afghanistan
28B3 **Andong** S Korea
15C1 **Andorra** *Principality* SW Europe
15C1 **Andorra-La-Vella** Andorra
7D4 **Andover** England
68E1 **Andover** New Hampshire, USA
68B1 **Andover** New York, USA
75B3 **Andradina** Brazil
19G1 **Andreapol'** Russian Federation
40B2 **Andreas,C** Cyprus
62B2 **Andrews** USA
16D2 **Andria** Italy
17E3 **Ándros** *I* Greece
57F4 **Andros** *I* The Bahamas
67C4 **Andros Town** Bahamas
44A3 **Androth** *I* India
15B2 **Andújar** Spain
51B5 **Andulo** Angola
48C3 **Anéfis** Mali
48C4 **Aného** Togo
33F3 **Aneityum** *I* Vanuatu
25M4 **Angarsk** Russian Federation
20A3 **Ånge** Sweden
70A2 **Angel de la Guarda** *I* Mexico
12G7 **Ängelholm** Sweden
34C1 **Angellala Creek** *R* Australia
66B1 **Angels Camp** USA
27G7 **Angemuk** *Mt* Indonesia
14B2 **Angers** France
13B3 **Angerville** France
30C3 **Angkor** *Hist Site* Cambodia
10C3 **Anglesey** *I* Wales
63C3 **Angleton** USA
Angmagssalik = Ammassalik
51E5 **Angoche** Mozambique
74B5 **Angol** Chile
64C2 **Angola** Indiana, USA
51B5 **Angola** *Republic* Africa
52J5 **Angola Basin** Atlantic Ocean
14C2 **Angoulême** France
48A1 **Angra do Heroismo** Azores
75D3 **Angra dos Reis** Brazil
69E3 **Anguilla** *I* Caribbean Sea
69B2 **Anguilla Cays** *Is* Caribbean Sea
43F4 **Angul** India
50C4 **Angumu** Zaïre
18C1 **Anholt** *I* Denmark
31C4 **Anhua** China
26F2 **Anhui** China
31D3 **Anhui** *Province* China
75B2 **Anhumas** Brazil
28A3 **Anhŭng** S Korea
54C3 **Aniak** USA

Anicuns Asturias

75C2 **Anicuns** Brazil
62A1 **Animas** *R* USA
62A2 **Animas Peak** *Mt* USA
61E2 **Anita** USA
26H2 **Aniva, Mys** *C* Russian Federation
13B3 **Anizy-le-Château** France
14B2 **Anjou** *Region* France
51E5 **Anjouan** *I* Comoros
51E5 **Anjozorobe** Madagascar
28B3 **Anju** N Korea
31B3 **Ankang** China
21E8 **Ankara** Turkey
51E5 **Ankaratra** *Mt* Madagascar
51E6 **Ankazoabo** Madagascar
51E5 **Ankazobe** Madagascar
61E2 **Ankeny** USA
18C2 **Anklam** Germany
30D3 **An Loc** Vietnam
31B4 **Anlong** China
31C3 **Anlu** China
64B3 **Anna** USA
16B3 **'Annaba** Algeria
40C3 **An Nabk** Saudi Arabia
40C3 **An Nabk** Syria
40D4 **An Nafūd** *Desert* Saudi Arabia
49E2 **An Nāfūrah** Libya
41D3 **An Najaf** Iraq
8D4 **Annan** Scotland
65D3 **Annapolis** USA
43E3 **Annapurna** *Mt* Nepal
64C2 **Ann Arbor** USA
45D1 **An Nāsirah** Syria
41E3 **An Nāsirīyah** Iraq
14D2 **Annecy** France
30D3 **An Nhon** Vietnam
31A5 **Anning** China
67A2 **Anniston** USA
48C4 **Annobon** *I* Equatorial Guinea
14C2 **Annonay** France
69J1 **Annotto Bay** Jamaica
31D3 **Anqing** China
31B2 **Ansai** China
18C3 **Ansbach** Germany
69C3 **Anse d'Hainault** Haiti
31E1 **Anshan** China
31B4 **Anshun** China
60D2 **Ansley** USA
62C2 **Anson** USA
27F8 **Anson B** Australia
48C3 **Ansongo** Mali
64C1 **Ansonville** Canada
64C3 **Ansted** USA
21F8 **Antakya** Turkey
51F5 **Antalaha** Madagascar
21E8 **Antalya** Turkey
21E8 **Antalya Körfezi** *B* Turkey
51E5 **Antananarivo** Madagascar
76G1 **Antarctic Circle** Antarctica
76G3 **Antarctic Pen** Antarctica
15B2 **Antequera** Spain
62A2 **Anthony** USA
48B1 **Anti-Atlas** *Mts* Morocco
55M5 **Anticosti, Ī. de** Canada
64B1 **Antigo** USA
69E3 **Antigua** *I* Caribbean Sea
Anti Lebanon = Sharqi, Jebel esh
59B3 **Antioch** USA
33G5 **Antipodes Is** New Zealand
63C2 **Antlers** USA
74B2 **Antofagasta** Chile
75C4 **Antonina** Brazil
62A1 **Antonito** USA
9C2 **Antrim** Northern Ireland
68E1 **Antrim** USA
9C2 **Antrim** *County* Northern Ireland
9C2 **Antrim Hills** Northern Ireland
51E5 **Antsirabe** Madagascar
51E5 **Antsirañana** Madagascar
51E5 **Antsohiny** Madagascar
28B2 **Antu** China
30D3 **An Tuc** Vietnam
13C2 **Antwerp** Belgium
Antwerpen = Antwerp
9C3 **An Uaimh** Irish Republic
28A3 **Anui** S Korea
42C3 **Anūpgarh** India
44C4 **Anuradhapura** Sri Lanka
Anvers = Antwerp
54B3 **Anvik** USA
25L5 **Anxi** China
31C2 **Anyang** China
31A3 **A'nyêmaqên Shan** *Mts* China
25S3 **Anyuysk** Russian Federation
24K4 **Anzhero-Sudzhensk** Russian Federation
16C2 **Anzio** Italy
33F2 **Aoba** *I* Vanuatu
29E2 **Aomori** Japan
16B1 **Aosta** Italy
48B3 **Aouker** *Desert Region* Mauritius
48C2 **Aoulef** Algeria
50B1 **Aozou** Chad
74E2 **Apa** *R* Brazil/Paraguay
57E4 **Apalachee B** USA
67B3 **Apalachicola** USA
67A3 **Apalachicola B** USA
72D3 **Apaporis** *R* Brazil/Colombia
75B3 **Aparecida do Taboado** Brazil
27F5 **Aparri** Philippines
17D1 **Apatin** Croatia
20E2 **Apatity** Russian Federation
70B3 **Apatzingan** Mexico
18B2 **Apeldoorn** Netherlands
33H2 **Apia** Western Samoa
75C3 **Apiaí** Brazil
73G2 **Apoera** Surinam
34B3 **Apollo Bay** Australia
67B3 **Apopka,L** USA
73H7 **Aporé** *R* Brazil
64A1 **Apostle Is** USA
57E3 **Appalachian Mts** USA
16C2 **Appennino Abruzzese** *Mts* Italy
16B2 **Appennino Ligure** *Mts* Italy
16D2 **Appennino Lucano** *Mts* Italy
16D2 **Appennino Napoletano** *Mts* Italy
16C2 **Appennino Tosco-Emilliano** *Mts* Italy
16C2 **Appennino Umbro-Marchigiano** *Mts* Italy
6C2 **Appleby** England
61D1 **Appleton** Minnesota, USA
64B2 **Appleton** Wisconsin, USA
21J7 **Apsheronskiy Poluostrov** *Pen* Azerbaijan
74F2 **Apucarana** Brazil
72E2 **Apure** *R* Venezuela
72D6 **Apurimac** *R* Peru
40C4 **'Aqaba** Jordan
40B4 **'Aqaba,G of** Egypt/Saudi Arabia
45C4 **'Aqaba, Wadi el** Egypt
41F3 **'Aqdā** Iran
73G8 **Aqidauana** Brazil
75A3 **Aquidabán** *R* Paraguay
74E2 **Aquidauana** Brazil
75A2 **Aquidauana** *R* Brazil
43E3 **Ara** India
67A2 **Arab** USA
45C1 **'Arab al Mulk** Syria
45C3 **'Araba, Wadi** Israel
36E4 **Arabian Basin** Indian Ocean
38E4 **Arabian Sea** SW Asia
45D2 **'Arab, Jabal al** *Mt* Syria
73L6 **Aracajú** Brazil
75A3 **Aracanguy,Mts de** Paraguay
73L4 **Aracati** Brazil
75D1 **Aracatu** Brazil
73H8 **Araçatuba** Brazil
15A2 **Aracena** Spain
73K7 **Araçuaí** Brazil
45C3 **'Arad** Israel
21C6 **Arad** Romania
50C2 **Arada** Chad
41F5 **'Arādah** UAE
32C1 **Arafura S** Indonesia/Australia
73H7 **Aragarças** Brazil
21G7 **Aragats** *Mt* Armenia
15B1 **Aragon** *R* Spain
15B1 **Aragón** *Region* Spain
75C1 **Araguaçu** Brazil
73H6 **Araguaia** *R* Brazil
73J5 **Araguaína** Brazil
73J7 **Araguari** Brazil
75C2 **Araguari** *R* Brazil
29C3 **Arai** Japan
45C3 **Araif el Naqa, Gebel** *Mt* Egypt
48C2 **Arak** Algeria
41E3 **Arāk** Iran
30A2 **Arakan Yoma** *Mts* Burma
44B3 **Arakkonam** India
41E2 **Araks** *R* Azerbaijan/Iran
24G5 **Aral S** Kazakhstan
24H5 **Aral'sk** Kazakhstan
15B1 **Aranda de Duero** Spain
10B2 **Aran I** Irish Republic
10B3 **Aran Is** Irish Republic
15B1 **Aranjuez** Spain
47B1 **Aranos** Namibia
63C3 **Aransas Pass** USA
28B4 **Arao** Japan
48B3 **Araouane** Mali
60D2 **Arapahoe** USA
74E4 **Arapey** *R* Uruguay
73L5 **Arapiraca** Brazil
75B3 **Araporgas** Brazil
74G3 **Ararangua** Brazil
73J8 **Araraquara** Brazil
75C3 **Araras** Brazil
32D4 **Ararat** Australia
41D2 **Ararat** Armenia
Ararat, Mt = Büyük Ağri Daği
75D3 **Araruama, Lagoa de** Brazil
40D3 **Ar'ar, Wadi** *Watercourse* Saudi Arabia
41D1 **Aras** *R* Turkey
21H8 **Aras** *R* Azerbaijan/Iran
29D3 **Arato** Japan
72E2 **Arauca** *R* Venezuela
72D2 **Arauea** Colombia
42C3 **Arāvalli Range** *Mts* India
33E1 **Arawa** Papua New Guinea
73J7 **Araxá** Brazil
21G8 **Araxes** *R* Iran
50D3 **Arba Minch** Ethiopia
16B3 **Arbatax** Sardinia,
21G8 **Arbil** Iraq
12H6 **Arbrå** Sweden
8D3 **Arbroath** Scotland
14B3 **Arcachon** France
68A1 **Arcade** USA
67B3 **Arcadia** USA
58B2 **Arcata** USA
66D1 **Arc Dome** *Mt* USA
20G3 **Archangel** Russian Federation
68C2 **Archbald** USA
59E3 **Arches Nat Pk** USA
13C3 **Arcis-sur-Aube** France
58D2 **Arco** USA
75C3 **Arcos** Brazil
15A2 **Arcos de la Frontera** Spain
55K2 **Arctic Bay** Canada
76C1 **Arctic Circle**
54E3 **Arctic Red** *R* Canada
54E3 **Arctic Red River** Canada
54D3 **Arctic Village** USA
76G2 **Arctowski** *Base* Antarctica
17F2 **Arda** *R* Bulgaria
21H8 **Ardabīl** Iran
21G7 **Ardahan** Turkey
12F6 **Årdal** Norway
48C2 **Ardar des Iforas** *Upland* Algeria/Mali
9C3 **Ardee** Irish Republic
41F3 **Ardekān** Iran
13C3 **Ardennes** *Department* France
18B2 **Ardennes** *Region* Belgium
41F3 **Ardestāh** Iran
40C3 **Ardh es Suwwan** *Desert Region* Jordan
15A2 **Ardila** *R* Portugal
34C2 **Ardlethan** Australia
56D3 **Ardmore** USA
8B3 **Ardnamurchan Pt** Scotland
13A2 **Ardres** France
8C3 **Ardrishaig** Scotland
8C4 **Ardrossan** Scotland
69D3 **Arecibo** Puerto Rico
73L4 **Areia Branca** Brazil
59B3 **Arena,Pt** USA
13D1 **Arenberg** *Region* Germany
12F7 **Arendal** Norway
72D7 **Arequipa** Peru
16C2 **Arezzo** Italy
16C2 **Argenta** Italy
14C2 **Argentan** France
13B3 **Argenteuil** France
71D7 **Argentina** *Republic* S America
52F7 **Argentine Basin** Atlantic Ocean
74B8 **Argentino, Lago** Argentina
14C2 **Argenton-sur-Creuse** France
17F2 **Argeş** *R* Romania
42B2 **Arghardab** *R* Afghanistan
17E3 **Argolikós Kólpos** *G* Greece
13C3 **Argonne** *Region* France
17E3 **Árgos** Greece
17E3 **Argostólion** Greece
66B3 **Arguello,Pt** USA
66D3 **Argus Range** *Mts* USA
32B2 **Argyle,L** Australia
8C3 **Argyll** Scotland
18C1 **Århus** Denmark
51C6 **Ariamsvlei** Namibia
48B3 **Aribinda** Burkina
74B1 **Arica** Chile
42C2 **Arifwala** Pakistan
Arihā = Jericho
60C3 **Arikaree** *R* USA
69L1 **Arima** Trinidad
75C2 **Arinos** Brazil
73G6 **Arinos** *R* Brazil
69L1 **Aripo,Mt** Trinidad
72F5 **Aripuanā** Brazil
72F5 **Aripuanã** *R* Brazil
8C3 **Arisaig** Scotland
45B3 **'Arîsh, Wadi el** *Watercourse* Egypt
56B3 **Arizona** *State* USA
12G7 **Årjäng** Sweden
25Q4 **Arka** Russian Federation
21G5 **Arkadak** Russian Federation
63D2 **Arkadelphia** USA
8C3 **Arkaig, L** Scotland
24H4 **Arkalyk** Kazakhstan
57D3 **Arkansas** *R* USA
57D3 **Arkansas** *State* USA
63C1 **Arkansas City** USA
29C2 **Arkhipovka** Russian Federation
25K2 **Arkipelag Nordenshelda** *Arch* Russian Federation
10B3 **Arklow** Irish Republic
15B1 **Arlanzón** *R* Spain
14C3 **Arles** France
61D2 **Arlington** S Dakota, USA
63C2 **Arlington** Texas, USA
65D3 **Arlington** Virginia, USA
58B1 **Arlington** Washington, USA
64B2 **Arlington Heights** USA
18B3 **Arlon** Belgium
Armageddon = Megiddo
9C2 **Armagh** Northern Ireland
9C2 **Armagh** *County* Northern Ireland
13B4 **Armançon** *R* France
21G7 **Armavir** Russian Federation
72C3 **Armenia** Colombia
21G7 **Armenia** *Republic* Europe
13B2 **Armentières** Belgium
32E4 **Armidale** Australia
55L3 **Arnaud** *R* Canada
40B2 **Arnauti** *C* Cyprus
62C1 **Arnett** USA
18B2 **Arnhem** Netherlands
32C2 **Arnhem,C** Australia
32C2 **Arnhem Land** Australia
66B1 **Arnold** USA
65D1 **Arnprior** Canada
13E2 **Arnsberg** Germany
47B2 **Aroab** Namibia
13E2 **Arolsen** Germany
33G1 **Arorae** *I* Kiribati
16B1 **Arosa** Switzerland
13B3 **Arpajon** France
75C1 **Arraias** Brazil
75C1 **Arraias, Serra de** *Mts* Brazil
41D3 **Ar Ramādī** Iraq
8C4 **Arran, I of** Scotland
40C2 **Ar Raqqah** Syria
49D2 **Ar Rāqūbah** Libya
14C1 **Arras** France
41D4 **Ar Rass** Saudi Arabia
45D1 **Ar Rastan** Syria
48A2 **Arrecife** Canary Islands
41E3 **Ar Rifā'ī** Iraq
41E3 **Ar Rihāb** *Desert Region* Iraq
Ar Riyād = Riyadh
8C3 **Arrochar** Scotland
75C1 **Arrojado** *R* Brazil
58C2 **Arrowrock Res** USA
35A2 **Arrowtown** New Zealand
66B3 **Arroyo Grande** USA
41F4 **Ar Ru'ays** Qatar
41G5 **Ar Rustāq** Oman
40D3 **Ar Rutbah** Iraq
41D5 **Ar Ruwaydah** Saudi Arabia
44B3 **Arsikere** India
20H4 **Arsk** Russian Federation
17E3 **Árta** Greece
28C2 **Artem** Russian Federation
25L4 **Artemovsk** Russian Federation
25N4 **Artemovskiy** Russian Federation
56C3 **Artesia** USA
35B2 **Arthurs P** New Zealand
74E4 **Artigas** Uruguay
54H3 **Artillery L** Canada
14C1 **Artois** *Region* France
19F3 **Artsiz** Ukraine
76G2 **Arturo Prat** *Base* Antarctica
21G7 **Artvin** Turkey
50D3 **Aru** Zaïre
73H6 **Aruanã** Brazil
69C4 **Aruba** *I* Caribbean Sea
27G7 **Aru, Kepulauan** *Arch* Indonesia
43F3 **Arun** *R* Nepal
43G3 **Arunāchal Pradesh** *Union Territory* India
44B4 **Aruppukkottai** India
50D4 **Arusha** Tanzania
50C3 **Aruwimi** *R* Zaïre
60B3 **Arvada** USA
26D2 **Arvayheer** Mongolia
55L5 **Arvida** Canada
12H5 **Arvidsjaur** Sweden
12G7 **Arvika** Sweden
59C3 **Arvin** USA
45C1 **Arwad** *I* Syria
20G4 **Arzamas** Russian Federation
15B2 **Arzew** Algeria
42C2 **Asadabad** Afghanistan
29B4 **Asahi** *R* Japan
29E2 **Asahi dake** *Mt* Japan
29E2 **Asahikawa** Japan
28A3 **Asan-man** *B* S Korea
43F4 **Asansol** India
49D2 **Asawanwah** *Well* Libya
20L4 **Asbest** Russian Federation
47C2 **Asbestos Mts** South Africa
65E2 **Asbury Park** USA
52H5 **Ascension** *I* Atlantic Ocean
70D3 **Ascensión, B de la** Mexico
18B3 **Aschaffenburg** Germany
18C2 **Aschersleben** Germany
16C2 **Ascoli Piceno** Italy
50E2 **Āseb** Ethiopia
48C2 **Asedjrad** *Upland* Algeria
50D3 **Asela** Ethiopia
12H6 **Åsele** Sweden
17E2 **Asenovgrad** Bulgaria
13C3 **Asfeld** France
20K4 **Asha** Russian Federation
7D3 **Ashbourne** England
67B2 **Ashburn** USA
33G5 **Ashburton** New Zealand
32A3 **Ashburton** *R* Australia
40B3 **Ashdod** Israel
63D2 **Ashdown** USA
67A1 **Asheboro** USA
57E3 **Asheville** USA
34D1 **Ashford** Australia
7E4 **Ashford** England
59D3 **Ash Fork** USA
29D2 **Ashibetsu** Japan
29D3 **Ashikaga** Japan
28B4 **Ashizuri-misaki** *Pt* Japan
24G6 **Ashkhabad** Turkmenistan
62C1 **Ashland** Kansas, USA
57E3 **Ashland** Kentucky, USA
60B1 **Ashland** Montana, USA
61D2 **Ashland** Nebraska, USA
64C2 **Ashland** Ohio, USA
56A2 **Ashland** Oregon, USA
65D3 **Ashland** Virginia, USA
61E1 **Ashland** Wisconsin, USA
34C1 **Ashley** Australia
60D1 **Ashley** USA
68C2 **Ashokan Res** USA
45C3 **Ashqelon** Israel
41D3 **Ash Shabakh** Iraq
41G4 **Ash Sha'm** UAE
41D2 **Ash Sharqāt** Iraq
41E3 **Ash Shatrah** Iraq
38C4 **Ash Shihr** Yemen
41E4 **Ash Shumlūl** Saudi Arabia
64C2 **Ashtabula** USA
55M4 **Ashuanipi L** Canada
21F8 **Asi** *R* Syria
15A2 **Asilah** Morocco
16B2 **Asinara** *I* Sardinia, Italy
24K4 **Asino** Russian Federation
50E1 **Asīr** *Region* Saudi Arabia
43E5 **Aska** India
40D2 **Aşkale** Turkey
12G7 **Askersund** Sweden
45B4 **Asl** Egypt
42C1 **Asmar** Afghanistan
50D2 **Asmera** Ethiopia
28B4 **Aso** Japan
50D2 **Asosa** Ethiopia
50D1 **Asoteriba, Jebel** *Mt* Sudan
62B2 **Aspermont** USA
35A2 **Aspiring,Mt** New Zealand
40C2 **As Sabkhah** Syria
41E5 **As Salamiyah** Saudi Arabia
40C2 **As Salamīyah** Syria
41D3 **As Salmān** Iraq
43G3 **Assam** *State* India
41E3 **As Samāwah** Iraq
41F5 **Aş Şanām** *Region* Saudi Arabia
45D2 **Aş Şanamayn** Syria
18B2 **Assen** Netherlands
18C1 **Assens** Denmark
49D1 **As Sidrah** Libya
54H5 **Assiniboia** Canada
54G4 **Assiniboine,Mt** Canada
73H8 **Assis** Brazil
40C3 **As Sukhnah** Syria
41E5 **Aş Şumman** *Region* Saudi Arabia
51E4 **Assumption** *I* Seychelles
40C3 **As Suwaydā'** Syria
41D3 **Aş Şuwayrah** Iraq
41E2 **Astara** Azerbaijan
16B2 **Asti** Italy
17F3 **Astipálaia** *I* Greece
15A1 **Astorga** Spain
56A2 **Astoria** USA
21H6 **Astrakhan'** Russian Federation
15A1 **Asturias** *Region* Spain

Asuka Ban Aranyaprathet

76F12 Asuka Base Antarctica
74E3 Asunción Paraguay
26H5 Asuncion I Marianas
50D3 Aswa R Uganda
40B5 Aswân Egypt
49F2 Aswân High Dam Egypt
49F2 Asyût Egypt
74C2 Atacama, Desierto de Desert Chile
33H1 Atafu I Tokelau Islands
45C3 Atā'ita, Jebel el Mt Jordan
48C4 Atakpamé Togo
27F7 Atambua Indonesia
55N3 Atangmik Greenland
45B4 Ataqa, Gebel Mt Egypt
48A2 Atar Mauritius
40C2 Atatirk Baraji Res Turkey
66B3 Atascadero USA
24J5 Atasu Kazakhstan
50D2 Atbara Sudan
24H4 Atbasar Kazakhstan
57D4 Atchafalaya B USA
57D3 Atchison USA
68C3 Atco USA
16C2 Atessa Italy
13B2 Ath Belgium
54G4 Athabasca Canada
54G4 Athabasca R Canada
54H4 Athabasca,L Canada
67A2 Athens Alabama, USA
57E3 Athens Georgia, USA
17E3 Athens Greece
64C3 Athens Ohio, USA
68B2 Athens Pennsylvania, USA
67B1 Athens Tennessee, USA
63C2 Athens Texas, USA
Athína = Athens
10B3 Athlone Irish Republic
45B1 Athna Cyprus
68D1 Athol USA
17E2 Áthos Mt Greece
9C3 Athy Irish Republic
50B2 Ati Chad
55J5 Atikoken Canada
25R3 Atka Russian Federation
21G5 Atkarsk Russian Federation
63D1 Atkins USA
57E3 Atlanta Georgia, USA
64C2 Atlanta Michigan, USA
61D2 Atlantic USA
57F3 Atlantic City USA
68C2 Atlantic Highlands USA
52H8 Atlantic-Indian Antarctic Basin Atlantic Ocean
52H7 Atlantic Indian Ridge Atlantic Ocean
Atlas Mts = Haut Atlas, Moyen Atlas
48C1 Atlas Saharien Mts Algeria
54E4 Atlin Canada
54E4 Atlin L Canada
45C2 'Atlit Israel
57E3 Atmore USA
51E6 Atofinandrahana Madagascar
63C2 Atoka USA
72C2 Atrato R Colombia
41F5 Attaf Region UAE
50E1 Aţ Ţā'if Saudi Arabia
45D2 At Tall Syria
67A2 Attalla USA
55K4 Attawapiskat Canada
55K4 Attawapiskat R Canada
41D3 At Taysīyah Desert Region Saudi Arabia
64B2 Attica Indiana, USA
68A1 Attica New York, USA
13C3 Attigny France
45B1 Attila Line Cyprus
65E2 Attleboro Massachusetts, USA
30D3 Attopeu Laos
40C4 At Tubayq Upland Saudi Arabia
12H7 Atvidaberg Sweden
66B2 Atwater USA
14D3 Aubagne France
13C3 Aube Department France
13C3 Aube R France
14C3 Aubenas France
67A2 Auburn Alabama, USA
59B3 Auburn California, USA
64B2 Auburn Indiana, USA
65E2 Auburn Maine, USA
61D2 Auburn Nebraska, USA
65D2 Auburn New York, USA
58B1 Auburn Washington, USA
14C3 Auch France
33G4 Auckland New Zealand
37K7 Auckland Is New Zealand
14C3 Aude R France
55K4 Auden Canada
61E2 Audubon USA
34C1 Augathella Australia
9C2 Aughnacloy Northern Ireland
47B2 Aughrabies Falls South Africa
18C3 Augsburg Germany
32A4 Augusta Australia
57E3 Augusta Georgia, USA
63C1 Augusta Kansas, USA
57G2 Augusta Maine, USA
58D1 Augusta Montana, USA
64A2 Augusta Wisconsin, USA
19E2 Augustow Poland
32A3 Augustus,Mt Australia
47B1 Auob R Namibia
42D3 Auraiya India
42D5 Aurangābād India
48C1 Aurès Mts Algeria
16B3 Aurès, Mt de l' Algeria
13D1 Aurich Germany
14C3 Aurillac France
56C3 Aurora Colorado, USA
64B2 Aurora Illinois, USA
64C3 Aurora Indiana, USA
63D1 Aurora Mississippi, USA
61D2 Aurora Nebraska, USA
47B2 Aus Namibia
64C2 Au Sable USA
48A2 Ausert Well Morocco
8D2 Auskerry, I Scotland
57D2 Austin Minnesota, USA
59C3 Austin Nevada, USA
68A2 Austin Pennsylvania, USA
56D3 Austin Texas, USA
32D4 Australian Alps Mts Australia
18C3 Austria Federal Republic Europe
70B3 Autlán Mexico
14C2 Autun France
14C2 Auvergne Region France
14C2 Auxerre France
13A2 Auxi-le-Château France
14C2 Avallon France
66C4 Avalon USA
55N5 Avalon Pen Canada
75C3 Avaré Brazil
13E1 Ave R Germany
45C3 Avedat Hist Site Israel
73G4 Aveiro Brazil
15A1 Aveiro Portugal
74E4 Avellaneda Argentina
16C2 Avellino Italy
66B3 Avenal USA
13B2 Avesnes-sur-Helpe France
12H6 Avesta Sweden
16C2 Avezzano Italy
8D3 Aviemore Scotland
35B2 Aviemore,L New Zealand
14C3 Avignon France
15B1 Avila Spain
15A1 Avilés Spain
61D2 Avoca Iowa, USA
68B1 Avoca New York, USA
34B3 Avoca R Australia
68B1 Avon USA
7C4 Avon County England
7D4 Avon R Dorset, England
7D3 Avon R Warwick, England
59D4 Avondale USA
7C4 Avonmouth Wales
67B3 Avon Park USA
13B3 Avre R France
17D2 Avtovac Bosnia & Herzegovina, Yugoslavia
45D2 A'waj R Syria
29D4 Awaji-shima I Japan
50E3 Awarē Ethiopia
35A2 Awarua Pt New Zealand
50E3 Awash Ethiopia
50E3 Awash R Ethiopia
29C3 Awa-shima I Japan
35B2 Awatere R New Zealand
49D2 Awbārī Libya
50C3 Aweil Sudan
8C3 Awe, Loch L Scotland
49E2 Awjilah Libya
55J1 Axel Heiberg I Canada
7C4 Axminster England
29C3 Ayabe Japan
74E5 Ayacucho Argentina
69C5 Ayacucho Colombia
72D6 Ayacucho Peru
24K5 Ayaguz Kazakhstan
39G2 Ayakkum Hu L China
15A2 Ayamonte Spain
25P4 Ayan Russian Federation
72D6 Ayaviri Peru
21D8 Aydin Turkey
17F3 Áyios Evstrátios I Greece
25N3 Aykhal Russian Federation
7D4 Aylesbury England
45D2 'Ayn al Fījah Syria
40D2 Ayn Zālah Iraq
49E2 Ayn Zuwayyah Well Libya
50D3 Ayod Sudan
32D2 Ayr Australia
8C4 Ayr Scotland
8C4 Ayr R Scotland
6B2 Ayre,Pt of Isle of Man, British Isles
17F2 Aytos Bulgaria
30C3 Ayutthaya Thailand
17F3 Ayvacik Turkey
17F3 Ayvalik Turkey
43E3 Āzamgarh India
48B3 Azaouad Desert Region Mali
48C3 Azaouak, Vallée de l' Niger
48D3 Azare Nigeria
40C2 A'zāz Syria
Azbine = Aïr
48A2 Azeffal Watercourse Mauritius
21H7 Azerbaijan Republic Europe
72C4 Azogues Ecuador
20H2 Azopol'ye Russian Federation
46B4 Azores Is Atlantic Ocean
50C2 Azoum R Chad
21F6 Azov, Sof Russian Federation/Ukraine
48B1 Azrou Morocco
62A1 Aztec USA
72B2 Azuero,Pen de Panama
74E5 Azul Argentina
75B1 Azul, Serra Mts Brazil
16B3 Azzaba Algeria
45D2 Az-Zabdānī Syria
41G5 Az Zāhirah Mts Oman
49D2 Az Zahrah Libya
40C3 Az Zilaf Syria
41D4 Az Zilfī Saudi Arabia
41E3 Az Zubayr Iraq

B

45C2 Ba'abda Lebanon
40C3 Ba'albek Lebanon
45C3 Ba'al Hazor Mt Israel
50E3 Baardheere Somalia
17F2 Babadag Romania
40A1 Babaeski Turkey
72C4 Babahoyo Ecuador
50E2 Bāb al Mandab Str Djibouti/Yemen
32B1 Babar, Kepulauan I Indonesia
50D4 Babati Tanzania
20F4 Babayevo Russian Federation
61E1 Babbitt USA
64C2 Baberton USA
54F4 Babine L Canada
32C1 Babo Indonesia
41F2 Bābol Iran
27F5 Babuyan Is Philippines
73J4 Bacabal Brazil
27F7 Bacan I Indonesia
21D6 Bacău Romania
30D1 Bac Can Vietnam
13D3 Baccarat France
34B3 Bacchus Marsh Australia
39F2 Bachu China
54J3 Back R Canada
30D1 Bac Ninh Vietnam
27F5 Bacolod Philippines
6C3 Bacup England
44B3 Badagara India
31A1 Badain Jaran Shamo Desert China
15A2 Badajoz Spain
15C1 Badalona Spain
40D3 Badanah Saudi Arabia
28B2 Badaohe China
13E3 Bad Bergzabern Germany
13D2 Bad Ems Germany
18B3 Baden-Baden Germany
13D3 Badenviller France
18B3 Baden-Württemberg State Germany
18C3 Badgastein Austria
66C2 Badger USA
18B2 Bad-Godesberg Germany
18B2 Bad Hersfeld Germany
13D2 Bad Honnef Germany
42B4 Badin Pakistan
16C1 Bad Ischl Austria
40C3 Badiyat ash Sham Desert Region Iraq/Jordan
18B3 Bad-Kreuznach Germany
60C1 Badlands Region USA
13E2 Bad Lippspringe Germany
13E2 Bad Nauheim Germany
13D2 Bad Nevenahr-Ahrweiler Germany
40C5 Badr Ḩunayn Saudi Arabia
13E2 Bad Ryrmont Germany
18C3 Bad Tolz Germany
44C4 Badulla Sri Lanka
13E2 Bad Wildungen Germany
13E3 Bad Wimpfen Germany
15B2 Baena Spain
48A3 Bafatá Guinea-Bissau
55L2 Baffin B Canada/Greenland
63C3 Baffin B USA
55L2 Baffin I Canada
50B3 Bafia Cameroon
48A3 Bafing R Mali
48A3 Bafoulabé Mali
50B3 Bafoussam Cameroon
41G3 Bāfq Iran
21F7 Bafra Burun Pt Turkey
41G4 Bāft Iran
50C3 Bafwasende Zaïre
43E3 Bagaha India
44B2 Bāgalkot India
51D4 Bagamoyo Tanzania
59D4 Bagdad USA
74F4 Bagé Brazil
60B2 Baggs USA
41D3 Baghdād Iraq
43F4 Bagherhat Bangladesh
41G3 Bāghīn Iran
42B1 Baghlan Afghanistan
61D1 Bagley USA
48B4 Bagnoa Ivory Coast
14C3 Bagnols-sur-Cèze France
48B3 Bagoé R Mali
28A2 Bag Tai China
27F5 Baguio Philippines
43F3 Bāhādurābād Bangladesh
57F4 Bahamas,The Is Caribbean Sea
43F4 Baharampur India
40A4 Bahariya Oasis Egypt
42C3 Bahawalnagar Pakistan
42C3 Bahawalpur Pakistan
42C3 Bahawalpur Division Pakistan
Bahia = Salvador
73K6 Bahia State Brazil
74D5 Bahía Blanca Argentina
70D3 Bahía, Islas de la Honduras
56B4 Bahia Kino Mexico
74C6 Bahias, Cabo dos Argentina
50D2 Bahir Dar Ethiopia
45A3 Bahra el Manzala L Egypt
43E3 Bahraich India
38D3 Bahrain Sheikhdom Arabian Pen
41D3 Bahr al Milh L Iraq
50C3 Bahr Aouk R Chad/Central African Republic
Bahrat Lut = Dead Sea
Bahr el Abiad = White Nile
50C3 Bahr el Arab Watercourse Sudan
Bahr el Azraq = Blue Nile
50D3 Bahr el Ghazal R Sudan
50B2 Bahr el Ghazal Watercourse Chad
45A3 Bahr Fâqûs R Egypt
15A2 Baia de Setúbal B Portugal
51B5 Baia dos Tigres Angola
21C6 Baia Mare Romania
50B3 Baïbokoum Chad
26F2 Baicheng China
55M5 Baie-Comeau Canada
45C2 Baie de St Georges B Lebanon
55L4 Baie-du-Poste Canada
65E1 Baie St Paul Canada
55N5 Baie-Verte Canada
31B3 Baihe China
31C3 Bai He R China
41D3 Ba'īji Iraq
25M4 Baikal, L Russian Federation
43E4 Baikunthpur India
Baile Atha Cliath = Dublin
17E2 Băileşti Romania
13B2 Bailleul France
31A3 Baima China
67B2 Bainbridge USA
54B3 Baird Mts USA
31D1 Bairin Youqi China
31D1 Bairin Zuoqi China
32D4 Bairnsdale Australia
43E3 Baitadi Nepal
28A2 Baixingt China
17D1 Baja Hungary
70A1 Baja California Pen Mexico
59C4 Baja California Norte State Mexico
70A2 Baja, Punta Pt Mexico
20K5 Bakal Russian Federation
50C3 Bakala Central African Republic
48A3 Bakel Senegal
59C3 Baker California, USA
56C2 Baker Montana, USA
56B2 Baker Oregon, USA
55J3 Baker Foreland Pt Canada
54J3 Baker L Canada
54J3 Baker Lake Canada
56A2 Baker,Mt USA
56B3 Bakersfield USA
7D3 Bakewell England
41G2 Bakharden Turkmenistan
41G2 Bakhardok Turkmenistan
21E5 Bakhmach Ukraine
12C1 Bakkaflói B Iceland
50D3 Bako Ethiopia
50C3 Bakouma Central African Republic
21H7 Baku Azerbaijan
40B2 Balâ Turkey
7C3 Bala Wales
27E6 Balabac I Philippines
27E6 Balabac Str Malaysia/Philippines
43E4 Bālāghāt India
34A2 Balaklava Australia
21H5 Balakovo Russian Federation
43E4 Balāngīr India
21G5 Balashov Russian Federation
43F4 Balasore India
17D1 Balaton L Hungary
9C3 Balbriggan Irish Republic
74E5 Balcarce Argentina
17F2 Balchik Bulgaria
33F5 Balclutha New Zealand
63D1 Bald Knob USA
7D4 Baldock England
67B2 Baldwin USA
58E1 Baldy Mt USA
56C3 Baldy Peak Mt USA
15C2 Balearic Is Spain
75E2 Baleia, Ponta da Pt Brazil
55M4 Baleine, Rivière de la R Canada
27F5 Baler Philippines
20J4 Balezino Russian Federation
32A1 Bali I Indonesia
40A2 Balikesir Turkey
40C2 Balīkh R Syria/Turkey
27E7 Balikpapan Indonesia
75B2 Baliza Brazil
42B1 Balkh Afghanistan
24J5 Balkhash Kazakhstan
24J5 Balkhash, L Kazakhstan
8C3 Ballachulish Scotland
8C4 Ballantrae Scotland
54G2 Ballantyne Str Canada
44B3 Ballāpur India
32D4 Ballarat Australia
8D3 Ballater Scotland
6B2 Ballaugh England
76G7 Balleny Is Antarctica
43E3 Ballia India
34D1 Ballina Australia
10B3 Ballina Irish Republic
62C2 Ballinger USA
9A4 Ballinskelligis B Irish Republic
13D4 Ballon d'Alsace Mt France
17D2 Ballsh Albania
68D1 Ballston Spa USA
9C2 Ballycastle Northern Ireland
9D2 Ballyclare Northern Ireland
9C4 Ballycotton B Irish Republic
9B3 Ballyhaunis Northern Ireland
9C2 Ballymena Northern Ireland
9C2 Ballymoney Northern Ireland
9C2 Ballynahinch Northern Ireland
9B2 Ballyshannon Irish Republic
9C3 Ballyteige B Irish Republic
34B3 Balmoral Australia
62B2 Balmorhea USA
42B3 Balochistān Region Pakistan
51B5 Balombo Angola
34C1 Balonn R Australia
42C3 Bālotra India
43E3 Balrāmpur India
32D4 Balranald Australia
73J5 Balsas Brazil
70B3 Balsas R Mexico
21D6 Balta Ukraine
12H7 Baltic S N Europe
40B3 Baltîm Egypt
57F3 Baltimore USA
43F3 Bālurghāt India
21J6 Balykshi Kazakhstan
41G4 Bam Iran
50B2 Bama Nigeria
48B3 Bamako Mali
50C3 Bambari Central African Republic
67B2 Bamberg USA
18C3 Bamberg Germany
50C3 Bambili Zaïre
75C3 Bambuí Brazil
50B3 Bamenda Cameroon
28A2 Bamiancheng China
50B3 Bamingui R Central African Republic
50B3 Bamingui Bangoran National Park Central African Republic
42B2 Bamiyan Afghanistan
33F1 Banaba I Kiribati
50C3 Banalia Zaïre
48B3 Banamba Mali
44E4 Bananga Nicobar Is, Indian Ocean
30C3 Ban Aranyaprathet Thailand

Belcher Is Bistcho L

55L4 **Belcher Is** Canada
42B1 **Belchiragh** Afghanistan
20J5 **Belebey** Russian Federation
50E3 **Beledweyne** Somalia
73J4 **Belém** Brazil
72C3 **Belén** Colombia
75A3 **Belén** Paraguay
56C3 **Belen** USA
33F2 **Bélep, Îles** Nouvelle Calédonie
16B3 **Belezma, Mts de** Algeria
9C2 **Belfast** Northern Ireland
47E2 **Belfast** South Africa
9C2 **Belfast Lough** *Estuary* Northern Ireland
60C1 **Belfield** USA
50D2 **Bēlfodiyo** Ethiopia
6D2 **Belford** England
14D2 **Belfort** France
44A2 **Belgaum** India
18A2 **Belgium** *Kingdom* NW Europe
21F5 **Belgorod** Russian Federation
21E6 **Belgorod Dnestrovskiy** Ukraine
58D1 **Belgrade** USA
17E2 **Belgrade** Serbia, Yugoslavia
49D2 **Bel Hedan** Libya
27D7 **Belitung** *I* Indonesia
70D3 **Belize** Belize
70D3 **Belize** *Republic* Central America
25P2 **Bel'kovskiy, Ostrov** *I* Russian Federation
14C2 **Bellac** France
54F4 **Bella Coola** Canada
63C3 **Bellaire** USA
44B2 **Bellary** India
34C1 **Bellata** Australia
68B2 **Bellefonte** USA
56C2 **Belle Fourche** USA
60C2 **Belle Fourche** *R* USA
14D2 **Bellegarde** France
13B4 **Bellegarde** France
67B3 **Belle Glade** USA
55N4 **Belle I** Canada
14B2 **Belle-Ile** *I* France
55N4 **Belle Isle,Str of** Canada
55L5 **Belleville** Canada
64B3 **Belleville** Illinois, USA
61D3 **Belleville** Kansas, USA
58D2 **Bellevue** Idaho, USA
64A2 **Bellevue** Iowa, USA
58B1 **Bellevue** Washington, USA
34D2 **Bellingen** Australia
6C2 **Bellingham** England
56A2 **Bellingham** USA
76G2 **Bellingshausen** *Base* Antarctica
76G3 **Bellingshausen S** Antarctica
16B1 **Bellinzona** Switzerland
72C2 **Bello** Colombia
33E3 **Bellona Reefs** Nouvelle Calédonie
66B1 **Bellota** USA
65E2 **Bellows Falls** USA
55K3 **Bell Pen** Canada
16C1 **Belluno** Italy
74D4 **Bell Ville** Argentina
68B1 **Belmont** USA
73L7 **Belmonte** Brazil
70D3 **Belmopan** Belize
26F1 **Belogorsk** Russian Federation
51E6 **Beloha** Madagascar
73K7 **Belo Horizonte** Brazil
61D3 **Beloit** Kansas, USA
57E2 **Beloit** Wisconsin, USA
20E3 **Belomorsk** Russian Federation
20K5 **Beloretsk** Russian Federation
20D5 **Belorussia** *Republic* Europe
51E5 **Belo-Tsiribihina** Madagascar
Beloye More *S* = **White Sea**
20F3 **Beloye Ozero** *L* Russian Federation
20F3 **Belozersk** Russian Federation
7D3 **Belper** England
64C3 **Belpre** USA
34A2 **Beltana** Australia
63C2 **Belton** USA
19F3 **Bel'tsy** Moldavia
24K5 **Belukha** *Mt* Russian Federation
20H2 **Belush'ye** Russian Federation
64B2 **Belvidere** Illinois, USA
68C2 **Belvidere** New Jersey, USA
24J2 **Belyy, Ostrov** *I* Russian Federation
51B4 **Bembe** Angola
48C3 **Bembéréké** Benin
57D2 **Bemidji** USA
63E1 **Bemis** USA
50C4 **Bena Dibele** Zaïre
34C3 **Benalla** Australia
8C3 **Ben Attow** *Mt* Scotland
15A1 **Benavente** Spain
8B3 **Benbecula** *I* Scotland
32A4 **Bencubbin** Australia
56A2 **Bend** USA
8C3 **Ben Dearg** *Mt* Scotland
50E3 **Bendarbeyla** Somalia
19F3 **Bendery** Moldavia
32D4 **Bendigo** Australia
18C3 **Benešov** Czechoslovakia
16C2 **Benevento** Italy
39G4 **Bengal,B of** Asia
49D1 **Ben Gardane** Tunisia
31D3 **Bengbu** China
49E1 **Benghazi** Libya
27D7 **Bengkulu** Indonesia
51B5 **Benguela** Angola
40B3 **Benha** Egypt
8C2 **Ben Hope** *Mt* Scotland
50C3 **Beni** Zaïre
72E6 **Béni** *R* Bolivia
48B1 **Beni Abbès** Algeria
15C1 **Benicarló** Spain
15B2 **Benidorm** Spain
15C2 **Beni Mansour** Algeria
49F2 **Beni Mazâr** Egypt
48B1 **Beni Mellal** Morocco
48C4 **Benin** *Republic* Africa
48C4 **Benin City** Nigeria
15B2 **Beni-Saf** Algeria
49F2 **Beni Suef** Egypt
60C3 **Benkelman** USA
8C2 **Ben Kilbreck** *Mt* Scotland
10C2 **Ben Lawers** *Mt* Scotland
8D3 **Ben Macdui** *Mt* Scotland
8B3 **Ben More** Scotland
8C2 **Ben More Assynt** *Mt* Scotland
35B2 **Benmore,L** New Zealand
25R2 **Bennetta, Ostrov** *I* Russian Federation
8C3 **Ben Nevis** *Mt* Scotland
65E2 **Bennington** USA
45C2 **Bennt Jbail** Lebanon
50B3 **Bénoué** *R* Cameroon
13E3 **Bensheim** Germany
56B3 **Benson** Arizona, USA
61D1 **Benson** Minnesota, USA
27F7 **Benteng** Indonesia
50C3 **Bentiu** Sudan
75A2 **Bento Gomes** *R* Brazil
63D2 **Benton** Arkansas, USA
66C2 **Benton** California, USA
64B3 **Benton** Kentucky, USA
64B2 **Benton Harbor** USA
48C4 **Benue** *R* Nigeria
8C3 **Ben Wyvis** *Mt* Scotland
31E1 **Benxi** China
Beograd = Belgrade
43E4 **Beohāri** India
28C4 **Beppu** Japan
17D2 **Berat** Albania
27G7 **Berau, Teluk** *B* Indonesia
50D2 **Berber** Sudan
50E2 **Berbera** Somalia
50B3 **Berbérati** Central African Republic
19F3 **Berdichev** Ukraine
21F6 **Berdyansk** Ukraine
64C3 **Berea** USA
48B4 **Berekum** Ghana
66B2 **Berenda** USA
40C5 **Berenice** Egypt
54J4 **Berens** *R* Canada
54J4 **Berens River** Canada
61D2 **Beresford** USA
19E3 **Berettyóújfalu** Hungary
19E2 **Bereza** Belorussia
19E3 **Berezhany** Ukraine
19F2 **Berezina** *R* Belorussia
20G3 **Bereznik** Russian Federation
20K4 **Berezniki** Russian Federation
21E6 **Berezovka** Ukraine
20L3 **Berezovo** Russian Federation
40A2 **Bergama** Turkey
16B1 **Bergamo** Italy
12F6 **Bergen** Norway
68B1 **Bergen** USA
13C2 **Bergen op Zoom** Netherlands
14C3 **Bergerac** France
13D2 **Bergisch-Gladbach** Germany
44C2 **Berhampur** India
25S4 **Beringa, Ostrov** *I* Russian Federation
25T3 **Beringovskiy** Russian Federation
37K2 **Bering S** Russian Federation/USA
76C6 **Bering Str** Russian Federation/USA
41G4 **Berīzak** Iran
15B2 **Berja** Spain
13D1 **Berkel** *R* Germany/ Netherlands
56A3 **Berkeley** USA
68A3 **Berkeley Spring** USA
7D4 **Berkhamsted** England
76F2 **Berkner I** Antarctica
17E2 **Berkovitsa** Bulgaria
7D4 **Berkshire** *County* England
68D1 **Berkshire Hills** USA
18C2 **Berlin** Germany
18C2 **Berlin** *State* Germany
65E2 **Berlin** New Hampshire, USA
72F8 **Bermejo** Bolivia
74E3 **Bermejo** *R* Argentina
53M5 **Bermuda** *I* Atlantic Ocean
Bern = Berne
62A1 **Bernalillo** USA
75B4 **Bernardo de Irigoyen** Argentina
68C2 **Bernardsville** USA
18C2 **Bernburg** Germany
16B1 **Berne** Switzerland
8B3 **Berneray, I** Scotland
55K2 **Bernier B** Canada
18C3 **Berounka** *R* Czechoslovakia
34B2 **Berri** Australia
48C1 **Berriane** Algeria
14C2 **Berry** *Region* France
66A1 **Berryessa,L** USA
57F4 **Berry Is** The Bahamas
68B3 **Berryville** USA
47B2 **Berseba** Namibia
60B3 **Berthoud P** USA
50B3 **Bertoua** Cameroon
33G1 **Beru** *I* Kiribati
65D2 **Berwick** USA
6C2 **Berwick-upon-Tweed** England
7C3 **Berwyn Mts** Wales
51E5 **Besalampy** Madagascar
14D2 **Besançon** France
19E3 **Beskidy Zachodnie** *Mts* Poland
40C2 **Besni** Turkey
45C3 **Besor** *R* Israel
67A2 **Bessemer** Alabama, USA
64B1 **Bessemer** Michigan, USA
51E5 **Betafo** Madagascar
15A1 **Betanzos** Spain
45C3 **Bet Guvrin** Israel
47D2 **Bethal** South Africa
47B2 **Bethanie** Namibia
61E2 **Bethany** Missouri, USA
63C1 **Bethany** Oklahoma, USA
54B3 **Bethel** Alaska, USA
68D2 **Bethel** Connecticut, USA
64C2 **Bethel Park** USA
65D3 **Bethesda** USA
45C3 **Bethlehem** Israel
47D2 **Bethlehem** South Africa
65D2 **Bethlehem** USA
47D3 **Bethulie** South Africa
14C1 **Béthune** France
51E6 **Betioky** Madagascar
34B1 **Betoota** Australia
50B3 **Betou** Congo
39E1 **Betpak Dala** *Steppe* Kazakhstan
51E6 **Betroka** Madagascar
55M5 **Betsiamites** Canada
64A2 **Bettendorf** USA
43E3 **Bettiah** India
42D4 **Betūl** India
13C2 **Betuwe** *Region* Netherlands
42D3 **Betwa** *R* India
7C3 **Betws-y-coed** Wales
13D2 **Betzdorf** Germany
7D3 **Beverley** England
68E1 **Beverly** USA
66C3 **Beverly Hills** USA
7E4 **Bexhill** England
40B2 **Bey Dağlari** Turkey
48B4 **Beyla** Guinea
44B3 **Beypore** India
Beyrouth = Beirut
40B2 **Beyşehir** Turkey
21E8 **Beysehir Gölü** *L* Turkey
45C2 **Beyt Shean** Israel
20F4 **Bezhetsk** Russian Federation
14C3 **Béziers** France
41G2 **Bezmein** Turkmenistan
26D1 **Beznosova** Russian Federation
43F3 **Bhadgaon** Nepal
44C2 **Bhadrāchalam** India
43F4 **Bhadrakh** India
44B3 **Bhadra Res** India
44B3 **Bhadrāvati** India
42B3 **Bhag** Pakistan
43F3 **Bhāgalpur** India
42C2 **Bhakkar** Pakistan
42D4 **Bhandāra** India
42D3 **Bharatpur** India
42C4 **Bharūch** India
43F4 **Bhātiāpāra Ghat** Bangladesh
42C2 **Bhatinda** India
44A3 **Bhatkal** India
43F4 **Bhātpāra** India
42C4 **Bhāvnagar** India
43E5 **Bhawānipatna** India
42C2 **Bhera** Pakistan
43E3 **Bheri** *R* Nepal
43E4 **Bhilai** India
42C3 **Bhīlwāra** India
44C2 **Bhīmavaram** India
42D3 **Bhind** India
42D3 **Bhiwāni** India
44B2 **Bhongir** India
42D4 **Bhopāl** India
43F4 **Bhubaneshwar** India
42B4 **Bhuj** India
42D4 **Bhusāwal** India
39H3 **Bhutan** *Kingdom* Asia
27G7 **Biak** *I* Indonesia
19E2 **Biala Podlaska** Poland
18D2 **Białogard** Poland
19E2 **Bialystok** Poland
12A1 **Biargtangar** *C* Iceland
41G2 **Biārjmand** Iran
14B3 **Biarritz** France
40B4 **Biba** Egypt
29E2 **Bibai** Japan
51B5 **Bibala** Angola
18B3 **Biberach** Germany
48B4 **Bibiani** Ghana
17F1 **Bicaz** Romania
7D4 **Bicester** England
59D3 **Bicknell** USA
48C4 **Bida** Nigeria
44B2 **Bīdar** India
41G5 **Bidbid** Oman
65E2 **Biddeford** USA
7C6 **Bideford** England
7B4 **Bideford B** England
48C2 **Bidon 5** Algeria
19E2 **Biebrza** *R* Poland
16B1 **Biel** Switzerland
18D2 **Bielawa** Poland
18B2 **Bielefeld** Germany
16B1 **Biella** Italy
19E2 **Bielsk Podlaski** Poland
30D3 **Bien Hoa** Vietnam
55L4 **Bienville, Lac** Canada
16C2 **Biferno** *R* Italy
40A1 **Biga** Turkey
17F3 **Bigadiç** Turkey
58D1 **Big Belt Mts** USA
62B3 **Big Bend Nat Pk** USA
63E2 **Big Black** *R* USA
61D2 **Big Blue** *R* USA
67B3 **Big Cypress Swamp** USA
54D3 **Big Delta** USA
8D4 **Biggar** Scotland
54H4 **Biggar Kindersley** Canada
34D1 **Biggenden** Australia
7D3 **Biggleswade** England
58D1 **Big Hole** *R* USA
60B1 **Bighorn** *R* USA
60B1 **Bighorn L** USA
60B2 **Bighorn Mts** USA
48C4 **Bight of Benin** *B* W Africa
48C4 **Bight of Biafra** *B* Cameroon
55L3 **Big I** Canada
62B2 **Big Lake** USA
48A3 **Bignona** Senegal
59C3 **Big Pine** USA
67B4 **Big Pine Key** USA
66C3 **Big Pine Mt** USA
64B2 **Big Rapids** USA
54H4 **Big River** Canada
58D1 **Big Sandy** USA
61D2 **Big Sioux** *R* USA
66D1 **Big Smokey V** USA
56C3 **Big Spring** USA
60C2 **Big Springs** USA
61D1 **Big Stone City** USA
64C3 **Big Stone Gap** USA
66B2 **Big Sur** USA
58E1 **Big Timber** USA
55J4 **Big Trout L** Canada
55K4 **Big Trout Lake** Canada
16D2 **Bihać** Bosnia & Herzegovina, Yugoslavia
43F3 **Bihār** India
43F4 **Bihār** *State* India
50D4 **Biharamulo** Tanzania
21C6 **Bihor** *Mt* Romania
48A3 **Bijagós, Arquipélago dos** *Is* Guinea-Bissau
44B2 **Bijāpur** India
44C2 **Bījāpur** India
41E2 **Bījār** Iran
43E3 **Bijauri** Nepal
17D2 **Bijeljina** Bosnia & Herzegovina, Yugoslavia
31B4 **Bijie** China
42D3 **Bijnor** India
42C3 **Bijnot** Pakistan
42C3 **Bīkāner** India
45C2 **Bikfaya** Lebanon
26G2 **Bikin** Russian Federation
50B4 **Bikoro** Zaïre
Bilbo = Bilbao
42C3 **Bilāra** India
42D2 **Bilāspur** India
43E4 **Bilāspur** India
30B3 **Bilauktaung Range** *Mts* Burma/Thailand
15B1 **Bilbao** Spain
45A3 **Bilbeis** Egypt
18D3 **Bílé** *R* Czechoslovakia
17D2 **Bileća** Yugoslavia
40B1 **Bilecik** Turkey
50C3 **Bili** *R* Zaïre
25S3 **Bilibino** Russian Federation
56C2 **Billings** USA
50B2 **Bilma** Niger
57E3 **Biloxi** USA
50C2 **Biltine** Chad
67C3 **Bimini Is** Bahamas
42D4 **Bīna-Etawa** India
51D5 **Bindura** Zimbabwe
51C5 **Binga** Zimbabwe
51D5 **Binga, Mt** Mozambique/ Zimbabwe
34D1 **Bingara** Australia
18B3 **Bingen** Germany
65F1 **Bingham** USA
57F2 **Binghamton** USA
40D2 **Bingöl** Turkey
31D3 **Binhai** China
15C2 **Binibeca, Cabo** *C* Spain
27D6 **Bintan** *I* Indonesia
27E6 **Bintulu** Malaysia
74B5 **Bió Bió** *R* Chile
48C4 **Bioko** *I* Equatorial Guinea
44B2 **Bīr** India
49E2 **Bîr Abu Husein** *Well* Egypt
49E2 **Bi'r al Harash** *Well* Libya
50C2 **Birao** Central African Republic
43F3 **Biratnagar** Nepal
34B3 **Birchip** Australia
61E1 **Birch L** USA
54G4 **Birch Mts** Canada
55J4 **Bird** Canada
32C3 **Birdsville** Australia
32C2 **Birdum** Australia
45A4 **Bîr el 'Agramîya** *Well* Egypt
45B3 **Bîr el Duweidâr** *Well* Egypt
43E3 **Birganj** Nepal
45B3 **Bîr Gifgâfa** *Well* Egypt
45A4 **Bîr Gindali** *Well* Egypt
45B3 **Bîr Hasana** *Well* Egypt
75B3 **Birigui** Brazil
45D1 **Bīrīn** Syria
41G3 **Bīrjand** Iran
40B4 **Birkat Qârun** *L* Egypt
13D3 **Birkenfeld** Germany
7C3 **Birkenhead** England
21D6 **Bîrlad** Romania
45B3 **Bîr Lahfân** *Well* Egypt
7C3 **Birmingham** England
57E3 **Birmingham** USA
49E2 **Bîr Misâha** *Well* Egypt
48A2 **Bir Moghrein** Mauritius
48C3 **Birnin-Kebbi** Nigeria
26G2 **Birobidzhan** Russian Federation
9C3 **Birr** Irish Republic
15C2 **Bir Rabalou** Algeria
34C1 **Birrie** *R* Australia
8D2 **Birsay** Scotland
20K4 **Birsk** Russian Federation
49E2 **Bîr Tarfâwi** *Well* Egypt
45B4 **Bîr Udelb** *Well* Egypt
25L4 **Biryusa** *R* Russian Federation
12J7 **Biržai** Lithuania
48B2 **Bir Zreigat** *Well* Mauritius
43K1 **Bisalpur** India
59E4 **Bisbee** USA
14A2 **Biscay,B of** France/Spain
67B3 **Biscayne B** USA
13D3 **Bischwiller** France
64C1 **Biscotasi L** Canada
31B4 **Bishan** China
39F1 **Bishkek** Kirgizia
56B3 **Bishop** USA
6D2 **Bishop Auckland** England
7C3 **Bishops Castle** England
7E4 **Bishop's Stortford** England
43E4 **Bishrāmpur** India
48C1 **Biskra** Algeria
56C2 **Bismarck** USA
32D1 **Bismarck Arch** Papua New Guinea
32D1 **Bismarck Range** *Mts* Papua New Guinea
32D1 **Bismarck S** Papua New Guinea
41E3 **Bīsotūn** Iran
48A3 **Bissau** Guinea-Bissau
57D1 **Bissett** Canada
54G4 **Bistcho L** Canada

Cagayan de Oro **Catanduanes**

27F6 **Cagayan de Oro** Philippines
16B3 **Cagliari** Sardinia, Italy
16B3 **Cagliari, G di** Sardinia, Italy
69D3 **Caguas** Puerto Rico
67A2 **Cahaba** *R* USA
9C3 **Cahir** Irish Republic
9C3 **Cahore Pt** Irish Republic
14C3 **Cahors** France
51D5 **Caia** Mozambique
73G6 **Caiabis, Serra dos** *Mts* Brazil
51C5 **Caianda** Angola
75B2 **Caiapó** *R* Brazil
75B2 **Caiapônia** Brazil
75B2 **Caiapó, Serra do** *Mts* Brazil
73L5 **Caicó** Brazil
69C2 **Caicos Is** Caribbean Sea
57F4 **Caicos Pass** The Bahamas
8D3 **Cairngorms** *Mts* Scotland
8C4 **Cairnryan** Scotland
32D2 **Cairns** Australia
40B3 **Cairo** Egypt
57E3 **Cairo** USA
8D2 **Caithness** Scotland
34B1 **Caiwarro** Australia
72C5 **Cajabamba** Peru
72C5 **Cajamarca** Peru
48C4 **Calabar** Nigeria
69D5 **Calabozo** Venezuela
17E2 **Calafat** Romania
74B8 **Calafate** Argentina
15B1 **Calahorra** Spain
14C1 **Calais** France
65F1 **Calais** USA
74C2 **Calama** Chile
72D3 **Calamar** Colombia
27E5 **Calamian Group** *Is* Philippines
51B4 **Calandula** Angola
27C6 **Calang** Indonesia
49E2 **Calanscio Sand Sea** Libya
27F5 **Calapan** Philippines
17F2 **Calarasi** Romania
15B1 **Calatayud** Spain
66B2 **Calaveras Res** USA
63D3 **Calcasieu L** USA
43F4 **Calcutta** India
15A2 **Caldas da Rainha** Portugal
73J7 **Caldas Novas** Brazil
74B3 **Caldera** Chile
56B2 **Caldwell** USA
47B3 **Caledon** South Africa
47D3 **Caledon** *R* South Africa
64A2 **Caledonia** Minnesota, USA
68B1 **Caledonia** New York, USA
74C7 **Caleta Olivia** Argentina
56B3 **Calexico** USA
54G4 **Calgary** Canada
67B2 **Calhoun** USA
67B2 **Calhoun Falls** USA
72C3 **Cali** Colombia
66C3 **Caliente** California, USA
56B3 **Caliente** Nevada, USA
62A1 **Caliente** New Mexico, USA
56A3 **California** *State* USA
66C3 **California Aqueduct** USA
70A1 **California, G de** Mexico
44B3 **Calimera,Pt** India
59C4 **Calipatria** USA
47C3 **Calitzdorp** South Africa
34B1 **Callabonna** *R* Australia
34A1 **Callabonna,L** Australia
65D1 **Callander** Canada
8C3 **Callander** Scotland
72C6 **Callao** Peru
68C2 **Callicoon** USA
67B3 **Caloosahatchee** *R* USA
34D1 **Caloundra** Australia
16C3 **Caltanissetta** Sicily, Italy
51B4 **Caluango** Angola
51B5 **Calulo** Angola
51B5 **Caluquembe** Angola
50F2 **Caluula** Somalia
16B2 **Calvi** Corsica, France
47B3 **Calvinia** South Africa
13E3 **Calw** Germany
75E1 **Camacari** Brazil
70E2 **Camagüey** Cuba
70E2 **Camagüey,Arch de** *Is* Cuba
75E1 **Camamu** Brazil
72D7 **Camaná** Peru
75B2 **Camapuã** Brazil
72E8 **Camargo** Bolivia
66C3 **Camarillo** USA
74C6 **Camarones** Argentina
58B1 **Camas** USA
51B4 **Camaxilo** Angola
51B4 **Cambatela** Angola
30C3 **Cambodia** *Republic* SE Asia
7B4 **Camborne** England
14C1 **Cambrai** France
66B3 **Cambria** USA
7C3 **Cambrian Mts** Wales
64C2 **Cambridge** Canada
7E3 **Cambridge** England
69H1 **Cambridge** Jamaica
65D3 **Cambridge** Maryland, USA
65E2 **Cambridge** Massachussets, USA
61E1 **Cambridge** Minnesota, USA
35C1 **Cambridge** New Zealand
64C2 **Cambridge** Ohio, USA
7D3 **Cambridge** *County* England
54H3 **Cambridge Bay** Canada
27F8 **Cambridge G** Australia
21F7 **Cam Burun** *Pt* Turkey
57D3 **Camden** Arkansas, USA
34D2 **Camden** Australia
65E3 **Camden** New Jersey, USA
68C1 **Camden** New York, USA
67B2 **Camden** South Carolina, USA
61E3 **Cameron** Missouri, USA
63C2 **Cameron** Texas, USA
54H2 **Cameron I** Canada
35A3 **Cameron Mts** New Zealand
50B3 **Cameroon** *Federal Republic* Africa
48C4 **Cameroun, Mt** Cameroon
73J4 **Cametá** Brazil
67B2 **Camilla** USA
66B1 **Camino** USA
72F8 **Camiri** Bolivia
51C4 **Camissombo** Angola
73K4 **Camocim** Brazil
32C2 **Camooweal** Australia
44E4 **Camorta** *I* Nicobar Is, Indian Ocean
74A7 **Campana** *I* Chile
47C2 **Campbell** South Africa
35B2 **Campbell,C** New Zealand
37K7 **Campbell I** New Zealand
54E3 **Campbell,Mt** Canada
42C2 **Campbellpore** Pakistan
54F5 **Campbell River** Canada
64B3 **Campbellsville** USA
55M5 **Campbellton** Canada
34D2 **Campbelltown** Australia
8C4 **Campbeltown** Scotland
70C3 **Campeche** Mexico
70C2 **Campeche, B de** Mexico
34B3 **Camperdown** Australia
73L5 **Campina Grande** Brazil
73J8 **Campinas** Brazil
75C2 **Campina Verde** Brazil
66C2 **Camp Nelson** USA
48C4 **Campo** Cameroon
16C2 **Campobasso** Italy
75C3 **Campo Belo** Brazil
75C2 **Campo Florido** Brazil
74D3 **Campo Gallo** Argentina
74F2 **Campo Grande** Brazil
73K4 **Campo Maior** Brazil
74F2 **Campo Mourão** Brazil
75D3 **Campos** Brazil
75C2 **Campos Altos** Brazil
59D4 **Camp Verde** USA
30D3 **Cam Ranh** Vietnam
54G4 **Camrose** Canada
51B5 **Camucuio** Angola
69K1 **Canaan** Tobago
68D1 **Canaan** USA
51B5 **Canacupa** Angola
53F3 **Canada** *Dominion* N America
74D4 **Cañada de Gómez** Argentina
68C2 **Canadensis** USA
62B1 **Canadian** USA
56C3 **Canadian** *R* USA
21D7 **Çanakkale** Turkey
68B1 **Canandaigua** USA
68B1 **Canandaigua L** USA
70A1 **Cananea** Mexico
75C4 **Cananeia** Brazil
Canarias, Islas = Canary Islands
52G3 **Canary Basin** Atlantic Ocean
48A2 **Canary Is** *Atlantic Ocean*
75C3 **Canastra, Serra da** *Mts* Brazil
70B2 **Canatlán** Mexico
57E4 **Canaveral,C** USA
73L7 **Canavieiras** Brazil
32D4 **Canberra** Australia
58B2 **Canby** California, USA
61D2 **Canby** Minnesota, USA
17F3 **Çandarli Körfezi** *B* Turkey
68D2 **Candlewood,L** USA
60D1 **Cando** USA
68B1 **Candor** USA
74E4 **Canelones** Uruguay
63C1 **Caney** USA
51C5 **Cangamba** Angola
51C5 **Cangombe** Angola
31D2 **Cangzhou** China
55M4 **Caniapiscau** *R* Canada
55M4 **Caniapiscau, Réservoir** *Res* Canada
16C3 **Canicatti** Sicily, Italy
73L4 **Canindé** Brazil
68B1 **Canisteo** USA
68B1 **Canisteo** *R* USA
62A1 **Canjilon** USA
40B1 **Çankiri** Turkey
8B3 **Canna** *I* Scotland
44B3 **Cannanore** India
14D3 **Cannes** France
7C3 **Cannock** England
60C1 **Cannonball** *R* USA
34C3 **Cann River** Australia
74F3 **Canõas** Brazil
75B4 **Canoinhas** Brazil
60B3 **Canon City** USA
34B2 **Canopus** Australia
54H4 **Canora** Canada
34C2 **Canowindra** Australia
15B1 **Cantabria** *Region* Spain
14A3 **Cantabrica, Cord** *Mts* Spain
7E4 **Canterbury** England
35B2 **Canterbury Bight** *B* New Zealand
35B2 **Canterbury Plains** New Zealand
30D4 **Can Tho** Vietnam
66D3 **Cantil** USA
Canton = Guangzhou
63E2 **Canton** Mississippi, USA
64A2 **Canton** Missouri, USA
57E2 **Canton** Ohio, USA
68B2 **Canton** Pensylvania, USA
61D2 **Canton** S Dakota, USA
33H1 **Canton** *I* Phoenix Islands
75B3 **Cantu, Serra do** *Mts* Brazil
62B2 **Canyon** USA
58C2 **Canyon City** USA
58D1 **Canyon Ferry L** USA
59E3 **Canyonlands Nat Pk** USA
58B2 **Canyonville** USA
51C4 **Canzar** Angola
30D1 **Cao Bang** Vietnam
28B2 **Caoshi** China
73J4 **Capanema** Brazil
75C3 **Capão Bonito** Brazil
75D3 **Caparaó, Serra do** *Mts* Brazil
14B3 **Capbreton** France
16B2 **Cap Corse** *C* Corsica, France
14B2 **Cap de la Hague** *C* France
65E1 **Cap-de-la-Madeleine** Canada
15C2 **Capdepera** Spain
34C4 **Cape Barren I** Australia
52J6 **Cape Basin** Atlantic Ocean
55N5 **Cape Breton I** Canada
Cape, Cabo etc: see also individual cape names
48B4 **Cape Coast** Ghana
65E2 **Cape Cod B** USA
55M3 **Cape Dyer** Canada
76F7 **Cape Evans** *Base* Antarctica
67C2 **Cape Fear** *R* USA
63E1 **Cape Girardeau** USA
74C8 **Cape Horn** Chile
36H4 **Cape Johnson Depth** Pacific Ocean
75D2 **Capelinha** Brazil
54B3 **Cape Lisburne** USA
51B5 **Capelongo** Angola
65E3 **Cape May** USA
54F5 **Cape Mendocino** USA
51B4 **Capenda Camulemba** Angola
54F2 **Cape Parry** Canada
47C3 **Cape Province** South Africa
47B3 **Cape Town** South Africa
52G4 **Cape Verde** *Is* Atlantic Ocean
52G4 **Cape Verde Basin** Atlantic Ocean
32D2 **Cape York Pen** Australia
69C3 **Cap-Haïtien** Haiti
73J4 **Capim** *R* Brazil
75A3 **Capitán Bado** Paraguay
59E3 **Capitol Reef Nat Pk** USA
75A2 **Capivari** *R* Brazil
9C3 **Cappoquin** Irish Republic
69P2 **Cap Pt** St Lucia
16C2 **Capri** *I* Italy
51C5 **Caprivi Strip** *Region* Namibia
72D4 **Caquetá** *R* Colombia
17E2 **Caracal** Romania
72F3 **Caracaraí** Brazil
72E1 **Caracas** Venezuela
75A3 **Caracol** Brazil
75C3 **Caraguatatuba** Brazil
74B5 **Carahue** Chile
75D2 **Caraí** Brazil
75D3 **Carandaí** Brazil
75A2 **Carandazal** Brazil
73K8 **Carangola** Brazil
17E1 **Caransebeş** Romania
69A3 **Caratasca** Honduras
70D3 **Caratasca, L de** *Lg* Honduras
75D2 **Caratinga** Brazil
15B2 **Caravaca de la Cruz** Spain
75E2 **Caravelas** Brazil
16B3 **Carbonara, C** Sardinia, Italy
64B3 **Carbondale** Illinois, USA
68C2 **Carbondale** Pennsylvania, USA
55N5 **Carbonear** Canada
16B3 **Carbonia** Sardinia, Italy
54G4 **Carcajou** Canada
50E2 **Carcar Mts** Somalia
14C3 **Carcassonne** France
54E3 **Carcross** Canada
30C3 **Cardamomes, Chaîne des** *Mts* Cambodia
70D2 **Cardenas** Cuba
7C4 **Cardiff** Wales
7B3 **Cardigan** Wales
7B3 **Cardigan B** Wales
75C4 **Cardoso, Ilha do** Brazil
17E1 **Carei** Romania
73G4 **Careiro** Brazil
64C2 **Carey** USA
14B2 **Carhaix-Plouguer** France
74D5 **Carhué** Argentina
73K8 **Cariacíca** Brazil
71C2 **Caribbean S** Central America
54J4 **Caribou** Canada
65F1 **Caribou** USA
54G4 **Caribou Mts** Alberta, Canada
54F4 **Caribou Mts** British Columbia, Canada
13C3 **Carignan** France
75D1 **Carinhanha** Brazil
75D1 **Carinhanha** *R* Brazil
72F1 **Caripito** Venezuela
65D1 **Carleton Place** Canada
47D2 **Carletonville** South Africa
58C2 **Carlin** USA
9C2 **Carlingford, L** Northern Ireland
64B3 **Carlinville** USA
6C2 **Carlisle** England
65D2 **Carlisle** USA
75D2 **Carlos Chagas** Brazil
9C3 **Carlow** Irish Republic
9C3 **Carlow** *County* Irish Republic
59C4 **Carlsbad** California, USA
56C3 **Carlsbad** New Mexico, USA
62B2 **Carlsbad Caverns Nat Pk** USA
36E4 **Carlsberg Ridge** Indian Ocean
54H5 **Carlyle** Canada
54E3 **Carmacks** Canada
7B4 **Carmarthen** Wales
7B4 **Carmarthen B** Wales
66B2 **Carmel** California, USA
68D2 **Carmel** New York, USA
7B3 **Carmel Hd** *Pt* Wales
45C2 **Carmel,Mt** Israel
66B2 **Carmel Valley** USA
56B4 **Carmen** *I* Mexico
74D6 **Carmen de Patagones** Argentina
64B3 **Carmi** USA
59B3 **Carmichael** USA
75C2 **Carmo do Paranaiba** Brazil
15A2 **Carmona** Spain
75E2 **Carnacá** Brazil
32A3 **Carnarvon** Australia
47C3 **Carnarvon** South Africa
9C2 **Carndonagh** Irish Republic
32B3 **Carnegie,L** Australia
44E4 **Car Nicobar** *I* Nicobar Is, Indian Ocean
50B3 **Carnot** Central African Republic
8D3 **Carnoustie** Scotland
9C3 **Carnsore Pt** Irish Republic
67B3 **Carol City** USA
73J5 **Carolina** Brazil
47E2 **Carolina** South Africa
67C2 **Carolina Beach** USA
27H6 **Caroline Is** Pacific Ocean
19F3 **Carpathian Mts** Romania
21C6 **Carpathians** *Mts* EEurope
32C2 **Carpentaria,G of** Australia
39H5 **Carpenter Ridge** Indian Ocean
14D3 **Carpentras** France
16C2 **Carpi** Italy
66C3 **Carpinteria** USA
67B3 **Carrabelle** USA
16C2 **Carrara** Italy
10B3 **Carrauntoohill** *Mt* Irish Republic
8C4 **Carrick** Scotland
9D2 **Carrickfergus** Northern Ireland
9C3 **Carrickmacross** Irish Republic
9C3 **Carrick-on-Suir** Irish Republic
34A2 **Carrieton** Australia
54J5 **Carrington** USA
15B1 **Carrión** *R* Spain
62C3 **Carrizo Springs** USA
62A2 **Carrizozo** USA
57D2 **Carroll** USA
67A2 **Carrollton** Georgia, USA
64B3 **Carrollton** Kentucky, USA
61E3 **Carrollton** Missouri, USA
9B2 **Carrowmore,L** *Irish Republic*
63E1 **Carruthersville** USA
21F7 **Carşamba** Turkey
21E8 **Carşamba** *R* Turkey
56B3 **Carson City** USA
64C2 **Carsonville** USA
8D4 **Carstairs** Scotland
69B4 **Cartagena** Colombia
15B2 **Cartagena** Spain
72C3 **Cartago** Colombia
70D4 **Cartago** Costa Rica
66C2 **Cartago** USA
35C2 **Carterton** New Zealand
63D1 **Carthage** Missouri, USA
65D2 **Carthage** New York, USA
63D2 **Carthage** Texas, USA
32B2 **Cartier I** Timor Sea
55N4 **Cartwright** Canada
73L5 **Caruaru** Brazil
72F1 **Carúpano** Venezuela
13B2 **Carvin** France
15A2 **Carvoeiro, Cabo** *C* Portugal
67C1 **Cary** USA
48B1 **Casablanca** Morocco
75C3 **Casa Branca** Brazil
56B3 **Casa Grande** USA
16B1 **Casale Monferrato** Italy
58D1 **Cascade** USA
35A2 **Cascade Pt** New Zealand
56A2 **Cascade Range** *Mts* USA
58C2 **Cascade Res** USA
74F2 **Cascavel** Brazil
16C2 **Caserta** Italy
76G9 **Casey** *Base* Antarctica
9C3 **Cashel** Irish Republic
33E3 **Casino** Australia
72C5 **Casma** Peru
66B3 **Casmalia** USA
15C1 **Caspe** Spain
56C2 **Casper** USA
21H7 **Caspian S** Asia/Europe
65D3 **Cass** USA
51C5 **Cassamba** Angola
13B2 **Cassel** France
61D1 **Casselton** USA
54E3 **Cassiar Mts** Canada
75B2 **Cassilândia** Brazil
16C2 **Cassino** Italy
61E1 **Cass Lake** USA
66C3 **Castaic** USA
14D3 **Castellane** France
16C2 **Castello, Città di** Italy
15C1 **Castellón de la Plana** Spain
73K5 **Castelo** Brazil
15A2 **Castelo Branco** Portugal
14C3 **Castelsarrasin** France
16C3 **Castelvetrano** Sicily, Italy
34B3 **Casterton** Australia
15B2 **Castilla la Mancha** *Region* Spain
15B1 **Castilla y León** *Region* Spain
10B3 **Castlebar** Irish Republic
8B3 **Castlebay** Scotland
9C2 **Castleblayney** Irish Republic
59D3 **Castle Dale** USA
8D4 **Castle Douglas** Scotland
6D3 **Castleford** England
58C1 **Castlegar** Canada
34B3 **Castlemaine** Australia
66B3 **Castle Mt** USA
58D2 **Castle Peak** *Mt* USA
34C2 **Castlereagh** *R* Australia
60C3 **Castle Rock** USA
6B2 **Castletown** England
9B4 **Castletown Bere** Irish Republic
14C3 **Castres-sur-l'Agout** France
69P2 **Castries** St Lucia
74B6 **Castro** Argentina
74F2 **Castro** Brazil
73L6 **Castro Alves** Brazil
16D3 **Castrovillari** Italy
66B2 **Castroville** USA
35A2 **Caswell Sd** New Zealand
70E2 **Cat** *I* The Bahamas
72B5 **Catacaos** Peru
75D3 **Cataguases** Brazil
63D2 **Catahoula L** USA
75C2 **Catalão** Brazil
15C1 **Cataluña** *Region* Spain
74C3 **Catamarca** Argentina
74C3 **Catamarca** *State* Argentina
51D5 **Catandica** Mozambique
27F5 **Catanduanes** *I* Philippines

Catanduva China L

74G2 Catanduva Brazil
75B4 Catanduvas Brazil
16D3 Catania Sicily, Italy
16D3 Catanzaro Italy
62C3 Catarina USA
27F5 Catarman Philippines
69C5 Catatumbo *R* Venezuela
68B2 Catawissa USA
27F5 Catbalogan Philippines
16B2 Cateraggio Corsica, France
51B4 Catete Angola
47D3 Cathcart South Africa
48A3 Catio Guinea-Bissau
55J4 Cat Lake Canada
33E3 Cato *I* Australia
70D2 Catoche,C Mexico
68B3 Catoctin Mt USA
65D3 Catonsville USA
65E2 Catskill USA
65E2 Catskill Mts USA
72D2 Cauca *R* Colombia
73L4 Caucaia Brazil
72C2 Caucasia Colombia
21G7 Caucasus *Mts* Georgia
13B2 Caudry France
51B4 Caungula Angola
74B5 Cauquenes Chile
65F1 Causapscal Canada
44B3 Cauvery *R* India
14D3 Cavaillon France
75C1 Cavalcante Brazil
61D1 Cavalier USA
48B4 Cavally *R* Liberia
9C3 Cavan Irish Republic
9C3 Cavan *County* Irish Republic
72D4 Caxias Brazil
73K4 Caxias Brazil
74F3 Caxias do Sul Brazil
51B4 Caxito Angola
67B2 Cayce USA
40D1 Çayeli Turkey
73H3 Cayenne French Guiana
70E3 Cayman Brac *I* Cayman Is, Caribbean Sea
69A3 Cayman Is Caribbean Sea
69A3 Cayman Trench Caribbean Sea
50E3 Caynabo Somalia
70E2 Cayo Romano *I* Cuba
70D3 Cayos Miskito *Is* Nicaragua
69A2 Cay Sal *I* Caribbean Sea
66B3 Cayucos USA
68B1 Cayuga L USA
68C1 Cazenovia USA
51C5 Cazombo Angola
Ceará = Fortaleza
73K5 Ceará *State* Brazil
27F5 Cebu Philippines
27F5 Cebu *I* Philippines
68C3 Cecilton USA
16C2 Cecina Italy
61E2 Cedar *R* USA
56B3 Cedar City USA
63C2 Cedar Creek Res USA
61E2 Cedar Falls USA
54H4 Cedar L Canada
66D1 Cedar Mts USA
57D2 Cedar Rapids USA
67A2 Cedartown USA
70A2 Cedros *I* Mexico
56B4 Cedros, Isla de Mexico
32C4 Ceduna Australia
50E3 Ceelbuur Somalia
50E2 Ceerigaabo Somalia
16C3 Cefalù Sicily, Italy
19D3 Cegléd Hungary
51B5 Cela Angola
70B2 Celaya Mexico
Celebes = Sulawesi
27F6 Celebes S SE Asia
64C2 Celina USA
16D1 Celje Slovenia
18C2 Celle Germany
7A4 Celtic S British Isles
7B3 Cemmaes Hd *Pt* Wales
27G7 Cendrawasih *Pen* Indonesia
63D2 Center USA
67A1 Center Hill L USA
68D2 Center Moriches USA
67A2 Center Point USA
62A2 Central USA
8C3 Central *Region* Scotland
50B3 Central African Republic Africa
61D2 Central City Nebraska, USA
68A2 Central City Pennsylvania, USA
68E2 Central Falls USA
64B3 Centralia Illinois, USA
56A2 Centralia Washington, USA
47C1 Central Kalahari Game Res Botswana
42A3 Central Makran Ra *Mts* Pakistan
58B2 Central Point USA
27H7 Central Range *Mts* Papua New Guinea
68B1 Central Square USA
67A2 Centreville Alabama, USA
68B3 Centreville Maryland, USA
Ceram = Seram
Ceram Sea = Seram Sea
73J7 Ceres Brazil
47B3 Ceres South Africa
66B2 Ceres USA
14C2 Cergy-Pontoise France
16D2 Cerignola Italy
21D7 Cernavodă Romania
13D4 Cernay France
56C4 Cerralvo *I* Mexico
72C6 Cerro de Pasco Peru
69D3 Cerro de Punta *Mt* Puerto Rico
69C4 Cerron *Mt* Venezuela
74C5 Cerros Colorados, Embalse *Res* Argentina
16C2 Cesena Italy
20D4 Cēsis Latvia
18C3 České Budějovice Czechoslovakia
18C3 České Zemé *Region* Czechoslovakia
18D3 Českomoravská Vysocina *Region* Czechoslovakia
17F3 Çeşme Turkey
32E4 Cessnock Australia
16D2 Cetina *R* Croatia
15A2 Ceuta NW Africa
40C2 Ceyhan Turkey
40C2 Ceyhan *R* Turkey
40C2 Ceylanpinar Turkey
44C4 Ceylon *I* Indian Ocean
Ceylon *Republic* = Sri Lanka
25L4 Chaa-Khol Russian Federation
14C2 Chaâteaudun France
13B4 Chablis France
72C5 Chachapoyas Peru
42C3 Chachran Pakistan
42C3 Chachro Pakistan
74D3 Chaco *State* Argentina
50B2 Chad *Republic* Africa
50B2 Chad, L C Africa
56C2 Chadron USA
28B3 Chaeryŏng N Korea
63E1 Chaffee USA
42A3 Chagai Pakistan
25P4 Chagda Russian Federation
42B2 Chaghcharan Afghanistan
36E5 Chagos Arch Indian Ocean
69L1 Chaguanas Trinidad
38E3 Chāh Bahār Iran
28A2 Ch'aho N Korea
30C2 Chai Badan Thailand
43F4 Chāībāsa India
30C2 Chaiyaphum Thailand
42C2 Chakwal Pakistan
72D7 Chala Peru
51D5 Chalabesa Zambia
42A2 Chalap Dalam *Mts* Afghanistan
57G2 Chaleurs, B des Canada
13C4 Chalindrey France
31C4 Chaling China
42D4 Chālisgaon India
27H5 Challenger Deep Pacific Ocean
13C3 Challerange France
58D2 Challis USA
13C3 Châlons-sur-Marne France
14C2 Chalon sur Saône France
28B2 Chaluhe China
18C3 Cham Germany
62A1 Chama USA
42B2 Chaman Pakistan
42D2 Chamba India
42D3 Chambal *R* India
60D2 Chamberlain USA
65D3 Chambersburg USA
14D2 Chambéry France
13B3 Chambly France
65E1 Chambord Canada
42A3 Chambor Kalat Pakistan
41F3 Chamgordan Iran
43E4 Chāmpa India
14C2 Champagne *Region* France
47D2 Champagne Castle *Mt* Lesotho
57E2 Champaign USA
43N2 Champaran *District* India
30D3 Champassak Laos
57F2 Champlain,L USA
44B3 Chāmrājnagar India
74B3 Chañaral Chile
54D3 Chandalar USA
54D3 Chandalar *R* USA
63E3 Chandeleur Is USA
42D2 Chandīgarh India
59D4 Chandler USA
43G4 Chandpur Bangladesh
42D5 Chandrapur India
47E1 Changane *R* Mozambique
51D5 Changara Mozambique
28B2 Changbai China
28B2 Changbai Shan *Mts* China
28B2 Changchun China
31C4 Changde China
28A3 Changdo N Korea
28A3 Changhai China
28A3 Changhang S Korea
28A3 Changhowan S Korea
26E4 Changhua Taiwan
28A4 Changhŭng S Korea
30D2 Changjiang China
31D3 Chang Jiang *R* China
28B2 Changjin N Korea
28A2 Changjin *R* N Korea
28A2 Changjin Res N Korea
28B3 Changnyŏn N Korea
31C4 Changsha China
31E3 Changshu China
31B2 Changwu China
28A3 Changyŏn N Korea
31C2 Changzhi China
31E3 Changzhou China
14B2 Channel Is British Isles
56B3 Channel Is USA
55N5 Channel Port-aux-Basques Canada
30C3 Chanthaburi Thailand
13B3 Chantilly France
55J3 Chantrey Inlet *B* Canada
63C1 Chanute USA
24J4 Chany, Ozero *L* Russian Federation
31D5 Chao'an China
31D3 Chao Hu *L* China
30C3 Chao Phraya *R* Thailand
15A2 Chaouen Morocco
31E1 Chaoyang China
73K6 Chapada Diamantina *Mts* Brazil
73K4 Chapadinha Brazil
70B2 Chapala, L de Mexico
21J5 Chapayevo Kazakhstan
74F3 Chapecó Brazil
7D3 Chapel-en-le-Frith England
67C1 Chapel Hill USA
69H1 Chapeltown Jamaica
55K5 Chapleau Canada
25U3 Chaplino, Mys *C* Russian Federation
20G5 Chaplygin Russian Federation
60C2 Chappell USA
76G3 Charcot I Antarctica
7C4 Chard England
38E2 Chardzhou Turkmenistan
14C2 Charente *R* France
50B2 Chari *R* Chad
50B2 Chari Baguirmi *Region* Chad
42B1 Charikar Afghanistan
61E2 Chariton *R* USA
73G2 Charity Guyana
42D3 Charkhāri India
13C2 Charleroi Belgium
57F3 Charles,C USA
64B3 Charleston Illinois, USA
63E1 Charleston Missouri, USA
57F3 Charleston S Carolina, USA
57E3 Charleston W Virginia, USA
59C3 Charleston Peak *Mt* USA
68B3 Charles Town USA
68D1 Charlestown USA
50C4 Charlesville Zaïre
32D3 Charleville Australia
14C2 Charleville-Mézières France
64B1 Charlevoix USA
64C2 Charlotte Michigan, USA
57E3 Charlotte N Carolina, USA
67B3 Charlotte Harbor *B* USA
57F3 Charlottesville USA
55M5 Charlottetown Canada
69K1 Charlotteville Tobago
34B3 Charlton Australia
57F1 Charlton I Canada
13D3 Charmes France
42C2 Charsadda Pakistan
32D3 Charters Towers Australia
14C2 Chartres France
74E5 Chascomús Argentina
28B2 Chasong N Korea
14B2 Châteaubriant France
14B2 Châteaulin France
13B4 Châteauneuf-sur-Loire France
14C2 Châteauroux France
13D3 Château-Salins France
14C2 Château-Thierry France
13C2 Châtelet Belgium
14C2 Châtellerault France
61E2 Chatfield USA
7F6 Chatham England
68E2 Chatham Massachusetts, USA
55M5 Chatham New Brunswick, Canada
68D1 Chatham New York, USA
64C2 Chatham Ontario, Canada
65D3 Chatham Virginia, USA
33H5 Chatham Is New Zealand
54E4 Chatham Str USA
14C2 Châtillon France
13B4 Châtillon-Coligny France
13C4 Châtillon-sur-Seine France
43E5 Chatrapur India
68C3 Chatsworth USA
67B2 Chattahoochee USA
67A2 Chattahoochee *R* USA
57E3 Chattanooga USA
30A1 Chauk Burma
43L2 Chauka *R* India
14D2 Chaumont France
13B3 Chauny France
30D3 Chau Phu Vietnam
44E4 Chaura *I* Nicobar Is, Indian Ocean
15A1 Chaves Portugal
20J4 Chaykovskiy Russian Federation
18C2 Cheb Czechoslovakia
20H4 Cheboksary Russian Federation
57E2 Cheboygan USA
19G2 Chechersk Belorussia
28B3 Chech'on S Korea
63C1 Checotah USA
7C4 Cheddar England
30A2 Cheduba I Burma
34B1 Cheepie Australia
48B2 Chegga Mauritius
51D5 Chegutu Zimbabwe
58B1 Chehalis USA
28B4 Cheju S Korea
28B4 Cheju Do *I* S Korea
28B4 Cheju Haehyŏp *Str* S Korea
25P4 Chekunda Russian Federation
58B1 Chelan,L USA
21J8 Cheleken Turkmenistan
16B3 Chélia, Dj *Mt* Algeria
15C2 Cheliff *R* Algeria
38D1 Chelkar Kazakhstan
19E2 Chełm Poland
19D2 Chełmno Poland
7E4 Chelmsford England
7C4 Cheltenham England
20L4 Chelyabinsk Russian Federation
25M2 Chelyuskin, Mys *C* Russian Federation
51D5 Chemba Mozambique
18C2 Chemnitz Germany
68B1 Chemung *R* USA
42D2 Chenab *R* India/Pakistan
48B2 Chenachen Algeria
68C1 Chenango *R* USA
58C1 Cheney USA
63C1 Cheney Res USA
31D1 Chengde China
31A3 Chengdu China
31E2 Chengshan Jiao *Pt* China
28A3 Chengzitan China
31C4 Chenxi China
31C4 Chen Xian China
31D3 Cheo Xian China
72C5 Chepén Peru
7C4 Chepstow Wales
64A1 Chequamegon B USA
14C2 Cher *R* France
67C2 Cheraw USA
14B2 Cherbourg France
15C2 Cherchell Algeria
20K3 Cherdyn Russian Federation
25M4 Cheremkhovo Russian Federation
20F4 Cherepovets Russian Federation
21E6 Cherkassy Ukraine
21G7 Cherkessk Russian Federation
21E5 Chernigov Ukraine
19G2 Chernobyl Ukraine
21D6 Chernovtsy Ukraine
20K4 Chernushka Russian Federation
20C5 Chernyakhovsk Russian Federation
21H6 Chernyye Zemli *Region* Russian Federation
61D2 Cherokee Iowa, USA
62C1 Cherokee Oklahoma, USA
63D1 Cherokees,L o'the USA
43G3 Cherrapunji India
33F2 Cherry *I* Solomon Islands
25S3 Cherskiy Russian Federation
25Q3 Cherskogo, Khrebet *Mts* Russian Federation
20D5 Cherven' Belorussia
19E2 Chervonograd Ukraine
65D3 Chesapeake USA
65D3 Chesapeake B USA
7D4 Chesham England
68D1 Cheshire USA
7C3 Cheshire *County* England
20H2 Chëshskaya Guba *B* Russian Federation
59B2 Chester California, USA
7C3 Chester England
64B3 Chester Illinois, USA
68D1 Chester Massachusets, USA
58D1 Chester Montana, USA
65D3 Chester Pennsylvania, USA
67B2 Chester S Carolina, USA
68D1 Chester Vermont, USA
68B3 Chester *R* USA
7D3 Chesterfield England
33E2 Chesterfield, Îles Nouvelle Calédonie
55J3 Chesterfield Inlet Canada
68B3 Chestertown USA
65F1 Chesuncook L USA
70D3 Chetumal Mexico
35B2 Cheviot New Zealand
10C2 Cheviots *Hills* England/Scotland
60C2 Cheyenne USA
60C2 Cheyenne *R* USA
60C3 Cheyenne Wells USA
43E3 Chhapra India
43G3 Chhātak Bangladesh
42D4 Chhatarpur India
42D4 Chhindwāra India
43F3 Chhukha Bhutan
51B5 Chiange Angola
30C2 Chiang Kham Thailand
30B2 Chiang Mai Thailand
31E5 Chiayi Taiwan
29E3 Chiba Japan
51B5 Chibia Angola
55L4 Chibougamau Canada
28B3 Chiburi-jima *I* Japan
47E1 Chibuto Mozambique
57E2 Chicago USA
64B2 Chicago Heights USA
54E4 Chichagof I USA
7D4 Chichester England
29C3 Chichibu Japan
26H4 Chichi-jima *I* Japan
57E3 Chickamauga L USA
63E2 Chickasawhay *R* USA
56D3 Chickasha USA
54D3 Chicken USA
72B5 Chiclayo Peru
56A3 Chico USA
74C6 Chico *R* Argentina
51D5 Chicoa Mozambique
65E2 Chicopee USA
55L5 Chicoutimi Canada
51D6 Chicualacuala Mozambique
44B3 Chidambaram India
55M3 Chidley,C Canada
67B3 Chiefland USA
48B4 Chiehn Liberia
51C4 Chiengi Zambia
13C3 Chiers *R* France
16C2 Chieti Italy
31D1 Chifeng China
73K7 Chifre, Serra do *Mts* Brazil
54C3 Chigmit Mts USA
47E1 Chigubo Mozambique
70B2 Chihuahua Mexico
62A3 Chihuahua *State* Mexico
44B3 Chik Ballāpur India
44B3 Chikmagalūr India
51D5 Chikwawa Malawi
30A1 Chi-kyaw Burma
44C2 Chilakalūrupet India
44B4 Chilaw Sri Lanka
34D1 Childers Australia
62B2 Childress USA
71C6 Chile *Republic* S America
51C5 Chililabombwe Zambia
43F5 Chilka L India
54F4 Chilko L Canada
74B5 Chillán Chile
61E3 Chillicothe Missouri, USA
64C3 Chillicothe Ohio, USA
43G3 Chilmari India
74B6 Chiloé, Isla de Chile
51D5 Chilongozi Zambia
58B2 Chiloquin USA
70C3 Chilpancingo Mexico
7D4 Chiltern Hills *Upland* England
64B2 Chilton USA
51D5 Chilumba Malawi
Chi-lung = Keelung
51D5 Chilwa, L Malawi
51D5 Chimanimani Zimbabwe
13C2 Chimay Belgium
24G5 Chimbay Uzbekistan
72C4 Chimborazo *Mt* Ecuador
72C5 Chimbote Peru
24H5 Chimkent Kazakhstan
51D5 Chimoio Mozambique
22F4 China *Republic* Asia
66D3 China L USA

Dahushan **Dilolo**

28A2 **Dahushan** China
43E3 **Dailekh** Nepal
Dairen = Lüda
40B4 **Dairût** Egypt
26G4 **Daitō Is** Pacific Ocean
32C3 **Dajarra** Australia
48A3 **Dakar** Senegal
48A2 **Dakhla** Morocco
49E2 **Dakhla Oasis** Egypt
48C3 **Dakoro** Niger
61D2 **Dakota City** USA
17E2 **Dakovica** Serbia, Yugoslavia
17D1 **Dakovo** Croatia
20B3 **Dal** *R* Sweden
51C5 **Dala** Angola
48A3 **Dalaba** Guinea
31D1 **Dalai Nur** *L* China
26D2 **Dalandzadgad** Mongolia
30D3 **Da Lat** Vietnam
31A1 **Dalay** Mongolia
8D4 **Dalbeattie** Scotland
32E3 **Dalby** Australia
67A1 **Dale Hollow L** USA
12F7 **Dalen** Norway
6C2 **Dales,The** *Upland* England
67A2 **Daleville** USA
56C3 **Dalhart** USA
65F1 **Dalhousie** Canada
54E2 **Dalhousie,C** Canada
31E2 **Dalian** China
8D4 **Dalkeith** Scotland
56D3 **Dallas** USA
58B1 **Dalles,The** USA
54E4 **Dall I** USA
43E4 **Dalli Rajhara** India
48C3 **Dallol** *Watercourse* Niger
8C3 **Dalmally** Scotland
16D2 **Dalmatia** *Region* Croatia
8C4 **Dalmellington** Scotland
26G2 **Dal'nerechensk** Russian Federation
48B4 **Daloa** Ivory Coast
31B4 **Dalou Shan** *Mts* China
8C4 **Dalry** Scotland
43E4 **Dāltenganj** India
6C2 **Dalton** England
67B2 **Dalton** Georgia, USA
68D1 **Dalton** Massachusetts, USA
55Q3 **Dalton, Kap** *C* Greenland
32C2 **Daly** *R* Australia
59B3 **Daly City** USA
32C2 **Daly Waters** Australia
42C4 **Damān** India
40B3 **Damanhûr** Egypt
32B1 **Damar** *I* Indonesia
50B3 **Damara** Central African Republic
32B1 **Damar, Kepulauan** *Is* Indonesia
40C3 **Damascus** Syria
68B3 **Damascus** USA
48D3 **Damaturu** Nigeria
41F2 **Damavand** Iran
51B4 **Damba** Angola
44C4 **Dambulla** Sri Lanka
41F2 **Damghan** Iran
Damietta = Dumyât
42D4 **Damoh** India
50E3 **Damot** Ethiopia
45C2 **Damour** Lebanon
32A3 **Dampier** Australia
45C3 **Danā** Jordan
66C2 **Dana,Mt** USA
48B4 **Danané** Liberia
30D2 **Da Nang** Vietnam
27C6 **Danau Toba** *L* Indonesia
27F7 **Danau Towuti** *L* Indonesia
31A3 **Danba** China
65E2 **Danbury** USA
68D1 **Danby** USA
43E3 **Dandeldhura** Nepal
44B2 **Dandeli** India
34C3 **Dandenong** Australia
28A2 **Dandong** China
47B3 **Danger Pt** *C* South Africa
50D2 **Dangila** Ethiopia
58D2 **Daniel** USA
55N4 **Daniel's Harbour** Canada
47C2 **Danielskuil** South Africa
55P3 **Dannebrogs Øy** *I* Greenland
35C2 **Dannevirke** New Zealand
68B1 **Dansville** USA
44C2 **Dantewāra** India
Danube *R* Bulgaria/Yugo **=Dunav R**
Danube *R* Romania **=Dunărea**
Danube *R* Austria/ Germany **=Donau**
57E2 **Danville** Illinois, USA
57E3 **Danville** Kentucky, USA
68B2 **Danville** Pennsylvania, USA
57F3 **Danville** Virginia, USA
Danzig = Gdańsk
31C4 **Dao Xian** China
31B4 **Daozhen** China
43H3 **Dapha Bum** *Mt* India
45B3 **Daphnae** *Hist Site* Egypt
26C3 **Da Qaidam** China
26F2 **Daqing** China
45D2 **Dar'a** Syria
40C3 **Dar'ā** Syria
41F4 **Dārāb** Iran
49D1 **Daraj** Libya
41F3 **Dārān** Iran
43F3 **Darbhanga** India
66C1 **Dardanelle** USA
63D1 **Dardanelle,L** USA
Dar-el-Beida = Casablanca
51D4 **Dar es Salaam** Tanzania
35B1 **Dargaville** New Zealand
67B2 **Darien** USA
69B5 **Darién, G of** Panama/ Colombia
Darjeeling = Dārjiling
43F3 **Dārjiling** India
32D4 **Darling** *R* Australia
34C1 **Darling Downs** Australia
55L1 **Darling Pen** Canada
34B2 **Darlington** Australia
6D2 **Darlington** England
67C2 **Darlington** USA
18B3 **Darmstadt** Germany
49E1 **Darnah** Libya
34B2 **Darnick** Australia
54F3 **Darnley B** Canada
76G10 **Darnley,C** Antarctica
15B1 **Daroca** Spain
50C3 **Dar Rounga** *Region* Central African Republic
7C4 **Dart** *R* England
7C4 **Dartmoor** England
55M5 **Dartmouth** Canada
7C4 **Dartmouth** England
32D1 **Daru** Papua New Guinea
16D1 **Daruvar** Croatia
6C3 **Darwen** England
32C2 **Darwin** Australia
41F4 **Daryācheh-ye Bakhtegan** *L* Iran
41F4 **Daryācheh-ye Mahārlū** *L* Iran
41F3 **Daryācheh-ye Namak** *Salt Flat* Iran
21H8 **Daryācheh-ye Orūmīyeh** *L* Iran
41F4 **Daryācheh-ye Tashk** *L* Iran
41G4 **Dārzīn** Iran
41F4 **Dās** *I* UAE
31C3 **Dashennongjia** *Mt* China
41G2 **Dasht** Iran
41F3 **Dasht-e-Kavir** *Salt Desert* Iran
41G3 **Dasht-e Lut** *Salt Desert* Iran
29D2 **Date** Japan
42D3 **Datia** India
31A2 **Datong** China
31C1 **Datong** China
31A2 **Datong He** *R* China
27D6 **Datuk, Tanjung** *C* Indonesia
19E1 **Daugava** *R* Latvia
20D4 **Daugavpils** Latvia
55M1 **Dauguard Jensen Land** *Region* Canada
42A1 **Daulatabad** Afghanistan
42B2 **Daulat Yar** Afghanistan
42D3 **Daulpur** India
13D2 **Daun** Germany
44A2 **Daund** India
54H4 **Dauphin** Canada
68B2 **Dauphin** USA
14D3 **Dauphiné** *Region* France
63E2 **Dauphin I** USA
48C3 **Daura** Nigeria
42D3 **Dausa** India
44B3 **Dāvangere** India
27F6 **Davao** Philippines
27F6 **Davao G** Philippines
66A2 **Davenport** California, USA
57D2 **Davenport** Iowa, USA
7D3 **Daventry** England
72B2 **David** Panama
54D3 **Davidson Mts** USA
59B3 **Davis** USA
76G10 **Davis** *Base* Antarctica
55M4 **Davis Inlet** Canada
55N3 **Davis Str** Canada/ Greenland
20K5 **Davlekanovo** Russian Federation
28A2 **Dawa** China
50E3 **Dawa** *R* Ethiopia
31A4 **Dawan** China
41F4 **Dawhat Salwah** *B* Qatar/ Saudi Arabia
30B2 **Dawna Range** *Mts* Burma/Thailand
54E3 **Dawson** Canada
67B2 **Dawson** Georgia, USA
60D1 **Dawson** N Dakota, USA
32D3 **Dawson** *R* Australia
54F4 **Dawson Creek** Canada
31A3 **Dawu** China
31C3 **Dawu** China
14B3 **Dax** France
31B3 **Daxian** China
31B5 **Daxin** China
31A3 **Daxue Shan** *Mts* China
31C4 **Dayong** China
45D2 **Dayr 'Alī** Syria
45D1 **Dayr 'Aṭīyah** Syria
40D2 **Dayr az Zawr** Syria
45D1 **Dayr Shumayyil** Syria
57E2 **Dayton** Ohio, USA
67A1 **Dayton** Tennessee, USA
63D3 **Dayton** Texas, USA
58C1 **Dayton** Washington, USA
57E4 **Daytona Beach** USA
31C4 **Dayu** China
31D2 **Da Yunhe** *R* China
58C2 **Dayville** USA
31B3 **Dazhu** China
47C3 **De Aar** South Africa
69C2 **Deadman's Cay** The Bahamas
40C3 **Dead S** Israel/Jordan
60C2 **Deadwood** USA
7E4 **Deal** England
47D2 **Dealesville** South Africa
64C2 **Dearborn** USA
54F3 **Dease Arm** *B* Canada
54E4 **Dease Lake** Canada
56B3 **Death V** USA
66D2 **Death Valley Nat Mon** USA
14C2 **Deauville** France
69L1 **Débé** Trinidad
19E2 **Debica** Poland
19E2 **Deblin** Poland
48B3 **Débo,L** Mali
50D3 **Debre Birhan** Ethiopia
19E3 **Debrecen** Hungary
50D2 **Debre Mark'os** Ethiopia
50D2 **Debre Tabor** Ethiopia
57E3 **Decatur** Alabama, USA
67B2 **Decatur** Georgia, USA
57E3 **Decatur** Illinois, USA
64C2 **Decatur** Indiana, USA
14C3 **Decazeville** France
65D1 **Decelles, Réservoir** Canada
47C1 **Deception** *R* Botswana
31A4 **Dechang** China
61E2 **Decorah** USA
48B3 **Dedougou** Burkina
51D5 **Dedza** Malawi
8C4 **Dee** *R* Dumfries and Galloway, Scotland
7C3 **Dee** *R* England/Wales
8D3 **Dee** *R* Grampian, Scotland
65D1 **Deep River** Canada
68D2 **Deep River** USA
66D2 **Deep Springs** USA
34D1 **Deepwater** Australia
55N5 **Deer Lake** Canada
56B2 **Deer Lodge** USA
58C2 **Deeth** USA
67A2 **De Funiak Springs** USA
26C3 **Dêgê** China
50E3 **Degeh Bur** Ethiopia
32A3 **De Grey** *R* Australia
50E2 **Dehalak Arch** *Is* Ethiopia
41F3 **Deh Bīd** Iran
42B1 **Dehi** Afghanistan
48D1 **Dehibat** Tunisia
44B4 **Dehiwala-Mt Lavinia** Sri Lanka
41E3 **Dehlorān** Iran
42D2 **Dehra Dūn** India
43E4 **Dehri** India
50C3 **Deim Zubeir** Sudan
45C2 **Deir Abu Sa'īd** Jordan
45D1 **Deir el Ahmar** Lebanon
21C6 **Dej** Romania
64B2 **De Kalb** Illinois, USA
63D2 **De Kalb** Texas, USA
25Q4 **De Kastri** Russian Federation
50C4 **Dekese** Zaïre
50B3 **Dekoa** Central African Republic
56B3 **Delano** USA
59D3 **Delano Peak** *Mt* USA
47D2 **Delareyville** South Africa
64C2 **Delaware** USA
65D2 **Delaware** *R* USA
57F3 **Delaware** *State* USA
57F3 **Delaware B** USA
34C3 **Delegate** Australia
13C1 **Delft** Netherlands
13D1 **Delfzijl** Netherlands
51E5 **Delgado, C** Mozambique
62B1 **Delhi** Colorado, USA
42D3 **Delhi** India
65E2 **Delhi** New York, USA
40B1 **Delice** Turkey
70B2 **Delicias** Mexico
41F3 **Delījān** Iran
61D2 **Dell Rapids** USA
15C2 **Dellys** Algeria
66D4 **Del Mar** USA
12F8 **Delmenhorst** Germany
25R2 **De-Longa, Ostrova** *Is* Russian Federation
54B3 **De Long Mts** USA
34C4 **Deloraine** Australia
54H5 **Deloraine** Canada
67B3 **Delray Beach** USA
56C4 **Del Rio** USA
56B3 **Delta** USA
68C1 **Delta Res** USA
50D3 **Dembī Dolo** Ethiopia
13C2 **Demer** *R* Belgium
19G1 **Demidov** Russian Federation
62A2 **Deming** USA
17F2 **Demirköy** Turkey
63E2 **Demopolis** USA
24H4 **Dem'yanskoye** Russian Federation
14C1 **Denain** France
39E2 **Denau** Uzbekistan
7C3 **Denbigh** Wales
13C2 **Dendermond** Belgium
50D3 **Dendi** *Mt* Ethiopia
13B2 **Dèndre** *R* Belgium
31B1 **Dengkou** China
31C3 **Deng Xian** China
Den Haag = The Hague
69H1 **Denham,Mt** Jamaica
18A2 **Den Helder** Netherlands
15C2 **Denia** Spain
32D4 **Deniliquin** Australia
58C2 **Denio** USA
61D2 **Denison** Iowa, USA
56D3 **Denison** Texas, USA
21D8 **Denizli** Turkey
12F7 **Denmark** *Kingdom* Europe
76C1 **Denmark Str** Greenland/ Iceland
69P2 **Dennery** St Lucia
8D2 **Dennis Head** *Pt* Scotland
27E7 **Denpasar** Indonesia
68C3 **Denton** Maryland, USA
56D3 **Denton** Texas, USA
32E1 **D'Entrecasteaux Is** Papua New Guinea
56C3 **Denver** USA
50B3 **Déo** *R* Cameroon
48D4 **Déo** *R* Cameroon/Nigeria
43F4 **Deoghar** India
42C5 **Deolāli** India
43M2 **Deoria** *District* India
42D1 **Deosai Plain** India
68A1 **Depew** USA
68C1 **Deposit** USA
25P3 **Deputatskiy** Russian Federation
63D2 **De Queen** USA
42B3 **Dera Bugti** Pakistan
42C3 **Dera Ghazi Khan** Pakistan
42C2 **Dera Ismail Khan** Pakistan
21H7 **Derbent** Russian Federation
32B2 **Derby** Australia
68D2 **Derby** Connecticut, USA
7D3 **Derby** England
63C1 **Derby** Kansas, USA
7D3 **Derby** *County* England
21F5 **Dergachi** Ukraine
10B3 **Derg, Lough** *L* Irish Republic
63D2 **De Ridder** USA
Derna = Darnah
9C3 **Derravaragh, L** Irish Republic
50E3 **Derri** Somalia
68E1 **Derry** USA
50D2 **Derudeb** Sudan
47C3 **De Rust** South Africa
68C1 **De Ruyter** USA
6D3 **Derwent** *R* England
34C4 **Derwent Bridge** Australia
72E7 **Desaguadero** *R* Bolivia
59C4 **Descanso** Mexico
58B2 **Deschutes** *R* USA
50D2 **Desē** Ethiopia
74C7 **Deseado** Argentina
74C7 **Deseado** *R* Argentina
48A1 **Deserta Grande** *I* Madeira
59C4 **Desert Center** USA
59D2 **Desert Peak** *Mt* USA
63D1 **Desloge** USA
57D2 **Des Moines** Iowa, USA
62B1 **Des Moines** New Mexico, USA
61E2 **Des Moines** *R* USA
21E5 **Desna** *R* Russian Federation
74B8 **Desolación** *I* Chile
64B2 **Des Plaines** USA
18C2 **Dessau** Germany
54E3 **Destruction Bay** Canada
17E1 **Deta** Romania
51C5 **Dete** Zimbabwe
13E2 **Detmold** Germany
57E2 **Detroit** USA
61D1 **Detroit Lakes** USA
30D3 **Det Udom** Thailand
17E1 **Deva** Romania
18B2 **Deventer** Netherlands
8D3 **Deveron** *R* Scotland
42C3 **Devikot** India
66C2 **Devil Postpile Nat Mon** USA
66C3 **Devils Den** USA
66C1 **Devils Gate** *P* USA
6E1 **Devil's Hole** *Region* N Sea
Devil's Island = Diable, Isla du
60D1 **Devils L** N Dakota, USA
62B3 **Devils L** Texas, USA
56D2 **Devils Lake** USA
7D4 **Devizes** England
42D3 **Devli** India
17E2 **Devoll** *R* Albania
7B4 **Devon** *County* England
55J2 **Devon I** Canada
32D5 **Devonport** Australia
43G3 **Dewangiri** Bhutan
42D4 **Dewās** India
47D2 **Dewetsdorp** South Africa
57E3 **Dewey Res** USA
63D2 **De Witt** USA
6D3 **Dewsbury** England
63E1 **Dexter** Missouri, USA
62B2 **Dexter** New Mexico, USA
31A3 **Deyang** China
41G3 **Deyhuk** Iran
41E3 **Dezfūl** Iran
31D2 **Dezhou** China
41E2 **Dezh Shāhpūr** Iran
45D3 **Dhab'i, Wadi edh** Jordan
41F4 **Dhahran** Saudi Arabia
43G4 **Dhākā** Bangladesh
45B1 **Dhali** Cyprus
44B3 **Dhamavaram** India
43E4 **Dhamtari** India
43F4 **Dhanbād** India
43E3 **Dhangarhi** Nepal
43M1 **Dhang Range** *Mts* Nepal
43F3 **Dhankuta** Nepal
42D4 **Dhār** India
44B3 **Dharmapuri** India
42D2 **Dharmsāla** India
48B3 **Dhar Oualata** *Desert Region* Mauritius
43E3 **Dhaulagiri** *Mt* Nepal
43F4 **Dhenkānāl** India
45C3 **Dhībān** Jordan
17F3 **Dhíkti Óri** *Mt* Greece
Dhodhekánisos = Dodecanese
17E3 **Dhomokós** Greece
44B2 **Dhone** India
42C4 **Dhoraji** India
42C4 **Dhrāngadhra** India
43F3 **Dhuburi** India
42C4 **Dhule** India
73H2 **Diable, Isle du** French Guiana
66B2 **Diablo,Mt** USA
59B3 **Diablo Range** *Mts* USA
73K7 **Diamantina** Brazil
32D3 **Diamantina** *R* Australia
75A1 **Diamantino** Brazil
43F4 **Diamond Harbour** India
66B1 **Diamond Springs** USA
58D2 **Diamondville** USA
41G4 **Dibā** UAE
51C4 **Dibaya** Zaïre
43G3 **Dibrugarh** India
62B2 **Dickens** USA
56C2 **Dickinson** USA
67A1 **Dickson** USA
65D2 **Dickson City** USA
21G8 **Dicle** *R* Turkey
42C3 **Dīdwāna** India
47E2 **Die Berg** *Mt* South Africa
48B3 **Diébougou** Burkina
13E3 **Dieburg** Germany
74C9 **Diego Ramírez, Islas** Chile
Diégo Suarez = Antsirañana
13D3 **Diekirch** Luxembourg
48B3 **Diéma** Mali
30C1 **Dien Bien Phu** Vietnam
18B2 **Diepholz** Germany
14C2 **Dieppe** France
13C2 **Diest** Belgium
13D3 **Dieuze** France
48D3 **Diffa** Niger
43H3 **Digboi** India
55M5 **Digby** Canada
14D3 **Digne** France
14C2 **Digoin** France
27F6 **Digos** Philippines
32C1 **Digul** *R* Indonesia
43G3 **Dihang** *R* China/India
Dijlah = Tigris
14C2 **Dijon** France
50B3 **Dik** Chad
50E2 **Dikhil** Djibouti
45A3 **Dikirnis** Egypt
13B2 **Diksmuide** Belgium
24K2 **Dikson** Russian Federation
38E2 **Dilaram** Afghanistan
27F7 **Dili** Indonesia
30D3 **Di Linh** Vietnam
13E2 **Dillenburg** Germany
62C3 **Dilley** USA
50C2 **Dilling** Sudan
54C4 **Dillingham** USA
56B2 **Dillon** USA
68B2 **Dillsburg** USA
51C5 **Dilolo** Zaïre

Dimāpur **East Branch Delaware**

43G3 **Dimāpur** India
Dimashq = Damascus
50C4 **Dimbelenge** Zaïre
48B4 **Dimbokro** Ivory Coast
17F2 **Dimitrovgrad** Bulgaria
20H5 **Dimitrovgrad** Russian Federation
45C3 **Dīmona** Israel
27F5 **Dinaget** *I* Philippines
43F3 **Dinajpur** India
14B2 **Dinan** France
13C2 **Dinant** Belgium
40B2 **Dinar** Turkey
50D2 **Dinder** *R* Sudan
44B3 **Dindigul** India
31B2 **Dingbian** China
43F3 **Dinggyê** China
10A3 **Dingle** Irish Republic
10A3 **Dingle B** Irish Republic
48A3 **Dinguiraye** Guinea
8C3 **Dingwall** Scotland
31A2 **Dingxi** China
31D2 **Ding Xian** China
30D1 **Dinh Lap** Vietnam
60B2 **Dinosaur** USA
66C2 **Dinuba** USA
48A3 **Dioulouloü** Senegal
43G3 **Diphu** India
50E3 **Dirē Dawa** Ethiopia
32A3 **Dirk Hartog** *I* Australia
50B2 **Dirkou** Niger
34C1 **Dirranbandi** Australia
74J8 **Disappointment,C** South Georgia
58B1 **Disappointment,C** USA
32B3 **Disappointment,L** Australia
34B3 **Discovery B** Australia
27E5 **Discovery Reef** S China Sea
52J7 **Discovery Tablemount** Atlantic Ocean
40B4 **Dishna** Egypt
55N3 **Disko** *I* Greenland
55N3 **Disko Bugt** *B* Greenland
55N3 **Diskofjord** Greenland
65D3 **Dismal Swamp** USA
19F1 **Disna** *R* Belorussia
67B3 **Disney World** USA
75C2 **Distrito Federal** Brazil
42C4 **Diu** India
73K8 **Divinópolis** Brazil
21G6 **Divnoye** Russian Federation
40C2 **Divriği** Turkey
66B1 **Dixon** California, USA
64B2 **Dixon** Illinois, USA
58D1 **Dixon** Montana, USA
54E4 **Dixon Entrance** *Sd* Canada/USA
41E3 **Diyālā** *R* Iraq
21G8 **Diyarbakir** Turkey
41E3 **Diz** *R* Iran
50B3 **Dja** *R* Cameroon
50B1 **Djado,Plat du** Niger
50B4 **Djambala** Congo
48C2 **Djanet** Algeria
48C1 **Djedi** *Watercourse* Algeria
48C1 **Djelfa** Algeria
50C3 **Djéma** Central African Republic
48B3 **Djenné** Mali
48B3 **Djibo** Burkina
50E2 **Djibouti** Djibouti
50E2 **Djibouti** *Republic* EAfrica
50C3 **Djolu** Zaïre
48C4 **Djougou** Benin
50B2 **Djourab, Erg du** *Desert Region* Chad
50D3 **Djugu** Zaïre
12C2 **Djúpivogur** Iceland
15C2 **Djurdjura** *Mts* Algeria
25P2 **Dmitriya Lapteva, Proliv** *Str* Russian Federation
20F4 **Dmitrov** Russian Federation
21E6 **Dnepr** *R* Ukraine
21E6 **Dneprodzerzhinsk** Ukraine
21F6 **Dnepropetrovsk** Ukraine
20D5 **Dneprovskaya Nizmennost'** *Region* Belorussia
21C6 **Dnestr** *R* Ukraine
20E4 **Dno** Russian Federation
50B3 **Doba** Chad
19E1 **Dobele** Latvia
32C1 **Dobo** Indonesia
17D2 **Doboj** Bosnia & Herzegovina, Yugoslavia
17F2 **Dobrich** Bulgaria
21E5 **Dobrush** Belorussia
73K7 **Doce** *R* Brazil
74D2 **Doctor P P Peña** Paraguay
44B3 **Dod** India
44B3 **Doda Betta** *Mt* India
17F3 **Dodecanese** *Is* Greece
56C3 **Dodge City** USA
64A2 **Dodgeville** USA
50D4 **Dodoma** Tanzania
64B1 **Dog L** Canada
64C1 **Dog L** Canada
29B3 **Dōgo** *I* Japan
48C3 **Dogondoutchi** Niger
41D2 **Doğubayazit** Turkey
41F4 **Doha** Qatar
43G3 **Doilungdêqên** China
13D1 **Dokkum** Netherlands
29F2 **Dokuchayevo, Mys** *C* Russian Federation
32C1 **Dolak** *I* Indonesia
61D2 **Doland** USA
55L5 **Dolbeau** Canada
14D2 **Dôle** France
7C3 **Dolgellau** Wales
68C1 **Dolgeville** USA
20K2 **Dolgiy, Ostrov** *I* Russian Federation
50E3 **Dolo Odo** Ethiopia
74E5 **Dolores** Argentina
60B3 **Dolores** *R* USA
54G3 **Dolphin and Union Str** Canada
74E8 **Dolphin,C** Falkland Islands
27G7 **Dom** *Mt* Indonesia
21K5 **Dombarovskiy** Russian Federation
12F6 **Dombås** Norway
13D3 **Dombasle-sur-Meurthe** France
17D1 **Dombóvár** Hungary
14B2 **Domfront** France
69E3 **Dominica** *I* Caribbean Sea
69C3 **Dominican Republic** Caribbean Sea
55L3 **Dominion,C** Canada
55N4 **Domino** Canada
26E1 **Domna** Russian Federation
16B1 **Domodossola** Italy
74B5 **Domuyo, Vol** Argentina
34D1 **Domville,Mt** Australia
8D3 **Don** *R* Scotland
21G6 **Don** *R* Russian Federation
9C2 **Donaghadee** Northern Ireland
Donau = Dunav Bulgaria
18C3 **Donau** *R* Austria/ Germany
13E4 **Donaueschingen** Germany
18C3 **Donauwörth** Germany
15A2 **Don Benito** Spain
7D3 **Doncaster** England
51B4 **Dondo** Angola
51D5 **Dondo** Mozambique
44C4 **Dondra Head** *C* Sri Lanka
10B3 **Donegal** Irish Republic
9C2 **Donegal** *County* Irish Republic
10B3 **Donegal B** Irish Republic
9C2 **Donegal Mts** Irish Republic
9B3 **Donegal Pt** Irish Republic
21F6 **Donetsk** Ukraine
31C4 **Dong'an** China
32A3 **Dongara** Australia
31A4 **Dongchuan** China
30D2 **Dongfang** China
28B2 **Dongfeng** China
32A1 **Donggala** Indonesia
26C3 **Donggi Cona** *L* China
28A3 **Donggou** China
31C5 **Donghai Dao** *I* China
31A1 **Dong He** *R* China
30D2 **Dong Hoi** Vietnam
31C5 **Dong Jiang** *R* China
28A2 **Dongliao He** *R* China
28C2 **Dongning** China
50D2 **Dongola** Sudan
31D5 **Dongshan** China
26E4 **Dongsha Qundao** *I* China
31C2 **Dongsheng** China
31E3 **Dongtai** China
31C4 **Dongting Hu** *L* China
31B5 **Dongxing** China
31D3 **Dongzhi** China
63D1 **Doniphan** USA
16D2 **Donji Vakuf** Bosnia & Herzegovina, Yugoslavia
12G5 **Dönna** *I* Norway
59B3 **Donner P** USA
13D3 **Donnersberg** *Mt* Germany
47D2 **Donnybrook** South Africa
Donostia = San Sebatián
66B2 **Don Pedro Res** USA
8C4 **Doon, Loch** *L* Scotland
31A3 **Do Qu** *R* China
14D2 **Dorbirn** Austria
7C4 **Dorchester** England
55L3 **Dorchester,C** Canada
14C2 **Dordogne** *R* France
18A2 **Dordrecht** Netherlands
47D3 **Dordrecht** South Africa
68D1 **Dorest Peak** *Mt* USA
48B3 **Dori** Burkina
47B3 **Doring** *R* South Africa
7D4 **Dorking** England
13B3 **Dormans** France
18B3 **Dornbirn** Austria
8C3 **Dornoch** Scotland
8D3 **Dornoch Firth** *Estuary* Scotland
12H6 **Dorotea** Sweden
34D2 **Dorrigo** Australia
58B2 **Dorris** USA
7C4 **Dorset** *County* England
55L3 **Dorset, Cape** Canada
13D2 **Dorsten** Germany
18B2 **Dortmund** Germany
50C3 **Doruma** Zaïre
25N4 **Dosatuy** Russian Federation
42B1 **Doshi** Afghanistan
66B2 **Dos Palos** USA
48C3 **Dosso** Niger
24G5 **Dossor** Kazakhstan
57E3 **Dothan** USA
14C1 **Douai** France
50A3 **Douala** Cameroon
34D1 **Double Island Pt** Australia
62B2 **Double Mountain Fork** *R* USA
66C3 **Double Mt** USA
14D2 **Doubs** *R* France
35A3 **Doubtful Sd** New Zealand
48B3 **Douentza** Mali
56C3 **Douglas** Arizona, USA
67B2 **Douglas** Georgia, USA
6B2 **Douglas** Isle of Man, British Isles
47C2 **Douglas** South Africa
56C2 **Douglas** Wyoming, USA
67B1 **Douglas L** USA
13C2 **Doulevant-le-Château** France
13B2 **Doullens** France
75B2 **Dourada, Serra** *Mts* Brazil
75C1 **Dourada, Serra** *Mts* Brazil
73H8 **Dourados** Brazil
75B3 **Dourados** *R* Brazil
75B3 **Dourados, Serra dos** *Mts* Brazil
13B3 **Dourdan** France
15A1 **Douro** *R* Portugal
7D3 **Dove** *R* England
62A1 **Dove Creek** USA
65D3 **Dover** Delaware, USA
7E4 **Dover** England
65E2 **Dover** New Hampshire, USA
68C2 **Dover** New Jersey, USA
64C2 **Dover** Ohio, USA
7E4 **Dover,Str of** England/ France
19G2 **Dovsk** Belorussia
9C2 **Down** *County* Northern Ireland
68C3 **Downingtown** USA
9D2 **Downpatrick** Northern Ireland
68C1 **Downsville** USA
68C2 **Doylestown** USA
28B3 **Dōzen** *I* Japan
65D1 **Dozois, Réservoir** Canada
48A2 **Dr'aa** *Watercourse* Morocco
75B3 **Dracena** Brazil
13D1 **Drachten** Netherlands
68E1 **Dracut** USA
14D3 **Draguignan** France
60C1 **Drake** USA
51D6 **Drakensberg** *Mts* South Africa
47D2 **Drakensberg** *Mt* South Africa
52E7 **Drake Passage** Atlantic O/ Pacific Ocean
17E2 **Dráma** Greece
12G7 **Drammen** Norway
12A1 **Drangajökull** *Ice cap* Iceland
16D1 **Drava** *R* Slovenia
13D1 **Drenthe** *Province* Netherlands
18C2 **Dresden** Germany
14C2 **Dreux** France
58C2 **Drewsey** USA
68A2 **Driftwood** USA
17E2 **Drin** *R* Albania
17D2 **Drina** *R* Bosnia & Herzegovina, Yugoslavia
19F1 **Drissa** *R* Belorussia
9C3 **Drogheda** Irish Republic
19E3 **Drogobych** Ukraine
9C3 **Droihead Nua** Irish Republic
7C3 **Droitwich** England
9C2 **Dromore** Northern Ireland
76F12 **Dronning Maud Land** *Region* Antarctica
54G4 **Drumheller** Canada
58D1 **Drummond** USA
64C1 **Drummond I** USA
65E1 **Drummondville** Canada
8C3 **Drumochter Pass** Scotland
19E2 **Druskininkai** Lithuania
25Q3 **Druzhina** Russian Federation
61E1 **Dryberry L** Canada
55J5 **Dryden** Canada
68B1 **Dryden** USA
69H1 **Dry Harbour Mts** Jamaica
30B3 **Duang** *I* Burma
40C4 **Dubā** Saudi Arabia
41G4 **Dubai** UAE
54H3 **Dubawnt** *R* Canada
54H3 **Dubawnt L** Canada
32D4 **Dubbo** Australia
9C3 **Dublin** Irish Republic
67B2 **Dublin** USA
9C3 **Dublin** *County* Irish Republic
20F4 **Dubna** Russian Federation
21D5 **Dubno** Ukraine
58D2 **Dubois** Idaho, USA
65D2 **Du Bois** USA
58E2 **Dubois** Wyoming, USA
19F3 **Dubossary** Moldavia
19F2 **Dubrovica** Ukraine
17D2 **Dubrovnik** Croatia
57D2 **Dubuque** USA
59D2 **Duchesne** USA
67A1 **Duck** *R* USA
66C3 **Ducor** USA
13D3 **Dudelange** Luxembourg
24K3 **Dudinka** Russian Federation
7C3 **Dudley** England
25L2 **Dudypta** *R* Russian Federation
48B4 **Duekoué** Ivory Coast
15B1 **Duero** *R* Spain
33F1 **Duff Is** Solomon Islands
8D3 **Dufftown** Scotland
16C2 **Dugi Otok** *I* Croatia
18B2 **Duisburg** Germany
47E1 **Duiwelskloof** South Africa
41E3 **Dūkan** Iraq
50D3 **Duk Faiwil** Sudan
41F4 **Dukhān** Qatar
31A4 **Dukou** China
26C3 **Dulan** China
70D4 **Dulce, Golfo** Costa Rica
43G4 **Dullabchara** India
13D2 **Dülmen** Germany
57D2 **Duluth** USA
7C4 **Dulverton** England
45D2 **Dūmā** Syria
27D6 **Dumai** Indonesia
56C3 **Dumas** USA
45D2 **Ḑumayr** Syria
8C4 **Dumbarton** Scotland
48B1 **Dumer Rbia** Morocco
8D4 **Dumfries** Scotland
8C4 **Dumfries and Galloway** *Region* Scotland
43F4 **Dumka** India
65D1 **Dumoine,L** Canada
76G8 **Dumont d'Urville** *Base* Antarctica
49F1 **Dumyat** Egypt
17F2 **Dunărea** *R* Romania
9C3 **Dunary Head** *Pt* Irish Republic
17E2 **Dunav** *R* Bulgaria
17D1 **Dunav** *R* Croatia/Serbia, Yugoslavia
28C2 **Dunay** Russian Federation
19F3 **Dunayevtsy** Ukraine
8D4 **Dunbar** Scotland
63C2 **Duncan** USA
68B2 **Duncannon** USA
44E3 **Duncan Pass** *Chan* Andaman Islands
8D2 **Duncansby Head** *Pt* Scotland
9C2 **Dundalk** Irish Republic
68B3 **Dundalk** USA
9C3 **Dundalk B** Irish Republic
55M2 **Dundas** Greenland
54G2 **Dundas Pen** Canada
27G8 **Dundas Str** Australia
47E2 **Dundee** South Africa
8D3 **Dundee** Scotland
68B1 **Dundee** USA
34B1 **Dundoo** Australia
9D2 **Dundrum B** Northern Ireland
43M2 **Dundwa Range** *Mts* Nepal
33G5 **Dunedin** New Zealand
67B3 **Dunedin** USA
34C2 **Dunedoo** Australia
8D3 **Dunfermline** Scotland
9C2 **Dungannon** Northern Ireland
42C4 **Dūngarpur** India
9C3 **Dungarvan** Irish Republic
7E4 **Dungeness** *Pen* England
34D2 **Dungog** Australia
50C3 **Dungu** Zaïre
50D1 **Dungunab** Sudan
28B2 **Dunhua** China
26C2 **Dunhuang** China
8D3 **Dunkeld** Scotland
Dunkerque = Dunkirk
13B2 **Dunkirk** France
57F2 **Dunkirk** USA
50D2 **Dunkur** Ethiopia
48B4 **Dunkwa** Ghana
10B3 **Dun Laoghaire** Irish Republic
9B4 **Dunmanus** Irish Republic
68C2 **Dunmore** USA
69B1 **Dunmore Town** The Bahamas
67C1 **Dunn** USA
8D2 **Dunnet Head** *Pt* Scotland
60C2 **Dunning** USA
8C4 **Dunoon** Scotland
8D4 **Duns** Scotland
60C1 **Dunseith** USA
58B2 **Dunsmuir** USA
35A2 **Dunstan Mts** New Zealand
13C3 **Dun-sur-Meuse** France
31D1 **Duolun** China
60C1 **Dupree** USA
64B3 **Du Quoin** USA
45C3 **Dura** Israel
14D3 **Durance** *R* France
64A2 **Durand** USA
70B2 **Durango** Mexico
15B1 **Durango** Spain
56C3 **Durango** USA
56D3 **Durant** USA
45D1 **Duraykīsh** Syria
74E4 **Durazno** Uruguay
47E2 **Durban** South Africa
13D2 **Duren** Germany
43E4 **Durg** India
43F4 **Durgapur** India
6D2 **Durham** England
57F3 **Durham** N Carolina, USA
68E1 **Durham** New Hampshire, USA
6D2 **Durham** *County* England
34B1 **Durham Downs** Australia
17D2 **Durmitor** *Mt* Montenegro, Yugoslavia
8C2 **Durness** Scotland
17D2 **Durrës** Albania
34B1 **Durrie** Australia
17F3 **Dursunbey** Turkey
35B2 **D'Urville I** New Zealand
41H2 **Dushak** Turkmenistan
31B4 **Dushan** China
39E2 **Dushanbe** Tajikistan
68B2 **Dushore** USA
35A3 **Dusky Sd** New Zealand
18B2 **Düsseldorf** Germany
59D3 **Dutton,Mt** USA
31B4 **Duyun** China
40B1 **Düzce** Turkey
20F2 **Dvinskaya Guba** *B* Russian Federation
42B4 **Dwārka** India
58C1 **Dworshak Res** USA
57E3 **Dyersburg** USA
7B3 **Dyfed** *County* Wales
21G7 **Dykh Tau** *Mt* Russian Federation
34B1 **Dynevor Downs** Australia
26C2 **Dzag** Mongolia
26E2 **Dzamïn Uüd** Mongolia
51E5 **Dzaoudzi** Mayotte, Indian Ocean
26C2 **Dzavhan Gol** *R* Mongolia
20G4 **Dzerzhinsk** Russian Federation
25O4 **Dzhalinda** Russian Federation
24J5 **Dzhambul** Kazakhstan
21E6 **Dzhankoy** Ukraine
24H5 **Dzhezkazgan** Kazakhstan
42B1 **Dzhilikul'** Tajikistan
25P4 **Dzhugdzhur, Khrebet** *Mts* Russian Federation
24J5 **Dzhungarskiy Alatau** *Mts* Kazakhstan
18D2 **Dzierzoniow** Poland
39G1 **Dzungaria Basin** China
25L5 **Dzüyl** Mongolia

E

55K4 **Eabamet L** Canada
60B3 **Eagle** Colorado, USA
60C1 **Eagle Butte** USA
58B2 **Eagle L** California, USA
65F1 **Eagle L** Maine, USA
65F1 **Eagle Lake** USA
63C2 **Eagle Mountain L** USA
56C4 **Eagle Pass** USA
62A2 **Eagle Peak** *Mt* USA
54E3 **Eagle Plain** Canada
59C3 **Earlimart** USA
8D3 **Earn** *R* Scotland
8C3 **Earn, Loch** *L* Scotland
59D4 **Earp** USA
62B2 **Earth** USA
6D2 **Easingwold** England
67B2 **Easley** USA
65D2 **East Aurora** USA
63E2 **East B** USA
7E4 **Eastbourne** England
68C1 **East Branch Delaware** *R* USA

Erzincan **Forel,Mt**

21F8 **Erzincan** Turkey
21G8 **Erzurum** Turkey
29D2 **Esan-misaki** *C* Japan
29D2 **Esashi** Japan
18B1 **Esbjerg** Denmark
59D3 **Escalante** USA
56C4 **Escalón** Mexico
57E2 **Escanaba** USA
70C3 **Escárcega** Mexico
13C3 **Esch** Luxembourg
59C4 **Escondido** USA
70B2 **Escuinapa** Mexico
70C3 **Escuintla** Guatemala
50B3 **Eséka** Cameroon
13D1 **Esens** Germany
14C3 **Esera** *R* Spain
15C1 **Esera** *R* Spain
41F3 **Eşfahān** Iran
47E2 **Eshowe** South Africa
45C3 **Esh Sharā** *Upland* Jordan
8D4 **Esk** *R* Scotland
35C1 **Eskdale** New Zealand
12C1 **Eskifjörður** Iceland
12H7 **Eskilstuna** Sweden
54E3 **Eskimo Lakes** Canada
55J3 **Eskimo Point** Canada
21E8 **Eskişehir** Turkey
15A1 **Esla** *R* Spain
15A1 **Esla, Embalse del** *Res* Spain
69B2 **Esmeralda** Cuba
74A7 **Esmeralda** *I* Chile
72C3 **Esmeraldas** Ecuador
14C3 **Espalion** France
64C1 **Espanola** Canada
62A1 **Espanola** USA
32B4 **Esperance** Australia
76G2 **Esperanza** *Base* Antarctica
15A2 **Espichel, Cabo** *C* Portugal
75D2 **Espinhaço, Serra do** *Mts* Brazil
75D2 **Espírito Santo** *State* Brazil
33F2 **Espiritu Santo** *I* Vanuatu
51D6 **Espungabera** Mozambique
74B6 **Esquel** Argentina
58B1 **Esquimalt** Canada
45D2 **Es Samrā** Jordan
48B1 **Essaouira** Morocco
18B2 **Essen** Germany
73G3 **Essequibo** *R* Guyana
7E4 **Essex** *County* England
64C2 **Essexville** USA
18B3 **Esslingen** Germany
13B3 **Essonne** *Department* France
13C3 **Essoyes** France
74D8 **Estados, Isla de los** Argentina
73L6 **Estância** Brazil
47D2 **Estcourt** South Africa
72A1 **Esteí** Nicaragua
13B3 **Esternay** France
66B3 **Estero B** USA
74D2 **Esteros** Paraguay
60B2 **Estes Park** USA
54H5 **Estevan** Canada
61E2 **Estherville** USA
67B2 **Estill** USA
13B3 **Estissac** France
20C4 **Estonia** *Republic* Europe
66B3 **Estrella** *R* USA
15A2 **Estremoz** Portugal
19D3 **Esztergom** Hungary
34A1 **Etadunna** Australia
55L2 **Etah** Canada
43K2 **Etah** India
13C3 **Etam** France
14C2 **Étampes** France
34A1 **Etamunbanie,L** Australia
42D3 **Etāwah** India
50D3 **Ethiopia** *Republic* Africa
8C3 **Etive, Loch** *Inlet* Scotland
16C3 **Etna** *Vol* Sicily, Italy
51B5 **Etosha Nat Pk** Namibia
51B5 **Etosha Pan** *Salt L* Namibia
67B2 **Etowah** *R* USA
13C3 **Ettelbruck** Luxembourg
33H3 **Eua** *I* Tonga
34C2 **Euabalong** Australia
17E3 **Euboea** *I* Greece
64C2 **Euclid** USA
34C3 **Eucumbene,L** Australia
34A2 **Eudunda** Australia
63C1 **Eufala L** USA
67A2 **Eufaula** USA
56A2 **Eugene** USA
70A2 **Eugenia, Punta** *Pt* Mexico
34C1 **Eulo** Australia
63D2 **Eunice** Louisiana, USA
62B2 **Eunice** New Mexico, USA
13D2 **Eupen** Germany
40D3 **Euphrates** *R* Iraq/Syria
63E2 **Eupora** USA
14C2 **Eure** *R* France
58B2 **Eureka** California, USA
55K1 **Eureka** Canada
58C1 **Eureka** Montana, USA
56B3 **Eureka** Nevada, USA
60D1 **Eureka** S Dakota, USA
59D3 **Eureka** Utah, USA
55K2 **Eureka Sd** Canada
66D2 **Eureka V** USA
34C3 **Euroa** Australia
34C1 **Eurombah** *R* Australia
51E6 **Europa** *I* Mozambique Channel
13C2 **Europoort** Netherlands
18B2 **Euskirchen** Germany
63E2 **Eutaw** USA
55K1 **Evans,C** Canada
55L4 **Evans,L** Canada
60B3 **Evans,Mt** Colorado, USA
58D1 **Evans,Mt** Montana, USA
55K3 **Evans Str** Canada
64B2 **Evanston** Illinois, USA
56B2 **Evanston** Wyoming, USA
57E3 **Evansville** Indiana, USA
60B2 **Evansville** Wyoming, USA
47D2 **Evaton** South Africa
32C4 **Everard,L** Australia
39G3 **Everest,Mt** China/Nepal
68A2 **Everett** Pennsylvania, USA
56A2 **Everett** Washington, USA
68D1 **Everett,Mt** USA
57E4 **Everglades,The** *Swamp* USA
67A2 **Evergreen** USA
7D3 **Evesham** England
50B3 **Evinayong** Equatorial Guinea
12F7 **Evje** Norway
15A2 **Évora** Portugal
14C2 **Evreux** France
Évvoia = Euboea
8C3 **Ewe, Loch** *Inlet* Scotland
50B4 **Ewo** Congo
66C1 **Excelsior Mt** USA
66C1 **Excelsior Mts** USA
61E3 **Excelsior Springs** USA
7C4 **Exe** *R* England
59C3 **Exeter** California, USA
7C4 **Exeter** England
65E2 **Exeter** New Hampshire, USA
7C4 **Exmoor** England
7C4 **Exmouth** England
15A2 **Extremadura** *Region* Spain
70E2 **Exuma Sd** The Bahamas
50D4 **Eyasi, L** Tanzania
8D4 **Eyemouth** Scotland
50E3 **Eyl** Somalia
32B4 **Eyre** Australia
32C3 **Eyre Creek** *R* Australia
32C3 **Eyre,L** Australia
32C4 **Eyre Pen** Australia
17F3 **Ezine** Turkey

F

54G3 **Faber L** Canada
12F7 **Fåborg** Denmark
16C2 **Fabriano** Italy
50B2 **Fachi** Niger
50C2 **Fada** Chad
48C3 **Fada N'Gourma** Burkina
25Q2 **Faddeyevskiy, Ostrov** *I* Russian Federation
16C2 **Faenza** Italy
55N3 **Færingehavn** Greenland
Færøerne = Faeroes
12D3 **Faeroes** *Is* N Atlantic Oc
50B3 **Fafa** *R* Central African Republic
50E3 **Fafan** *R* Ethiopia
17E1 **Făgăraş** Romania
13C2 **Fagnes** *Region* Belgium
48B3 **Faguibine,L** Mali
41G5 **Fahūd** Oman
48A1 **Faiol** *I* Azores
62A2 **Fairacres** USA
54D3 **Fairbanks** USA
64C3 **Fairborn** USA
56D2 **Fairbury** USA
68B3 **Fairfax** USA
59B3 **Fairfield** California, USA
68D2 **Fairfield** Connecticut, USA
58D2 **Fairfield** Idaho, USA
58D1 **Fairfield** Montana, USA
64C3 **Fairfield** Ohio, USA
9C2 **Fair Head** *Pt* Northern Ireland
10C2 **Fair Isle** *I* Scotland
35B2 **Fairlie** New Zealand
61E2 **Fairmont** Minnesota, USA
64C3 **Fairmont** W Virginia, USA
68B1 **Fairport** USA
62C1 **Fairview** USA
54E4 **Fairweather,Mt** USA
27H6 **Fais** *I* Pacific Ocean
42C2 **Faisalabad** Pakistan
60C1 **Faith** USA
8E1 **Faither,The** *Pen* Scotland
33H1 **Fakaofo** *I* Tokelau Islands
7E3 **Fakenham** England
32C1 **Fakfak** Indonesia
28A2 **Faku** China
43G4 **Falam** Burma
70C2 **Falcon Res** Mexico/USA
48A3 **Falémé** *R* Mali/Senegal/Guinea
62C3 **Falfurrias** USA
12G7 **Falkenberg** Sweden
8D4 **Falkirk** Scotland
74D8 **Falkland Is** *Dependency* S Atlantic
74E8 **Falkland Sd** Falkland Islands
12G7 **Falköping** Sweden
66D4 **Fallbrook** USA
56B3 **Fallon** USA
65E2 **Fall River** USA
60B2 **Fall River P** USA
61D2 **Falls City** USA
7B4 **Falmouth** England
69H1 **Falmouth** Jamaica
65E2 **Falmouth** Maine, USA
68E2 **Falmouth** Massachusetts, USA
7B4 **Falmouth Bay** England
47B3 **False B** South Africa
70A2 **Falso,C** Mexico
18C2 **Falster** *I* Denmark
17F1 **Fălticeni** Romania
12H6 **Falun** Sweden
40B2 **Famagusta** Cyprus
45B1 **Famagusta B** Cyprus
13C2 **Famenne** *Region* Belgium
66C3 **Famoso** USA
30B2 **Fang** Thailand
50D3 **Fangak** Sudan
31E5 **Fangliao** Taiwan
8C3 **Fannich, L** Scotland
16C2 **Fano** Italy
45A3 **Fâqûs** Egypt
76G3 **Faraday** *Base* Antarctica
50C3 **Faradje** Zaïre
51E6 **Farafangana** Madagascar
49E2 **Farafra Oasis** Egypt
38E2 **Farah** Afghanistan
27H5 **Farallon de Medinilla** *I* Pacific Ocean
26H4 **Farallon de Pajaros** *I* Marianas
48A3 **Faranah** Guinea
50E2 **Farasan Is** Saudi Arabia
27H6 **Faraulep** *I* Pacific Ocean
55J5 **Farbault** USA
7D4 **Fareham** England
55O4 **Farewell,C** Greenland
33G5 **Farewell,C** New Zealand
35B2 **Farewell Spit** *Pt* New Zealand
56D2 **Fargo** USA
45C2 **Fari'a** *R* Israel
57D2 **Faribault** USA
43F4 **Faridpur** Bangladesh
41G2 **Farīmān** Iran
45A3 **Fâriskûr** Egypt
65E2 **Farmington** Maine, USA
63D1 **Farmington** Missouri, USA
68E1 **Farmington** New Hampshire, USA
56C3 **Farmington** New Mexico, USA
58D2 **Farmington** Utah, USA
66B2 **Farmington Res** USA
6D2 **Farne Deep** N Sea
15A2 **Faro** Portugal
12H7 **Fårö** *I* Sweden
46K9 **Farquhar Is** Indian Ocean
8C3 **Farrar** *R* Scotland
64C2 **Farrell** USA
43K2 **Farrukhabad** *District* India
17E3 **Fársala** Greece
75B4 **Fartura, Serra de** *Mts* Brazil
62B2 **Farwell** USA
41F4 **Fasā** Iran
21D5 **Fastov** Ukraine
43K2 **Fatehgarh** India
43E3 **Fatehpur** India
73H7 **Fatima du Sul** Brazil
58C1 **Fauquier** Canada
47D2 **Fauresmith** South Africa
12H5 **Fauske** Norway
7E4 **Faversham** England
55K4 **Fawn** *R* Canada
12H6 **Fax** *R* Sweden
12A2 **Faxaflói** *B* Iceland
50B2 **Faya** Chad
63E2 **Fayette** USA
57D3 **Fayetteville** Arkansas, USA
57F3 **Fayetteville** N Carolina, USA
67A1 **Fayetteville** Tennessee, USA
45B3 **Fâyid** Egypt
41E4 **Faylakah** *I* Kuwait
42C2 **Fāzilka** India
48A2 **Fdérik** Mauritius
57F3 **Fear,C** USA
66B1 **Feather** *R* USA
59B3 **Feather Middle Fork** *R* USA
14C2 **Fécamp** France
18C2 **Fehmarn** *I* Germany
75D3 **Feia, Lagoa** Brazil
72D5 **Feijó** Brazil
31C5 **Feilai Xai Bei Jiang** *R* China
35C2 **Feilding** New Zealand
51D5 **Feira** Zambia
73L6 **Feira de Santan** Brazil
40C2 **Feke** Turkey
13D4 **Feldberg** *Mt* Germany
18B3 **Feldkirch** Austria
10D3 **Felixstowe** England
12G6 **Femund** *L* Norway
28A2 **Fengcheng** China
31B4 **Fengdu** China
31B3 **Fengjie** China
31D1 **Fengning** China
31B3 **Feng Xian** China
31C1 **Fengzhen** China
31C2 **Fen He** *R* China
51E5 **Fenoarivo Atsinanana** Madagascar
21F7 **Feodosiya** Ukraine
41G3 **Ferdow** Iran
13B3 **Fère-Champenoise** France
39F1 **Fergana** Uzbekistan
61D1 **Fergus Falls** USA
48B4 **Ferkessedougou** Ivory Coast
9C2 **Fermanagh** *County* Northern Ireland
67B2 **Fernandina Beach** USA
73M4 **Fernando de Noronha, Isla** Brazil
75B3 **Fernandópolis** Brazil
Fernando Poo *I* **=Bioko**
58B1 **Ferndale** USA
58C1 **Fernie** Canada
59C3 **Fernley** USA
16C2 **Ferrara** Italy
15B2 **Ferrat, Cap** *C* Algeria
72C5 **Ferreñafe** Peru
63D2 **Ferriday** USA
13B3 **Ferrières** France
48B1 **Fès** Morocco
63D1 **Festus** USA
17F2 **Feteşti** Romania
9C3 **Fethard** Irish Republic
40A2 **Fethiye** Turkey
21J7 **Fetisovo** Kazakhstan
8E1 **Fetlar** *I* Scotland
55L4 **Feuilles, Rivière aux** *R* Canada
24J6 **Feyzabad** Afghanistan
7C3 **Ffestiniog** Wales
51E6 **Fianarantsoa** Madagascar
50D3 **Fichē** Ethiopia
47D2 **Ficksburg** South Africa
45C3 **Fidan, Wadi** Jordan
17D2 **Fier** Albania
8D3 **Fife** *Region* Scotland
8D3 **Fife Ness** *Pen* Scotland
14C3 **Figeac** France
15A1 **Figueira da Foz** Portugal
Figueres = Figueras
15C1 **Figueras** Spain
48B1 **Figuig** Morocco
33G2 **Fiji** *Is* Pacific Ocean
15B2 **Filabres, Sierra de los** *Mts* Spain
73G8 **Filadelfia** Paraguay
6D2 **Filey** England
17E2 **Filiaşi** Romania
17E3 **Filiatrá** Greece
16C3 **Filicudi** *I* Italy
59C4 **Fillmore** California, USA
59D3 **Fillmore** Utah, USA
8C3 **Findhorn** *R* Scotland
57E2 **Findlay** USA
65D2 **Finger Lakes** USA
51D5 **Fingoè** Mozambique
21E8 **Finike** Turkey
15A1 **Finisterre, Cabo** *C* Spain
32C3 **Finke** *R* Australia
20C3 **Finland** *Republic* N Europe
12J7 **Finland,G of** N Europe
54F4 **Finlay** *R* Canada
54F4 **Finlay Forks** Canada
34C3 **Finley** Australia
9C2 **Finn** *R* Irish Republic
12H5 **Finnsnes** Norway
27H7 **Finschhafen** Papua New Guinea
12H7 **Finspång** Sweden
18C2 **Finsterwalde** Germany
9C2 **Fintona** Northern Ireland
35A3 **Fiordland Nat Pk** New Zealand
45C2 **Fiq** Syria
21F8 **Firat** *R* Turkey
66B2 **Firebaugh** USA
Firenze = Florence
42D3 **Firozābād** India
42C2 **Firozpur** India
8C4 **Firth of Clyde** *Estuary* Scotland
8D3 **Firth of Forth** *Estuary* Scotland
8B3 **Firth of Lorn** *Estuary* Scotland
10C2 **Firth of Tay** *Estuary* Scotland
41F4 **Firūzābād** Iran
47B2 **Fish** *R* Namibia
47C3 **Fish** *R* South Africa
66C2 **Fish Camp** USA
68D2 **Fishers I** USA
55K3 **Fisher Str** Canada
7B4 **Fishguard** Wales
55N3 **Fiskenæsset** Greenland
13B3 **Fismes** France
65E2 **Fitchburg** USA
8E2 **Fitful Head** *Pt* Scotland
67B2 **Fitzgerald** USA
32B2 **Fitzroy** *R* Australia
32B2 **Fitzroy Crossing** Australia
64C1 **Fitzwilliam I** Canada
Fiume = Rijeka
50C4 **Fizi** Zaïre
47D3 **Flagstaff** South Africa
56B3 **Flagstaff** USA
65E1 **Flagstaff L** USA
6D2 **Flamborough Head** *C* England
56C2 **Flaming Gorge Res** USA
27G7 **Flamingo, Teluk** *B* Indonesia
13B2 **Flandres, Plaine des** Belgium/France
8B2 **Flannan Isles** Scotland
56B2 **Flathead L** USA
63D1 **Flat River** USA
27H8 **Flattery,C** Australia
56A2 **Flattery,C** USA
6C3 **Fleetwood** England
12F7 **Flekkefjord** Norway
26H4 **Fleming Deep** Pacific Ocean
68C2 **Flemington** USA
18B2 **Flensburg** Germany
32C4 **Flinders** *I* Australia
32D5 **Flinders** *I* Australia
32D2 **Flinders** *R* Australia
32C4 **Flinders Range** *Mts* Australia
54H4 **Flin Flon** Canada
57E2 **Flint** USA
7C3 **Flint** Wales
57E3 **Flint** *R* USA
13B2 **Flixecourt** France
64A1 **Floodwood** USA
67A2 **Florala** USA
57E3 **Florence** Alabama, USA
59D4 **Florence** Arizona, USA
60B3 **Florence** Colorado, USA
16C2 **Florence** Italy
63C1 **Florence** Kansas, USA
58B2 **Florence** Oregon, USA
57F3 **Florence** S Carolina, USA
66C2 **Florence L** USA
72C3 **Florencia** Colombia
74C6 **Florentine Ameghino, Embalse** *Res* Argentina
13C3 **Florenville** Belgium
70D3 **Flores** Guatemala
48A1 **Flores** *I* Azores
32B1 **Flores** *I* Indonesia
27E7 **Flores S**Indonesia
73K5 **Floriano** Brazil
74G3 **Florianópolis** Brazil
74E4 **Florida** Uruguay
70D2 **Florida** *State* USA
67B3 **Florida B** USA
67B3 **Florida City** USA
33E1 **Florida Is** Solomon Islands
57E4 **Florida Keys** *Is* USA
57E4 **Florida,Strs of** USA
17E2 **Flórina** Greece
12F6 **Florø** Norway
62B2 **Floydada** USA
32D1 **Fly** *R* Papua New Guinea
17F1 **Focşani** Romania
16D2 **Foggia** Italy
48A4 **Fogo** *I* Cape Verde
14C3 **Foix** France
64C1 **Foleyet** Canada
55L3 **Foley I** Canada
16C2 **Foligno** Italy
7E4 **Folkestone** England
67B2 **Folkston** USA
16C2 **Follonica** Italy
66B1 **Folsom** USA
68C1 **Fonda** USA
54H4 **Fond-du-Lac** Canada
57E2 **Fond du Lac** USA
70D3 **Fonseca, G de** Honduras
14C2 **Fontainbleau** France
14B2 **Fontenay-le-Comte** France
17D1 **Fonyód** Hungary
Foochow = Fuzhou
54C3 **Foraker, Mt** USA
13D3 **Forbach** France
34C2 **Forbes** Australia
48C4 **Forcados** Nigeria
66C3 **Ford City** USA
12F6 **Førde** Norway
7D4 **Fordingbridge** England
34C1 **Fords Bridge** Australia
63D2 **Fordyce** USA
48A4 **Forécariah** Guinea
55P3 **Forel,Mt** Greenland

Foremost **Gedaref**

58D1 **Foremost** Canada
64C2 **Forest** Canada
63E2 **Forest** USA
61E2 **Forest City** Iowa, USA
68C2 **Forest City** Pennsylvania, USA
7C4 **Forest of Dean** England
67B2 **Forest Park** USA
66A1 **Forestville** USA
13B3 **Forêt d'Othe** France
8D3 **Forfar** Scotland
62B1 **Forgan** USA
58B1 **Forks** USA
16C2 **Forlì** Italy
7C3 **Formby** England
15C2 **Formentera** *I* Spain
15C1 **Formentor, Cabo** *C* Spain
16C2 **Formia** Italy
48A1 **Formigas** *I* Azores
Formosa = Taiwan
74E3 **Formosa** Argentina
73J7 **Formosa** Brazil
74D2 **Formosa** *State* Argentina
Formosa Channel = Taiwan Str
73G6 **Formosa, Serra** *Mts* Brazil
75C1 **Formoso** Brazil
75C1 **Formoso** *R* Brazil
8D3 **Forres** Scotland
32B4 **Forrest** Australia
57D3 **Forrest City** USA
32D2 **Forsayth** Australia
12J6 **Forssa** Finland
34D2 **Forster** Australia
63D1 **Forsyth** Missouri, USA
60B1 **Forsyth** Montana, USA
42C3 **Fort Abbas** Pakistan
55K4 **Fort Albany** Canada
73L4 **Fortaleza** Brazil
8C3 **Fort Augustus** Scotland
47D3 **Fort Beaufort** South Africa
58D1 **Fort Benton** USA
59B3 **Fort Bragg** USA
62C1 **Fort Cobb Res** USA
56C2 **Fort Collins** USA
65D1 **Fort Coulonge** Canada
62B2 **Fort Davis** USA
69E4 **Fort-de-France** Martinique
67A2 **Fort Deposit** USA
57D2 **Fort Dodge** USA
32A3 **Fortescue** *R* Australia
57D2 **Fort Frances** Canada
54F3 **Fort Franklin** Canada
54F3 **Fort Good Hope** Canada
34B1 **Fort Grey** Australia
8C3 **Forth** *R* Scotland
62A2 **Fort Hancock** USA
55K4 **Fort Hope** Canada
8F3 **Forties** *Oilfield* N Sea
65F1 **Fort Kent** USA
48C1 **Fort Lallemand** Algeria
Fort Lamy = Ndjamena
60C2 **Fort Laramie** USA
57E4 **Fort Lauderdale** USA
54F3 **Fort Liard** Canada
54G4 **Fort Mackay** Canada
54G5 **Fort Macleod** Canada
54G4 **Fort McMurray** Canada
54E3 **Fort McPherson** Canada
64A2 **Fort Madison** USA
56C2 **Fort Morgan** USA
57E4 **Fort Myers** USA
54F4 **Fort Nelson** Canada
54F3 **Fort Norman** Canada
67A2 **Fort Payne** USA
60B1 **Fort Peck** USA
56C2 **Fort Peck Res** USA
57E4 **Fort Pierce** USA
60C2 **Fort Pierre** USA
68C1 **Fort Plain** USA
54G3 **Fort Providence** Canada
54G3 **Fort Resolution** Canada
50B4 **Fort Rousset** Congo
54F4 **Fort St James** Canada
54F4 **Fort St John** Canada
63D1 **Fort Scott** USA
54E3 **Fort Selkirk** Canada
55K4 **Fort Severn** Canada
21J7 **Fort Shevchenko** Kazakhstan
54F3 **Fort Simpson** Canada
54G3 **Fort Smith** Canada
57D3 **Fort Smith** USA
54F3 **Fort Smith** *Region* Canada
56C3 **Fort Stockton** USA
62B2 **Fort Sumner** USA
62C1 **Fort Supply** USA
58B2 **Fortuna** California, USA
60C1 **Fortuna** N Dakota, USA
54G4 **Fort Vermilion** Canada
67A2 **Fort Walton Beach** USA
57E2 **Fort Wayne** USA
8C3 **Fort William** Scotland
62A1 **Fort Wingate** USA
56D3 **Fort Worth** USA
54D3 **Fort Yukon** USA
31C5 **Foshan** China
55K2 **Fosheim Pen** Canada
61D1 **Fosston** USA
50B4 **Fougamou** Gabon
14B2 **Fougères** France
8D1 **Foula** *I* Scotland
7E4 **Foulness I** England
35B2 **Foulwind,C** New Zealand
50B3 **Foumban** Cameroon
48B2 **Foum el Alba** *Region* Mali
14C1 **Fourmies** France
17F3 **Foúrnoi** *I* Greece
48A3 **Fouta Djallon** *Mts* Guinea
33F5 **Foveaux Str** New Zealand
7B4 **Fowey** England
62B1 **Fowler** USA
64B2 **Fox** *R* USA
55K3 **Foxe Basin** *G* Canada
55K3 **Foxe Chan** Canada
55L3 **Foxe Pen** Canada
60B2 **Foxpark** USA
35C2 **Foxton** New Zealand
10B2 **Foyle, Lough** *Estuary* Irish Republic/Northern Ireland
51B5 **Foz do Cuene** Angola
74F3 **Foz do Iguaçu** Brazil
68B2 **Frackville** USA
15C1 **Fraga** Spain
68E1 **Framingham** USA
73J8 **Franca** Brazil
14C2 **France** *Republic* Europe
14D2 **Franche Comté** *Region* France
47D1 **Francistown** Botswana
58E2 **Francs Peak** *Mt* USA
13E2 **Frankenberg** Germany
64B2 **Frankfort** Indiana, USA
57E3 **Frankfort** Kentucky, USA
68C1 **Frankfort** New York, USA
47D2 **Frankfort** South Africa
18B2 **Frankfurt am Main** Germany
18C2 **Frankfurt an-der-Oder** Germany
18C3 **Fränkischer Alb** *Upland* Germany
58D2 **Franklin** Idaho, USA
64B3 **Franklin** Indiana, USA
63D3 **Franklin** Louisiana, USA
68E1 **Franklin** Massachusetts, USA
67B1 **Franklin** N Carolina, USA
68E1 **Franklin** New Hampshire, USA
68C2 **Franklin** New Jersey, USA
65D2 **Franklin** Pennsylvania, USA
67A1 **Franklin** Tennessee, USA
65D3 **Franklin** Virginia, USA
54F2 **Franklin B** Canada
58C1 **Franklin D Roosevelt** *L* USA
54F3 **Franklin Mts** Canada
54J2 **Franklin Str** Canada
68A1 **Franklinville** USA
35B2 **Franz Josef Glacier** New Zealand
Franz-Josef-Land = Zemlya Frantsa Josifa
54F5 **Fraser** *R* Canada
47C3 **Fraserburg** South Africa
8D3 **Fraserburgh** Scotland
34D1 **Fraser I** Australia
68C3 **Frederica** USA
18B1 **Fredericia** Denmark
65D3 **Frederick** Maryland, USA
62C2 **Frederick** Oklahoma, USA
62C2 **Fredericksburg** Texas, USA
65D3 **Fredericksburg** Virginia, USA
64A3 **Fredericktown** USA
55M5 **Fredericton** Canada
55N3 **Frederikshåp** Greenland
12G7 **Frederikshavn** Denmark
65D2 **Fredonia** USA
12G7 **Fredrikstad** Norway
68C2 **Freehold** USA
66C1 **Freel Peak** *Mt* USA
61D2 **Freeman** USA
64B2 **Freeport** Illinois, USA
63C3 **Freeport** Texas, USA
69B1 **Freeport** The Bahamas
62C3 **Freer** USA
48A4 **Freetown** Sierra Leone
18B3 **Freiburg** Germany
13D3 **Freiburg im Breisgau** Germany
18C3 **Freistadt** Austria
32A4 **Fremantle** Australia
66B2 **Fremont** California, USA
61D2 **Fremont** Nebraska, USA
64C2 **Fremont** Ohio, USA
73H3 **French Guiana** *Dependency* S America
60B1 **Frenchman** *R* USA
34C4 **Frenchmans Cap** *Mt* Australia
37M5 **French Polynesia** *Is* Pacific Ocean
15C2 **Frenda** Algeria
70B2 **Fresnillo** Mexico
56B3 **Fresno** USA
66C2 **Fresno** *R* USA
58D1 **Fresno Res** USA
13E3 **Freudenstadt** Germany
13B2 **Frévent** France
34C4 **Freycinet Pen** Australia
48A3 **Fria** Guinea
66C2 **Friant** USA
66C2 **Friant Dam** USA
16B1 **Fribourg** Switzerland
13E2 **Friedberg** Germany
18B3 **Friedrichshafen** Germany
13C1 **Friesland** *Province* Netherlands
62C3 **Frio** *R* USA
75D3 **Frio, Cabo** *C* Brazil
62B2 **Friona** USA
55M3 **Frobisher B** Canada
55M3 **Frobisher Bay** Canada
54H4 **Frobisher L** Canada
21G6 **Frolovo** Russian Federation
7C4 **Frome** England
7C4 **Frome** *R* England
32C4 **Frome,L** Australia
63D1 **Frontenac** USA
70C3 **Frontera** Mexico
65D3 **Front Royal** USA
16C2 **Frosinone** Italy
60B3 **Fruita** USA
31C5 **Fuchuan** China
31E4 **Fuding** China
70B2 **Fuerte** *R* Mexico
75A3 **Fuerte Olimpo** Brazil
74E2 **Fuerte Olimpo** Paraguay
48A2 **Fuerteventura** *I* Canary Islands
31C2 **Fugu** China
26B2 **Fuhai** China
41G4 **Fujairah** UAE
29C3 **Fuji** Japan
31D4 **Fujian** *Province* China
26G2 **Fujin** China
29C3 **Fujinomiya** Japan
29D3 **Fuji-san** *Mt* Japan
29C3 **Fujisawa** Japan
29C3 **Fuji-Yoshida** Japan
29D2 **Fukagawa** Japan
24K5 **Fukang** China
29D3 **Fukuchiyama** Japan
28A4 **Fukue** Japan
28A4 **Fukue** *I* Japan
29D3 **Fukui** Japan
28C4 **Fukuoka** Japan
29E3 **Fukushima** Japan
29C4 **Fukuyama** Japan
61D2 **Fulda** USA
18B2 **Fulda** Germany
18B2 **Fulda** *R* Germany
31B4 **Fuling** China
69L1 **Fullarton** Trinidad
66D4 **Fullerton** USA
6F1 **Fulmar** *Oilfield* N Sea
64A2 **Fulton** Illinois, USA
64B3 **Fulton** Kentucky, USA
65D2 **Fulton** New York, USA
13C2 **Fumay** France
29D3 **Funabashi** Japan
33G1 **Funafuti** *I* Tuvalu
48A1 **Funchal** Madeira
75D2 **Fundão** Brazil
55M5 **Fundy,B of** Canada
51D6 **Funhalouro** Mozambique
31B5 **Funing** China
31D3 **Funing** China
48C3 **Funtua** Nigeria
31D4 **Fuqing** China
51D5 **Furancungo** Mozambique
29D2 **Furano** Japan
41G4 **Fūrg** Iran
75B2 **Furnas, Serra das** *Mts* Brazil
32D5 **Furneaux Group** *Is* Australia
13D1 **Fürstenau** Germany
18C2 **Fürstenwalde** Germany
18C3 **Fürth** Germany
29D2 **Furubira** Japan
29E3 **Furukawa** Japan
55K3 **Fury and Hecla Str** Canada
28A2 **Fushun** China
31A4 **Fushun** Sichuan, China
28B2 **Fusong** China
18C3 **Füssen** Germany
31E2 **Fu Xian** China
31E1 **Fuxin** China
31D3 **Fuyang** China
31E1 **Fuyuan** Liaoning, China
31A4 **Fuyuan** Yunnan, China
26B2 **Fuyun** China
31D4 **Fuzhou** China
28A3 **Fuzhoucheng** China
18C1 **Fyn** *I* Denmark
8C3 **Fyne, Loch** *Inlet* Scotland

G

50E3 **Gaalkacyo** Somalia
59C3 **Gabbs** USA
66C1 **Gabbs Valley Range** *Mts* USA
51B5 **Gabela** Angola
48D1 **Gabès, G de** Tunisia
66B2 **Gabilan Range** *Mts* USA
50B4 **Gabon** *Republic* Africa
47D1 **Gaborone** Botswana
15A1 **Gabriel y Galán, Embalse** *Res* Spain
17F2 **Gabrovo** Bulgaria
41F3 **Gach Sārān** Iran
44B2 **Gadag** India
67A2 **Gadsden** Alabama, USA
59D4 **Gadsden** Arizona, USA
16C2 **Gaeta** Italy
27H6 **Gaferut** *I* Pacific Ocean
67B1 **Gaffney** USA
45A3 **Gafra, Wadi el** Egypt
48C1 **Gafsa** Tunisia
20E4 **Gagarin** Russian Federation
55M4 **Gagnon** Canada
21G7 **Gagra** Georgia
43F3 **Gaibanda** Bangladesh
74C6 **Gaimán** Argentina
67B3 **Gainesville** Florida, USA
67B2 **Gainesville** Georgia, USA
63C2 **Gainesville** Texas, USA
7D3 **Gainsborough** England
32C4 **Gairdner, L** Australia
8C3 **Gairloch** Scotland
68B3 **Gaithersburg** USA
28A2 **Gai Xian** China
44B2 **Gajendragarh** India
31D4 **Ga Jiang** *R* China
47C2 **Gakarosa** *Mt* South Africa
50D4 **Galana** *R* Kenya
72N **Galapagos Is** Pacific Ocean
Gálápagos, Islas = Galapagos Islands
8D4 **Galashiels** Scotland
17F1 **Galaţi** Romania
64C3 **Galax** USA
62A2 **Galeana** Mexico
54C3 **Galena** Alaska, USA
64A2 **Galena** Illinois, USA
63D1 **Galena** Kansas, USA
69L1 **Galeota Pt** Trinidad
69L1 **Galera Pt** Trinidad
64A2 **Galesburg** USA
68B2 **Galeton** USA
20G4 **Galich** Russian Federation
15A1 **Galicia** *Region* Spain
Galilee,S of = Tiberias,L
69J1 **Galina Pt** Jamaica
50D2 **Gallabat** Sudan
67A1 **Gallatin** USA
58D1 **Gallatin** *R* USA
44C4 **Galle** Sri Lanka
62A3 **Gallego** Mexico
15B1 **Gállego** *R* Spain
72D1 **Gallinas, Puerta** Colombia
Gallipoli = Gelibolu
17D2 **Gallipoli** Italy
20C2 **Gällivare** Sweden
8C4 **Galloway** *District* Scotland
8C4 **Galloway,Mull of** *C* Scotland
62A1 **Gallup** USA
66B1 **Galt** USA
9B3 **Galty Mts** Irish Republic
70C2 **Galveston** USA
57D4 **Galveston B** USA
10B3 **Galway** Irish Republic
10B3 **Galway B** Irish Republic
43F3 **Gamba** China
48B3 **Gambaga** Ghana
54A3 **Gambell** USA
48A3 **Gambia** *R* Senegal/The Gambia
48A3 **Gambia,The** *Republic* Africa
37N6 **Gambier, Îles** Pacific Ocean
50B4 **Gamboma** Congo
51B5 **Gambos** Angola
44C4 **Gampola** Sri Lanka
59E3 **Ganado** USA
50E3 **Ganale Dorya** *R* Ethiopia
65D2 **Gananoque** Canada
Gand = Gent
51B5 **Ganda** Angola
51C4 **Gandajika** Zaïre
43N2 **Gandak** *R* India/Nepal
43M2 **Gandak Dam** Nepal
42B3 **Gandava** Pakistan
55N5 **Gander** Canada
42B4 **Gāndhīdhām** India
42C4 **Gāndhīnagar** India
42D4 **Gāndhi Sāgar** *L* India
15B2 **Gandia** Spain
75E1 **Gandu** Brazil
Ganga *R* **=Ganges**
42C3 **Ganganagar** India
43G4 **Gangaw** Burma
31A2 **Gangca** China
39G2 **Gangdise Shan** *Mts* China
22F4 **Ganges** *R* India
43F4 **Ganges, Mouths of the** Bangladesh/India
28B2 **Gangou** China
43F3 **Gangtok** India
31B3 **Gangu** China
58E2 **Gannett Peak** *Mt* USA
31B2 **Ganquan** China
12K8 **Gantsevichi** Belorussia
31D4 **Ganzhou** China
48C3 **Gao** Mali
31A2 **Gaolan** China
31C2 **Gaoping** China
48B3 **Gaoua** Burkina
48A3 **Gaoual** Guinea
31D3 **Gaoyou Hu** *L* China
31C5 **Gaozhou** China
14D3 **Gap** France
42D2 **Gar** China
9C3 **Gara,L** Irish Republic
34C1 **Garah** Australia
73L5 **Garanhuns** Brazil
59B2 **Garberville** USA
75C3 **Garça** Brazil
15A2 **Garcia de Sola, Embalse de** *Res* Spain
75B3 **Garcias** Brazil
16C1 **Garda, L di** Italy
62B1 **Garden City** USA
64B1 **Garden Pen** USA
42B2 **Gardez** Afghanistan
58D1 **Gardiner** USA
68D2 **Gardiners I** USA
68E1 **Gardner** USA
33H1 **Gardner** *I* Phoenix Islands
66C1 **Gardnerville** USA
16D2 **Gargano, Monte** *Mt* Italy
16D2 **Gargano, Prom. del** Italy
42D4 **Garhākota** India
43K1 **Garhmuktesar** India
20L4 **Gari** Russian Federation
47B3 **Garies** South Africa
50D4 **Garissa** Kenya
63C2 **Garland** USA
18C3 **Garmisch-Partenkirchen** Germany
41F2 **Garmsar** Iran
63C1 **Garnett** USA
56B2 **Garnett Peak** *Mt* USA
14C3 **Garonne** *R* France
49D4 **Garoua** Cameroon
49D4 **Garoua Boulai** Cameroon
60C1 **Garrison** USA
9D2 **Garron** *Pt* Northern Ireland
8C3 **Garry** *R* Scotland
54H3 **Garry L** Canada
43E4 **Garwa** India
64B2 **Gary** USA
39G2 **Garyarsa** China
63C2 **Garza-Little Elm** *Res* USA
41F2 **Gasan Kuli** Turkmenistan
14B3 **Gascogne** *Region* France
63D1 **Gasconade** *R* USA
32A3 **Gascoyne** *R* Australia
50B3 **Gashaka** Nigeria
48D3 **Gashua** Nigeria
57G2 **Gaspé** Canada
57G2 **Gaspé,C de** Canada
57G2 **Gaspé, Peninsule de** Canada
67B1 **Gastonia** USA
67C1 **Gaston,L** USA
45B1 **Gata, C** Cyprus
15B2 **Gata, Cabo de** *C* Spain
20D4 **Gatchina** Russian Federation
8C4 **Gatehouse of Fleet** Scotland
6D2 **Gateshead** England
63C2 **Gatesville** USA
13B3 **Gâtinais** *Region* France
65D1 **Gatineau** Canada
65D1 **Gatineau** *R* Canada
67B1 **Gatlinburg** USA
34D1 **Gatton** Australia
33F2 **Gaua** *I* Vanuatu
43G3 **Gauhāti** India
19E1 **Gauja** *R* Latvia
43E3 **Gauri Phanta** India
17E4 **Gávdhos** *I* Greece
75D1 **Gavião** *R* Brazil
66B3 **Gaviota** USA
12H6 **Gävle** Sweden
32C4 **Gawler Ranges** *Mts* Australia
31A1 **Gaxun Nur** *L* China
43E4 **Gaya** India
48C3 **Gaya** Niger
48C3 **Gaya** Nigeria
28B2 **Gaya He** *R* China
64C1 **Gaylord** USA
34D1 **Gayndah** Australia
20J3 **Gayny** Russian Federation
19F3 **Gaysin** Ukraine
40B3 **Gaza** Israel
40C2 **Gaziantep** Turkey
48B4 **Gbaringa** Liberia
48D1 **Gbbès** Tunisia
19D2 **Gdańsk** Poland
19D2 **Gdańsk,G of** Poland
12K7 **Gdov** Russian Federation
19D2 **Gdynia** Poland
45A4 **Gebel el Galâla el Bahariya** *Desert* Egypt
50D2 **Gedaref** Sudan

Grand Falls **Hāflong**

55M5 **Grand Falls** New Brunswick, Canada
55N5 **Grand Falls** Newfoundland, Canada
58C1 **Grand Forks** Canada
61D1 **Grand Forks** USA
68C1 **Grand Gorge** USA
64B2 **Grand Haven** USA
60D2 **Grand Island** USA
63E2 **Grand Isle** USA
60B3 **Grand Junction** USA
63D3 **Grand L** USA
64A1 **Grand Marais** USA
65E1 **Grand Mère** Canada
15A2 **Grândola** Portugal
54G4 **Grand Prairie** Canada
54J4 **Grand Rapids** Canada
64B2 **Grand Rapids** Michigan, USA
64A1 **Grand Rapids** Minnesota, USA
16B1 **Grand St Bernard, Col du** *P* Italy/Switzerland
56B2 **Grand Teton** *Mt* USA
58D2 **Grand Teton Nat Pk** USA
60B3 **Grand Valley** USA
58C1 **Grangeville** USA
58E1 **Granite Peak** *Mt* Montana, USA
59D2 **Granite Peak** *Mt* Utah, USA
15C1 **Granollérs** Spain
16B1 **Gran Paradiso** *Mt* Italy
7D3 **Grantham** England
66C1 **Grant,Mt** USA
8D3 **Grantown-on-Spey** Scotland
62A1 **Grants** USA
58B2 **Grants Pass** USA
14B2 **Granville** France
68D1 **Granville** USA
54H4 **Granville L** Canada
75D2 **Grão Mogol** Brazil
66C3 **Grapevine** USA
66D2 **Grapevine Mts** USA
47E1 **Graskop** South Africa
54G3 **Gras, Lac de** Canada
14D3 **Grasse** France
6D2 **Grassington** England
58E1 **Grassrange** USA
59B3 **Grass Valley** USA
74F4 **Gravatai** Brazil
54H5 **Gravelbourg** Canada
13B2 **Gravelines** France
51D6 **Gravelotte** South Africa
65D2 **Gravenhurst** Canada
58D1 **Grave Peak** *Mt* USA
34D1 **Gravesend** Australia
7E4 **Gravesend** England
58B1 **Grays Harbour** *B* USA
58D2 **Grays L** USA
64C3 **Grayson** USA
64B3 **Grayville** USA
18D3 **Graz** Austria
69H1 **Great** *R* Jamaica
57F4 **Great Abaco** *I* The Bahamas
32B4 **Great Australian Bight** *G* Australia
68E1 **Great B** New Hampshire, USA
68C3 **Great B** New Jersey, USA
70E2 **Great Bahama Bank** The Bahamas
35C1 **Great Barrier I** New Zealand
32D2 **Great Barrier Reef** *Is* Australia
68D1 **Great Barrington** USA
59C2 **Great Basin** USA
54F3 **Great Bear L** Canada
62C1 **Great Bend** USA
45B3 **Great Bitter L** Egypt
68A3 **Great Cacapon** USA
44E3 **Great Coco I** Burma
32D3 **Great Dividing Range** *Mts* Australia
6D2 **Great Driffield** England
68C3 **Great Egg Harbor** *B* USA
76F10 **Greater Antarctica** *Region* Antarctica
69B2 **Greater Antilles** *Is* Caribbean Sea
7D4 **Greater London** *Metropolitan County* England
7C3 **Greater Manchester** *Metropolitan County* England
70E2 **Great Exuma** *I* The Bahamas
58D1 **Great Falls** USA
47D3 **Great Fish** *R* South Africa
8C3 **Great Glen** *V* Scotland
43F3 **Great Himalayan Range** *Mts* Asia
57F4 **Great Inagua** *I* The Bahamas
47C3 **Great Karoo** *Mts* South Africa
47D3 **Great Kei** *R* South Africa
34C4 **Great L** Australia
7C3 **Great Malvern** England
51B6 **Great Namaland** *Region* Namibia
44E4 **Great Nicobar** *I* Indian Ocean
7C3 **Great Ormes Head** *C* Wales
68E2 **Great Pt** USA
57F4 **Great Ragged** *I* The Bahamas
51D4 **Great Ruaha** *R* Tanzania
65E2 **Great Sacandaga L** USA
58D2 **Great Salt L** USA
58D2 **Great Salt Lake Desert** USA
49E2 **Great Sand Sea** Egypt/Libya
32B3 **Great Sandy Desert** Australia
56A2 **Great Sandy Desert** USA
Great Sandy I = Fraser I
54G3 **Great Slave L** Canada
67B1 **Great Smoky Mts** USA
67B1 **Great Smoky Mts Nat Pk** USA
68D2 **Great South B** USA
47C3 **Great Tafelberg** *Mt* South Africa
32B3 **Great Victoria Desert** Australia
31B2 **Great Wall** China
7E3 **Great Yarmouth** England
48C2 **Gréboun, Mont** Niger
45C1 **Greco, C** Cyprus
15A1 **Gredos, Sierra de** *Mts* Spain
65D2 **Greece** USA
17E3 **Greece** *Republic* Europe
60C2 **Greeley** USA
55K1 **Greely Fjord** Canada
24H1 **Greem Bell, Ostrov** *I* Russian Federation
64B3 **Green** *R* Kentucky, USA
59D3 **Green** *R* Utah, USA
64B1 **Green B** USA
64B2 **Green Bay** USA
64B3 **Greencastle** Indiana, USA
68B3 **Greencastle** Pennsylvania, USA
68C1 **Greene** USA
67B1 **Greeneville** USA
66B2 **Greenfield** California, USA
66C3 **Greenfield** California, USA
68D1 **Greenfield** Massachusetts, USA
64B2 **Greenfield** Wisconsin, USA
55O2 **Greenland** *Dependency* N Atlantic Ocean
52F1 **Greenland** *I* Atlantic Ocean
52H1 **Greenland Basin** Greenland Sea
76B1 **Greenland Sea** Greenland
8D4 **Greenlaw** Scotland
8C4 **Greenock** Scotland
68D2 **Greenport** USA
59D3 **Green River** Utah, USA
58E2 **Green River** Wyoming, USA
68C3 **Greensboro** Maryland, USA
67C1 **Greensboro** N Carolina, USA
62C1 **Greensburg** Kansas, USA
64B3 **Greensburg** Kentucky, USA
65D2 **Greensburg** Pennsylvania, USA
8C3 **Greenstone Pt** Scotland
64B3 **Greenup** USA
59D4 **Green Valley** USA
67A2 **Greenville** Alabama, USA
48B4 **Greenville** Liberia
63D2 **Greenville** Mississippi, USA
67C1 **Greenville** N Carolina, USA
68E1 **Greenville** New Hampshire, USA
64C2 **Greenville** Ohio, USA
67B2 **Greenville** S Carolina, USA
63C2 **Greenville** Texas, USA
67B2 **Greenville** Florida, USA
27H8 **Greenville,C** Australia
7E4 **Greenwich** England
68D2 **Greenwich** USA
68C3 **Greenwood** Delaware, USA
63D2 **Greenwood** Mississippi, USA
67B2 **Greenwood** S Carolina, USA
63D1 **Greers Ferry L** USA
60D2 **Gregory** USA
34A1 **Gregory,L** Australia
32D2 **Gregory Range** *Mts* Australia
18C2 **Greifswald** Germany
20F2 **Gremikha** Russian Federation
18C1 **Grenå** Denmark
63E2 **Grenada** USA
69E4 **Grenada** *I* Caribbean Sea
69E4 **Grenadines,The** *Is* Caribbean Sea
34C2 **Grenfell** Australia
14D2 **Grenoble** France
69M2 **Grenville** Grenada
32D2 **Grenville,C** Australia
58B1 **Gresham** USA
63D3 **Gretna** USA
35B2 **Grey** *R* New Zealand
58E2 **Greybull** USA
55N4 **Grey Is** Canada
68D1 **Greylock,Mt** USA
35B2 **Greymouth** New Zealand
32D3 **Grey Range** *Mts* Australia
9C3 **Greystones** Irish Republic
47E2 **Greytown** South Africa
67B2 **Griffin** USA
34C2 **Griffith** Australia
32D5 **Grim,C** Australia
65D2 **Grimsby** Canada
7D3 **Grimsby** England
12B1 **Grimsey** *I* Iceland
12F7 **Grimstad** Norway
61E2 **Grinnell** USA
55J2 **Grinnell Pen** Canada
55K2 **Grise Fjord** Canada
20J3 **Griva** Russian Federation
12J7 **Grobina** Latvia
47D2 **Groblersdal** South Africa
19E2 **Grodno** Belorussia
43E3 **Gromati** *R* India
13D1 **Gronan** Germany
18B2 **Groningen** Netherlands
13D1 **Groningen** *Province* Netherlands
62B1 **Groom** USA
47C3 **Groot** *R* South Africa
32C2 **Groote Eylandt** *I* Australia
51B5 **Grootfontein** Namibia
47B2 **Groot-Karasberge** *Mts* Namibia
47C1 **Groot Laagte** *R* Botswana/Namibia
47C2 **Groot Vloer** *Salt L* South Africa
69P2 **Gros Islet** St Lucia
13E2 **Grosser Feldberg** *Mt* Germany
16C2 **Grosseto** Italy
13E3 **Gross-Gerau** Germany
18C3 **Grossglockner** *Mt* Austria
58D2 **Gros Ventre Range** *Mts* USA
61D1 **Groton** USA
64C1 **Groundhog** *R* Canada
63E2 **Grove Hill** USA
66B2 **Groveland** USA
66B3 **Grover City** USA
65E2 **Groveton** USA
21H7 **Groznyy** Russian Federation
19D2 **Grudziadz** Poland
47B2 **Grünau** Namibia
8E2 **Grutness** Scotland
21G5 **Gryazi** Russian Federation
20G4 **Gryazovets** Russian Federation
74J8 **Grytviken** South Georgia
69B2 **Guacanayabo, G de** Cuba
75D3 **Guaçuí** Brazil
70B2 **Guadalajara** Mexico
15B1 **Guadalajara** Spain
33E1 **Guadalcanal** *I* Solomon Islands
15B2 **Guadalimar** *R* Spain
15B1 **Guadalope** *R* Spain
15B2 **Guadalquivir** *R* Spain
70B2 **Guadalupe** Mexico
66B3 **Guadalupe** USA
53G6 **Guadalupe** *I* Mexico
62C3 **Guadalupe** *R* USA
62B2 **Guadalupe Mtns Nat Pk** USA
62B2 **Guadalupe Peak** *Mt* USA
15A2 **Guadalupe, Sierra de** *Mts* Spain
15B1 **Guadarrama, Sierra de** *Mts* Spain
69E3 **Guadeloupe** *I* Caribbean Sea
15B2 **Guadian** *R* Spain
15A2 **Guadiana** *R* Portugal
15B2 **Guadiana** *R* Spain
15B2 **Guadix** Spain
75B3 **Guaira** Brazil
72E6 **Guajará Mirim** Brazil
72D1 **Guajira,Pen de** Colombia
69C4 **Guajiri, Península de la** Colombia
72C4 **Gualaceo** Ecuador
27H5 **Guam** *I* Pacific Ocean
74D5 **Guaminí** Argentina
30C5 **Gua Musang** Malaysia
69A2 **Guanabacoa** Cuba
75D1 **Guanambi** Brazil
72E2 **Guanare** Venezuela
28B2 **Guandi** China
70D2 **Guane** Cuba
31C5 **Guangdong** *Province* China
31A3 **Guanghan** China
31C3 **Guanghua** China
31A4 **Guangmao Shan** *Mt* China
31A5 **Guangnan** China
31B5 **Guangxi** *Province* China
31B3 **Guangyuan** China
31D4 **Guangze** China
31C5 **Guangzhou** China
75D2 **Guanhães** Brazil
72E3 **Guania** *R* Colombia/Venezuela
69E5 **Guanipa** *R* Venezuela
69B2 **Guantánamo** Cuba
31D1 **Guanting Shuiku** *Res* China
31A3 **Guan Xian** China
72C2 **Guapá** Colombia
72F6 **Guaporé** *R* Bolivia/Brazil
72E7 **Guaquí** Bolivia
75D1 **Guará** *R* Brazil
72C4 **Guaranda** Ecuador
75B4 **Guarapuava** Brazil
75C4 **Guaraqueçaba** Brazil
15B1 **Guara, Sierra de** *Mts* Spain
75C3 **Guaratinguetá** Brazil
75C4 **Guaratuba, B** Brazil
15A1 **Guarda** Portugal
75C2 **Guarda Mor** Brazil
56C4 **Guasave** Mexico
70C3 **Guatemala** Guatemala
70C3 **Guatemala** *Republic* Central America
72D3 **Guaviare** *R* Colombia
75C3 **Guaxupé** Brazil
69L1 **Guayaguayare** Trinidad
72B4 **Guayaquil** Ecuador
72B4 **Guayaquil, Golfo de** Ecuador
70A2 **Guaymas** Mexico
51C5 **Guba** Zaïre
25P2 **Guba Buorkhaya** *B* Russian Federation
50E3 **Guban** *Region* Somalia
18C2 **Gubin** Poland
15B1 **Gudar, Sierra de** *Mts* Spain
44B3 **Güdür** India
13D4 **Guebwiller** France
16B3 **Guelma** Algeria
64C2 **Guelph** Canada
48A2 **Guelta Zemmur** Morocco
50C2 **Guéréda** Chad
14C2 **Guéret** France
60C2 **Guernsey** USA
14B2 **Guernsey** *I* Channel Islands
50D3 **Gughe** *Mt* Ethiopia
25O4 **Gugigu** China
27H5 **Guguan** *I* Pacific Ocean
49D4 **Guider** Cameroon
31C4 **Guidong** China
48B4 **Guiglo** Ivory Coast
47E1 **Guijá** Mozambique
31C5 **Gui Jiang** *R* China
7D4 **Guildford** England
31C4 **Guilin** China
31A2 **Guinan** China
66A1 **Guinda** USA
48A3 **Guinea** *Republic* Africa
52H4 **Guinea Basin** Atlantic Ocean
48A3 **Guinea-Bissau** *Republic* Africa
48C4 **Guinea,G of** W Africa
69A2 **Güines** Cuba
48B3 **Guir** *Well* Mali
75B2 **Guiratinga** Brazil
72F1 **Güiria** Venezuela
6D2 **Guisborough** England
13B3 **Guise** France
27F5 **Guiuan** Philippines
31B5 **Gui Xian** China
31B4 **Guiyang** China
31B4 **Guizhou** *Province* China
42C4 **Gujarāt** *State* India
42C2 **Gujranwala** Pakistan
42C2 **Gujrat** Pakistan
34C2 **Gulargambone** Australia
44B2 **Gulbarga** India
19F1 **Gulbene** Latvia
44B2 **Guledagudda** India
63E2 **Gulfport** USA
38D3 **Gulf,The** SW Asia
34C2 **Gulgong** Australia
31B4 **Gulin** China
17F3 **Güllük Körfezi** *B* Turkey
50D3 **Gulu** Uganda
34C1 **Guluguba** Australia
48C3 **Gumel** Nigeria
43E4 **Gumla** India
13D2 **Gummersbach** Germany
40C1 **Gümüşhane** Turkey
42D4 **Guna** India
50D2 **Guna** *Mt* Ethiopia
34C3 **Gundagai** Australia
50B4 **Gungu** Zaïre
55Q3 **Gunnbjørn Fjeld** *Mt* Greenland
34D2 **Gunnedah** Australia
60B3 **Gunnison** USA
60B3 **Gunnison** *R* USA
44B2 **Guntakal** India
67A2 **Guntersville** USA
67A2 **Guntersville L** USA
44C2 **Guntūr** India
30C5 **Gunung Batu Puteh** *Mt* Malaysia
30C5 **Gunung Tahan** *Mt* Malaysia
51B5 **Gunza** Angola
31D3 **Guoyang** China
42D2 **Gurdāspur** India
42D3 **Gurgaon** India
72F2 **Guri, Embalse de** *Res* Venezuela
43E3 **Gurkha** Nepal
40C2 **Gürün** Turkey
73J4 **Gurupi** *R* Brazil
51D5 **Guruve** Zimbabwe
31A1 **Gurvan Sayhan Uul** *Upland* Mongolia
21J6 **Gur'yev** Kazakhstan
48C3 **Gusau** Nigeria
19E2 **Gusev** Russian Federation
28A3 **Gushan** China
20G4 **Gus' Khrustalnyy** Russian Federation
55P3 **Gustav Holm, Kap** *C* Greenland
54E4 **Gustavus** USA
66B2 **Gustine** USA
57E3 **Guston** USA
18B2 **Gütersloh** Germany
64B3 **Guthrie** Kentucky, USA
63C1 **Guthrie** Oklahoma, USA
62B2 **Guthrie** Texas, USA
61E2 **Guttenberg** USA
73G3 **Guyana** *Republic* S America
52F4 **Guyana Basin** Atlantic Ocean
31C1 **Guyang** China
14B3 **Guyenne** *Region* France
62B1 **Guymon** USA
34D2 **Guyra** Australia
31B2 **Guyuan** China
62A2 **Guzmán, Laguna** *L* Mexico
43G5 **Gwa** Burma
34C2 **Gwabegar** Australia
38E3 **Gwadar** Pakistan
42D3 **Gwalior** India
47D1 **Gwanda** Zimbabwe
50C3 **Gwane** Zaïre
7C4 **Gwent** *County* Wales
51C5 **Gweru** Zimbabwe
34C1 **Gwydir** *R* Australia
7C3 **Gwynedd** Wales
21H7 **Gyandzha** Azerbaijan
43F3 **Gyangzê** China
26C3 **Gyaring Hu** *L* China
24J2 **Gydanskiy Poluostrov** *Pen* Russian Federation
43F3 **Gyirong** China
55O3 **Gyldenløves Fjord** Greenland
34D1 **Gympie** Australia
19D3 **Gyöngyös** Hungary
19D3 **Györ** Hungary

H

33H2 **Ha'apai Group** *Is* Tonga
12K6 **Haapajärvi** Finland
20C4 **Haapsalu** Estonia
18A2 **Haarlem** Netherlands
13D2 **Haarstrang** *Region* Germany
Habana, La = Havana
43G4 **Habiganj** Bangladesh
29D4 **Hachijō-jima** *I* Japan
29C3 **Hachiman** Japan
29E2 **Hachinohe** Japan
29C3 **Hachioji** Japan
68C2 **Hackettstown** USA
34A2 **Hack** *Mt* Australia
8D4 **Haddington** Scotland
34B1 **Haddon Corner** Australia
34B1 **Haddon Downs** Australia
48D3 **Hadejia** Nigeria
48C3 **Hadejia** *R* Nigeria
45C2 **Hadera** Israel
18B1 **Haderslev** Denmark
38D4 **Hadiboh** Socotra
54H2 **Hadley B** Canada
28A3 **Hadong** S Korea
31B5 **Hadong** Vietnam
38C4 **Ḥadramawt** *Region* Yemen
18C1 **Hadsund** Denmark
28B3 **Haeju** N Korea
28A3 **Haeju-man** *B* N Korea
28A4 **Haenam** S Korea
41E4 **Hafar al Bātin** Saudi Arabia
55M2 **Haffners Bjerg** *Mt* Greenland
42C2 **Hafizabad** Pakistan
43G3 **Hāflong** India

Hafnarfjörður Herradura

12A2 Hafnarfjörður Iceland
18B2 Hagen Germany
68B3 Hagerstown USA
28B4 Hagi Japan
31A5 Ha Giang Vietnam
13D3 Hagondange France
13D3 Haguenan France
48A2 Hagunia *Well* Morocco
26H4 Haha-jima *I* Japan
26C3 Hah Xil Hu *L* China
28A2 Haicheng China
30D1 Hai Duong Vietnam
45C2 Haifa Israel
45C2 Haifa,B of Israel
31D2 Hai He *R* China
31C5 Haikang China
30E1 Haikou China
40D4 Hā'il Saudi Arabia
43G4 Hailākāndi India
25N5 Hailar China
28B2 Hailong China
26F2 Hailun China
12J5 Hailuoto *I* Finland
30D2 Hainan *I* China
54E4 Haines USA
54E3 Haines Junction Canada
18D3 Hainfeld Austria
31B5 Haiphong Vietnam
28A2 Haisgai China
69C3 Haiti *Republic* Caribbean Sea
66D2 Haiwee Res USA
50D2 Haiya Sudan
31A2 Haiyan China
31B2 Haiyuan China
19E3 Hajdúböszörmény Hungary
29C3 Hajiki-saki *Pt* Japan
43G4 Haka Burma
66E5 Hakalau Hawaiian Islands
41D2 Hakkâri Turkey
29E2 Hakodate Japan
29C3 Hakui Japan
29C3 Haku-san *Mt* Japan
Ḩalab = Aleppo
41E2 Halabja Iraq
50D1 Halaib Egypt
45B3 Halâl, Gebel *Mt* Egypt
45D1 Halba Lebanon
26C2 Halban Mongolia
18C2 Halberstadt Germany
12G7 Halden Norway
43F4 Haldia India
42D3 Haldwāni India
55M5 Halifax Canada
6D3 Halifax England
65D3 Halifax USA
45D1 Halīmah, Jabal *Mt* Lebanon/Syria
8D2 Halkirk Scotland
28A4 Halla-san *Mt* S Korea
55M1 Hall Basin *Sd* Canada/Greenland
55K3 Hall Beach Canada
13C2 Halle Belgium
18C2 Halle Germany
76F1 Halley *Base* Antarctica
65D1 Halleybury Canada
60C1 Halliday USA
12F6 Hallingdal *R* Norway
61D1 Hallock USA
55M3 Hall Pen Canada
32B2 Hall's Creek Australia
68C2 Hallstead USA
27F6 Halmahera *Is* Indonesia
12G7 Halmstad Sweden
16C3 Halq el Qued Tunisia
18B2 Haltern Germany
20C2 Halti *Mt* Finland/Norway
8D4 Haltwhistle England
41F4 Halul *I* Qatar
45C3 Haluza *Hist Site* Israel
28B4 Hamada Japan
48C2 Hamada de Tinrhert *Desert Region* Algeria
48B2 Hamada du Dra *Upland* Algeria
41E3 Hamadān Iran
48B2 Hamada Tounassine *Region* Algeria
21F8 Ḩamāh Syria
29C4 Hamamatsu Japan
12G6 Hamar Norway
40C5 Hamâta, Gebel *Mt* Egypt
29D1 Hama-Tombetsu Japan
44C4 Hambantota Sri Lanka
63D2 Hamburg Arkansas, USA
61D2 Hamburg Iowa, USA
68A1 Hamburg New York, USA
68C2 Hamburg Pennsylvania, USA
18B2 Hamburg Germany
68D2 Hamden USA
12J6 Hämeenlinna Finland
13E1 Hameln Germany
32A3 Hamersley Range *Mts* Australia
28B2 Hamgyong Sanmaek *Mts* N Korea
28B3 Hamhŭng N Korea
26C2 Hami China
45C1 Ḩamīdīyah Syria
63E2 Hamilton Alabama, USA
34B3 Hamilton Australia
65D2 Hamilton Canada
58D1 Hamilton Montana, USA
68C1 Hamilton New York, USA
35C1 Hamilton New Zealand
64C3 Hamilton Ohio, USA
8C4 Hamilton Scotland
66B2 Hamilton,Mt USA
12K6 Hamina Finland
43E3 Hamīrpur India
28A3 Hamju N Korea
18B2 Hamm Germany
49D2 Hammādāh al Hamrā *Upland* Libya
16C3 Hammamet Tunisia
16C3 Hammamet, Golfe de Tunisia
12H6 Hammerdal Sweden
12J4 Hammerfest Norway
64B2 Hammond Illinois, USA
63D2 Hammond Louisiana, USA
60C1 Hammond Montana, USA
68C3 Hammonton USA
35B3 Hampden New Zealand
7D4 Hampshire *County* England
63D2 Hampton Arkansas, USA
61E2 Hampton Iowa, USA
68E1 Hampton New Hampshire, USA
65D3 Hampton Virginia, USA
38D3 Hāmūn-e-Jāz-Mūriān *L* Iran
42B3 Hamun-i-Lora *Salt L* Pakistan
28A3 Han *R* S Korea
66E5 Hana Hawaiian Islands
66E5 Hanalei Hawaiian Islands
29E3 Hanamaki Japan
13E2 Hanau Germany
31C2 Hancheng China
31C3 Hanchuan China
65D3 Hancock Maryland, USA
64B1 Hancock Michigan, USA
68C2 Hancock New York, USA
29C4 Handa Japan
8C2 Handa, I Scotland
31C2 Handan China
50D4 Handeni Tanzania
66C2 Hanford USA
31B2 Hanggin Qi China
12J7 Hangö Finland
31E3 Hangzhou China
31E3 Hangzhou Wan *B* China
61D1 Hankinson USA
59D3 Hanksville USA
35B2 Hanmer Springs New Zealand
54G4 Hanna Canada
61E3 Hannibal USA
18B2 Hannover Germany
12G7 Hanöbukten *B* Sweden
30D1 Hanoi Vietnam
47C3 Hanover South Africa
68B3 Hanover USA
74B8 Hanover *I* Chile
31C3 Han Shui *R* China
42D3 Hānsi India
26D2 Hantay Mongolia
31B3 Hanzhong China
43F4 Hāora India
12J5 Haparanda Sweden
28A3 Hapch'on S Korea
43G3 Hāpoli India
43J1 Hapur India
40C4 Ḩaql Saudi Arabia
41E5 Ḩaradh Saudi Arabia
45C4 Harad, Jebel el *Mt* Jordan
50E3 Hara Fanna Ethiopia
29D3 Haramachi Japan
51D5 Harare Zimbabwe
50C2 Harazé Chad
26F2 Harbin China
64C2 Harbor Beach USA
42D4 Harda India
12F6 Hardangerfjord *Inlet* Norway
13D1 Härdenberg Netherlands
13C1 Harderwijk Netherlands
60B1 Hardin USA
43L2 Hardoi India
13D3 Hardt *Region* Germany
63D1 Hardy USA
45C3 Hareidin, Wadi Egypt
50E3 Harēr Ethiopia
50E3 Hargeysa Somalia
45C3 Har Hakippa *Mt* Israel
26C3 Harhu *L* China
27D7 Hari *R* Indonesia
29B4 Harima-nada *B* Japan
64C3 Harlan USA
7B3 Harlech Wales
58E1 Harlem USA
7E3 Harleston England
18B2 Harlingen Netherlands
63C3 Harlingen USA
7E4 Harlow England
58E1 Harlowtown USA
45C2 Har Meron *Mt* Israel
58C2 Harney Basin USA
58C2 Harney L USA
12H6 Härnösand Sweden
48B4 Harper Liberia
66D3 Harper L USA
65D3 Harpers Ferry USA
13E1 Harpstedt Germany
45C3 Har Ramon *Mt* Israel
40C4 Harrat al 'Uwayrid *Region* Saudi Arabia
40D5 Ḩarrāt Kishb *Region* Saudi Arabia
55L4 Harricanaw *R* Canada
67B1 Harriman USA
68D1 Harriman Res USA
68C3 Harrington USA
55N4 Harrington Harbour Canada
8B3 Harris *District* Scotland
64B3 Harrisburg Illinois, USA
68B2 Harrisburg Pennsylvania, USA
47D2 Harrismith South Africa
63D1 Harrison USA
65D3 Harrisonburg USA
55N4 Harrison,C Canada
61E3 Harrisonville USA
8B3 Harris,Sound of *Chan* Scotland
64C2 Harrisville USA
6D2 Harrogate England
45C3 Har Saggi *Mt* Israel
45D2 Ḩarsīr, Wadi al Syria
12H5 Harstad Norway
28A2 Hartao China
47C2 Hartbees *R* South Africa
12F6 Hårteigen *Mt* Norway
68D2 Hartford Connecticut, USA
64B2 Hartford Michigan, USA
61D2 Hartford S Dakota, USA
12G6 Hartkjølen *Mt* Norway
65F1 Hartland Canada
7B4 Hartland England
7B4 Hartland Pt England
6D2 Hartlepool England
62B1 Hartley USA
67A2 Hartselle USA
63C2 Hartshorne USA
67B2 Hartwell Res USA
47C2 Hartz *R* South Africa
45C3 Hārūn, Jebel *Mt* Jordan
25L5 Har Us Nuur *L* Mongolia
38E2 Harut *R* Afghanistan
60B3 Harvard,Mt USA
60C1 Harvey USA
7E4 Harwich England
42D3 Haryāna *State* India
45C3 Hāsā Jordan
45B3 Hasana, Wadi Egypt
45C3 Hāsā, Wadi el Jordan
45C2 Hāsbaiya Lebanon
13E1 Hase *R* Germany
13D1 Haselünne Germany
29C4 Hashimoto Japan
41E2 Hashtpar Iran
41E2 Hashtrūd Iran
62C2 Haskell USA
7D4 Haslemere England
44B3 Hassan India
18B2 Hasselt Belgium
48C2 Hassi Inifel Algeria
48B2 Hassi Mdakane *Well* Algeria
48C1 Hassi Messaoud Algeria
12G7 Hässleholm Sweden
34C3 Hastings Australia
7E4 Hastings England
61E2 Hastings Minnesota, USA
56D2 Hastings Nebraska, USA
35C1 Hastings New Zealand
63E1 Hatchie *R* USA
34B2 Hatfield Australia
42D3 Hāthras India
30D2 Ha Tinh Vietnam
34B2 Hattah Australia
57F3 Hatteras,C USA
63E2 Hattiesburg USA
19D3 Hatvan Hungary
30D3 Hau Bon Vietnam
50E3 Haud *Region* Ethiopia
12F7 Haugesund Norway
35C1 Hauhungaroa Range *Mts* New Zealand
35B1 Hauraki G New Zealand
35A3 Hauroko,L New Zealand
48B1 Haut Atlas *Mts* Morocco
50C3 Haute Kotto *Region* Central African Republic
13C3 Haute-Marne *Department* France
13D4 Haute-Saône *Department* France
13C2 Hautes Fagnes *Mts* Belgium/Germany
65F2 Haut, Isle au USA
13C2 Hautmont France
13D4 Haut-Rhin *Department* France
42A2 Hauz Qala Afghanistan
70D2 Havana Cuba
64A2 Havana USA
44B4 Havankulam Sri Lanka
59D4 Havasu L USA
67C2 Havelock USA
35C1 Havelock North New Zealand
7E3 Haverhill England
68E1 Haverhill USA
44B3 Hāveri India
68D2 Haverstraw USA
18D3 Havlíčkův Brod Czechoslovakia
58E1 Havre USA
68B3 Havre de Grace USA
55M4 Havre-St-Pierre Canada
17F2 Havsa Turkey
66E5 Hawaii *Is, State* Pacific Ocean
66E5 Hawaii Volcanoes Nat Pk Hawaiian Islands
35A2 Hawea,L New Zealand
35B1 Hawera New Zealand
66E5 Hawi Hawaiian Islands
8D4 Hawick Scotland
35A2 Hawkdun Range *Mts* New Zealand
35C1 Hawke B New Zealand
34D2 Hawke,C Australia
34A2 Hawker Australia
68C2 Hawley USA
30B1 Hawng Luk Burma
41D3 Hawr al Habbaniyah *L* Iraq
41E3 Hawr al Hammár *L* Iraq
40D3 Ḩawrān, Wadi *R* Iraq
66C1 Hawthorne USA
34B2 Hay Australia
7C3 Hay England
54G3 Hay *R* Canada
13C3 Hayange France
54B3 Haycock USA
59D4 Hayden Arizona, USA
60B2 Hayden Colorado, USA
55J4 Hayes *R* Canada
55M2 Hayes Halvø *Region* Greenland
54D3 Hayes, Mt USA
7B4 Hayle England
7D4 Hayling *I* England
68B3 Haymarket USA
54G3 Hay River Canada
60D3 Hays USA
63C1 Haysville USA
66A2 Hayward California, USA
64A1 Hayward Wisconsin, USA
7D4 Haywards Heath England
42A2 Hazarajat *Region* Afghanistan
64C3 Hazard USA
43F4 Hazārībāg India
13B2 Hazebrouck France
63D2 Hazelhurst USA
54F4 Hazelton Canada
54B3 Hazen B USA
55L1 Hazen L Canada
54G2 Hazen Str Canada
45C3 Hazeva Israel
68C2 Hazleton USA
66A1 Healdsburg USA
34C3 Healesville Australia
36E7 Heard I Indian Ocean
63C2 Hearne USA
57E2 Hearst Canada
60C1 Heart *R* USA
62C3 Hebbronville USA
31D2 Hebei *Province* China
34C1 Hebel Australia
58D2 Heber City USA
58D2 Hebgen L USA
31C2 Hebi China
31C2 Hebian China
55M4 Hebron Canada
45C3 Hebron Israel
60C1 Hebron N Dakota, USA
61D2 Hebron Nebraska, USA
54E4 Hecate Str Canada
31B5 Hechi China
13E3 Hechingen Germany
54G2 Hecla and Griper B Canada
35C2 Hector,Mt New Zealand
12G6 Hede Sweden
12H6 Hedemora Sweden
58C1 He Devil Mt USA
18B2 Heerenveen Netherlands
13C2 Heerlen Netherlands
Hefa = Haifa
31D3 Hefei China
31B4 Hefeng China
26G2 Hegang China
29C3 Hegura-jima *I* Japan
30B1 Heho Burma
45C3 Heidan *R* Jordan
18B2 Heide Germany
47C3 Heidelberg Cape Province, South Africa
47D2 Heidelberg Transvaal, South Africa
18B3 Heidelberg Germany
18C3 Heidenheim Germany
25O4 Heihe China
47D2 Heilbron South Africa
18B3 Heilbronn Germany
18C2 Heiligenstadt Germany
12K6 Heinola Finland
28A2 Heishan China
31B4 Hejiang China
55R3 Hekla *Mt* Iceland
30C1 Hekou Vietnam
31A5 Hekou Yaozou Zizhixian China
31B2 Helan China
31B2 Helan Shan *Mt* China
63D2 Helena Arkansas, USA
58D1 Helena Montana, USA
66D3 Helendale USA
27G6 Helen Reef Pacific Ocean
8C3 Helensburgh Scotland
45A3 Heliopolis Egypt
41F4 Helleh *R* Iran
15B2 Hellín Spain
58C1 Hells Canyon *R* USA
13D2 Hellweg *Region* Germany
66B2 Helm USA
38E2 Helmand *R* Afghanistan/Iran
47B2 Helmeringhausen Namibia
13C2 Helmond Netherlands
8D2 Helmsdale Scotland
51F5 Helodrano Antongila *B* Madagascar
28B2 Helong China
12G7 Helsingborg Sweden
Helsingfors = Helsinki
18C1 Helsingør Denmark
12J6 Helsinki Finland
7B4 Helston England
9C3 Helvick Hd *Pt* Irish Republic
40B4 Helwân Egypt
7D4 Hemel Hempstead England
63C2 Hempstead USA
12H7 Hemse Sweden
31A3 Henan China
31C3 Henan *Province* China
35B1 Hen and Chickens Is New Zealand
29C2 Henashi-zaki *C* Japan
64B3 Henderson Kentucky, USA
67C1 Henderson N Carolina, USA
59D3 Henderson Nevada, USA
63D2 Henderson Texas, USA
67B1 Hendersonville N Carolina, USA
67A1 Hendersonville Tennessee, USA
47D3 Hendrik Verwoerd Dam South Africa
31E5 Hengchun Taiwan
26C4 Hengduan Shan *Mts* China
18B2 Hengelo Netherlands
31B2 Hengshan China
31D2 Hengshui China
30D1 Heng Xian China
31C4 Hengyang China
30A4 Henhoaha Nicobar Is, India
7D4 Henley-on-Thames England
68C3 Henlopen,C USA
68E1 Henniker USA
62C2 Henrietta USA
55K4 Henrietta Maria,C Canada
59D3 Henrieville USA
63C1 Henryetta USA
55M3 Henry Kater Pen Canada
47A1 Henties Bay Namibia
26D2 Hentiyn Nuruu *Mts* Mongolia
30B2 Henzada Burma
31B5 Hepu China
38E2 Herat Afghanistan
54H4 Herbert Canada
35C2 Herbertville New Zealand
13E2 Herborn Germany
69A4 Heredia Costa Rica
7C3 Hereford England
62B2 Hereford USA
7C3 Hereford & Worcester *County* England
13C2 Herentals Belgium
13E1 Herford Germany
61D3 Herington USA
35A3 Heriot New Zealand
68C1 Herkimer USA
8E1 Herma Ness *Pen* Scotland
47B3 Hermanus South Africa
34C2 Hermidale Australia
35B2 Hermitage New Zealand
32D1 Hermit Is Papua New Guinea
45C2 Hermon, Mt Lebanon/Syria
70A2 Hermosillo Mexico
75B4 Hernandarias Paraguay
68B2 Herndon USA
66C2 Herndon USA
13D2 Herne Germany
7E4 Herne Bay England
18B1 Herning Denmark
41E2 Herowābad Iran
75A4 Herradura Argentina

Kent Kohyon

7E4 **Kent** *County* England
64B2 **Kentland** USA
64C2 **Kenton** USA
54H3 **Kent Pen** Canada
64C3 **Kentucky** *R* USA
57E3 **Kentucky** *State* USA
57E3 **Kentucky L** USA
63D2 **Kentwood** Louisiana, USA
64B2 **Kentwood** Michigan, USA
50D3 **Kenya** *Republic* Africa
50D4 **Kenya,Mt** Kenya
64A2 **Keokuk** USA
43E4 **Keonchi** India
43F4 **Keonjhargarh** India
19D2 **Kepno** Poland
44B3 **Kerala** *State* India
34B3 **Kerang** Australia
12K6 **Kerava** Finland
21F6 **Kerch'** Ukraine
20J3 **Kerchem'ya** Russian Federation
32D1 **Kerema** Papua New Guinea
58C1 **Keremeos** Canada
50D2 **Keren** Ethiopia
36E7 **Kerguelen** *Is* Indian Ocean
36E7 **Kerguelen Ridge** Indian Ocean
50D4 **Kericho** Kenya
27D7 **Kerinci** *Mt* Indonesia
50D3 **Kerio** *R* Kenya
48D1 **Kerkenna, Îles** Tunisia
38E2 **Kerki** Turkmenistan
Kérkira = Corfu
33H3 **Kermadec Is** Pacific Ocean
33H4 **Kermadec Trench** Pacific Ocean
41G3 **Kermān** Iran
66B2 **Kerman** USA
41E3 **Kermānshāh** Iran
62B2 **Kermit** USA
59C3 **Kern** *R* USA
66C3 **Kernville** USA
20J3 **Keros** Russian Federation
62C2 **Kerrville** USA
9B3 **Kerry Hd** Irish Republic
67B2 **Kershaw** USA
25N5 **Kerulen** *R* Mongolia
48B2 **Kerzaz** Algeria
17F2 **Keşan** Turkey
43N2 **Kesariya** India
29E3 **Kesennuma** Japan
21G7 **Kesir Dağlari** *Mt* Turkey
12L5 **Kesten'ga** Russian Federation
6C2 **Keswick** England
48C4 **Kéta** Ghana
27E7 **Ketapang** Indonesia
54E4 **Ketchikan** USA
42B4 **Keti Bandar** Pakistan
19E2 **Kętrzyn** Poland
7D3 **Kettering** England
64C3 **Kettering** USA
58C1 **Kettle** *R* Canada
66C2 **Kettleman City** USA
58C1 **Kettle River Range** *Mts* USA
55L3 **Kettlestone B** Canada
68B1 **Keuka L** USA
41G3 **Kevir-i-Namak** *Salt Flat* Iran
64B2 **Kewaunee** USA
64B1 **Keweenaw B** USA
64B1 **Keweenaw Pen** USA
64C1 **Key Harbour** Canada
67B3 **Key Largo** USA
57E4 **Key West** USA
25M4 **Kezhma** Russian Federation
45D2 **Khabab** Syria
26G2 **Khabarovsk** Russian Federation
21G8 **Khabūr, al** *R* Syria
42B3 **Khairpur** Pakistan
42B3 **Khairpur** *Division* Pakistan
47C1 **Khakhea** Botswana
45B3 **Khalig el Tîna** *B* Egypt
38D4 **Khalīj Maşīrah** *G* Oman
17F3 **Khálki** *I* Greece
17E2 **Khalkidhíki** *Pen* Greece
17E3 **Khalkís** Greece
20L2 **Khal'mer-Yu** Russian Federation
20H4 **Khalturin** Russian Federation
42C4 **Khambhāt,G of** India
42D4 **Khāmgaon** India
30C2 **Kham Keut** Laos
44C2 **Khammam** India
45B3 **Khamsa** Egypt
41E2 **Khamseh** *Mts* Iran
30C2 **Khan** *R* Laos
42B1 **Khanabad** Afghanistan
41E3 **Khānaqīn** Iraq
42D4 **Khandwa** India
42C2 **Khanewal** Pakistan
45D3 **Khan ez Zabīb** Jordan
30D4 **Khanh Hung** Vietnam
17E3 **Khaniá** Greece
26G2 **Khanka, Ozero** *L* China/ Russian Federation
Khankendy = Stepanakert
42C3 **Khanpur** Pakistan
45D1 **Khān Shaykhūn** Syria
24H3 **Khanty-Mansiysk** Russian Federation
45C3 **Khan Yunis** Israel
42D1 **Khapalu** India
26E2 **Khapcheranga** Russian Federation
21H6 **Kharabali** Russian Federation
43F4 **Kharagpur** India
42B3 **Kharan** Pakistan
41G4 **Khārān** *R* Iran
41F3 **Kharānaq** Iran
41F4 **Khārg** *I* Iran
49F2 **Khârga Oasis** Egypt
42D4 **Khargon** India
45B3 **Kharîm, Gebel** *Mt* Egypt
21F6 **Khar'kov** Ukraine
20F2 **Kharlovka** Russian Federation
17F2 **Kharmanli** Bulgaria
20G4 **Kharovsk** Russian Federation
50D2 **Khartoum** Sudan
50D2 **Khartoum North** Sudan
28C2 **Khasan** Russian Federation
50D2 **Khashm el Girba** Sudan
43G3 **Khasi-Jaintia Hills** India
17F2 **Khaskovo** Bulgaria
25M2 **Khatanga** Russian Federation
25N2 **Khatangskiy Zaliv** *Estuary* Russian Federation
25T3 **Khatyrka** Russian Federation
30B3 **Khawsa** Burma
40C4 **Khaybar** Saudi Arabia
40B5 **Khazzan an-Nasr** *L* Egypt
30C2 **Khe Bo** Vietnam
42C4 **Khed Brahma** India
15C2 **Khemis** Algeria
16B3 **Khenchela** Algeria
48B1 **Khenifra** Morocco
43L1 **Kheri** *District* India
15D2 **Kherrata** Algeria
21E6 **Kherson** Ukraine
25N4 **Khilok** Russian Federation
17F3 **Khíos** Greece
17F3 **Khíos** *I* Greece
21D6 **Khmel'nitskiy** Ukraine
19E3 **Khodorov** Ukraine
39E1 **Khodzhent** Tajikistan
42B1 **Kholm** Afghanistan
19G1 **Kholm** Russian Federation
47B1 **Khomas Hochland** *Mts* Namibia
30D3 **Khong** Laos
41F4 **Khonj** Iran
26G2 **Khor** Russian Federation
41F5 **Khōr Duwayhin** *B* UAE
42C1 **Khorog** Tajikistan
41E3 **Khorramābad** Iran
41E3 **Khorramshahr** Iran
41G3 **Khosf** Iran
42B2 **Khost** Pakistan
21D6 **Khotin** Ukraine
21D5 **Khoyniki** Belorussia
41G2 **Khrebet Kopet Dag** *Mts* Iran/Turkmenistan
20L2 **Khrebet Pay-khoy** *Mts* Russian Federation
45B1 **Khrysokhou B** Cyprus
20L3 **Khulga** *R* Russian Federation
43F4 **Khulna** Bangladesh
42D1 **Khunjerāb P** China/India
41F3 **Khunsar** Iran
41E4 **Khurays** Saudi Arabia
43F4 **Khurda** India
42D3 **Khurja** India
42C2 **Khushab** Pakistan
45C2 **Khushnīyah** Syria
45D4 **Khush Shah, Wadi el** Jordan
19E3 **Khust** Ukraine
50C2 **Khuwei** Sudan
42B3 **Khuzdar** Pakistan
21H5 **Khvalynsk** Russian Federation
41G3 **Khvor** Iran
41F4 **Khvormūj** Iran
21G8 **Khvoy** Iran
42C1 **Khwaja Muhammad Ra** *Mts* Afghanistan
42C2 **Khyber P** Afghanistan/ Pakistan
51C4 **Kiambi** Zaïre
63C2 **Kiamichi** *R* USA
50B4 **Kibangou** Congo
50D4 **Kibaya** Tanzania
50C4 **Kibombo** Zaïre
50D4 **Kibondo** Tanzania
50D4 **Kibungu** Rwanda
17E2 **Kicevo** Macedonia, Yugoslavia
54G4 **Kicking Horse P** Canada
48C3 **Kidal** Mali
7C3 **Kidderminster** England
48A3 **Kidira** Senegal
35C1 **Kidnappers,C** New Zealand
18C2 **Kiel** Germany
19E2 **Kielce** Poland
6C2 **Kielder Res** England
18C2 **Kieler Bucht** *B* Germany
21E5 **Kiev** Ukraine
38E2 **Kifab** Uzbekistan
48A3 **Kiffa** Mauritius
50D4 **Kigali** Rwanda
50C4 **Kigoma** Tanzania
66E5 **Kiholo** Hawaiian Islands
29C4 **Kii-sanchi** *Mts* Japan
29C4 **Kii-suidō** *Str* Japan
25R4 **Kikhchik** Russian Federation
17E1 **Kikinda** Serbia, Yugoslavia
Kikládhes = Cyclades
32D1 **Kikon** Papua New Guinea
29D2 **Kikonai** Japan
27H7 **Kikori** Papua New Guinea
50B4 **Kikwit** Zaïre
66E5 **Kilauea Crater** *Vol* Hawaiian Islands
8C4 **Kilbrannan Sd** Scotland
54C3 **Kilbuck Mts** USA
28B2 **Kilchu** N Korea
34D1 **Kilcoy** Australia
9C3 **Kildare** Irish Republic
9C3 **Kildare** *County* Irish Republic
63D2 **Kilgore** USA
50E4 **Kilifi** Kenya
50D4 **Kilimanjaro** *Mt* Tanzania
51D4 **Kilindoni** Tanzania
40C2 **Kilis** Turkey
19F3 **Kiliya** Ukraine
9D2 **Kilkeel** Northern Ireland
9C3 **Kilkenny** Irish Republic
9C3 **Kilkenny** *County* Irish Republic
17E2 **Kilkís** Greece
34D1 **Killarney** Australia
10B3 **Killarney** Irish Republic
63C2 **Killeen** USA
8C3 **Killin** Scotland
17E3 **Killíni** *Mt* Greece
9B3 **Killorglin** Irish Republic
9D2 **Killyleagh** Northern Ireland
8C4 **Kilmarnock** Scotland
20J4 **Kil'mez** Russian Federation
9C3 **Kilmichael Pt** Irish Republic
51D4 **Kilosa** Tanzania
10B3 **Kilrush** Irish Republic
8C4 **Kilsyth** Scotland
51C4 **Kilwa** Zaïre
51D4 **Kilwa Kisiwani** Tanzania
51D4 **Kilwa Kivinje** Tanzania
60C2 **Kimball** USA
54G5 **Kimberley** Canada
47C2 **Kimberley** South Africa
32B2 **Kimberley Plat** Australia
28B2 **Kimch'aek** N Korea
28B3 **Kimch'ŏn** S Korea
28A3 **Kimhae** S Korea
17E3 **Kími** Greece
28A3 **Kimje** S Korea
20F4 **Kimry** Russian Federation
28A3 **Kimwha** N Korea
27E6 **Kinabalu** *Mt* Malaysia
8D2 **Kinbrace** Scotland
64C2 **Kincardine** Canada
63D2 **Kinder** USA
48A3 **Kindia** Guinea
50C4 **Kindu** Zaïre
20J5 **Kinel'** Russian Federation
20G4 **Kineshma** Russian Federation
34D1 **Kingaroy** Australia
59B3 **King City** USA
54F4 **Kingcome Inlet** Canada
63C1 **Kingfisher** USA
76H4 **King George I** Antarctica
55L4 **King George Is** Canada
32D5 **King I** Australia
32B2 **King Leopold Range** *Mts* Australia
56B3 **Kingman** USA
50C4 **Kingombe** Zaïre
66C2 **Kingsburg** USA
59C3 **Kings Canyon Nat Pk** USA
32B2 **King Sd** Australia
64B1 **Kingsford** USA
67B2 **Kingsland** USA
7E3 **King's Lynn** England
33G1 **Kingsmill Group** *Is* Kiribati
68D2 **Kings Park** USA
56B2 **Kings Peak** *Mt* USA
67B1 **Kingsport** USA
32C4 **Kingston** Australia
55L5 **Kingston** Canada
70E3 **Kingston** Jamaica
65E2 **Kingston** New York, USA
35A3 **Kingston** New Zealand
68C2 **Kingston** Pennsylvania, USA
69N2 **Kingstown** St Vincent
56D4 **Kingsville** USA
7C3 **Kington** England
8C3 **Kingussie** Scotland
54J3 **King William I** Canada
47D3 **King William's Town** South Africa
50B4 **Kinkala** Congo
12G7 **Kinna** Sweden
8D3 **Kinnairds Head** *Pt* Scotland
29C3 **Kinomoto** Japan
8D3 **Kinross** Scotland
50B4 **Kinshasa** Zaïre
62C1 **Kinsley** USA
67C1 **Kinston** USA
27E7 **Kintap** Indonesia
8C4 **Kintyre** *Pen* Scotland
50D3 **Kinyeti** *Mt* Sudan
17E3 **Kiparissía** Greece
17E3 **Kiparissiakós Kólpos** *G* Greece
65D1 **Kipawa,L** Canada
51D4 **Kipili** Tanzania
9C3 **Kippure** *Mt* Irish Republic
51C5 **Kipushi** Zaïre
25M4 **Kirensk** Russian Federation
24J5 **Kirgizia Republic** Asia
39F1 **Kirgizskiy Khrebet** *Mts* Kirgizia
50B4 **Kiri** Zaïre
33G1 **Kiribati** *Is, Republic* Pacific Ocean
21E8 **Kirikkale** Turkey
40B2 **Kirikkale** Turkey
20E4 **Kirishi** Russian Federation
42B3 **Kirithar Range** *Mts* Pakistan
17F3 **Kirkağaç** Turkey
21H8 **Kirk Bulāg Dāgh** *Mt* Iran
6C2 **Kirkby** England
8D3 **Kirkcaldy** Scotland
8C4 **Kirkcudbright** Scotland
12K5 **Kirkenes** Norway
6C3 **Kirkham** England
55K5 **Kirkland Lake** Canada
40A1 **Kirklareli** Turkey
6C2 **Kirkoswald** England
76E7 **Kirkpatrick,Mt** Antarctica
57D2 **Kirksville** USA
41D2 **Kirkūk** Iraq
8D2 **Kirkwall** Scotland
47D3 **Kirkwood** South Africa
61E3 **Kirkwood** USA
20E5 **Kirov** Russian Federation
20H4 **Kirov** Russian Federation
41D1 **Kirovakan** Armenia
20K4 **Kirovgrad** Russian Federation
21E6 **Kirovograd** Ukraine
20E2 **Kirovsk** Russian Federation
25R4 **Kirovskiy** Kamchatka, Russian Federation
8D3 **Kirriemuir** Scotland
20J4 **Kirs** Russian Federation
40B2 **Kirşehir** Turkey
18C2 **Kiruna** Sweden
29C3 **Kiryū** Japan
50C3 **Kisangani** Zaïre
29C3 **Kisarazu** Japan
43F3 **Kishanganj** India
42C3 **Kishangarh** India
19F3 **Kishinev** Moldavia
29C4 **Kishiwada** Japan
50D4 **Kisii** Kenya
51D4 **Kisiju** Tanzania
17D1 **Kiskunfélegyháza** Hungary
19D3 **Kiskunhalas** Hungary
21G7 **Kislovodsk** Russian Federation
50E4 **Kismaayo** Somalia
29C3 **Kiso-sammyaku** *Mts* Japan
48B4 **Kissidougou** Guinea
67B3 **Kissimmee,L** USA
50D4 **Kisumu** Kenya
19E3 **Kisvárda** Hungary
48B3 **Kita** Mali
24H6 **Kitab** Uzbekistan
29D3 **Kitakami** Japan
29D3 **Kitakami** *R* Japan
29D3 **Kitakata** Japan
28C4 **Kita-Kyūshū** Japan
50D3 **Kitale** Kenya
26H4 **Kitalo** *I* Japan
29E2 **Kitami** Japan
29D2 **Kitami-Esashi** Japan
60C3 **Kit Carson** USA
55K5 **Kitchener** Canada
50D3 **Kitgum** Uganda
17E3 **Kíthira** *I* Greece
17E3 **Kíthnos** *I* Greece
45B1 **Kiti, C** Cyprus
54G2 **Kitikmeot** *Region* Canada
54F4 **Kitimat** Canada
12K5 **Kitinen** *R* Finland
28B4 **Kitsuki** Japan
65D2 **Kittanning** USA
65E2 **Kittery** USA
12J5 **Kittilä** Finland
67C1 **Kitty Hawk** USA
51D4 **Kitunda** Tanzania
51C5 **Kitwe** Zambia
18C3 **Kitzbühel** Austria
18C3 **Kitzingen** Germany
50C4 **Kiumbi** Zaïre
54B3 **Kivalina** USA
19F2 **Kivercy** Ukraine
50C4 **Kivu,L** Rwanda/Zaïre
54B3 **Kiwalik** USA
Kiyev = Kiev
19G2 **Kiyevskoye Vodokhranilishche** *Res* Ukraine
20K4 **Kizel** Russian Federation
20G3 **Kizema** Russian Federation
40C2 **Kizil** *R* Turkey
38D2 **Kizyl'-Arvat** Turkmenistan
21J8 **Kizyl-Atrek** Turkmenistan
18C2 **Kladno** Czechoslovakia
18C3 **Klagenfurt** Austria
20C4 **Klaipēda** Lithuania
58B2 **Klamath** *R* USA
56A2 **Klamath Falls** USA
58B2 **Klamath Mts** USA
18C3 **Klatovy** Czechoslovakia
45C1 **Kleiat** Lebanon
47B2 **Kleinsee** South Africa
47D2 **Klerksdorp** South Africa
19G2 **Kletnya** Russian Federation
13D2 **Kleve** Germany
19G2 **Klimovichi** Belorussia
20F4 **Klin** Russian Federation
19D1 **Klintehamn** Sweden
21E5 **Klintsy** Russian Federation
47C3 **Klipplaat** South Africa
16D2 **Ključ** Bosnia & Herzegovina, Yugoslavia
18D2 **Kłodzko** Poland
54D3 **Klondike Plat** Canada/ USA
18D3 **Klosterneuburg** Austria
19D2 **Kluczbork** Poland
6D2 **Knaresborough** England
7C3 **Knighton** Wales
16D2 **Knin** Croatia
32A4 **Knob,C** Australia
9B3 **Knockmealdown Mts** Irish Republic
13B2 **Knokke-Heist** Belgium
76G9 **Knox Coast** Antarctica
61E2 **Knoxville** Iowa, USA
57E3 **Knoxville** Tennessee, USA
55Q3 **Knud Rasmussens Land** *Region* Greenland
7C3 **Knutsford** England
47C3 **Knysna** South Africa
55O3 **Kobberminebugt** *B* Greenland
29D4 **Kōbe** Japan
København = Copenhagen
18B2 **Koblenz** Germany
19E2 **Kobrin** Belorussia
27G7 **Kobroör** *I* Indonesia
54B3 **Kobuk** *R* USA
17E2 **Kočani** Macedonia, Yugoslavia
28B3 **Kochang** S Korea
28B3 **Koch'ang** S Korea
30C3 **Ko Chang** *I* Thailand
43F3 **Koch Bihār** India
55L3 **Koch I** Canada
44B4 **Kochi** India
29C4 **Kōchi** Japan
54C4 **Kodiak** USA
54C4 **Kodiak I** USA
44B3 **Kodikkarai** India
50D3 **Kodok** Sudan
29D2 **Kodomari-misaki** *C* Japan
19F3 **Kodyma** Ukraine
66D3 **Koehn L** USA
47B2 **Koes** Namibia
47D2 **Koffiefontein** South Africa
48B4 **Koforidua** Ghana
29D3 **Kofu** Japan
29C3 **Koga** Japan
12G7 **Køge** Denmark
42C2 **Kohat** Pakistan
42B2 **Koh-i-Baba** *Mts* Afghanistan
42B1 **Koh-i-Hisar** *Mts* Afghanistan
42B2 **Koh-i-Khurd** *Mt* Afghanistan
43G3 **Kohima** India
42B2 **Koh-i-Mazar** *Mt* Afghanistan
42B3 **Kohlu** Pakistan
20D4 **Kohtla Järve** Estonia
28A4 **Kohung** S Korea
28A4 **Kohyon** S Korea

Koide Kutcharo-ko

29C3 **Koide** Japan
30A4 **Koihoa** Nicobar Is, India
28A2 **Koin** N Korea
28B4 **Koje Dŏ** *I* S Korea
29C2 **Ko-jima** *I* Japan
24H4 **Kokchetav** Kazakhstan
12J6 **Kokemäki** *L* Finland
12J6 **Kokkola** Finland
32D1 **Kokoda** Papua New Guinea
64B2 **Kokomo** USA
27G7 **Kokonau** Indonesia
26B2 **Kokpekty** Kazakhstan
28A3 **Koksan** N Korea
55M4 **Koksoak** *R* Canada
28A3 **Koksŏng** S Korea
47D3 **Kokstad** South Africa
30C3 **Ko Kut** *I* Thailand
20E2 **Kola** Russian Federation
27F7 **Kolaka** Indonesia
30B4 **Ko Lanta** *I* Thailand
44B3 **Kolār** India
44B3 **Kolār Gold Fields** India
48A3 **Kolda** Senegal
12F7 **Kolding** Denmark
20H2 **Kolguyev, Ostrov** *I* Russian Federation
44A2 **Kolhāpur** India
18D2 **Kolín** Czechoslovakia
44B4 **Kollam** India
Köln = Cologne
19D2 **Koło** Poland
66E5 **Koloa** Hawaiian Islands
18D2 **Kołobrzeg** Poland
48B3 **Kolokani** Mali
20F4 **Kolomna** Russian Federation
21D6 **Kolomyya** Ukraine
25R4 **Kolpakovskiy** Russian Federation
24K4 **Kolpashevo** Russian Federation
17F3 **Kólpos Merabéllou** *B* Greece
17E2 **Kólpos Singitikós** *G* Greece
17E2 **Kólpos Strimonikós** *G* Greece
17E2 **Kólpos Toronaíos** *G* Greece
20F2 **Kol'skiy Poluostrov** *Pen* Russian Federation
20K2 **Kolva** *R* Russian Federation
12G6 **Kolvereid** Norway
51C5 **Kolwezi** Zaïre
25R3 **Kolyma** *R* Russian Federation
25R3 **Kolymskaya Nizmennost'** *Lowland* Russian Federation
25S3 **Kolymskoye Nagor'ye** *Mts* Russian Federation
17E2 **Kom** *Mt* Bulgaria/Serbia, Yugoslavia
50D3 **Koma** Ethiopia
29D3 **Koma** Japan
48D3 **Komadugu Gana** *R* Nigeria
29D2 **Komaga take** *Mt* Japan
25S4 **Komandorskiye Ostrova** *Is* Russian Federation
19D3 **Komárno** Czechoslovakia
47E2 **Komati** *R* South Africa/Swaziland
47E2 **Komati Poort** South Africa
29D3 **Komatsu** Japan
29B4 **Komatsushima** Japan
20J3 **Komi Republic** Russian Federation
26B1 **Kommunar** Russian Federation
27E7 **Komodo** *I* Indonesia
27G7 **Komoran** *I* Indonesia
29C3 **Komoro** Japan
17F2 **Komotiní** Greece
47C3 **Kompasberg** *Mt* South Africa
30D3 **Kompong Cham** Cambodia
30C3 **Kompong Chhnang** Cambodia
30C3 **Kompong Som** Cambodia
30D3 **Kompong Thom** Cambodia
30D3 **Kompong Trabek** Cambodia
19F3 **Komrat** Moldavia
47C3 **Komsberg** *Mts* South Africa
25L1 **Komsomolets, Ostrov** *I* Russian Federation
20L2 **Komsomol'skiy** Russian Federation
25P4 **Komsomol'sk na Amure** Russian Federation
24H4 **Konda** *R* Russian Federation
43E5 **Kondagaon** India
50D4 **Kondoa** Tanzania
20E3 **Kondopoga** Russian Federation
44B2 **Kondukūr** India
20F3 **Konevo** Russian Federation
55P3 **Kong Christian IX Land** *Region* Greenland
55O3 **Kong Frederik VI Kyst** *Region* Greenland
28A3 **Kongju** S Korea
24D2 **Kong Karls Land** *Is* Svalbard
50C4 **Kongolo** Zaïre
12F7 **Kongsberg** Norway
12G6 **Kongsvinger** Norway
Königsberg = Kaliningrad
19D2 **Konin** Poland
17D2 **Konjic** Bosnia & Herzegovina, Yugoslavia
20G3 **Konosha** Russian Federation
29C3 **Konosu** Japan
21E5 **Konotop** Ukraine
19E2 **Końskie** Poland
18B3 **Konstanz** Germany
48C3 **Kontagora** Nigeria
30D3 **Kontum** Vietnam
21E8 **Konya** Turkey
58C1 **Kootenay L** Canada
42C5 **Kopargaon** India
55R3 **Kópasker** Iceland
12A2 **Kópavogur** Iceland
16C1 **Koper** Slovenia
38D2 **Kopet Dag** *Mts* Iran/Turkmenistan
20L4 **Kopeysk** Russian Federation
30C4 **Ko Phangan** *I* Thailand
30B4 **Ko Phuket** *I* Thailand
12H7 **Köping** Sweden
28A3 **Kopo-ri** S Korea
44B2 **Koppal** India
16D1 **Koprivnica** Croatia
42B4 **Korangi** Pakistan
44C2 **Koraput** India
43E4 **Korba** India
18B2 **Korbach** Germany
17E2 **Korçë** Albania
16D2 **Korčula** *I* Croatia
31E2 **Korea B** China/Korea
28B2 **Korea, North** *Republic* Asia
28B3 **Korea, South** *Republic* Asia
26F3 **Korea Strait** Japan/Korea
19F2 **Korec** Ukraine
25S3 **Korf** Russian Federation
40B1 **Körğlu Tepesi** *Mt* Turkey
48B4 **Korhogo** Ivory Coast
42B4 **Kori Creek** India
Kórinthos = Corinth
29E3 **Kōriyama** Japan
20L5 **Korkino** Russian Federation
25R3 **Korkodon** Russian Federation
25R3 **Korkodon** *R* Russian Federation
40B2 **Korkuteli** Turkey
39G1 **Korla** China
45B1 **Kormakiti, C** Cyprus
16D2 **Kornat** *I* Croatia
21E7 **Köroğlu Tepesi** *Mt* Turkey
50D4 **Korogwe** Tanzania
34B3 **Koroit** Australia
27G6 **Koror** Palau, Pacific Ocean
19E3 **Körös** *R* Hungary
21D5 **Korosten** Ukraine
19F2 **Korostyshev** Ukraine
50B2 **Koro Toro** Chad
26H2 **Korsakov** Russian Federation
12G7 **Korsør** Denmark
20J3 **Kortkeros** Russian Federation
18A2 **Kortrijk** Belgium
25S3 **Koryakskoye Nagor'ye** *Mts* Russian Federation
28A3 **Koryong** S Korea
17F3 **Kós** *I* Greece
30C4 **Ko Samui** *I* Thailand
28A3 **Kosan** N Korea
19D2 **Kościerzyna** Poland
63E2 **Kosciusko** USA
32D4 **Kosciusko** *Mt* Australia
43J2 **Kosi** India
43K1 **Kosi** *R* India
19E3 **Košice** Czechoslovakia
20J2 **Kosma** *R* Russian Federation
28B3 **Kosŏng** N Korea
17E2 **Kosovo** *Region* Serbia, Yugoslavia
48B4 **Kossou** *L* Ivory Coast
47D2 **Koster** South Africa
50D2 **Kosti** Sudan
19F2 **Kostopol'** Ukraine
20G4 **Kostroma** Russian Federation
18C2 **Kostrzyn** Poland
20K2 **Kos'yu** *R* Russian Federation
12H8 **Koszalin** Poland
42D3 **Kota** India
30C4 **Kota Bharu** Malaysia
42C2 **Kot Addu** Pakistan
27E6 **Kota Kinabalu** Malaysia
44C2 **Kotapad** India
20H4 **Kotel'nich** Russian Federation
21G6 **Kotel'nikovo** Russian Federation
25P2 **Kotel'nyy, Ostrov** *I* Russian Federation
12K6 **Kotka** Finland
20H3 **Kotlas** Russian Federation
54B3 **Kotlik** USA
17D2 **Kotor** Montenegro, Yugoslavia
21D6 **Kotovsk** Ukraine
42B3 **Kotri** Pakistan
44C2 **Kottagūdem** India
44B4 **Kottayam** India
50C3 **Kotto** *R* Central African Republic
44B3 **Kottūru** India
25L3 **Kotuy** *R* Russian Federation
54B3 **Kotzebue** USA
54B3 **Kotzebue Sd** USA
48C3 **Kouandé** Benin
50C3 **Kouango** Central African Republic
48B3 **Koudougou** Burkina
47C3 **Kougaberge** *Mts* South Africa
50B4 **Koulamoutou** Gabon
48B3 **Koulikoro** Mali
48B3 **Koupéla** Burkina
73H2 **Kourou** French Guiana
48B3 **Kouroussa** Guinea
50B2 **Kousséri** Cameroon
12K6 **Kouvola** Finland
12L5 **Kovdor** Russian Federation
12L5 **Kovdozero, Ozero** *L* Russian Federation
19E2 **Kovel** Ukraine
Kovno = Kaunas
20G4 **Kovrov** Russian Federation
20G5 **Kovylkino** Russian Federation
20F3 **Kovzha** *R* Russian Federation
30C4 **Ko Way** *I* Thailand
31C5 **Kowloon** Hong Kong
28A3 **Kowŏn** N Korea
42B2 **Kowt-e-Ashrow** Afghanistan
40A2 **Köyceğiz** Turkey
20G2 **Koyda** Russian Federation
44A2 **Koyna Res** India
20H3 **Koynas** Russian Federation
54C3 **Koyukuk** USA
40C2 **Kozan** Turkey
17E2 **Kozańi** Greece
44B3 **Kozhikode** India
20K2 **Kozhim** Russian Federation
20H4 **Koz'modemyansk** Russian Federation
29C4 **Kōzu-shima** *I* Japan
48C4 **Kpalimé** Togo
47D3 **Kraai** *R* South Africa
12F7 **Kragerø** Norway
17E2 **Kragujevac** Serbia, Yugoslavia
30B3 **Kra, Isthmus of** Burma/Malaysia
45D1 **Krak des Chevaliers** *Hist Site* Syria
Kraków = Cracow Poland
17E2 **Kraljevo** Serbia, Yugoslavia
21F6 **Kramatorsk** Ukraine
12H6 **Kramfors** Sweden
16C1 **Kranj** Slovenia
20H3 **Krasavino** Russian Federation
20J1 **Krasino** Russian Federation
28C2 **Kraskino** Russian Federation
19E2 **Kraśnik** Poland
21H5 **Krasnoarmeysk** Russian Federation
21F6 **Krasnodar** Russian Federation
20K4 **Krasnokamsk** Russian Federation
20L4 **Krasnotur'insk** Russian Federation
20K4 **Krasnoufimsk** Russian Federation
20K5 **Krasnousol'skiy** Russian Federation
20K3 **Krasnovishersk** Russian Federation
21J7 **Krasnovodsk** Turkmenistan
25L4 **Krasnoyarsk** Russian Federation
19E2 **Krasnystaw** Poland
21H5 **Krasnyy Kut** Russian Federation
21F6 **Krasnyy Luch** Ukraine
21H6 **Krasnyy Yar** Russian Federation
30D3 **Kratie** Cambodia
55N2 **Kraulshavn** Greenland
18B2 **Krefeld** Germany
21E6 **Kremenchug** Ukraine
21E6 **Kremenchugskoye Vodokhranilische** *Res* Ukraine
19F2 **Kremenets** Ukraine
60B2 **Kremming** USA
48C4 **Kribi** Cameroon
20E5 **Krichev** Belorussia
44B2 **Krishna** *R* India
44B3 **Krishnagiri** India
43F4 **Krishnanagar** India
12F7 **Kristiansand** Norway
12G7 **Kristianstad** Sweden
24B3 **Kristiansund** Norway
12J6 **Kristiinankaupunki** Finland
12G7 **Kristinehamn** Sweden
Kríti = Crete
21E6 **Krivoy Rog** Ukraine
16C1 **Krk** *I* Croatia
47D1 **Krokodil** *R* South Africa
25S4 **Kronotskaya Sopka** *Mt* Russian Federation
25S4 **Kronotskiy, Mys** *C* Russian Federation
55P3 **Kronprins Frederik Bjerge** *Mts* Greenland
12K7 **Kronshtadt** Russian Federation
47D2 **Kroonstad** South Africa
21G6 **Kropotkin** Russian Federation
47E1 **Kruger Nat Pk** South Africa
47D2 **Krugersdorp** South Africa
17D2 **Kruje** Albania
Krung Thep = Bangkok
19F2 **Krupki** Belorussia
17E2 **Kruševac** Serbia, Yugoslavia
12K7 **Krustpils** Latvia
Krym = Crimea
21F7 **Krymsk** Russian Federation
18D2 **Krzyz** Poland
15C2 **Ksar El Boukhari** Algeria
15A2 **Ksar-el-Kebir** Morocco
48C1 **Ksour, Mts des** Algeria
27C6 **Kuala** Indonesia
30C5 **Kuala Dungun** Malaysia
30C4 **Kuala Kerai** Malaysia
30C5 **Kuala Kubu Baharu** Malaysia
30C5 **Kuala Lipis** Malaysia
30C5 **Kuala Lumpur** Malaysia
30C4 **Kuala Trengganu** Malaysia
27F6 **Kuandang** Indonesia
28A2 **Kuandian** China
30C5 **Kuantan** Malaysia
21H7 **Kuba** Azerbaijan
27H7 **Kubor** *Mt* Papua New Guinea
27E6 **Kuching** Malaysia
27E6 **Kudat** Malaysia
20J4 **Kudymkar** Russian Federation
18C3 **Kufstein** Austria
41G3 **Kuh Duren** *Upland* Iran
41F3 **Kūh-e Dinar** *Mt* Iran
41G2 **Kūh-e-Hazār Masjed** *Mts* Iran
41G4 **Kūh-e Jebāl Barez** *Mts* Iran
41F3 **Kūh-e Karkas** *Mts* Iran
41G4 **Kūh-e Laleh Zar** *Mt* Iran
41E2 **Kūh-e Sahand** *Mt* Iran
38E3 **Kuh-e-Taftān** *Mt* Iran
21H9 **Kūhhaye Alvand** *Mts* Iran
21H8 **Kūhhaye Sabalan** *Mts* Iran
41E3 **Kūhhā-ye Zāgros** *Mts* Iran
12K6 **Kuhmo** Finland
41F3 **Kūhpāyeh** Iran
41G3 **Kūhpāyeh** *Mt* Iran
41G4 **Kūh-ye Bashākerd** *Mts* Iran
41E2 **Kūh-ye Sabalan** *Mt* Iran
47B2 **Kuibis** Namibia
47B1 **Kuiseb** *R* Namibia
51B5 **Kuito** Angola
28A3 **Kujang** N Korea
29E2 **Kuji** Japan
28B4 **Kuju-san** *Mt* Japan
17E2 **Kukës** Albania
30C5 **Kukup** Malaysia
41G4 **Kūl** *R* Iran
17F3 **Kula** Turkey
21K6 **Kulakshi** Kazakhstan
50D3 **Kulal,Mt** Kenya
17E2 **Kulata** Bulgaria
20C4 **Kuldīga** Latvia
20G2 **Kulov** *R* Russian Federation
21J6 **Kul'sary** Kazakhstan
42D2 **Kulu** India
40B2 **Kulu** Turkey
24J4 **Kulunda** Russian Federation
34B2 **Kulwin** Australia
21H7 **Kuma** *R* Russian Federation
29C3 **Kumagaya** Japan
27E7 **Kumai** Indonesia
21L5 **Kumak** Russian Federation
28C4 **Kumamoto** Japan
29C4 **Kumano** Japan
17E2 **Kumanovo** Macedonia, Yugoslavia
48B4 **Kumasi** Ghana
48C4 **Kumba** Cameroon
44B3 **Kumbakonam** India
28A3 **Kŭmch'ŏn** N Korea
20K5 **Kumertau** Russian Federation
28A3 **Kumgang** N Korea
12H7 **Kumla** Sweden
28A4 **Kŭmnyŏng** S Korea
28A4 **Kŭmo-do** *I* S Korea
44A3 **Kumta** India
39G1 **Kumüx** China
28B3 **Kumwha** S Korea
42C2 **Kunar** *R* Afghanistan
29F2 **Kunashir, Ostrov** *I* Russian Federation
12K7 **Kunda** Estonia
42C4 **Kundla** India
42B1 **Kunduz** Afghanistan
Kunene *R* **= Cunene R**
12G7 **Kungsbacka** Sweden
20K4 **Kungur** Russian Federation
30B1 **Kunhing** Burma
39G2 **Kunlun Shan** *Mts* China
31A4 **Kunming** China
20M3 **Kunovat** *R* Russian Federation
28B3 **Kunsan** S Korea
12K6 **Kuopio** Finland
16D1 **Kupa** *R* Bosnia & Herzegovina, Yugoslavia/Croatia
32B2 **Kupang** Indonesia
32D2 **Kupiano** Papua New Guinea
54E4 **Kupreanof I** USA
21F6 **Kupyansk** Ukraine
39G1 **Kuqa** China
21H8 **Kura** *R* Azerbaijan
29C3 **Kurabe** Japan
29C4 **Kurashiki** Japan
29B3 **Kurayoshi** Japan
41E2 **Kurdistan** *Region* Iran
17F2 **Kŭrdzhali** Bulgaria
28C4 **Kure** Japan
20C4 **Kuressaare** Estonia
25L3 **Kureyka** *R* Russian Federation
24H4 **Kurgan** Russian Federation
12J6 **Kurikka** Finland
25Q5 **Kuril Is** Russian Federation
Kuril'skiye Ostrova *Is* **= Kuril Islands**
36J2 **Kuril Trench** Pacific Ocean
21H8 **Kurinskaya Kosa** *Sand Spit* Azerbaijan
44B2 **Kurnool** India
29D2 **Kuroishi** Japan
29D3 **Kuroiso** Japan
35B2 **Kurow** New Zealand
34D2 **Kurri Kurri** Australia
21F5 **Kursk** Russian Federation
26B2 **Kuruktag** *R* China
47C2 **Kuruman** South Africa
47C2 **Kuruman** *R* South Africa
28C4 **Kurume** Japan
44C3 **Kurunegala** Sri Lanka
24K5 **Kurunktag** *R* China
20K3 **Kur'ya** Russian Federation
20K4 **Kusa** Russian Federation
17F3 **Kuşadasi Kōrfezi** *B* Turkey
17F2 **Kus Golü** *L* Turkey
29D4 **Kushimoto** Japan
29E2 **Kushiro** Japan
38E2 **Kushka** Afghanistan
43F4 **Kushtia** Bangladesh
21J5 **Kushum** *R* Kazakhstan
20K4 **Kushva** Russian Federation
54B3 **Kuskokwim** *R* USA
54C3 **Kuskokwim Mts** USA
43E3 **Kusma** Nepal
28B3 **Kusŏng** N Korea
24H4 **Kustanay** Kazakhstan
27E7 **Kuta** *R* Indonesia
21D8 **Kütahya** Turkey
21G7 **Kutaisi** Georgia
29D2 **Kutchan** Japan
29E2 **Kutcharo-ko** *L* Japan

Leichhardt **Long B**

32C2 **Leichhardt** *R* Australia
18A2 **Leiden** Netherlands
13B2 **Leie** *R* Belgium
32C4 **Leigh Creek** Australia
7E4 **Leigh on Sea** England
7D4 **Leighton Buzzard** England
18B2 **Leine** *R* Germany
9C3 **Leinster** *Region* Irish Republic
18C2 **Leipzig** Germany
15A2 **Leiria** Portugal
12F7 **Leirvik** Norway
8D4 **Leith** Scotland
31C4 **Leiyang** China
31B5 **Leizhou Bandao** *Pen* China
31C5 **Leizhou Wan** *B* China
18A2 **Lek** *R* Netherlands
16B3 **Le Kef** Tunisia
63D2 **Leland** USA
17D2 **Lelija** *Mt* Bosnia & Herzegovina, Yugoslavia
16B1 **Léman, Lac** France/ Switzerland
14C2 **Le Mans** France
61D2 **Le Mars** USA
13E1 **Lemgo** Germany
58D2 **Lemhi Range** *Mts* USA
55M3 **Lemieux Is** Canada
56C2 **Lemmon** USA
59D4 **Lemmon,Mt** USA
59C3 **Lemoore** USA
14C2 **Lempdes** France
43G4 **Lemro** *R* Burma
16D2 **Le Murge** *Region* Italy
25O3 **Lena** *R* Russian Federation
20E3 **Lendery** Russian Federation
13D1 **Lengerich** Germany
31C4 **Lengshuijiang** China
21G7 **Leninakan** Armenia
Leningrad = St Petersburg
76F7 **Leningradskaya** *Base* Antarctica
20J5 **Leninogorsk** Russian Federation
26B1 **Leninogorsk** Kazakhstan
24K4 **Leninsk-Kuznetskiy** Russian Federation
26G2 **Leninskoye** Russian Federation
21H8 **Lenkoran'** Azerbaijan
13E2 **Lenne** *R* Germany
67B1 **Lenoir** USA
68D1 **Lenox** USA
13B2 **Lens** France
25N3 **Lensk** Russian Federation
16C3 **Lentini** Sicily, Italy
30B3 **Lenya** *R* Burma
16C1 **Leoben** Austria
7C3 **Leominster** England
68E1 **Leominster** USA
70B2 **León** Mexico
72A1 **León** Nicaragua
15A1 **León** Spain
47B1 **Leonardville** Namibia
45C1 **Leonarisso** Cyprus
32B3 **Leonora** Australia
75D3 **Leopoldina** Brazil
Léopoldville = Kinshasa
20D5 **Lepel** Belorussia
31D4 **Leping** China
14C2 **Le Puy** France
50B3 **Léré** Chad
47D2 **Leribe** Lesotho
15C1 **Lérida** Spain
17F3 **Léros** *I* Greece
68B1 **Le Roy** USA
10C1 **Lerwick** Scotland
69C3 **Les Cayes** Haiti
65F1 **Les Escoumins** Canada
31A4 **Leshan** China
17E2 **Leskovac** Serbia, Yugoslavia
47D2 **Leslie** South Africa
20J4 **Lesnoy** Russian Federation
25L4 **Lesosibirsk** Russian Federation
47D2 **Lesotho** *Kingdom* South Africa
26G2 **Lesozavodsk** Russian Federation
14B2 **Les Sables-d'Olonne** France
76E4 **Lesser Antarctica** *Region* Antarctica
69E3 **Lesser Antilles** *Is* Caribbean Sea
17F3 **Lésvos** *I* Greece
18D2 **Leszno** Poland
47E1 **Letaba** *R* South Africa
43G4 **Letha Range** *Mts* Burma
54G5 **Lethbridge** Canada
73G3 **Lethem** Guyana
19F3 **Letichev** Ukraine
72E4 **Letícia** Colombia
32B1 **Leti, Kepulauan** *I* Indonesia
47D1 **Letlhakeng** Botswana
7E4 **le Touquet-Paris-Plage** France
30B2 **Letpadan** Burma
25N4 **Let Oktyabr'ya** Russian Federation
14C1 **Le Tréport** France
9C2 **Letterkenny** Irish Republic
27C6 **Leuser** *Mt* Indonesia
18A2 **Leuven** Belgium
17E3 **Levádhia** Greece
12G6 **Levanger** Norway
62B2 **Levelland** USA
8D3 **Leven** Scotland
8D3 **Leven, Loch** *L* Scotland
27F8 **Lévèque,C** Australia
13D2 **Leverkusen** Germany
19D3 **Levice** Czechoslovakia
35C2 **Levin** New Zealand
55L5 **Lévis** Canada
65E2 **Levittown** USA
17E3 **Lévka Óri** *Mt* Greece
17E3 **Levkás** Greece
17E3 **Levkás** *I* Greece
32B2 **Lévêque,C** Australia
17F2 **Levski** Bulgaria
7E4 **Lewes** England
62C1 **Lewis** USA
10B2 **Lewis** *I* Scotland
68B2 **Lewisburg** USA
35B2 **Lewis P** New Zealand
56B2 **Lewis Range** *Mts* USA
67A2 **Lewis Smith,L** USA
56B2 **Lewiston** Idaho, USA
57F2 **Lewiston** Maine, USA
56C2 **Lewistown** Montana, USA
65D2 **Lewistown** Pennsylvania, USA
63D2 **Lewisville** USA
57E3 **Lexington** Kentucky, USA
61E3 **Lexington** Missouri, USA
67B1 **Lexington** N Carolina, USA
60D2 **Lexington** Nebraska, USA
65D3 **Lexington** Virginia, USA
65D3 **Lexington Park** USA
6D2 **Leyburn** England
27F5 **Leyte** *I* Philippines
17D2 **Lezhe** Albania
39H3 **Lhasa** China
43F3 **Lhazê** China
27C6 **Lhokseumawe** Indonesia
43G3 **Lhozhag** China
26C4 **Lhunze** China
Liancourt Rocks = Tok-do
28B2 **Liangbingtai** China
31B3 **Liangdang** China
31C5 **Lianjiang** China
31C5 **Lianping** China
31C5 **Lian Xian** China
31D3 **Lianyungang** China
31E1 **Liaodong Bandao** *Pen* China
31E1 **Liaodong Wan** *B* China
31E1 **Liao He** *R* China
28A2 **Liaoning** *Province* China
31E1 **Liaoyang** China
28A2 **Liaoyangwopu** China
31E1 **Liaoyuan** China
28A2 **Liaozhong** China
54F3 **Liard** *R* Canada
54F4 **Liard River** Canada
13C3 **Liart** France
45C2 **Liban, Jebel** *Mts* Lebanon
58C1 **Libby** USA
50B3 **Libenge** Zaïre
56C3 **Liberal** USA
18C2 **Liberec** Czechoslovakia
48A4 **Liberia** *Republic* Africa
61E3 **Liberty** Missouri, USA
65E2 **Liberty** New York, USA
68B2 **Liberty** Pennsylvania, USA
63D2 **Liberty** Texas, USA
45B3 **Libni, Gebel** *Mt* Egypt
14B3 **Libourne** France
48C4 **Libreville** Equatorial Guinea
49D2 **Libya** *Republic* Africa
49E2 **Libyan Desert** Egypt/ Libya/Sudan
49E1 **Libyan Plat** Egypt
16C3 **Licata** Sicily, Italy
7D3 **Lichfield** England
51D5 **Lichinga** Mozambique
47D2 **Lichtenburg** South Africa
64C3 **Licking** *R* USA
66B2 **Lick Observatory** USA
16C2 **Licosa, Punta** *Pt* Italy
66D2 **Lida** USA
20D5 **Lida** Belorussia
12G7 **Lidköping** Sweden
16C2 **Lido di Ostia** Italy
16B1 **Liechtenstein** *Principality* Europe
18B2 **Liège** Belgium
19E1 **Lielupe** *R* Latvia
50C3 **Lienart** Zaïre
18C3 **Lienz** Austria
12J7 **Liepāja** Latvia
13C2 **Lier** Belgium
65E1 **Lièvre** *R* Canada
18C3 **Liezen** Austria
9C3 **Liffey** *R* Irish Republic
9C2 **Lifford** Irish Republic
33F3 **Lifu** *I* Nouvelle Calédonie
34C1 **Lightning Ridge** Australia
13C3 **Ligny-en-Barrois** France
51D5 **Ligonha** *R* Mozambique
16B2 **Ligurian S** Italy
33E1 **Lihir Group** *Is* Papua New Guinea
66E5 **Lihue** Hawaiian Islands
51C5 **Likasi** Zaïre
14C1 **Lille** France
12G6 **Lillehammer** Norway
13B2 **Lillers** France
12G7 **Lillestrøm** Norway
51D5 **Lilongwe** Malawi
17D2 **Lim** *R* Montenegro/ Serbia, Yugoslavia
72C6 **Lima** Peru
57E2 **Lima** USA
15A1 **Lima** *R* Portugal
58D2 **Lima Res** USA
40B3 **Limassol** Cyprus
9C2 **Limavady** Northern Ireland
48C4 **Limbe** Cameroon
51D5 **Limbe** Malawi
18B2 **Limburg** Germany
73J8 **Limeira** Brazil
10B3 **Limerick** Irish Republic
18B1 **Limfjorden** *L* Denmark
32C2 **Limmen Bight** *B* Australia
17F3 **Límnos** *I* Greece
73L5 **Limoeiro** Brazil
14C2 **Limoges** France
70D4 **Limón** Costa Rica
56C3 **Limon** USA
14C2 **Limousin** *Region* France
14C2 **Limousin, Plateaux de** France
47E1 **Limpopo** *R* Mozambique
74B5 **Linares** Chile
56D4 **Linares** Mexico
15B2 **Linares** Spain
26C4 **Lincang** China
74D4 **Lincoln** Argentina
7D3 **Lincoln** England
64B2 **Lincoln** Illinois, USA
65F1 **Lincoln** Maine, USA
56D2 **Lincoln** Nebraska, USA
65E2 **Lincoln** New Hampshire, USA
35B2 **Lincoln** New Zealand
7D3 **Lincoln** *County* England
58B2 **Lincoln City** USA
64C2 **Lincoln Park** USA
76A2 **Lincoln Sea** Greenland
16B2 **L'Incudine** *Mt* Corsica, France
18B3 **Lindau** Germany
73G2 **Linden** Guyana
12F7 **Lindesnes** *C* Norway
51D4 **Lindi** Tanzania
50C3 **Lindi** *R* Zaïre
47D2 **Lindley** South Africa
17F3 **Lindos** Greece
66C2 **Lindsay** California, USA
65D2 **Lindsay** Canada
60B1 **Lindsay** Montana, USA
37M4 **Line Is** Pacific Ocean
31C2 **Linfen** China
30D2 **Lingao** China
27F5 **Lingayen** Philippines
18B2 **Lingen** Germany
27D7 **Lingga** *I* Indonesia
60C2 **Lingle** USA
31C4 **Lingling** China
31B5 **Lingshan** China
31C2 **Lingshi** China
48A3 **Linguère** Senegal
31E4 **Linhai** Zhejiang, China
73L7 **Linhares** Brazil
31B1 **Linhe** China
28B2 **Linjiang** China
28A2 **Linjiatai** China
12H7 **Linköping** Sweden
8C3 **Linnhe, Loch** *Inlet* Scotland
31D2 **Linqing** China
75C3 **Lins** Brazil
31A2 **Lintao** China
60C1 **Linton** USA
26E2 **Linxi** China
31A2 **Linxia** China
18C3 **Linz** Austria
14C3 **Lion, Golfe du** *G* France
16C3 **Lipari** *I* Italy
16C3 **Lipari, Isole** *Is* Italy
21F5 **Lipetsk** Russian Federation
17E1 **Lipova** Romania
18B2 **Lippe** *R* Germany
13E2 **Lippstadt** Germany
50D3 **Lira** Uganda
50B4 **Liranga** Congo
50C3 **Lisala** Zaïre
Lisboa = Lisbon
15A2 **Lisbon** Portugal
61D1 **Lisbon** USA
9C2 **Lisburn** Northern Ireland
31D4 **Lishui** China
31C4 **Li Shui** *R* China
21F6 **Lisichansk** Ukraine
14C2 **Lisieux** France
21F5 **Liski** Russian Federation
13B3 **L'Isle-Adam** France
33E3 **Lismore** Australia
9C3 **Lismore** Irish Republic
31B5 **Litang** China
45C2 **Lītāni** *R* Lebanon
73H3 **Litani** *R* Surinam
64B3 **Litchfield** Illinois, USA
61E1 **Litchfield** Minnesota, USA
32E4 **Lithgow** Australia
20C4 **Lithuania** *Republic* Europe
68B2 **Lititz** USA
26G2 **Litovko** Russian Federation
63C2 **Little** *R* USA
57F4 **Little Abaco** *I* The Bahamas
44E3 **Little Andaman** *I* Andaman Islands
67C3 **Little Bahama Bank** Bahamas
35C1 **Little Barrier I** New Zealand
58D1 **Little Belt Mts** USA
45B3 **Little Bitter L** Egypt
70D3 **Little Cayman** *I* Cayman Is, Caribbean Sea
68C3 **Little Egg Harbor** *B* USA
61E1 **Little Falls** Minnesota, USA
68C1 **Little Falls** New York, USA
62B2 **Littlefield** USA
61E1 **Littlefork** USA
61E1 **Little Fork** *R* USA
8E2 **Little Halibut Bank** *Sand-bank* Scotland
7D4 **Littlehampton** England
69C2 **Little Inagua** *I* The Bahamas
47C3 **Little Karoo** *Mts* South Africa
66D3 **Little Lake** USA
60C1 **Little Missouri** *R* USA
30A4 **Little Nicobar** *I* Nicobar Is, India
57D3 **Little Rock** USA
66D3 **Littlerock** USA
68B3 **Littlestown** USA
60B3 **Littleton** Colorado, USA
65E2 **Littleton** New Hampshire, USA
28B2 **Liuhe** China
31B2 **Liupan Shan** *Upland* China
31B5 **Liuzhou** China
17E3 **Livanátais** Greece
19F1 **Līvāni** Latvia
67B2 **Live Oak** USA
59B3 **Livermore** USA
62B2 **Livermore,Mt** USA
55M5 **Liverpool** Canada
7C3 **Liverpool** England
54E2 **Liverpool B** Canada
7C3 **Liverpool B** England
55L2 **Liverpool,C** Canada
34D2 **Liverpool Range** *Mts* Australia
56B2 **Livingston** Montana, USA
67A1 **Livingston** Tennessee, USA
63D2 **Livingston** Texas, USA
8D4 **Livingstone** Scotland
51C5 **Livingstone** Zambia
63C2 **Livingston,L** USA
16D2 **Livno** Bosnia & Herzegovina, Yugoslavia
21F5 **Livny** Russian Federation
64C2 **Livonia** USA
16C2 **Livorno** Italy
75D1 **Livramento do Brumado** Brazil
51D4 **Liwale** Tanzania
7B5 **Lizard Pt** England
16C1 **Ljubljana** Slovenia
12G6 **Ljungan** *R* Sweden
12G7 **Ljungby** Sweden
12H6 **Ljusdal** Sweden
20B3 **Ljusnan** *R* Sweden
7C4 **Llandeilo** Wales
7C4 **Llandovery** Wales
7C3 **Llandrindod Wells** Wales
7C3 **Llandudno** Wales
7D4 **Llanelli** Wales
7C3 **Llangollen** Wales
62C2 **Llano** USA
62C2 **Llano** *R* USA
56C3 **Llano Estacado** *Plat* USA
72D2 **Llanos** *Region* Colombia/ Venezuela
72F7 **Llanos de Chiquitos** *Region* Bolivia
7C4 **Llantrisant** Wales
7C3 **Llanwrst** Wales
Lleida = Lérida
15A2 **Llerena** Spain
7B3 **Lleyn** *Pen* Wales
54F4 **Lloyd George,Mt** Canada
54H4 **Lloydminster** Canada
74C2 **Llullaillaco** *Mt* Argentina/ Chile
74C2 **Loa** *R* Chile
50B4 **Loange** *R* Zaïre
47D2 **Lobatse** Botswana
50B3 **Lobaye** *R* Central African Republic
51B5 **Lobito** Angola
8B3 **Lochboisdale** Scotland
8C3 **Lochearnhead** Scotland
14C2 **Loches** France
8C3 **Lochgoilhead** Scotland
8C2 **Lochinver** Scotland
8D4 **Lochmaben** Scotland
8B3 **Lochmaddy** Scotland
8D3 **Lochnagar** *Mt* Scotland
8C3 **Loch Ness** Scotland
58C1 **Lochsa** *R* USA
8C3 **Lochy, Loch** *L* Scotland
8D4 **Lockerbie** Scotland
65D2 **Lock Haven** USA
65D2 **Lockport** USA
30D3 **Loc Ninh** Vietnam
16D3 **Locri** Italy
45C3 **Lod** Israel
34B3 **Loddon** *R* Australia
20E3 **Lodeynoye Pole** Russian Federation
58E1 **Lodge Grass** USA
42C3 **Lodhran** Pakistan
16B1 **Lodi** Italy
59B3 **Lodi** USA
50C4 **Lodja** Zaïre
50D3 **Lodwar** Kenya
19D2 **Łódź** Poland
47B3 **Loeriesfontein** South Africa
12G5 **Lofoten** *Is* Norway
6D2 **Loftus** England
62B1 **Logan** New Mexico, USA
56B2 **Logan** Utah, USA
54D3 **Logan,Mt** Canada
64B2 **Logansport** Indiana, USA
15D3 **Logansport** Louisiana, USA
68B2 **Loganton** USA
50B2 **Logone** *R* Cameroon/ Chad
15B1 **Logroño** Spain
43E4 **Lohārdaga** India
12J6 **Lohja** Finland
30B2 **Loikaw** Burma
12J6 **Loimaa** Finland
13B3 **Loing** *R* France
14C2 **Loir** *R* France
14C2 **Loire** *R* France
13B4 **Loiret** *Department* France
72C4 **Loja** Ecuador
15B2 **Loja** Spain
12K5 **Lokan Tekojärvi** *Res* Finland
13B2 **Lokeren** Belgium
27F7 **Lokialaki, G** *Mt* Indonesia
50D3 **Lokitaung** Kenya
19F1 **Loknya** Russian Federation
50C4 **Lokolo** *R* Zaïre
50C4 **Lokoro** *R* Zaïre
55M3 **Loks Land** *I* Canada
18C2 **Lolland** *I* Denmark
58D1 **Lolo P** USA
17E2 **Lom** Bulgaria
51C4 **Lomami** *R* Zaïre
48A4 **Loma Mts** Guinea/Sierra Leone
27F7 **Lomblen** *I* Indonesia
27E7 **Lombok** *I* Indonesia
48C4 **Lomé** Togo
50C4 **Lomela** Zaïre
50C4 **Lomela** *R* Zaïre
8C3 **Lomond, Loch** *L* Scotland
20D4 **Lomonosov** Russian Federation
59B4 **Lompoc** USA
19E2 **Łomza** Poland
44A2 **Lonāvale** India
74B5 **Loncoche** Chile
55K5 **London** Canada
7D4 **London** England
64C3 **London** USA
9C2 **Londonderry** Northern Ireland
9C2 **Londonderry** *County* Northern Ireland
74B9 **Londonderry** *I* Chile
32B2 **Londonderry,C** Australia
74C3 **Londres** Argentina
74F2 **Londrina** Brazil
66D1 **Lone Mt** USA
66C2 **Lone Pine** USA
27H7 **Long** *I* Papua New Guinea
57F4 **Long** *I* The Bahamas
25T2 **Longa, Proliv** *Str* Russian Federation
69H2 **Long B** Jamaica

Long B Mafraq

67C2 **Long B** USA
56B3 **Long Beach** California, USA
65E2 **Long Beach** New York, USA
65E2 **Long Branch** USA
31D5 **Longchuan** China
58C2 **Long Creek** USA
7D3 **Long Eaton** England
34C4 **Longford** Australia
9C3 **Longford** Irish Republic
9C3 **Longford** *County* Irish Republic
8E3 **Long Forties** *Region* N Sea
28B2 **Longgang Shan** *Mts* China
31D1 **Longhua** China
57F4 **Long I** Bahamas
55L4 **Long I** Canada
32D1 **Long I** Papua New Guinea
57F2 **Long I** USA
68D2 **Long Island Sd** USA
28B2 **Longjing** China
64B1 **Long L** Canada
60C1 **Long L** USA
55K4 **Longlac** Canada
31B5 **Longlin** China
8C3 **Long, Loch** *Inlet* Scotland
7E3 **Long Melford** England
56C2 **Longmont** USA
13C3 **Longny** France
61E1 **Long Prairie** USA
32D3 **Longreach** Australia
31A2 **Longshou Shan** *Upland* China
60B2 **Longs Peak** *Mt* USA
7E3 **Long Sutton** England
6C2 **Longtown** England
65E1 **Longueuil** Canada
13C3 **Longuyon** France
57D3 **Longview** Texas, USA
56A2 **Longview** Washington, USA
14D2 **Longwy** France
31A3 **Longxi** China
30D3 **Long Xuyen** Vietnam
31D4 **Longyan** China
31B5 **Longzhou** China
13D1 **Löningen** Germany
74B5 **Lonquimay** Chile
14D2 **Lons-le-Saunier** France
7B4 **Looe** England
57F3 **Lookout,C** USA
50D4 **Loolmalasin** *Mt* Tanzania
25R4 **Lopatka, Mys** *C* Russian Federation
30C3 **Lop Buri** Thailand
26C2 **Lop Nur** *L* China
15A2 **Lora del Rio** Spain
57E2 **Lorain** USA
42B2 **Loralai** Pakistan
15B2 **Lorca** Spain
41F3 **Lordegān** Iran
33E4 **Lord Howe** *I* Australia
37K6 **Lord Howe Rise** Pacific Ocean
55J3 **Lord Mayor B** Canada
56C3 **Lordsburg** USA
75C3 **Lorena** Brazil
14B2 **Lorient** France
34B3 **Lorne** Australia
18B3 **Lörrach** Germany
13C3 **Lorraine** *Region* France
56C3 **Los Alamos** USA
66B3 **Los Alamos** USA
74B5 **Los Angeles** Chile
66B3 **Los Angeles** USA
66C3 **Los Angeles Aqueduct** USA
59B3 **Los Banos** USA
59B3 **Los Gatos** USA
16C2 **Lošinj** *I* Croatia
74B5 **Los Lagos** Chile
62A2 **Los Lunas** USA
70B2 **Los Mochis** Mexico
66B3 **Los Olivos** USA
72E1 **Los Roques, Islas** Venezuela
8D3 **Lossie** *R* Scotland
8D3 **Lossiemouth** Scotland
69E4 **Los Testigos** *Is* Venezuela
66C3 **Lost Hills** USA
58D1 **Lost Trail P** USA
74B4 **Los Vilos** Chile
14C3 **Lot** *R* France
8D4 **Lothian** *Region* Scotland
50D3 **Lotikipi Plain** Kenya/Sudan
50C4 **Loto** Zaïre
47D1 **Lotsane** *R* Botswana
12K5 **Lotta** *R* Finland/Russian Federation
14B2 **Loudéac** France
48A3 **Louga** Senegal
7D3 **Loughborough** England
54H2 **Lougheed I** Canada
64C3 **Louisa** USA
27E6 **Louisa Reef** S China Sea
33E2 **Louisiade Arch** Papua New Guinea
57D3 **Louisiana** *State* USA
47D1 **Louis Trichardt** South Africa
67B2 **Louisville** Georgia, USA
57E3 **Louisville** Kentucky, USA
63E2 **Louisville** Mississippi, USA
20E2 **Loukhi** Russian Federation
61D2 **Loup** *R* USA
14B3 **Lourdes** France
Lourenço Marques = Maputo
34C2 **Louth** Australia
7D3 **Louth** England
9C3 **Louth** *County* Irish Republic
Louvain = Leuven
14C2 **Louviers** France
20E4 **Lovat** *R* Russian Federation
17E2 **Lovech** Bulgaria
60B2 **Loveland** USA
60B3 **Loveland P** USA
58E2 **Lovell** USA
59C2 **Lovelock** USA
16C1 **Lóvere** Italy
62B2 **Lovington** USA
20F2 **Lovozero** Russian Federation
55K3 **Low,C** Canada
57F2 **Lowell** Massachusetts, USA
58B2 **Lowell** Oregon, USA
68E1 **Lowell** USA
58C1 **Lower Arrow L** Canada
35B2 **Lower Hutt** New Zealand
66A1 **Lower Lake** USA
61D1 **Lower Red L** USA
7E3 **Lowestoft** England
19D2 **Łowicz** Poland
34B2 **Loxton** Australia
47C3 **Loxton** South Africa
68B2 **Loyalsock Creek** *R* USA
33F3 **Loyalty Is** New Caledonia
17D2 **Loznica** Serbia, Yugoslavia
24H3 **Lozva** *R* Russian Federation
51C5 **Luacano** Angola
51C4 **Luachimo** Angola
50C4 **Lualaba** *R* Zaïre
51C5 **Luampa** Zambia
51C5 **Luân** Angola
31D3 **Lu'an** China
51B4 **Luanda** Angola
51B5 **Luando** *R* Angola
51C5 **Luanginga** *R* Angola
30C1 **Luang Namtha** Laos
30C2 **Luang Prabang** Laos
51B4 **Luangue** *R* Angola
51D5 **Luangwa** *R* Zambia
31D1 **Luan He** *R* China
31D1 **Luanping** China
51C5 **Luanshya** Zambia
51C5 **Luapula** *R* Zaïre
15A1 **Luarca** Spain
51B4 **Lubalo** Angola
19F2 **L'uban** Belorussia
51B5 **Lubango** Angola
56C3 **Lubbock** USA
18C2 **Lübeck** Germany
50C4 **Lubefu** Zaïre
50C4 **Lubefu** *R* Zaïre
50C3 **Lubero** Zaïre
51C4 **Lubilash** *R* Zaïre
19E2 **Lublin** Poland
21E5 **Lubny** Ukraine
51C4 **Lubudi** Zaïre
51C4 **Lubudi** *R* Zaïre
27D7 **Lubuklinggau** Indonesia
51C5 **Lubumbashi** Zaïre
50C4 **Lubutu** Zaïre
75A1 **Lucas** Brazil
67C3 **Lucaya** Bahamas
16C2 **Lucca** Italy
8C4 **Luce B** Scotland
63E2 **Lucedale** USA
19D3 **Lucenec** Czechoslovakia
Lucerne = Luzern
62A2 **Lucero** Mexico
31C5 **Luchuan** China
66B2 **Lucia** USA
18C2 **Luckenwalde** Germany
47C2 **Luckhoff** South Africa
43E3 **Lucknow** India
51C5 **Lucusse** Angola
13D2 **Lüdenscheid** Germany
47B2 **Lüderitz** Namibia
42D2 **Ludhiana** India
64B2 **Ludington** USA
59C4 **Ludlow** California, USA
7C3 **Ludlow** England
68D1 **Ludlow** Vermont, USA
17F2 **Ludogorie** *Upland* Bulgaria
67B2 **Ludowici** USA
17E1 **Luduş** Romania
12H6 **Ludvika** Sweden
18B3 **Ludwigsburg** Germany
18B3 **Ludwigshafen** Germany
18C2 **Ludwigslust** Germany
50C4 **Luebo** Zaïre
50C4 **Luema** *R* Zaïre
51C4 **Luembe** *R* Angola
51B5 **Luena** Angola
51C5 **Luene** *R* Angola
31B3 **Lüeyang** China
31D5 **Lufeng** China
57D3 **Lufkin** USA
20D4 **Luga** Russian Federation
20D4 **Luga** *R* Russian Federation
16B1 **Lugano** Switzerland
51D5 **Lugela** Mozambique
51D5 **Lugenda** *R* Mozambique
9C3 **Lugnaquillia,Mt** Irish Republic
15A1 **Lugo** Spain
17E1 **Lugoj** Romania
45D2 **Luhfi, Wadi** Jordan
31A3 **Luhuo** China
51B4 **Lui** *R* Angola
51C5 **Luiana** Angola
51C5 **Luiana** *R* Angola
Luichow Peninsula = Leizhou Bandao
20D2 **Luiro** *R* Finland
51C5 **Luishia** Zaïre
26C4 **Luixi** China
51C4 **Luiza** Zaïre
31D3 **Lujiang** China
50B4 **Lukenie** *R* Zaïre
59D4 **Lukeville** USA
50B4 **Lukolela** Zaïre
19E2 **Łuków** Poland
50C4 **Lukuga** *R* Zaïre
51C5 **Lukulu** Zambia
20C2 **Lule** *R* Sweden
12J5 **Luleå** Sweden
17F2 **Lüleburgaz** Turkey
31C2 **Lüliang Shan** *Mts* China
63C3 **Luling** USA
50C3 **Lulonga** *R* Zaïre
Luluabourg = Kananga
51C5 **Lumbala Kaquengue** Angola
57F3 **Lumberton** USA
20G2 **Lumbovka** Russian Federation
43G3 **Lumding** India
51C5 **Lumeje** Angola
35A3 **Lumsden** New Zealand
12G7 **Lund** Sweden
51D5 **Lundazi** Zambia
51D6 **Lundi** *R* Zimbabwe
7B4 **Lundy** *I* England
18C2 **Lüneburg** Germany
13D3 **Lunéville** France
51C5 **Lunga** *R* Zambia
43G4 **Lunglei** India
51B5 **Lungue Bungo** *R* Angola
19F2 **Luninec** Belorussia
66C1 **Luning** USA
50B4 **Luobomo** Congo
31B5 **Luocheng** China
31C5 **Luoding** China
31C3 **Luohe** China
31C3 **Luo He** *R* Henan, China
31B2 **Luo He** *R* Shaanxi, China
31C4 **Luoxiao Shan** *Hills* China
31C3 **Luoyang** China
50B4 **Luozi** Zaïre
51C5 **Lupane** Zimbabwe
51D5 **Lupilichi** Mozambique
Lu Qu *R* **= Tao He**
74E3 **Luque** Paraguay
13D4 **Lure** France
9C2 **Lurgan** Northern Ireland
51D5 **Lurio** *R* Mozambique
41E3 **Luristan** *Region* Iran
51C5 **Lusaka** Zambia
50C4 **Lusambo** Zaïre
17D2 **Lushnjë** Albania
50D4 **Lushoto** Tanzania
26C4 **Lushui** China
31E2 **Lüshun** China
60C2 **Lusk** USA
7D4 **Luton** England
21D5 **Lutsk** Ukraine
50E3 **Luuq** Somalia
61D2 **Luverne** USA
51C4 **Luvua** *R* Zaïre
51D4 **Luwegu** *R* Tanzania
51D5 **Luwingu** Zambia
27F7 **Luwuk** Indonesia
14D2 **Luxembourg** Luxembourg
13D3 **Luxembourg** *Grand Duchy* NW Europe
13D4 **Luxeuil-les-Bains** France
31A5 **Luxi** China
49F2 **Luxor** Egypt
20H3 **Luza** Russian Federation
20H3 **Luza** *R* Russian Federation
16B1 **Luzern** Switzerland
68D1 **Luzerne** USA
31B5 **Luzhai** China
31B4 **Luzhi** China
31B4 **Luzhou** China
75C2 **Luziânia** Brazil
27F5 **Luzon** *I* Philippines
27F5 **Luzon Str** Philippines
19E3 **L'vov** Ukraine
8D2 **Lybster** Scotland
12H6 **Lycksele** Sweden
7E4 **Lydd** England
51C6 **Lydenburg** South Africa
56B3 **Lyell,Mt** USA
68B2 **Lykens** USA
58D2 **Lyman** USA
7C4 **Lyme B** England
7C4 **Lyme Regis** England
7D4 **Lymington** England
57F3 **Lynchburg** USA
34A2 **Lyndhurst** Australia
65E2 **Lynn** USA
67A2 **Lynn Haven** USA
54H4 **Lynn Lake** Canada
7C4 **Lynton** England
54H3 **Lynx L** Canada
14C2 **Lyon** France
67B2 **Lyons** Georgia, USA
68B1 **Lyons** New York, USA
32A3 **Lyons** *R* Australia
20K4 **Lys'va** Russian Federation
6C3 **Lytham St Anne's** England
35B2 **Lyttelton** New Zealand
66A1 **Lytton** USA
19F2 **Lyubeshov** Ukraine
20F4 **Lyublino** Russian Federation

M

30C1 **Ma** *R* Laos/Vietnam
45C2 **Ma'agan** Jordan
45C2 **Ma'alot Tarshīhā** Israel
40C3 **Ma'ān** Jordan
31D3 **Ma'anshan** China
45D1 **Ma'arrat an Nu'mān** Syria
13C2 **Maas** *R* Netherlands
13C2 **Maaseik** Belgium
18B2 **Maastricht** Belgium
47E1 **Mabalane** Mozambique
73G2 **Mabaruma** Guyana
7E3 **Mablethorpe** England
51D6 **Mabote** Mozambique
19E2 **Mabrita** Belorussia
75D3 **Macaé** Brazil
56D3 **McAlester** USA
56D4 **McAllen** USA
51D5 **Macaloge** Mozambique
73H3 **Macapá** Brazil
75D2 **Macarani** Brazil
72C4 **Macas** Ecuador
73L5 **Macaú** Brazil
31C5 **Macau** *Dependency* SE Asia
75D1 **Macaúbas** Brazil
50C3 **M'Bari** *R* Central African Republic
58C2 **McCall** USA
62B2 **McCamey** USA
58D2 **McCammon** USA
7C3 **Macclesfield** England
55K1 **McClintock B** Canada
54H2 **McClintock Chan** Canada
68B2 **McClure** USA
66B2 **McClure,L** USA
54G2 **McClure Str** Canada
63D2 **McComb** USA
60C2 **McConaughy,L** USA
68B3 **McConnellsburg** USA
56C2 **McCook** USA
55L2 **Macculloch,C** Canada
54F4 **McDame** Canada
58C2 **McDermitt** USA
58D1 **McDonald Peak** *Mt* USA
32C3 **Macdonnell Ranges** *Mts* Australia
8D3 **MacDuff** Scotland
15A1 **Macedo de Cavaleiros** Portugal
17E2 **Macedonia** *Republic* Yugoslavia
73L5 **Maceió** Brazil
48B4 **Macenta** Guinea
16C2 **Macerata** Italy
63D2 **McGehee** USA
59D3 **McGill** USA
54C3 **McGrath** USA
58D1 **McGuire,Mt** USA
75C3 **Machado** Brazil
51D6 **Machaíla** Mozambique
50D4 **Machakos** Kenya
72C4 **Machala** Ecuador
51D6 **Machaze** Mozambique
44B2 **Mācherla** India
45C2 **Machgharab** Lebanon
65F2 **Machias** USA
44C2 **Machilīpatnam** India
72D1 **Machiques** Venezuela
72D6 **Machu-Picchu** *Hist Site* Peru
7C3 **Machynlleth** Wales
51D6 **Macia** Mozambique
Macias Nguema *I* **= Bioko**
60C1 **McIntosh** USA
34C1 **MacIntyre** *R* Australia
60B3 **Mack** USA
32D3 **Mackay** Australia
58D2 **Mackay** USA
32B3 **Mackay,L** Australia
33H1 **McKean** *I* Phoenix Islands
65D2 **McKeesport** USA
54F3 **Mackenzie** *R* Canada
54E3 **Mackenzie B** Canada
54G2 **Mackenzie King I** Canada
54E3 **Mackenzie Mts** Canada
64C1 **Mackinac,Str of** USA
64C1 **Mackinaw City** USA
54C3 **McKinley, Mt** USA
63C2 **McKinney** USA
55L2 **Mackinson Inlet** *B* Canada
66C3 **McKittrick** USA
34D2 **Macksville** Australia
60C1 **McLaughlin** USA
34D1 **Maclean** Australia
47D3 **Maclear** South Africa
54G4 **McLennan** Canada
54G3 **McLeod B** Canada
32A3 **McLeod,L** Australia
58B2 **McLoughlin,Mt** USA
54E3 **Macmillan** *R* Canada
62B2 **McMillan,L** USA
58B1 **McMinnville** Oregon, USA
67A1 **McMinnville** Tennessee, USA
76F7 **McMurdo** *Base* Antarctica
59E4 **McNary** USA
64A2 **Macomb** USA
16B2 **Macomer** Sardinia, Italy
51D5 **Macomia** Mozambique
14C2 **Mâcon** France
57E3 **Macon** Georgia, USA
61E3 **Macon** Missouri, USA
51C5 **Macondo** Angola
63C1 **McPherson** USA
34C2 **Macquarie** *R* Australia
34C4 **Macquarie Harbour** *B* Australia
36J7 **Macquarie Is** Australia
34D2 **Macquarie,L** Australia
67B2 **McRae** USA
76F11 **Mac Robertson Land** *Region* Antarctica
54G3 **McTavish Arm** *B* Canada
54F3 **McVicar Arm** *B* Canada
45C3 **Mādabā** Jordan
50C2 **Madadi** *Well* Chad
46J9 **Madagascar** *I* Indian Ocean
36D6 **Madagascar Basin** Indian Ocean
50B1 **Madama** Niger
32D1 **Madang** Papua New Guinea
48C3 **Madaoua** Niger
43G4 **Madaripur** Bangladesh
41F2 **Madau** Turkmenistan
65D1 **Madawaska** *R* Canada
48A1 **Madeira** *I* Atlantic Ocean
72F5 **Madeira** *R* Brazil
19F2 **M'adel** Belorussia
55M5 **Madeleine Îles de la** Canada
61E2 **Madelia** USA
70B2 **Madera** Mexico
59B3 **Madera** USA
44A2 **Madgaon** India
43F3 **Madhubani** India
43E4 **Madhya Pradesh** *State* India
44B3 **Madikeri** India
50B4 **Madimba** Zaïre
50B4 **Madingo Kayes** Congo
50B4 **Madingou** Congo
57E3 **Madison** Indiana, USA
61D1 **Madison** Minnesota, USA
61D2 **Madison** Nebraska, USA
61D2 **Madison** S Dakota, USA
57E2 **Madison** Wisconsin, USA
58D1 **Madison** *R* USA
64B3 **Madisonville** Kentucky, USA
63C2 **Madisonville** Texas, USA
50D3 **Mado Gashi** Kenya
44C3 **Madras** India
58B2 **Madras** USA
74A8 **Madre de Dios** *I* Chile
72E6 **Madre de Dios** *R* Bolivia
70C2 **Madre, Laguna** Mexico
63C3 **Madre, Laguna** USA
15B1 **Madrid** Spain
15B2 **Madridejos** Spain
27E7 **Madura** *I* Indonesia
44B4 **Madurai** India
29C3 **Maebashi** Japan
30B3 **Mae Khlong** *R* Thailand
30B4 **Mae Luang** *R* Thailand
30C2 **Mae Nam Mun** *R* Thailand
30B2 **Mae Nam Ping** *R* Thailand
28A3 **Maengsan** N Korea
51E5 **Maevatanana** Madagascar
33F2 **Maewo** *I* Vanuatu
47D2 **Mafeteng** Lesotho
34C3 **Maffra** Australia
51D4 **Mafia I** Tanzania
47D2 **Mafikeng** South Africa
74G3 **Mafra** Brazil
40C3 **Mafraq** Jordan

Merriman **Monclova**

60C2 **Merriman** USA
67B3 **Merritt Island** USA
34D2 **Merriwa** Australia
50E3 **Mersa Fatma** Ethiopia
7E4 **Mersea** *I* England
15B2 **Mers el Kebir** Algeria
7C3 **Mersey** *R* England
7C3 **Merseyside** *Metropolitan County* England
21E8 **Mersin** Turkey
30C5 **Mersing** Malaysia
42C3 **Merta** India
7C4 **Merthyr Tydfil** Wales
15A2 **Mertola** Portugal
13B3 **Méru** France
50D4 **Meru** *Mt* Tanzania
21F7 **Merzifon** Turkey
13D3 **Merzig** Germany
56B3 **Mesa** USA
62A1 **Mesa Verde Nat Pk** USA
13E2 **Meschede** Germany
40D1 **Mescit Dağ** *Mt* Turkey
50C3 **Meshra'er Req** Sudan
17E3 **Mesolóngion** Greece
59D3 **Mesquite** Nevada, USA
63C2 **Mesquite** Texas, USA
51D5 **Messalo** *R* Mozambique
47D1 **Messina** South Africa
16D3 **Messina** Sicily, Italy
16D3 **Messina, Stretto de** *Str* Italy/Sicily
17E3 **Messíni** Greece
17E3 **Messiniakós Kólpos** *G* Greece
Mesta *R* = **Néstos**
17E2 **Mesta** *R* Bulgaria
16C1 **Mestre** Italy
72D3 **Meta** *R* Colombia/Venezuela
20E4 **Meta** *R* Russian Federation
55M3 **Meta Incognita Pen** Canada
63D3 **Metairie** USA
58C1 **Metaline Falls** USA
74D3 **Metán** Argentina
51D5 **Metangula** Mozambique
16D2 **Metaponto** Italy
8D3 **Methil** Scotland
68E1 **Methuen** USA
35B2 **Methven** New Zealand
54E4 **Metlakatla** USA
64B3 **Metropolis** USA
44B3 **Mettūr** India
14D2 **Metz** France
27C6 **Meulaboh** Indonesia
13D3 **Meurthe** *R* France
13D3 **Meurthe-et-Moselle** *Department* France
13C3 **Meuse** *Department* France
13C2 **Meuse** *R* Belgium
14D2 **Meuse** *R* France
7D3 **Mexborough** England
63C2 **Mexia** USA
70A1 **Mexicali** Mexico
59E3 **Mexican Hat** USA
70C3 **México** Mexico
61E3 **Mexico** USA
70B2 **Mexico** *Federal Republic* Central America
70C2 **Mexico,G of** Central America
24H6 **Meymaneh** Afghanistan
45C3 **Mezada** *Hist Site* Israel
20G2 **Mezen'** Russian Federation
20H3 **Mezen'** *R* Russian Federation
14C3 **Mézenc, Mount** France
19G1 **Mezha** *R* Russian Federation
20J1 **Mezhdusharskiy, Ostrov** *I* Russian Federation
42D4 **Mhow** India
59D4 **Miami** Arizona, USA
57E4 **Miami** Florida, USA
63D1 **Miami** Oklahoma, USA
57E4 **Miami Beach** USA
21H8 **Miandowāb** Iran
51E5 **Miandrivazo** Madagascar
21H8 **Mīāneh** Iran
42C2 **Mianwali** Pakistan
31A3 **Mianyang** China
31C3 **Mianyang** China
31A3 **Mianzhu** China
31E2 **Miaodao Qundao** *Arch* China
31B4 **Miao Ling** *Upland* China
20L5 **Miass** Russian Federation
19E3 **Michalovce** Czechoslovakia
58D1 **Michel** Canada
69D3 **Miches** Dominican Republic
57E2 **Michigan** *State* USA
64B2 **Michigan City** USA
57E2 **Michigan,L** USA
64C1 **Michipicoten** Canada
55K5 **Michipicoten I** Canada
17F2 **Michurin** Bulgaria
21G5 **Michurinsk** Russian Federation
27H6 **Micronesia** *Is* Pacific Ocean
36J4 **Micronesia** *Region* Pacific Ocean
52F4 **Mid Atlantic Ridge** Atlantic Ocean
47C3 **Middelburg** Cape Province, South Africa
13B2 **Middelburg** Netherlands
47D2 **Middelburg** Transvaal, South Africa
58B2 **Middle Alkali L** USA
37O4 **Middle America Trench** Pacific Ocean
44E3 **Middle Andaman** *I* Indian Ocean
68E2 **Middleboro** USA
68B2 **Middleburg** Pennsylvania, USA
68B3 **Middleburg** Virginia, USA
68C1 **Middleburgh** USA
65E2 **Middlebury** USA
57E3 **Middlesboro** USA
6D2 **Middlesbrough** England
68D2 **Middletown** Connecticut, USA
68C3 **Middletown** Delaware, USA
65E2 **Middletown** New York, USA
64C3 **Middletown** Ohio, USA
68B2 **Middletown** Pennsylvania, USA
68C1 **Middleville** USA
7C3 **Middlewich** England
48B1 **Midelt** Morocco
7C4 **Mid Glamorgan** *County* Wales
50E2 **Mīdī** Yemen
36E5 **Mid Indian Basin** Indian Ocean
36E5 **Mid Indian Ridge** Indian Ocean
55L5 **Midland** Canada
64C2 **Midland** Michigan, USA
56C3 **Midland** Texas, USA
9B4 **Midleton** Irish Republic
51E6 **Midongy Atsimo** Madagascar
37K4 **Mid Pacific Mts** Pacific Ocean
58C2 **Midvale** USA
37L3 **Midway Is** Pacific Ocean
60B2 **Midwest** USA
63C1 **Midwest City** USA
40D2 **Midyat** Turkey
17E2 **Midžor** *Mt* Serbia, Yugoslavia
19E2 **Mielec** Poland
17F1 **Miercurea-Ciuc** Romania
15A1 **Mieres** Spain
68B2 **Mifflintown** USA
13B4 **Migennes** France
28B4 **Mihara** Japan
17E2 **Mikhaylovgrad** Bulgaria
21G5 **Mikhaylovka** Russian Federation
28C2 **Mikhaylovka** Russian Federation
24J4 **Mikhaylovskiy** Russian Federation
45C4 **Mikhrot Timna** Israel
12K6 **Mikkeli** Finland
17F3 **Mikonos** *I* Greece
18D3 **Mikulov** Czechoslovakia
51D4 **Mikumi** Tanzania
20J3 **Mikun** Russian Federation
29D3 **Mikuni-sammyaku** *Mts* Japan
29C4 **Mikura-jima** *I* Japan
61E1 **Milaca** USA
72C4 **Milagro** Ecuador
16B1 **Milan** Italy
63E1 **Milan** USA
51D5 **Milange** Mozambique
Milano = Milan
21D8 **Milas** Turkey
61D1 **Milbank** USA
32D4 **Mildura** Australia
31A5 **Mile** China
41D3 **Mileh Tharthār** *L* Iraq
32E3 **Miles** Australia
56C2 **Miles City** USA
16C2 **Miletto, Monte** *Mt* Italy
68D2 **Milford** Connecticut, USA
65D3 **Milford** Delaware, USA
61D2 **Milford** Nebraska, USA
68E1 **Milford** New Hampshire, USA
68C2 **Milford** Pennsylvania, USA
59D3 **Milford** Utah, USA
7B4 **Milford Haven** Wales
7B4 **Milford Haven** *Sd* Wales
61D3 **Milford L** USA
35A2 **Milford Sd** New Zealand
15C2 **Miliana** Algeria
54G4 **Milk** *R* Canada/USA
60B1 **Milk** *R* USA
25R4 **Mil'kovo** Russian Federation
50C2 **Milk, Wadi el** *Watercourse* Sudan
14C3 **Millau** France
68D2 **Millbrook** USA
67B2 **Milledgeville** USA
61E1 **Mille Lacs L** USA
61E1 **Mille Lacs, Lac des** Canada
60D2 **Miller** USA
21G6 **Millerovo** Russian Federation
68B2 **Millersburg** USA
68D1 **Millers Falls** USA
68D2 **Millerton** USA
66C2 **Millerton L** USA
65E2 **Millford** Massachusetts, USA
34B3 **Millicent** Australia
63E1 **Millington** USA
65F1 **Millinocket** USA
34D1 **Millmerran** Australia
6C2 **Millom** England
8C4 **Millport** Scotland
9B3 **Millstreet** Irish Republic
65F1 **Milltown** Canada
58D1 **Milltown** USA
66A2 **Mill Valley** USA
65E3 **Millville** USA
55Q2 **Milne Land** *I* Greenland
66E5 **Milolii** Hawaiian Islands
17E3 **Milos** *I* Greece
32D3 **Milparinka** Australia
68B2 **Milroy** USA
67A2 **Milton** Florida, USA
35A3 **Milton** New Zealand
68B2 **Milton** Pennsylvania, USA
7D3 **Milton Keynes** England
57E2 **Milwaukee** USA
29D2 **Mimmaya** Japan
66C1 **Mina** USA
15C2 **Mina** *R* Algeria
41E4 **Mīnā' al Aḥmadī** Kuwait
41G4 **Mīnāb** Iran
74E4 **Minas** Uruguay
73J7 **Minas Gerais** *State* Brazil
75D2 **Minas Novas** Brazil
70C3 **Minatitlán** Mexico
30A1 **Minbu** Burma
30A1 **Minbya** Burma
8B3 **Minch,Little** *Sd* Scotland
8B2 **Minch,North** *Sd* Scotland
10B2 **Minch,The** *Sd* Scotland
27F6 **Mindanao** *I* Philippines
63D2 **Minden** Louisiana, USA
66C1 **Minden** Nevada, USA
18B2 **Minden** Germany
34B2 **Mindona L** Australia
27F5 **Mindoro** *I* Philippines
27F5 **Mindoro Str** Philippines
7C4 **Minehead** England
73H7 **Mineiros** Brazil
63C2 **Mineola** USA
62C2 **Mineral Wells** USA
68B2 **Minersville** USA
34B2 **Mingary** Australia
21H7 **Mingechaurskoye Vodokhranilische** *Res* Azerbaijan
8B3 **Mingulay, I** Scotland
31A2 **Minhe** China
44A4 **Minicoy** *I* India
31D4 **Min Jiang** *R* Fujian, China
31A4 **Min Jiang** *R* Sichuan, China
66C2 **Minkler** USA
34A2 **Minlaton** Australia
31A2 **Minle** China
48C4 **Minna** Nigeria
57D2 **Minneapolis** USA
54J4 **Minnedosa** Canada
61D2 **Minnesota** *R* USA
57D2 **Minnesota** *State* USA
15A1 **Miño** *R* Spain
15C1 **Minorca** *I* Spain
56C2 **Minot** USA
31A2 **Minqin** China
31A3 **Min Shan** *Upland* China
20D5 **Minsk** Belorussia
19E2 **Minsk Mazowiecki** Poland
54G2 **Minto Inlet** *B* Canada
55L4 **Minto,L** Canada
60B3 **Minturn** USA
26C1 **Minusinsk** Russian Federation
31A3 **Min Xian** China
45A3 **Minya el Qamn** Egypt
55N5 **Miquelon** *I* France
66D3 **Mirage L** USA
40D3 **Mīrah, Wadi al** *Watercourse* Iraq/Saudi Arabia
44A2 **Miraj** India
74E5 **Miramar** Argentina
42B2 **Miram Shah** Pakistan
75A3 **Miranda** Brazil
75A2 **Miranda** *R* Brazil
15B1 **Miranda de Ebro** Spain
75B3 **Mirante, Serra do** *Mts* Brazil
42B2 **Mīr Bachchen Kūt** Afghanistan
13C3 **Mirecourt** France
27E6 **Miri** Malaysia
48A3 **Mirik,C** Mauritius
74F4 **Mirim, Lagoa** *L* Brazil/Uruguay
25K3 **Mirnoye** Russian Federation
25N3 **Mirnyy** Russian Federation
76G9 **Mirnyy** *Base* Antarctica
19G3 **Mironovka** Ukraine
42C2 **Mirpur** Pakistan
42B3 **Mirpur Khas** Pakistan
17E3 **Mirtoan S** Greece
28B3 **Miryang** S Korea
43E3 **Mirzāpur** India
42C1 **Misgar** Pakistan
64B2 **Mishawaka** USA
28B4 **Mi-shima** *I* Japan
43H3 **Mishmi Hills** India
33E2 **Misima** *I* Papua New Guinea
74F3 **Misiones** *State* Argentina
19E3 **Miskolc** Hungary
45D2 **Mismīyah** Syria
27G7 **Misoōl** *I* Indonesia
49D1 **Misrātah** Libya
55K5 **Missinaibi** *R* Canada
64C1 **Missinaibi L** Canada
60C2 **Mission** S Dakota, USA
62C3 **Mission** Texas, USA
58B1 **Mission City** Canada
65D2 **Mississauga** Canada
57D3 **Mississippi** *R* USA
57D3 **Mississippi** *State* USA
63E3 **Mississippi Delta** USA
56B2 **Missoula** USA
48B1 **Missour** Morocco
57D3 **Missouri** *R* USA
57D3 **Missouri** *State* USA
61D2 **Missouri Valley** USA
57F1 **Mistassini,Lac** Canada
72D7 **Misti** *Mt* Peru
34C1 **Mitchell** Australia
56D2 **Mitchell** USA
32D2 **Mitchell** *R* Australia
57E3 **Mitchell,Mt** USA
27H8 **Mitchell River** Australia
45A3 **Mīt el Nasâra** Egypt
45A3 **Mīt Ghamr** Egypt
42C3 **Mithankot** Pakistan
17F3 **Mitilíni** Greece
45B3 **Mitla Pass** Egypt
29E3 **Mito** Japan
33G2 **Mitre** *I* Solomon Islands
50D2 **Mits'iwa** Ethiopia
13D1 **Mittel Land Kanal** Germany
72D3 **Mitú** Colombia
51C4 **Mitumba, Chaine des** *Mts* Zaïre
50C4 **Mitumbar Mts** Zaïre
51C4 **Mitwaba** Zaïre
50B3 **Mitzic** Gabon
29C3 **Miura** Japan
31C3 **Mi Xian** China
26G3 **Miyake** *I* Japan
29C4 **Miyake-jima** *I* Japan
29E3 **Miyako** Japan
26F4 **Miyako** *I* Ryukyu Is, Japan
29C3 **Miyazu** Japan
28C4 **Miyoshi** Japan
31D1 **Miyun** China
31D1 **Miyun Shuiku** *Res* China
29D2 **Mi-zaki** *Pt* Japan
50D3 **Mīzan Teferī** Ethiopia
49D1 **Mizdah** Libya
17F1 **Mizil** Romania
43G4 **Mizo Hills** India
43G4 **Mizoram** *Union Territory* India
45C3 **Mizpe Ramon** Israel
29E3 **Mizusawa** Japan
12H7 **Mjölby** Sweden
51C5 **Mkushi** Zambia
47E2 **Mkuzi** South Africa
18C2 **Mladá Boleslav** Czechoslovakia
19E2 **Mława** Poland
17D2 **Mljet** *I* Croatia
47D2 **Mmabatho** South Africa
48A4 **Moa** *R* Sierra Leone
56C3 **Moab** USA
45C3 **Moab** *Region* Jordan
47E2 **Moamba** Mozambique
50B4 **Moanda** Congo
50B4 **Moanda** Gabon
9C3 **Moate** Irish Republic
51C4 **Moba** Zaïre
29D3 **Mobara** Japan
50C3 **Mobaye** Central African Republic
50C3 **Mobayi** Zaïre
57D3 **Moberly** USA
57E3 **Mobile** USA
57E3 **Mobile B** USA
63E2 **Mobile Pt** USA
56C2 **Mobridge** USA
51E5 **Moçambique** Mozambique
Moçâmedes = Namibe
30C1 **Moc Chau** Vietnam
Mocha = Al Mukhā
47D1 **Mochudi** Botswana
51E5 **Mocimboa da Praia** Mozambique
72C3 **Mocoa** Colombia
75C3 **Mococa** Brazil
51D5 **Mocuba** Mozambique
47D2 **Modder** *R* South Africa
16C2 **Modena** Italy
13D3 **Moder** *R* France
56A3 **Modesto** USA
66B2 **Modesto Res** USA
16C3 **Modica** Sicily,
18D3 **Mödling** Austria
8D4 **Moffat** Scotland
42D2 **Moga** India
50E3 **Mogadishu** Somalia
75C3 **Mogi das Cruzes** Brazil
19G2 **Mogilev** Belorussia
21D6 **Mogilev Podol'skiy** Ukraine
75C3 **Mogi-Mirim** Brazil
51E5 **Mogincual** Mozambique
26E1 **Mogocha** Russian Federation
24K4 **Mogochin** Russian Federation
47D1 **Mogol** *R* South Africa
15A2 **Moguer** Spain
35C1 **Mohaka** *R* New Zealand
47D3 **Mohale's Hoek** Lesotho
60C1 **Mohall** USA
15C2 **Mohammadia** Algeria
43G4 **Mohanganj** Bangladesh
59D3 **Mohave,L** USA
68C1 **Mohawk** USA
65E2 **Mohawk** *R* USA
51E5 **Mohéli** *I* Comoros
51D4 **Mohoro** Tanzania
24J5 **Mointy** Kazakhstan
12G5 **Mo i Rana** Norway
14C3 **Moissac** France
59C3 **Mojave** USA
66D3 **Mojave** *R* USA
56B3 **Mojave Desert** USA
43F3 **Mokama** India
35B1 **Mokau** *R* New Zealand
66B1 **Mokelumne** *R* USA
66B1 **Mokelumne Aqueduct** USA
66B1 **Mokelumne Hill** USA
47D2 **Mokhotlong** Lesotho
16C3 **Moknine** Tunisia
43G3 **Mokokchūng** India
50B2 **Mokolo** Cameroon
28B4 **Mokp'o** S Korea
20G5 **Moksha** *R* Russian Federation
17E3 **Moláoi** Greece
7C3 **Mold** Wales
21D6 **Moldavia** *Republic* Europe
12F6 **Molde** Norway
17E1 **Moldoveanu** *Mt* Romania
47D1 **Molepolole** Botswana
13D3 **Molesheim** France
16D2 **Molfetta** Italy
72D7 **Mollendo** Peru
20D5 **Molodechno** Belorussia
76G11 **Molodezhnaya** *Base* Antarctica
66E5 **Molokai** *I* Hawaiian Islands
20H4 **Moloma** *R* Russian Federation
34C2 **Molong** Australia
47C2 **Molopo** *R* Botswana/South Africa
50B3 **Molounddu** Cameroon
56D1 **Molson L** Canada
32B1 **Molucca S**Indonesia
27F7 **Moluccas** *Is* Indonesia
51D5 **Moma** Mozambique
73K5 **Mombaça** Brazil
50D4 **Mombasa** Kenya
29D2 **Mombetsu** Japan
75B2 **Mombuca, Serra da** *Mts* Brazil
50C3 **Mompono** Zaïre
18C2 **Mon** *I* Denmark
8B3 **Monach Is** Scotland
14D3 **Monaco** *Principality* Europe
8C3 **Monadhliath Mts** Scotland
9C2 **Monaghan** Irish Republic
9C2 **Monaghan** *County* Irish Republic
62B2 **Monahans** USA
69D3 **Mona Pass** Caribbean Sea
60B3 **Monarch P** USA
54G4 **Monashee Mts** Canada
10B3 **Monastereven** Irish Republic
16C3 **Monastir** Tunisia
29D2 **Monbetsu** Japan
73J4 **Monção** Brazil
12L5 **Monchegorsk** Russian Federation
18B2 **Mönchen-gladbach** Germany
70B2 **Monclova** Mexico

Mungindi **Negolu**

34C1 **Mungindi** Australia
18C3 **Munich** Germany
64B1 **Munising** USA
74B8 **Muñoz Gamero,Pen** Chile
28A3 **Munsan** S Korea
13D3 **Munster** France
18B2 **Münster** Germany
13D2 **Münsterland** *Region* Germany
17E1 **Munţii Apuseni** *Mts* Romania
17E1 **Munţii Călimani** *Mts* Romania
17E1 **Munţii Carpaţii Meridionali** *Mts* Romania
17E1 **Munţii Rodnei** *Mts* Romania
17E1 **Munţii Zarandului** *Mts* Romania
40C2 **Munzur Silsilesi** *Mts* Turkey
30C1 **Muong Khoua** Laos
30D3 **Muong Man** Vietnam
30D2 **Muong Nong** Laos
30C1 **Muong Ou Neua** Laos
30C1 **Muong Sai** Laos
30C2 **Muong Sen** Vietnam
30C1 **Muong Sing** Laos
30C1 **Muong Son** Laos
12J5 **Muonio** Finland
12J5 **Muonio** *R* Finland/Sweden
28A3 **Muping** China
Muqdisho = Mogadishu
16C1 **Mur** *R* Austria
29D3 **Murakami** Japan
74B7 **Murallón** *Mt* Argentina/Chile
20H4 **Murashi** Russian Federation
40D2 **Murat** *R* Turkey
16B3 **Muravera** Sardinia, Italy
29D3 **Murayama** Japan
41F3 **Murcheh Khvort** Iran
35B2 **Murchison** New Zealand
32A3 **Murchison** *R* Australia
15B2 **Murcia** Spain
15B2 **Murcia** *Region* Spain
60C2 **Murdo** USA
17E1 **Mureş** *R* Romania
67C1 **Murfreesboro** N Carolina, USA
67A1 **Murfreesboro** Tennessee, USA
13E3 **Murg** *R* Germany
24H6 **Murgab** *R* Turkmenistan
42A1 **Murghab** *R* Afghanistan
42B2 **Murgha Kibzai** Pakistan
34D1 **Murgon** Australia
43F4 **Muri** India
75D3 **Muriaé** Brazil
51C4 **Muriege** Angola
20E2 **Murmansk** Russian Federation
20G4 **Murom** Russian Federation
29E2 **Muroran** Japan
15A1 **Muros** Spain
29C4 **Muroto** Japan
29B4 **Muroto-zaki** *C* Japan
58C2 **Murphy** Idaho, USA
67B1 **Murphy** N Carolina, USA
66B1 **Murphys** USA
64B3 **Murray** Kentucky, USA
58D2 **Murray** Utah, USA
34B2 **Murray** *R* Australia
34A3 **Murray Bridge** Australia
27H7 **Murray,L** Papua New Guinea
67B2 **Murray,L** USA
47C3 **Murraysburg** South Africa
37M3 **Murray Seacarp** Pacific Ocean
34B2 **Murrumbidgee** *R* Australia
34C2 **Murrumburrah** Australia
34D2 **Murrurundi** Australia
34B3 **Murtoa** Australia
28A2 **Muruin Sum** *R* China
35C1 **Murupara** New Zealand
43E4 **Murwāra** India
34D1 **Murwillimbah** Australia
27E7 **Muryo** *Mt* Indonesia
40D2 **Muş** Turkey
17E2 **Musala** *Mt* Bulgaria
28B2 **Musan** N Korea
41G4 **Musandam Pen** Oman
38D3 **Muscat** Oman
61E2 **Muscatine** USA
32C3 **Musgrave Range** *Mts* Australia
50B4 **Mushie** Zaïre
68E2 **Muskeget Chan** USA
64B2 **Muskegon** USA
64B2 **Muskegon** *R* USA
63C1 **Muskogee** USA
65D2 **Muskoka,L** Canada
50D2 **Musmar** Sudan
50D4 **Musoma** Tanzania
32D1 **Mussau** *I* Papua New Guinea
58E1 **Musselshell** *R* USA
51B5 **Mussende** Angola
14C3 **Mussidan** France
17F2 **Mustafa-Kemalpasa** Turkey
43E3 **Mustang** Nepal
74C7 **Musters, Lago** Argentina
28A2 **Musu-dan** *C* N Korea
34D2 **Muswellbrook** Australia
49E2 **Mut** Egypt
75E1 **Mutá, Ponta do** *Pt* Brazil
51D5 **Mutarara** Mozambique
51D5 **Mutare** Zimbabwe
20K2 **Mutnyy Materik** Russian Federation
51D5 **Mutoko** Zimbabwe
51E5 **Mutsamudu** Comoros
51C5 **Mutshatsha** Zaïre
29E2 **Mutsu** Japan
29E2 **Mutsu-wan** *B* Japan
75C1 **Mutunópolis** Brazil
31B2 **Mu Us Shamo** *Desert* China
51B4 **Muxima** Angola
25N4 **Muya** Russian Federation
20E3 **Muyezerskiy** Russian Federation
50D4 **Muyinga** Burundi
51C4 **Muyumba** Zaïre
39E1 **Muyun Kum** *Desert* Kazakhstan
42C2 **Muzaffarābad** Pakistan
42C2 **Muzaffargarh** Pakistan
42D3 **Muzaffarnagar** India
43F3 **Muzaffarpur** India
24H3 **Muzhi** Russian Federation
39G2 **Muzlag** *Mt* China
39F2 **Muztagala** *Mt* China
51D5 **Mvuma** Zimbabwe
50D4 **Mwanza** Tanzania
51C4 **Mwanza** Zaïre
50C4 **Mweka** Zaïre
51C4 **Mwene Ditu** Zaïre
51D6 **Mwenezi** Zimbabwe
47E1 **Mwenezi** *R* Zimbabwe
50C4 **Mwenga** Zaïre
51C4 **Mweru, L** Zaïre/Zambia
51C5 **Mwinilunga** Zambia
30B2 **Myanaung** Burma
Myanma = Burma
18D3 **M'yaróvár** Hungary
30B1 **Myingyan** Burma
30B3 **Myinmoletkat** *Mt* Burma
30B3 **Myitta** Burma
43G4 **Mymensingh** Bangladesh
7C3 **Mynydd Eppynt** Wales
26G3 **Myojin** *I* Japan
28A2 **Myongchon** N Korea
28A2 **Myonggan** N Korea
12F6 **Myrdal** Norway
12B2 **Myrdalsjökull** *Mts* Iceland
67C2 **Myrtle Beach** USA
58B2 **Myrtle Creek** USA
12G7 **Mysen** Norway
20G2 **Mys Kanin Nos** *C* Russian Federation
19D3 **Myślenice** Poland
18C2 **Mysliborz** Poland
44B3 **Mysore** India
21E7 **Mys Sarych** *C* Ukraine
25U3 **Mys Shmidta** Russian Federation
20F2 **Mys Svyatoy Nos** *C* Russian Federation
68E2 **Mystic** USA
21J7 **Mys Tyub-Karagan** *Pt* Kazakhstan
24H2 **Mys Zhelaniya** *C* Russian Federation
30D3 **My Tho** Vietnam
58B2 **Mytle Point** USA
51D5 **Mzimba** Malawi
51D5 **Mzuzú** Malawi

N

66E5 **Naalehu** Hawaiian Islands
12J6 **Naantali** Finland
9C3 **Naas** Irish Republic
29C4 **Nabari** Japan
20J4 **Naberezhnyye Chelny** Russian Federation
16C3 **Nabeul** Tunisia
75A3 **Nabileque** *R* Brazil
45C2 **Nablus** Israel
51E5 **Nacala** Mozambique
58B1 **Naches** USA
51D5 **Nachingwea** Tanzania
66B3 **Nacimiento** *R* USA
66B3 **Nacimiento Res** USA
63D2 **Nacogdoches** USA
70B1 **Nacozari** Mexico
13E2 **Nadel** *Mt* Germany
42C4 **Nadiād** India
15B2 **Nador** Morocco
41F3 **Nadūshan** Iran
20E3 **Nadvoitsy** Russian Federation
19E3 **Nadvornaya** Ukraine
18C1 **Naestved** Denmark
49E2 **Nafoora** Libya
27F5 **Naga** Philippines
28B4 **Nagahama** Japan
43H3 **Naga Hills** India
29C3 **Nagai** Japan
43G3 **Nāgāland** *State* India
29D3 **Nagano** Japan
29D3 **Nagaoka** Japan
44B3 **Nāgappattinam** India
42C4 **Nagar Parkar** Pakistan
28B4 **Nagasaki** Japan
29C4 **Nagashima** Japan
28B4 **Nagato** Japan
42C3 **Nāgaur** India
44B4 **Nāgercoil** India
42B3 **Nagha Kalat** Pakistan
42D3 **Nagīna** India
13E3 **Nagold** Germany
29D3 **Nagoya** Japan
42D4 **Nāgpur** India
39H2 **Nagqu** China
18D3 **Nagykanizsa** Hungary
19D3 **Nagykörös** Hungary
26F4 **Naha** Okinawa, Japan
42D2 **Nāhan** India
54F3 **Nahanni Butte** Canada
45C2 **Nahariya** Israel
41E3 **Nahāvand** Iran
13D3 **Nahe** *R* Germany
31D2 **Nahpu** China
74B6 **Nahuel Haupí, Lago** Argentina
31E1 **Naimen Qi** China
55M4 **Nain** Canada
41F3 **Nā'īn** Iran
42D3 **Naini Tal** India
43E4 **Nainpur** India
8D3 **Nairn** Scotland
50D4 **Nairobi** Kenya
41F3 **Najafābād** Iran
40C4 **Najd** *Region* Saudi Arabia
28C2 **Najin** N Korea
50E2 **Najrān** Saudi Arabia
28A3 **Naju** S Korea
28A4 **Nakadori-jima** Japan
28B4 **Nakama** Japan
29E3 **Nakaminato** Japan
28B4 **Nakamura** Japan
29C3 **Nakano** Japan
29B3 **Nakano-shima** *I* Japan
28C4 **Nakatsu** Japan
29C3 **Nakatsu-gawa** Japan
50D2 **Nak'fa** Ethiopia
21H8 **Nakhichevan** Azerbaijan
45B4 **Nakhl** Egypt
28C2 **Nakhodka** Russian Federation
30C3 **Nakhon Pathom** Thailand
30C3 **Nakhon Ratchasima** Thailand
30C4 **Nakhon Si Thammarat** Thailand
55K4 **Nakina** Ontario, Canada
54C4 **Naknek** USA
12G8 **Nakskov** Denmark
28A3 **Naktong** *R* S Korea
50D4 **Nakuru** Kenya
21G7 **Nal'chik** Russian Federation
44B2 **Nalgonda** India
44B2 **Nallamala Range** *Mts* India
49D1 **Nālūt** Libya
47E2 **Namaacha** Mozambique
24G6 **Namak** *L* Iran
41G3 **Namakzar-e Shadad** *Salt Flat* Iran
24J5 **Namangan** Uzbekistan
51D5 **Namapa** Mozambique
51B7 **Namaqualand** *Region* South Africa
34D1 **Nambour** Australia
34D2 **Nambucca Heads** Australia
30D4 **Nam Can** Vietnam
39H2 **Nam Co** *L* China
30D1 **Nam Dinh** Vietnam
51D5 **Nametil** Mozambique
47A1 **Namib Desert** Namibia
51B5 **Namibe** Angola
51B6 **Namibia** *Republic* Africa
27F7 **Namlea** Indonesia
43F3 **Namling** China
34C2 **Namoi** *R* Australia
58C2 **Nampa** USA
48B3 **Nampala** Mali
30C2 **Nam Phong** Thailand
28B3 **Namp'o** N Korea
51D5 **Nampula** Mozambique
12G6 **Namsos** Norway
30B1 **Namton** Burma
25O3 **Namtsy** Russian Federation
51D5 **Namuno** Mozambique
13C2 **Namur** Belgium
51B5 **Namutoni** Namibia
56A2 **Nanaimo** Canada
28B2 **Nanam** N Korea
34D1 **Nanango** Australia
29D3 **Nanao** Japan
29C3 **Nanatsu-jima** *I* Japan
31B3 **Nanbu** China
31D4 **Nanchang** China
31B3 **Nanchong** China
44E4 **Nancowry** *I* Nicobar Is, Indian Ocean
14D2 **Nancy** France
43E2 **Nanda Devi** *Mt* India
44B2 **Nānded** India
34D2 **Nandewar Range** *Mts* Australia
42C4 **Nandurbār** India
44B2 **Nandyāl** India
50B3 **Nanga Eboko** Cameroon
42C1 **Nanga Parbat** *Mt* Pakistan
27E7 **Nangapinon** Indonesia
13B3 **Nangis** France
28A2 **Nangnim** N Korea
28B2 **Nangnim Sanmaek** *Mts* N Korea
43G3 **Nang Xian** China
44B3 **Nanjangūd** India
31D3 **Nanjing** China
Nanking = Nanjing
29B4 **Nankoku** Japan
31C4 **Nan Ling** *Region* China
30D1 **Nanliu** *R* China
31B5 **Nanning** China
55O3 **Nanortalik** Greenland
31A5 **Nanpan Jiang** *R* China
43E3 **Nānpāra** India
31D4 **Nanping** China
28B2 **Nanping** China
55J1 **Nansen Sd** Canada
27E5 **Nanshan** *I* S China Sea
50D4 **Nansio** Tanzania
14B2 **Nantes** France
68C2 **Nanticoke** USA
31E3 **Nantong** China
68E2 **Nantucket** USA
68E2 **Nantucket I** USA
68E2 **Nantucket Sd** USA
7C3 **Nantwich** England
33G1 **Nanumanga** *I* Tuvalu
33G1 **Nanumea** *I* Tuvalu
75D2 **Nanuque** Brazil
31C3 **Nanyang** China
31D2 **Nanyang Hu** *L* China
50D3 **Nanyuki** Kenya
28A2 **Nanzamu** China
15C2 **Nao, Cabo de la** *C* Spain
29D3 **Naoetsu** Japan
42B4 **Naokot** Pakistan
66A1 **Napa** USA
65D2 **Napanee** Canada
24K4 **Napas** Russian Federation
55N3 **Napassoq** Greenland
30D2 **Nape** Laos
35C1 **Napier** New Zealand
67B3 **Naples** Florida, USA
16C2 **Naples** Italy
68B1 **Naples** New York, USA
63D2 **Naples** Texas, USA
31B5 **Napo** China
72D4 **Napo** *R* Ecuador/Peru
60D1 **Napoleon** USA
Napoli = Naples
41E2 **Naqadeh** Iran
45C3 **Naqb Ishtar** Jordan
29C4 **Nara** Japan
48B3 **Nara** Mali
32D4 **Naracoorte** Australia
44B2 **Narasarāopet** India
30C4 **Narathiwat** Thailand
43G4 **Narayanganj** Bangladesh
44B2 **Nārāyenpet** India
14C3 **Narbonne** France
30A3 **Narcondam** *I* Indian Ocean
42D2 **Narendranagar** India
55L2 **Nares Str** Canada
19E2 **Narew** *R* Poland
28B2 **Narhong** China
29D3 **Narita** Japan
42C4 **Narmada** *R* India
42D3 **Nārnaul** India
20F4 **Naro Fominsk** Russian Federation
50D4 **Narok** Kenya
19F2 **Narovl'a** Belorussia
42C2 **Narowal** Pakistan
32D4 **Narrabri** Australia
34C1 **Narran** *R* Australia
34C2 **Narrandera** Australia
34C1 **Narran L** Australia
32A4 **Narrogin** Australia
34C2 **Narromine** Australia
64C3 **Narrows** USA
68C2 **Narrowsburg** USA
42D4 **Narsimhapur** India
44C2 **Narsīpatnam** India
55O3 **Narssalik** Greenland
55O3 **Narssaq** Greenland
55O3 **Narssarssuaq** Greenland
47B2 **Narubis** Namibia
29D3 **Narugo** Japan
29B4 **Naruto** Japan
20D4 **Narva** Russian Federation
12H5 **Narvik** Norway
42D3 **Narwāna** India
20J2 **Nar'yan Mar** Russian Federation
34B1 **Narylico** Australia
24J5 **Naryn** Kirgizia
48C4 **Nasarawa** Nigeria
52D6 **Nasca Ridge** Pacific Ocean
68E1 **Nashua** USA
63D2 **Nashville** Arkansas, USA
67A1 **Nashville** Tennessee, USA
17D1 **Našice** Croatia
42C4 **Nāsik** India
50D3 **Nasir** Sudan
69B1 **Nassau** The Bahamas
68D1 **Nassau** USA
49F2 **Nasser,L** Egypt
12G7 **Nässjö** Sweden
55L4 **Nastapoka Is** Canada
51C6 **Nata** Botswana
73L5 **Natal** Brazil
27C6 **Natal** Indonesia
47E2 **Natal** *Province* South Africa
36C6 **Natal Basin** Indian Ocean
41F3 **Natanz** Iran
55M4 **Natashquan** Canada
55M4 **Natashquan** *R* Canada
63D2 **Natchez** USA
63D2 **Natchitoches** USA
34C3 **Nathalia** Australia
55Q2 **Nathorsts Land** *Region* Greenland
59C4 **National City** USA
29D3 **Natori** Japan
50D4 **Natron, L** Tanzania
40A3 **Natrun, Wadi el** *Watercourse* Egypt
32A4 **Naturaliste,C** Australia
18C2 **Nauen** Germany
68D2 **Naugatuck** USA
18C2 **Naumburg** Germany
45C3 **Naur** Jordan
33F1 **Nauru** *I, Republic* Pacific Ocean
25M4 **Naushki** Russian Federation
47B2 **Naute Dam** *Res* Namibia
56C3 **Navajo Res** USA
15A2 **Navalmoral de la Mata** Spain
25T3 **Navarin, Mys** *C* Russian Federation
74C9 **Navarino** *I* Chile
15B1 **Navarra** *Province* Spain
63C2 **Navasota** USA
63C2 **Navasota** *R* USA
8C2 **Naver, L** Scotland
15A1 **Navia** *R* Spain
42C4 **Navlakhi** India
21E5 **Navlya** Russian Federation
70B2 **Navojoa** Mexico
17E3 **Návpaktos** Greece
17E3 **Návplion** Greece
42C4 **Navsāri** India
45D2 **Nawá** Syria
42B3 **Nawabshah** Pakistan
43F4 **Nawāda** India
42B2 **Nawah** Afghanistan
31B4 **Naxi** China
17F3 **Náxos** *I* Greece
41F4 **Nāy Band** Iran
41G3 **Nāy Band** Iran
29E2 **Nayoro** Japan
75E1 **Nazaré** Brazil
45C2 **Nazareth** Israel
72D6 **Nazca** Peru
40A2 **Nazilli** Turkey
25L4 **Nazimovo** Russian Federation
50D3 **Nazrēt** Ethiopia
41G5 **Nazwa'** Oman
24J4 **Nazyvayevsk** Russian Federation
51B4 **Ndalatando** Angola
50C3 **Ndélé** Central African Republic
50B4 **Ndendé** Gabon
33F2 **Ndende** *I* Solomon Islands
50B2 **Ndjamena** Chad
50B4 **Ndjolé** Gabon
51C5 **Ndola** Zambia
34C1 **Neabul** Australia
10B3 **Neagh, Lough** *L* Northern Ireland
17E3 **Neápolis** Greece
7C4 **Neath** Wales
34C1 **Nebine** *R* Australia
24G6 **Nebit Dag** Turkmenistan
56C2 **Nebraska** *State* USA
61D2 **Nebraska City** USA
16C3 **Nebrodi, Monti** *Mts* Sicily, Italy
63C2 **Neches** *R* USA
74E5 **Nechochea** Argentina
43G3 **Nedong** China
7E3 **Needham Market** England
59D4 **Needles** USA
7D4 **Needles** *Pt* England
64B2 **Neenah** USA
54J4 **Neepawa** Canada
13C2 **Neerpelt** Belgium
25M4 **Neftelensk** Russian Federation
50D3 **Negelē** Ethiopia
45C3 **Negev** *Desert* Israel
75A3 **Negla** *R* Paraguay
21C6 **Negolu** *Mt* Romania

Negombo **Northallerton**

44B4 **Negombo** Sri Lanka
30A2 **Negrais,C** Burma
72B4 **Negritos** Peru
72F4 **Negro** *R* Amazonas, Brazil
74D5 **Negro** *R* Argentina
75A2 **Negro** *R* Mato Grosso do Sul, Brazil
75A3 **Negro** *R* Paraguay
74F4 **Negro** *R* Brazil/Uruguay
15A2 **Negro, Cap** *C* Morocco
27F6 **Negros** *I* Philippines
17F2 **Negru Vodă** Romania
31B4 **Neijiang** China
64A2 **Neillsville** USA
Nei Monggol Zizhiqu = Inner Mongolia Aut. Region
72C3 **Neiva** Colombia
50D3 **Nejo** Ethiopia
50D3 **Nek'emte** Ethiopia
20E4 **Nelidovo** Russian Federation
61D2 **Neligh** USA
44B3 **Nellore** India
26G2 **Nel'ma** Russian Federation
54G5 **Nelson** Canada
6C3 **Nelson** England
35B2 **Nelson** New Zealand
34B3 **Nelson,C** Australia
47E2 **Nelspruit** South Africa
48B3 **Néma** Mauritius
31A1 **Nemagt Uul** *Mt* Mongolia
16B3 **Nementcha, Mts Des** Algeria
17F1 **Nemira** *Mt* Romania
13B3 **Nemours** France
19E1 **Nemunas** *R* Lithuania
29F2 **Nemuro** Japan
29F2 **Nemuro-kaikyō** *Str* Japan/Russian Federation
25O5 **Nen** *R* China
10B3 **Nenagh** Irish Republic
54D3 **Nenana** USA
7D3 **Nene** *R* England
26F2 **Nenjiang** China
63C1 **Neodesha** USA
63D1 **Neosho** USA
25M4 **Nepa** Russian Federation
39G3 **Nepal** *Kingdom* Asia
43E3 **Nepalganj** Nepal
59D3 **Nephi** USA
45C3 **Neqarot** *R* Israel
26E1 **Nerchinsk** Russian Federation
17D2 **Neretva** *R* Bosnia & Herzegovina, Yugoslavia/Croatia
27H5 **Nero Deep** Pacific Ocean
20G2 **Nes'** Russian Federation
12C1 **Neskaupstaður** Iceland
13B3 **Nesle** France
62C1 **Ness City** USA
8C3 **Ness, Loch** *L* Scotland
17E2 **Néstos** *R* Greece
45C2 **Netanya** Israel
68C2 **Netcong** USA
18B2 **Netherlands** *Kingdom* Europe
53M7 **Netherlands Antilles** *Is* Caribbean Sea
43G4 **Netrakona** Bangladesh
55L3 **Nettilling L** Canada
18C2 **Neubrandenburg** Germany
16B1 **Neuchâtel** Switzerland
13C3 **Neufchâteau** Belgium
13C3 **Neufchâteau** France
14C2 **Neufchâtel** France
18B2 **Neumünster** Germany
16D1 **Neunkirchen** Austria
13D3 **Neunkirchen** Germany
74C5 **Neuquén** Argentina
74C5 **Neuquén** *R* Argentina
74B5 **Neuquén** *State* Argentina
18C2 **Neuruppin** Germany
67C1 **Neuse** *R* USA
13D2 **Neuss** Germany
18C2 **Neustadt** Germany
13E3 **Neustadt an der Weinstrasse** Germany
13E1 **Neustadt a R** Germany
13E4 **Neustadt im Schwarzwald** Germany
18C2 **Neustrelitz** Germany
13E1 **Neuwerk** *I* Germany
13D2 **Neuwied** Germany
63D1 **Nevada** USA
56B3 **Nevada** *State* USA
15B2 **Nevada, Sierra** *Mts* Spain
45C3 **Nevatim** Israel
20D4 **Nevel'** Russian Federation
14C2 **Nevers** France
34C2 **Nevertire** Australia
Nevis = St Kitts-Nevis
40B2 **Nevşehir** Turkey
20L4 **Nev'yansk** Russian Federation
64C3 **New** *R* USA
51D5 **Newala** Tanzania
64B3 **New Albany** Indiana, USA
63E2 **New Albany** Mississippi, USA
73G2 **New Amsterdam** Guyana
34C1 **New Angledool** Australia
65D3 **Newark** Delaware, USA
57F2 **Newark** New Jersey, USA
68B1 **Newark** New York, USA
64C2 **Newark** Ohio, USA
7D3 **Newark-upon-Trent** England
65E2 **New Bedford** USA
58B1 **Newberg** USA
67C1 **New Bern** USA
67B2 **Newberry** USA
47C3 **New Bethesda** South Africa
69B2 **New Bight** The Bahamas
64C3 **New Boston** USA
62C3 **New Braunfels** USA
68D2 **New Britain** USA
32E1 **New Britain** *I* Papua New Guinea
32E1 **New Britain Trench** Papua New Guinea
68C2 **New Brunswick** USA
55M5 **New Brunswick** *Province* Canada
68C2 **Newburgh** USA
7D4 **Newbury** England
68E1 **Newburyport** USA
33F3 **New Caledonia** *I* SW Pacific Ocean
68D2 **New Canaan** USA
34D2 **Newcastle** Australia
64B3 **New Castle** Indiana, USA
9D2 **Newcastle** Northern Ireland
64C2 **New Castle** Pennsylvania, USA
47D2 **Newcastle** South Africa
60C2 **Newcastle** Wyoming, USA
8D4 **New Castleton** Scotland
7C3 **Newcastle under Lyme** England
6D2 **Newcastle upon Tyne** England
32C2 **Newcastle Waters** Australia
66C3 **New Cuyama** USA
42D3 **New Delhi** India
34D2 **New England Range** *Mts* Australia
68A1 **Newfane** USA
7D4 **New Forest,The** England
55N5 **Newfoundland** *I* Canada
55M4 **Newfoundland** *Province* Canada
52F2 **Newfoundland Basin** Atlantic Ocean
61E3 **New Franklin** USA
8C4 **New Galloway** Scotland
33E1 **New Georgia** *I* Solomon Islands
55M5 **New Glasgow** Canada
32D1 **New Guinea** *I* SE Asia
66C3 **Newhall** USA
57F2 **New Hampshire** *State* USA
61E2 **New Hampton** USA
47E2 **New Hanover** South Africa
32E1 **New Hanover** *I* Papua New Guinea
7E4 **Newhaven** England
65E2 **New Haven** USA
33F3 **New Hebrides Trench** Pacific Ocean
63D2 **New Iberia** USA
32E1 **New Ireland** *I* Papua New Guinea
57F2 **New Jersey** *State* USA
62B2 **Newkirk** USA
55L5 **New Liskeard** Canada
68D2 **New London** USA
32A3 **Newman** Australia
66B2 **Newman** USA
7E3 **Newmarket** England
65D3 **New Market** USA
58C2 **New Meadows** USA
56C3 **New Mexico** *State* USA
68D2 **New Milford** Connecticut, USA
68C2 **New Milford** Pennsylvania, USA
67B2 **Newnan** USA
34C4 **New Norfolk** Australia
57D3 **New Orleans** USA
68C2 **New Paltz** USA
64C2 **New Philadelphia** USA
35B1 **New Plymouth** New Zealand
63D1 **Newport** Arkansas, USA
7D4 **Newport** England
64C3 **Newport** Kentucky, USA
68D1 **Newport** New Hampshire, USA
58B2 **Newport** Oregon, USA
68B2 **Newport** Pennsylvania, USA
65E2 **Newport** Rhode Island, USA
65E2 **Newport** Vermont, USA
7C4 **Newport** Wales
58C1 **Newport** Washington, USA
66D4 **Newport Beach** USA
57F3 **Newport News** USA
69B1 **New Providence** *I* The Bahamas
7B4 **Newquay** England
7B3 **New Quay** Wales
55L3 **New Quebec Crater** Canada
7C3 **New Radnor** Wales
7E4 **New Romney** England
9C3 **New Ross** Irish Republic
9C2 **Newry** Northern Ireland
New Siberian Is = Novosibirskye Ostrova
67B3 **New Smyrna Beach** USA
32D4 **New South Wales** *State* Australia
61E2 **Newton** Iowa, USA
63C1 **Newton** Kansas, USA
68E1 **Newton** Massachusetts, USA
63E2 **Newton** Mississippi, USA
68C2 **Newton** New Jersey, USA
9D2 **Newtonabbey** Northern Ireland
7C4 **Newton Abbot** England
9C2 **Newton Stewart** Northern Ireland
8C4 **Newton Stewart** Scotland
60C1 **New Town** USA
7C3 **Newtown** Wales
9D2 **Newtownards** Northern Ireland
61E2 **New Ulm** USA
68B2 **Newville** USA
54F5 **New Westminster** Canada
57F2 **New York** USA
57F2 **New York** *State* USA
33G5 **New Zealand** *Dominion* SWPacific Ocean
37K7 **New Zealand Plat** Pacific Ocean
20G4 **Neya** Russian Federation
41F4 **Neyrīz** Iran
41G2 **Neyshābūr** Iran
21E5 **Nezhin** Ukraine
50B4 **Ngabé** Congo
51C6 **Ngami, L** Botswana
49D4 **Ngaoundéré** Cameroon
30A1 **Ngape** Burma
35C1 **Ngaruawahia** New Zealand
35C1 **Ngaruroro** *R* New Zealand
35C1 **Ngauruhoe,Mt** New Zealand
50B4 **Ngo** Congo
30D2 **Ngoc Linh** *Mt* Vietnam
50B3 **Ngoko** *R* Cameroon/ Central African Republic/Congo
26C3 **Ngoring Hu** *L* China
50D4 **Ngorongoro Crater** Tanzania
50B4 **N'Gounié** *R* Gabon
50B2 **Nguigmi** Niger
27G6 **Ngulu** *I* Pacific Ocean
48D3 **Nguru** Nigeria
30D3 **Nha Trang** Vietnam
75A2 **Nhecolândia** Brazil
34B3 **Nhill** Australia
47E2 **Nhlangano** Swaziland
30D2 **Nhommarath** Laos
32C2 **Nhulunbuy** Australia
48B3 **Niafounké** Mali
64B1 **Niagara** USA
65D2 **Niagara Falls** Canada
65D2 **Niagara Falls** USA
27E6 **Niah** Malaysia
48B4 **Niakaramandougou** Ivory Coast
48C3 **Niamey** Niger
50C3 **Niangara** Zaïre
50C3 **Nia Nia** Zaïre
27E6 **Niapa** *Mt* Indonesia
27C6 **Nias** *I* Indonesia
70D3 **Nicaragua** *Republic* Central America
70D3 **Nicaragua, L de** Nicaragua
16D3 **Nicastro** Italy
14D3 **Nice** France
69B1 **Nicholl's Town** The Bahamas
68C2 **Nicholson** USA
39H5 **Nicobar Is** India
45B1 **Nicosia** Cyprus
72A2 **Nicoya, Golfo de** Costa Rica
70D3 **Nicoya,Pen de** Costa Rica
6D2 **Nidd** *R* England
13E2 **Nidda** *R* Germany
19E2 **Nidzica** Poland
13D3 **Niederbronn** France
18B2 **Niedersachsen** *State* Germany
50C4 **Niemba** Zaïre
18B2 **Nienburg** Germany
13D2 **Niers** *R* Germany
48B4 **Niete,Mt** Liberia
73G2 **Nieuw Amsterdam** Surinam
73G2 **Nieuw Nickerie** Surinam
47B3 **Nieuwoudtville** South Africa
13B2 **Nieuwpoort** Belgium
40B2 **Niğde** Turkey
48B3 **Niger** *R* W Africa
48C3 **Niger** *Republic* Africa
48C4 **Nigeria** *Federal Republic* Africa
48C4 **Niger, Mouths of the** Nigeria
43L1 **Nighasan** India
64C1 **Nighthawk L** Canada
17E2 **Nigríta** Greece
29D3 **Nihommatsu** Japan
29D3 **Niigata** Japan
29C4 **Niihama** Japan
29C4 **Nii-jima** *I* Japan
29B4 **Niimi** Japan
29D3 **Niitsu** Japan
45C3 **Nijil** Jordan
18B2 **Nijmegen** Netherlands
20E2 **Nikel'** Russian Federation
48C4 **Nikki** Benin
29D3 **Nikko** Japan
21E6 **Nikolayev** Ukraine
21H6 **Nikolayevsk** Russian Federation
25Q4 **Nikolayevsk-na-Amure** Russian Federation
20H5 **Nikol'sk** Penza, Russian Federation
20H4 **Nikol'sk** Russian Federation
21E6 **Nikopol** Ukraine
40C1 **Niksar** Turkey
38A1 **Nikšić** Yugoslavia
17D2 **Nikšić** Montenegro, Yugoslavia
33G1 **Nikunau** *I* Kiribati
27F7 **Nila** *I* Indonesia
38B3 **Nile** *R* NE Africa
64B2 **Niles** USA
44B3 **Nilgiri Hills** India
42C4 **Nimach** India
14C3 **Nîmes** France
34C3 **Nimmitabel** Australia
50D3 **Nimule** Sudan
39F5 **Nine Degree Chan** Indian Ocean
36F5 **Ninety-East Ridge** Indian Ocean
34C3 **Ninety Mile Beach** Australia
31D4 **Ningde** China
31D4 **Ningdu** China
26C3 **Ningjing Shan** *Mts* China
30D1 **Ningming** China
31A4 **Ningnan** China
31B2 **Ningxia** *Province* China
31B2 **Ning Xian** China
31B5 **Ninh Binh** Vietnam
32D1 **Ninigo Is** Papua New Guinea
75A3 **Nioaque** Brazil
60C2 **Niobrara** *R* USA
50B4 **Nioki** Zaïre
48B3 **Nioro du Sahel** Mali
14B2 **Niort** France
54H4 **Nipawin** Canada
55K5 **Nipigon** Canada
64B1 **Nipigon B** Canada
55K5 **Nipigon,L** Canada
64C1 **Nipissing,L** Canada
66B3 **Nipomo** USA
59C3 **Nipton** USA
75C1 **Niquelândia** Brazil
44B2 **Nirmal** India
43F3 **Nirmāli** India
17E2 **Niš** Serbia, Yugoslavia
38C4 **Nişāb** Yemen
26H4 **Nishino-shima** *I* Japan
28C3 **Nishino-shima** *I* Japan
28A4 **Nishi-suidō** *Str* S Korea
29B4 **Nishiwaki** Japan
33E1 **Nissan Is** Papua New Guinea
55L4 **Nitchequon** Canada
73K8 **Niterói** Brazil
8D4 **Nith** *R* Scotland
19D3 **Nitra** Czechoslovakia
64C3 **Nitro** USA
33J2 **Niue** *I* Pacific Ocean
33G2 **Niulakita** *I* Tuvalu
27E6 **Niut** *Mt* Indonesia
33G1 **Niutao** *I* Tuvalu
28A2 **Niuzhuang** China
13C2 **Nivelles** Belgium
14C2 **Nivernais** *Region* France
12L5 **Nivskiy** Russian Federation
44B2 **Nizāmābād** India
45C3 **Nizana** *Hist Site* Israel
26C1 **Nizhneudinsk** Russian Federation
20K4 **Nizhniye Sergi** Russian Federation
20G5 **Nizhniy Lomov** Russian Federation
20G4 **Nizhiny Novgorod** Russian Federation
20J3 **Nizhniy Odes** Russian Federation
20K4 **Nizhniy Tagil** Russian Federation
25L3 **Nizhnyaya Tunguska** *R* Russian Federation
20G2 **Nizhnyaya Zolotitsa** Russian Federation
40C2 **Nizip** Turkey
12C1 **Njarðvik** Iceland
51C5 **Njoko** *R* Zambia
51D4 **Njombe** Tanzania
50B3 **Nkambé** Cameroon
51D5 **Nkhata Bay** Malawi
50B3 **Nkongsamba** Cameroon
48C3 **N'Konni** Niger
43G4 **Noakhali** Bangladesh
54B3 **Noatak** USA
54B3 **Noatak** *R* USA
28C4 **Nobeoka** Japan
29D2 **Noboribetsu** Japan
75A1 **Nobres** Brazil
63C2 **Nocona** USA
70A1 **Nogales** Sonora, Mexico
59D4 **Nogales** USA
28B4 **Nogata** Japan
13C3 **Nogent-en-Bassigny** France
13B3 **Nogent-sur-Seine** France
20F4 **Noginsk** Russian Federation
42C3 **Nohar** India
29D2 **Noheji** Japan
14B2 **Noirmoutier, Ile de** *I* France
47C1 **Nojane** Botswana
29C4 **Nojima-zaki** *C* Japan
50B3 **Nola** Central African Republic
20H4 **Nolinsk** Russian Federation
68E2 **Nomans Land** *I* USA
54B3 **Nome** USA
13D3 **Nomeny** France
31B1 **Nomgon** Mongolia
28A4 **Nomo-saki** *Pt* Japan
54H3 **Nonacho L** Canada
30C2 **Nong Khai** Thailand
47E2 **Nongoma** South Africa
33G1 **Nonouti** *I* Kiribati
28A3 **Nonsan** S Korea
13C1 **Noord Holland** *Province* Netherlands
47B2 **Noordoewer** Namibia
13C1 **Noordoost Polder** Netherlands
13C1 **Noordzeekanal** Netherlands
54B3 **Noorvik** USA
50B4 **Noqui** Angola
55L5 **Noranda** Canada
13B2 **Nord** *Department* France
24D2 **Nordaustlandet** *I* Svalbard
13D1 **Norden** Germany
13E1 **Nordenham** Germany
13D1 **Norderney** *I* Germany
12F6 **Nordfjord** *Inlet* Norway
12F8 **Nordfriesische** *Is* Germany
18C2 **Nordhausen** Germany
13D1 **Nordhorn** Germany
18B2 **Nordrhein Westfalen** *State* Germany
12J4 **Nordkapp** *C* Norway
55N3 **Nordre Strømfyord** *Fyord* Greenland
12G5 **Nord Storfjället** *Mt* Sweden
25N2 **Nordvik** Russian Federation
9C3 **Nore** *R* Irish Republic
61D2 **Norfolk** Nebraska, USA
65D3 **Norfolk** Virginia, USA
7E3 **Norfolk** *County* England
33F3 **Norfolk I** Pacific Ocean
37K6 **Norfolk I Ridge** Pacific Ocean
63D1 **Norfolk L** USA
25K3 **Noril'sk** Russian Federation
64B2 **Normal** USA
63C1 **Norman** USA
14B2 **Normandie** *Region* France
67B1 **Norman,L** USA
32D2 **Normanton** Australia
54F3 **Norman Wells** Canada
20B2 **Norra Storfjället** *Mt* Sweden
67B1 **Norris L** USA
65D2 **Norristown** USA
12H7 **Norrköping** Sweden
12H6 **Norrsundet** Sweden
12H7 **Norrtälje** Sweden
32B4 **Norseman** Australia
26F1 **Norsk** Russian Federation
75A1 **Nortelândia** Brazil
6D2 **Northallerton** England

Okoja Pacific Grove

48C4 **Okoja** Nigeria
47B1 **Okombahe** Namibia
50B4 **Okondja** Gabon
29D2 **Okoppe** Japan
50B4 **Okoyo** Congo
48C4 **Okpara** *R* Benin/Nigeria
20A2 **Okstindan** *Mt* Norway
21K6 **Oktyabr'sk** Kazakhstan
20J5 **Oktyabr'skiy** Bashkirskaya, Russian Federation
26J1 **Oktyabr'skiy** Kamchatka, Russian Federation
20M3 **Oktyabr'skoye** Russian Federation
25L2 **Oktyabrskoy Revolyutsii, Ostrov** *I* Russian Federation
29D2 **Okushiri-tō** Japan
47C1 **Okwa** *R* Botswana
12B1 **Olafsjorðr** Iceland
66D2 **Olancha** USA
66C2 **Olancha Peak** *Mt* USA
12H7 **Öland** *I* Sweden
34B2 **Olary** Australia
61E3 **Olathe** USA
74D5 **Olavarría** Argentina
16B2 **Olbia** Sicily, Italy
68A1 **Olcott** USA
54E3 **Old Crow** Canada
18B2 **Oldenburg** Niedersachsen, Germany
18C2 **Oldenburg** Schleswig-Holstein, Germany
68C2 **Old Forge** USA
7C3 **Oldham** England
10B3 **Old Head of Kinsale** *C* Irish Republic
68D2 **Old Lyme** USA
8D3 **Oldmeldrum** Scotland
54G4 **Olds** Canada
65F2 **Old Town** USA
31B1 **Öldziyt**
68A1 **Olean** USA
25O4 **Olekma** *R* Russian Federation
25O3 **Olekminsk** Russian Federation
20E2 **Olenegorsk** Russian Federation
25N3 **Olenek** Russian Federation
25O2 **Olenek** *R* Russian Federation
19F2 **Olevsk** Ukraine
29D2 **Ol'ga** Russian Federation
47C3 **Olifants** *R* Cape Province, South Africa
47B1 **Olifants** *R* Namibia
47E1 **Olifants** *R* Transvaal, South Africa
47C2 **Olifantshoek** South Africa
17E2 **Ólimbos** *Mt* Greece
75C3 **Olímpia** Brazil
73M5 **Olinda** Brazil
74C4 **Olivares** *Mt* Argentina/Chile
75D3 **Oliveira** Brazil
61E2 **Olivia** USA
74C2 **Ollagüe** Chile
74C2 **Ollagüe, Vol** Bolivia
7D3 **Ollerton** England
64B3 **Olney** Illinois, USA
62C2 **Olney** Texas, USA
26E1 **Olochi** Russian Federation
12G7 **Olofström** Sweden
50B4 **Olombo** Congo
18D3 **Olomouc** Czechoslovakia
20E3 **Olonets** Russian Federation
14B3 **Oloron-Ste-Marie** France
26E1 **Olovyannaya** Russian Federation
13D2 **Olpe** Germany
19E2 **Olsztyn** Poland
16B1 **Olten** Switzerland
17E2 **Olt** *R* Romania
58B1 **Olympia** USA
58B1 **Olympic Nat Pk** USA
Olympus *Mt* = **Ólimbos**
45B1 **Olympus,Mt** Cyprus
58B1 **Olympus,Mt** USA
25T4 **Olyutorskiy, Mys** *C* Russian Federation
29C3 **Omachi** Japan
29C4 **Omae-zaki** *C* Japan
9C2 **Omagh** Northern Ireland
61D2 **Omaha** USA
58C1 **Omak** USA
38D4 **Oman** *Sultanate* Arabian Pen
38D3 **Oman,G of** UAE
47B1 **Omaruru** Namibia
47A1 **Omaruru** *R* Namibia
29D2 **Ōma-saki** *C* Japan
50A4 **Omboué** Gabon
50D2 **Omdurman** Sudan
50D2 **Om Häjer** Ethiopia
29D2 **Ōminato** Japan
54F4 **Omineca Mts** Canada
29C3 **Omiya** Japan
54H2 **Ommanney B** Canada
50D3 **Omo** *R* Ethiopia
16B2 **Omodeo, L** Sardinia, Italy
25R3 **Omolon** *R* Russian Federation
25P3 **Omoloy** *R* Russian Federation
29D3 **Omono** *R* Japan
24J4 **Omsk** Russian Federation
29D2 **Ōmu** Japan
28C4 **Omura** Japan
47C1 **Omuramba Eiseb** *R* Botswana
28C4 **Ōmuta** Japan
20J4 **Omutninsk** Russian Federation
64A2 **Onalaska** USA
65D3 **Onancock** USA
43K1 **Onandausi** India
64C1 **Onaping L** Canada
61D2 **Onawa** USA
51B5 **Oncócua** Angola
51B5 **Ondangua** Namibia
19E3 **Ondava** *R* Czechoslovakia
48C4 **Ondo** Nigeria
26E2 **Öndörhaan** Mongolia
39F5 **One and Half Degree Chan** Indian Ocean
42F3 **Onega** Russian Federation
20F3 **Onega** *R* Russian Federation
20F3 **Onega, L** Russian Federation
68C1 **Oneida** USA
68B1 **Oneida L** USA
60D2 **O'Neill** USA
26J2 **Onekotan** *I* Kuril Is, Russian Federation
50C4 **Onema** Zaïre
68C1 **Oneonta** USA
17F1 **Oneşti** Romania
20F3 **Onezhskaya Guba** *B* Russian Federation
Onezhskoye, Oz *L* = **Onega, L**
47C3 **Ongers** *R* South Africa
51B5 **Ongiva** Angola
28B3 **Ongjin** N Korea
31D1 **Ongniud Qi** China
44C2 **Ongole** India
51E6 **Onilahy** *R* Madagascar
48C4 **Onitsha** Nigeria
26D2 **Onjüül** Mongolia
29C3 **Ono** Japan
29C4 **Ōnohara-jima** *I* Japan
29C4 **Onomichi** Japan
33G1 **Onotoa** *I* Kiribati
32A3 **Onslow** Australia
67C2 **Onslow B** USA
29C3 **Ontake-san** *Mt* Japan
66D3 **Ontario** California, USA
58C2 **Ontario** Oregon, USA
55J4 **Ontario** *Province* Canada
65D2 **Ontario,L** Canada/USA
15B2 **Onteniente** Spain
33E1 **Ontong Java Atoll** Solomon Islands
28A3 **Onyang** S Korea
66C3 **Onyx** USA
32C3 **Oodnadatta** Australia
32C4 **Ooldea** Australia
63C1 **Oologah L** USA
13C1 **Oostelijk Flevoland** *Polder* Netherlands
13B2 **Oostende** Belgium
13B2 **Oosterschelde** *Estuary* Netherlands
44B3 **Ootacamund** India
25R4 **Opala** Russian Federation
50C4 **Opala** Zaïre
44C4 **Opanake** Sri Lanka
20H4 **Oparino** Russian Federation
19D3 **Opava** Czechoslovakia
67A2 **Opelika** USA
63D2 **Opelousas** USA
60B1 **Opheim** USA
19F1 **Opochka** Russian Federation
19D2 **Opole** Poland
15A1 **Oporto** Portugal
35C1 **Opotiki** New Zealand
67A2 **Opp** USA
12F6 **Oppdal** Norway
35B1 **Opunake** New Zealand
17E1 **Oradea** Romania
12B2 **Öræfajökull** *Mts* Iceland
42D3 **Orai** India
15B2 **Oran** Algeria
72F8 **Orán** Argentina
28A2 **Orang** N Korea
34C2 **Orange** Australia
66D4 **Orange** California, USA
14C3 **Orange** France
63D2 **Orange** Texas, USA
47B2 **Orange** *R* South Africa
67B2 **Orangeburg** USA
73H3 **Orange, Cabo** *C* Brazil
61D2 **Orange City** USA
47D2 **Orange Free State** *Province* South Africa
67B2 **Orange Park** USA
64C2 **Orangeville** Canada
18C2 **Oranienburg** Germany
47B2 **Oranjemund** Namibia
47D1 **Orapa** Botswana
27F5 **Oras** Philippines
17E1 **Orăştie** Romania
17E1 **Oraviţa** Romania
16C2 **Orbetello** Italy
68B2 **Orbisonia** USA
34C3 **Orbost** Australia
13B2 **Orchies** France
66B3 **Orcutt** USA
60D2 **Ord** USA
32B2 **Ord** *R* Australia
59D3 **Orderville** USA
32B2 **Ord,Mt** Australia
25M6 **Ordos** *Desert* China
40C1 **Ordu** Turkey
62B1 **Ordway** USA
12H7 **Örebro** Sweden
64C2 **Oregon** USA
56A2 **Oregon** *State* USA
58B1 **Oregon City** USA
12H6 **Öregrund** Sweden
20F4 **Orekhovo Zuyevo** Russian Federation
21F5 **Orel** Russian Federation
59D2 **Orem** USA
21J5 **Orenburg** Russian Federation
15A1 **Orense** Spain
18C1 **Oresund** *Str* Denmark/Sweden
35A3 **Oreti** *R* New Zealand
19F3 **Orgeyev** Moldavia
17F3 **Orhaneli** *R* Turkey
26D2 **Orhon Gol** *R* Mongolia
34B1 **Orientos** Australia
15B2 **Orihuela** Spain
65D2 **Orillia** Canada
72F2 **Orinoco** *R* Venezuela
68C1 **Oriskany Falls** USA
43E4 **Orissa** *State* India
16B3 **Oristano** Sicily, Italy
16B3 **Oristano, G. di** Sardinia, Italy
12K6 **Orivesi** *L* Finland
73G4 **Oriximiná** Brazil
70C3 **Orizaba** Mexico
75C2 **Orizona** Brazil
8D2 **Orkney** *Is, Region* Scotland
75C3 **Orlândia** Brazil
67B3 **Orlando** USA
14C2 **Orléanais** *Region* France
14C2 **Orléans** France
68E2 **Orleans** USA
25L4 **Orlik** Russian Federation
67B3 **Ormond Beach** USA
7C3 **Ormskirk** England
13C3 **Ornain** *R* France
14B2 **Orne** *R* France
12H6 **Örnsköldsvik** Sweden
28A2 **Oro** N Korea
72D3 **Orocué** Colombia
58C1 **Orofino** USA
45C3 **Oron** Israel
8B3 **Oronsay, I** Scotland
Orontes = **Asi**
19E3 **Orosháza** Hungary
25R3 **Orotukan** Russian Federation
59B3 **Oroville** California, USA
58C1 **Oroville** Washington, USA
19G2 **Orsha** Belorussia
21K5 **Orsk** Russian Federation
12F6 **Ørsta** Norway
14B3 **Orthez** France
15A1 **Ortigueira** Spain
14E2 **Ortles** *Mt* Italy
69L1 **Ortoire** *R* Trinidad
61D1 **Ortonville** USA
25O3 **Orulgan, Khrebet** *Mts* Russian Federation
72E7 **Oruro** Bolivia
7E3 **Orwell** *R* England
20K4 **Osa** Russian Federation
61E2 **Osage** Iowa, USA
60C2 **Osage** Wyoming, USA
63D1 **Osage** *R* USA
29D4 **Ōsaka** Japan
70D4 **Osa,Pen de** Costa Rica
63E1 **Osceola** Arkansas, USA
61E2 **Osceola** Iowa, USA
58C2 **Osgood Mts** USA
29D2 **Oshamambe** Japan
65D2 **Oshawa** Canada
29D4 **Ō-shima** *I* Japan
60C2 **Oshkosh** Nebraska, USA
55K5 **Oshkosh** USA
64B2 **Oshkosh** Wisconsin, USA
21H8 **Oshnovīyeh** Iran
48C4 **Oshogbo** Nigeria
50B4 **Oshwe** Zaïre
17D1 **Osijek** Croatia
24K4 **Osinniki** Russian Federation
19F2 **Osipovichi** Belorussia
61E2 **Oskaloosa** USA
20B4 **Oskarshamn** Sweden
12G6 **Oslo** Norway
40C2 **Osmaniye** Turkey
18B2 **Osnabrück** Germany
74B6 **Osorno** Chile
15B1 **Osorno** Spain
58C1 **Osoyoos** Canada
32D5 **Ossa,Mt** Australia
64A2 **Osseo** USA
68D2 **Ossining** USA
25S4 **Ossora** Russian Federation
20E4 **Ostashkov** Russian Federation
13E1 **Oste** *R* Germany
Ostend = **Oostende**
12G6 **Østerdalen** *V* Norway
13E1 **Osterholz-Scharmbeck** Germany
12G6 **Östersund** Sweden
13D1 **Ostfriesland** *Region* Germany
12H6 **Östhammär** Sweden
16C2 **Ostia** Italy
19D3 **Ostrava** Czechoslovakia
19D2 **Ostróda** Poland
19E2 **Ostrołeka** Poland
20D4 **Ostrov** Russian Federation
19D2 **Ostrów** Poland
19E2 **Ostrowiec** Poland
19E2 **Ostrów Mazowiecka** Poland
15A2 **Osuna** Spain
65D2 **Oswego** USA
68B1 **Oswego** *R* USA
7C3 **Oswestry** England
19D3 **Oświęcim** Poland
29C3 **Ota** Japan
35B3 **Otago Pen** New Zealand
35C2 **Otaki** New Zealand
29E2 **Otaru** Japan
72C3 **Otavalo** Ecuador
51B5 **Otavi** Namibia
29D3 **Otawara** Japan
68C1 **Otego** USA
58C1 **Othello** USA
17E3 **Óthris** *Mt* Greece
60C2 **Otis** Colorado, USA
68D1 **Otis** Massachusetts, USA
68C2 **Otisville** USA
47B1 **Otjimbingwe** Namibia
51B6 **Otjiwarongo** Namibia
6D3 **Otley** England
31B2 **Otog Qi** China
29D2 **Otoineppu** Japan
35C1 **Otorohanga** New Zealand
12F7 **Otra** *R* Norway
17D2 **Otranto** Italy
17D2 **Otranto,Str of** *Chan* Albania/Italy
64B2 **Otsego** USA
68C1 **Otsego L** USA
29C3 **Ōtsu** Japan
12F6 **Otta** Norway
65D1 **Ottawa** Canada
64B2 **Ottawa** Illinois, USA
63C1 **Ottawa** Kansas, USA
65D1 **Ottawa** *R* Canada
55K4 **Ottawa Is** Canada
13E1 **Otterndorf** Germany
55K4 **Otter Rapids** Canada
55K1 **Otto Fjord** Canada
47D2 **Ottosdal** South Africa
64A2 **Ottumwa** USA
13D3 **Ottweiler** Germany
48C4 **Oturkpo** Nigeria
72C5 **Otusco** Peru
34B3 **Otway,C** Australia
19E2 **Otwock** Poland
30C1 **Ou** *R* Laos
63D2 **Ouachita** *R* USA
63D2 **Ouachita,L** USA
63D2 **Ouachita Mts** USA
48A2 **Ouadane** Mauritius
50C3 **Ouadda** Central African Republic
50C2 **Ouaddai** *Desert Region* Chad
48B3 **Ouagadougou** Burkina
48B3 **Ouahigouya** Burkina
50C3 **Ouaka** *R* Central African Republic
48C3 **Oualam** Niger
48C2 **Ouallen** Algeria
50C3 **Ouanda Djallé** Central African Republic
13B4 **Ouanne** *R* France
48A2 **Ouarane** *Region* Mauritius
48C1 **Ouargla** Algeria
48B2 **Ouarkziz, Jbel** *Mts* Morocco
50C3 **Ouarra** *R* Central African Republic
15C2 **Ouarsenis, Massif de l'** *Mts* Algeria
48B1 **Ouarzazate** Morocco
15C2 **Ouassel** *R* Algeria
50B3 **Oubangui** *R* Central African Republic/Congo/Zaïre
13B2 **Oudenaarde** Belgium
47C3 **Oudtshoorn** South Africa
15B2 **Oued Tlělat** Algeria
48B1 **Oued Zem** Morocco
40B4 **Ouena, Wadi** *Watercourse* Egypt
14A2 **Ouessant, Ile d'** *I* France
50B3 **Ouesso** Congo
48B1 **Ouezzane** Morocco
9C2 **Oughter, L** Irish Republic
50B3 **Ouham** *R* Chad
48C4 **Ouidah** Benin
48B1 **Oujda** Morocco
12J6 **Oulainen** Finland
15C3 **Ouled Nail, Monts des** Algeria
12K5 **Oulu** Finland
12K6 **Oulu** *R* Finland
12K6 **Oulujärvi** *L* Finland
50C2 **Oum Chalouba** Chad
16B3 **Oumel Bouaghi** Algeria
50B2 **Oum Hadjer** Chad
50C2 **Oum Haouach** *Watercourse* Chad
12K5 **Ounas** *R* Finland
20C2 **Ounastunturi** *Mt* Finland
50C2 **Ounianga Kebir** Chad
13D2 **Our** *R* Germany
62A1 **Ouray** USA
13C3 **Ource** *R* France
13B3 **Ourcq** *R* France
Ourense = **Orense**
73K5 **Ouricurí** Brazil
75C3 **Ourinhos** Brazil
75D3 **Ouro Prêto** Brazil
13C2 **Ourthe** *R* Belgium
7E3 **Ouse** *R* Norfolk, England
6D2 **Ouse** *R* N Yorks, England
10B2 **Outer Hebrides** *Is* Scotland
66C4 **Outer Santa Barbara** *Chan* USA
51B6 **Outjo** Namibia
12K6 **Outokumpu** Finland
34B3 **Ouyen** Australia
16B2 **Ovada** Italy
74B4 **Ovalle** Chile
51B5 **Ovamboland** *Region* Namibia
13D1 **Overijssel** *Province* Netherlands
59D3 **Overton** USA
12J5 **Övertorneå** Sweden
60C2 **Ovid** Colorado, USA
68B1 **Ovid** New York, USA
15A1 **Oviedo** Spain
12F6 **Øvre** Norway
21D5 **Ovruch** Ukraine
25O4 **Ovsyanka** Russian Federation
35A3 **Owaka** New Zealand
68B1 **Owasco L** USA
29C4 **Owase** Japan
61E2 **Owatonna** USA
68B1 **Owego** USA
66C2 **Owens** *R* USA
64B3 **Owensboro** USA
66D2 **Owens L** USA
64C2 **Owen Sound** Canada
32D1 **Owen Stanley Range** *Mts* Papua New Guinea
48C4 **Owerri** Nigeria
58E2 **Owl Creek Mts** USA
48C4 **Owo** Nigeria
64C2 **Owosso** USA
58C2 **Owyhee** USA
58C2 **Owyhee** *R* USA
58C2 **Owyhee Mts** USA
72C6 **Oxapampa** Peru
12H7 **Oxelösund** Sweden
7D3 **Oxford** England
68E1 **Oxford** Massachusetts, USA
63E2 **Oxford** Mississippi, USA
68C1 **Oxford** New York, USA
7D4 **Oxford** *County* England
66C3 **Oxnard** USA
29D3 **Oyama** Japan
50B3 **Oyen** Gabon
8C3 **Oykel** *R* Scotland
25Q3 **Oymyakon** Russian Federation
34C4 **Oyster B** Australia
27F6 **Ozamiz** Philippines
19F2 **Ozarichi** Belorussia
67A2 **Ozark** USA
63D1 **Ozark Plat** USA
63D1 **Ozarks,L of the** USA
19E3 **Ózd** Hungary
62B2 **Ozona** USA
40D1 **Ozurgety** Georgia

P

47B3 **Paarl** South Africa
8B3 **Pabbay** *I* Scotland
19D2 **Pabianice** Poland
43F4 **Pabna** Bangladesh
19F1 **Pabrade** Lithuania
72F3 **Pacaraima, Serra** *Mts* Brazil/Venezuela
72C5 **Pacasmayo** Peru
70C2 **Pachuca** Mexico
66B1 **Pacific** USA
37N7 **Pacific-Antarctic Ridge** Pacific Ocean
66B2 **Pacific Grove** USA

Pulau Kolepom **Razim**

27G7 **Pulau Kolepom** *I* Indonesia
27C7 **Pulau Pulau Batu** *Is* Indonesia
Pulau Pulau Macan - Kepulauan = Takabonerate
19E2 **Pulawy** Poland
44C3 **Pulicat L** India
42B1 **Pul-i-Khumri** Afghanistan
44B4 **Puliyangudi** India
58C1 **Pullman** USA
27G6 **Pulo Anna** *I* Pacific Ocean
12L5 **Pulozero** Russian Federation
19E2 **Pultusk** Poland
74C3 **Puna de Atacama** Argentina
72B4 **Puná, Isla** Ecuador
43F3 **Punakha** Bhutan
42C2 **Pūnch** Pakistan
47E1 **Punda Milia** South Africa
44A2 **Pune** India
28A2 **Pungsan** N Korea
28A2 **Pungso** N Korea
50C4 **Punia** Zaïre
74B4 **Punitaqui** Chile
42C2 **Punjab** *Province* Pakistan
42D2 **Punjab** *State* India
72D7 **Puno** Peru
74D5 **Punta Alta** Argentina
74B8 **Punta Arenas** Chile
59C4 **Punta Banda, Cabo** *C* Mexico
74F4 **Punta del Este** Uruguay
70D3 **Punta Gorda** Belize
67B3 **Punta Gorda** USA
72B1 **Puntarenas** Costa Rica
31C4 **Puqi** China
24J3 **Pur** *R* Russian Federation
72C3 **Purace, Vol** Colombia
63C1 **Purcell** USA
62B1 **Purgatoire** *R* USA
43F5 **Puri** India
44B2 **Pūrna** India
43F3 **Pūrnia** India
30C3 **Pursat** Cambodia
72F4 **Purus** *R* Brazil
63E2 **Purvis** USA
27D7 **Purwokerto** Indonesia
28B2 **Puryŏng** N Korea
42D5 **Pusad** India
28B3 **Pusan** S Korea
20E4 **Pushkin** Russian Federation
20F3 **Pushlakhta** Russian Federation
19F1 **Pustoshka** Russian Federation
43H3 **Putao** Burma
35C1 **Putaruru** New Zealand
31D4 **Putian** China
27E7 **Puting, Tanjung** *C* Indonesia
68E2 **Putnam** USA
68D1 **Putney** USA
44B4 **Puttalam** Sri Lanka
18C2 **Puttgarden** Germany
72C4 **Putumayo** *R* Colombia/ Ecuador/Peru
27E6 **Putussiban** Indonesia
12K6 **Puulavesi** *L* Finland
58B1 **Puyallup** USA
35A3 **Puysegur Pt** New Zealand
51C4 **Pweto** Zaïre
7B3 **Pwllheli** Wales
20F3 **Pyal'ma** Russian Federation
20E2 **Pyaozero, Ozero** *L* Russian Federation
30B2 **Pyapon** Burma
25K2 **Pyasina** *R* Russian Federation
21G7 **Pyatigorsk** Russian Federation
12K6 **Pyhäselkä** *L* Finland
30B2 **Pyinmana** Burma
28A2 **Pyŏktong** N Korea
28A3 **Pyonggang** N Korea
28A3 **Pyŏnggok-dong** S Korea
28A3 **P'yŏngsan** N Korea
28A3 **P'yŏngt'aek** S Korea
28B3 **P'yŏngyang** N Korea
34B3 **Pyramid Hill** Australia
59C2 **Pyramid L** USA
35A2 **Pyramid,Mt** New Zealand
14B3 **Pyrénées** *Mts* France/ Spain
19F1 **Pytalovo** Russian Federation
30B2 **Pyu** Burma

Q

45D4 **Qa'ash Shubyk, Wadi** Jordan
45C2 **Qabatiya** Israel
45D3 **Qā'el Hafira** *Mud Flats* Jordan
45D3 **Qa'el Jinz** *Mud Flats* Jordan
55O3 **Qagssimiut** Greenland
26C3 **Qaidam Pendi** *Salt Flat* China
45D2 **Qa Khanna** *Salt Marsh* Jordan
50D2 **Qala'en Nahl** Sudan
42B2 **Qalat** Afghanistan
45D1 **Qal'at al Ḩişn** Syria
45C1 **Qal'at al Marqab** *Hist Site* Syria
50E2 **Qal'at Bīshah** Saudi Arabia
41E3 **Qal'at Sālih** Iraq
26C3 **Qamdo** Tibet, China
Qaqortoq = Julianehåb
50E2 **Qandala** Somalia
49E2 **Qara** Egypt
50E3 **Qardho** Somalia
21H8 **Qareh Dāgh** *Mts* Iran
41E4 **Qaryat al Ulyā** Saudi Arabia
45C3 **Qasr ed Deir, Jebel** *Mt* Jordan
45D3 **Qasr el Kharana** Jordan
41E3 **Qāşr e Shīrīn** Iran
49E2 **Qasr Farâfra** Egypt
45D2 **Qaţanā** Syria
41F4 **Qatar** *Emirate* Arabian Pen
45C4 **Qatim, Jebel** *Mt* Jordan
45D3 **Qatrāna** Jordan
49E2 **Qattâra Depression** Egypt
41G3 **Qāyen** Iran
41F2 **Qazvīn** Iran
40B4 **Qena** Egypt
Qeqertarsuaq = Julianehåb
41E2 **Qeydār** Iran
41F4 **Qeys** *I* Iran
21H8 **Qezel Owzan** *R* Iran
45C3 **Qeziot** Israel
31B5 **Qian Jiang** *R* China
31E1 **Qian Shan** *Upland* China
31E3 **Qidong** China
31B4 **Qijiang** China
26C2 **Qijiaojing** China
42B2 **Qila Saifullah** Pakistan
31A2 **Qilian** China
26C3 **Qilian Shan** China
25L6 **Qilian Shan** *Mts* China
31B3 **Qin'an** China
31E2 **Qingdao** China
28A3 **Qingduizi** China
31A2 **Qinghai** *Province* China
26C3 **Qinghai Hu** *L* China
31D3 **Qingjiang** Jiangsu, China
31D4 **Qingjiang** Jiangxi, China
31B3 **Qing Jiang** *R* China
31C2 **Qingshuihe** China
31B2 **Qingshui He** *R* China
31B2 **Qingtongxia** China
31B2 **Qingyang** China
28A2 **Qingyuan** China
31D4 **Qingyuan** Zhejiang, China
39G2 **Qing Zang** *Upland* China
31B5 **Qingzhou** China
31D2 **Qinhuangdao** China
31B3 **Qin Ling** *Mts* China
30D1 **Qinzhou** China
30E2 **Qionghai** China
31A3 **Qionglai Shan** *Upland* China
30D1 **Qiongzhou Haixia** *Str* China
26F2 **Qiqihar** China
45C3 **Qiraîya, Wadi** Egypt
45C2 **Qiryat Ata** Israel
45C3 **Qiryat Gat** Israel
45C2 **Qiryat Shemona** Israel
45C2 **Qiryat Yam** Israel
45C2 **Qishon** *R* Israel
25K5 **Qitai** China
31C4 **Qiyang** China
31B1 **Qog Qi** China
41F2 **Qolleh-ye Damavand** *Mt* Iran
41F3 **Qom** Iran
41F3 **Qomisheh** Iran
Qomolangma Feng *Mt* = **Everest,Mt**
45D1 **Qornet es Saouda** *Mt* Lebanon
55N3 **Qôrnoq** Greenland
41E2 **Qorveh** Iran
41G4 **Qotbābad** Iran
21H8 **Qotur** *R* Iran
68D1 **Quabbin Res** USA
47C2 **Quaggablat** South Africa
13D1 **Quakenbrück** Germany
68C2 **Quakertown** USA
30C3 **Quam Phu Quoc** *I* Vietnam
62C2 **Quanah** USA
30D2 **Quang Ngai** Vietnam
30D2 **Quang Tri** Vietnam
30D4 **Quan Long** Vietnam
31D5 **Quanzhou** Fujian, China
31C4 **Quanzhou** Guangxi, China
54H4 **Qu' Appelle** *R* Canada
59D4 **Quartzsite** USA
41G2 **Quchan** Iran
34C3 **Queanbeyan** Australia
65E1 **Québec** Canada
55L4 **Quebec** *Province* Canada
75C2 **Quebra-Anzol** *R* Brazil
74F3 **Quedas do Iguaçu** *Falls* Argentina/Brazil
68C3 **Queen Anne** USA
54E4 **Queen Charlotte Is** Canada
54F4 **Queen Charlotte Sd** Canada
54F4 **Queen Charlotte Str** Canada
54H1 **Queen Elizabeth Is** Canada
76F9 **Queen Mary Land** *Region* Antarctica
54H3 **Queen Maud G** Canada
76E6 **Queen Maud Mts** Antarctica
68D2 **Queens** *Borough* New York, USA
27F8 **Queen's Ch** Australia
34B3 **Queenscliff** Australia
32D3 **Queensland** *State* Australia
34C4 **Queenstown** Australia
35A3 **Queenstown** New Zealand
47D3 **Queenstown** South Africa
68B3 **Queenstown** USA
51B4 **Quela** Angola
51D5 **Quelimane** Mozambique
62A2 **Quemado** USA
70B2 **Querétaro** Mexico
42B2 **Quetta** Pakistan
70C3 **Quezaltenango** Guatemala
27F5 **Quezon City** Philippines
51B5 **Quibala** Angola
51B4 **Quibaxe** Angola
72C2 **Quibdó** Colombia
14B2 **Quiberon** France
51B4 **Quicama Nat Pk** Angola
75A4 **Quiindy** Paraguay
72D6 **Quillabamba** Peru
72E7 **Quillacollo** Bolivia
14C3 **Quillan** France
54H4 **Quill Lakes** Canada
74B4 **Quillota** Chile
34B1 **Quilpie** Australia
51B4 **Quimbele** Angola
14B2 **Quimper** France
14B2 **Quimperlé** France
59B3 **Quincy** California, USA
64A3 **Quincy** Illinois, USA
68E1 **Quincy** Massachusetts, USA
30D3 **Qui Nhon** Vietnam
15B2 **Quintanar de la Orden** Spain
51B5 **Quirima** Angola
34D2 **Quirindi** Australia
51E5 **Quissanga** Mozambique
51D6 **Quissico** Mozambique
72C4 **Quito** Ecuador
73L4 **Quixadá** Brazil
31A4 **Qujing** China
47D3 **Qumbu** South Africa
32C4 **Quorn** Australia
40B4 **Qus** Egypt
40B4 **Quseir** Egypt
55N3 **Qutdligssat** Greenland
Quthing = Moyeni
31B3 **Qu Xian** Sichuan, China
31D4 **Qu Xian** Zhejiang, China
30D2 **Quynh Luu** Vietnam
31C2 **Quzhou** China
43G3 **Qūzū** China

R

12J6 **Raahe** Finland
8B3 **Raasay** *I* Scotland
8B3 **Raasay,Sound of** *Chan* Scotland
50F2 **Raas Caseyr** Somalia
16C2 **Rab** *I* Croatia
27E7 **Raba** Indonesia
18D3 **Rába** *R* Hungary
48B1 **Rabat** Morocco
32E1 **Rabaul** Papua New Guinea
45C3 **Rabba** Jordan
40C5 **Rābigh** Saudi Arabia
55N5 **Race,C** Canada
68E1 **Race Pt** USA
45C2 **Rachaya** Lebanon
18C3 **Rachel** *Mt* Germany
30D3 **Rach Gia** Vietnam
64B2 **Racine** USA
19F3 **Rădăuţi** Romania
64B3 **Radcliff** USA
64C3 **Radford** USA
42C4 **Radhanpur** India
69L1 **Radix,Pt** Trinidad
19E2 **Radom** Poland
19D2 **Radomsko** Poland
19F2 **Radomyshl'** Ukraine
18C3 **Radstad** Austria
19E1 **Radviliškis** Lithuania
54G3 **Rae** Canada
43E3 **Rāe Bareli** India
55K3 **Rae Isthmus** Canada
54G3 **Rae L** Canada
35C1 **Raetihi** New Zealand
74D4 **Rafaela** Argentina
45C3 **Rafah** Egypt
50C3 **Rafai** Central African Republic
41D3 **Rafhā** Saudi Arabia
41G3 **Rafsanjān** Iran
50C3 **Raga** Sudan
69Q2 **Ragged Pt** Barbados
16C3 **Ragusa** Sicily, Italy
50D2 **Rahad** *R* Sudan
42C3 **Rahimyar Khan** Pakistan
41F3 **Rāhjerd** Iran
44B2 **Rāichur** India
43E4 **Raigarh** India
34B3 **Rainbow** Australia
67A2 **Rainbow City** USA
58B1 **Rainier** USA
58B1 **Rainier,Mt** USA
61E1 **Rainy** *R* Canada/USA
55J5 **Rainy L** Canada
61E1 **Rainy L** Canada/USA
61E1 **Rainy River** Canada
43E4 **Raipur** India
44C2 **Rājahmundry** India
27E6 **Rajang** *R* Malaysia
42C3 **Rajanpur** Pakistan
44B4 **Rājapālaiyam** India
42C3 **Rājasthān** *State* India
42D4 **Rājgarh** Madhya Pradesh, India
42D3 **Rājgarh** Rājasthān, India
42C4 **Rājkot** India
43F4 **Rājmahāl Hills** India
43E4 **Raj Nāndgaon** India
42C4 **Rājpīpla** India
43F4 **Rajshahi** Bangladesh
42D4 **Rājur** India
35B2 **Rakaia** *R* New Zealand
39G3 **Raka Zangbo** *R* China
19E3 **Rakhov** Ukraine
42A3 **Rakhshan** *R* Pakistan
47C1 **Rakops** Botswana
19F2 **Rakov** Belorussia
67C1 **Raleigh** USA
45C4 **Ram** Jordan
45C2 **Rama** Israel
75D1 **Ramalho, Serra do** *Mts* Brazil
45C3 **Ramallah** Israel
44B4 **Rāmanāthapuram** India
26H3 **Ramapo Deep** Pacific Ocean
45C2 **Ramat Gan** Israel
13D3 **Rambervillers** France
14C2 **Rambouillet** France
43F4 **Rāmgarh** Bihār, India
42C3 **Rāmgarh** Rājasthān, India
41E3 **Rāmhormoz** Iran
45C4 **Ram, Jebel** *Mt* Jordan
45C3 **Ramla** Israel
59C4 **Ramona** USA
42D3 **Rāmpur** India
42D4 **Rāmpura** India
43G5 **Ramree I** Burma
21J8 **Rāmsar** Iran
6B2 **Ramsey** Isle of Man, British Isles
68C2 **Ramsey** USA
7B4 **Ramsey I** Wales
7E4 **Ramsgate** England
45D2 **Ramtha** Jordan
32D1 **Ramu** *R* Papua New Guinea
27E6 **Ranau** Malaysia
74B4 **Rancagua** Chile
60B2 **Ranchester** USA
43F4 **Rānchi** India
43E4 **Rānchi Plat** India
74B6 **Ranco, Lago** Chile
47D2 **Randburg** South Africa
12F7 **Randers** Denmark
47D2 **Randfontein** South Africa
65E2 **Randolph** Vermont, USA
66D3 **Randsburg** USA
35B3 **Ranfurly** New Zealand
43G4 **Rangamati** Bangladesh
60B2 **Rangely** USA
35B2 **Rangiora** New Zealand
35C1 **Rangitaiki** *R* New Zealand
35B2 **Rangitata** *R* New Zealand
35C1 **Rangitikei** *R* New Zealand
30B2 **Rangoon** Burma
43F3 **Rangpur** Bangladesh
44B3 **Rānībennur** India
43F4 **Rānīganj** India
55J3 **Rankin Inlet** Canada
34C2 **Rankins Springs** Australia
8C3 **Rannoch, Loch** *L* Scotland
42B4 **Rann of Kachchh** *Flood Area* India
30B4 **Ranong** Thailand
27C6 **Rantauparapat** Indonesia
27F7 **Rantekombola, G** *Mt* Indonesia
64B2 **Rantoul** USA
75B1 **Ranuro** *R* Brazil
13D3 **Raon-l'Etape** France
33H3 **Raoul** *I* Pacific Ocean
16B2 **Rapallo** Italy
55M3 **Raper,C** Canada
60C2 **Rapid City** USA
64B1 **Rapid River** USA
65D3 **Rappahannock** *R* USA
43M2 **Rapti** *R* India
68C2 **Raritan B** USA
40C5 **Ras Abû Dâra** *C* Egypt
40C5 **Ra's Abu Madd** *C* Saudi Arabia
50D1 **Ras Abu Shagara** *C* Sudan
40D2 **Ra's al 'Ayn** Syria
41G4 **Ras al Khaimah** UAE
38D4 **Ra's al Madrakah** *C* Oman
50E2 **Ras Andadda** *C* Ethiopia
41E4 **Ra's az Zawr** *C* Saudi Arabia
40C5 **Râs Banâs** *C* Egypt
45B3 **Râs Burûn** *C* Egypt
50D2 **Ras Dashan** *Mt* Ethiopia
41E3 **Ra's-e Barkan** *Pt* Iran
45A3 **Ras el Barr** *C* Egypt
16B3 **Ras El Hadid** Algeria
40A3 **Râs el Kenâyis** *Pt* Egypt
45C4 **Râs el Nafas** *Mt* Egypt
45B4 **Râs el Sudr** *C* Egypt
45C4 **Ras en Naqb** *Upland* Jordan
38D4 **Ra's Fartak** *C* Yemen
40B4 **Râs Ghârib** Egypt
50D2 **Rashad** Sudan
45C3 **Rashādīya** Jordan
40B3 **Rashîd** Egypt
41E2 **Rasht** Iran
45C1 **Ra's ibn Hāni'** *C* Syria
50E2 **Ras Khanzira** *C* Somalia
42B3 **Ras Koh** *Mt* Pakistan
45B4 **Ras Matarma** *C* Egypt
40B4 **Râs Muhammad** *C* Egypt
48A2 **Ras Nouadhibou** *C* Mauritius/Morocco
26J2 **Rasshua** *I* Kuril Is, Russian Federation
21G5 **Rasskazovo** Russian Federation
41E4 **Ra's Tanāqib** *C* Saudi Arabia
41F4 **Ra's Tannūrah** Saudi Arabia
18B3 **Rastatt** Germany
Ras Uarc = Tres Forcas, Cabo
45C4 **Ras Um Seisabān** *Mt* Jordan
50E2 **Ras Xaafuun** *C* Somalia
42C3 **Ratangarh** India
30B3 **Rat Buri** Thailand
42D3 **Rāth** India
18C2 **Rathenow** Germany
9C2 **Rathfriland** Northern Ireland
9C2 **Rathlin I** Northern Ireland
9C2 **Rathmelton** Irish Republic
45D4 **Ratiyah, Wadi** Jordan
42C4 **Ratlām** India
44A2 **Ratnāgiri** India
44C4 **Ratnapura** Sri Lanka
19E2 **Ratno** Ukraine
62B1 **Raton** USA
12H6 **Rättvik** Sweden
35C1 **Raukumara Range** *Mts* New Zealand
75D3 **Raul Soares** Brazil
12J6 **Rauma** Finland
43E4 **Raurkela** India
41E3 **Ravānsar** Iran
41G3 **Rāvar** Iran
19E2 **Rava Russkaya** Ukraine
68D1 **Ravena** USA
16C2 **Ravenna** Italy
18B3 **Ravensburg** Germany
32D2 **Ravenshoe** Australia
6E2 **Ravenspurn** *Oilfield* N Sea
42C2 **Ravi** *R* Pakistan
55Q3 **Ravn Kap** *C* Greenland
42C2 **Rawalpindi** Pakistan
41D2 **Rawāndiz** Iraq
18D2 **Rawicz** Poland
32B4 **Rawlinna** Australia
56C2 **Rawlins** USA
74D6 **Rawson** Argentina
6C3 **Rawtenstall** England
44B3 **Rāyadurg** India
44C2 **Rāyagada** India
45D2 **Rayak** Lebanon
55N5 **Ray,C** Canada
41G4 **Rāyen** Iran
66C2 **Raymond** California, USA
58D1 **Raymond** Canada
68E1 **Raymond** New Hampshire, USA
58B1 **Raymond** Washington, USA
34D2 **Raymond Terrace** Australia
63C3 **Raymondville** USA
41E2 **Razan** Iran
19G3 **Razdel'naya** Ukraine
28C2 **Razdol'noye** Russian Federation
17F2 **Razgrad** Bulgaria
17F2 **Razim** *L* Romania

Reading **Rotoiti,L**

7D4 **Reading** England
68C2 **Reading** USA
54G3 **Read Island** Canada
68D1 **Readsboro** USA
49E2 **Rebiana** *Well* Libya
49E2 **Rebiana Sand Sea** Libya
12L6 **Reboly** Russian Federation
29E1 **Rebun-tō** *I* Japan
32B4 **Recherche,Arch of the** *Is* Australia
19G2 **Rechitsa** Belorussia
73M5 **Recife** Brazil
47D3 **Recife,C** South Africa
75E2 **Recifes da Pedra Grande** *Arch* Brazil
33F2 **Récifs d'Entrecasteaux** New Caledonia
13D2 **Recklinghausen** Germany
74E3 **Reconquista** Argentina
61D1 **Red** *R* Canada/USA
63D2 **Red** *R* USA
30C4 **Redang** *I* Malaysia
68C2 **Red Bank** New Jersey, USA
67A1 **Red Bank** Tennessee, USA
59B2 **Red Bluff** USA
62B2 **Red Bluff L** USA
6D2 **Redcar** England
34D1 **Redcliffe** Australia
34B2 **Red Cliffs** Australia
60D2 **Red Cloud** USA
54G4 **Red Deer** Canada
54G4 **Red Deer** *R* Canada
58B2 **Redding** USA
7D3 **Redditch** England
60D2 **Redfield** USA
7D4 **Redhill** England
62C1 **Red Hills** USA
57D2 **Red L** USA
55J4 **Red Lake** Canada
61D1 **Red Lake** *R* USA
66D3 **Redlands** USA
68B3 **Red Lion** USA
58E1 **Red Lodge** USA
58B2 **Redmond** USA
66D3 **Red Mountain** USA
61D2 **Red Oak** USA
14B2 **Redon** France
66C4 **Redondo Beach** USA
31B5 **Red River Delta** Vietnam
7B4 **Redruth** England
38B3 **Red Sea** Africa/Arabian Pen
54G4 **Redwater** Canada
61E2 **Red Wing** USA
66A2 **Redwood City** USA
61D2 **Redwood Falls** USA
64B2 **Reed City** USA
66C2 **Reedley** USA
58B2 **Reedsport** USA
65D3 **Reedville** USA
35B2 **Reefton** New Zealand
10B3 **Ree, Lough** *L* Irish Republic
6D2 **Reeth** England
40C2 **Refahiye** Turkey
63C3 **Refugio** USA
75E2 **Regência** Brazil
18C3 **Regensburg** Germany
48C2 **Reggane** Algeria
16D3 **Reggio di Calabria** Italy
16C2 **Reggio nell'Emilia** Italy
17E1 **Reghin** Romania
54H4 **Regina** Canada
42A2 **Registan** *Region* Afghanistan
47B1 **Rehoboth** Namibia
65D3 **Rehoboth Beach** USA
45C3 **Rehovot** Israel
67C1 **Reidsville** USA
7D4 **Reigate** England
14B2 **Ré, Ile de** *I* France
13B3 **Reims** France
74B8 **Reina Adelaida, Archipiélago de la** Chile
61E2 **Reinbeck** USA
54H4 **Reindeer L** Canada
15B1 **Reinosa** Spain
68B3 **Reisterstown** USA
47D2 **Reitz** South Africa
54H3 **Reliance** Canada
58E2 **Reliance** USA
15C2 **Relizane** Algeria
34A2 **Remarkable,Mt** Australia
27E7 **Rembang** Indonesia
13D3 **Remiremont** France
13D2 **Remscheid** Germany
68C1 **Remsen** USA
12G6 **Rena** Norway
64B3 **Rend L** USA
18B2 **Rendsburg** Germany
65D1 **Renfrew** Canada
8C4 **Renfrew** Scotland
27D7 **Rengat** Indonesia
19F3 **Reni** Ukraine
50D2 **Renk** Sudan
55Q2 **Renland** *Pen* Greenland
34B2 **Renmark** Australia
33F2 **Rennell** *I* Solomon Islands
14B2 **Rennes** France
59C3 **Reno** USA
16C2 **Reno** *R* Italy
68B2 **Renovo** USA
68D1 **Rensselaer** USA
58B1 **Renton** USA
27F7 **Reo** Indonesia
19G2 **Repki** Ukraine
75C3 **Reprêsa de Furnas** *Dam* Brazil
75C2 **Reprêsa Três Marias** *Dam* Brazil
58C1 **Republic** USA
60D2 **Republican** *R* USA
55K3 **Repulse Bay** Canada
41F2 **Reshteh-ye Alborz** *Mts* Iran
31A2 **Reshui** China
74E3 **Resistencia** Argentina
17E1 **Reşiţa** Romania
55J2 **Resolute** Canada
35A3 **Resolution I** New Zealand
55M3 **Resolution Island** Canada
47E2 **Ressano Garcia** Mozambique
13C3 **Rethel** France
17E3 **Réthimnon** Greece
36D6 **Réunion** *I* Indian Ocean
15C1 **Reus** Spain
18B3 **Reutlingen** Germany
20K4 **Revda** Russian Federation
54G4 **Revelstoke** Canada
13C3 **Revigny-sur-Ornain** France
70A3 **Revillagigedo** *Is* Mexico
37O4 **Revilla Gigedo, Islas** Pacific Ocean
13C3 **Revin** France
45C3 **Revivim** Israel
43E4 **Rewa** India
42D3 **Rewāri** India
58D2 **Rexburg** USA
12A2 **Reykjavik** Iceland
70C2 **Reynosa** Mexico
14B2 **Rezé** France
19F1 **Rezekne** Latvia
20L4 **Rezh** Russian Federation
7C3 **Rhayader** Wales
45C1 **Rhazīr** Lebanon
13E2 **Rheda Wiedenbrück** Germany
18B2 **Rhein** *R* WEurope
18B2 **Rheine** Germany
14D2 **Rheinland Pfalz** *Region* Germany
Rhine *R* = **Rhein**
68D2 **Rhinebeck** USA
64B1 **Rhinelander** USA
65E2 **Rhode Island** *State* USA
68E2 **Rhode Island Sd** USA
17F3 **Rhodes** Greece
17F3 **Rhodes** *I* Greece
47D1 **Rhodes Drift** *Ford* Botswana/South Africa
58D1 **Rhodes Peak** *Mt* USA
7C4 **Rhondda** Wales
14C3 **Rhône** *R* France
7C3 **Rhyl** Wales
73L6 **Riachão do Jacuipe** Brazil
75D1 **Riacho de Santana** Brazil
15A1 **Ria de Arosa** *B* Spain
15A1 **Ria de Betanzos** *B* Spain
15A1 **Ria de Corcubion** *B* Spain
15A1 **Ria de Lage** *B* Spain
15A1 **Ria de Sta Marta** *B* Spain
15A1 **Ria de Vigo** *B* Spain
42C2 **Riāsi** Pakistan
27D6 **Riau, Kepulauan** *Is* Indonesia
15A1 **Ribadeo** Spain
75B3 **Ribas do Rio Pardo** Brazil
51D5 **Ribauè** Mozambique
6C3 **Ribble** *R* England
75C3 **Ribeira** Brazil
75C3 **Ribeirão Prêto** Brazil
72E6 **Riberalta** Bolivia
65D2 **Rice L** Canada
64A1 **Rice Lake** USA
47E2 **Richard's Bay** South Africa
63C2 **Richardson** USA
54E3 **Richardson Mts** Canada
59D3 **Richfield** USA
68C1 **Richfield Springs** USA
66C3 **Richgrove** USA
58C1 **Richland** USA
64C3 **Richlands** USA
66A2 **Richmond** California, USA
47C3 **Richmond** Cape Province, South Africa
6D2 **Richmond** England
64C3 **Richmond** Kentucky, USA
47E2 **Richmond** Natal, South Africa
34D2 **Richmond** New South Wales, Australia
35B2 **Richmond** New Zealand
32D3 **Richmond** Queensland, Australia
65D3 **Richmond** Virginia, USA
35B2 **Richmond Range** *Mts* New Zealand
68C1 **Richmondville** USA
7D4 **Rickmansworth** England
65D2 **Rideau Lakes** Canada
67B2 **Ridgeland** USA
68A2 **Ridgway** USA
69D4 **Riecito** Venezuela
18C2 **Riesa** Germany
74B8 **Riesco** *I* Chile
47C2 **Riet** *R* South Africa
16C2 **Rieti** Italy
15B2 **Rif** *Mts* Morocco
48B1 **Rif** *R* Morocco
60B3 **Rifle** USA
19E1 **Riga** Latvia
11H2 **Riga,G of** Estonia/Latvia
Rīgas Jūrās Līcis = **Gulf of Riga**
58D2 **Rigby** USA
58C1 **Riggins** USA
55N4 **Rigolet** Canada
Riia Laht = **Gulf of Riga**
12J6 **Riihimaki** Finland
16C1 **Rijeka** Croatia
29D3 **Rikuzen-Tanaka** Japan
12H7 **Rimbo** Sweden
16C2 **Rimini** Italy
17F1 **Rîmnicu Sărat** Romania
17E1 **Rîmnicu Vîlcea** Romania
57G2 **Rimouski** Canada
12F7 **Ringkøbing** Denmark
27E7 **Rinjani** *Mt* Indonesia
8B4 **Rinns Point** Scotland
13E1 **Rinteln** Germany
72C4 **Riobamba** Ecuador
48C4 **Rio Benito** Equatorial Guinea
72E5 **Rio Branco** Brazil
75C4 **Rio Branco do Sul** Brazil
62C3 **Rio Bravo** Mexico
70B1 **Rio Bravo del Norte** *R* Mexico/USA
75B3 **Rio Brilhante** Brazil
75C3 **Rio Claro** Brazil
69L1 **Rio Claro** Trinidad
74D4 **Ríocuarto** Argentina
75D3 **Rio de Janeiro** Brazil
75D3 **Rio de Janeiro** *State* Brazil
48A2 **Rio de Oro, Bahia de** *B* Morocco
74C8 **Río Gallegos** Argentina
74C8 **Río Grande** Argentina
74F4 **Rio Grande** Brazil
69A4 **Río Grande** Nicaragua
70B2 **Rio Grande** *R* Mexico/USA
70D3 **Rio Grande** *R* Nicaragua
62C3 **Rio Grande City** USA
70B2 **Rio Grande de Santiago** *R* Mexico
73L5 **Rio Grande do Norte** *State* Brazil
74F3 **Rio Grande Do Sul** *State* Brazil
52G6 **Rio Grande Rise** Atlantic Ocean
69C4 **Ríohacha** Colombia
14C2 **Riom** France
72E7 **Rio Mulatos** Bolivia
75C4 **Rio Negro** Brazil
74C5 **Río Negro** *State* Argentina
74E4 **Rio Negro, Embalse de** *Res* Uruguay
74F3 **Rio Pardo** Brazil
74B8 **Rio Turbio** Argentina
75B2 **Rio Verde** Brazil
75B2 **Rio Verde de Mato Grosso** Brazil
7D3 **Ripley** England
64C3 **Ripley** Ohio, USA
63E1 **Ripley** Tennessee, USA
64C3 **Ripley** West Virginia, USA
6D2 **Ripon** England
66B2 **Ripon** USA
29E1 **Rishiri-tō** *I* Japan
45C3 **Rishon le Zion** Israel
68B3 **Rising Sun** USA
12F7 **Risør** Norway
44E3 **Ritchie's Arch** *Is* Andaman Islands
55N2 **Ritenbenk** Greenland
66C2 **Ritter,Mt** USA
58C1 **Ritzville** USA
74B3 **Rivadavia** Chile
72A1 **Rivas** Nicaragua
74E4 **Rivera** Uruguay
66B2 **Riverbank** USA
48B4 **River Cess** Liberia
66C2 **Riverdale** USA
68D2 **Riverhead** USA
34B3 **Riverina** *Region* Australia
35A3 **Riversdale** New Zealand
47C3 **Riversdale** South Africa
66D4 **Riverside** USA
35A3 **Riverton** New Zealand
58E2 **Riverton** USA
67B3 **Riviera Beach** USA
65F1 **Riviére-du-Loup** Canada
28A2 **Riwon** N Korea
41E5 **Riyadh** Saudi Arabia
40D1 **Rize** Turkey
31D2 **Rizhao** China
45C1 **Rizokaipaso** Cyprus
16D3 **Rizzuto, C** Italy
12F7 **Rjukan** Norway
8B2 **Roag, Loch** *Inlet* Scotland
55K2 **Roanes Pen** Canada
14C2 **Roanne** France
67A2 **Roanoke** Alabama, USA
65D3 **Roanoke** Virginia, USA
65D3 **Roanoke** *R* USA
67C1 **Roanoke Rapids** USA
59D3 **Roan Plat** USA
58D2 **Roberts** USA
59C3 **Roberts Creek Mt** USA
12J6 **Robertsfors** Sweden
63D1 **Robert S Kerr Res** USA
47B3 **Robertson** South Africa
48A4 **Robertsport** Liberia
55L5 **Roberval** Canada
6D2 **Robin Hood's Bay** England
34B2 **Robinvale** Australia
63C3 **Robstown** USA
15A2 **Roca, Cabo de** *C* Portugal
70A3 **Roca Partida** *I* Mexico
73M4 **Rocas** *I* Brazil
74F4 **Rocha** Uruguay
7C3 **Rochdale** England
75B2 **Rochedo** Brazil
14B2 **Rochefort** France
64B2 **Rochelle** USA
54G3 **Rocher River** Canada
34B3 **Rochester** Australia
55L5 **Rochester** Canada
7E4 **Rochester** England
61E2 **Rochester** Minnesota, USA
68E1 **Rochester** New Hampshire, USA
68B1 **Rochester** New York, USA
64B2 **Rock** *R* USA
52H2 **Rockall** *I* UK
64B2 **Rockford** USA
67B2 **Rock Hill** USA
67C2 **Rockingham** USA
64A2 **Rock Island** USA
64B1 **Rockland** Michigan, USA
34B3 **Rocklands Res** Australia
67B3 **Rockledge** USA
63C3 **Rockport** USA
61D2 **Rock Rapids** USA
60B2 **Rock River** USA
60B1 **Rock Springs** Montana, USA
62B2 **Rocksprings** Texas, USA
58E2 **Rock Springs** Wyoming, USA
35B2 **Rocks Pt** New Zealand
34C3 **Rock,The** Australia
68D2 **Rockville** Connecticut, USA
64B3 **Rockville** Indiana, USA
68B3 **Rockville** Maryland, USA
65F1 **Rockwood** USA
62B1 **Rocky Ford** USA
64C1 **Rocky Island L** Canada
67C1 **Rocky Mount** USA
60B2 **Rocky Mountain Nat Pk** USA
56B1 **Rocky Mts** Canada/USA
18C2 **Rødbyhavn** Denmark
14C3 **Rodez** France
Ródhos = **Rhodes**
16D2 **Rodi Garganico** Italy
17E2 **Rodopi Planina** *Mts* Bulgaria
32A3 **Roebourne** Australia
47D1 **Roedtan** South Africa
13D2 **Roer** *R* Netherlands
13C2 **Roermond** Netherlands
13B2 **Roeselare** Belgium
55K3 **Roes Welcome Sd** Canada
19F2 **Rogachev** Belorussia
72E6 **Rogaguado, Lago** Bolivia
63D1 **Rogers** USA
64C1 **Rogers City** USA
66D3 **Rogers L** USA
64C3 **Rogers,Mt** USA
58D2 **Rogerson** USA
47B3 **Roggeveldberge** *Mts* South Africa
58B2 **Rogue** *R* USA
42B3 **Rohri** Pakistan
42D3 **Rohtak** India
19E1 **Roja** Latvia
70C2 **Rojo, Cabo** *C* Mexico
75B3 **Rolândia** Brazil
63D1 **Rolla** USA
58D1 **Rollins** USA
Roma = **Rome**
34C1 **Roma** Australia
67C2 **Romain,C** USA
17F1 **Roman** Romania
52H5 **Romanche Gap** Atlantic Ocean
27F7 **Romang** *I* Indonesia
21C6 **Romania** *Republic* E Europe
67B3 **Romano,C** USA
14D2 **Romans-sur-Isère** France
27F5 **Romblon** Philippines
67A2 **Rome** Georgia, USA
16C2 **Rome** Italy
68C1 **Rome** New York, USA
65D2 **Rome** USA
14C2 **Romilly-sur-Seine** France
65D3 **Romney** USA
21E5 **Romny** Ukraine
18B1 **Rømø** *I* Denmark
14C2 **Romoratin** France
8C3 **Rona, I** Scotland
8B3 **Ronay, I** Scotland
75B1 **Roncador, Serra do** *Mts* Brazil
15A2 **Ronda** Spain
15A2 **Ronda, Sierra de** *Mts* Spain
72F6 **Rondônia** Brazil
72F6 **Rondônia** *State* Brazil
75B2 **Rondonópolis** Brazil
31B4 **Rong'an** China
31B4 **Rongchang** China
31E2 **Rongcheng** China
54H4 **Ronge, Lac la** Canada
31B4 **Rongjiang** China
31B4 **Rong Jiang** *R* China
30A1 **Rongklang Range** *Mts* Burma
12G7 **Rønne** Denmark
12H7 **Ronneby** Sweden
76F2 **Ronne Ice Shelf** Antarctica
13B2 **Ronse** Belgium
13D1 **Roodeschool** Netherlands
56C3 **Roof Butte** *Mt* USA
42D3 **Roorkee** India
13C2 **Roosendaal** Netherlands
59D2 **Roosevelt** USA
76E6 **Roosevelt I** Antarctica
61E2 **Root** *R* USA
32C2 **Roper** *R* Australia
8D2 **Rora Head** *Pt* Scotland
72F2 **Roraima** *Mt* Brazil/Guyana/Venezuela
72F3 **Roraima** *State* Brazil
12G6 **Røros** Norway
12G6 **Rorvik** Norway
19G3 **Ros'** *R* Ukraine
69Q2 **Rosalie** Dominica
66C3 **Rosamond** USA
66C3 **Rosamond L** USA
74D4 **Rosario** Argentina
73K4 **Rosário** Brazil
75A3 **Rosario** Paraguay
75A1 **Rosário Oeste** Brazil
68C2 **Roscoe** USA
14B2 **Roscoff** France
10B3 **Roscommon** Irish Republic
9C3 **Roscrea** Irish Republic
69Q2 **Roseau** Dominica
34C4 **Rosebery** Australia
60B1 **Rosebud** USA
58B2 **Roseburg** USA
63C3 **Rosenberg** USA
18C3 **Rosenheim** Germany
54H4 **Rosetown** Canada
66B1 **Roseville** USA
12G7 **Roskilde** Denmark
20E5 **Roslavl'** Russian Federation
20G4 **Roslyatino** Russian Federation
17E2 **Roşorii de Vede** Romania
35B2 **Ross** New Zealand
16D3 **Rossano** Italy
10B3 **Rossan Pt** Irish Republic
63E2 **Ross Barnett Res** USA
65D1 **Rosseau L** Canada
33E2 **Rossel** *I* Papua New Guinea
76E6 **Ross Ice Shelf** Antarctica
58B1 **Ross L** USA
9C3 **Rosslare** Irish Republic
35C2 **Ross,Mt** New Zealand
48A3 **Rosso** Mauritius
16B2 **Rosso, C** Corsica, France
7C4 **Ross-on-Wye** England
21F5 **Rossosh** Russian Federation
54E3 **Ross River** Canada
76F6 **Ross S**Antarctica
41F4 **Rostāq** Iran
18C2 **Rostock** Germany
20F4 **Rostov** Russian Federation
21F6 **Rostov-na-Donu** Russian Federation
67B2 **Roswell** Georgia, USA
62B2 **Roswell** New Mexico, USA
27H5 **Rota** *I* Pacific Ocean
27F8 **Rote** *I* Indonesia
18B2 **Rotenburg** Niedersachsen, Germany
13E2 **Rothaar-Geb** *Region* Germany
6D2 **Rothbury** England
76G3 **Rothera** *Base* Antarctica
7D3 **Rotherham** England
8C4 **Rothesay** Scotland
8D3 **Rothes-on-Spey** Scotland
34C2 **Roto** Australia
35B2 **Rotoiti,L** New Zealand

Salem **São João do Paraíso**

68D1 **Salem** New York, USA
58B2 **Salem** Oregon, USA
64C3 **Salem** Virginia, USA
12G6 **Sälen** Sweden
16C2 **Salerno** Italy
7C3 **Salford** England
17D1 **Salgót** Hungary
19D3 **Salgótarján** Hungary
73L5 **Salgueiro** Brazil
60B3 **Salida** USA
17F3 **Salihli** Turkey
51D5 **Salima** Malawi
61D3 **Salina** Kansas, USA
59D3 **Salina** Utah, USA
16C3 **Salina** *I* Italy
70C3 **Salina Cruz** Mexico
75D2 **Salinas** Brazil
66B2 **Salinas** USA
66B2 **Salinas** *R* USA
15C2 **Salinas, Cabo de** *C* Spain
74D3 **Salinas Grandes** *Salt Pans* Argentina
62A2 **Salinas Peak** *Mt* USA
63D2 **Saline** *R* Arkansas, USA
60C3 **Saline** *R* Kansas, USA
69M2 **Salines,Pt** Grenada
66D2 **Saline V** USA
73J4 **Salinópolis** Brazil
Salisbury = Harare
7D4 **Salisbury** England
65D3 **Salisbury** Maryland, USA
67B1 **Salisbury** North Carolina, USA
55L3 **Salisbury I** Canada
7D4 **Salisbury Plain** England
45D2 **Şalkhad** Syria
12K5 **Salla** Finland
63D1 **Sallisaw** USA
55L3 **Salluit** Canada
43E3 **Sallyana** Nepal
41D2 **Salmas** Iran
12L6 **Salmi** Russian Federation
58C1 **Salmo** Canada
58D1 **Salmon** USA
58C1 **Salmon** *R* USA
54G4 **Salmon Arm** Canada
58C1 **Salmon River Mts** USA
12J6 **Salo** Finland
14D3 **Salon-de-Provence** France
Salonica = Thessaloníki
17E1 **Salonta** Romania
12K6 **Salpausselkä** *Region* Finland
21G6 **Sal'sk** Russian Federation
45C2 **Salt** Jordan
47C3 **Salt** *R* South Africa
59D4 **Salt** *R* USA
74C2 **Salta** Argentina
74C2 **Salta** *State* Argentina
7B4 **Saltash** England
9C3 **Saltee, I** Irish Republic
70B2 **Saltillo** Mexico
58D2 **Salt Lake City** USA
72D3 **Salto Angostura** *Waterfall* Colombia
75E2 **Salto da Divisa** Brazil
75B3 **Salto das Sete Quedas** Brazil
72F2 **Salto del Angel** *Waterfall* Venezuela
74E2 **Salto del Guaíra** *Waterfall* Brazil
72D4 **Salto Grande** *Waterfall* Colombia
59C4 **Salton S** USA
75B4 **Saltos do Iguaçu** *Waterfall* Argentina
74E4 **Salto Tacuarembó** Uruguay
42C2 **Salt Range** *Mts* Pakistan
69H2 **Salt River** Jamaica
67B2 **Saluda** USA
44C2 **Sālūr** India
73L6 **Salvador** Brazil
63D3 **Salvador,L** USA
41F5 **Salwah** Qatar
30B1 **Salween** *R* Burma
21H8 **Sal'yany** Azerbaijan
64C3 **Salyersville** USA
18C3 **Salzburg** Austria
18C2 **Salzgitter** Germany
18C2 **Salzwedel** Germany
26C1 **Samagaltay** Russian Federation
69D3 **Samaná** Dominican Republic
40C2 **Samandaği** Turkey
42B1 **Samangan** Afghanistan
29D2 **Samani** Japan
45A3 **Samannûd** Egypt
27F5 **Samar** *I* Philippines
20J5 **Samara** Russian Federation
32E2 **Samarai** Papua New Guinea
27E7 **Samarinda** Indonesia
38E2 **Samarkand** Uzbekistan
41D3 **Sāmarrā'** Iraq
43E4 **Sambalpur** India
27D6 **Sambas** Indonesia
51F5 **Sambava** Madagascar
42D3 **Sambhal** India
19E3 **Sambor** Ukraine
13B2 **Sambre** *R* France
28B3 **Samch'ŏk** S Korea
28A4 **Samch'ŏnp'o** S Korea
28A3 **Samdŭng** N Korea
50D4 **Same** Tanzania
51C5 **Samfya** Zambia
30B1 **Samka** Burma
30C1 **Sam Neua** Laos
33H2 **Samoan Is** Pacific Ocean
17F3 **Sámos** *I* Greece
17F2 **Samothráki** *I* Greece
27E7 **Sampit** Indonesia
63D2 **Sam Rayburn Res** USA
30C3 **Samrong** Cambodia
18C1 **Samsø** *I* Denmark
28A2 **Samsu** N Korea
40C1 **Samsun** Turkey
48B3 **San** Mali
30D3 **San** *R* Cambodia
19E2 **San** *R* Poland
50E2 **San'ā** Yemen
50B3 **Sanaga** *R* Cameroon
74C4 **San Agustín** Argentina
52D6 **San Ambrosia, Isla** Pacific Ocean
41E2 **Sanandaj** Iran
66B1 **San Andreas** USA
69A4 **San Andres, Isla de** Caribbean Sea
62A2 **San Andres Mts** USA
70C3 **San Andrés Tuxtla** Mexico
62B2 **San Angelo** USA
16B3 **San Antioco** Sardinia, Italy
16B3 **San Antioco** *I* Sardinia, Italy
56B4 **San Antonia, Pt** Mexico
74B4 **San Antonio** Chile
62A2 **San Antonio** New Mexico, USA
62C3 **San Antonio** Texas, USA
66B2 **San Antonio** *R* California, USA
63C3 **San Antonio** *R* Texas, USA
15C2 **San Antonio Abad** Spain
69A2 **San Antonio, Cabo** *C* Cuba
62B2 **San Antonio de Bravo** Mexico
69A2 **San Antonio de los Banos** Cuba
66D3 **San Antonio,Mt** USA
74D6 **San Antonio Oeste** Argentina
66B3 **San Antonio Res** USA
66B2 **San Ardo** USA
42D4 **Sanāwad** India
70A3 **San Benedicto** *I* Mexico
63C3 **San Benito** USA
66B2 **San Benito** *R* USA
66B2 **San Benito Mt** USA
66D3 **San Bernardino** USA
74B4 **San Bernardo** Chile
59C4 **San Bernardo Mts** USA
67A3 **San Blas,C** USA
70E4 **San Blas, Puerta** *Pt* Panama
74E3 **San Borja** Brazil
74B5 **San Carlos** Chile
72B1 **San Carlos** Nicaragua
59D4 **San Carlos** USA
74B6 **San Carlos de Bariloche** Argentina
20H4 **Sanchursk** Russian Federation
66D4 **San Clemente** USA
59C4 **San Clemente I** USA
70C3 **San Cristóbal** Mexico
72D2 **San Cristóbal** Venezuela
33F2 **San Cristobal** *I* Solomon Islands
70E2 **Sancti Spíritus** Cuba
14C2 **Sancy, Puy de** *Mt* France
47D1 **Sand** *R* South Africa
8C4 **Sanda, I** Scotland
27E6 **Sandakan** Malaysia
8D2 **Sanday** *I* Scotland
62B2 **Sanderson** USA
7E4 **Sandgate** England
59C4 **San Diego** USA
74C8 **San Diego, Cabo** Argentina
40B2 **Sandikli** Turkey
43E3 **Sandīla** India
12F7 **Sandnes** Norway
12G5 **Sandnessjøen** Norway
51C4 **Sandoa** Zaïre
19E2 **Sandomierz** Poland
43G5 **Sandoway** Burma
7D4 **Sandown** England
12D3 **Sandoy** *I* Faeroes
58C1 **Sandpoint** USA
63C1 **Sand Springs** USA
32A3 **Sandstone** Australia
61E1 **Sandstone** USA
31C4 **Sandu** China
64C2 **Sandusky** USA
12H6 **Sandviken** Sweden
68E2 **Sandwich** USA
55J4 **Sandy L** Canada
75A3 **San Estanislao** Paraguay
56B3 **San Felipe** Baja Cal, Mexico
74B4 **San Felipe** Chile
69D4 **San Felipe** Venezuela
15C1 **San Feliu de Guixols** Spain
52D6 **San Felix, Isla** Pacific Ocean
74B4 **San Fernando** Chile
27F5 **San Fernando** Philippines
15A2 **San Fernando** Spain
69L2 **San Fernando** Trinidad
66C3 **San Fernando** USA
72E2 **San Fernando** Venezuela
67B3 **Sanford** Florida, USA
65E2 **Sanford** Maine, USA
67C1 **Sanford** N Carolina, USA
57E4 **Sanford** USA
54D3 **Sanford, Mt** USA
74D4 **San Francisco** Argentina
69C3 **San Francisco** Dominican Republic
66A2 **San Francisco** USA
66A2 **San Francisco B** USA
70B2 **San Francisco del Oro** Mexico
66D3 **San Gabriel Mts** USA
42C5 **Sangamner** India
64B3 **Sangamon** *R* USA
25O3 **Sangar** Russian Federation
44B2 **Sangāreddi** India
66C2 **Sanger** USA
31C2 **Sanggan He** *R* China
27E6 **Sanggau** Indonesia
50B3 **Sangha** *R* Congo
42B3 **Sanghar** Pakistan
27F6 **Sangir** *I* Indonesia
27F6 **Sangir, Kepulauan** *Is* Indonesia
30B3 **Sangkhla Buri** Thailand
27E6 **Sangkulirang** Indonesia
44A2 **Sāngli** India
50B3 **Sangmélima** Cameroon
56B3 **San Gorgonio Mt** USA
62A1 **Sangre de Cristo Mts** USA
66A2 **San Gregorio** USA
42D2 **Sangrūr** India
47E1 **Sangutane** *R* Mozambique
74E3 **San Ignacio** Argentina
72D2 **San Jacinto** Colombia
59C4 **San Jacinto Peak** *Mt* USA
28A2 **Sanjiangkou** China
29D3 **Sanjō** Japan
74H2 **San João del Rei** Brazil
66B2 **San Joaquin** *R* USA
66B2 **San Joaquin Valley** USA
62B1 **San Jon** USA
74C7 **San Jorge, Golfo** *G* Argentina
15C1 **San Jorge, Golfo de** *G* Spain
72B1 **San José** Costa Rica
70C3 **San José** Guatemala
66B2 **San Jose** USA
56B4 **San José** *I* Mexico
72F7 **San José de Chiquitos** Bolivia
56C4 **San José del Cabo** Mexico
74G2 **San José do Rio Prêto** Brazil
70B2 **San Joseé del Cabo** Mexico
28A3 **Sanju** S Korea
74C4 **San Juan** Argentina
69D3 **San Juan** Puerto Rico
69L1 **San Juan** Trinidad
72E2 **San Juan** Venezuela
69B2 **San Juan** *Mt* Cuba
66B3 **San Juan** *R* California, USA
70D3 **San Juan** *R* Costa Rica/Nicaragua
59D3 **San Juan** *R* Utah, USA
74C4 **San Juan** *State* Argentina
74E3 **San Juan Bautista** Paraguay
66B2 **San Juan Bautista** USA
70D3 **San Juan del Norte** Nicaragua
69D4 **San Juan de los Cayos** Venezuela
70D3 **San Juan del Sur** Nicaragua
58B1 **San Juan Is** USA
62A1 **San Juan Mts** USA
74C7 **San Julián** Argentina
50C4 **Sankuru** *R* Zaïre
66A2 **San Leandro** USA
40C2 **Sanliurfa** Turkey
72C3 **San Lorenzo** Colombia
72B4 **San Lorenzo, Cabo** *C* Ecuador
15B1 **San Lorenzo de Escorial** Spain
66B2 **San Lucas** USA
74C4 **San Luis** Argentina
59D4 **San Luis** USA
74C4 **San Luis** *State* Argentina
66B2 **San Luis Canal** USA
66B3 **San Luis Obispo** USA
66B3 **San Luis Obispo B** USA
70B2 **San Luis Potosí** Mexico
66B2 **San Luis Res** USA
16B3 **Sanluri** Sardinia, Italy
72E2 **San Maigualida** *Mts* Venezuela
63C3 **San Marcos** USA
76G3 **San Martin** *Base* Antarctica
74B7 **San Martin, Lago** Argentina/Chile
66A2 **San Mateo** USA
73G7 **San Matías** Bolivia
74D6 **San Matías, Golfo** *G* Argentina
31C3 **Sanmenxia** China
70D3 **San Miguel** El Salvador
66B3 **San Miguel** USA
66B3 **San Miguel** *I* USA
74C3 **San Miguel de Tucumán** Argentina
74F3 **San Miguel d'Oeste** Brazil
31D4 **Sanming** China
74D4 **San Nicolas** Argentina
56B3 **San Nicolas** *I* USA
47D2 **Sannieshof** South Africa
48B4 **Sanniquellie** Liberia
19E3 **Sanok** Poland
69B5 **San Onofore** Colombia
66D4 **San Onofre** USA
27F5 **San Pablo** Philippines
66A1 **San Pablo B** USA
48B4 **San Pédro** Ivory Coast
74D2 **San Pedro** Jujuy, Argentina
74E2 **San Pedro** Paraguay
59D4 **San Pedro** *R* USA
66C4 **San Pedro Chan** USA
56C4 **San Pedro de los Colonias** Mexico
70D3 **San Pedro Sula** Honduras
16B3 **San Pietro** *I* Sardinia, Italy
8D4 **Sanquar** Scotland
70A1 **San Quintin** Mexico
74C4 **San Rafael** Argentina
66A2 **San Rafael** USA
66C3 **San Rafael Mts** USA
16B2 **San Remo** Italy
62C2 **San Saba** *R* USA
71B2 **San Salvador** El Salvador
69C2 **San Salvador** *I* The Bahamas
74C2 **San Salvador de Jujuy** Argentina
15B1 **San Sebastián** Spain
16D2 **San Severo** Italy
66B3 **San Simeon** USA
72E7 **Santa Ana** Bolivia
70C3 **Santa Ana** Guatemala
66D4 **Santa Ana** USA
66D4 **Santa Ana Mts** USA
62C2 **Santa Anna** USA
70B2 **Santa Barbara** Mexico
66C3 **Santa Barbara** USA
66C4 **Santa Barbara** *I* USA
66B3 **Santa Barbara Chan** USA
66C3 **Santa Barbara Res** USA
66C4 **Santa Catalina** *I* USA
66C4 **Santa Catalina,G of** USA
74F3 **Santa Catarina** *State* Brazil
74G3 **Santa Catarina, Isla de** Brazil
69B2 **Santa Clara** Cuba
66B2 **Santa Clara** USA
66C3 **Santa Clara** *R* USA
74C8 **Santa Cruz** Argentina
72F7 **Santa Cruz** Bolivia
27F5 **Santa Cruz** Philippines
66A2 **Santa Cruz** USA
66C4 **Santa Cruz** *I* USA
59D4 **Santa Cruz** *R* USA
74B7 **Santa Cruz** *State* Argentina
75E2 **Santa Cruz Cabrália** Brazil
66C3 **Santa Cruz Chan** USA
48A2 **Santa Cruz de la Palma** Canary Islands
69B2 **Santa Cruz del Sur** Cuba
48A2 **Santa Cruz de Tenerife** Canary Islands
51C5 **Santa Cruz do Cuando** Angola
75C3 **Santa Cruz do Rio Pardo** Brazil
33F2 **Santa Cruz Is** Solomon Islands
66A2 **Santa Cruz Mts** USA
72F3 **Santa Elena** Venezuela
74D4 **Santa Fe** Argentina
62A1 **Santa Fe** USA
74D3 **Santa Fe** *State* Argentina
75B2 **Santa Helena de Goiás** Brazil
31B3 **Santai** China
74B8 **Santa Inés** *I* Chile
33E1 **Santa Isabel** *I* Solomon Islands
66B2 **Santa Lucia Range** *Mts* USA
48A4 **Santa Luzia** *I* Cape Verde
66B3 **Santa Margarita** USA
66D4 **Santa Margarita** *R* USA
70A2 **Santa Margarita, Isla** Mexico
74F3 **Santa Maria** Brazil
66B3 **Santa Maria** USA
48A1 **Santa Maria** *I* Azores
62A2 **Santa Maria** *R* Chihuahua, Mexico
47E2 **Santa Maria, Cabo de** *C* Mozambique
75D1 **Santa Maria da Vitória** Brazil
17D3 **Santa Maria di Leuca, Capo** *C* Italy
62A2 **Santa María Laguna de** *L* Mexico
69C4 **Santa Marta** Colombia
72D1 **Santa Marta, Sierra Nevada de** *Mts* Colombia
66C3 **Santa Monica** USA
66C4 **Santa Monica B** USA
75D1 **Santana** Brazil
74E4 **Santana do Livramento** Brazil
72C3 **Santander** Colombia
15B1 **Santander** Spain
15C2 **Santañy** Spain
66C3 **Santa Paula** USA
73K4 **Santa Quitéria** Brazil
73H4 **Santarém** Brazil
15A2 **Santarém** Portugal
75B2 **Santa Rita do Araguaia** Brazil
74D5 **Santa Rosa** Argentina
66A1 **Santa Rosa** California, USA
70D3 **Santa Rosa** Honduras
62B2 **Santa Rosa** New Mexico, USA
66B3 **Santa Rosa** *I* USA
70A2 **Santa Rosalía** Mexico
58C2 **Santa Rosa Range** *Mts* USA
73L5 **Santa Talhada** Brazil
75D2 **Santa Teresa** Brazil
16B2 **Santa Teresa di Gallura** Sardinia, Italy
66B3 **Santa Ynez** *R* USA
66B3 **Santa Ynez Mts** USA
67C2 **Santee** *R* USA
74B4 **Santiago** Chile
69C3 **Santiago** Dominican Republic
72B2 **Santiago** Panama
72C4 **Santiago** *R* Peru
15A1 **Santiago de Compostela** Spain
69B2 **Santiago de Cuba** Cuba
74D3 **Santiago del Estero** Argentina
74D3 **Santiago del Estero** *State* Argentina
66D4 **Santiago Peak** *Mt* USA
33F2 **Santo** Vanuatu
75C3 **Santo Amaro, Ilha** Brazil
75B3 **Santo Anastatácio** Brazil
74F3 **Santo Angelo** Brazil
48A4 **Santo Antão** *I* Cape Verde
75B3 **Santo Antônio da Platina** Brazil
75E1 **Santo Antônio de Jesus** Brazil
75A2 **Santo Antônio do Leverger** Brazil
69D3 **Santo Domingo** Dominican Republic
75C3 **Santos** Brazil
75D3 **Santos Dumont** Brazil
59C4 **Santo Tomas** Mexico
74E3 **Santo Tomé** Argentina
74B7 **San Valentin** *Mt* Chile
16C3 **San Vito, C** Sicily, Italy
28B2 **Sanyuanpu** China
51B4 **Sanza Pomba** Angola
75C3 **São Carlos** Brazil
75C1 **São Domingos** Brazil
73H5 **São Félix** Mato Grosso, Brazil
75D3 **São Fidélis** Brazil
75D2 **São Francisco** Brazil
73L5 **São Francisco** *R* Brazil
74G3 **São Francisco do Sul** Brazil
75C4 **São Francisco, Ilha de** Brazil
75C2 **São Gotardo** Brazil
51D4 **Sao Hill** Tanzania
75A2 **São Jerônimo, Serra de** *Mts* Brazil
75D3 **São João da Barra** Brazil
75C3 **São João da Boa Vista** Brazil
75C1 **São João d'Aliança** Brazil
75D2 **São João da Ponte** Brazil
75D3 **São João del Rei** Brazil
75D2 **São João do Paraíso** Brazil

Skokie Stapleton

64B2 Skokie USA
17E3 Skópelos I Greece
17E2 Skopje Macedonia, Yugoslavia
12G7 Skövde Sweden
25O4 Skovorodino Russian Federation
65F2 Skowhegan USA
47E1 Skukuza South Africa
54C3 Skwentna USA
18D2 Skwierzyna Poland
10B2 Skye I Scotland
12G7 Slagelse Denmark
27D7 Slamet Mt Indonesia
9C3 Slaney R Irish Republic
17E2 Slatina Romania
54G3 Slave R Canada
19G2 Slavgorod Belorussia
24J4 Slavgorod Russian Federation
19F2 Slavuta Ukraine
21F6 Slavyansk Ukraine
18D2 Sławno Poland
7D3 Sleaford England
8C3 Sleat,Sound of Chan Scotland
54C3 Sleetmute USA
63E2 Slidell USA
68C2 Slide Mt USA
9B3 Slieve Aughty Mts Irish Republic
9C3 Slieve Bloom Mts Irish Republic
10B3 Sligo Irish Republic
10B3 Sligo B Irish Republic
17F2 Sliven Bulgaria
59C3 Sloan USA
17F2 Slobozia Romania
19F2 Slonim Belorussia
7D4 Slough England
66B2 Slough R USA
16C1 Slovenia Republic Europe
19D3 Slovensko Region Czechoslovakia
18C2 Słubice Poland
19F2 Sluch' R Ukraine
18D2 Słupsk Poland
19F2 Slutsk Belorussia
19F2 Slutsk R Belorussia
10A3 Slyne Head Pt Irish Republic
25M4 Slyudyanka Russian Federation
55M4 Smallwood Res Canada
48A2 Smara Morocco
17E2 Smederevo Serbia, Yugoslavia
17E2 Smederevska Palanka Serbia, Yugoslavia
21E6 Smela Ukraine
68A2 Smethport USA
66C1 Smith USA
54F3 Smith Arm B Canada
54F4 Smithers Canada
67C1 Smithfield N Carolina, USA
47D3 Smithfield South Africa
58D2 Smithfield Utah, USA
55L3 Smith I Canada
65D2 Smiths Falls Canada
34C4 Smithton Australia
60C3 Smoky R USA
34D2 Smoky C Australia
60D3 Smoky Hills USA
58D2 Smoky Mts USA
12F6 Smøla I Norway
20E5 Smolensk Russian Federation
17E2 Smólikas Mt Greece
17E2 Smolyan Bulgaria
19F2 Smorgon' Belorussia
Smyrna = Izmir
68C3 Smyrna Delaware, USA
67B2 Smyrna Georgia, USA
12B2 Snæfell Mt Iceland
6B2 Snaefell Mt Isle of Man, British Isles
58C1 Snake R USA
56B2 Snake River Canyon USA
58D2 Snake River Plain USA
33F5 Snares Is New Zealand
18B2 Sneek Netherlands
66B2 Snelling USA
18D2 Sněžka Mt Czechoslovakia/Poland
8B3 Snizort, Loch Inlet Scotland
12F6 Snøhetta Mt Norway
58B1 Snohomish USA
58B1 Snoqualmie P USA
30D3 Snoul Cambodia
7B3 Snowdon Mt Wales
7B3 Snowdonia Nat Pk Wales
54G3 Snowdrift Canada
59D4 Snowflake USA
54H4 Snow Lake Canada
68B2 Snow Shoe USA
34A2 Snowtown Australia
58D2 Snowville USA
34C3 Snowy Mts Australia
62B2 Snyder USA
28B4 Soan Kundo Is S Korea
8B3 Soay, I Scotland
28A3 Sobaek Sanmaek Mts S Korea
50D3 Sobat R Sudan
73K4 Sobral Brazil
19E2 Sochaczew Poland
21F7 Sochi Russian Federation
28A3 Söch'on S Korea
37M5 Société, Îles de la Pacific Ocean
49D2 Socna Libya
62A2 Socorro USA
70A3 Socorro I Mexico
38D4 Socotra I Yemen
66C3 Soda L USA
12K5 Sodankylä Finland
58D2 Soda Springs USA
50D3 Soddo Ethiopia
12H6 Söderhamn Sweden
12H7 Södertälje Sweden
50C2 Sodiri Sudan
50D3 Sodo Ethiopia
68B1 Sodus Point USA
13E2 Soest Germany
51D5 Sofala Mozambique
17E2 Sofia Bulgaria
Sofiya = Sofia
20E2 Sofporog Russian Federation
26H4 Sofu Gan I Japan
72D2 Sogamoso Colombia
12F6 Sognefjorden Inlet Norway
28A4 Sögwi-ri S Korea
39H2 Sog Xian China
40B4 Sohâg Egypt
33E1 Sohano Papua New Guinea
13B2 Soignies Belgium
13B3 Soissons France
42C3 Sojat India
28A3 Sokcho S Korea
40A2 Söke Turkey
19E2 Sokołka Poland
48C4 Sokodé Togo
20G4 Sokol Russian Federation
48B3 Sokolo Mali
55Q3 Søkongens Øy I Greenland
48C3 Sokoto Nigeria
48C3 Sokoto R Nigeria
35A3 Solander I New Zealand
44B2 Solāpur India
69C4 Soledad Colombia
66B2 Soledad USA
7D4 Solent Sd England
13B2 Solesmes France
19F2 Soligorsk Belorussia
20K4 Solikamsk Russian Federation
21J5 Sol'Iletsk Russian Federation
72D4 Solimões Peru
13D2 Solingen Germany
47B1 Solitaire Namibia
12H6 Sollefteå Sweden
27D7 Solok Indonesia
33E1 Solomon Is Pacific Ocean
64A1 Solon Springs USA
20F2 Solovetskiye, Ostrova I Russian Federation
12F8 Soltau Germany
66B3 Solvang USA
68B1 Solvay USA
8D4 Solway Firth Estuary England/Scotland
51C5 Solwezi Zambia
29D3 Sōma Japan
17F3 Soma Turkey
38C5 Somalia Republic EAfrica
36D4 Somali Basin Indian Ocean
17D1 Sombor Serbia, Yugoslavia
44E4 Sombrero Chan Nicobar Is, Indian Ocean
32D2 Somerset Australia
64C3 Somerset Kentucky, USA
68E2 Somerset Massachusetts, USA
65D2 Somerset Pennsylvania, USA
7C4 Somerset County England
47D3 Somerset East South Africa
55J2 Somerset I Canada
68D1 Somerset Res USA
68C3 Somers Point USA
68E1 Somersworth USA
68C2 Somerville USA
63C2 Somerville Res USA
17E1 Someş R Romania
13B3 Somme Department France
13B3 Somme R France
13C3 Sommesous France
72A1 Somoto Nicaragua
43E4 Son R India
28A3 Sönch'ŏn N Korea
47D3 Sondags R South Africa
12F8 Sønderborg Denmark
55N3 Søndre Strømfjord Greenland
55N2 Søndre Upernavik Greenland
14D2 Sondrio Italy
30D3 Song Ba R Vietnam
30D3 Song Cau Vietnam
28A3 Söngch'on N Korea
51D5 Songea Tanzania
28A2 Songgan N Korea
26F2 Songhua R China
31E3 Songjiang China
28A3 Songjŏng S Korea
30C4 Songkhla Thailand
30C5 Sông Pahang R Malaysia
31A3 Songpan China
28A4 Söngsan-ni S Korea
31C1 Sonid Youqi China
42D3 Sonīpat India
30C1 Son La Vietnam
42B3 Sonmiani Pakistan
42B3 Sonmiani Bay Pakistan
59D4 Sonoita Mexico
66A1 Sonoma USA
66B2 Sonora California, USA
62B2 Sonora Texas, USA
70A2 Sonora R Mexico
59D4 Sonora State Mexico
56B3 Sonoran Desert USA
66C1 Sonora P USA
70D3 Sonsonate El Salvador
27G6 Sonsorol I Pacific Ocean
57E2 Soo Canals Canada/USA
19D2 Sopot Poland
18D3 Sopron Hungary
66B2 Soquel USA
16C2 Sora Italy
45C3 Sored R Israel
65E1 Sorel Canada
34C4 Sorell Australia
40C2 Sorgun Turkey
15B1 Soria Spain
24C2 Sørkapp I Barents Sea
12J5 Sørkjosen Norway
21J6 Sor Mertvyy Kultuk Plain Kazakhstan
75C3 Sorocaba Brazil
20J5 Sorochinsk Moldavia
19F3 Soroki Russian Federation
27H6 Sorol I Pacific Ocean
29D2 Soroma-ko L Japan
27G7 Sorong Indonesia
50D3 Soroti Uganda
12J4 Sørøya I Norway
16C2 Sorrento Italy
12K5 Sorsatunturi Mt Finland
12H5 Sorsele Sweden
20E3 Sortavala Russian Federation
28B3 Sŏsan S Korea
19D2 Sosnowiec Poland
20L4 Sos'va Russian Federation
50B3 Souanké Congo
48B4 Soubré Ivory Coast
68C2 Souderton USA
69P2 Soufrière St Lucia
69N2 Soufrière Mt St Vincent
14C3 Souillac France
16B3 Souk Ahras Algeria
Sŏul = Seoul
15C2 Soummam R Algeria
Sour = Tyre
47D2 Sources,Mt aux Lesotho
60C1 Souris Manitoba, Canada
60C1 Souris R Canada/USA
73L5 Sousa Brazil
16C3 Sousse Tunisia
51C7 South Africa Republic Africa
68C2 S Amboy USA
64C2 Southampton Canada
7D4 Southampton England
68D2 Southampton USA
55K3 Southampton I Canada
44E3 South Andaman I Indian Ocean
55M4 South Aulatsivik I Canada
32C3 South Australia State Australia
36H6 South Australian Basin Indian Ocean
63E2 Southaven USA
62A2 South Baldy Mt USA
67B3 South Bay USA
64C1 South Baymouth Canada
64B2 South Bend Indiana, USA
58B1 South Bend Washington, USA
65D3 South Boston USA
68E1 Southbridge USA
South Cape = Ka Lae
57E3 South Carolina State USA
27E5 South China S SE Asia
56C2 South Dakota State USA
68D1 South Deerfield USA
7D4 South Downs England
34C4 South East C Australia
37O7 South East Pacific Basin Pacific Ocean
54H4 Southend Canada
7E4 Southend-on-Sea England
35A2 Southern Alps Mts New Zealand
32A4 Southern Cross Australia
54J4 Southern Indian L Canada
67C1 Southern Pines USA
69H2 Southfield Jamaica
37K6 South Fiji Basin Pacific Ocean
7E4 South Foreland Pt England
62A1 South Fork USA
66B1 South Fork R California, USA
66B1 South Fork American R USA
66C3 South Fork Kern R USA
71G9 South Georgia I S Atlantic Ocean
7C4 South Glamorgan County Wales
64B2 South Haven USA
54J3 South Henik L Canada
65D3 South Hill USA
36J3 South Honshu Ridge Pacific Ocean
35A2 South I New Zealand
68D2 Southington USA
28B3 South Korea Republic S Korea
59B3 South Lake Tahoe USA
36D6 South Madagascar Ridge Indian Ocean
76G8 South Magnetic Pole Antarctica
67B3 South Miami USA
68B3 South Mt USA
54F3 South Nahanni R Canada
69G1 South Negril Pt Jamaica
52F8 South Orkney Is Atlantic Ocean
71B5 South Pacific O
60C2 South Platte R USA
76E South Pole Antarctica
64C1 South Porcupine Canada
7C3 Southport England
69Q2 South Pt Barbados
68C2 South River USA
8D2 South Ronaldsay I Scotland
52G7 South Sandwich Trench Atlantic Ocean
66A2 South San Francisco USA
54H4 South Saskatchewan R Canada
6D2 South Shields England
35B1 South Taranaki Bight B New Zealand
8B3 South Uist I Scotland
South West Africa = Namibia
32D5 South West C Australia
36D6 South West Indian Ridge Indian Ocean
37M6 South West Pacific Basin Pacific Ocean
52D5 South West Peru Ridge Pacific Ocean
7E3 Southwold England
7D3 South Yorkshire County England
47D1 Soutpansberg Mts South Africa
19E1 Sovetsk Russian Federation
20H4 Sovetsk Russian Federation
26G2 Sovetskaya Gavan' Russian Federation
20L3 Sovetskiy Russian Federation
47D2 Soweto South Africa
29D1 Sōya-misaki C Japan
51B4 Soyo Congo Angola
19G2 Sozh R Belorussia
13C2 Spa Belgium
15 Spain Kingdom SW Europe
Spalato = Split
7D3 Spalding England
64C1 Spanish R Canada
59D2 Spanish Fork USA
69J1 Spanish Town Jamaica
59C3 Sparks USA
64A2 Sparta USA
67B2 Spartanburg USA
17E3 Spartí Greece
16D3 Spartivento, C Italy
26G2 Spassk Dal'niy Russian Federation
60C2 Spearfish USA
62B1 Spearman USA
69R2 Speightstown Barbados
54D3 Spenard USA
55J3 Spence Bay Canada
64B3 Spencer Indiana, USA
61D2 Spencer Iowa, USA
32C4 Spencer G Australia
55L3 Spencer Is Canada
35B2 Spenser Mts New Zealand
9C2 Sperrin Mts Northern Ireland
8D3 Spey R Scotland
18B3 Speyer Germany
69K1 Speyside Tobago
58C1 Spirit Lake USA
54G4 Spirit River Canada
24C2 Spitsbergen I Svalbard, Norway
Spitsbergen Is = Svalbard
18C3 Spittal Austria
13D1 Spjekeroog I Germany
12F6 Spjelkavik Norway
16D2 Split Croatia
58C1 Spokane USA
64A1 Spooner USA
Sporádhes Is = Dodecanese
27E6 Spratly I S China Sea
27E6 Spratly Is S China Sea
58C2 Spray USA
18C2 Spree R Germany
47B2 Springbok South Africa
63D1 Springdale USA
62B1 Springer USA
59E4 Springerville USA
62B1 Springfield Colorado, USA
64B3 Springfield Illinois, USA
68D1 Springfield Massachusetts, USA
61E2 Springfield Minnesota, USA
63D1 Springfield Missouri, USA
64C3 Springfield Ohio, USA
58B2 Springfield Oregon, USA
67A1 Springfield Tennessee, USA
65E2 Springfield Vermont, USA
47D3 Springfontein South Africa
59C3 Spring Mts USA
47D2 Springs South Africa
68A1 Springville New York, USA
59D2 Springville Utah, USA
68B1 Springwater USA
58D2 Spruce Mt USA
7E3 Spurn Head C England
58B1 Spuzzum Canada
16D3 Squillace, G di Italy
25S4 Sredinnyy Khrebet Mts Russian Federation
25R3 Srednekolymsk Russian Federation
20F5 Sredne-Russkaya Vozvyshennost' Upland Russian Federation
25M3 Sredne Sibirskoye Ploskogorye Tableland Russian Federation
20K4 Sredniy Ural Mts Russian Federation
30D3 Srepok R Cambodia
26E1 Sretensk Russian Federation
30C3 Sre Umbell Cambodia
44C2 Srīkākulam India
44B3 Sri Kālahasti India
39G5 Sri Lanka Republic SAsia
42C2 Srīnagar Pakistan
44A2 Srīvardhan India
18D2 Sroda Poland
8C2 Stack Skerry I Scotland
13E1 Stade Germany
13E1 Stadthagen Germany
8B3 Staffa I Scotland
7C3 Stafford England
7C3 Stafford County England
68D2 Stafford Springs USA
Stalingrad = Volgograd
47B3 Stallberg Mt South Africa
55J1 Stallworthy,C Canada
19E2 Stalowa Wola Poland
68D2 Stamford Connecticut, USA
7D3 Stamford England
68C1 Stamford New York, USA
62C2 Stamford Texas, USA
47B1 Stampriet Namibia
47D2 Standerton South Africa
64C2 Standish USA
58D1 Stanford USA
47E2 Stanger South Africa
6C2 Stanhope England
66B2 Stanislaus R USA
17E2 Stanke Dimitrov Bulgaria
34C4 Stanley Australia
74E8 Stanley Falkland Islands
58D2 Stanley Idaho, USA
60C1 Stanley N Dakota, USA
44B3 Stanley Res India
Stanleyville = Kisangani
70D3 Stann Creek Belize
26F1 Stanovoy Khrebet Mts Russian Federation
34D1 Stanthorpe Australia
8A3 Stanton Banks Sand-bank Scotland
60C2 Stapleton USA

Texas **Toya-ko**

34D1 **Texas** Australia
56C3 **Texas** *State* USA
63D3 **Texas City** USA
18A2 **Texel** *I* Netherlands
62B1 **Texhoma** USA
63C2 **Texoma,L** USA
47D2 **Teyateyaneng** Lesotho
42A2 **Teyvareh** Afghanistan
43G3 **Tezpur** India
30C1 **Tha** *R* Laos
47D2 **Thabana Ntlenyana** *Mt* Lesotho
47D2 **Thaba Putsoa** *Mt* Lesotho
47D1 **Thabazimbi** South Africa
30B3 **Thagyettaw** Burma
30D1 **Thai Binh** Vietnam
30C2 **Thailand** *Kingdom* SE Asia
30C3 **Thailand,G of** Thailand
30D1 **Thai Nguyen** Vietnam
30D2 **Thakhek** Laos
42C2 **Thal** Pakistan
30C4 **Thale Luang** *L* Thailand
34C1 **Thallon** Australia
35C1 **Thames** New Zealand
7E4 **Thames** *R* England
21G8 **Thamhar, Wadi ath** *R* Iraq
44A2 **Thāne** India
30D2 **Thanh Hoa** Vietnam
44B3 **Thanjāvūr** India
13D4 **Thann** France
42C3 **Thar Desert** India
34B1 **Thargomindah** Australia
17E2 **Thásos** *I* Greece
30B2 **Thaton** Burma
30A2 **Thayetmyo** Burma
7E3 **The Broads** England
54F5 **The Dalles** USA
60C2 **Thedford** USA
48A3 **The Gambia** *Republic* W Africa
41F4 **The Gulf** SW Asia
18A2 **The Hague** Netherlands
54H3 **Thelon** *R* Canada
7E4 **The Naze** *Pt* England
32E3 **Theodore** Australia
59D4 **Theodore Roosevelt L** USA
72F6 **Theodore Roosevelt, R** Brazil
54H4 **The Pas** Canada
17E2 **Thermaïkós Kólpos** *G* Greece
58E2 **Thermopolis** USA
54F2 **Thesiger B** Canada
64C1 **Thessalon** Canada
17E2 **Thessaloníki** Greece
7E3 **Thetford** England
65E1 **Thetford Mines** Canada
47D2 **Theunissen** South Africa
63D3 **Thibodaux** USA
54J4 **Thicket Portage** Canada
61D1 **Thief River Falls** USA
58B2 **Thielsen,Mt** USA
14C2 **Thiers** France
48A3 **Thiès** Senegal
50D4 **Thika** Kenya
43F3 **Thimphu** Bhutan
14D2 **Thionville** France
17F3 **Thíra** *I* Greece
6D2 **Thirsk** England
44B4 **Thiruvananthapuram** India
12F7 **Thisted** Denmark
27E5 **Thitu** S China Sea
17E3 **Thívai** Greece
14C2 **Thiviers** France
66C2 **Thomas A Edison,L** USA
67B2 **Thomaston** Georgia, USA
65F2 **Thomaston** Maine, USA
9C3 **Thomastown** Irish Republic
63E2 **Thomasville** Alabama, USA
67B2 **Thomasville** Georgia, USA
67C1 **Thomasville** N Carolina, USA
55J2 **Thom Bay** Canada
54J4 **Thompson** Canada
61E2 **Thompson** *R* USA
58C1 **Thompson Falls** USA
54G3 **Thompson Landing** Canada
68D2 **Thompsonville** USA
67B2 **Thomson** USA
32D3 **Thomson** *R* Australia
30C3 **Thon Buri** Thailand
30B2 **Thongwa** Burma
62A1 **Thoreau** USA
6D2 **Thornaby** England
7D3 **Thorne** England
8D4 **Thornhill** Scotland
14B2 **Thouars** France
65D2 **Thousand Is** Canada/USA
58D1 **Three Forks** USA
64B1 **Three Lakes** USA
30B2 **Three Pagodas P** Thailand
48B4 **Three Points, C** Ghana
66C2 **Three Rivers** California, USA
64B2 **Three Rivers** Michigan, USA
62C3 **Three Rivers** Texas, USA
58B2 **Three Sisters** *Mt* USA
55M2 **Thule** Greenland
16B1 **Thun** Switzerland
64B1 **Thunder Bay** Canada
30B4 **Thung Song** Thailand
18C2 **Thüringen** *State* Germany
18C2 **Thüringer Wald** *Upland* Germany
9C3 **Thurles** Irish Republic
8D2 **Thurso** Scotland
76F4 **Thurston I** Antarctica
34B1 **Thylungra** Australia
31B5 **Tiandong** China
31B5 **Tian'e** China
31D2 **Tianjin** China
31B5 **Tianlin** China
28B2 **Tianqiaoling** China
24J5 **Tian Shan** *Mts* China/Kirgizia
31B3 **Tianshui** China
31A2 **Tianzhu** China
15C2 **Tiaret** Algeria
75B3 **Tibagi** *R* Brazil
48D4 **Tibati** Cameroon
45C2 **Tiberias** Israel
45C2 **Tiberias,L** Israel
Tiber,R = Tevere,R
58D1 **Tiber Res** USA
50B1 **Tibesti** *Mountain Region* Chad
39G2 **Tibet** *Autonomous Region* China
34B1 **Tibooburra** Australia
43E3 **Tibrikot** Nepal
70A2 **Tiburón** *I* Mexico
48B3 **Tichitt** Mauritius
48A2 **Tichla** Morocco
65E2 **Ticonderoga** USA
70D2 **Ticul** Mexico
48C2 **Tidikelt, Plaine du** *Desert Region* Algeria
48A3 **Tidjikja** Mauritius
48A3 **Tidra, Isla** Mauritius
13C2 **Tiel** Netherlands
28A2 **Tieling** China
13B2 **Tielt** Belgium
13C2 **Tienen** Belgium
13E4 **Tiengen** Germany
Tientsin = Tianjin
12H6 **Tierp** Sweden
62A1 **Tierra Amarilla** USA
70C3 **Tierra Blanca** Mexico
71C9 **Tierra del Fuego** *I* Argentina/Chile
74C8 **Tierra del Fuego** *Territory* Argentina
74C8 **Tierra del Fuego, Isla Grande de** Argentina/Chile
75C3 **Tietê** Brazil
75B3 **Tiete** *R* Brazil
64C2 **Tiffin** USA
67B2 **Tifton** USA
25R4 **Tigil** Russian Federation
72C4 **Tigre** *R* Peru
72F2 **Tigre** *R* Venezuela
50D2 **Tigre** *Region* Ethiopia
41E3 **Tigris** *R* Iraq
45B4 **Tīh, Gebel el** *Upland* Egypt
59C4 **Tijuana** Mexico
42D4 **Tikamgarh** India
21G6 **Tikhoretsk** Russian Federation
20E4 **Tikhvin** Russian Federation
33F2 **Tikopia** *I* Solomon Islands
41D3 **Tikrīt** Iraq
25O2 **Tiksi** Russian Federation
13C2 **Tilburg** Netherlands
7E4 **Tilbury** England
74C2 **Tilcara** Argentina
34B1 **Tilcha** Australia
48C3 **Tilemis, Vallée du** Mali
43K2 **Tilhar** India
30A1 **Tilin** Burma
48C3 **Tillabéri** Niger
58B1 **Tillamook** USA
44E4 **Tillanchong** *I* Nicobar Is, Indian Ocean
48C3 **Tillia** Niger
6D2 **Till, R** England
17F3 **Tílos** *I* Greece
34B2 **Tilpa** Australia
8D3 **Tilt** *R* Scotland
20H2 **Timanskiy Kryazh** *Mts* Russian Federation
35B2 **Timaru** New Zealand
21F6 **Timashevsk** Russian Federation
17E3 **Timbákion** Greece
63D3 **Timbalier B** USA
48B3 **Timbédra** Mauritius
Timbuktu = Tombouctou
48B3 **Timétrine Monts** *Mts* Mali
48C3 **Timia** Niger
17E1 **Timiş** *R* Romania
48C2 **Timimoun** Algeria
17E1 **Timişoara** Romania
64C1 **Timmins** Canada
32B1 **Timor** *I* Indonesia
32B2 **Timor S** Australia/Indonesia
45B3 **Timsâh,L** Egypt
67A1 **Tims Ford L** USA
27F6 **Tinaca Pt** Philippines
69D5 **Tinaco** Venezuela
44B3 **Tindivanam** India
48B2 **Tindouf** Algeria
66C2 **Tinemaha Res** USA
48B2 **Tinfouchy** Algeria
48C2 **Tin Fouye** Algeria
55O3 **Tingmiarmiut** Greenland
72C5 **Tingo María** Peru
48B3 **Tingrela** Ivory Coast
43F3 **Tingri** China
75E1 **Tinharé, Ilha de** Brazil
27H5 **Tinian** Pacific Ocean
74C3 **Tinogasta** Argentina
17F3 **Tínos** *I* Greece
43H3 **Tinsukia** India
7B4 **Tintagel Head** *Pt* England
48C2 **Tin Tarabine** *Watercourse* Algeria
34B3 **Tintinara** Australia
48C2 **Tin Zaouaten** Algeria
60C1 **Tioga** USA
68B2 **Tioga** *R* USA
66C2 **Tioga P** USA
30C5 **Tioman** *I* Malaysia
68B1 **Tioughnioga** *R* USA
10B3 **Tipperary** Irish Republic
9C3 **Tipperary** *County* Irish Republic
66C2 **Tipton** California, USA
61E3 **Tipton** Missouri, USA
44B3 **Tiptūr** India
17D2 **Tiranë** Albania
19F3 **Tiraspol** Moldavia
45A3 **Tir'at el Ismâilîya** *Canal* Egypt
17F3 **Tire** Turkey
40C1 **Tirebolu** Turkey
8B3 **Tiree** *I* Scotland
17F2 **Tîrgovişte** Romania
17E1 **Tîrgu Jiu** Romania
17E1 **Tîrgu Mureş** Romania
42C1 **Tirich Mir** *Mt* Pakistan
48A2 **Tiris** *Region* Morocco
20K5 **Tirlyanskiy** Russian Federation
17E1 **Tîrnăveni** Romania
17E3 **Tírnavos** Greece
42D4 **Tirodi** India
16B2 **Tirso** *R* Sardinia, Italy
44B4 **Tiruchchendūr** India
44B3 **Tiruchchirāppalli** India
44B4 **Tirunelveli** India
44B3 **Tirupati** India
44B3 **Tiruppattūr** India
44B3 **Tiruppur** India
44B3 **Tiruvannāmalai** India
63C2 **Tishomingo** USA
45D2 **Tisīyah** Syria
19E3 **Tisza** *R* Hungary
72E7 **Titicaca, Lago** Bolivia/Peru
43E4 **Titlagarh** India
17D2 **Titograd** Montenegro, Yugoslavia
17E2 **Titova Mitrovica** Serbia, Yugoslavia
17D2 **Titovo Užice** Serbia, Yugoslavia
17E2 **Titov Veles** Montenegro, Yugoslavia
50C3 **Titule** Zaïre
67B3 **Titusville** USA
8B2 **Tiumpan Head** *Pt* Scotland
7C4 **Tiverton** England
16C2 **Tivoli** Italy
70D2 **Tizimín** Mexico
15C2 **Tizi Ouzou** Algeria
48B2 **Tiznit** Morocco
48B1 **Tlemcen** Algeria
51E5 **Toamasina** Madagascar
29C4 **Toba** Japan
42B2 **Toba and Kakar Ranges** *Mts* Pakistan
69E4 **Tobago** *I* Caribbean Sea
27F6 **Tobelo** Indonesia
64C1 **Tobermory** Canada
8B3 **Tobermory** Scotland
27G6 **Tobi** *I* Pacific Ocean
59C2 **Tobin,Mt** USA
29C3 **Tobi-shima** *I* Japan
27D7 **Toboah** Indonesia
24H4 **Tobol** *R* Russian Federation
27F7 **Toboli** Indonesia
24H4 **Tobol'sk** Russian Federation
Tobruk = Tubruq
20J2 **Tobseda** Russian Federation
73J4 **Tocantins** *R* Brazil
73J6 **Tocantins** *State* Brazil
67B2 **Toccoa** USA
74B2 **Tocopilla** Chile
74C2 **Tocorpuri** Bolivia/Chile
72E1 **Tocuyo** *R* Venezuela
42D3 **Toda** India
28B3 **Todong** S Korea
73L6 **Todos os Santos, Baia de** *B* Brazil
56B4 **Todos Santos** Mexico
59C4 **Todos Santos,B de** Mexico
33H2 **Tofua** *I* Tonga
32B1 **Togian, Kepulauan** *I* Indonesia
48C4 **Togo** *Republic* W Africa
31C1 **Togtoh** China
62A1 **Tohatchi** USA
29E2 **Tokachi** *R* Japan
29C3 **Tokamachi** Japan
50D2 **Tokar** Sudan
26F4 **Tokara Retto** *Arch* Japan
40C1 **Tokat** Turkey
28B3 **Tok-do** *I* S Korea
33H1 **Tokelau Is** Pacific Ocean
39F1 **Tokmak** Kirgizia
35C1 **Tokomaru Bay** New Zealand
26F4 **Tokuno** *I* Ryukyu Is, Japan
29C4 **Tokushima** Japan
28B4 **Tokuyama** Japan
29D3 **Tōkyō** Japan
35C1 **Tolaga Bay** New Zealand
51E6 **Tôlañaro** Madagascar
73H8 **Toledo** Brazil
15B2 **Toledo** Spain
64C2 **Toledo** USA
63D2 **Toledo Bend Res** USA
51E6 **Toliara** Madagascar
72C2 **Tolima** *Mt* Colombia
19F2 **Tolochin** Belorussia
15B1 **Tolosa** Spain
28A4 **Tolsan-do** *I* S Korea
74B5 **Toltén** Chile
70C3 **Toluca** Mexico
20H5 **Tol'yatti** Russian Federation
64A2 **Tomah** USA
64B1 **Tomahawk** USA
29E2 **Tomakomai** Japan
15A2 **Tomar** Portugal
19E2 **Tomaszów Mazowiecka** Poland
63E2 **Tombigbee** *R* USA
51B4 **Tomboco** Angola
75D3 **Tombos** Brazil
48B3 **Tombouctou** Mali
59E4 **Tombstone** USA
51B5 **Tombua** Angola
47D1 **Tomburke** South Africa
74B5 **Tomé** Chile
15B2 **Tomelloso** Spain
28A4 **Tomie** Japan
8D3 **Tomintoul** Scotland
32B3 **Tomkinson Range** *Mts* Australia
25O4 **Tommot** Russian Federation
17E2 **Tomorrit** *Mt* Albania
24K4 **Tomsk** Russian Federation
68C3 **Toms River** USA
70C3 **Tonalá** Mexico
58C1 **Tonasket** USA
7E4 **Tonbridge** England
33H3 **Tonga** *Is, Kingdom* Pacific Ocean
47E2 **Tongaat** South Africa
33H3 **Tongatapu** *I* Tonga
33H3 **Tongatapu Group** *Is* Tonga
33H3 **Tonga Trench** Pacific Ocean
28A2 **Tongchang** N Korea
31D3 **Tongcheng** China
31B2 **Tongchuan** China
31A2 **Tongde** China
13C2 **Tongeren** Belgium
30E2 **Tonggu Jiao** *I* China
31A5 **Tonghai** China
28B2 **Tonghua** China
28B3 **Tongjosŏn-Man** *S* N Korea
30D1 **Tongkin,G of** China/Vietnam
31E1 **Tongliao** China
31D3 **Tongling** China
28A3 **Tongnae** S Korea
34B2 **Tongo** Australia
31B4 **Tongren** Guizhou, China
31A2 **Tongren** Qinghai, China
43G3 **Tongsa** Bhutan
30B1 **Tongta** Burma
26C3 **Tongtian He** *R* China
8C2 **Tongue** Scotland
60B1 **Tongue** *R* USA
31D2 **Tong Xian** China
31B2 **Tongxin** China
28A2 **Tongyuanpu** China
31B4 **Tongzi** China
25L5 **Tonhil** Mongolia
56C4 **Tónichi** Mexico
50C3 **Tonj** Sudan
42D3 **Tonk** India
63C1 **Tonkawa** USA
30C3 **Tonle Sap** *L* Cambodia
13C4 **Tonnerre** France
29D3 **Tono** Japan
59C3 **Tonopah** USA
58D2 **Tooele** USA
34D1 **Toogoolawah** Australia
34B1 **Toompine** Australia
34D1 **Toowoomba** Australia
66C1 **Topaz L** USA
61D3 **Topeka** USA
59D4 **Topock** USA
56C4 **Topolobampo** Mexico
20E2 **Topozero, Ozero** *L* Russian Federation
58B1 **Toppenish** USA
68E1 **Topsfield** USA
50D3 **Tor** Ethiopia
17F3 **Torbali** Turkey
41G2 **Torbat-e-Heydarīyeh** Iran
15A1 **Tordesillas** Spain
18C2 **Torgau** Germany
13B2 **Torhout** Belgium
26H3 **Tori** *I* Japan
Torino = Turin
50D3 **Torit** Sudan
75B2 **Torixoreu** Brazil
15A1 **Tormes** *R* Spain
12J5 **Torne** *R* Sweden
12H5 **Torneträsk** *L* Sweden
55M4 **Torngat** *Mts* Canada
12J5 **Tornio** Finland
74C3 **Toro, Cerro del** *Mt* Argentina/Chile
65D2 **Toronto** Canada
20E4 **Toropets** Russian Federation
50D3 **Tororo** Uganda
Toros, Dağlari = Taurus Mts
7C4 **Torquay** England
66C4 **Torrance** USA
15A2 **Torrão** Portugal
15C1 **Torreblanca** Spain
16C2 **Torre del Greco** Italy
15B1 **Torrelavega** Spain
15B2 **Torremolinos** Spain
32C4 **Torrens, L** Australia
56C4 **Torreón** Mexico
33F2 **Torres Is** Vanuatu
32D2 **Torres Str** Australia
15A2 **Torres Vedras** Portugal
7B4 **Torridge** *R* England
8C3 **Torridon, Loch** *Inlet* Scotland
68D2 **Torrington** Connecticut, USA
60C2 **Torrington** Wyoming, USA
12D3 **Tórshavn** Faeroes
15C1 **Tortosa** Spain
15C1 **Tortosa, Cabo de** *C* Spain
72C3 **Tortugas, Golfo de** Colombia
41G2 **Torūd** Iran
19D2 **Toruń** Poland
10B2 **Tory I** Irish Republic
9B2 **Tory Sol** Irish Republic
20E4 **Torzhok** Russian Federation
29B4 **Tosa** Japan
28C4 **Tosashimizu** Japan
29C4 **Tosa-Wan** *B* Japan
29C4 **To-shima** *I* Japan
12L7 **Tosno** Russian Federation
28B4 **Tosu** Japan
40B1 **Tosya** Turkey
15B2 **Totana** Spain
20G4 **Tot'ma** Russian Federation
7C4 **Totnes** England
73G2 **Totness** Surinam
34C2 **Tottenham** Australia
29C3 **Tottori** Japan
48B4 **Touba** Ivory Coast
48A3 **Touba** Senegal
48B1 **Toubkal** *Mt* Morocco
13B4 **Toucy** France
48B3 **Tougan** Burkina
48C1 **Touggourt** Algeria
48A3 **Tougué** Guinea
13C3 **Toul** France
14D3 **Toulon** France
14C3 **Toulouse** France
48B4 **Toumodi** Ivory Coast
30B2 **Toungoo** Burma
13B2 **Tourcoing** France
48A2 **Tourine** Mauritius
13B2 **Tournai** Belgium
14C2 **Tours** France
47C3 **Touws River** South Africa
29E2 **Towada** Japan
29E2 **Towada-ko** *L* Japan
68B2 **Towanda** USA
66D2 **Towne P** USA
60C1 **Towner** USA
58D1 **Townsend** USA
32D2 **Townsville** Australia
68B3 **Towson** USA
7C4 **Towy** *R* Wales
62B2 **Toyah** USA
29D2 **Toya-ko** *L* Japan

Washburn,Mt Wittlich

58D2 **Washburn,Mt** USA
42D4 **Wāshīm** India
57F3 **Washington** District of Columbia, USA
67B2 **Washington** Georgia, USA
64B3 **Washington** Indiana, USA
61E2 **Washington** Iowa, USA
61E3 **Washington** Missouri, USA
67C1 **Washington** N Carolina, USA
68C2 **Washington** New Jersey, USA
64C2 **Washington** Pennsylvania, USA
59D3 **Washington** Utah, USA
56A2 **Washington** *State* USA
64C3 **Washington Court House** USA
55M1 **Washington Land** *Region* Canada
65E2 **Washington,Mt** USA
62C1 **Washita** *R* USA
7E3 **Wash,The** *B* England
42A3 **Washuk** Pakistan
51L4 **Waskaganish** Canada
69A4 **Waspán** Nicaragua
66C1 **Wassuk Range** *Mts* USA
13C3 **Wassy** France
27F7 **Watampone** Indonesia
47D3 **Waterberge** *Mts* South Africa
68D2 **Waterbury** USA
10B3 **Waterford** Irish Republic
9C3 **Waterford** *County* Irish Republic
9C3 **Waterford Harbour** Irish Republic
13C2 **Waterloo** Belgium
61E2 **Waterloo** USA
64B1 **Watersmeet** USA
58D1 **Waterton-Glacier International Peace Park** USA
65D2 **Watertown** New York, USA
61D2 **Watertown** S Dakota, USA
64B2 **Watertown** Wisconsin, USA
47E2 **Waterval-Boven** South Africa
65F2 **Waterville** Maine, USA
68C1 **Waterville** New York, USA
68D1 **Watervliet** USA
54G4 **Waterways** Canada
7D4 **Watford** England
60C1 **Watford City** USA
68B1 **Watkins Glen** USA
62C1 **Watonga** USA
56C1 **Watrous** Canada
62B1 **Watrous** USA
50C3 **Watsa** Zaïre
54F3 **Watson Lake** Canada
66B2 **Watsonville** USA
27H7 **Wau** Papua New Guinea
50C3 **Wau** Sudan
34D2 **Wauchope** Australia
67B3 **Wauchula** USA
64B2 **Waukegan** USA
64B2 **Waukesha** USA
64B2 **Waupaca** USA
64B2 **Waupun** USA
63C2 **Waurika** USA
64B2 **Wausau** USA
64B2 **Wauwatosa** USA
32C2 **Wave Hill** Australia
7E3 **Waveney** *R* England
60E2 **Waverly** Iowa, USA
68B1 **Waverly** New York, USA
64C3 **Waverly** Ohio, USA
13C2 **Wavre** Belgium
64C1 **Wawa** Canada
49D2 **Wāw Al Kabīr** Libya
49D2 **Wāw an Nāmūs** *Well* Libya
66C2 **Wawona** USA
63C2 **Waxahachie** USA
67B2 **Waycross** USA
61D2 **Wayne** USA
67B2 **Waynesboro** Georgia, USA
63E2 **Waynesboro** Mississippi, USA
68B3 **Waynesboro** Pennsylvania, USA
65D3 **Waynesboro** Virginia, USA
63D1 **Waynesville** Missouri, USA
67B1 **Waynesville** N Carolina, USA
42B2 **Wazi Khwa** Afghanistan
8E1 **W Burra** *I* Scotland
7E4 **Weald,The** *Upland* England
6C2 **Wear** *R* England
62C1 **Weatherford** Oklahoma, USA
63C2 **Weatherford** Texas, USA
58B2 **Weaverville** USA
64C1 **Webbwood** Canada
68B1 **Webster** New York, USA
61D1 **Webster** S Dakota, USA
68E1 **Webster** USA
61E2 **Webster City** Massachusetts, USA
64A3 **Webster Groves** USA
74D8 **Weddell** *I* Falkland Islands
76G2 **Weddell Sea** Antarctica
58B2 **Weed** USA
68A2 **Weedville** USA
47E2 **Weenen** South Africa
34C2 **Wee Waa** Australia
31D1 **Weichang** China
18C3 **Weiden** Germany
31D2 **Weifang** China
31E2 **Weihai** China
31C3 **Wei He** *R* Henan, China
31C2 **Wei He** *R* Shaanxi, China
34C1 **Weilmoringle** Australia
13E3 **Weinheim** Germany
31A4 **Weining** China
32D2 **Weipa** Australia
64C2 **Weirton** USA
58C2 **Weiser** USA
31D3 **Weishan Hu** *L* China
18C2 **Weissenfels** Germany
67A2 **Weiss L** USA
64C3 **Welch** USA
50E2 **Weldiya** Ethiopia
66C3 **Weldon** USA
47D2 **Welkom** South Africa
65D2 **Welland** Canada
7D3 **Welland** *R* England
32C2 **Wellesley Is** Australia
68E2 **Wellfleet** USA
7D3 **Wellingborough** England
34C2 **Wellington** Australia
60C2 **Wellington** Colorado, USA
7C4 **Wellington** England
63C1 **Wellington** Kansas, USA
66C1 **Wellington** Nevada, USA
35B2 **Wellington** New Zealand
47B3 **Wellington** South Africa
62B2 **Wellington** Texas, USA
55J2 **Wellington Chan** Canada
74B7 **Wellington, Isla** Chile
7C4 **Wells** England
58D2 **Wells** Nevada, USA
68C1 **Wells** New York, USA
68B2 **Wellsboro** USA
35B1 **Wellsford** New Zealand
32B3 **Wells,L** Australia
7E3 **Wells-next-the-Sea** England
68B1 **Wellsville** USA
18C3 **Wels** Austria
7C3 **Welshpool** Wales
7D4 **Welwyn Garden City** England
55L4 **Wemindji** Canada
58B1 **Wenatchee** USA
58C1 **Wenatchee** *R* USA
48B4 **Wenchi** Ghana
31E2 **Wendeng** China
58D2 **Wendover** USA
31E4 **Wenling** China
31A5 **Wenshan** China
6D2 **Wensleydale** England
7E3 **Wensum** *R* England
34B2 **Wentworth** Australia
31A3 **Wen Xian** China
31E4 **Wenzhou** China
31C4 **Wenzhu** China
47D2 **Wepener** South Africa
47C2 **Werda** Botswana
50E3 **Werder** Ethiopia
18C2 **Werra** *R* Germany
34D2 **Werris Creek** Australia
13D2 **Wesel** Germany
18B2 **Weser** *R* Germany
60C3 **Weskan** USA
63C3 **Weslaco** USA
55N5 **Wesleyville** Canada
32C2 **Wessel Is** Australia
60D2 **Wessington Springs** USA
64B2 **West Allis** USA
36F5 **West Australian Basin** Indian Ocean
36F6 **West Australian Ridge** Indian Ocean
63E3 **West B** USA
43F4 **West Bengal** *State* India
68C1 **West Branch Delaware** *R* USA
68A2 **West Branch Susquehanna** *R* USA
7D3 **West Bromwich** England
65E2 **Westbrook** USA
64A2 **Westby** USA
68C3 **West Chester** USA
67C3 **West End** Bahamas
66D3 **Westend** USA
13D2 **Westerburg** Germany
18B2 **Westerland** Germany
68E2 **Westerly** USA
32B3 **Western Australia** *State* Australia
44A2 **Western Ghats** *Mts* India
8B3 **Western Isles** *Region* Scotland
48A2 **Western Sahara** *Region* Morocco
33H2 **Western Samoa** *Is* Pacific Ocean
13B2 **Westerschelde** *Estuary* Netherlands
13D1 **Westerstede** Germany
13D2 **Westerwald** *Region* Germany
14D1 **Westfalen** *Region* Germany
74D8 **West Falkland** *Is* Falkland Islands
68D1 **Westfield** Massachusetts, USA
65D2 **Westfield** New York, USA
68B2 **Westfield** Pennsylvania, USA
64B3 **West Frankfort** USA
34C1 **Westgate** Australia
7C4 **West Glamorgan** *County* Wales
65F1 **West Grand L** USA
52E3 **West Indies** *Is* Caribbean Sea
64C3 **West Liberty** USA
64C2 **West Lorne** Canada
9C3 **Westmeath** *County* Irish Republic
63D1 **West Memphis** USA
7D3 **West Midlands** *County* England
7D4 **Westminster** England
68B3 **Westminster** Maryland, USA
67B2 **Westminster** S Carolina, USA
47D1 **West Nicholson** Zimbabwe
27E6 **Weston** Malaysia
64C3 **Weston** USA
7C4 **Weston-super-Mare** England
67B3 **West Palm Beach** USA
63D1 **West Plains** USA
66B1 **West Point** California, USA
63E2 **West Point** Mississippi, USA
61D2 **West Point** Nebraska, USA
68D2 **West Point** New York, USA
35B2 **Westport** New Zealand
10C2 **Westray** *I* Scotland
6E3 **West Sole** *Oilfield* N Sea
57E3 **West Virginia** *State* USA
66C1 **West Walker** *R* USA
34C2 **West Wyalong** Australia
58D2 **West Yellowstone** USA
7D3 **West Yorkshire** *County* England
27F7 **Wetar** *I* Indonesia
54G4 **Wetaskiwin** Canada
50D4 **Wete** Tanzania
13E2 **Wetter** *R* Germany
13E2 **Wetzlar** Germany
Wevok = Lisburne, Cape
32D1 **Wewak** Papua New Guinea
63C1 **Wewoka** USA
9C3 **Wexford** Irish Republic
9C3 **Wexford** *County* Irish Republic
7D4 **Weybridge** England
54H5 **Weyburn** Canada
7C4 **Weymouth** England
68E1 **Weymouth** USA
35C1 **Whakatane** New Zealand
35C1 **Whakatane** *R* New Zealand
8E1 **Whalsay** *I* Scotland
35B1 **Whangarei** New Zealand
6D3 **Wharfe** *R* England
63C3 **Wharton** USA
60B2 **Wheatland** USA
68B3 **Wheaton** Maryland, USA
61D1 **Wheaton** Minnesota, USA
59D3 **Wheeler Peak** *Mt* Nevada, USA
62A1 **Wheeler Peak** *Mt* New Mexico, USA
66C3 **Wheeler Ridge** USA
64C2 **Wheeling** USA
65D2 **Whitby** Canada
6D2 **Whitby** England
7C3 **Whitchurch** England
63D1 **White** *R* Arkansas, USA
60B2 **White** *R* Colorado, USA
64B3 **White** *R* Indiana, USA
60C2 **White** *R* S Dakota, USA
55N4 **White B** Canada
60C1 **White Butte** *Mt* USA
34B2 **White Cliffs** Australia
10C2 **White Coomb** *Mt* Scotland
58D1 **Whitefish** USA
64B1 **Whitefish Pt** USA
55M4 **Whitegull L** Canada
65E2 **Whitehall** New York, USA
68C2 **Whitehall** Pennsylvania, USA
64A2 **Whitehall** Wisconsin, USA
6C2 **Whitehaven** England
54E3 **Whitehorse** Canada
35C1 **White I** New Zealand
63D3 **White L** USA
34C4 **Whitemark** Australia
59C3 **White Mountain Peak** *Mt* USA
66C2 **White Mts** California, USA
65E2 **White Mts** New Hampshire, USA
50D2 **White Nile** *R* Sudan
68D2 **White Plains** USA
55K5 **White River** Canada
60C2 **White River** USA
65E2 **White River Junction** USA
White Russia = Belorussia
58B1 **White Salmon** USA
20F2 **White Sea** Russian Federation
58D1 **White Sulphur Springs** USA
67C2 **Whiteville** USA
48B4 **White Volta** W Africa
64B2 **Whitewater** USA
8C4 **Whithorn** Scotland
67B2 **Whitmire** USA
66C2 **Whitney,Mt** USA
66C4 **Whittier** California, USA
7D3 **Whittlesey** England
54H3 **Wholdaia** Canada
32C4 **Whyalla** Australia
64C2 **Wiarton** Canada
8B3 **Wiay, I** Scotland
60C1 **Wibaux** USA
63C1 **Wichita** USA
62C2 **Wichita** *R* USA
62C2 **Wichita Falls** USA
62C2 **Wichita Mts** USA
8D2 **Wick** Scotland
59D4 **Wickenburg** USA
9C3 **Wicklow** Irish Republic
9C3 **Wicklow** *County* Irish Republic
9C3 **Wicklow Hd** *Pt* Irish Republic
9C3 **Wicklow Mts** Irish Republic
34C1 **Widgeegoara** *R* Australia
7C3 **Widnes** England
13D2 **Wied** *R* Germany
19D2 **Wielun** Poland
Wien = Vienna
18D3 **Wiener Neustadt** Austria
19E2 **Wieprz** *R* Poland
13E2 **Wiesbaden** Germany
13D4 **Wiese** *R* Germany
7C3 **Wigan** England
63E2 **Wiggins** USA
7D4 **Wight, I of** *County* England
6C2 **Wigton** England
8C4 **Wigtown** Scotland
8C4 **Wigtown B** Scotland
58C1 **Wilbur** USA
34B2 **Wilcannia** Australia
59C3 **Wildcat Peak** *Mt* USA
13E1 **Wildeshausen** Germany
16C1 **Wildspitze** *Mt* Austria
67B3 **Wildwood** Florida, USA
68C3 **Wildwood** New Jersey, USA
62B1 **Wiley** USA
47D2 **Wilge** *R* South Africa
32D1 **Wilhelm,Mt** Papua New Guinea
18B2 **Wilhelmshaven** Germany
68C2 **Wilkes-Barre** USA
76F8 **Wilkes Land** *Region* Antarctica
58B2 **Willamette** *R* USA
34B2 **Willandra** *R* Australia
58B1 **Willapa B** USA
59E4 **Willcox** USA
69D4 **Willemstad** Curaçao
34B3 **William,Mt** Australia
59D3 **Williams** Arizona, USA
59B3 **Williams** California, USA
65D3 **Williamsburg** USA
54F4 **Williams Lake** Canada
64C3 **Williamson** USA
68B2 **Williamsport** USA
67C1 **Williamston** USA
68D1 **Williamstown** Massachusetts, USA
64C3 **Williamstown** W Virginia, USA
68D2 **Willimantic** USA
68C2 **Willingboro** USA
32E2 **Willis Group** *Is* Australia
67B3 **Williston** Florida, USA
60C1 **Williston** N Dakota, USA
47C3 **Williston** South Africa
61D1 **Willmar** USA
34A3 **Willoughby,C** Australia
60B1 **Willow Bunch** Canada
47C3 **Willowmore** South Africa
58B2 **Willow Ranch** USA
59B3 **Willows** USA
63D1 **Willow Springs** USA
34A2 **Wilmington** Australia
68C3 **Wilmington** Delaware, USA
67C2 **Wilmington** N Carolina, USA
68D1 **Wilmington** Vermont, USA
60D3 **Wilson** Kansas, USA
67C1 **Wilson** N Carolina, USA
68A1 **Wilson** New York, USA
57F3 **Wilson** USA
34B1 **Wilson** *R* Australia
55K3 **Wilson,C** Canada
60D3 **Wilson L** USA
66C3 **Wilson,Mt** California, USA
62A1 **Wilson,Mt** Colorado, USA
58B1 **Wilson,Mt** Oregon, USA
34C3 **Wilson's Promontory** *Pen* Australia
13E1 **Wilstedt** Germany
7D4 **Wiltshire** *County* England
13C3 **Wiltz** Luxembourg
32B3 **Wiluna** Australia
64B2 **Winamac** USA
47D2 **Winburg** South Africa
7C4 **Wincanton** England
68D1 **Winchendon** USA
65D1 **Winchester** Canada
7D4 **Winchester** England
64C3 **Winchester** Kentucky, USA
68D1 **Winchester** New Hampshire, USA
65D3 **Winchester** Virginia, USA
58E2 **Wind** *R* USA
60C2 **Wind Cave Nat Pk** USA
6C2 **Windermere** England
6C2 **Windermere** *L* England
47B1 **Windhoek** Namibia
61D2 **Windom** USA
32D3 **Windorah** Australia
58E2 **Wind River Range** *Mts* USA
34D2 **Windsor** Australia
68D2 **Windsor** Connecticut, USA
7D4 **Windsor** England
67C1 **Windsor** N Carolina, USA
55M5 **Windsor** Nova Scotia, Canada
64C2 **Windsor** Ontario, Canada
65E1 **Windsor** Quebec, Canada
67B2 **Windsor Forest** USA
68D2 **Windsor Locks** USA
69E4 **Windward Is** Caribbean Sea
69C3 **Windward Pass** Caribbean Sea
63E2 **Winfield** Alabama, USA
63C1 **Winfield** Kansas, USA
34D2 **Wingham** Australia
55K4 **Winisk** *R* Canada
55K4 **Winisk L** Canada
30B2 **Winkana** Burma
58B1 **Winlock** USA
48B4 **Winneba** Ghana
61E2 **Winnebago** USA
64B2 **Winnebago,L** USA
58C2 **Winnemucca** USA
60D2 **Winner** USA
63D2 **Winnfield** USA
61E1 **Winnibigoshish L** USA
54J4 **Winnipeg** Canada
54J4 **Winnipeg,L** Canada
54J4 **Winnipegosis** Canada
65E2 **Winnipesaukee,L** USA
61E2 **Winona** Minnesota, USA
63E2 **Winona** Mississippi, USA
55J5 **Winona** USA
65E2 **Winooski** USA
13D1 **Winschoten** Netherlands
59D4 **Winslow** USA
68D2 **Winsted** USA
67B1 **Winston-Salem** USA
13E2 **Winterberg** Germany
67B3 **Winter Garden** USA
67B3 **Winter Park** USA
66B1 **Winters** USA
13D2 **Winterswijk** Netherlands
16B1 **Winterthur** Switzerland
61E2 **Winthrop** USA
32D3 **Winton** Australia
35A3 **Winton** New Zealand
7E3 **Wisbech** England
64A2 **Wisconsin** *R* USA
57E2 **Wisconsin** *State* USA
64B2 **Wisconsin Dells** USA
55K5 **Wisconsin Rapids** USA
54C3 **Wiseman** USA
19D2 **Wisła** *R* Poland
18C2 **Wismar** Germany
13D3 **Wissembourg** France
73G2 **Witagron** Surinam
47D2 **Witbank** South Africa
56D3 **Witchita Falls** USA
7E3 **Witham** England
7D3 **Witham** *R* England
6E3 **Withernsea** England
7D4 **Witney** England
13D2 **Witten** Germany
18C2 **Wittenberg** Germany
16B1 **Wittenberg** France/Italy
18C2 **Wittenberge** Germany
32A3 **Wittenoom** Australia
13D2 **Wittlich** Germany

ACKNOWLEDGEMENTS

PICTURE CREDITS
The sources for the
photographs and illustrations
appearing in the atlas are
listed below.

page
48-61   Physical maps by
Duncan Mackay,
copyright © Times
Books., London

62   *Mercury* NSSDC/NASA
Venus NASA/Science Photo Library
Mars NASA/Science Photo Library
Neptune NASA/Science Photo Library
Uranus Jet Propulsion Laboratory/NASA
Saturn NASA

63   *Rock and
Hydrological Cycles*
Encyclopaedia Universalis
Editeur, Paris

90   *Manhattan* Adapted
from map by
Nicholson
Publications Ltd.

94-99   Robert Harding
Picture Library Ltd.

Rear   G.L. Fitzpatrick and M.J.
Endpaper   Modlin: *Direct Line Distances.
International Edition* Metuchen
N.J. and London, 1986

ABU DHABI	5167	3260	14244	4975	5142	5972	4637	2003	10735	5158	13534	2367	3471	7498	11688	4845	2317	4903	4892	6071	13865	2987	2043	5478	1348
	AMSTERDAM	2164	18728	9185	1237	7841	577	6864	5575	174	11424	3282	7620	9647	6628	623	6368	690	367	9300	11676	2213	3350	359	896
		ATHENS	16775	7933	1822	7633	1803	5179	7639	2092	11677	1120	6325	7979	8765	2136	5019	1710	2026	8560	13439	562	1256	2394	111
			AUCKLAND	9566	19204	10388	17743	12294	14478	18279	10372	16573	11176	11796	13181	17525	12482	18609	17813	9121	7052	17042	16287	18330	1047
3211				**BANGKOK**	9692	3291	8613	3010	13733	9263	16885	7279	1610	10144	13789	8628	2917	9249	8824	1723	10634	7477	6895	9544	1331
2026	1345				**BARCELONA**	8822	1500	7044	5881	1063	10447	2897	8084	8502	7101	1760	6782	624	1473	10087	12766	2238	3122	1138	967
8851	11637	10424				**BEIJING**	7375	4760	10860	7983	19265	7557	3271	12947	10626	7218	3788	8223	7492	1972	8171	7072	7135	8160	1008
3091	5707	4930	5944				**BERLIN**	6298	6098	654	11890	2891	7045	9588	7103	355	5791	876	255	8770	11782	1739	2903	934	933
3195	769	1132	11933	6023				**BOMBAY**	12275	6891	14937	4363	1664	8216	12976	6430	1156	6725	6544	4311	12928	4818	4017	7205	1402
3711	4872	4743	6455	2045	5482				**BOSTON**	5598	8619	8737	12517	12411	1369	5904	11504	5929	5843	12831	8191	7783	8884	5280	417
2881	358	1120	11025	5352	932	4583				**BRUSSELS**	11282	3212	7689	9490	6679	769	6427	533	491	9416	11825	2185	3302	320	905
1245	4265	3218	7639	1870	4377	2958	3914				**BUENOS AIRES**	11811	16535	6891	8978	12046	15800	11045	11773	18463	12160	12235	12236	11105	982
6671	3464	4747	8996	8534	3654	6748	3789	7628				**CAIRO**	5708	7208	9881	3206	4436	2816	3125	8158	14239	1234	426	3513	1222
3205	108	1300	11358	5756	661	4961	406	4282	3479				**CALCUTTA**	9684	12861	7083	1307	7651	7264	2654	11357	5867	5314	7978	1314
8410	7099	7256	6445	10492	6492	11971	7388	9282	5356	7011				**CAPE TOWN**	13658	9942	9284	8958	9725	11867	18562	8367	7481	9635	1605
1471	2039	696	10298	4523	1800	4696	1796	2711	5429	1996	7339				**CHICAGO**	6860	12047	7069	6850	12560	6849	8834	9978	6371	281
2157	4735	3930	6945	1000	5023	2033	4378	1034	7778	4778	10275	3547				**COPENHAGEN**	5857	1145	289	8688	11428	2021	3191	958	902
4659	5995	4958	7330	6303	5283	8045	5958	5105	7712	5897	4282	4479	6018				**DELHI**	6363	6020	3770	11930	4560	4032	6724	1288
7263	4119	5447	8191	8568	4413	6603	4414	8063	851	4150	5579	6140	7992	8487				**GENEVA**	862	9544	12358	1921	2959	748	951
3011	387	1327	10890	5361	1094	4485	221	3996	3669	478	7485	1992	4401	6178	4263				**HAMBURG**	8934	11629	1988	3150	723	909
1440	3957	3119	7756	1813	4214	2354	3599	718	7148	3994	9818	2757	812	5769	7486	3640				**HONG KONG**	8945	8034	7740	9646	1167
3047	429	1063	11563	5747	388	5110	544	4179	3684	331	6863	1750	4754	5566	4393	712	3954				**HONOLULU**	13068	13969	11653	412
3040	228	1259	11069	5483	915	4655	159	4066	3631	305	7291	1942	4514	6043	4257	180	3741	536				**ISTANBUL**	1170	2504	1104
3772	5779	5319	5668	1071	6268	1225	5450	2679	7973	5851	11473	5069	1649	7374	7805	5399	2343	5931	5552				**JERUSALEM**	3615	1221
8616	7255	8351	4382	6608	7933	5077	7321	8033	5090	7348	7556	8848	7057	11534	4256	7101	7413	7679	7226	5558				**LONDON**	877
1856	1375	349	10590	4646	1391	4394	1081	2994	4836	1358	7603	767	3646	5199	5489	1256	2834	1194	1235	4992	8120				**LOS ANGELES**
1270	2082	781	10121	4285	1940	4434	1804	2496	5520	2052	7603	265	3302	4649	6200	1983	2505	1839	1957	4810	8680	727			
3404	223	1488	11390	5931	707	5071	580	4477	3281	199	6901	2183	4957	5987	3959	595	4178	465	449	5994	7241	1556	2246		
8377	5570	6909	6512	8276	6013	6265	5799	8713	2597	5627	6107	7595	8166	9976	1746	5609	8005	5915	5653	7254	2563	6862	7587	5455	
3500	921	1475	12174	6336	314	5744	1163	4688	3410	818	6229	2085	5337	5304	4191	1289	4529	637	1111	6562	7874	1705	2238	785	5833
7263	10280	9289	1634	4573	10458	5650	9924	6096	10521	10325	7226	8678	5547	6424	9673	9930	6333	10271	10057	4593	5507	9090	8521	10503	7930
8932	5739	7024	6802	9739	5909	7754	6056	9739	2279	5757	4577	7700	9504	8515	1691	5921	9121	5962	5898	8796	3789	7114	7800	5560	1549
2893	514	910	11482	5614	452	5031	523	4029	3838	434	6943	1599	4619	5493	4542	720	3816	155	560	5823	7764	1041	1685	597	6051
6616	3428	4737	8935	8337	3677	6518	3740	7522	251	3451	5593	5427	7615	7919	744	3606	7013	3677	3581	7744	4918	4803	5502	3256	2469
2321	1337	1386	10063	4393	1873	3610	1002	3129	4498	1404	8365	1801	3443	6277	4984	971	2702	1504	1109	4672	7048	1091	1660	1557	6085
2126	4133	2828	8678	4485	3652	5727	3948	2816	7190	4066	6472	2186	3839	2542	8010	4155	3373	3764	4080	5449	10741	2952	2276	4229	9664
6860	3654	4937	8816	8668	3842	6843	3979	7808	191	3669	5276	5618	7936	7799	713	3857	7319	3874	3820	8068	4969	5026	5711	3471	2451
4808	5742	5797	5532	2615	6421	1110	5494	3956	6871	5840	9786	5796	2955	8906	6500	5363	3415	6036	5541	1549	4104	5448	5535	5919	5724
6692	3512	4825	8835	8353	3772	6509	3820	7582	313	3536	5612	5516	7649	8010	645	3682	7061	3766	3661	7734	4819	4887	5588	3342	2366
3260	266	1306	11521	5877	517	5118	547	4365	3446	163	6853	1998	4892	5783	4143	639	4102	257	464	5996	7449	1405	2075	212	5658
5614	8779	7628	3312	3301	8788	4944	8427	4514	11621	8793	7839	6992	4163	5416	10979	8499	4877	8660	8579	3728	6777	7467	6850	8989	9337
7310	5937	6033	7636	9993	5294	10766	6207	8338	4829	5844	1223	6141	9372	3775	5284	6321	8749	5673	6147	11005	8291	6380	6405	5750	6294
2674	804	655	11433	5494	534	5061	735	3845	4102	729	6919	1327	4495	5230	4821	951	3684	433	813	5779	8038	857	1435	891	6346
8145	5468	6792	6517	7930	5963	5918	567	8405	2699	5532	6453	7466	7828	10245	1859	5474	7693	5833	5533	6910	4261	672	7436	5369	347
9097	7452	7797	6021	10968	6923	11842	7772	9984	5217	7375	705	7954	10961	4946	5294	7835	10518	7274	7677	11607	6861	8136	2005	7240	5578
7527	6077	6221	7483	10196	5452	10933	6356	8558	4795	5985	1044	6345	9592	3949	5209	6462	8967	5826	6290	11221	8090	6567	6610	5885	6149
4299	5332	5305	5963	2312	5982	595	5064	3488	6815	5425	12073	5284	2514	8519	6546	4948	2920	5601	5123	1303	4549	4956	5023	5519	5968
4068	5530	5318	5815	1784	6119	669	5233	3131	7314	5616	12190	5199	2113	8053	7081	5143	2640	5753	5310	755	4955	4973	4934	5731	6507
3669	6526	5629	5227	887	6767	2775	6169	2428	9410	6566	9873	5199	1794	6009	9375	6195	2574	6525	6306	1600	6726	5376	4924	6748	8784
2978	701	1497	10565	5143	1417	4179	505	3878	3753	799	7793	2115	4204	6421	4286	325	3467	1032	505	5122	6872	1352	2064	892	5531
6085	2875	9523	1343	4675	10677	5545	9998	6305	10092	10404	7345	8957	5668	6856	9242	9963	6472	10422	10111	4566	5065	9286	8778	10557	7497
5018	5788	5922	5475	2865	6487	1307	5556	4195	6718	5888	11412	5957	3200	9157	6311	5415	3640	6101	5594	1798	3858	5574	5699	5956	5486
6905	3728	5044	8624	8480	3989	6594	4035	7777	431	3754	5545	5734	7810	8134	437	3896	7243	3985	3877	7815	4659	5103	5806	3560	2176
2635	582	797	11094	5251	1026	4647	326	3721	4045	570	7328	1480	4262	5653	4698	541	3465	500	462	5437	7634	794	1504	769	6116
7063	3858	5141	8621	8806	4044	6941	4181	8002	395	3873	5194	5822	8102	7892	595	4058	7501	4075	4023	8163	4838	5231	5915	3676	2300

MILES